T0214754

Lecture Notes in Computer Science 12531

More information about this subseries at http://www.springer.com/series/7408

Shang-Wei Lin · Zhe Hou ·
Brendan Mahony (Eds.)

Formal Methods
and Software Engineering

22nd International Conference
on Formal Engineering Methods, ICFEM 2020
Singapore, Singapore, March 1–3, 2021
Proceedings

Springer

Editors
Shang-Wei Lin ⓘ
Nanyang Technological University
Singapore, Singapore

Brendan Mahony
Defence Science and Technology Group
Edinburgh, SA, Australia

Zhe Hou ⓘ
School of Information
and Communication Technology
Griffith University
Nathan Campus, QLD, Australia

ISSN 0302-9743   ISSN 1611-3349 (electronic)
Lecture Notes in Computer Science
ISBN 978-3-030-63405-6   ISBN 978-3-030-63406-3 (eBook)
https://doi.org/10.1007/978-3-030-63406-3

LNCS Sublibrary: SL2 – Programming and Software Engineering

This Springer imprint is published by the registered company Springer Nature Switzerland AG
The registered company address is: Gewerbestrasse 11, 6330 Cham, Switzerland

Preface

The International Conference on Formal Engineering Methods (ICFEM) gathers researchers and practitioners interested in the recent development in the use and development of formal engineering methods for software and system development. It records the latest development in formal engineering methods.

ICFEM 2020 – the 22nd edition of ICFEM – was planned for late October 2020, but due to the COVID-19 pandemic, the conference was delayed and postponed to Singapore during March 1–3, 2021. ICFEM 2020 received 41 submissions covering theory and applications in formal engineering methods together with case studies. Each paper was reviewed by at least three reviewers, and the Program Committee accepted 16 regular papers and 4 short papers, leading to an attractive scientific program.

After the success of the doctoral symposium of the previous edition, we decided to host a doctoral symposium again at ICFEM 2020. The doctoral symposium Program Committee (chaired by Lei Ma from Kyushu University, Japan; Weiyi Shang from Concordia University, Canada; and Xiaoning Du from Monash University, Australia) accepted one doctoral symposium paper, included in the back matter of ICFEM 2020 proceedings.

ICFEM 2020 would not have been successful without the contribution and involvement of the Program Committee members and the external reviewers who contributed to the review process (with more than 120 reviews) and the selection of the best contributions. This event would not exist if authors and contributors did not submit their proposals. We address our thanks to every person, reviewer, author, Programme Committee member and Organizing Committee member involved in the success of ICFEM 2020.

The EasyChair system was set up for the management of ICFEM 2020 supporting submission, review, and volume preparation processes. It proved to be a powerful framework.

ICFEM 2020 had one affiliated workshop: the 10th International Workshop on SOFL + MSVL for Reliability and Security (SOFL+MSVL 2020), which brought in additional participants to the ICFEM week and helped make it an interesting and successful event. We thank all the workshop organizers for their hard work.

ICFEM 2020 was hosted and sponsored by the National University of Singapore. The Local Organizing Committee offered all the facilities to run the conference in a lovely and friendly atmosphere. Many thanks to all the local organizers.

We wish to express our special thanks to the general co-chairs, the Steering Committee members and in particular Shaoying Liu and Jin Song Dong for their valuable support.

September 2020

Shang-Wei Lin
Zhe Hou
Brendan Mahony

The original version of the book was revised: the surname of the editor was misspelled. The surname has been corrected. The correction to the book is available at https://doi.org/10.1007/978-3-030-63406-3_21

Organization

General Co-chairs

Jin Song Dong   National University of Singapore, Singapore,
                                    and Griffith University, Australia

Jim McCarthy   Defence Science and Technology, Australia

Program Co-chairs

Zhe Hou   Griffith University, Australia
Shang-Wei Lin   Nanyang Technological University, Singapore
Brendan Mahony   Defence Science and Technology, Australia

Finance Co-chairs

Yang Liu   Nanyang Technological University, Singapore
Jun Sun   Singapore University of Technology and Design,
                                    Singapore

Workshop Chair

Hadrien Bride   Griffith University, Australia

Doctoral Symposium Co-chairs

Xiaoning Du   Nanyang Technological University, Singapore
Lei Ma   Kyushu University, Japan
Weiyi Shang   Concordia University, Canada

Steering Committee

Keijiro Araki   Kyushu University, Japan
David Basin   ETH Zurich, Switzerland
Michael Butler   University of Southampton, UK
Jin Song Dong   National University of Singapore, Singapore,
                                    and Griffith University, Australia
Jifeng He   Shanghai Academy of AI Industrial Technology, China
Mike Hinchey   University of Limerick, Ireland
Shaoying Liu   Hosei University, Japan
Kazuhiro Ogata   JAIST, Japan
Shengchao Qin   Teesside University, UK

Program Committee

Yamine Ait Ameur	IRIT, INPT-ENSEEIHT, France
Étienne André	University of Lorraine, France
Cyrille Artho	KTH Royal Institute of Technology, Sweden
Christian Attiogbe	University of Nantes, France
Guangdong Bai	The University of Queensland, Australia
Christel Baier	TU Dresden, Germany
Richard Banach	The University of Manchester, UK
Luis Barbosa	University of Minho, Portugal
Hadrien Bride	Griffith University, Australia
Michael Butler	University of Southampton, UK
Franck Cassez	Macquarie University, Australia
Ana Cavalcanti	University of York, UK
Yuting Chen	Shanghai Jiao Tong University, China
Zhenbang Chen	National University of Defense Technology, China
Yu-Fang Chen	Academia Sinica, Taiwan
Yean-Ru Chen	National Cheng Kung University, Taiwan
Wei-Ngan Chin	National University of Singapore, Singapore
Ranald Clouston	The Australian National University, Australia
Sylvain Conchon	Université Paris-Sud, France
Florin Craciun	Babes-Bolyai University, Romania
Jeremy Dawson	The Australian National University, Australia
Frank De Boer	Centrum Wiskunde & Informatica (CWI), The Netherlands
Yuxin Deng	East China Normal University, China
Jin Song Dong	National University of Singapore, Singapore, and Griffith University, Australia
Naipeng Dong	The University of Queensland, Australia
Zhenhua Duan	Xidian University, China
Marc Frappier	Université de Sherbrooke, Canada
Lindsay Groves	Victoria University of Wellington, New Zealand
Ichiro Hasuo	National Institute of Informatics, Japan
Xudong He	Florida International University, USA
Zhé Hóu	Griffith University, Australia
Pao-Ann Hsiung	National Chung Cheng University, Taiwan
Fuyuki Ishikawa	National Institute of Informatics, Japan
Fabrice Kordon	LIP6, Sorbonne Université, CNRS, France
Yi Li	Nanyang Technological University, Singapore
Xuandong Li	Nanjing University, China
Shang-Wei Lin	Nanyang Technological University, Singapore
Yang Liu	Nanyang Technological University, Singapore
Zhiming Liu	Southwest University, China
Shuang Liu	Tianjin University, China
Brendan Mahony	Defence Science and Technology, Australia
Jim McCarthy	Defence Science and Technology, Australia

Contents

Formal Languages

Other Applications of Formal Methods

Short Papers

Doctoral Symposium Paper

Safety and Security

Hackers vs. Security: Attack-Defence Trees as Asynchronous Multi-agent Systems

Jaime Arias[1], Carlos E. Budde[2(✉)], Wojciech Penczek[3],
Laure Petrucci[1], Teofil Sidoruk[3,5], and Mariëlle Stoelinga[2,4]

[1] LIPN, CNRS UMR 7030, Université Sorbonne Paris Nord,
Sorbonne Paris Cité, Villetaneuse, France
[2] Formal Methods and Tools, University of Twente, Enschede, The Netherlands
`c.e.budde@utwente.nl`
[3] Institute of Computer Science, Polish Academy of Sciences, Warsaw, Poland
[4] Department of Software Science, Radboud University, Nijmegen, The Netherlands
[5] Warsaw University of Technology, Warsaw, Poland

Abstract. Attack-Defence Trees (ADTrees) are a well-suited formalism to assess possible attacks to systems and the efficiency of countermeasures. This paper extends the available ADTree constructs with reactive patterns that cover further security scenarios, and equips all constructs with attributes such as time and cost to allow for quantitative analyses. We model ADTrees as (an extension of) Asynchronous Multi-Agents Systems: EAMAS. The ADTree–EAMAS transformation allows us to quantify the impact of different agents configurations on metrics such as attack time. Using EAMAS also permits parametric verification: we derive constraints for property satisfaction, e.g. the maximum time a defence can take to block an attack. Our approach is exercised on several case studies using the Uppaal and IMITATOR tools. We developed the open-source tool adt2amas implementing our transformation.

1 Introduction

Over the past ten years of security analysis, multiple formalisms have been developed to study interactions between attacker and defender parties [16,19,22,26, 28]. Among these, *Attack-Defence Trees* (ADTrees [22]) stand out as a graphical, straightforward formalism of great modelling versatility. However, research is thus far focused on bipartite graph characterisations, where nodes belong to either the attacker or defender party [8,14,22,23]. This can model interactions between opposing players, but lacks expressiveness to analyse potential sources of parallelism when each party is itself formed of multiple agents.

Agents distribution over the tree nodes, i.e. which agent performs which task for which goal, can determine not only the performance but also the feasibility of

---

This work was partially funded by the NWO project SEQUOIA, the PHC van Gogh project PAMPAS, the BQR project AMoJAS, and the IEA project PARTIES.

S.-W. Lin et al. (Eds.): ICFEM 2020, LNCS 12531, pp. 3–19, 2020.
https://doi.org/10.1007/978-3-030-63406-3_1

an attack or defence strategy. For instance, a monitored double-locked gate may require two concurrent burglars, to steal goods before the alerted police arrives. Likewise, distributed DoS attacks exploit multiplicity to overcome standard DoS countermeasures. Clearly, studying agents distribution *within the operations of an attack/defence party* is crucial to assess attacks and effective countermeasures. However and to our surprise, we find no literature studies focused in this topic.

To fill this gap we hereby model ADTrees in an agent-aware formalism, and study the mechanics of different agents distributions. Our approach permits quantifying performance metrics (e.g. cost and time) of attack/defence strategies under distinct agents coalitions. Employing modern verification tools—IMITA-TOR [4] and UPPAAL [11]—we *reason about the impact of coalition strategies*, and *synthesise the value of the attributes that make them feasible*, such as the maximum time allowed for a defence mechanism to be triggered. In this way, we make an important step towards the analysis of more complex security scenarios.

Contributions. Concretely, in this paper we introduce: (*i*) a unified scheme for ADTree representation with counter- and sequential-operators, including a new construct to negate sequences; (*ii*) EAMAS: formal semantics to model ADTrees, where *all* nodes have attributes and can be operated by *agents*; (*iii*) compositional, sound and complete *pattern transformation rules* from ADTree to EAMAS, which can model ADTrees with shared subtrees; (*iv*) the open-source tool adt2amas [1] to translate ADTree models into EAMAS and generate IMI-TATOR models; (*v*) measurements of the impact of different *agents coalitions* on attack performance metrics, such as cost, exercised on several case studies; (*vi*) *synthesis of ADTree attributes* (e.g. time) that enable attack/defence strategies.

Outline. In Sects. 2 and 3 we review the basic notions of ADTrees and AMAS. Sect. 4 extends AMAS with attributes, to model ADTrees via the graph-based transformation patterns introduced in Sect. 5. The effectiveness of our approach is shown in Sect. 6, where we analyse three case studies from the literature, and demonstrate scalability. We conclude in Sect. 7 and discuss future research.

Related Work. Attack-Defence Trees [22] extend Attack Trees with defensive counter-actions. Several analysis frameworks implement this formalism as Priced Timed Automata (PTA) [14], I/O-IMCs [7], Bayesian Networks (BN) [15], stochastic games [9], and so on—see surveys [23,30]. Each framework computes queries for the underlying semantics: conditional probabilities for BNs, time of attacks/defences for PTAs, etc. In [25] a model driven approach is proposed to inter-operate across these frameworks. However, none of them analyses agent distributions *within* the attack/defence parties. Such studies are at the core of this work. Furthermore, most analyses operate on fully described models, where the attributes of all basic attack and defence nodes are known a priori. Instead we extend the work of [5] to ADTrees, *synthesising* (constraints for the) values of attributes that yield a successful attack or defence. Moreover, our EAMAS formalism offers a succinct representation amenable to state space reduction techniques [21]. This deploys lightweight analyses in comparison to other highly expressive formalisms, such as Attack-Defence Diagrams [16]. Via EAMAS we extend the work on Attack Trees in [18]: we give formal semantics to sequential order operators in ADTrees, that keep the order of events but abstract away their exact occurrence point in time, as usual in the literature [10,18,20,23,25,28].

2   Attack-Defence Trees

2.1   The Basic ADTree Model

Attack Trees are graphical tree-like representations of attack scenarios. They allow for evaluating the security of complex systems to the desired degree of refinement. The *root* of the tree is the goal of the attacker, and the children of a node represent refinements of the node's goal into sub-goals. The tree *leaves* are (possibly quantified) basic attack actions. For instance, Fig. 1a shows a simplistic Attack Tree where the goal is to $\underline{S}$teal $\underline{J}$ewels from a museum (SJ), for which burglars must $\underline{b}$reak $\underline{i}$n (node bi, an *attack leaf*) and $\underline{f}$orce a $\underline{d}$isplay (fd). Nodes in the tree whose state depends on other nodes are called *gates*: SJ is an AND gate with two children.

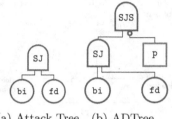

(a) Attack Tree (b) ADTree

Fig. 1. Steal jewels

Attack-Defence Trees [22] can model counter-actions of a defender: they represent an interplay between the actions of both attacker and defender. This can model mechanisms triggered by the occurrence of opposite actions. So for instance in the ADTree in Fig. 1b, the jewels burglary will succeed (SJS) only if all attack actions are performed, and the alerted police (node p, a *defence leaf*) does not stop them.

We define ADTree structures as shown in Table 1. The formal semantics of each construct will be later given in Sect. 5 in terms of (specialised) Multi-Agent Systems; here we simply give a natural language interpretation of such semantics. Since constructs are symmetric for attack and defence goals, Table 1 shows a comprehensive selection of structures. Here $D, d, d_1, \cdots, d_n \in \Sigma_d$ and $A, a, a_1, \cdots, a_n \in \Sigma_a$, where Σ_d and Σ_a are sets of defence and attack nodes, respectively. Graphically, triangular nodes stand for arbitrary subtrees that are children of a gate, and circular (resp. rectangular) nodes represent attack (resp. defence) leaves, i.e. basic actions that are no further refined. Table 1 thus reinterprets [22] using a unified gate notation along the lines of [25], including CAND gates that express counter-attacks or -defences, e.g. *counter defence* in the table.

Table 1 also introduces operators for a *choice* between a successful attack and a failing defence (named *no defence*), and vice-versa (*inhibiting attack*). These constructs, less usual in the literature [23], model realistic scenarios such as attack goals succeeding by security negligence rather than by performing costly attack. This is of interest for quantitative analyses of e.g. cost and probability.

Moreover, we consider sequential operators, which lack a standard interpretation for ADTrees. For Attack Trees, [18] proposes a sequentially ordered conjunction (SAND) where attacks succeed as soon as all children took place in the required order. This abstracts away the occurrence time point of events, and

Table 1. ADTree constructs (selection) and their informal semantics

Name	Graphics	Semantics	Name	Graphics	Semantics
Attack	a	$a \equiv$ "basic attack *action a* done"	No defence	A / a d	$A \equiv$ "either attack a done or else defence d not done"
Defence	d	$d \equiv$ "basic defence *action d* done"			
And attack	A / $a_1 \cdots a_n$	$A \equiv$ "attacks a_1 through a_n done"	Inhibiting attack	D / d a	$D \equiv$ "either defence d done or else attack a not done"
Or defence	D / $d_1 \cdots d_n$	$D \equiv$ "one of the defences d_1 through d_n done"	Sequential and attack	A / $a_1 \cdots a_n$	$A \equiv$ "done attack a_1, then attack a_2, ... then attack a_n"
Counter defence	A / a d	$A \equiv$ "attack a done and defence d not done"	Failed reactive defence	A / a d	$A \equiv$ "done attack a and then did not do defence d"

describes instead the *order* in which events must take place. Thus, SAND gates *enforce* sequential events and rule out parallel executions: this is a fundamental construct in multi-agent systems. For instance, Steal Jewels (SJ) in Fig. 1 is modelled with an AND gate. Let break-in (bi) take 10 min and force the display (fd) 5 min. If two attackers cooperate, an ADTree analysis could conclude that attack SJ succeeds after 10 min. But fd depends logically on bi, since the display can only be forced after breaking in. Using instead a SAND gate for SJ enforces this sequentiality so that attacks cannot take less than 15 min. We integrate such SAND gates in our ADTree framework, as the *sequential and attack* in Table 1.

We further introduce SCAND gates: sequential gates that have attacks and defences as children. To the best of our knowledge, this is novel in a typed setting where subtrees (rather than leaves) can be assigned attack/defence goals. This contribution is conservative: it extends the SAND gates of [18] to coincide with previous works on sequential operators in defence-aware representations, e.g. Attack-Defence Diagrams [16]. We distinguish two scenarios: a successful attack followed by a failed counter defence (*failed reactive defence* in Table 1), and vice versa. We disregard the second scenario as uninteresting—it models defence goals which depend on attacks failing by themselves—and focus on the first one. SCANDs then model an attack goal that must overcome some counter defence, triggered only after the incoming attack has been detected.

2.2 Attributes and Agents for ADTrees

Attributes (also "parameters" and "gains" [8,10,25]) are numeric properties of attack/defence nodes that allow for quantitative analyses. Typical attributes include cost and time: in the Steal Jewels example, the 10 min to break in is a time attribute of this attack leaf. In general, attributes are associated only with tree leaves, and used to compute e.g. the min/max time required by an attack.

General Attributes. We extend attributes, from leaves, to all nodes in ADTrees, because a node need not be fully described by its children. An attribute is then given by a node's *intrinsic value*, and a *computation function*. For example, refine bi to be an AND gate between pick main lock (pml, 7 min) and saw padlock (sp, 2 min). Then it may take an extra minute to enter and locate the correct display, counted after pml and sp finished. In general, when the goal of a gate is successful, its attribute value is the result of its computation function applied to its intrinsic value and to the attributes of its children. For bi, if two burglars cooperate, the computation function is $init\_time(\texttt{bi}) + \max(init\_time(\texttt{pml}), init\_time(\texttt{sp}))$. This allows for flexibility in describing different kinds of attributes, and gains special relevance when considering coalitions of agents, as we will further illustrate in Sect. 2.3. Moreover, attributes can be *parameters* as in [5]. We can synthesise constraints over parameters, such as $init\_time(\texttt{bi}) \leqslant 1$ min, e.g. to determine which attribute values make an attack successful.

Agents. Each action described by an ADTree construct can be performed by a particular *agent*. Different attacks/defences could be handled by one or multiple agents, which allows to express properties on agents coalitions. For instance, in the Steal Jewels example of Fig. 1b, the minimal number of burglars required to minimise the SJS attack time is two: one to do bi and another to parallelly perform fd. If the SJ gate is changed to a SAND, then one burglar suffices, since bi and fd cannot be parallelised. Upon using the refinement bi = AND(pml, sp), then again a coalition of two burglars minimises the attack time, since pml and sp can be parallelised. Each node in the ADTree will thus be assigned to an agent, and a single agent can handle multiple nodes. In the general case, the only constraint is that no agent handles both attack and defence nodes. Notice that even modern formalisms for ADTrees such as [13] are oblivious of agents distributions: encoding them requires modifying the tree structure, e.g. changing an AND for a SAND to enforce the sequential occurrence of actions (i.e. they are carried out by the same agent). As we show in Sect. 4 and demonstrate empirically in Sect. 6, our semantics decouples the attack structure from the agent distribution. This permits to analyse and synthesise which distribution optimises a goal, e.g. achieve the fastest attack, without tampering with the ADTree model. Users can thus focus exclusively on the relevant studies of agent coalitions: this entails less error-prone and shorter computation times than in formalisms where agent distributions must be hacked into the ADTree structure.

Conditional Counter Measures. It may happen that a countering node has a successful or unsuccessful outcome depending on the attributes of its children. We therefore associate *conditions* with countering nodes, which are Boolean functions over the attributes of the ADTree. When present, the condition then comes as an additional constraint for the node operation to be successful.

2.3 Example: Treasure Hunters

Our simple running example in Fig. 2 features thieves that try to steal a treasure in a museum. To achieve their goal, they first must access the treasure room, which involves bribing a guard (b), and forcing the secure door (f). Both actions are costly and take some time. Two coalitions are possible: either a single thief has to carry out both actions, or a second thief could be hired to parallelise b and f. After these actions succeed the attacker/s can steal the treasure (ST), which takes a little time for opening its display stand and putting it in a bag. If the two-thieves coalition is used, we encode in ST an extra € 90 to hire the second thief—the computation function of the gate can handle this plurality—else ST incurs no extra cost. Then the thieves are ready to flee (TF), choosing an escape route to get away (GA): this can be a spectacular escape in a helicopter (h), or a mundane one via the emergency exit (e). The helicopter is expensive but fast while the emergency exit is slower but at no cost. Furthermore, the time to perform a successful escape could depend on the number of agents involved in the robbery. Again, this can be encoded via computation functions in gate GA.

As soon as the treasure room is penetrated (i.e. after b and f but before ST) an alarm goes off at the police station, so while the thieves flee the police hurries to intervene (p). The treasure is then successfully stolen iff the thieves have fled and the police failed to arrive or does so too late. This last possibility is captured by the condition associated with the treasure stolen gate (TS), which states that the arrival time of the police must be greater than the time for the thieves to steal the treasure and go away.

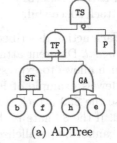

(a) ADTree

Name	Cost	Time
TS (treasure stolen)		
p (police)	€ 100	10 min
TF (thieves fleeing)		
ST (steal treasure)	€ {0, 90}	2 min
b (bribe gatekeeper)	€ 500	1 h
f (force arm. door)	€ 100	2 h
GA (get away)		
h (helicopter)	€ 500	3 min
e (emergency exit)		10 min

Condition for TS:
$init\_time(p) > init\_time(ST) + time(GA)$

(b) Attributes of nodes

Fig. 2. The treasure hunters

3 AMAS

Asynchronous Multi-Agent Systems (AMAS [17]) are a modern semantic model for the study of agents' strategies in asynchronous systems. They provide an analysis framework with efficient reachability checks even on non-trivial models. Technically, AMAS are similar to networks of automata that synchronise on shared actions, and interleave local transitions to execute asynchronously [12,17,27]. However, to deal with agents coalitions, automata semantics (e.g. for ADTrees) must resort to algorithms and additional attributes. In contrast, by linking protocols to agents, AMAS are a natural compositional formalism to analyse multi-agent systems.

Definition 1 (Asynchronous Multi-Agent Systems [17]**).** *An asynchronous multi-agent system (AMAS) consists of n agents $A = \{1, \ldots, n\}$, where
each agent has an associated tuple $A_i = (L_i, \iota_i, Act_i, P_i, T_i)$ including (i) a set of
local states $L_i = \{l_i^1, l_i^2, \ldots, l_i^{n_i}\}$; (ii) an initial state $\iota_i \in L_i$; (iii) a set of actions
$Act_i = \{a_i^1, a_i^2, \ldots, a_i^{m_i}\}$; (iv) a local protocol $P_i: L_i \rightarrow 2^{Act_i}$ which selects the
actions available at each local state; and (v) a (partial) local transition function
$T_i \subseteq L_i \times Act_i \times L_i$ s.t. $(l_i, a, l_i') \in T_i$ for some $l_i' \in L_i$ iff $a \in P_i(l_i)$.*

Sets Act_i need not be disjoint. $Act = \bigcup_{i \in A} Act_i$ and $Loc = \bigcup_{i \in A} L_i$ are
resp. the set of all actions and all local states. For each action $a \in Act$, set
$Agent(a) = \{i \in A \mid a \in Act_i\}$ has all agents that can perform action a. The
parallel composition of AMAS is given by Interleaved Interpreted Systems,
which extend AMAS with propositional variables and define *global-states* and
-transitions.

Definition 2 (Interleaved Interpreted System [17]**).** *Let PV be a set of
propositional variables. An* interleaved interpreted system (IIS)*is an AMAS
extended with (i) a set of global states $S \subseteq \prod_{i=1}^n L_i$; (ii) an initial state $\iota \in S$;
(iii) a (partial) global transition function $T: S \times Act \rightarrow S$ s.t. $\forall i \in Agent(a)$,
$T(s_1, a) = s_2$ iff $T_i(s_1^i, a) = s_2^i$, whereas $\forall i \in A \backslash Agent(a)$, $s_1^i = s_2^i$, where s_1^i is
the i-th local state of s_1; and (iv) a valuation function $V: S \rightarrow 2^{PV}$.*

4 Extending the AMAS Model

As defined in [17], AMAS do not include attributes. Therefore, to model ADTrees
we now define *Extended AMAS*, associating attributes with local transitions.

Definition 3 (Extended Asynchronous Multi-Agent Systems). *An*
Extended Asynchronous Multi-Agent System (EAMAS) *is an AMAS where
each local transition function $t \in LT = \bigcup_{i \in A} T_i$ has a finite set of variables
$AT_t = \{v_t^1, \ldots, v_t^k\}$ (attributes) over a domain $D_t = d_t^1 \times \cdots \times d_t^k$.*

*Let $AT = \bigcup_{t \in T} AT_t$ and $D = \prod_{t \in T} D_t$. Let Guards be the set of formulæ
of the form $\beta \sim 0$, where β is a linear expression over attributes of AT and
$\sim \in \{<, \leqslant, =, \geqslant, >\}$. Let M be the set of all messages, FUN be all functions
taking arguments in AT, and $EXP(AT, FUN)$ be linear expressions over AT
and FUN. Each transition $t \in LT$ has associated: (i) a message $f_M(t) \in (\{!, ?\} \times
M) \cup \{\perp\}$; (ii) a guard $f_G(t) \in Guards$; (iii) an update function $f_t: AT_t \rightarrow
EXP(AT, FUN)$.*

Item (i) indicates whether transition t does not synchronise ($\perp$), or sends
(marked with !) or receives (?) a message m. For ADTrees, $m \in M = \{ok, nok\}$.
Guards in item (ii) constrain transitions. item (iii) states how taking a transition
modifies the associated attributes. To model ADTrees we further extend IIS.

Definition 4 (Extended Interleaved Interpreted System). *Let PV be
a set of propositional variables, $\mathbf{v}: AT \rightarrow D$ a valuation of the attributes, and
$\mathbf{v}_0$ an initial valuation. An* extended interleaved interpreted system (EIIS), *or*

a model, is an EAMAS extended with (i) a set of global states $S \subseteq L_1 \times \cdots \times L_n \times D$; *(ii) an* initial state $s_0 = \langle(\iota_1,\ldots,\iota_n),\mathbf{v}_0\rangle \in S$; *(iii) a* global transition relation $T \subseteq S \times Act \times S$ *s.t.* $\langle(l_1,\ldots,l_n,\mathbf{v}),a,(l'_1,\ldots,l'_n,\mathbf{v}')\rangle \in T$ *iff: either A):* $|Agent(a)| = 1 \wedge \exists t_i = (l_i,a,l'_i) \in T_i$ *for* $i \in Agent(a) \wedge \forall k \in A\backslash\{i\}$ $l_k = l'_k \wedge \mathbf{v} \models f_G(t_i) \wedge \mathbf{v}' = \mathbf{v}[AT_{t_i}]$; *or B):* **(a)** $\exists i,j \in Agent(a) \wedge \exists t_i = (l_i,a,l'_i) \in T_i \wedge \exists t_j = (l_j,a,l'_j) \in T_j$ *s.t.* $f_M(t_i) = (!,m) \wedge f_M(t_j) = (?,m)$; **(b)** $\forall k \in A\backslash\{i,j\}$ $l_k = l'_k$; **(c)** $\mathbf{v} \models f_G(t_i) \wedge f_G(t_j)$; **(d)** $\mathbf{v}' = \mathbf{v}[AT_{t_i}][AT_{t_j}]$, *where* AT_{t_i} *and* AT_{t_j} *are disjoint; and (iv) a* valuation function $V : S \to 2^{PV}$. *In item* **(d)**, $\mathbf{v}[AT_{t_i}][AT_{t_j}]$ *indicates the substitution of attributes in the valuation* $\mathbf{v}$ *according to transitions* t_i *and* t_j, *that is* $\mathbf{v}' = \mathbf{v}\left[\bigwedge_{v_{t_i} \in AT_{t_i}} v_{t_i} := f_{t_i}(v_{t_i})\right]\left[\bigwedge_{v_{t_j} \in AT_{t_j}} v_{t_j} := f_{t_j}(v_{t_j})\right]$.

In the definition of the global transition relation T, item **(a)** specifies the synchronisation of transition t_i (with a sending action) and t_j (with a receiving action) that share the message m. Item **(b)** ensures that agents other than i and j do not change their states in such a synchronisation. Item **(c)** guarantees that the guards of t_i and t_j hold for the valuation $\mathbf{v}$. Finally, item **(d)** indicates how $\mathbf{v}'$ is obtained by updating $\mathbf{v}$ with the attributes values modified by t_i and t_j.

5   EAMAS Transformation of ADTrees

We give formal semantics to ADTrees as EIIS. For that, we model ADTree nodes as EAMAS via *transformation patterns*. The resulting EAMAS synchronise with each other via shared actions. Note that unlike formalisms such as Timed Automata where clocks let time elapse, time in EAMAS is an attribute.

We show that this compositional approach is correct, i.e. *complete*—all relevant ADTree paths are captured by the model—and *sound*—no new paths are introduced leading to a node's goal. Moreover, these semantics are amenable to state-space reductions [21], and naturally support shared subtrees in the ADTree, all of which favours its use in practical scenarios.

5.1   Transformation Patterns

Table 2 shows each ADTree construct transformed into one agent (sub-) model. In this compositional modelling approach, agents communicate via the blue transitions. Transformations are symmetrical for attack and defence nodes: Table 2 shows attack patterns. A leaf signals action a iff it succeeds. Self-loops in states l_A, l_N synchronise with all nodes that depend on this node (leaf or gate). Thus our semantics can model ADTrees where gates share children. An AND gate succeeds when all actions occur, in any order. Then attack A occurs, followed by a broadcast of signal $!A\_ok$ by the AND gate. The AND fails if any action of a child fails. OR, CAND, and COR operate in the expected analogous way. Models for SAND and SCAND enforce the absence of parallelism, as per their semantics in Sect. 2.1.

Table 2. ADTree nodes and corresponding agent models

To go from the initial to a final state, EAMAS patterns in Table 2 use one order of actions. We now show that this order represents all orderings of actions that make the attack/defence succeed. That is, our semantics is complete, in that it captures all paths of successful attacks/defences—see also [6].

Theorem 1 (Completeness). *Let $a_1, \ldots, a_n$ be the children of the ADTree gate A with EAMAS models $M_{a_1}, \ldots, M_{a_n}, M_A$ resp. Let A succeed when $a_{i_1} \cdots a_{i_m}$ finalise (succeeding or failing) in that order. If the EAMAS models $M_{a_{i_j}}$ finalise in the same order, then M_A transits from its initial state l_0 to its final state l_A.*

Proof. First note that if node x finalises, its EAMAS model will send *either* $!x\_ok$ or $!x\_nok$. Moreover, due to the self-loops in the end states, this happens infinitely often. Thus, if nodes $a_{i_1} a_{i_2} \cdots a_{i_m}$ finalise, actions $!a_{i_1}\_ok, !a_{i_2}\_ok, \ldots,$ $!a_{i_m}\_ok$ (or the corresponding $!a_*\_nok$) will be signaled infinitely often. By hypothesis, gate A succeeds when $a_{i_1} \cdots a_{i_m}$ finalise in that order. All patterns in Table 2 have (at least) one sequence of actions $?a_{j_1}\_ok \cdots ?a_{j_k}\_ok$ (or $?a_*\_nok$) that take it from l_0 to l_A. By the first argument, all actions in the sequence of M_A are signaled infinitely often. M_A will then transit from l_0 to l_A.

This covers *expected* actions that a parent must receive from its children to achieve its goal. For *unexpected* sequences of signals, a parent may not react to all information from its children—e.g. a CAND gate that after $?a\_ok$ receives (unexpectedly) $?d\_ok$. In such scenarios the model cannot reach its final state, entering a deadlock. This means that the model of A cannot signal its $!A\_ok$ action. Notice that this is exactly what should happen, because such unexpected sequences actually inhibit the goal of node A. To formally complete this argument, we now prove that the transformations of Table 2 are sound. That is, that all paths (of actions) that make the model of a node A signal $!A\_ok$, correspond to an ordered sequence of finalising children of A that make it reach its goal.

Theorem 2 Soundness). *Let $a_1, \ldots, a_n$ be the children of the ADTree gate A with EAMAS models $M_{a_1}, \ldots, M_{a_n}, M_A$ respectively. Let the sequence of actions $?a_{i_1}\_s_{i_1} ?a_{i_2}\_s_{i_2} \cdots ?a_{i_m}\_s_{i_m}$ take M_A from its initial state l_0 to its final state l_A, where $s_j \in \{ok, nok\}$. Then the corresponding ordered success or failure of the children $a_{i_1}, \ldots, a_{i_m}$ make the ADTree gate A succeed.*

Proof. First, observe that the reduced models in Table 2 are subsets of the *full models*—which consider all possible interleavings of synchronisation messages from child nodes. Thus, any path π in a reduced model also appears in the corresponding full model. Moreover, inspecting Tables 1 and 2 shows that, in the full model $\overline{M}_A$ of gate A, a path of actions $?a_i\_s_i$ (from children a_i of A) that transit from l_0 to l_A, encodes the ordered finalisation of these children that make the ADTree A succeed. Our hypothesis is the existence of a path π of actions in (the reduced model) M_A, that take this EAMAS from l_0 to l_A. By the first argument, π is also a path in (the full model) $\overline{M}_A$. By the second argument, π encodes the ordered finalisation of children c of A that make this gate succeed.

5.2   Adding Node Attributes

Transformation patterns in Table 2 concern only an ADTree *structure*. To take the value of *attributes* into account, a child must transmit these to all parents.

Attributes and Computation Functions. Attributes attached to a node are given by the intrinsic value and computation function of the node—see Sect. 2.2 and the EAMAS update function in item (iii) of Definition 3. For example, the cost of an AND gate is typically its own cost plus those of all children. Attributes values are computed only after all the preconditions of the node are satisfied. OR gates involve a choice among children: here, computation happens upon receiving the message from one child. Conditions associated with ADTree countering nodes (e.g. TS in Fig. 2) are added as guards to the corresponding action transition.

Distribution of Agents over Nodes. Computation functions are a versatile solution to analyse agents coalitions. For instance, the attack time of an AND gate can depend on the number of agents (within the attack party) that cooperate to execute its children. This can be different for the attack *cost* of the same AND gate, and for the attack time of a SAND gate. We illustrate this in the following.

Example 1. In our running example—Fig. 2—the computation function for the attack time of the gate $ST = AND(b, f)$ can be generically expressed with binary functions f and g as $f(init\_time(ST), g(init\_time(b), init\_time(f)))$, where:

▶ $f = +$, since ST depends logically on the completion of both children nodes;
▶ g depends on the agent coalition: if we use a single thief for b and f then $g = +$, if we use two thieves then $g = \max$.

This duality of g is precisely the kind of analyses that our approach enables. ◆

In the general case, the children of a binary gate will be subtrees L and R rather than leaves, which allows for more complex computations of potential parallelism between the agents in L and R. For example, to model a worst-case scenario in an AND gate with a set of agents A, let $A_L \subseteq A$ (resp. $A_R \subseteq A$) be all agents from subtree L (resp. R). Then let the attack time of the AND be either:

▶ *the sum* of the times of L and R if $A_L \cap A_R \neq \varnothing$, because then some agent is used in both children and thus full parallelism cannot be ensured;
▶ *the maximum* between these times otherwise, since L and R are independent.

Notice that these considerations also cover cases where gates share children, e.g. $A_L \cap A_R \neq \varnothing$ above. The main advantage of computations functions—and our semantics in general—w.r.t. other approaches in the literature is that agents coalitions that are internal to an attack or defence party can be modelled in any desired way. In [6] and https://up13.fr/?VvxUgNCK we give more examples.

6   Experiments

Two state-of-the-art verification tools are used to exercise our approach and provide an empirical demonstration of its capabilities:

– UPPAAL [11] is a model-checker for real-time systems. Automata templates are declared in its GUI and given semantics as Priced Time Automata. A full model is an automata network built from the instantiation of the templates, which can be queried using PCTL-like formulæ.

– IMITATOR [4] is a model-checker for Parametric Timed Automata [3], that implements full-synchronisation semantics on the shared transition labels of the automata in the model. Moreover, IMITATOR can synthesise parameter constraints e.g. to find the values of attributes so that an attack is feasible.

The GUI of UPPAAL permits straightforward implementations of our transformation patterns: compare the pattern for the SCAND gate (last row in Table 2) with its corresponding UPPAAL template (Fig. 3). Furthermore, the instantiation of

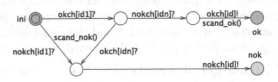

Fig. 3. UPPAAL template for SCAND pattern

templates to define the full model ("system declarations") makes it easy to describe the ADTree structure, as well as the agents distribution via an array. Our UPPAAL models are available as XML files in https://up13.fr/?VvxUgNCK.

In turn, the open source tool IMITATOR [2] can use symbolic computations to find out the values of attributes that permit or prevent an attack. So for instance, instead of stating that the police takes 10 min to arrive, our running example could have the time t_p set as a parameter variable. Checking when the attack fails results in IMITATOR outputting a set of constraints, e.g. $\{t_p \leqslant 5\}$.

We implemented the tool adt2amas [1] to execute our transformation process automatically. The tool receives as input the ADTree model and recursively applies the transformation rules. Then, it compiles the generated EAMAS model into the format of the tool IMITATOR. Our tool also generates a PDF file with the EAMAS model—see e.g. Fig. 5 in [6] and also https://up13.fr/?VvxUgNCK.

6.1   Case Studies

The two above mentioned tools were used to analyse 3 literature case studies, detailed in https://up13.fr/?VvxUgNCK and [6]. These case studies were chosen so that their ADTree structures are easy to present and grasp by the readers. Notice that our approach can scale to much larger state spaces as shown in [21].

Forestalling a software release is based on a real-world attack to the intellectual property of a company from a competitor that wants to be "the first to market" [10]. We follow [24] where software extraction and deployment by the competitor must occur before the lawful company deploys its own product.

Compromise IoT device describes an attack to an Internet-of-Things device via wireless or wired LAN. The attacker accesses the LAN, acquires credentials, and then exploits software vulnerabilities to run a malicious script. Our ADTree adds defence nodes on top of the attack trees used in [25].

Obtain admin privileges models a hacker trying to escalate privileges in a UNIX system, via physical access to an already logged-in CLI or remote access (attacking SysAdmin). This well known case study [19,23,24,29] has a branching structure: all gates but one are OR in the original tree of [29]. We enrich this with the SAND gates of [24], and further add reactive defences.

Table 3. Quantitative results for ADTrees implementations: ORIGIN VS. EAMAS

Number of attack agents:		Time of an attack				Cost of an attack			
		min		max		min		max	
		1	2	1	2	1	2	1	2
treasure hunters	ORIGIN	–	125 min	–	132 min	–	€690	–	€1190
	EAMAS	185 min	125 min	185 min	125 min	€1100	€1190	€1100	€1190
forestall	ORIGIN	–	43 days	–	55 days	–	€4k	–	€10.5k
	EAMAS	43 days	43 days	55 days	55 days	€4k	€4k	€7.5k	€7.5k
iot-dev	ORIGIN	–	694 min	–	695 min	–	€270	–	€380
	EAMAS	784 min	694 min	1114 min	694 min	€270	€270	€320	€320
gain-admin	ORIGIN	–	2942 min	–	23070 min	–	€100	–	€15820
	EAMAS	2942 min	2942 min	23070 min	23070 min	€100	€100	€6000	€6000

6.2 Experimentation Setup

We computed the cost and time of attacks of four ADTrees: one corresponding to our running example, plus one for each case study. Each tree was implemented: 1) in IMITATOR using the patterns of Table 2 (we call this "EAMAS"); 2) in UPPAAL using the same patterns (also "EAMAS"); and 3) in UPPAAL using the original templates of [24, 25] that employ clocks and time constraints, extended to fit Sect. 6.1 ("ORIGIN"). Such triple implementation pursues two goals:

(a) *verify correctness*, checking that the results of reachability ("can the attack succeed?") and quantitative queries ("what is the time of the fastest possible attack?", "what is the lowest cost incurred?") coincide between the ORIGIN and EAMAS implementations, regardless of the tool used;
(b) *demonstrate our contributions*: studying the impact of agent coalitions on quantitative metrics such as minimal attack time/cost; and synthesising the parameter valuations rendering an attack feasible.

6.3 Verifying Correctness

To achieve goal (a) we queried the min/max time and cost of attacks for each ADTree: Table 3 summarises our results. For all ADTrees, all queries on the EAMAS implementations in IMITATOR and in UPPAAL yielded the same values, thus the joint name "EAMAS". In the running example, adding the constraint on the police (associated with TS) would impact the structure of the ORIGIN model too much, and thus this constraint was only implemented in the EAMAS versions.

Six values in Table 3 (underlined) differ between the EAMAS and ORIGIN implementations of an ADTree. For max cost this is because the ORIGIN models consider all possible actions for maximisation, unnecessary for e.g. OR gates. An EAMAS model by default considers a single attack in such cases, but it can mimic ORIGIN if one forces the occurrence of all attacks (even for OR gates).

The correct max time of iot-dev with 2 agents is the one for EAMAS: 694 min, via attacks CPN, GVC, esv, and rms. We suspect that the ORIGIN UPPAAL implementation yields an imprecise result due to the use of non-discrete clocks and our remark *i)* on UPPAAL's time abstractions when clock variables are used.

In treasure hunters, the time condition for TS (see Fig. 2) is much more difficult to model in UPPAAL with clocks than in the EAMAS model where time is an attribute. The value € 690 in the ORIGIN model is incorrect because it uses e (emergency gate), which would be too slow to get away from an alerted police.

Table 3 also shows initial experiments with agents: we used one or two attackers, in the latter case setting the time-optimal agent distribution. This distribution was chosen according to the structure of the tree; so for instance when two attackers are used in the iot-dev case study, we set different agents for the leaves of gate APN, allowing attacks CPN and GVC to run in parallel.

Such agents coalitions were easily encoded (as arrays) in the EAMAS models. In contrast, the ORIGIN ADTree implementations use clock variables and constraints to encode the duration of attacks/defences. This approach—standard in verification of real time systems—has two drawbacks when analysing ADTrees:

i) UPPAAL uses abstractions and approximations for time zones that rule out decidability in the general case. Thus, queries (e.g. "is an attack feasible?") result in "may be true/false". In contrast, EAMAS transformations are untimed and verification is exact. The price to pay is a larger state space (which we did not reduce but see [21]) and approx. thrice-longer computation times.

ii) Unless explicitly encoded in each gate, time elapses simultaneously for all clocks. This is equivalent to having an agent for each tree node. Thus, modelling dependent node executions requires e.g. using a SAND gate rather than an AND gate. This contaminates the structure of the ADTree with the distribution of the agents that perform the actions. In contrast, EAMAS can keep the ADTree structure unmodified while studying agents coalitions.

Remark *ii)* makes it impossible to analyse one-agent coalitions in the ORIGIN implementations. Therefore, for each ADTree of Table 3, ORIGIN entries only have results for the maximum number of time-parallelisable agents in that tree.

6.4 Playing with Agents Coalitions

In the running example, the min/max times differ for one and two agents, and an extra cost (€ 90) is incurred when the second agent is used. In contrast, the forestall and gain-admin case studies are intrinsically sequential, hence attack times (and cost) are unaffected by the number of agents.

The iot-dev case study behaves similar to the running example when adding an extra agent. However, the minimal time decreases when an agent handles the CPN subtree while the other one is assigned to gc. Since gc has a longer duration than any option in the CPN subtree, the choice it makes does not change the operation time. With one agent, both gc and an option of CPN are achieved by the same agent, leading to different min and max times, depending on the choice.

Figure 4 shows attack times for a different ADTree (that can be found in https://up 13.fr/?VvxUgNCK and also in [6]) where changing the agents coalition has a larger impact in attack metrics. The chart shows the fastest and slowest attack times achieved with different assign-

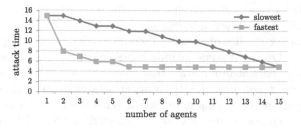

Fig. 4. Scaling w.r.t. the assignment of agents

ments of agents to nodes, where all nodes take 1 time unit to complete.

These times coincide when there is a single agent, or one agent per node, since then there is only one way to assign agents to nodes. Instead, in the middle cases, the difference between fastest and slowest attack varies substantially for different agents coalitions. Such difference would be exacerbated by more heterogeneous time attributes in the nodes. The analyses enabled by our approach show that the fastest attack can be achieved using only 6 agents.

6.5   Parameter Synthesis

We also experimented with the parametric capabilities offered by IMITATOR:

Treasure Hunters: "To catch the thieves, what is the maximum time the police can take to arrive?" Answering this question requires synthesising a value for the time attribute of the p node, which becomes a model *parameter*. IMITATOR computed that the police can take at most 5 min to prevent the burglary.

Case Studies: an attack is successful if its associated defence was slower. (*i*) for forestall, id should take at most 1 day to block NA—since NAS is a *failed reactive defence*, id is triggered as soon as heb succeeds, and must finish faster than the intrinsic time of NA; (*ii*) for iot-dev, inc is effective iff it takes at most 3 min; (*iii*) for gain-admin we proved that whatever the time for tla, an attack is feasible (as GSAP is a disjunction), hence the other defences are required.

7   Conclusion and Future Work

We revisited Attack-Defence Trees under a unified syntax, extending the usual constructs with a new sequential counter-operator (SCAND). More importantly we introduced EAMAS, an agent-aware formalism to model ADTrees, and trans-formation patters from the latter to the former that are sound, complete, and preserve the compositionality of ADTrees, naturally covering cases with shared subtrees. The impact of different agent coalitions on attack time and cost was evaluated using UPPAAL and IMITATOR. Finally, the feasibility of an attack was evaluated through parameter synthesis with IMITATOR, to obtain the attribute values of ADTree nodes that make an attack succeed. Our experiments show that (and how) different agent distributions affect the time of attacks/defence strategies, possibly rendering some infeasible. We expect this will open the gate to richer studies of security scenarios, with multiple agents that can collaborate.

Our next goals include logics to express properties in EAMAS, and adapting the *partial order reduction* from [17] as well as the *state space reduction for tree topologies* of [21] to agent strategies in EAMAS, including extensions to parametric timing information. This will allow for studying the strategic abilities of agents, ultimately in a parametric setting. Finally, we will add support for agents assignment to our tool `adt2amas` that transforms ADTrees into EAMAS.

References

1. ADT2AMAS. https://depot.lipn.univ-paris13.fr/parties/tools/adt2amas
2. IMITATOR. https://www.imitator.fr
3. Alur, R., Henzinger, T., Vardi, M.: Parametric real-time reasoning. In: ACM Symposium on Theory of Computing, pp. 592–601. ACM (1993). https://doi.org/10.1145/167088.167242
4. André, É., Fribourg, L., Kühne, U., Soulat, R.: IMITATOR 2.5: a tool for analyzing robustness in scheduling problems. In: Giannakopoulou, D., Méry, D. (eds.) FM 2012. LNCS, vol. 7436, pp. 33–36. Springer, Heidelberg (2012). https://doi.org/10.1007/978-3-642-32759-9_6
5. André, É., Lime, D., Ramparison, M., Stoelinga, M.: Parametric analyses of attack-fault trees. In: ACSD 2019, pp. 33–42. IEEE (2019). https://doi.org/10.1109/ACSD.2019.00008
6. Arias, J., Budde, C.E., Penczek, W., Petrucci, L., Sidoruk, T., Stoelinga, M.: Hackers vs. security: attack-defence trees as asynchronous multi-agent systems. HAL (2020). https://hal.archives-ouvertes.fr/hal-02902348
7. Arnold, F., Guck, D., Kumar, R., Stoelinga, M.: Sequential and parallel attack tree modelling. In: Koornneef, F., van Gulijk, C. (eds.) SAFECOMP 2015. LNCS, vol. 9338, pp. 291–299. Springer, Cham (2015). https://doi.org/10.1007/978-3-319-24249-1_25
8. Aslanyan, Z., Nielson, F.: Pareto efficient solutions of attack-defence trees. In: Focardi, R., Myers, A. (eds.) POST 2015. LNCS, vol. 9036, pp. 95–114. Springer, Heidelberg (2015). https://doi.org/10.1007/978-3-662-46666-7_6
9. Aslanyan, Z., Nielson, F., Parker, D.: Quantitative verification and synthesis of attack-defence scenarios. In: CSF 2016, pp. 105–119. IEEE (2016). https://doi.org/10.1109/CSF.2016.15
10. Buldas, A., Laud, P., Priisalu, J., Saarepera, M., Willemson, J.: Rational choice of security measures via multi-parameter attack trees. In: Lopez, J. (ed.) CRITIS 2006. LNCS, vol. 4347, pp. 235–248. Springer, Heidelberg (2006). https://doi.org/10.1007/11962977_19
11. David, A., Larsen, K.G., Legay, A., Mikuvcionis, M., Poulsen, D.B.: UPPAAL SMC tutorial. Int. J. Softw. Tools Technol. Transf. **17**(4), 397–415 (2015). https://doi.org/10.1007/s10009-014-0361-y
12. Fagin, R., Halpern, J., Moses, Y., Vardi, M.: Reasoning About Knowledge. MIT Press, Cambridge (1995)
13. Fila, B., Widel, W.: Efficient attack-defense tree analysis using Pareto attribute domains. In: CSF 2019, pp. 200–215. IEEE (2019). https://doi.org/10.1109/CSF.2019.00021

14. Gadyatskaya, O., Hansen, R.R., Larsen, K.G., Legay, A., Olesen, M.C., Poulsen, D.B.: Modelling attack-defense trees using timed automata. In: Fränzle, M., Markey, N. (eds.) FORMATS 2016. LNCS, vol. 9884, pp. 35–50. Springer, Cham (2016). https://doi.org/10.1007/978-3-319-44878-7_3

15. Gribaudo, M., Iacono, M., Marrone, S.: Exploiting Bayesian networks for the analysis of combined attack trees. ENTCS **310**, 91–111 (2015). https://doi.org/10.1016/j.entcs.2014.12.014

16. Hermanns, H., Krämer, J., Krvcál, J., Stoelinga, M.: The value of attack-defence diagrams. In: Piessens, F., Viganò, L. (eds.) POST 2016. LNCS, vol. 9635, pp. 163–185. Springer, Heidelberg (2016). https://doi.org/10.1007/978-3-662-49635-0_9

17. Jamroga, W., Penczek, W., Dembinski, P., Mazurkiewicz, A.: Towards partial order reductions for strategic ability. In: AAMAS 2018, pp. 156–165. ACM (2018)

18. Jhawar, R., Kordy, B., Mauw, S., Radomirović, S., Trujillo-Rasua, R.: Attack trees with sequential conjunction. In: Federrath, H., Gollmann, D. (eds.) SEC 2015. IAICT, vol. 455, pp. 339–353. Springer, Cham (2015). https://doi.org/10.1007/978-3-319-18467-8_23

19. Jürgenson, A., Willemson, J.: Computing exact outcomes of multi-parameter attack trees. In: Meersman, R., Tari, Z. (eds.) OTM 2008. LNCS, vol. 5332, pp. 1036–1051. Springer, Heidelberg (2008). https://doi.org/10.1007/978-3-540-88873-4_8

20. Khand, P.: System level security modeling using attack trees. In: 2nd International Conference on Computer, Control and Communication, pp. 1–6 (2009). https://doi.org/10.1109/IC4.2009.4909245

21. Knapik, M., Penczek, W., Petrucci, L., Sidoruk, T.: Squeezing state spaces of (attack-defence) trees. In: ICECCS 2019. IEEE Computer Society (2019)

22. Kordy, B., Mauw, S., Radomirović, S., Schweitzer, P.: Attack-defense trees. J. Log. Comput. **24**(1), 55–87 (2014). https://doi.org/10.1093/logcom/exs029

23. Kordy, B., Piètre-Cambacédès, L., Schweitzer, P.: DAG-based attack and defense modeling: don't miss the forest for the attack trees. Comput. Sci. Rev. **13–14**, 1–38 (2014). https://doi.org/10.1016/j.cosrev.2014.07.001

24. Kumar, R., Ruijters, E., Stoelinga, M.: Quantitative attack tree analysis via priced timed automata. In: Sankaranarayanan, S., Vicario, E. (eds.) FORMATS 2015. LNCS, vol. 9268, pp. 156–171. Springer, Cham (2015). https://doi.org/10.1007/978-3-319-22975-1_11

25. Kumar, R., et al.: Effective analysis of attack trees: a model-driven approach. In: Russo, A., Schürr, A. (eds.) FASE 2018. LNCS, vol. 10802, pp. 56–73. Springer, Cham (2018). https://doi.org/10.1007/978-3-319-89363-1_4

26. Kumar, R., Stoelinga, M.: Quantitative security and safety analysis with attack-fault trees. In: HASE 2017, pp. 25–32. IEEE (2017)

27. Lomuscio, A., Penczek, W., Qu, H.: Partial order reductions for model checking temporal epistemic logics over interleaved multi-agent systems. In: AAMAS 2010, vol. 1–3, pp. 659–666. IFAAMAS (2010)

28. Sheyner, O., Haines, J., Jha, S., Lippmann, R., Wing, J.: Automated generation and analysis of attack graphs. In: Proceedings 2002 IEEE Symposium on Security and Privacy, pp. 273–284 (2002). https://doi.org/10.1109/SECPRI.2002.1004377

29. Weiss, J.: A system security engineering process. In: Proceedings of the 14th National Computer Security Conference, pp. 572–581 (1991)

30. Widel, W., Audinot, M., Fila, B., Pinchinat, S.: Beyond 2014: formal methods for attack tree-based security modeling. ACM Comp. Surv. **52**(4), 75:1–75:36 (2019). https://doi.org/10.1145/3331524

Robustness and Failure Detection in Epistemic Gossip Protocols

Kosei Fujishiro[✉] and Koji Hasebe

Department of Computer Science, University of Tsukuba,
1-1-1, Tennodai, Tsukuba 305-8573, Japan
fujishiro@mas.cs.tsukuba.ac.jp, hasebe@cs.tsukuba.ac.jp

Abstract. Gossip problem is an information dissemination problem in which networked agents (nodes) must share their secrets by the minimum number of calls. In recent years, to solve the problem, various epistemic gossip protocols have been proposed, where the agents decide who to call based on the higher-order knowledge about the possession of secrets. Although most previous studies on the epistemic gossip protocol have restricted their scope to the environments including only reliable agents, from the practical viewpoint, it is worthwhile investigating robust protocols against agent failure. In this paper, we assume the existence of unreliable agents and analyze the robustness of some existing protocols using epistemic logic. In our model, when an agent fails, it loses the secrets and telephone numbers gained by previous calls and returns to its initial state. In addition, during each call, agents share not only their possessing secrets but also the history of the transmission path of each secret. For these settings, we show that the protocols ANY and PIG are successful (i.e., the protocols always lead to the state where every agent knows all secrets). We also show that the protocol CO is not immediately successful under the assumption that agents can fail, but it becomes successful if the protocol execution satisfies some conditions. Furthermore, we clarify sufficient conditions for agents to detect the failure of other agent, which are useful for designing robust protocols.

1 Introduction

A gossip protocol determines a one-to-one communication (call) to share secrets among networked agents (nodes). This network is represented as a directed graph, where the edge from agent a to agent b indicates the relation that a knows the telephone number of b, i.e. a can call b. Initially, each agent only knows its own secret, and during each call, two agents share their secrets gained by previous calls. One of the main challenges with the gossip protocol is to find the shortest sequence of calls that leads to everyone knowing all secrets. The minimum length of sequence depends on the initial graph, and according to the early studies [9,11], it is $2n - 4$ for the complete graph, and $2n - 3$ for the other connected graphs for agents $n > 3$.

© Springer Nature Switzerland AG 2020
S.-W. Lin et al. (Eds.): ICFEM 2020, LNCS 12531, pp. 20–35, 2020.
https://doi.org/10.1007/978-3-030-63406-3_2

Recently, to solve the problem, various epistemic gossip protocols have been proposed [5,6]. In these protocols, an agent decides who to call based not only on the agent's knowledge about its possessing secrets and telephone numbers, but also on higher-order knowledge (i.e., the knowledge that the agent has about the knowledge of other agents). These studies also analyzed the conditions for the protocols to be successful (i.e., the protocols must achieve the state where every agent knows all secrets) using epistemic logic [8]. The results provide useful information for designing epistemic gossip protocols. However, most previous studies on epistemic gossip protocols have been limited to models consisting of only reliable agents, which were not realistic from a practical viewpoint. Therefore, to enhance the reliability of the protocols, it is worthwhile investigating the robustness against agent failure.

In this paper, we assume the existence of unreliable agents and analyze the robustness of some existing protocols in such a model using epistemic logic. Specifically, here we focus on the dynamic gossip protocols [6], where agents exchange not only their possessing secrets but also their telephone numbers when making a call. In our proposed model, when an agent fails, it loses the secrets previously learnt and returns to its initial state. In addition, during each call, agents share not only the secrets but also the history of the transmission path of each secret.

For these settings, we analyzed the protocols ANY (ANY call), PIG (Possible Information Growth), and CO (Call me Once), which were originally introduced by [6]. For the former two, we prove that these are successful even in the environment where agents can fail. On the other hand, for the latter protocol, we prove that it is not immediately successful, but it becomes successful if its execution satisfies some conditions. Furthermore, we clarify sufficient conditions for agents to detect the failure of other agents.

The contribution of this paper is twofold. First, we give a new model to analyze the robustness of epistemic gossip protocols. Second, we demonstrate a logical analysis of some epistemic gossip protocols and prove properties about the robustness and failure detection. Although we do not present a concrete robust protocol, our method is still useful in protocol verification and design.

The structure of this paper is as follows. Section 2 presents related work. Section 3 defines our model and the logic used for the protocol analysis. Section 4 shows some properties about robustness and failure detection in some existing epistemic gossip protocols. Finally, Sect. 5 concludes the paper and presents possible future directions.

2   Related Work

The earliest studies of the gossip problem date back to the 1970s [9,11]. (See also [10] for a survey summarizing results on the classic gossip problem and its variants as well as techniques to schedule centralized optimal calls).

In recent years, as an approach to the gossip problem, there have been a number of studies on the epistemic gossip protocol. Attamah et al. [2] have proposed a method for the autonomous distributed control of calls by epistemic gossip protocol and investigated its various extensions. Van Ditmarsch et al. [6,7] have presented some epistemic gossip protocols with dynamic setting, in which agents exchange both their secrets and telephone numbers when making a call. In [6,7], they introduced some successful protocols named ANY, CO, LNS, and PIG. Our model and analysis presented in this paper are extensions of the method proposed in the studies [6,7].

Apt et al. [1] provides a framework for formally analyzing the validity and termination of the epistemic gossip protocol of the merge-then-learn method and presents the protocol for complete graphs and ring graphs. On the other hand, in our study and in [6], the learn-then-merge method is adopted in which the information sent by each agent is acquired and then merged.

Cooper et al. [5] have extended the gossip problem by paying attention to epistemic depth. Specifically, they set a state about higher-order knowledge as a goal and investigate the optimal call scheduling for it. Unlike our research, their focus is on centralized scheduling.

Similar to our research, van den Berg [3] has assumed the existence of unreliable agents in the setting of dynamic gossip and investigated their effects and how to identify them. However, as a possible application, unlike our research, the prevention of the spread of fake news is emphasized. Therefore, the modeling of agent "unreliability" is different with ours. In that setting, there is a result that is similar to the one in this research that the existing protocol called LNS will not succeed owing to the existence of unreliable agents. It also describes the counterintuitive and interesting results about the difficulty of identifying unreliable agents.

This paper also analyzes the failure detection in an environment where agents can fail. Failure detection is a central research issue for ensuring the reliability of distributed systems. As an early important study, Chandra and Toueg [4] have argued the importance of failure detectors in distributed systems. This study defines two classes of failure detectors with the notions of completeness and correctness, and shows how they can be used to solve consensus problems in asynchronous systems where crash failures can occur.

3   Basic Concepts

In this section, we define our proposed model including unreliable agents and introduce epistemic logic used in protocol specification and analysis.

3.1   Modeling Agent Failure

Our model is obtained by adding events of agent failure to the model defined by [6]. We first define the set of events as follows.

Definition 1 (Event). Let xy denote the call from agent x to agent y and $[x_1 \ldots x_k]$ denote the simultaneous failure of agents $x_1, \ldots, x_k$. We write either

xy or yx as $\overline{xy}$. A call or an agent's failure is called an event. Let C and F be the sets of calls and failures, respectively. The set of events E is defined as $E = C \cup F$. We write $x \in e$ to denote that agent x is involved in the event e.

Protocol execution is modeled as a sequence of events defined below.

Definition 2 (Event sequence). The expression $e_1; e_2; \ldots; e_n$ is used to denote the sequence $e_1, e_2, \ldots, e_n$ of n events. E^* is the set of all event sequences. Throughout we also use some notations defined below.

- Empty sequence is denoted by ϵ.
- Semi-colon is also used to concatenate events or event sequences.
- $\sigma \sqsubseteq \tau$ indicates that either σ is a prefix of τ or $\sigma = \tau$.
- σ_n is used to denote the n-th event in the sequence of $\sigma \in E^*$
- $\sigma|n$ is used to denote the prefix of σ up to the n-th event.
- For each $x \in A$, σ_x is used to denote the subsequence of σ consisting of all σ_n which x is involved in.

In [6], during a call, agents exchange their secrets and telephone numbers gained by previous calls, while in our model, we assume that the history of the transmission path of each secret is also exchanged. This history is represented by a tree structure, called a memory tree, and is defined below.

Definition 3 (Memory tree). A memory tree is a binary tree defined as follows.

- Base Case: $\langle x \rangle$ is a memory tree for any $x \in A$.
- Ind. Step: if T and T' are memory trees, then $\langle T, xy, T' \rangle$ is a memory tree for any call xy.

We denote the root of a memory tree T by $r(T)$ and the set of all leaves by $leaves(T)$. For the memory tree T_x of agent x, $leaves(T_x)$ is the set of secrets owned by x. For $T = \langle T_1, xy, T_2 \rangle$, we define T_L and T_R as $T_L = T_1$ and $T_R = T_2$, respectively. We denote that T is a subtree of T' by $T \subseteq T'$.

Next, we define the gossip graph. The gossip graph is a directed graph indicating the agents' knowledge about their telephone numbers at a certain point in time. Formally, a gossip graph consists of a set A of agents, a binary relation N over A representing the agents' knowledge about telephone numbers, and a class $\{T_x\}_{x \in A}$ each of which represents the set of memory trees stored by an agent. Similar to the definition of [6], $(x, y) \in N$ means that x knows the telephone number of y. Throughout, we also use the notations Nxy and N_x to denote $(x, y) \in N$ and $\{y \in A \mid Nxy\}$, respectively.

Definition 4 (Gossip graph). A gossip graph is a tuple $G = (A, N, \{T_x\}_{x \in A})$, where A is a finite set of agents, N is a subset of $A \times A$ and T_x is a memory tree belonging to x. A gossip graph which satisfies $T_x = \langle x \rangle$ and $(x, x) \in N$ for any x is called an initial gossip graph. A gossip graph is weakly connected if in the graph (A, N) for any $x, y \in A$ there exists a directed path from x to y. A gossip graph is complete if $N = A \times A$. Agent x is called expert if $leaves(T_x) = A$.

A gossip graph that represents the initial state is called the initial gossip graph. Along with a protocol execution, a gossip graph starts with one of the initial gossip graphs and changes every time an event occurs. Intuitively, when a call occurs between agents, all information contained in each other's memory tree is shared, whereas when an agent fails, it loses the stored memory tree and returns to the initial state. These processes are formally defined as follows.

Definition 5 (Event-induced gossip graph). For an initial gossip graph $G = (A, N, \{T_x\}_{x \in A})$ and an event sequence σ, a new gossip graph $G^\sigma = (A, N^\sigma, \{T_x^\sigma\}_{x \in A})$ obtained by executing σ in G is defined as follows.

- Base Case: if $\sigma = \epsilon$, then $N^\epsilon = N$ and $T_x^\epsilon = T_x$ for all x. (Therefore, $G^\epsilon = G$).
- Ind. Step: if $\sigma = \sigma'; e$,
  - for the case where e is a call xy,

$$N_z^{\sigma';xy} = \begin{cases} N_x^{\sigma'} \cup N_y^{\sigma'} & (z \in \{x, y\}) \\ N_z^{\sigma'} & \text{(otherwise)} \end{cases}$$

$$T_z^{\sigma';xy} = \begin{cases} \langle T_x^{\sigma'}, xy, T_y^{\sigma'} \rangle & (z \in \{x, y\}) \\ T_z^{\sigma'} & \text{(otherwise)} \end{cases}$$

  - for the case where e is a failure $e = [x_1 \ldots x_k]$,

$$N_z^{\sigma';[x_1\ldots x_k]} = \begin{cases} N & (z \in \{x_1, \ldots, x_k\}) \\ N_z^{\sigma'} & \text{(otherwise)} \end{cases}$$

$$T_z^{\sigma';[x_1\ldots x_k]} = \begin{cases} T_z & (z \in \{x_1, \ldots, x_k\}) \\ T_z^{\sigma'} & \text{(otherwise)} \end{cases}$$

A call xy is said to be valid if the gossip graph $G = (A, N, \{T_x\}_{x \in A})$ satisfies Nxy. In addition, we consider the failure $[x_1 \ldots x_k]$ to be valid at G for any gossip graph G. Thus, it is assumed that the failure (in some cases, consecutively) occurs at any timing between calls. However, consecutive failures are regarded as one simultaneous failure. For example, $[x_1]; [x_2]; [x_3]$ is regarded to be the same as $[x_1x_2x_3]$. When any element σ_n of the sequence σ of events is valid in $G^{\sigma|n-1}$, σ is said to be valid in G.

Example 1. Consider the sequence $ab; [b]; ca$. Figure 1 shows event-induced graph G^σ for each prefix $\sigma \sqsubseteq ab; [b]; ca$. In the graphs of the leftmost column, each node labeled x represents agent x. Each dashed arrow from x to y represents Nxy, and solid one represents $y \in leaves(T_x^\sigma)$. Arrows to oneself is omitted. Each row corresponds to $G^\sigma = (A, N^\sigma, \{T_x^\sigma\}_{x \in A})$ for the same prefix σ.

The Gossip graph partially represents the knowledge of agents, but not the higher-order knowledge. Therefore, the higher-order knowledge of the agents in the epistemic gossip protocol is represented by the Kripke model (cf. [8]). A state (possible world) in the model is called a gossip state.

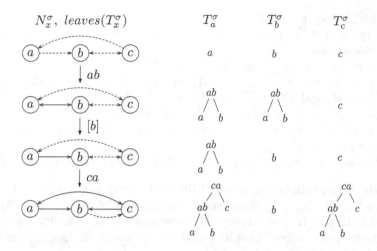

Fig. 1. Event-induced graphs for each prefix $\sigma \sqsubseteq ab; [b]; ca$

Definition 6 (Gossip state). A gossip state is a pair (G, σ) of an initial gossip graph G and a finite event sequence σ that is valid in G.

In our model, each agent assumes the initial gossip graph and the event sequence that realize the current gossip state on the basis of the following common knowledge.

- The set of agents is A.
- The gossip graph changes depending on events, as defined in the Definition 5.
- The graph when no event has occurred yet is one of the initial gossip graphs.
- When no event has occurred yet, each agent does not know the telephone numbers that the other agents know.
- Each agent does not know the protocols followed by the other agents.

The last statement being common knowledge means that the agent considers any valid sequence to be executable, although in reality not all valid sequences may be executed depending on the given protocol.

Based on the assumptions stated above, the notion of accessibility relation is defined below. Here, different relations are given for two types of call modes, asynchronous and synchronous call. Asynchronous call cannot be recognized by agents other than the calling agents. However, synchronous are recognized by all agents, but it is impossible to know who is calling. In either call mode, the failure of the other agents cannot be recognized. Furthermore, if (3) in Definitions 7 and 8 are assumed, the failure of oneself cannot be recognized.

Definition 7 (Asynchronous accessibility relation). Let $G = (A, N, \{T_x\}_{x \in A})$ and $H = (A, O, \{U_x\}_{x \in A})$ be initial gossip graphs, and let σ and τ be valid event sequences in G and H, respectively. The asynchronous accessibility relation $\sim_x$ is the reflexive, symmetric, transitive closure of binary relation $\sim'_x$ on gossip graphs defined as follows.

(1) $(G, \epsilon) \sim'_x (H, \epsilon)$ if $N_x = O_x$.
(2) For any $(\sigma, \tau) \neq (\epsilon, \epsilon)$, we have $(G, \sigma) \sim'_x (H, \tau)$ if any one of the following conditions hold:
  (a) $\sigma = \sigma'; yz$, $x \notin \{y, z\}$, and $(G, \sigma') \sim'_x (H, \tau)$;
  (b) $\sigma = \sigma'; yz$, $\tau = \tau'; yz$, $x \in \{y, z\}$, for each $u \in \{y, z\}$ it is the case that $N_u^{\sigma'} = O_u^{\tau'}$ and $T_u^{\sigma'} = U_u^{\tau'}$, and $(G, \sigma') \sim'_x (H, \tau')$;
  (c) $\sigma = \sigma'; [x_1 \ldots x_k]$, $x \notin \{x_1, \ldots, x_k\}$, and $(G, \sigma') \sim'_x (H, \tau)$;
  (d) $\sigma = \sigma'; [x_1 \ldots x_k]$, $\tau = \tau'; [y_1 \ldots y_l]$, $x \in \{x_1, \ldots, x_k\} \cap \{y_1, \ldots, y_l\}$, and $(G, \sigma') \sim'_x (H, \tau')$.
(3) (Optional) If $\sigma = \sigma'; [x_1 \ldots x_k]$ and $x \in \{x_1, \ldots, x_k\}$, then $(G, \sigma) \sim'_x (G, \epsilon)$.

Definition 8 (Synchronous accessibility relation). Let $G = (A, N, \{T_x\}_{x \in A})$ and $H = (A, O, \{U_x\}_{x \in A})$ be initial gossip graphs, and let σ and τ be valid event sequences in G and H, respectively. The synchronous accessibility relation $\approx_x$ is the reflexive, symmetric, transitive closure of binary relation $\approx'_x$ on gossip graphs defined as follows.

(1) $(G, \epsilon) \approx'_x (H, \epsilon)$ if $N_x = O_x$.
(2) For any $(\sigma, \tau) \neq (\epsilon, \epsilon)$ we have $(G, \sigma) \approx'_x (H, \tau)$ if any one of the following conditions hold:
  (a) $\sigma = \sigma'; yz$, $\tau = \tau'; uv$, $x \notin \{y, z, u, v\}$, and $(G, \sigma') \approx'_x (H, \tau')$;
  (b) $\sigma = \sigma'; yz$, $\tau = \tau'; yz$, $x \in \{y, z\}$, for each $u \in \{y, z\}$ it is the case that $N_u^{\sigma'} = O_u^{\tau'}$ and $T_u^{\sigma'} = U_u^{\tau'}$, and $(G, \sigma') \approx'_x (H, \tau')$;
  (c) $\sigma = \sigma'; [x_1 \ldots x_k]$, $x \notin \{x_1, \ldots, x_k\}$, and $(G, \sigma') \approx'_x (H, \tau)$;
  (d) $\sigma = \sigma'; [x_1 \ldots x_k]$, $\tau = \tau'; [y_1 \ldots y_l]$, $x \in \{x_1, \ldots, x_k\} \cap \{y_1, \ldots, y_l\}$, and $(G, \sigma') \approx'_x (H, \tau')$.
(3) (Optional) If $\sigma = \sigma'; [x_1 \ldots x_k]$ and $x \in \{x_1, \ldots, x_k\}$, then $(G, \sigma) \approx'_x (G, \epsilon)$.

The Kripke model, which is based on the accessibility relation and the gossip state defined above, is called the gossip model.

Definition 9 (Gossip model). Given a set of agents A, the asynchronous gossip model and the synchronous gossip model are respectively the tuples

$$\mathcal{G}^\sim = (\mathcal{G}, \langle \sim_a \rangle_{a \in A}, \langle \xrightarrow{e} \rangle_{e \in E}) \quad \text{and} \quad \mathcal{G}^\approx = (\mathcal{G}, \langle \approx_a \rangle_{a \in A}, \langle \xrightarrow{e} \rangle_{e \in E}),$$

where

 - $\mathcal{G}$ is the set of gossip states;
 - $\sim_a$ and $\approx_a$ are relations defined in 7 and 8;
 - $\xrightarrow{e}$ is the relation on $\mathcal{G}$ such that for any G where event e is valid and for any σ it is the case that $(G, \sigma) \xrightarrow{e} (G, \sigma; e)$.

3.2 Epistemic Logic

To specify and analyse protocols, we use epistemic logic defined below.

Definition 10 (Language). Given a set of agents A, the language $\mathcal{L}$ used to specify conditions of protocols is defined by the following BNF:

$$\varphi ::= \mathtt{N}(a,b) \mid \mathtt{S}(a,b) \mid \mathtt{C}(ab,c) \mid \mathtt{F}(a) \mid \neg\varphi \mid (\varphi \wedge \varphi) \mid K_a\varphi$$

where $a,b,c \in A$. We define connectives $\rightarrow$, $\vee$ and $\leftrightarrow$ in a standard way and denote the dual of K_a by $\hat{K}_a$.

Intuitively, $\mathtt{N}(a,b)$ means that a knows the telephone number of b. $\mathtt{S}(a,b)$ means that a knows the secret of b. $\mathtt{C}(ab,c)$ means that ab is included in the call involving c. $\mathtt{C}(ab,c)$ is false whenever c is neither a nor b, and $\mathtt{C}(ab,a)$ and $\mathtt{C}(ab,b)$ are true at (G,σ) when σ contains ab. $\mathtt{F}(a)$ indicates that a has failed at least once. $K_a\varphi$ means that a knows φ, and $\hat{K}_a\varphi$ means that a considers φ to be possible.

Formally, the truth conditions for the formulas are defined as follows.

Definition 11 (Semantics). Let $\mathcal{G}^{\sim} = (\mathcal{G}, \langle\sim_a\rangle_{a\in A}, \langle\xrightarrow{ab}\rangle_{a,b\in A})$ be an asynchronous gossip model. For any $(G,\sigma) \in \mathcal{G}$ with $G = (A, N, \{T_x\}_{x\in A})$ and for any formula φ in $\mathcal{L}$, we define $\mathcal{G}^{\sim}, (G,\sigma) \models \varphi$ by induction on φ as follows.

$$
\begin{aligned}
&\mathcal{G}^{\sim}, (G,\sigma) \models \top &&\text{iff}\quad \text{always} \\
&\mathcal{G}^{\sim}, (G,\sigma) \models \mathtt{N}(a,b) &&\text{iff}\quad N^{\sigma}ab \\
&\mathcal{G}^{\sim}, (G,\sigma) \models \mathtt{S}(a,b) &&\text{iff}\quad b \in leaves(T_a^{\sigma}) \\
&\mathcal{G}^{\sim}, (G,\sigma) \models \mathtt{C}(ab,c) &&\text{iff}\quad ab \in \sigma_c \\
&\mathcal{G}^{\sim}, (G,\sigma) \models \mathtt{F}(a) &&\text{iff}\quad [x_1\ldots x_k] \in \sigma \text{ and } a \in \{x_1,\ldots,x_k\} \\
&\mathcal{G}^{\sim}, (G,\sigma) \models \neg\varphi &&\text{iff}\quad \text{not } \mathcal{G}^{\sim}, (G,\sigma) \models \varphi \\
&\mathcal{G}^{\sim}, (G,\sigma) \models (\varphi_1 \wedge \varphi_2) &&\text{iff}\quad \mathcal{G}^{\sim}, (G,\sigma) \models \varphi_1 \text{ and } \mathcal{G}^{\sim}, (G,\sigma) \models \varphi_2 \\
&\mathcal{G}^{\sim}, (G,\sigma) \models K_a\varphi &&\text{iff}\quad \text{for any } (H,\tau) \text{ with } (G,\sigma) \sim_a (H,\tau), \\
& && \phantom{\text{iff}\quad} \text{we have } \mathcal{G}^{\sim}, (H,\tau) \models \varphi
\end{aligned}
$$

We define $\mathcal{G}^{\approx}, (G,\sigma) \models \varphi$ by replacing $\sim_a$ with $\approx_a$ in the above condition on $K_a\varphi$.

The algorithm that specifies the behavior the agent should follow in the epistemic gossip protocol is defined below. In this study, we assume that all agents follow the same protocol.

Definition 12 (Gossip protocol). A gossip protocol is the nondeterministic algorithm of the following form:

> **while** not all agents are experts and there are $u, v \in A$ s.t. $\varphi(u,v)$ is satisfied and call uv is valid;
> **select** $u, v \in A$ s.t. $\varphi(u,v)$ is satisfied and call uv is valid;
> **execute** call uv;

where $\varphi(u,v)$ is a formula in the language $\mathcal{L}$.

For a given protocol P, all possible sequences of events that can be executed according to that protocol are called the P$^\sim$-permitted sequence. A set of P$^\sim$-permitted sequences is called extensions.

Definition 13 (Permitted sequence). Let P be a protocol given by condition $\varphi(x, y)$ and G be an initial gossip graph.

- A call ab is P$^\sim$-permitted in (G, σ) if $\mathcal{G}^\sim, (G, \sigma) \models \varphi(a, b)$, call ab is valid in G^σ and not all agents are experts in G^σ.
- A failure $[x_1 \ldots x_k]$ is P$^\sim$-permitted in (G, σ) if there exists a P$^\sim$-permitted call in (G, σ).
- An event sequence σ is P$^\sim$-permitted in G if each event σ_{n+1} is P$^\sim$-permitted in $(G, \sigma|n)$.
- The extension of P in G is the set of all P$^\sim$-permitted event sequences in G, denoted by P$^\sim_G$.
- A sequence $\sigma \in$ P$^\sim_G$ is P$^\sim$-maximal on G if it is infinite or there is no event e such that $\sigma; e \in$ P$^\sim_G$.

P$^\approx$-permitted, P$^\approx_G$ and P$^\approx$-maximal are defined similarly. When we discuss both P$^\sim$ and P$^\approx$ together, we simply write P.

Given an initial gossip graph and a protocol, the more number of sequences are included in the extension of the protocol that succeed in spreading the secret, the more the protocol is considered to be successful. Thus, protocols are classified into the following four types, depending on their level of success.

Definition 14 (Successful). Let G be an initial gossip graph and P be a protocol.

- A sequence $\sigma \in$ P$_G$ is successful if it is finite and in G^σ all agents are experts.
- A sequence $\sigma \in$ P$_G$ is fair if it is finite or for any call xy the following condition holds.
    If for any $i \in \mathbb{N}$ there exists $j \geq i$ such that xy is P-permitted in $G^{\sigma|j}$, then for any $i \in \mathbb{N}$ there exists $j \geq i$ such that $\sigma_j = xy$.
- P is strongly successful on G if all maximal $\sigma \in$ P$_G$ are successful.
- P is fairly successful on G if all fair and maximal $\sigma \in$ P$_G$ are successful.
- P is weakly successful on G if there exists $\sigma \in$ P$_G$ which is maximal and successful.
- P is unsuccessful on G if there is no $\sigma \in$ P$_G$ which is maximal and successful.

4   Analysis of Robustness and Failure Detection

In this section, we present the results of our protocol analysis.

4.1   Properties on Robustness

We analyze the following three protocols [6].

ANY (ANY Call) $\varphi(x,y) := \top$
 While not every agent knows all secrets, randomly select a pair xy such that x knows y's number and let x call y.

PIG (Possible Information Growth) $\varphi(x,y) := \hat{K}_x \bigvee_{z \in A}(S(x,z) \leftrightarrow \neg S(y,z))$
 Call xy can be made if x knows y's number and if x considers it possible that there is a secret known by one of x,y but not the other.

CO (Call Me Once) $\varphi(x,y) := \neg C(xy,x) \wedge \neg C(yx,x)$
 Agent x may call agent y if x knows y's number and there was no prior call between x and y.

Here, we assume that the number of failures is finite. Thus, for protocol P, we restrict P_G to a set of sequences, each of which contains a finite number of failures.

First, we confirm that for the protocols ANY and PIG, the properties shown in [6] also hold even if the agents fail.

Theorem 1. *Protocol ANY is fairly successful on G iff G is weakly connected.*

Proof. We can prove the statement in a way similar to [7]. We prove only $\Leftarrow$ part because the converse is obvious. Let σ be an ANY-permitted and fair sequence. It suffices to show that σ is not infinite. For contradiction, we assume that σ is infinite. Now that we assume that σ contains only a finite number of failures, there is a finite prefix $\tau \sqsubseteq \sigma$ such that for any $\tau'(\tau \sqsubseteq \tau' \sqsubseteq \sigma)$, we have $N^\tau = N^{\tau'}$ and $leaves(T_x^\tau) = leaves(T_x^{\tau'})$ for any $x \in A$. Since σ is not successful, there are $x, y \in A$ such that Nxy and $leaves(T_x^\tau) \neq leaves(T_y^\tau)$ (Otherwise σ is successful because G is weakly connected). However, since σ is fair, in σ the call xy is executed after τ. This is a contradiction.   □

Theorem 2. *Protocol PIG$^\sim$ is fairly successful on G iff G is weakly connected.*

Proof. We can prove the statement by similar argument of [7]. We prove only $\Leftarrow$ direction because the converse is obvious. Let σ be a PIG$^\sim$-maximal sequence.

 We first show that if σ is infinite, it is not fair. Since we assume that σ contains only a finite number of failures, there is a finite prefix $\tau \sqsubseteq \sigma$ such that for any $\tau'(\tau \sqsubseteq \tau' \sqsubseteq \sigma)$, we have $N^\tau = N^{\tau'}$ and $leaves(T_x^\tau) = leaves(T_x^{\tau'})$ for any $x \in A$. Further, since σ is not successful, there are $x, y \in A$ such that Nxy and $leaves(T_x^\tau) \neq leaves(T_y^\tau)$. This implies that after τ the call xy is always PIG$^\sim$-permitted. However, xy is not executed after τ. Therefore, σ is not fair.

 We next show that if σ is finite, it is successful. The sequence σ is finite only if all agents are experts in G^σ or for any $x, y \in A$ it is the case that $\mathcal{G}^\sim, (G,\sigma) \not\models \hat{K}_x \bigvee_{z \in A}(S(x,z) \leftrightarrow \neg S(y,z))$. In the former case, σ is successful by definition. In the latter case, by definition of $\hat{K}_x$, we have $\mathcal{G}^\sim, (G,\sigma) \models$

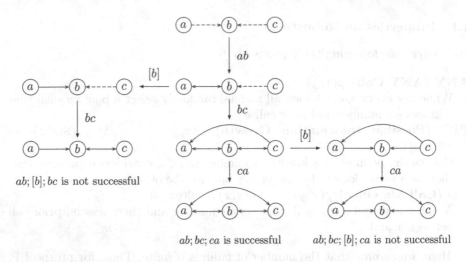

Fig. 2. A counter example of Theorem 13 in [7]

$K_x \neg \bigvee_{z \in A}(\mathsf{S}(x,z) \leftrightarrow \neg \mathsf{S}(y,z))$. This implies that for any $x, y \in A$ it is the case that $leaves(T_x^\sigma) = leaves(T_y^\sigma)$. Therefore, σ is successful.

Finally, it remains to show that there exists a successful σ. Let σ be a successful ANY-permitted sequence of minimum length. We show that σ is also PIG$^\sim$-permitted. Clearly, in σ there is no call between two experts. The prefix $\sigma|1$ is PIG$^\sim$-permitted. We need to show that each σ_{n+1} is PIG$^\sim$-permitted in $G^{\sigma|n}$. If σ_{n+1} is a failure, then it is clearly PIG$^\sim$-permitted in $G^{\sigma|n}$. Thus, we assume σ_{n+1} is a call xy. In the case $leaves(T_x^{\sigma|n}) = A$, we have $leaves(T_y^{\sigma|n}) \neq A$ Therefore, xy is PIG$^\sim$-permitted in $G^{\sigma|n}$. In the case $leaves(T_x^{\sigma|n}) \neq A$, let $z \in A \setminus leaves(T_x^{\sigma|n})$. Then we have $(G, \sigma|n) \sim_x (G, \sigma|n; zy)$ and $leaves(T_x^{\sigma|n}) \neq leaves(T_y^{\sigma|n;zy})$. Therefore, xy is PIG$^\sim$-permitted in $G^{\sigma|n}$. □

The reason why these theorems hold is that ANY and PIG are the "careful" protocol for failures. In other words, in these protocols, agents are forced to repeatedly exchange information in case of failure. A careful protocol assumes the worst case and decides who to call, regardless of whether or not the other agent actually fails. Therefore, if fairness is not assumed, redundant calls may be repeated.

Unlike ANY and PIG, the property shown in [6] does not hold for CO. More precisely, CO is successful in a weakly connected graph when there is no agent failure (cf. Theorem 13 in [7]) but it does not when failure may occur. As a counterexample of this theorem in our model, in Fig. 2, we show a sequence of events beginning with a weakly connected initial gossip graph but do not achieve a successful state.

The result shown above is obtained because CO, unlike ANY and PIG, is a protocol that reduces too much redundancy and, thus, fails to fully recover failures. A closer look at the cause yields two useful suggestions. The first suggestion is obtained from the counterexample sequence $ab; bc; [b]; ca$, which suggests that agents who may fail should not be experts first. This occurs because the information owned by such agents may be lost owing to a failure in the future. The other suggestion is obtained from the counterexample sequence $ab; [b]; bc$, which suggests that information should not be routed through an agent who may fail. This occurs because the transmission of information may fail depending on the timing of the agent failure.

The following theorem shows that a successful sequence can be achieved if we schedule the partial sequence of calls to avoid the undesired steps presented in the counterexamples above.

Theorem 3. *For an initial gossip graph $G = (A, N, \{T_x\}_{x \in A})$, we assume the following.*

- *A single agent a is the only agent who can fail.*
- *There are at least two agents who do not fail.*
- *The restriction of G to $A \setminus \{a\}$ is weakly connected.*
- *There is $x \in A \setminus \{a\}$ such that Nxa.*

Then the sequence $xa; \sigma; ya$ obtained by the following procedure is CO-permitted and successful (even if σ contains a finite number of a's failures).

(1) Execute a call xa.
(2) Execute CO among the agents in $A \setminus \{a\}$ (let us denote the event sequence executed in this step by σ, which may contain some $[a]$).
(3) Select an agent $y \in A \setminus \{a\}$ other than x and then execute a call ya.

Proof. By executing the call xa in (1), x obtains the secret and the telephone number of a. Since CO is strongly successful in a weakly connected graph when there is no agent failure (cf. Theorem 13 in [7]), σ is finite and after the execution of σ, all $z \in A \setminus \{a\}$ are experts. Since there are at least two agents who do not fail, there is an agent $y \in A \setminus \{a\}$ other than x. By the call ya in (3), a lastly becomes an expert. Therefore, $xa; \sigma; ya$ is successful. Moreover, since there is no calls which a is involved in, $xa; \sigma; ya$ is CO-permitted.   □

However, in the framework of epistemic gossip protocol, such scheduling cannot be realized directly. This fact suggests to us, as an alternative approach, to design a protocol with the level of carefulness that reconciles the trade-off relationship between the protocol CO and the protocol ANY or PIG. This is an ideal protocol that is able to detect failures and recover lost information when needed. In the next subsection, as a first step in designing such protocol, we investigate sufficient conditions in the sequence of calls that allow agents to detect failures.

4.2   Analysis of Failure Detection

In this subsection, we assume that the following are common knowledge between agents: gossip graph G is complete; only one particular agent (say, a) can fail; failure can occur only once. Formally, assuming these three things to be common knowledge means that we consider $\mathcal{G}$, which consists of only gossip state (G, σ) for which the three facts stated above hold. Also, $\approx_x$ is used as the reachability relation. Under these assumptions, we use the notation $\sigma \approx_x \tau$ to denote $(G, \sigma) \approx_x (G, \tau)$ and the notation $\sigma \models \phi$ to denote $\mathcal{G}^{\approx}, (G, \sigma) \models \phi$.

For a given protocol P and agents $a, x \in A$, if $\sigma \models K_x F(a)$, agent x is said to detect a's failure in $\sigma \in P_G$. By the definition of $\models$, this is equivalent to $[a] \in \tau$ for any τ that satisfies $\sigma \approx_x \tau$. A counterexample τ of this condition, namely τ that satisfies $\sigma \approx_x \tau$ and $[a] \notin \tau$, is called an optimistic path. The formal definition is given below.

Definition 15 (Optimistic path). For an event sequence σ, an optimistic path of x for σ is a sequence τ such that $\sigma \approx_x \tau$ and $[a] \notin \tau$. Let $opt_x : \mathsf{E}^* \to 2^{\mathsf{E}^*}$ be the function which maps an event sequence σ to the set of optimistic paths of x for σ. That is, we define opt_x as follows.

$$opt_x(\sigma) := \{\tau \mid \sigma \approx_x \tau \text{ and } [a] \notin \tau\}.$$

In order to show that $\sigma \models K_x F(a)$ holds, it suffices to show that the set $opt_x(\sigma)$ is empty. By the definition of $\approx_x$, the set $opt_x(\sigma)$ can be calculated by induction on σ:

- Base Case: If $\sigma = \epsilon$, then $opt_x(\sigma) = \{\epsilon\}$.
- Ind. Step: If $\sigma = \sigma'; \mathsf{c}$ and $\mathsf{c} \in \mathsf{C}$,
  - For the case $x \in \mathsf{c}$, let $\mathsf{c} = \overline{xy}$. Then it follows that

$$opt_x(\sigma) = \{\tau; \mathsf{c} \mid \tau \in opt_x(\sigma') \text{ and } T_y^{\sigma'} = T_y^\tau\}.$$

  - For the case $x \notin \mathsf{c}$, it follows that

$$opt_x(\sigma) = \{\tau; \mathsf{c}' \mid \tau \in opt_x(\sigma') \text{ and } x \notin \mathsf{c}'\}.$$

If $\sigma = \sigma'; [a]$, then $opt_x(\sigma) = opt_x(\sigma')$.

Here we note that no assumptions about telephone number appear in the calculations presented above, because we assume that G is a complete graph. In addition, optimistic path is usually calculated bottom-up beginning with $\tau = \epsilon$.

Example 2. For $\sigma = ax; [a]; ab; bx$, the set $opt_x(\sigma)$ can be calculated by the following steps:

$$
\begin{aligned}
opt_x(\epsilon) &= \{\epsilon\} \\
opt_x(ax) &= \{\epsilon; ax \mid T_a^\epsilon = T_a^\epsilon\} = \{ax\} \\
opt_x(ax; [a]) &= \{ax\} \\
opt_x(ax; [a]; ab) &= \{ax; \mathsf{c} \mid x \notin \mathsf{c}\} \\
opt_x(ax; [a]; ab; bx) &= \{ax; \mathsf{c}; bx \mid x \notin \mathsf{c} \text{ and } T_b^{ax;[a];ab} = T_b^{ax;\mathsf{c}}\}.
\end{aligned}
$$

Since there is no call c such that $x \notin \mathsf{c}$ and $T_b^{ax;\{a\};ab} = T_b^{ax;\mathsf{c}}$, we have $opt_x(\sigma) = \emptyset$. Therefore, after the execution of σ, agent x can detect the failure of a. In a similar way, we can determine whether $\sigma \models K_x F(a)$ is true or not, given $\sigma \in \mathsf{E}^*$.

From now on, we consider a more general pattern of σ that satisfies $\sigma \models K_x F(a)$. The pattern of σ, shown in Theorem 4 below, is a generalization of σ presented in Example 2. The underlying idea is that an agent can detect the failure by comparing information before and after the a's failure. Before proving the theorem, we provide some lemmas. Hereafter, we use $sub_a(T)$ to denote $\{T' \subseteq T \mid a \in r(T')\}$.

Lemma 1. *If a finite event sequence σ satisfies $[a] \notin \sigma$, then for any $x \in A$ and for any $T \in sub_a(T_x^\sigma)$ there is $\tau \sqsubseteq \sigma$ such that $T = T_a^\tau$.*

Proof. We prove this by induction on σ.

- Base Case: If $\sigma = \epsilon$, for any $x \in A$ it is the case that $T_x^\sigma = T_x^\epsilon = \langle x \rangle$. Thus, the statement holds for $\sigma = \epsilon$.
- Ind. Step: Let $\sigma = \sigma'$; c and c $\in$ C. We fist consider the case $a \notin$ c. Let c $= yz$. Then it follows that

$$sub_a(T_x^\sigma) = \begin{cases} sub_a(T_y^{\sigma'}) \cup sub_a(T_z^{\sigma'}) & \text{if } x \in \{y, z\}, \\ sub_a(T_x^{\sigma'}) & \text{otherwise.} \end{cases}$$

Therefore, by the induction hypothesis, we have the statement. We then consider the case $a \in$ c. Let c $= \overline{a}y$. Then it follows that

$$sub_a(T_x^\sigma) = \begin{cases} sub_a(T_a^{\sigma'}) \cup sub_a(T_y^{\sigma'}) \cup \{T_a^\sigma\} & \text{if } x \in \{a, y\}, \\ sub_a(T_x^{\sigma'}) & \text{otherwise.} \end{cases}$$

We can take $\tau = \sigma$ for T_a^σ. Therefore, together with the induction hypothesis, we have the statement. $\square$

Lemma 2. *If an event sequence σ satisfies $[a] \notin \sigma$, then for any $x \in A$ and for any $T, T' \in sub_a(T_x^\sigma)$ it is the case that $T \subseteq T'$ or $T' \subseteq T$.*

Proof. By Lemma 1, for any $x \in A$ and for any $T, T' \in sub_a(T_x^\sigma)$ there are $\tau, \tau' \sqsubseteq \sigma$ such that $T = T_a^\tau$ and $T' = T_a^{\tau'}$. If $\tau \sqsubseteq \tau'$, then $T_a^\tau \subseteq T_a^{\tau'}$, that is, $T \subseteq T'$. If $\tau' \sqsubseteq \tau$, then $T_a^{\tau'} \subseteq T_a^\tau$, that is, $T' \subseteq T$. $\square$

Lemma 3. *For any event sequence σ and any $x \in A$, if $[a] \notin \sigma$ and $r(T_x^\sigma) = ax$ (xa, resp.), then for any $T \in sub_a(T_{x,R}^\sigma)$ ($sub_a(T_{x,L}^\sigma)$, resp.), it is the case that $T \subseteq T_{x,L}^\sigma$ ($T_{x,R}^\sigma$, resp.).*

Proof. Since we assume $r(T_x^\sigma) = ax$ (xa, resp.), there is a prefix $\tau \sqsubseteq \sigma$ such that $\tau = \tau'$; ax and $T_x^\sigma - T_x^\tau$. Furthermore, we have $T_{x,L}^\sigma = T_{x,L}^\tau = T_a^{\tau'}$ ($T_x^{\tau'}$, resp.) and $T_{x,R}^\sigma = T_{x,R}^\tau = T_x^{\tau'}$ ($T_a^{\tau'}$, resp.). Since $[a] \notin \sigma$ implies $[a] \notin \tau'$, using Lemma 1, for any $T \in sub_a(T_x^{\tau'})$ there is a prefix $\rho \sqsubseteq \tau'$ such that $T = T_a^\rho$. Moreover, since $\rho \sqsubseteq \tau'$, we have $T_a^\rho \subseteq T_a^{\tau'}$, that is, $T \subseteq T_a^{\tau'}$. Therefore, for any $T \in sub_a(T_{x,R}^\sigma)$ ($sub_a(T_{x,L}^\sigma)$, resp.), we have $T \subseteq T_{x,L}^\sigma$ ($T_{x,R}^\sigma$, resp.). $\square$

Theorem 4. *When agent x obtains agent a's secret distributed before and after a's failure from two paths which do not share any nodes, x can detect a's failure. Formally, if $\{b_1,\ldots,b_k\}, \{c_1,\ldots,c_l\} \subseteq A$ and $\{b_1,\ldots,b_k\} \cap \{c_1,\ldots,c_l\} = \emptyset$ with $k,l \geq 0$, and if σ is a sequence consisting of the following events:*

$$\overline{ab_1}, \overline{b_1 b_2}, \ldots, \overline{b_{k-1} b_k}, \overline{b_k x}, \overline{ac_1}, \overline{c_1 c_2}, \ldots, \overline{c_{l-1} c_l}, \overline{c_l x}, [a],$$

and if

$$\overline{ab_1} \prec \overline{b_1 b_2} \prec \cdots \prec \overline{b_{k-1} b_k} \prec \overline{b_k x} \tag{1}$$

$$\overline{ac_1} \prec \overline{c_1 c_2} \prec \cdots \prec \overline{c_{l-1} c_l} \prec \overline{c_l x} \tag{2}$$

$$\overline{ab_1} \prec [a] \prec \overline{ac_1} \tag{3}$$

where $\mathsf{e}_1 \prec \mathsf{e}_2$ means that e_1 is executed earlier than e_2 in σ, then $\sigma \models K_x F(a)$.

Proof. We divide the proof according to whether k and l are equal to 0 or not, respectively.

- For $k = l = 0$, we have $\sigma = \overline{ax}; [a]; \overline{ax}$. Then $opt_x(\sigma) = \{\overline{ax}; \overline{ax} \mid T_a^{\overline{ax};[a]} = T_a^{\overline{ax}}\}$. Since $T_a^{\overline{ax};[a]} \neq T_a^{\overline{ax}}$, we have $opt_x(\sigma) = \emptyset$. Therefore, $\sigma \models K_x F(a)$.
- For $k > 0$ and $l = 0$, we have $\sigma = \sigma'; \overline{ax}$ or $\sigma = \sigma'; \overline{b_k x}$. If $\sigma = \sigma'; \overline{ax}$, then $r(T_x^\sigma) = \overline{ax}$. By the conditions (1), (2) and (3), it is the case that $T_a^{\sigma'} = \langle a \rangle$ and $T_x^{\sigma'}$ has $\langle\langle a \rangle, ab_1, \langle b_1 \rangle\rangle$ or $\langle\langle b_1 \rangle, b_1 a, \langle a \rangle\rangle$ as a subtree. Since T_x^σ is $\langle T_a^{\sigma'}, ax, T_x^{\sigma'} \rangle$ or $\langle T_x^{\sigma'}, xa, T_a^{\sigma'} \rangle$, using Lemma 3, we have $\sigma \models K_x F(a)$. If $\sigma = \sigma'; \overline{b_k x}$, by the conditions (1), (2) and (3), the tree $T_{b_k}^{\sigma'}$ has $\langle\langle a \rangle, ab_1, \langle b_1 \rangle\rangle$ or $\langle\langle b_1 \rangle, b_1 a, \langle a \rangle\rangle$ as a subtree, and $T_x^{\sigma'}$ is $\langle\langle a \rangle, ax, \langle x \rangle\rangle$ or $\langle\langle x \rangle, xa, \langle a \rangle\rangle$. Since the tree T_x^σ is $\langle T_{b_k}^{\sigma'}, b_k x, T_x^{\sigma'} \rangle$ or $\langle T_x^{\sigma'}, x b_k, T_{b_k}^{\sigma'} \rangle$, using Lemma 2, we have $\sigma \models K_x F(a)$.
- For $k = 0$ and $l > 0$, we have $\sigma = \overline{ax}; [a]; \overline{ac_1}; \overline{c_1 c_2}; \ldots; \overline{c_{l-1} c_l}; \overline{c_l x}$. Let $\sigma = \sigma'; \overline{c_l x}$. Then $T_{c_l}^{\sigma'}$ has $\langle\langle a \rangle, ac_1, \langle c_1 \rangle\rangle$ or $\langle\langle c_1 \rangle, c_1 a, \langle a \rangle\rangle$ as a subtree, and $T_x^{\sigma'}$ has $\langle\langle a \rangle, ax, \langle x \rangle\rangle$ or $\langle\langle x \rangle, xa, \langle a \rangle\rangle$ as a subtree. Since the tree T_x^σ is $\langle T_{c_l}^{\sigma'}, c_l x, T_x^{\sigma'} \rangle$ or $\langle T_x^{\sigma'}, x c_l, T_{c_l}^{\sigma'} \rangle$, using Lemma 2, we have $\sigma \models K_x F(a)$.
- For $k > 0$ and $l > 0$, we have $\sigma = \sigma'; \overline{b_k x}$ or $\sigma = \sigma'; \overline{c_l x}$. If $\sigma = \sigma'; \overline{b_k x}$, by the assumption that $\{b_1,\ldots,b_k\} \cap \{c_1,\ldots,c_l\} = \emptyset$ and the conditions (1), (2) and (3), it is the case that $T_{b_k}^{\sigma'} = T_{b_k}^{\overline{ab_1}; \overline{b_1 b_2}; \ldots; \overline{b_{k-1} b_k}}$ and $T_x^{\sigma'} = T_x^{\overline{ac_1}; \overline{c_1 c_2}; \ldots; \overline{c_{l-1} c_l}; \overline{c_l x}}$. Since $\{b_1,\ldots,b_k\} \cap \{c_1,\ldots,c_l\} = \emptyset$, it follows that $\langle b_1 \rangle \subseteq T_{b_k}^{\sigma'}$ and $\langle b_1 \rangle \not\subseteq T_x^{\sigma'}$. Using Lemma 2, we have $\sigma \models K_x F(a)$. If $\sigma = \sigma'; \overline{c_l x}$, By the assumption that $\{b_1,\ldots,b_k\} \cap \{c_1,\ldots,c_l\} = \emptyset$ and the conditions (1), (2) and (3), it is the case that $T_{c_l}^{\sigma'} = T_{c_l}^{\overline{ac_1}; \overline{c_1 c_2}; \ldots; \overline{c_{l-1} c_l}}$ and $T_x^{\sigma'} = T_x^{\overline{ab_1}; \overline{b_1 b_2}; \ldots; \overline{b_{k-1} b_k}; \overline{b_k x}}$. Since $\{b_1,\ldots,b_k\} \cap \{c_1,\ldots,c_l\} = \emptyset$, it follows that $\langle c_1 \rangle \subseteq T_{c_l}^{\sigma'}$ and $\langle c_1 \rangle \not\subseteq T_x^{\sigma'}$. Using Lemma 2, we have $\sigma \models K_x F(a)$. $\square$

5   Conclusions and Future Work

In this paper, in order to increase the reliability of epistemic gossip protocols, we proposed a logical analysis method of robustness against agent failure. In our model, when agent fails, it loses the secrets and telephone numbers gained by previous calls and returns to the initial state. In addition, during each call, agent share not only the secrets but also the history of the transmission path of each secret.

For this settings, we showed that the protocols ANY and PIG are fairly successful if the graphs were connected, as in the case where no failure is assumed. On the other hand, for the protocol CO, we showed that there exists a sequence of calls that is not successful in a weakly connected graph. These results suggest the need for a failure detection mechanism. Therefore, in this paper, we also showed the sufficient condition of the sequence of calls for an agent to detect the failure of other agents in PIG. Our results provide useful information to make the protocol robust against agent failure.

There are still issues to be addressed as an extension of this study. Although condition that the sequence of calls must satisfy to detect other agent's failure, we have not achieved a concrete protocol that allows the sequence that satisfies this condition. Moreover, currently, we have only obtained a sufficient condition. Thus, there should be a more general form of a sequence of calls where someone can detect a failure. From a more practical point of view, the robustness against various other types of failures such as the Byzantine failure of agents and communication failures has not yet been clarified. We plan to address these research issues by extending the framework given in this study.

References

1. Apt, K.R., Grossi, D., van der Hoek, W.: Epistemic protocols for distributed gossiping. Electron. Proc. Theor. Comput. Sci. **215**, 51–66 (2016)
2. Attamah, M., Van Ditmarsch, H., Grossi, D., van der Hoek, W.: Knowledge and gossip. In: ECAI, pp. 21–26 (2014)
3. van den Berg, L.: Unreliable gossip. Master's thesis, Universiteit van Amsterdam (2018)
4. Chandra, T.D., Toueg, S.: Unreliable failure detectors for reliable distributed systems. J. ACM (JACM) **43**(2), 225–267 (1996)
5. Cooper, M.C., Herzig, A., Maffre, F., Maris, F., Régnier, P.: The epistemic gossip problem. Discrete Math. **342**(3), 654–663 (2019)
6. van Ditmarsch, H., van Eijck, J., Pardo, P., Ramezanian, R., Schwarzentruber, F.: Epistemic protocols for dynamic gossip. J. Appl. Log. **20**, 1–31 (2017)
7. van Ditmarsch, H., van Eijck, J., Pardo, P., Ramezanian, R., Schwarzentruber, F.: Dynamic gossip. Bull. Iran. Math. Soc. **45**(3), 701–728 (2019)
8. Fagin, R., Moses, Y., Halpern, J.Y., Vardi, M.Y.: Reasoning About Knowledge. MIT Press, Cambridge (1995)
9. Hajnal, A., Milner, E.C., Szemerédi, E.: A cure for the telephone disease. Can. Math. Bull. **15**(3), 447–450 (1972)
10. Hedetniemi, S.M., Hedetniemi, S.T., Liestman, A.L.: A survey of gossiping and broadcasting in communication networks. Networks **18**(4), 319–349 (1988)
11. Tijdeman, R.: On a telephone problem. Nieuw Arch. voor Wiskunde **3**(19), 188–192 (1971)

Reasoning with Failures

Hamid Jahanian[✉] and Annabelle McIver

Macquarie University, Sydney, Australia
hamid.jahanian@hdr.mq.edu.au, annabelle.mciver@mq.edu.au

Abstract. Safety Instrumented Systems (SIS) protect major hazard facilities, e.g. power plants, against catastrophic accidents. An SIS consists of hardware components and a controller software – the "program". Current safety analyses of SIS' include the construction of a fault tree, summarising potential faults of the components and how they can arise within an SIS. The exercise of identifying faults typically relies on the experience of the safety engineer. Unfortunately the program part is often too complicated to be analysed in such a "by hand" manner and so the impact it has on the resulting safety analysis is not accurately captured. In this paper we demonstrate how a formal model for faults and failure modes can be used to analyse the impact of an SIS program. We outline the underlying concepts of *Failure Mode Reasoning* and its application in safety analysis, and we illustrate the ideas on a practical example.

1 Introduction

Plant accidents can have catastrophic consequences. An explosion at a chemical plant in eastern China killed over 70 people and injured more than 600 in 2019. Safety Instrumented Systems (SIS) are protection mechanisms against major plant accidents [16]. Failure of SIS components can result in the SIS being unavailable to respond to hazardous situations. It is therefore crucial to analyse and address such failures. A typical SIS comprises physical components to interact with plant, and a software program[1] that analyses the information and initiates safety actions. Such software can be highly complex, and even when it is not itself faulty still propagate input faults from the sensors to the safety actuators. This paper concerns a current omission in the standard safety engineering process: that of an accurate fault analysis of complex SIS program.

Well established methods, such as Fault Tree Analysis (FTA), already exist in the industry for analysing and quantifying SIS failure modes [32]. FTA is a deductive method that uses fault trees for quantitative and qualitative analysis of failure scenarios. A fault tree is a graphical representation of the conditions that contribute to the occurrence of a predefined failure event. A fault tree will be created by a safety analyst and based on their knowledge and understanding of the failure behaviours in a system. Not only are such by-hand analyses inherently subject to human-error, they also require expertise, time and effort.

---

[1] In this paper the term *program* refers to the software code run by SIS CPU; also known in safety standards as SIS Application Program [16].

© Springer Nature Switzerland AG 2020
S.-W. Lin et al. (Eds.): ICFEM 2020, LNCS 12531, pp. 36–52, 2020.
https://doi.org/10.1007/978-3-030-63406-3_3

A new method, Failure Mode Reasoning (FMR), was recently introduced to circumvent the need for by-hand analysis of parts of SIS [17]. Using a special calculus built on failure modes, FMR analyses the SIS program to identify the hardware faults at SIS inputs that can result in a given failure at its output. The main outcome of FMR is a short list of failure modes, which can also be used to calculate the probability of failure. In this paper we show how to use ideas from formal methods to justify FMR. We use an abstraction to model failures directly, and we show that such an abstraction can be used to track failures within the SIS program so that potential output failures can be linked to the potential input failures that cause them. We prove the soundness of the technique and illustrate it on a practical example.

The rest of this paper is organised as follows: Sect. 2 provides a brief explanation of the context and how FMR can enhance safety analysis. Section 3 formalises the underlying ideas of analysis of failures for SIS programs. Based on these concepts, Sects. 4 and 5 formulate the concepts for composing the individual elements in FMR and the reasoning process on the interactions between these elements. Section 6 includes descriptions of how FMR is applied in practice and in particular in large scale projects. Finally Sects. 7 and 8 wrap up the paper with a review of FMR's position with respect to other research works and potential research in future.

2   SIS and FMR

An SIS consists of sensors, a logic solver, and final elements. The sensors collect data about the environment (such as temperature and pressure) and the logic solver processes the sensor readings and controls the final elements to intervene and prevent a hazard. Such interventions can include shutting down the (industrial) plant and they are referred to as Safety Instrumented Functions (SIFs). Figure 1b illustrates a simple SIS consisting of two sensors, one logic solver and one final element. This SIS performs only one SIF, which is to protect the downstream process against high pressure in the upstream gas pipe. The sensors measure the gas pressure and the logic solver initiates a command to close the valve if the gas pressure exceeds a threshold limit.

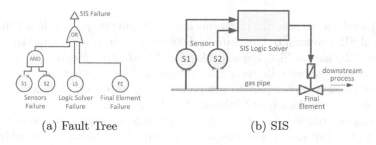

(a) Fault Tree   (b) SIS

Fig. 1. An example SIS and its corresponding fault tree model

SIS faults are typically modelled by using fault trees. For an accurate analysis a fault tree must reflect all potential faults caused by all components in the SIS. Clearly incorrect sensor readings are a significant factor in safety analysis as they can lead to hazardous scenarios. One of the problems in safety analysis is to understand how such deviations can be propagated by the SIS program and lead to faults at SIS outputs. If done by hand, such understandings depends critically on the analyst's knowledge of the details of the SIS program.

Consider, for example the fault tree in Fig. 1a, which is meant to summarise the failures of SIS in Fig. 1b: the SIS fails if both sensors fail or if the logic solver fails or if the final element fails. The fault tree is built on the assumption that the two sensors provide redundancy, which means that provided one of the two sensors is in a healthy state, that is sufficient to detect potential hazards. However, the validity of this assumption, and thus the validity of the fault tree, directly depends on the details of SIS program and how it computes the output from the input. For example, if the two inputs from sensors are averaged first and then compared to the high pressure limit as shown in Fig. 2a, the proposed fault tree (Fig. 1a) is incorrect; because failure of one sensor will affect the average of the two. But if each sensor reading is separately compared to the threshold limit first (as in Fig. 2b), the sensors can be considered redundant and the fault tree would summarise the failures accurately. While the two programs deliver the same functionality, they do not show the same failure behaviour; and the proposed fault tree can correspond to only one of them.

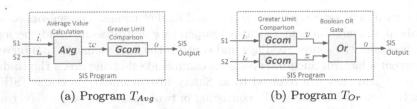

(a) Program T_{Avg} (b) Program T_{Or}

For variables $i_1, i_2, w \in \mathbb{R}$ and $v, z, o \in \mathbb{B}$, and parameter $K \in \mathbb{R}$: $w = Avg(i_1, i_2) = (i_1 + i_2)/2$, $o = Gcom_K(w) = (w > K)$ and $o = Or(v, z) = v \vee z$.

Fig. 2. Two possible implementations for the Logic Solver in Fig. 1a

In real world scenarios, SIS programs are large and complex. It is not unusual for a typical SIS program to have hundreds of inputs like i_1 and i_2 and thousands of Function Blocks [15] like Avg and $Gcom_K$. Conducting a detailed analysis of program of such scales will be a real challenge for a human analyst, but it nonetheless plays a crucial part in producing accurate results. In such scenarios an automated method such as FMR can be of a great help.

FMR is a technique for enabling the details of SIS programs to be accurately reflected in the full safety analysis of a system. The challenge we address is identifying the SIS input "failure modes" that cause a given SIS output failure mode by analysing the SIS program that reads those inputs and produces that output. The results can then be incorporated in an overall safety analysis of SIS.

SIS programs are commonly developed in the form of Function Block Diagrams (FBD) [15]. Figure 2 showed two very simple examples of FBDs. An FBD consists of function blocks and their interconnections, which we label with variable names. In Fig. 2a, o, w, i_1 and i_2 are the variables and Avg and $Gcom_K$ are the function blocks. We will use this FBD as a worked example through this paper to demonstrate the FMR process.

The SIS program given at Fig. 2a is supposed to initiate a command to close the gas value when the pressure rises above a given threshold. In normal circumstances, when all inputs report correct measurements from the sensor readings, an output of t causes the correct shut down command to be delivered when the pressure is high. Suppose however that the inputs i_1, i_2 are incorrectly recording the pressure. These inaccuracies propagate through the program and lead to an f at the output, meaning that the SIS will not initiate the safety action required to prevent the hazardous event.

In simple terms, this is how FMR analyses such output deviations: from o being f by fault we can conclude that w must be less than the threshold limit set in $Gcom_K$: $(o = \mathsf{f}) \Rightarrow (w \le K)$. Sentence $(w \le K)$ in turn implies that the average value of i_1 and i_2 must be less than the threshold limit: $(w \le K) \Rightarrow ((i_1 + i_2)/2 \le K)$. Assuming that this is due to an input fault, we can conclude that either input i_1 must be reading lower than what it should, or input i_2. Overall, we can conclude:

$$(o \text{ being f by fault}) \Rightarrow (i_1 \text{ reads too low}) \vee (i_2 \text{ reads too low}) \qquad (1)$$

Notice that the actual values of inputs are not required, but only their categories in terms of whether they are "too high", or "too low". It turns out that we can take advantage of this abstraction to simplify the overall analysis. In the next section we describe a simple model of failures from which we derive an analysis that uses "failure modes" explicitly.[2]

FMR completes the SIS safety analysis by incorporating the functionally most important part of the system – the program, and it does this by analysing the actual program rather than a synthesised model. The process is automated and thus it saves time and effort, and offers accuracy and certainty. The purpose of FMR is similar to fault tree analysis, but it adds rigour to the consideration of fault propagation in the SIS program.

3   Modelling Failures

In this section we formalise the ideas underlying the identification and analysis of potential failures for SIS programs. In particular the result of the analysis should be the identification of potential faults and, in addition, to categorise

---

[2] Note that in Fig. 2b the FMR analysis would produce a different result, i.e. $(o \text{ being f by fault}) \Rightarrow (i_1 \text{ reads too low}) \wedge (i_2 \text{ reads too low})$.

them in terms of their "modes of failure". This is an essential step in any safety engineering exercise.

In what follows we use well known constructions from relational-style modelling. Our contribution is to apply those ideas in this new setting for SIS programs. Let V be an abstract state space; we use $\mathbb{P}\mathcal{X}$ for the power set over $\mathcal{X}$. A partition of a set $\mathcal{X}$ is a set of pairwise non-intersecting subsets in $\mathbb{P}\mathcal{X}$.

We begin with a simple abstract model for a generic SIS function. It is a function which takes inputs to outputs over an (abstract) type V.

Definition 1. *An abstract model for an SIS function is a function of type* $V \to V$.

An SIS function can be a function block (FB), a combination of FBs or the entire SIS program. As described above, the safety analyst can only access information about the safety status of the system through the SIS program variables. The challenge is that this reported status (i.e. the sensor readings) might be inaccurate or wrong. To model such faults we need to keep track of the values recorded in the SIS program variables *and* the value that *should* have been reported. When these values are not the same we say that there is a fault. The next definition shows how to keep track of these faults within a particular SIS setting.

Definition 2. *Given an SIS function $f : V \to V$, a failure model is a function* $\langle f \rangle : V^2 \to V^2$ *defined by*

$$\langle f \rangle (m, a) \quad := \quad (f(m), f(a)).$$

For the pair $(m, a) \in V^2$, the first component m models the value reported by the SIS program variables, and the second component a is the actual value that should be reported. We say that (m, a) is a failure state *whenever $m \neq a$.*[3]

For example, in Fig. 2a we model the simple SIS program as a function T_{Avg} of type $\mathbb{R}^2 \to \mathbb{B}$, where the input (pair) corresponds to the readings of the variables i_1, i_2, and the output corresponds to the value of the output variable o.[4] There are two possible output failure states wrt. $\langle T_{Avg} \rangle \in (\mathbb{R}^2)^2 \to (\mathbb{B})^2$, and they are (t, f) and (f, t).

Observe however from Definition 2 that the only way an output failure state can occur is if the corresponding input is also a failure state (since we are assuming that no additional failures are caused by the SIS program itself). Given a function f, we say that failure output state (m', a') was *caused by* input failure state (m, a) if $\langle f \rangle (m, a) = (m', a')$.

In the case of Fig. 2a, the failure state (f, t) can only be caused by input failure state $((m_1, m_2), (a_1, a_2))$ if either $m_1 < a_1$ or $m_2 < a_2$. Here the values m_1, a_1 correspond to the variable i_1 and m_2, a_2 correspond to the variable i_2 in the figure. In scenarios where e.g. $m_1 < a_1$ there is always some reported value

---

[3] In our abstract model we use a single type V for simplicity of presentation.

[4] Note here that we are distinguishing the types in the example.

for m_2 such that the reported average $(m_1+m_2)/2$ is below the fixed threshold in $Gcom_K$, thus there exists a scenario satisfying the identified input constraints such that:

$$\langle T_{Avg}\rangle((m_1, a_1), (m_2, a_2)) = (\mathsf{f}, \mathsf{t}).$$

From this example we can see there are potentially infinitely many values for a failure state (m, a) whenever m, a can take real values. Rather than a safety engineer needing to know these precise values, what is more relevant is a report of the (usually) finite number of classes or *modes* describing the kinds of failure.

Definition 3. *Given a set of states $V \times V$ wrt. a failure model, the failure modes are defined by a partition $\mathscr{P}$ of $V \times V$. Each subset in $\mathscr{P}$ defines a failure mode (relative to $\mathscr{P}$). Two states (m, a) and (m', a') satisfy the same failure mode if and only if they belong to the same partition subset of $\mathscr{P}$.*

Given a partition $\mathscr{P}$ defining a set of failure modes we define $md_{\mathscr{P}} : V \times V \to \mathscr{P}$ which maps failure states to their relevant failure mode (partition subset).

Examples of failure modes are normally described by constraints on variables. For instance in Fig. 2a the failure modes for the initial failure state $((m_1, m_2), (a_1, a_2))$ are summarised by "either i_1 is reading too low or i_2 is reading too low". In terms of Definition 3 this can be characterised by part of a partition that includes ℓ_1, ℓ_2 and ℓ, where ℓ_1 is the set of failure states such that $m_1 < a_1 \wedge m_2 \geq a_2$; ℓ_2 is the set of failure states such that $m_1 \geq a_1 \wedge m_2 < a_2$ and ℓ is the set of failure states such that $m_1 < a_1 \wedge m_2 < a_2$.

Given an output failure mode, we would like to compute all initial failure modes that could cause that final failure mode. We say that an initial failure mode e (to an SIS function) *causes* an output failure mode e' (of an SIS function) if there exists a failure state satisfying e such that the output of the SIS function given that initial state satisfies e'.

For a given SIS function f, one way to do this is to compute all relevant failure states for $\langle f \rangle$, and then use $md_{\mathscr{P}}$ to interpret the failure modes for each failure state. Our first observation is that, given a partition $\mathscr{P}$ defining the failure modes, we can simplify this procedure significantly by abstracting the behaviour of f to act directly in terms of the failure modes rather than failure states.

Definition 4. *Let $f : V \to V$ be an SIS function, and $\mathscr{P}$ be a partition of V^2 defining the set of failure modes as in Definition 3.*

We define $[f]_{\mathscr{P}} : \mathscr{P} \to \mathbb{P}\mathscr{P}$ to be the failure mode abstraction of f as the (possibly nondeterministic) function satisfying the following constraint for any input $(m, a) \in V^2$:

$$md_{\mathscr{P}} \circ \langle f \rangle(m, a) \in [f]_{\mathscr{P}} \circ md_{\mathscr{P}}(m, a).$$

In Fig. 2a, where the initial failure modes are ℓ_1, ℓ_2 and ℓ explained above, and final failure modes are $f = \{(\mathsf{f}, \mathsf{t})\}$ and $t = \{(\mathsf{t}, \mathsf{f})\}$, we can see that $[T_{Avg}]_{\mathscr{P}}(\ell_1)$

contains f, where we are writing $\mathscr{P}$ to represent the partition defined by all initial and final variables.[5]

We shall show below that there are a variety of functions that have well-defined failure mode abstractions. Our next task however, is to show that the abstraction defined by Definition 4 is compositional, i.e. the abstraction of $f; g$ of SIS functions f and g can be computed from the composition of their abstractions. We recall the well-known Kleisli lifting of set-valued [24,25] functions as follows. We write the composition $f; g$ to mean first f is executed, and then g, or as functions the output from initial s is $g(f(s))$.

Let $\rho : \mathcal{T} \to \mathbb{P}\mathcal{T}$, define $\rho^\dagger : \mathbb{P}\mathcal{T} \to \mathbb{P}\mathcal{T}$

$$\rho^\dagger(K) := \bigcup_{k \in K} \rho(k). \tag{2}$$

Lemma 1. *Let f, g be SIS functions which have well-defined failure-mode abstractions as given by Definition 4. The failure-mode abstraction for the composition $[f; g]_\mathscr{P}$ is equal to $[g]_\mathscr{P}^\dagger \circ [f]_\mathscr{P}$, where $[g]_\mathscr{P}^\dagger : \mathbb{P}\mathscr{P} \to \mathbb{P}\mathscr{P}$ is the standard lifting set out at Eq. 2 above.*[6]

Proof. (Sketch) We show, for any input (m, a), that:

$$\mathsf{md}_\mathscr{P} \circ \langle g \rangle \circ \langle f \rangle (m, a) \in [g]_\mathscr{P}^\dagger \circ [f]_\mathscr{P} \circ \mathsf{md}_\mathscr{P}(m, a) \ ,$$

and that all failure modes arise in this way. The result follows from Definition 4, and standard manipulations of set-valued functions [1,25].

The failure mode abstractions $[f]_\mathscr{P}$ enable a significant simplification in the identification of possible failures in an SIS program. For example we shall see that $[T_{Avg}]_\mathscr{P} = [Gcom_K]_\mathscr{P}^\dagger \circ [Avg]_\mathscr{P}$ for abstractions of the function blocks $[Gcom_K]_\mathscr{P}$ and $[Avg]_\mathscr{P}$.

In general a safety analyst considers possible output failure modes and asks for the inputs that potentially cause them. In some circumstances some failure modes can never be satisfied by any input, and are deemed *unreachable*. The analyst is thus able to concentrate on *reachable* failure modes, defined next.

Definition 5. *Given an SIS function f, and abstraction defined by Definition 4. A failure mode $m \in \mathscr{P}$ is reachable (wrt. f) if there is some input failure state (i, i') such that $\mathsf{md}_\mathscr{P} \circ \langle f \rangle (i, i') = m$.*

Failure Mode Reasoning is based on backwards calculational reasoning. We use a weak transformer to compute all input failure modes which can possibly cause a given output failure mode. This is similar to the dual transformer of dynamic logic [7] and the conjugate transformer [26] for the well-known guarded command language [11].

---

[5] More precisely we would define failure modes separately on inputs and outputs, and indeed this is what happens in practice. To simplify the presentation however we assume that there is a single partition which serves to define failure modes on a single set, without distinguishing between inputs and outputs.

[6] Recall that for simplicity we assume that the function modes $\mathscr{P}$ applies to both functions f and g.

Definition 6. *Given SIS function* [7] f, *we define the* inverse failure transformer $[f]^-_{\mathscr{P}} : \mathbb{P}\mathscr{P} \to \mathbb{P}\mathscr{P}$ *as*

$$[f]^-_{\mathscr{P}}(K) := \{k \mid [f]_{\mathscr{P}}(k) \cap K \neq \phi\}. \tag{3}$$

Definition 6 satisfies two properties. The first is that any initial failure modes computed from final failure modes are the ones that could cause the selected final failure modes. The second is that inverse failure transformers compute all initial failure modes from final reachable failure modes. The next two definitions formalise these properties.

Definition 7. *Given SIS function* f, *we say an inverse failure transformer* t *is* sound *wrt.* f *if all* $k \in t(\mathcal{K})$ *implies* $[f]_{\mathscr{P}}(k) \cap \mathcal{K} \neq \phi$.

Definition 8. *Given SIS function* f, *we say an inverse failure transformer* t *is* complete *if for any set of reachable failure modes* $\mathcal{F}$ *and (initial) failure modes* $\mathcal{I}$, *we have the following:*

$$\mathcal{I} \subseteq t(\mathcal{F}) \quad \Leftrightarrow \quad (\forall i \in \mathcal{I} \cdot [f]_{\mathscr{P}}(i) \cap \mathcal{F} \neq \phi) . \tag{4}$$

Observe that given failure modes m and m' such that $m \in t\{m'\}$, then m' is reachable if there is some (i, i') such that $\mathrm{md}_{\mathscr{P}}(i, i') = m$. In general the safety engineer is not concerned with "unrealistic" failure modes in the sense that no corresponding scenario comprised of failure states can be constructed.

It is clear from Definition 6 that $[f]^-_{\mathscr{P}}$ is a sound and complete transformer relative to f. The definition of completeness is important because it means, for the safety engineer, that all potential failure modes are accounted for by the abstraction. The next lemma records the fact that soundness and completeness is conserved by function composition.

Lemma 2. *Let* f, g *be SIS functions, and let* $\mathscr{P}$ *determine the failure modes so that* $[f]^-_p$ *and* $[g]^-_p$ *are sound and complete transformers. Then their composition* $[f]^-_p \circ [g]^-_p$ *is also sound and complete for the composition SIS function* $f; g$.

Proof. Follows from Definition 6 and standard facts about functions and their transformers [25, 26].

In this section we have set out a formal methods treatment of failure modes for SIFs in SIS programs. We have demonstrated a simple model for failures and shown how this "application-oriented" approach supports a rigorous analysis of failure modes and how they are propagated in SIS programs. In the following sections we show how this can be used to justify the use of standard backwards-reasoning to compute all input failure modes that cause reachable failure modes.

---

[7] We do not treat non-termination nor partial functions.

4   Failure Mode Reasoning

In this section we show how to apply the failures model introduced in Section 3 to the typical safety analysis.

Recall T_{Avg} defined in Fig. 2a. In this example, the failure modes of interest relate to whether the readings of the various sensors accurately record the physical environment or not, and when they do not, which combinations of deviant readings have the potential to result in a hazard.

The safety analysis begins with the identification of hazardous outputs: these are outputs from the SIS program which would directly cause a hazard if it is not correct, in the sense that it deviates from the "true" result which would have been output had all the sensors accurately recorded the status of the plant.

For simplicity we assume that all readings are real-valued, thus we identify "True" with "1" and "False" with "0". Following Definition 3 we set $V = \mathbb{R}$ and identify a partition on $\mathbb{R} \times \mathbb{R}$ given as follows.

Definition 9. *Define the* failures partition *as follows. Let* $\hbar, \ell, m$ *respectively partition* $\mathbb{R} \times \mathbb{R}$ *defined by:*

$$(r, r') \in \hbar \quad iff \quad r > r' \quad ; \quad (r, r') \in m \quad iff \quad r = r' \quad ; \quad (r, r') \in \ell \quad iff \quad r < r'.$$

Here we have identified the common failure modes "reading too high", corresponding to $\hbar$ and "reading too low" corresponding to ℓ. We have also included "reading correct" corresponding to m which is not strictly speaking a "failure", but is useful in the formal analysis. From our gas pressure example, the situation where the input recorded on i_1 is lower than the real pressure in the pipe is modelled by pairs of values that lie in ℓ.

Safety engineers want to know the input failure modes that "cause" particular reachable output failures. Definition 8 and Lemma 2 above support a standard backwards reasoning method on failure modes directly.

For each variable s in an SIS program we use $\hat{s}$ for a corresponding variable taking failure modes for values, which in this case is $\{\hbar, \ell, m\}$.

Definition 10. *Given an SIS function f and a partition $\mathscr{P}$ defining the failure modes. A* failure triple *is written*

$$\{ \hat{s} \in \mathcal{A} \} \ f \ \{ \hat{s}' \in \mathcal{A}' \} , \tag{5}$$

where $\mathcal{A}, \mathcal{A}' \subseteq \{\hbar, \ell, m\}$. *The triple Eq. 5 is* valid *if, for each failure mode $e \in \mathcal{A}$ there exists (m, m') such that* $\mathsf{md}_{\mathscr{P}}(m, m') = e$ *and* $\mathsf{md}_{\mathscr{P}}(\langle f \rangle(m, m')) \cap \mathcal{A}' \neq \phi$.

Note that as a special case where $\mathcal{A}$ is a singleton set $\{a\}$ we write "$\hat{s} = a$" rather than "$\hat{s} \in \mathcal{A}$".

Definition 5 is reminiscent of a standard Hoare Triple for failure modes, however a failure triple is based on Definition 6. More importantly Definition 5 corresponds with the scenarios relevant for the assessment of failures. Whenever f corresponds to an SIS function for example, the valid triple given by Eq. 5

means that the initial failure mode corresponding to a *causes* the final failure mode a'. This effectively enables the identification of failure mode propagation, summarised in the next result.

Theorem 1. *Let f be an SIS function and $\mathscr{P}$ define the relevant failure modes. Let a' be a reachable final failure mode wrt. f. Then for all $a \in [f]_{\mathscr{P}}^-\{a'\}$*

$$\{\ \hat{s} = a\ \}\ f\ \{\ \hat{s}' = a'\ \}$$

is a valid failure triple.

Proof. Definition of $[f]_{\mathscr{P}}^-$, Definition 6.

Backwards Reasoning for Failure Modes: As mentioned above we can use Theorem 1 to compute the failure modes that are the cause of a given reachable final failure mode. A complex SIS program determining a SIF typically comprises multiple function blocks with clearly defined "input" variables and "output" variables, where the outputs are determined by the values on the inputs. The architecture of the SIS program is then equated with a composition of a series of function blocks. Now that we have a formal description in terms of failure triples, we are able to use the standard composition rule:

$$\{\ \hat{s} = a\ \}\ f_1\ \{\ \hat{s}_1 = b\ \}\ \wedge\ \{\ \hat{s}_1 = b\ \}\ f_2\ \{\ \hat{s}' = a'\ \}$$
$$\Rightarrow\ \{\ \hat{s} = a\ \}\ f_1; f_2\ \{\ \hat{s}' = a'\ \}\ .$$

From this we can now deduce failure triples of a complex SIS program by reasoning about failure triples for component function blocks. We illustrate this for Avg and $Gcom_K$ in the next section.

5   Individual Function Blocks

A typical SIS program library, from which function blocks (FBs) are chosen, may include 100 types of FBs [31]. For each FB the relationships between FB input failure modes and FB output failure modes, can be summarised in a Failure Mode Block (FMB). An FMB is proposed based on the well-defined function of its corresponding FB. In this section we will propose FMBs for SIS functions Avg and $Gcom_K$, which we used in our gas pressure example, and we will prove the soundness and completeness of the proposed FMBs. More sample FMBs are proposed and proven in the appendix of [18].

The Avg function block takes two inputs and computes the average. The relevant output failures therefore are whether the output reads too high or too low. The abstraction for failure modes is given below.

Definition 11. *Let Avg be the function defined by: $Avg(i_1, i_2) := (i_1 + i_2)/2$. Its associated FMB, FAvg, is defined as follows:*

$$\{\hat{i}_1 = h \vee \hat{i}_2 = h\} \quad Avg \quad \{\hat{o} = h\}$$
$$\{\hat{i}_1 = \ell \vee \hat{i}_2 = \ell\} \quad Avg \quad \{\hat{o} = \ell\}$$

$$\left. \begin{array}{l} \hat{i}_1 = h \wedge \hat{i}_2 = \ell \vee \\ \hat{i}_1 = \ell \wedge \hat{i}_2 = h \vee \\ \hat{i}_1 = m \wedge \hat{i}_2 = m \end{array} \right\} \quad Avg \quad \{\hat{o} = m\}$$

Definition 11 tells us that if the output reads too high, then it must be because one of the two inputs also reads too high. Similarly, if the output reads too low then it can only be because one of the two inputs also reads too low. On the other hand the output can deliver an accurate result for scenarios where one input reads too high and the other reads too low. At the qualitative level of abstraction, however, all of these possibilities must be accounted for.

$Gcom_K$ is another typical function block which compares the input with a given threshold and reports whether the input meets the given threshold.

Definition 12. *Let $Gcom_K$ be the function defined by: $Gcom_K(i) := (i > K)$. Its associated FMB, FGcom, is defined as follows:*

$$\{\hat{i} = h\} \qquad Gcom_K \quad \{\hat{o} = t\}$$
$$\{\hat{i} = \ell\} \qquad Gcom_K \quad \{\hat{o} = f\}$$
$$\{\hat{i} = \ell \vee \hat{i} = m \vee \hat{i} = h\} \quad Gcom_K \quad \{\hat{o} = m\}$$

Definition 12 tells us that the output reading f when it should read t can only happen when the input is delivering a lower value than it should, and similarly the output reading t when it should read f can only happen when the input reading is falsely reporting a high value. Notice that this definition is actually independent of K, which is why K is suppressed in the FMB model.

The following theorem confirms that Definition 11 and Definition 12 are sound and complete in respect of their operational definitions.

Theorem 2. *The FAvg and FGcom models Definitions 11 and 12 are the sound and complete failure models of Avg and $Gcom_K$ (for all real-valued K).*

Proof. Individual FMBs can be proven by using truth-tables. All possible combinations of faults at the inputs and outputs of a corresponding FB can be defined, based on which the soundness and completeness conditions can be examined. Detailed proof is given in the appendix of [18].

6　FMR in Practice

The FMR process consists of four main stages: composition, substitution, simplification and calculation. In the composition stage, FMBs and failure mode variables are defined and connected in accordance with the SIS program. The model for our example SIS program (Fig. 2a) will include two FMBs: $FAvg$ and $FGcom$. Similarly, variables o, w, i_1 and i_2 in SIS program will have their own corresponding failure mode variables $\hat{o}, \hat{w}, \hat{i}_1$ and $\hat{i}_2$ in the model.

The reasoning process begins at the last FB, i.e. the one that produces the SIS output. In our gas pressure example, the given output fault is $\hat{o} = f$. Taking into account the function of $Gcom_K$ from Definition 12, we can say:

$$\{\hat{w} = \ell\} \quad Gcom_K \quad \{\hat{o} = f\} \tag{6}$$

Statement (6) suggests that output o being f by fault implies that the input to the greater comparison FB, w, is reading lower than what it should.

The reasoning process continues through the SIS program until all the conclusion parts of the implication statements include no more intermediate variables. In our example, the next FB is Avg. Considering the function of Avg, if the fault $\hat{w} = \ell$ occurs at its output, we can conclude that from Definition 11:

$$\{\hat{i}_1 = \ell \vee \hat{i}_2 = \ell\} \quad Avg \quad \{\hat{w} = \ell\} \tag{7}$$

This statement suggests that if the reported value at w is lower than its intended value, then either input i_1 or i_2 may be reading lower. The reasoning sequence terminates here as the left hand side of (7) only includes SIS inputs.

In the second stage of FMR we use the logical composition rules to eliminate intermediate variables in order to reduce the set of FB failure reasons to only one relation that links SIS inputs to its outputs. In our example, the only internal variable is $\hat{w}$. By substituting (7) in (6) we can conclude:

$$\{\hat{i}_1 = \ell \vee \hat{i}_2 = \ell\} \quad Avg; Gcom_K \quad \{\hat{o} = f\} \tag{8}$$

which is very similar to the result (1) of our earlier informal description of FMR.

The third stage of FMR is simplification, where we use standard rules of propositional logic [6] to simplify (8) and create the FMR short list of failure triples. As (8) is already minimal, we can easily see that our short list of faults comprises $\hat{i}_1 = \ell$ and $\hat{i}_2 = \ell$.

Having the input failure modes identified, we can implement the last stage of analysis, calculation, in which we would assign probability values to individual failure events and calculate the overall probability of failure. We skip this stage for this simple example. A comprehensive safety analysis for a realistic case study is described in other work [17].

In a more recent project [19] we examined a larger case study where we integrated FMR with other model-base analysis methods HiP-HOPS [27] and CFT [21]. We demonstrated that not only is FMR able to handle larger examples with precision, but its output can also be of value to other safety analysis tools that are designed to model generic systems but not programs. The process we examined in this case study is briefly shown in Fig. 3: a SIS that protects a gas-fired industrial boiler against high level of water. The SIS program in this example consists of over 2170 function blocks. With close to 100 inputs and

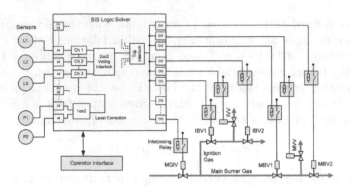

Fig. 3. SIS configuration

over 25 outputs, the SIS performs a total of 34 safety functions (SIFs). The SIS program in this project was developed in FBD and saved in XML format.

The FMR analysis produced two short lists of failure modes, one for Dangerous Undetected (DU) failure and one for Spurious Trip (ST). The lists included a total of 39 failure scenarios. In the quantitative stage the failure data of SIS inputs were entered and the aggregated probability measures for DU and ST failures were calculated.

Provided that failure data are readily available, the whole analysis process for an SIS of this scale takes less than an hour to complete, using the experimental system incorporating FMR analysis [19]. Conducting similar analysis by hand would take days. To visualise the extent of work, consider manual implementation of a fault tree with around 3500 gates. Even if the analyst is prepared for such a challenge, the implemented model, and thus its outcome, will be prone to human error. In comparison, FMR is fast, accurate, consistent, and reliable.

7   Discussion and Related Works

Reasoning about faults is not a new research topic. Diagnostics based on systematic inference was extensively studied in the 1980's. Some of the frequently cited articles include [8,14,28]. Generally speaking, the studies were aimed at answering one question: given an observed deviation at the output of a system, how can we identify the (potentially) faulty components by reasoning based on the knowledge of system structure and/or system function? Logic circuits, in particular, would make an interesting application as they typically consist of complex yet well-defined, logical structures. Unlike inference-based diagnostics, FMR is primarily designed to target probable *input faults*, rather than faulty system components. Input faults are external to the system and do not represent system failure scenarios.

FMR uses abstraction techniques, which is also a well-established area, particularly in formal methods [5]. One may find similarities between the abstraction in FMR and that of Qualitative Reasoning (QR), where quantitative aspects of physical systems are replaced with qualitative representations [2,9]. It should be noted however that QR is a method for expressing physical entities, and with an application in AI; whereas FMR is a technique for reasoning about failures, and (at least, currently) focused on conventional safety systems.

FMR is in some respects similar to FTA. Both methods look at the root causes that can result in a given top event. Parts of the computation techniques are similar between the two methods as well. However, FMR and FTA are different in some conceptual respects. FTA is a generic method that can be applied to any fault in any type of system, whereas FMR is specifically designed for analysing SIS programs. FTA computes a Boolean state of failure-success, but FMR computes multiple failure modes. The top event in FTA is a single event, but the program output in FMR can be an array of variables. The main question FMR tries to answer is that: given an abstracted state of output and given the function that produces it, what are the possible (abstracted) states of inputs to that function. This is obviously different to FTA in which we "know" the failure behaviour of a system and we build a model (fault tree) to summarise our understanding. FTA relies on the knowledge and skills of the analyst whereas FMR extracts information directly from the system. In a general term, FTA is a failure modeling method while FMR is a mode calculation method.

FTA was first introduced in 1961 to study a missile launch control system. In almost six decades, many extensions and variations of the method have been introduced to solve other types of problems. Useful surveys are conducted on FTA and its extensions in recent years [20,29]. Thanks to the growing capabilities of today's technology, attention has shifted towards modularity and automatic synthesis of fault trees, which can greatly assist with solving complex problems at less effort. Various model-based dependability analysis methods have been developed, such as HiP-HOPS [27,30], AADL [13] and AltaRica [23], which use FTA as their primary means and automate the synthesis process to some degrees. More recently, the concept of contract-based design has also been used for automatic generation of hierarchical fault trees from formal models [3].

The common concept in automatic hierarchical synthesis of fault trees is that if we have the typical definition of component fault trees, we can synthesise the system level fault tree by interconnecting the smaller fault trees of components. At a conceptual level, this idea is utilised by FMR too; however, the *components* in FMR are the FBs, as opposed to the other methods that analyse physical systems. Also, while FMR uses the actual SIS program for its analysis, the other methods rely on separate models or specifications in order to generate fault trees. The actual running program in SIS is always the most accurate, detailed, and specific source of information on the behaviour of system, and having that FMR does not require any additional models.

Model checking has been used in SIS related applications too (see [12,22] as examples). In model checking a formal specification of system (model) is checked against a formal specification of requirements. Such methods focus on verifying the program against the requirements, as opposed to FMR which aims to identify failure modes.

Satisfiability Modulo Theories (SMT) is about determining whether a first order formula is satisfiable with respect to some logical theory [4,10]. SMT solvers are used in various applications in the field of computer and formal verification. With respect to FMR, SMT can potentially help with determining the SIS input values that can result in a given output value. While this makes a potential area for further research; our experiments so far indicate that any SMT analysis will require post-processing in order to transform the results into failure modes.

8   Conclusion

In this paper we have shown how techniques from traditional formal methods can be brought to bear on a challenging problem in safety engineering: that of determining with precision how faults arising from incorrect sensor readings propagate through complex SIS programs. Within the safety engineering discipline, FMR is a novel way to analyse failure modes in Safety Instrumented Systems. Future work will include more complex constructs for function blocks, including looping, timing and probabilistic analysis. Moreover, we are working on implementing FMR for identify systematic failures in SIS programs, where the input to the program is correct but the output is faulty due to a pre-existing error in program.

References

1. Berghammer, R., Zierer, H.: Relational algebraic semantics of deterministic and nondeterministic programs. Theoret. Comput. Sci. **43**, 123–147 (1986)
2. Bobrow, D.G.: Qualitative reasoning about physical systems: an introduction. Artif. Intell. **24**(1–3), 1–5 (1984)
3. Bozzano, M., Cimatti, A., Mattarei, C., Tonetta, S.: Formal safety assessment via contract-based design. In: Cassez, F., Raskin, J.-F. (eds.) ATVA 2014. LNCS, vol. 8837, pp. 81–97. Springer, Cham (2014). https://doi.org/10.1007/978-3-319-11936-6_7
4. Clarke, E.M., Henzinger, T.A., Veith, H., Bloem, R.: Handbook of model checking, vol. 10. Springer, Heidelberg (2018). https://doi.org/10.1007/978-3-319-10575-8
5. Cousot, P., Cousot, R.: Abstract interpretation frameworks. J. Log. Comput. **2**(4), 511–547 (1992)
6. Crama, Y., Hammer, P.L.: Boolean Functions: Theory, Algorithms, and Applications. Cambridge University Press, Cambridge (2011)
7. Harel, D.K.D., Tiuryn, J.: Dynamic Logic. Foundations of Computing. MIT Press, Cambridge (2000)
8. Davis, R.: Diagnostic reasoning based on structure and behavior. Artif. Intell. **24**(1–3), 347–410 (1984)
9. De Kleer, J., Brown, J.S.: A qualitative physics based on confluences. Artif. Intell. **24**(1–3), 7–83 (1984)
10. de Moura, L., Bjørner, N.: Satisfiability modulo theories: an appetizer. In: Oliveira, M.V.M., Woodcock, J. (eds.) SBMF 2009. LNCS, vol. 5902, pp. 23–36. Springer, Heidelberg (2009). https://doi.org/10.1007/978-3-642-10452-7_3

11. Dijkstra, E.W.: A Discipline of Programming, vol. 1. Prentice-Hall, Englewood Cliffs (1976)
12. Fantechi, A., Gnesi, S.: On the adoption of model checking in safety-related software industry. In: Flammini, F., Bologna, S., Vittorini, V. (eds.) SAFECOMP 2011. LNCS, vol. 6894, pp. 383–396. Springer, Heidelberg (2011). https://doi.org/10.1007/978-3-642-24270-0_28
13. Feiler, P., Delange, J.: Automated fault tree analysis from aadl models. ACM SIGAda Ada Lett. **36**(2), 39–46 (2017)
14. Genesereth, M.R.: The use of design descriptions in automated diagnosis. Artif. Intell. **24**(1–3), 411–436 (1984)
15. IEC: Programmable controllers - Part 3: Programming languages (2013)
16. IEC: Functional safety-Safety instrumented systems for the process industry sector - Part 1: Framework, definitions, system, hardware and application programming requirements (2016)
17. Jahanian, H.: Failure mode reasoning. In: 2019 4th International Conference on System Reliability and Safety (ICSRS), pp. 295–303. IEEE (2019)
18. Jahanian, H., McIver, A.: Reasoning with failures. arXiv preprint arXiv:2007.10841 (2020)
19. Jahanian, H., Parker, D., Zeller, M., McIver, A., Papadopoulos, Y.: Failure mode reasoning in model based safety analysis. In: 7th International Symposium on Model-Based Safety and Assessment (2020)
20. Kabir, S.: An overview of fault tree analysis and its application in model based dependability analysis. Expert Syst. Appl. **77**, 114–135 (2017)
21. Kaiser, B., Liggesmeyer, P., Mäckel, O.: A new component concept for fault trees. In: Proceedings of the 8th Australian Workshop on Safety Critical Systems and Software, vol. 33, pp. 37–46. ACS Inc. (2003)
22. Lahtinen, J., Valkonen, J., Björkman, K., Frits, J., Niemelä, I., Heljanko, K.: Model checking of safety-critical software in the nuclear engineering domain. Reliab. Eng. Syst. Saf. **105**, 104–113 (2012)
23. Li, S., Li, X.: Study on generation of fault trees from altarica models. Proc. Eng. **80**, 140–152 (2014)
24. Mac Lane, S.: Categories for the Working Mathematician. Springer, Heidelberg (1978). https://doi.org/10.1007/978-1-4757-4721-8
25. McIver, A.K., Morgan, C., Sanders, J.W.: Application-oriented program semantics. In: South African Computer Society (SAICSIT) (1997)
26. Morgan, C.: Of wp and CSP. In: Feijen, W.H.J., van Gasteren, A.J.M., Gries, D., Misra, J. (eds.) Beauty is Our Business. Texts and Monographs in Computer Science, pp. 319–326. Springer, New York (1990). https://doi.org/10.1007/978-1-4612-4476-9_37
27. Papadopoulos, Y., McDermid, J.A.: Hierarchically performed hazard origin and propagation studies. In: Felici, M., Kanoun, K. (eds.) SAFECOMP 1999. LNCS, vol. 1698, pp. 139–152. Springer, Heidelberg (1999). https://doi.org/10.1007/3-540-48249-0_13
28. Reiter, R.: A theory of diagnosis from first principles. Artif. Intell. **32**(1), 57–95 (1987)
29. Ruijters, E., Stoelinga, M.: Fault tree analysis: a survey of the state-of-the-art in modeling, analysis and tools. Comput. Sci. Rev. **15**, 29–62 (2015)

30. Sharvia, S., Papadopoulos, Y.: Integrating model checking with HiP-HOPS in model-based safety analysis. Reliab. Eng. Syst. Saf. **135**, 64–80 (2015)
31. Siemens: Industrial software S7 F/FH Systems - Configuring and Programming. Siemens (2015)
32. Vesely, W.E., Goldberg, F.F., Roberts, N.H., Haasl, D.F.: Fault tree handbook (NUREG-0492). US Nuclear Regulatory Commission (1981)

Program Verification

Verification of Programs with Pointers in SPARK

Georges-Axel Jaloyan[1,2]($\boxtimes$), Claire Dross[3], Maroua Maalej[3], Yannick Moy[3], and Andrei Paskevich[4,5]

[1] École normale supérieure, PSL University, Paris, France
georges-axel.jaloyan@ens.fr
[2] CEA, DAM, DIF, 91297 Arpajon, France
[3] AdaCore, Paris, France
[4] LRI, Université Paris-Sud, CNRS, 91405 Orsay, France
[5] Inria Saclay, Université Paris Saclay, 91120 Palaiseau, France

Abstract. In the field of deductive software verification, programs with pointers present a major challenge due to pointer aliasing. In this paper, we introduce pointers to SPARK, a well-defined subset of the Ada language, intended for formal verification of mission-critical software. Our solution uses a permission-based static alias analysis method inspired by Rust's *borrow-checker* and *affine types*. To validate our approach, we have implemented it in the SPARK GNATprove formal verification toolset for Ada. In the paper, we give a formal presentation of the analysis rules for a core version of SPARK and discuss their implementation and scope.

1 Introduction

SPARK [1] is a subset of the Ada programming language targeted at safety- and security-critical applications. SPARK restrictions ensure that the behavior of a SPARK program is unambiguously defined, and simple enough that formal verification tools can perform an automatic diagnosis of conformance between a program specification and its implementation. As a consequence, it forbids the use of features that either prevent automatic proof, or make it possible only at the expense of extensive user annotation effort. The lack of support for pointers is the main example of this choice.

Among the various problems related to the use of pointers in the context of formal program verification, the most difficult problem is that two names may refer to overlapping memory locations, a.k.a. aliasing. Formal verification platforms that support pointer aliasing like Frama-C [?] require users to annotate programs to specify when pointers are not aliased. This can take the form of inequalities between pointers when a typed memory model is used, or the form of separation predicates between memory zones when an untyped memory model is

This work is partly supported by the Joint Laboratory ProofInUse (ANR-13-LAB3-0007) and project VECOLIB (ANR-14-CE28-0018) of the French National Research Agency (ANR).

S.-W. Lin et al. (Eds.): ICFEM 2020, LNCS 12531, pp. 55–72, 2020.
https://doi.org/10.1007/978-3-030-63406-3_4

used. In both cases, the annotation burden is acceptable for leaf functions which manipulate single-level pointers, and quickly becomes overwhelming for functions that manipulate pointer-rich data structures. In parallel to the increased cost of annotations, the benefits of automation decrease, as automatic provers have difficulties reasoning explicitly with these inequalities and separation predicates.

Programs often rely on non-aliasing in general for correctness, when such aliasing would introduce interferences between two unrelated names. We call aliasing *potentially harmful* when a memory location modified through one name could be read through another name, within the scope of a verification condition. Otherwise, the aliasing is *benign*, when the memory location is only read through both names. A reasonable approach to formal program verification is thus to detect and forbid potentially harmful aliasing of names. Although this restricted language fragment cannot include all pointer-manipulating programs, it still allows us to introduce pointers to SPARK with minimal overhead for its program verification engine.

In this paper, we provide a formal description of the inclusion of pointers in the Ada language subset supported in SPARK, generalizing intuitions that can be found in [3,4] or on Adacore's blog [5,6]. As our main contribution, we show that it is possible to borrow and adapt the ideas underlying the safe support for pointers in permission-based languages like Rust, to safely restrict the use of pointers in usual imperative languages like Ada.

The rest of the paper is organized as follows. In Sect. 2, we give an informal description of our approach. Section 3 introduces a small formal language for which we define the formal alias analysis rules in Sect. 4. In Sect. 5, we describe the implementation of the analysis in GNATProve, a formal verification tool for Ada, and discuss some limitations with the help of various examples. We survey related works in Sect. 6 and future works in Sect. 7.

2 Informal Overview of Alias Analysis in SPARK

In Ada, the access to memory areas is given through *paths* that start with an identifier (a variable name) and follow through record fields, array indices, or through a special field all, which corresponds to pointer dereferencing. In what follows, we only consider record and pointer types, and discuss the treatment of arrays in Sect. 5.

As an example, we use the following Ada type, describing singly linked lists where each node carries a Boolean flag and a pointer to a shared integer value.

```
type List is record
   Flag : Boolean;
   Key  : access Integer;
   Next : access List;
end record;
```

Given a variable A : List, the paths A.Flag, A.Key.all, A.Next.all.Key are valid and their respective types are Boolean, Integer, and access Integer (a pointer to an Integer). The important difference between pointers and records in Ada is that—similarly to C—assignment of a record copies the values of fields, whereas assignment of a pointer only copies the address and creates an alias.

The alias analysis procedure runs after the type checking. The idea is to associate one of the four permissions—RW, R, W or NO—to each possible path (starting from the available variables) at each sequence point in the program. A set of rules ensures that for any two aliased pointers, at most one has the ownership of the underlying memory area, that means the ability to read and modify it.

The absence of permission is denoted as the NO permission. Any modification or access to the value accessible from the path is forbidden. This typically applies to aliased memory areas that have lost the ownership over their stored values.

The *read-only* permission R allows us to read any value accessible from the path: use it in a computation, or pass it as an in parameter in a procedure call. As a consequence, if a given path has the R permission, then each valid extension of this path also has it.

The *write-only* permission W allows us to modify memory occupied by the value: use it on the left-hand side in an assignment or pass it as an out parameter in a procedure call. For example, having a write permission for a path of type List allows us to modify the Flag field or to change the addresses stored in the pointer fields Key and Next. However, this does not necessarily give us the permission to modify memory accessible from those pointers. Indeed, to dereference a pointer, we must read the address stored in it, which requires the read permission. Thus, the W permission only propagates to path extensions that do not dereference pointers, i.e., do not contain additional all fields.

The *read-write* permission RW combines the properties of the R and W permissions and grants the full ownership of the path and every value accessible from it. In particular, the RW permission propagates to all valid path extensions including those that dereference pointers. The RW permission is required to pass a value as an in out parameter in a procedure call.

Execution of program statements changes permissions. A simple example of this is procedure call: all out parameters must be assigned by the callee and get the RW permission after the call. The assignment statement is more complicated and several cases must be considered. If we assign a value that does not contain pointers (say, an integer or a pointer-free record), the whole value is copied into the left-hand side, and we only need to check that we have the appropriate permissions: W or RW for the left-hand side and R or RW for the right-hand side. However, whenever we copy a pointer, an alias is created. We want to make the left-hand side the new full owner of the value (i.e., give it the RW permission), and therefore, after the permission checks, we must revoke the permissions from the right-hand side, to avoid potentially harmful aliasing. The permission checks are also slightly different in this case, as we require the right-hand side to have the RW permission in order to move it to the left-hand side.

Let us now consider several simple programs and see how the permission checks allow us to detect potentially harmful aliasing.

```
procedure P1                          procedure P2
  (A,B: in out List) is                 (A,B: in out access Integer) is
begin                                 begin
  A := B;                               while B.all > 0 loop
  B.Flag := True;                         A.all := A.all + 1;
  B.Key.all := 42;                        B.all := B.all - 1;
  -- A.Key.all == 42?                     A := B;
end P1;                                 end loop;
                                        -- loop terminates?
                                      end P2;
```

Fig. 1. Examples of potentially harmful aliasing, with some verification conditions that require tracking aliases throughout the program to be checked.

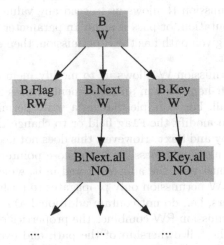

Fig. 2. Graphical representation of the permissions attributed to B and its extensions after assignment A := B; in P1.

Procedure P1 in Fig. 1 receives two in out parameters A and B of type List. At the start of the procedure, all in out parameters assume permission RW. In particular, this implies that each in out parameter is separated from all other parameters, in the sense that no memory area can be reached from two different parameters. The first assignment copies the structure B into A. Thus, the paths A.Flag, A.Key, and A.Next are separated, respectively, from B.Flag, B.Key, and B.Next. However, the paths A.Key.all and B.Key.all are aliased, and A.Next.all and B.Next.all are aliased as well.

The first assignment does not change the permissions of A and its extensions: they retain the RW permission and keep the full ownership of their respective memory areas, even if the areas themselves have changed. The paths under B, however, must relinquish (some of) their permissions, as shown in Fig. 2. The paths B.Key.all and B.Next.all as well as all their extensions get the NO permission, that is, lose both read and write permissions. This is necessary, as the ownership over their memory areas is transferred to the corresponding paths under A. The paths B, B.Key, and B.Next lose the read permission but keep the write-only W permission. Indeed, we forbid reading from memory that can be altered through a concurrent path. However, it is allowed to "redirect" the pointers B.Key and B.Next, either by assigning those fields directly or by copying some different record into B. The field B.Flag is not aliased, nor has aliased extensions, and thus retains the initial RW permission. This RW permission allows us to perform the assignment B.Flag := True on the next line.

The third assignment, however, is now illegal, since B.Key.all does not have the write permission anymore. What is more, at the end of the procedure the in out parameters A and B are not separated. This is forbidden, as the caller assumes that all out and in out parameters are separated after the call just as they were before.

Procedure P2 in Fig. 1 receives two pointers A and B, and manipulates them inside a while loop. Since the permissions are assigned statically, we must ensure that at the end of a single iteration, we did not lose the permissions necessary for the next iteration. This requirement is violated in the example: after the last assignment A := B, the path B receives permission W and the path B.all, permission NO, as B.all is now an alias of A.all. The new permissions for B and B.all are thus weaker than the original ones (RW for both), and the procedure is rejected. Should it be accepted, we would have conflicting memory modifications from two aliased paths at the beginning of the next iteration.

3 μSPARK Language

For the purposes of formal presentation, we introduce μSPARK, a small subset of SPARK featuring pointers, records, loops, and procedure calls. We present the syntax of μSPARK, and define the rules of alias safety.

The data types of μSPARK are as follows:

type ::= Integer | Real | Boolean		scalar type
| access *type*		access type (pointer)
| *ident*		record type

Every μSPARK program starts with a list of record type declarations:

record ::= type *ident* is record *field** end

field ::= *ident* : *type*

We require all field names to be distinct. The field types must not refer to the record types declared later in the list. Nevertheless, a record type R can be made recursive by adding a field whose type is a pointer to R (written access R). We discuss the handling of array types in Sect. 5.

The syntax of μSPARK statements is defined by the following rules:

$$
\begin{array}{rlll}
path & ::= & ident & \text{variable} \\
 & | & path \,.\, ident & \text{record field} \\
 & | & path \,.\, \mathtt{all} & \text{pointer dereference} \\[4pt]
expr & ::= & path & \text{l-value} \\
 & | & \mathtt{42} \mid \mathtt{3.14} \mid \mathtt{True} \mid \mathtt{False} \mid \dots & \text{scalar value} \\
 & | & expr \ (\, \mathtt{+} \mid \mathtt{-} \mid \mathtt{<} \mid \mathtt{=} \mid \dots \,) \ expr & \text{binary operator} \\
 & | & \mathtt{null} & \text{null pointer} \\[4pt]
stmt & ::= & path \ \mathtt{:=} \ expr & \text{assignment} \\
 & | & path \ \mathtt{:=} \ \mathtt{new} \ type & \text{allocation} \\
 & | & \mathtt{if} \ expr \ \mathtt{then} \ stmt^\star \ \mathtt{else} \ stmt^\star \ \mathtt{end} & \text{conditional} \\
 & | & \mathtt{while} \ expr \ \mathtt{loop} \ stmt^\star \ \mathtt{end} & \text{``while'' loop} \\
 & | & ident \ (\ expr^\star \ ) & \text{procedure call}
\end{array}
$$

Following the record type declarations, a μSPARK program contains a set of mutually recursive procedure declarations:

$$
\begin{array}{rll}
procedure & ::= & \mathtt{procedure} \ ident \ (\ param^\star \ ) \ \mathtt{is} \ local^\star \ \mathtt{begin} \ stmt^\star \ \mathtt{end} \\
param & ::= & ident \ : \ (\, \mathtt{in} \mid \mathtt{in} \ \mathtt{out} \mid \mathtt{out} \,) \ type \\
local & ::= & ident \ : \ type
\end{array}
$$

We require all formal parameters and local variables in a procedure to have distinct names. A procedure call can only pass left-values (i.e., paths) for **in out** and **out** parameters. The execution starts from a procedure named Main with the empty parameter list.

The type system for μSPARK is rather standard and we do not show it here in full. We assume that binary operators only operate on scalar types. The null pointer can have any pointer type access τ. The dereference operator .all converts access τ to τ. Allocation $p := \mathtt{new} \ \tau$ requires path p to have type access τ. In what follows, we only consider well-typed μSPARK programs. A formal semantics for μSPARK statements is given in Appendix A.

On the semantic level, we need to distinguish the units of allocation, such as whole records, from the units of access, such as individual record fields. We use the term *location* to refer to the memory area occupied by an allocated value. We treat locations as elements of an abstract infinite set, and denote them with letter ℓ. We use the term *address* to designate either a location, denoted ℓ, or a specific component inside the location of a record, denoted $\ell.f.g$, where f and g are field names (assuming that at ℓ we have a record whose field f is itself a record with a field g). A *value* is either a scalar, an address, a null pointer or a record, that is, a finite mapping from field names to values.

A μSPARK program is executed in the context defined by a *binding* Υ that maps variable names to addresses and a *store* Σ that maps locations to values. By a slight abuse of notation, we apply Σ to arbitrary addresses, so that $\Sigma(\ell.f)$ is $\Sigma(\ell)(f)$, the value of the field f of the record value stored in Σ at ℓ.

The evaluation of expressions is effect-free and is denoted $\llbracket e \rrbracket_\Sigma^\Upsilon$. We also need to evaluate l-values to the corresponding addresses in the store, written $\langle p \rangle_\Sigma^\Upsilon$, where p is the evaluated path. Illicit operations, such as dereferencing a null pointer, cannot be evaluated and stall the execution (*blocking semantics*). In the formal rules below, c stands for a scalar constant and $\odot$, for a binary operator:

$$\langle x \rangle_\Sigma^\Upsilon = \Upsilon(x) \qquad\qquad \langle p.f \rangle_\Sigma^\Upsilon = \langle p \rangle_\Sigma^\Upsilon.f \qquad\qquad \langle p.\texttt{all} \rangle_\Sigma^\Upsilon = \llbracket p \rrbracket_\Sigma^\Upsilon$$

$$\llbracket c \rrbracket_\Sigma^\Upsilon = c \qquad\qquad \llbracket p \rrbracket_\Sigma^\Upsilon = \Sigma(\langle p \rangle_\Sigma^\Upsilon) \qquad\qquad \llbracket \texttt{null} \rrbracket_\Sigma^\Upsilon = \texttt{null}$$

$$\llbracket e_1 \odot e_2 \rrbracket_\Sigma^\Upsilon = \llbracket e_1 \rrbracket_\Sigma^\Upsilon \odot \llbracket e_2 \rrbracket_\Sigma^\Upsilon$$

4   Access Policies, Transformers, and Alias Safety Rules

We denote paths with letters p and q. We write $p \sqsubset q$ to denote that p is a strict *prefix* of q or, equivalently, q is a strict *extension* of p. In what follows, we always mean strict prefixes and extensions, unless explicitly said otherwise.

In the typing context of a given procedure, a well-typed path is said to be *deep* if it has a non-strict extension of an access type, otherwise it is called *shallow*. We extend these notions to types: a type τ is deep (resp. shallow) if and only if a τ-typed path is deep (resp. shallow). In other words, a path or a type is deep if a pointer can be reached from it, and shallow otherwise. For example, the `List` type in Sect. 2 is a deep type, and so is `access Integer`, whereas any scalar type or any record with scalar fields only is shallow.

An extension q of a path p is called a *near extension* if it has as many pointer dereferences as p, otherwise it is a *far extension*. For instance, given a variable `A` of type `List`, the paths `A.Flag`, `A.Key`, and `A.Next` are the near extensions of `A`, whereas `A.Key.all`, `A.Next.all`, and their extensions are far extensions, since they all create an additional pointer dereference by passing through `all`.

We say that *sequence points* are the program points before or after a given statement. For each sequence point in a given μSPARK program, we statically compute an *access policy*: a partial function that maps each well-typed path to one of the four *permissions*: RW, R, W, and NO, which form a diamond lattice: RW > R|W > NO. We denote permissions by π and access policies by Π.

Permission transformers modify policies at a given path, as well as its prefixes and extensions. Symbolically, we write $\Pi \xrightarrow{T}_p \Pi'$ to denote that policy Π' results from application of transformer T to Π at path p. We define a composition operation $\Pi \xrightarrow{T_1}_{p_1} \,\mathring{,}\, \xrightarrow{T_2}_{p_2} \Pi'$ that allows chaining the application of permission transformers T_1 at path p_1 and T_2 at path p_2 to Π resulting in the policy Π'. We write $\Pi \xrightarrow{T_1 \,\mathring{,}\, T_2}_p \Pi'$ as an abbreviation for $\Pi \xrightarrow{T_1}_p \,\mathring{,}\, \xrightarrow{T_2}_p \Pi'$ (that is, for some Π'', $\Pi \xrightarrow{T_1}_p \Pi'' \xrightarrow{T_2}_p \Pi'$). We write $\Pi \xrightarrow{T}_{p,q} \Pi'$ as an abbreviation for $\Pi \xrightarrow{T}_p \,\mathring{,}\, \xrightarrow{T}_q \Pi'$.

Permission transformers can also apply to expressions, which consists in updating the policy for every path in the expression. This only includes paths that occur as sub-expressions: in an expression `X.f.g + Y.h`, only the paths

X.f.g and Y.h are concerned, whereas X, X.f and Y are not. The order in which
the individual paths are treated must not affect the final result.

$$\frac{\Pi \xrightarrow{\text{move}}_e \ \overset{\circ}{,} \ \xrightarrow{\text{check W } \overset{\circ}{,} \text{ fresh RW } \overset{\circ}{,} \text{ lift}}_p \Pi'}{\Pi \cdot p := e \rightarrow \Pi'} \quad \text{(P-ASSIGN)}$$

$$\frac{\Pi \xrightarrow{\text{check W } \overset{\circ}{,} \text{ fresh RW } \overset{\circ}{,} \text{ lift}}_p \Pi'}{\Pi \cdot p := \textbf{new} \ \tau \rightarrow \Pi'} \quad \text{(P-ALLOC)}$$

$$\frac{\Pi \xrightarrow{\text{check R}}_e \Pi \quad \Pi \cdot \bar{s}_1 \rightarrow \Pi_1 \quad \Pi \cdot \bar{s}_2 \rightarrow \Pi_2 \quad \forall p. \ \Pi'(p) = \Pi_1(p) \wedge \Pi_2(p)}{\Pi \cdot \textbf{if} \ e \ \textbf{then} \ \bar{s}_1 \ \textbf{else} \ \bar{s}_2 \ \textbf{end} \rightarrow \Pi'} \quad \text{(P-IF)}$$

$$\frac{\Pi \xrightarrow{\text{check R}}_e \Pi \quad \Pi \cdot \bar{s} \rightarrow \Pi' \quad \forall \pi. \ \Pi'(\pi) \geqslant \Pi(\pi)}{\Pi \cdot \textbf{while} \ e \ \textbf{loop} \ \bar{s} \ \textbf{end} \rightarrow \Pi} \quad \text{(P-WHILE)}$$

$$\textbf{procedure} \ P \ (\ a_1 : \textbf{in} \ \tau_{a_1} ; \ldots ; b_1 : \textbf{in out} \ \tau_{b_1} ; \ldots ; c_1 : \textbf{out} \ \tau_{c_1} ; \ldots)$$
$$\text{is} \cdots \textbf{begin} \ \bar{s} \ \textbf{end} \ \text{is declared in the program}$$

$$\frac{\Pi \xrightarrow{\text{check R } \overset{\circ}{,} \text{ observe}}_{e_{a_1}, \ldots} \overset{\circ}{,} \xrightarrow{\text{check RW } \overset{\circ}{,} \text{ borrow}}_{p_{b_1}, \ldots} \overset{\circ}{,} \xrightarrow{\text{check W } \overset{\circ}{,} \text{ borrow}}_{q_{c_1}, \ldots} \Pi'' \quad \Pi \xrightarrow{\text{fresh RW } \overset{\circ}{,} \text{ lift}}_{p_{b_1}, \ldots} \overset{\circ}{,} \xrightarrow{\text{fresh RW } \overset{\circ}{,} \text{ lift}}_{q_{c_1}, \ldots} \Pi'}{\Pi \cdot P(e_{a_1}, \ldots, p_{b_1}, \ldots, q_{c_1}, \ldots) \rightarrow \Pi'} \quad \text{(P-CALL)}$$

Fig. 3. Alias safety rules for statements.

We define the rules of alias safety for μSPARK statements in the context of
a current access policy. An *alias-safe* statement yields an updated policy which
is used to check the subsequent statement. We write $\Pi \cdot s \rightarrow \Pi'$ to denote that
statement s is safe with respect to policy Π and yields the updated policy Π'.
We extend this notation to sequences of statements in an obvious way, as the
reflexive-transitive closure of the update relation on Π. The rules for checking
the alias safety of statements are given in Fig. 3. These rules use a number of
permission transformers such as 'fresh', 'check', 'move', 'observe', and 'borrow',
which we define and explain below.

Let us start with the (P-ASSIGN) rule. Assignments grant the full ownership
over the copied value to the left-hand side. If we copy a value of a shallow
type, we merely have to ensure that the right-hand side has the read permission.
Whenever we copy a deep-typed value, aliases may be created, and we must
check that the right-hand side is initially the sole owner of the copied value
(that is, possesses the RW permission) and revoke the ownership from it.

To define the 'move' transformer that handles permissions for the right-hand
side of an assignment, we need to introduce several simpler transformers.

Definition 1. *Permission transformer* check π *does not modify the access policy
and only verifies that a given path p has permission π or greater. In other words,*
$\Pi \xrightarrow{\text{check } \pi}_p \Pi'$ *if and only if $\Pi(p) \geqslant \pi$ and $\Pi = \Pi'$. This transformer also*

applies to expressions: $\Pi \xrightarrow{\text{check } \pi}_e \Pi'$ *states that* $\Pi \xrightarrow{\text{check } \pi}_p \Pi'(= \Pi)$ *for every path p occurring in e.*

Definition 2. *Permission transformer* fresh π *assigns permission* π *to a given path p and all its extensions.*

Definition 3. *Permission transformer* cut *assigns restricted permissions to a deep path p and its extensions: the path p and its near deep extensions receive permission* W, *the near shallow extensions keep their current permissions, and the far extensions receive permission* NO.

Going back to the procedure P1 in Fig. 1, the change of permissions on the right-hand side after the assignment A := B corresponds to the definition of 'cut'. In the case where the right-hand side of an assignment is a deep path, we also need to change permissions of the prefixes, to reflect the ownership transfer.

Definition 4. *Permission transformer* block *propagates the loss of the read permission from a given path to all its prefixes. Formally, it is defined by the following rules, where x stands for a variable and f for a field name:*

$$\frac{}{\Pi \xrightarrow{\text{block}}_x \Pi} \qquad \frac{\Pi[p \mapsto W] \xrightarrow{\text{block}}_p \Pi'}{\Pi \xrightarrow{\text{block}}_{p.\text{all}} \Pi'}$$

$$\frac{\Pi(p) = \text{NO}}{\Pi \xrightarrow{\text{block}}_{p.f} \Pi} \qquad \frac{\Pi(p) \geqslant W \quad \Pi[p \mapsto W] \xrightarrow{\text{block}}_p \Pi'}{\Pi \xrightarrow{\text{block}}_{p.f} \Pi'}$$

Definition 5. *Permission transformer* move *applies to expressions:*

- *if e has a shallow type, then* $\Pi \xrightarrow{\text{move}}_e \Pi' \Leftrightarrow \Pi \xrightarrow{\text{check R}}_e \Pi'$,
- *if e is a deep path p, then* $\Pi \xrightarrow{\text{move}}_e \Pi' \Leftrightarrow \Pi \xrightarrow{\text{check RW } \mathring{,} \text{ cut } \mathring{,} \text{ block}}_p \Pi'$,
- *if e is* null, *then* $\Pi \xrightarrow{\text{move}}_e \Pi' \Leftrightarrow \Pi' = \Pi$.

To further illustrate the 'move' transformer, let us consider two variables P and Q of type access List and an assignment P := Q.all.Next. We assume that Q and all its extensions have full ownership (RW) before the assignment. We apply the second case in the definition of 'move' to the deep path Q.all.Next. The 'check RW' condition is verified, and the 'cut' transformer sets the permission for Q.all.Next to W and the permission for Q.all.Next.all and all its extensions to NO. Indeed, P.all becomes an alias of Q.all.Next.all and steals the full ownership for this memory area. However, we still can reassign Q.all.Next to a different address. Moreover, we still can write some new values into Q.all or Q, without compromising safety. This is enforced by the application of the 'block' transformer at the end. We cannot keep the read permission for Q or Q.all, since it implies the read access to the data under Q.all.Next.all.

Finally, we need to describe the change of permissions on the left-hand side of an assignment, in order to reflect the gain of the full ownership. The idea is that as soon as we have the full ownership for each field of a record, we can assume the full ownership of the whole record, and similarly for pointers.

Definition 6. *Permission transformer* lift *propagates the* RW *permission from a given path to its prefixes, wherever possible:*

$$\frac{}{\Pi \xrightarrow{\text{lift}}_x \Pi}$$

$$\frac{\Pi[p \mapsto \text{RW}] \xrightarrow{\text{lift}}_p \Pi'}{\Pi \xrightarrow{\text{lift}}_{p.all} \Pi'}$$

$$\frac{\forall q \sqsupseteq p. \, \Pi(q) = \text{RW} \quad \Pi[p \mapsto \text{RW}] \xrightarrow{\text{lift}}_p \Pi'}{\Pi \xrightarrow{\text{lift}}_{p.f} \Pi'}$$

$$\frac{\exists q \sqsupseteq p. \, \Pi(q) \neq \text{RW}}{\Pi \xrightarrow{\text{lift}}_{p.f} \Pi}$$

In the (P-ASSIGN) rule, we revoke the permissions from the right-hand side of an assignment before granting the ownership to the left-hand side. This is done in order to prevent creation of circular data structures. Consider an assignment `A.Next.all := A`, where `A` has type `List`. According to the definition of 'move', all far extensions of the right-hand side, notably `A.Next.all`, receive permission NO. This makes the left-hand side fail the write permission check.

Allocations `p := new τ` are handled by the (P-ALLOC) rule. We grant the full permission on the newly allocated memory, as it cannot possibly be aliased.

In a conditional statement, the policies at the end of the two branches are merged selecting the most restrictive permission for each path. Loops require that no permissions are lost at the end of a loop iteration, compared to the entry, as explained above for procedure P2 in Fig. 1.

Procedure calls guarantee to the callee that every argument with mode in, in out, or out has at least permission R, RW or W, respectively. To ensure the absence of potentially harmful aliasing, we revoke the necessary permissions using the 'observe' and 'borrow' transformers.

Definition 7. *Permission transformer* borrow *assigns permission* NO *to a given path p and all its prefixes and extensions.*

Definition 8. *Permission transformer* freeze *removes the write permission from a given path p and all its prefixes and extensions. In other words,* freeze *assigns to each path q comparable to p the minimum permission* $\Pi(q) \wedge R$.

Definition 9. *Permission transformer* observe *applies to expressions:*

- *if e has a shallow type, then* $\Pi \xrightarrow{\text{observe}}_e \Pi' \Leftrightarrow \Pi' = \Pi$,
- *if e is a deep path p, then* $\Pi \xrightarrow{\text{observe}}_e \Pi' \Leftrightarrow \Pi \xrightarrow{\text{freeze}}_p \Pi'$,
- *if e is* **null**, *then* $\Pi \xrightarrow{\text{observe}}_e \Pi' \Leftrightarrow \Pi' = \Pi$.

We remove the write permission from the deep-typed in parameters using the 'observe' transformer, in order to allow aliasing between the read-only paths. As for the in out and out parameters, we transfer the full ownership over them to the callee, which is reflected by dropping every permission on the caller's side using 'borrow'.

In the (P-CALL) rule, we revoke permissions right after checking them for each parameter. In this way, we cannot pass, for example, the same path as an in and in out parameter in the same call. Indeed, the 'observe' transformer will remove the write permission, which is required by 'check RW' later in the transformer chain. At the end of the call, the callee transfers to the caller the full ownership over each in out and out parameter.

We apply our alias safety analysis to each procedure declaration. We start with an empty access policy, denoted $\varnothing$. Then we fill the policy with the permissions for the formal parameters and the local variables and check the procedure body. At the end, we verify that every in out and out parameter has the RW permission. Formally, this is expressed with the following rule:

$$\cfrac{\varnothing \xrightarrow{\text{fresh R}}_{a_1,\dots}\; \S\; \xrightarrow{\text{fresh RW}}_{b_1,\dots}\; \S\; \xrightarrow{\text{fresh W}\; \S\; \text{cut}}_{c_1,\dots}\; \S\; \xrightarrow{\text{fresh RW}}_{d_1,\dots}\; \Pi' \qquad \Pi' \cdot \bar{s} \to \Pi'' \qquad \Pi''(b_1) = \dots = \Pi''(c_1) = \dots = \text{RW}}{\begin{array}{c}\textbf{procedure } P\ (\,a_1 : \textbf{in}\,\tau_{a_1}\,;\dots;\,b_1 : \textbf{in out}\,\tau_{b_1}\,;\dots;\,c_1 : \textbf{out}\,\tau_{c_1}\,;\dots)\\ \textbf{is } d_1 : \tau_{d_1}\,;\dots \textbf{begin } \bar{s} \textbf{ end} \quad \text{is alias-safe}\end{array}}$$

We say that a μSPARK program is *alias-safe* if all its procedures are.

By the end of the analysis, an alias-safe program has an access policy associated to each sequence point in it. We say that an access policy Π is *consistent* whenever it satisfies the following conditions for all valid paths π, $\pi.f$, $\pi.\texttt{all}$:

$$\Pi(\pi) = \text{RW} \implies \Pi(\pi.f) = \text{RW} \qquad \Pi(\pi) = \text{RW} \implies \Pi(\pi.\texttt{all}) = \text{RW} \qquad (1)$$
$$\Pi(\pi) = \text{R} \implies \Pi(\pi.f) = \text{R} \qquad \Pi(\pi) = \text{R} \implies \Pi(\pi.\texttt{all}) = \text{R} \qquad (2)$$
$$\Pi(\pi) = \text{W} \implies \Pi(\pi.f) \geq \text{W} \qquad\qquad\qquad\qquad\qquad (3)$$

These invariants correspond to the informal explanations given in Sect. 2. Invariant (1) states that the full ownership over a value propagates to all values reachable from it. Invariant (2) states that the read-only permission must also propagate to all extensions. Indeed, a modification of a reachable component can be observed from any prefix. Invariant (3) states that write permission over a record value implies a write permission over each of its fields. However, the write permission does not necessarily propagate across pointer dereference.

Lemma 1 (Policy Consistency). *The alias safety rules in Fig. 3 preserve policy consistency.*

When, during an execution, we arrive at a given sequence point with the set of variable bindings Υ, store Σ, and statically computed and consistent access policy Π, we say that the state of the execution respects the *Concurrent Read, Exclusive Write* condition (CREW), if and only if for any two distinct valid paths p and q, $\langle p \rangle^\Upsilon_\Sigma = \langle q \rangle^\Upsilon_\Sigma \wedge \Pi(p) \geq \text{W} \implies \Pi(q) = \text{NO}$.

The main result about the soundness of our approach is as follows.

Theorem 1 (Soundness). *A terminating evaluation of a well-typed alias-safe μSPARK program respects the CREW condition at every sequence point.*

The full proof, for a slightly different definition of μSPARK, is given in [7]. The argument proceeds by induction on the evaluation derivation, following the rules provided in Appendix A. The only difficult cases are assignment, where the required permission withdrawal is ensured by the 'move' transformer, and procedure call, where the chain of 'observe' and 'borrow' transformers, together with the corresponding checks, on the caller's side, ensures that the CREW condition is respected at the beginning of the callee.

For the purposes of verification, an alias-safe program can be treated with no regard for sharing. More precisely, we can safely transform access types into records with a single field that contains either null or the referenced value. Since records are copied on assignment, we obtain a program that can be verified using the standard rules of Floyd-Hoare logic or weakest-precondition calculus (as the rules have also ensured the absence of aliasing between procedure parameters).

Indeed, consider an assignment A := B where A and B are pointers. In an alias-safe program, B loses its ownership over the referenced value and cannot be used anymore without being reassigned. Then, whenever we modify that value through A.all, we do not need to update B.all in the verification condition. In other words, we can safely treat A := B as a *deep copy* of B.all into A.all. The only adjustment that needs to be made to the verification condition generator consists in adding checks against the null pointer dereferencement, which is not handled by our rules.

5   Implementation and Evaluation

The alias safety rules presented above have been implemented in the SPARK proof tool, called GNATprove. The real SPARK subset differs from μSPARK in several respects: arrays, functions, additional loop constructs, and global variables. For arrays, permission rules apply to all elements, without taking into account the exact index of an element, which may not be known statically in the general case. Functions return values and cannot perform side effects. They only take in parameters and may be called inside expressions. To avoid creating aliases between the function parameters and the returned value, the full RW permission is required on the latter at the end of the callee. The rules for loops have been extended to handle for-loops and plain loops (which have no exit condition), and also the exit (break) statements inside loops. Finally, global variables are considered as implicit parameters of subprograms that access them, with mode depending on whether the subprogram reads and/or modifies the variable.

Though our alias safety rules are constraining, we feel that they significantly improve the expressive power of the SPARK subset. To demonstrate it, let us go over some examples.[1] One of the main uses of pointers is to serve as references to avoid copying potentially big data structures. We believe this use case is supported as long as the CREW condition is respected. We demonstrate this on a small procedure that swaps two pointers.

---

[1] https://github.com/GAJaloyan/SPARKExamples.

```
type Int_Ptr is access Integer;

procedure Swap (X, Y: in out Int_Ptr) is
  T : Int_Ptr := X; -- ownership of X is moved to T, X gets 'W'
begin
  X := Y; -- ownership of Y is moved to X, Y gets 'W', X gets 'RW'
  Y := T; -- ownership of T is moved to Y, T gets 'W', Y gets 'RW'
  return; -- when exiting Swap, X and Y should be 'RW'
end Swap; -- local variable T is not required to have any permission
```

This code is accepted by our alias safety rules. We can provide it with a contract, which can then be verified by the SPARK proof tool.

```
procedure Swap (X, Y: in out Int_Ptr) with
  Pre  => X /= null and Y /= null,
  Post => X.all = Y.all'Old and Y.all = X.all'Old;
```

Another common use case for pointers in Ada is to store indefinite types (that is, the types whose size is not known statically, such as String) inside aggregate data structures like arrays or records. The usual workaround consists in storing pointers to indefinite elements instead. This usage is also supported by our alias analysis, as illustrated by an implementation of word sets, which is accepted and fully verified by SPARK.

```
type Red_Black is (Red, Black);        procedure Insert_Rec
type Tree;                               (T: in out Tree_Ptr;
type Tree_Ptr is access Tree;            V: Integer) is
type Tree is record                    begin
  Value : Integer;                       if T = null then
  Color : Red_Black;                       T := new Tree'(
  Left  : Tree_Ptr;                          Value => V,
  Right : Tree_Ptr;                          Color => Red,
end record;                                  Left  => null,
                                             Right => null);
procedure Rotate_Left                    elsif T.Value = V then
  (T: in out Tree_Ptr)                     return;
is                                       elsif T.Value > V then
  X: Tree := T.Right;                      Insert_Rec (T.Left, V);
begin                                    else
  T.Right := X.Left;                       Insert_Rec (T.Right, V);
  X.Left := T;                           end if;
  T := X;                                Balance (T);
end Rotate_Left;                       end Insert_Rec;
```

The last use case that we want to consider is the implementation of recursive data structures such as lists and trees. While alias safety rules exclude structures whose members do not have a single owner like doubly linked lists or arbitrary graphs, they are permissive enough for many non-trivial tree data structures, for example, red-black trees. To insert a value in a red-black tree, the tree is first traversed top-down to find the correct leaf for the insertion, and then it is traversed again bottom-up to reestablish balancing. Doing this traversal iteratively requires storing a link to the parent node in children, which is not allowed as it would introduce an alias. Therefore, we went for a recursive implementation, partially shown above. The rotating functions, which are used by the `Balance` procedure (not shown here) can be implemented straightforwardly, since rotation moves pointers around without creating any cycles.

This example passes alias safety analysis successfully (*i.e.* without errors from the tool) and can be verified to be free of runtime exceptions (such as dereferences of null pointers) by the SPARK proof tool.

6   Related Work

The recent adoption of permission-based typing systems by programming languages is the culmination of several decades of research in this field. Going back as early as 1987 for Girard's linear logic [8] and 1983 for Ada's limited types [9], Baker was the first to suggest using linear types in programming languages [10], formalised in 1998 by Clarke et al. [11]. More recent works focus on Java, such as Javari and Uno [12,13].

Separation logic [14] is an extension of Hoare-Floyd logic that allows reasoning about pointers. In general, it is difficult to integrate into automated deductive verification: in particular, it is not directly supported by SMT provers, although some recent attempts try to have it mended [15,16].

Permission-based programming languages generalize the issue of avoiding harmful aliasing to the more general problem of preventing harmful sharing of resources (memory, but also network connections, files, etc.).

Cyclone and Rust achieve absence of harmful aliasing by enforcing an ownership type system on the memory pointed to by objects [17,18]. Furthermore, Rust has many sophisticated lifetime checks, that prevent dangling pointers, double free, and null pointer dereference. In SPARK, those checks are handled by separate analysis passes of the toolset. Even though there is still no formal description of Rust's borrow-checker, we must note a significant recent effort to provide a rigorous formal description of the foundations of Rust [19].

Dafny associates each object with its *dynamic frame*, the set of pointers that it owns [20]. This dynamic version of ownership is enforced by modeling the ownership of pointers in logic, generating verification conditions to detect violations of the single-owner model, and proving them using SMT provers. In Spec#, ownership is similarly enforced by proof, to detect violations of the so-called Boogie methodology [21].

In our work, we use a permission-based mechanism for detecting potentially harmful aliasing, in order to make the presence of pointers transparent for automated provers. In addition, our approach does not require additional user annotations, that are required in some of the previously mentioned techniques. We thus expect to achieve high automation and usability, which was our goal for supporting pointers in SPARK.

7 Future Work

The GNAT+SPARK Community release in 2020 contains support for pointers, as defined in Sect. 3.10 of the SPARK Reference Manual [22], with two important improvement not discussed in this paper: local observe/borrow operations and support for proof of absence of memory leaks.

Both these features require extensive changes to the generation of verification conditions. Support for local borrows requires special mechanisms to report changes on the borrower to the borrowee at the end of the borrow, as shown by recent work on Rust [23]. Support for proof of absence of memory leaks requires special mechanisms to track values that are either null or moved so that we can make sure that all values going out of scope are in this case.

8 Conclusion

In this paper, we have presented the rules for alias safety analysis that allow implementing and verifying in SPARK a wide range of programs using pointers and dynamic allocation. To the best of our knowledge, this is a novel approach to control aliasing introduced by arbitrary pointers in a programming language supported by proof. Our approach does not require additional user annotations or proof of additional verification conditions, which makes it much simpler to adopt. We provided a formalization of our rules for a subset of SPARK in order to mathematically prove the safety of our analysis.

In the future, we plan to extend our formalism and proof to non-terminating executions. For that purpose, we can provide a co-inductive definition of the big-step semantics and perform a similar co-inductive soundness proof, as described by Leroy and Grall [24].

Another long-term goal would be extending our analysis so that it could handle automatic reclamation, parallelism, initialization and lifetime checks, instead of relying on external checks.

A   Semantics for μSPARK statements

We use big-step operational semantics and write $\Upsilon \cdot \Sigma \cdot s \Downarrow \Sigma'$ to denote that μSPARK statement s, when evaluated under binding Υ and store Σ, terminates with the state of the store Σ'. We extend this notation to sequences of statements in an obvious way, as the reflexive-transitive closure of the evaluation relation on Σ. Similarly, we write $\Sigma[\ell.f \mapsto v]$ to denote an update of a single field in a record, that is, $\Sigma[\ell \mapsto \Sigma(\ell)[f \mapsto v]]$. In this paper, we do not consider diverging statements.

Allocation adds a fresh address to the store, mapping it to a default value for the corresponding type: 0 for Integer, False for Boolean, null for the access types, and for the record types, a record value where each field has the default value. Notice that since pointers are initialised to null, there is no deep allocation. We write $\Box_\tau$ to denote the default value of type τ.

$$\frac{[\![e]\!]_\Sigma^\Upsilon = v}{\Upsilon \cdot \Sigma \cdot p := e \Downarrow \Sigma[\langle p \rangle_\Sigma^\Upsilon \mapsto v]} \quad \text{(E-ASSIGN)}$$

$$\frac{\ell \notin dom\ \Sigma}{\Upsilon \cdot \Sigma \cdot p := \mathbf{new}\,\tau \Downarrow \Sigma[\langle p \rangle_\Sigma^\Upsilon \mapsto \ell, \ell \mapsto \Box_\tau]} \quad \text{(E-ALLOC)}$$

$$\frac{[\![e]\!]_\Sigma^\Upsilon = \mathbf{True} \qquad \Upsilon \cdot \Sigma \cdot \bar{s}_1 \Downarrow \Sigma'}{\Upsilon \cdot \Sigma \cdot \mathbf{if}\ e\ \mathbf{then}\ \bar{s}_1\ \mathbf{else}\ \bar{s}_2 \Downarrow \Sigma'} \quad \text{(E-IFTRUE)}$$

$$\frac{[\![e]\!]_\Sigma^\Upsilon = \mathbf{False} \qquad \Upsilon \cdot \Sigma \cdot \bar{s}_2 \Downarrow \Sigma'}{\Upsilon \cdot \Sigma \cdot \mathbf{if}\ e\ \mathbf{then}\ \bar{s}_1\ \mathbf{else}\ \bar{s}_2 \Downarrow \Sigma'} \quad \text{(E-IFFALSE)}$$

$$\frac{[\![e]\!]_\Sigma^\Upsilon = \mathbf{True} \qquad \Upsilon \cdot \Sigma \cdot (\bar{s}\ ;\ \mathbf{while}\ e\ \mathbf{loop}\ \bar{s}\ \mathbf{end}) \Downarrow \Sigma'}{\Upsilon \cdot \Sigma \cdot \mathbf{while}\ e\ \mathbf{loop}\ \bar{s}\ \mathbf{end} \Downarrow \Sigma'} \quad \text{(E-WHILETRUE)}$$

$$\frac{[\![e]\!]_\Sigma^\Upsilon = \mathbf{False}}{\Upsilon \cdot \Sigma \cdot \mathbf{while}\ e\ \mathbf{loop}\ \bar{s}\ \mathbf{end} \Downarrow \Sigma} \quad \text{(E-WHILEFALSE)}$$

$$\frac{\begin{array}{c} \mathbf{procedure}\ P\ (\,a_1 : \mathbf{in}\ \tau_{a_1};\dots;\,b_1 : \mathbf{in\ out}\ \tau_{b_1};\dots;\,c_1 : \mathbf{out}\ \tau_{c_1};\dots) \\ \mathbf{is}\ d_1 : \tau_{d_1};\dots\ \mathbf{begin}\ \bar{s}\ \mathbf{end}\ \text{is declared in the program} \\ \ell_{a_1},\dots,\ell_{d_1},\dots \notin dom\ \Sigma \qquad [\![e_{a_1}]\!]_\Sigma^\Upsilon = v_{a_1},\dots \\ \Upsilon_P = [\,a_1 \mapsto \ell_{a_1},\dots,b_1 \mapsto \langle p_{b_1} \rangle_\Sigma^\Upsilon,\dots,c_1 \mapsto \langle q_{c_1} \rangle_\Sigma^\Upsilon,\dots,d_1 \mapsto \ell_{d_1},\dots] \\ \Sigma_P = \Sigma[\ell_{a_1} \mapsto v_{a_1},\dots,\ell_{d_1} \mapsto \Box_{\tau_{d_1}},\dots] \qquad \Upsilon_P \cdot \Sigma_P \cdot \bar{s} \Downarrow \Sigma' \end{array}}{\Upsilon \cdot \Sigma \cdot P(e_{a_1},\dots,p_{b_1},\dots,q_{c_1},\dots) \Downarrow \{\ell_{a_1},\dots,\ell_{d_1},\dots\} \lhd \Sigma'} \quad \text{(E-CALL)}$$

Fig. 4. Semantics of μSPARK (terminating statements).

The evaluation rules are given in Fig. 4. In the (E-CALL) rule, we evaluate the procedure body in the dedicated context $\Upsilon_P \cdot \Sigma_P$. This context binds the **in** parameters to fresh locations containing the values of the respective expression arguments, binds the **in out** and **out** parameters to the addresses of the respective l-value arguments, and allocates memory for the local variables. At the end of the call, the memory allocated for the **in** parameters and local variables is reclaimed: the operation $\lhd$ stands for domain anti-restriction, meaning that locations $\ell_{a_1},\dots,\ell_{d_1},\dots$ are removed from Σ'. As there is no possibility to take the address of a local variable, there is no risk of dangling pointers.

References

1. McCormick, J., Chapin, P.: Building High Integrity Applications with SPARK. Cambridge University Press, Cambridge (2015)
2. Kirchner, F., Kosmatov, N., Prevosto, V., Signoles, J., Yakobowski, B.: Frama-C: a software analysis perspective. Formal Aspects Comput. **27**(3), 573–609 (2015). https://doi.org/10.1007/s00165-014-0326-7

3. Maalej, M., Taft, T., Moy, Y.: Safe dynamic memory management in ada and SPARK. In: Casimiro, A., Ferreira, P.M. (eds.) Ada-Europe 2018. LNCS, vol. 10873, pp. 37–52. Springer, Cham (2018). https://doi.org/10.1007/978-3-319-92432-8_3

4. Dross, C., Kanig, J.: Recursive data structures in SPARK. In: Lahiri, S.K., Wang, C. (eds.) CAV 2020. LNCS, vol. 12225, pp. 178–189. Springer, Cham (2020). https://doi.org/10.1007/978-3-030-53291-8_11

5. Dross, C.: Using pointers in spark (2019). https://blog.adacore.com/using-pointers-in-spark

6. Dross, C.: Pointer based data-structures in spark (2019). https://blog.adacore.com/pointer-based-data-structures-in-spark

7. Jaloyan, G.A.: Internship report: safe pointers in SPARK 2014 (2017). https://arxiv.org/pdf/1710.07047

8. Girard, J.Y.: Linear logic. Theoret. Comput. Sci. **50**(1), 1–101 (1987)

9. AdaLRM: Reference manual for the Ada(R) programming language. ANSI/MIL-STD-1815A-1983 (1983)

10. Baker, H.: 'Use-once' variables and linear objects: storage management, reflection and multi-threading. SIGPLAN Not. **30**(1), 45–52 (1995)

11. Clarke, D., Potter, J., Noble, J.: Ownership types for flexible alias protection. In: Proceedings of the 13th ACM SIGPLAN Conference on Object-oriented Programming, Systems, Languages, and Applications, pp. 48–64. ACM, New York (1998)

12. Tschantz, M., Ernst, M.: Javari: adding reference immutability to Java. In: Proceedings of the 20th Annual ACM SIGPLAN Conference on Object-oriented Programming, Systems, Languages, and Applications, pp. 211–230. ACM, New York (2005)

13. Ma, K.K., Foster, J.: Inferring aliasing and encapsulation properties for Java. In: Proceedings of the 22nd Annual ACM SIGPLAN Conference on Object-oriented Programming Systems and Applications, pp. 423–440. ACM, New York (2007)

14. Reynolds, J.: Separation logic: a logic for shared mutable data structures. In: Proceedings of the 17th Annual IEEE Symposium on Logic in Computer Science, Washington, DC, USA, pp. 55–74. IEEE Computer Society (2002)

15. Distefano, D., Parkinson, M.: jStar: towards practical verification for Java. In: Proceedings of the 23rd ACM SIGPLAN Conference on Object-oriented Programming Systems Languages and Applications, pp. 213–226. ACM, New York (2008)

16. Bakst, A., Jhala, R.: Predicate abstraction for linked data structures. In: Jobstmann, B., Leino, K.R.M. (eds.) VMCAI 2016. LNCS, vol. 9583, pp. 65–84. Springer, Heidelberg (2016). https://doi.org/10.1007/978-3-662-49122-5_3

17. Grossman, D., Morrisett, G., Jim, T., Hicks, M., Wang, Y., Cheney, J.: Region-based memory management in Cyclone. SIGPLAN Not. **37**(5), 282–293 (2002)

18. Balasubramanian, A., Baranowski, M., Burtsev, A., Panda, A., Rakamarić, Z., Ruzhyk, L.: System programming in rust: beyond safety. SIGOPS Oper. Syst. Rev. **51**(1), 94–99 (2017)

19. Jung, R., Jourdan, J.H., Krebbers, R., Dreyer, D.: RustBelt: securing the foundations of the rust programming language. Proc. ACM Program. Lang. **2**(POPL), 66:1–66:34 (2018)

20. Leino, K.R.M.: Dafny: an automatic program verifier for functional correctness. In: Clarke, E.M., Voronkov, A. (eds.) LPAR 2010. LNCS (LNAI), vol. 6355, pp. 348–370. Springer, Heidelberg (2010). https://doi.org/10.1007/978-3-642-17511-4_20

21. Barnett, M., Chang, B.-Y.E., DeLine, R., Jacobs, B., Leino, K.R.M.: Boogie: a modular reusable verifier for object-oriented programs. In: de Boer, F.S., Bonsangue, M.M., Graf, S., de Roever, W.-P. (eds.) FMCO 2005. LNCS, vol. 4111, pp. 364–387. Springer, Heidelberg (2006). https://doi.org/10.1007/11804192_17
22. AdaCore and Altran UK Ltd: SPARK 2014 Reference Manual (2019)
23. Astrauskas, V., Müller, P., Poli, F., Summers, A.J.: Leveraging rust types for modular specification and verification. Technical report, ETH Zurich (2018)
24. Leroy, X., Grall, H.: Coinductive big-step operational semantics. Inf. Comput. 207(2), 284–304 (2009)

Automated Temporal Verification
of Integrated Dependent Effects

Yahui Song$^{(\boxtimes)}$ and Wei-Ngan Chin$^{(\boxtimes)}$

School of Computing, National University of Singapore, Singapore, Singapore
{yahuis,chinwn}@comp.nus.edu.sg

Abstract. Existing approaches to temporal verification have either sacrificed compositionality in favor of achieving automation or vice-versa. To exploit the best of both worlds, we present a new solution to ensure temporal properties via a Hoare-style verifier and a term rewriting system (T.r.s) on *Integrated Dependent Effects*. The first contribution is a novel effects logic capable of integrating value-dependent finite and infinite traces into a single disjunctive form, resulting in more concise and expressive specifications. As a second contribution, by avoiding the complex translation into automata, our purely algebraic T.r.s efficiently checks the language inclusion, relying on both inductive and coinductive definitions. We demonstrate the feasibility of our method using a prototype system and a number of case studies. Our experimental results show that our implementation outperforms the automata-based model checker PAT by 31.7% of the average computation time.

1   Introduction

We are interested in automatic verification using finite-state, yet possibly nonterminating models of systems, with the underlying assumption that linear-time system behavior can be represented as a set of traces representing all the possible histories. In this model, verification consists of checking for language inclusion: the implementation describes a set of actual traces, in an automaton $\mathcal{A}$; and the specification gives the set of allowed traces, in an automaton $\mathcal{B}$; the implementation meets the specification if every actual trace is allowed, i.e., $\mathcal{L}(\mathcal{A}) \subseteq \mathcal{L}(\mathcal{B})$.

In this paper, we specify system behaviors in the form of *Integrated Dependent Effects*, which integrates the basic and ω-regular expressions with dependent values and arithmetic constraints, gaining the expressive power beyond finite-state machines. Specifically, our novel effects provide insights of: (i) Definite finite traces: we use symbolic values to present finite repetitions, which can be dependent on program inputs; (ii) Definite infinite traces constructed by infinity operator (ω); (iii) Possibly finite and possibly infinite traces constructed by Kleene star ($\star$). For example, we express, the effects of method **send(n)** as:

$$\Phi^{\text{send(n)}} \triangleq (\text{n}{\geq}0 \land \underline{\textbf{Send}}^{\text{n}} \cdot \underline{\textbf{Done}}) \lor (\text{n}{<}0 \land \underline{\textbf{Send}}^{\omega})$$

The **send** method takes a parameter **n**, and recursively sends out **n** messages. The above specification of **send(n)** indicates the fact that for non-negative values of

© Springer Nature Switzerland AG 2020
S.-W. Lin et al. (Eds.): ICFEM 2020, LNCS 12531, pp. 73–90, 2020.
https://doi.org/10.1007/978-3-030-63406-3_5

the parameter n, the send method generates a finite trace comprising a sequence with n times of event **Send**, followed by a final event **Done**. For the case when the parameter is negative, it generates an infinite trace of event **Send**. Note that (i) the integrated effects can express both finite traces and infinite traces in one single formula, separated by arithmetic constraints, and (ii) n is a parameter to send, making the effects *dependent* w.r.t the value of send's parameter. Furthermore, by allowing events to be parametrised with symbolic values, the effects are defined as languages over potentially infinite alphabets of the form $\Sigma \times \mathbb{Z}$, where Σ is a finite event set, and $\mathbb{Z}$ is the infinite integer set.

Deciding the inclusion between two regular sets is PSPACE-complete. The standard approaches to the problem are based on the following steps: (i) translate each regular expression into an equivalent NFA, (ii) convert those NFAs to equivalent DFAs and finally (iii) minimize those DFAs to $\mathcal{M}_A$ and $\mathcal{M}_B$, and then check emptiness of $\mathcal{M}_A \cap \neg \mathcal{M}_B$. However, any efficient algorithm[9] based on such translation potentially gives rise to an exponential blow-up.

As an alternative approach, Antimirov and Mosses [5] presented a term rewriting system (T.r.s) for deciding the inclusion of regular expressions based on a complete axiomatic algorithm of the algebra of regular sets. A T.r.s is a refutation method that normalizes regular expressions in such a way that checking their inclusion corresponds to an iterated process of checking the inclusion of their *partial derivatives* [4]. Works based on such a T.r.s [3,5,11,12] show its feasibility and suggest that this method is a better average-case algorithm than those based on the comparison of minimal DFAs.

In this paper, we present a new solution of extensive temporal verification, which deploys a decision procedure inspired by Antimirov and Mosses' algorithm but solving the language inclusions between more expressive Integrated Dependent Effects. Our main contributions are:

1. **Temporal Effects Specification:** We define the syntax and semantics of our novel effects, which escapes LTL, μ-calculus and prior effects (Sect. 3).
2. **Automated Verification System:** Targeting a core language, we develop a Hoare-style forward verifier to accumulate effects from the source code, as the front-end (Sect. 4); and a sound decision procedure (our T.r.s) to solve the effects inclusions, as the back-end (Sect. 5).
3. **Implementation and Evaluation:** We prototype the novel effects logic on top of the HIP/SLEEK system [8] [2]. We further provide case studies and experimental results to show the feasibility of our method (Sect. 6).

Organization. Section 2 gives a straightforward motivation example to highlight the key methodologies and contributions. Section 3 formally specifies the syntax of the target language, and the syntax and semantics of our integrated dependent effects. Section 4 presents the forward verifier for the target language. Section 5 illustrates the effects inclusion checking procedure, by presenting a set of inference rules, and displays the essential auxiliary functions. Section 6 demonstrates the implementation, case studies and experimental results as the evaluation of our T.r.s. We discuss related works in Sect. 7 and conclude in

Sect. 8. Termination and soundness proofs can be found in the extended technical report [2].

2 Overview

We now give a summary of our techniques, using the example shown in Table 1-
(a). Our integrated dependent effects can be illustrated with send and server,
which simulate a server who continuously sends messages to all its clients.

Table 1. (a) Source code and (b) pre/post effects specifications for the methods.

(a) Source Code	(b) Effects Specifications
| ```
1  void send (int n){
2     if (n==0) {
3        event["Done"];
4     }else{
5        event["Send"]; send (n-1);
6     }}
7  void server (int n){
8     event["Ready"];
9     send(n);
10    server(n);}
``` | $\Phi_{pre}^{send(n)} \triangleq \text{True} \wedge \underline{\text{Ready}} \cdot \_^*$ <br> $\Phi_{post}^{send(n)} \triangleq (n \geq 0 \wedge \underline{\text{Send}}^n \cdot \underline{\text{Done}}) \vee (n < 0 \wedge \underline{\text{Send}}^\omega)$ <br><br> $\Phi_{pre}^{server(n)} \triangleq n \geq 0 \wedge \epsilon$ <br> $\Phi_{post}^{server(n)} \triangleq n \geq 0 \wedge (\underline{\text{Ready}} \cdot \underline{\text{Send}}^n \cdot \underline{\text{Done}})^\omega$ |

Here, event[a] is a primitive in our target language (cf. Sect. 3), used to
trigger a single event a. This method server takes an integer parameter n,
triggers an event **Ready**, then calls the method send, making a boolean choice
depending on input n: in one case it triggers an event **Done**; otherwise it triggers
an event **Send**, then makes a recursive call with parameter n-1. Finally server
recurs.

2.1 Integrated Dependent Effects

The effects specifications for server and send are given in Table 1-(b). We
define Hoare-triple style specifications for each of the programs, which leads
to a more compositional verification strategy, where temporal reasoning can be
done locally. Method send's precondition, denoted by $\Phi_{pre}^{send(n)}$, requires the event
Ready to have happened at some point of the effects history; and it guarantees
the final effects/postcondition, denoted by $\Phi_{post}^{send(n)}$.

Method server's precondition, $\Phi_{pre}^{server(n)}$, requires the input value be non
negative while the pre-trace is required to be empty (ϵ); its postcondition ensures
the final effects $\Phi_{post}^{server(n)}$ – an infinite repetition of a trace consisting of an event
Ready followed by n times of **Send** followed by **Done**. Directly from the specifi-
cations, we are aware of (i) termination properties: server *must* not terminate,
while send *may* not terminate; (ii) branching properties: different arithmetic
conditions on the input parameters lead to different temporal effects; and (iii)
```

required history traces: by defining the prior effects in precondition. The examples already show that our effects provide more detail information than classical LTL or μ-calculus, and in fact, it cannot be fully captured by any prior works [10,13,15,17]. Nevertheless, the gain in expressive power comes at the efforts of a more dedicated verification process, namely handled by our T.r.s.

2.2   Forward Verification

As shown in Fig. 1, we demonstrate the forward verification process of method send. The current effects states of a program is captured in the form of $\{\Phi_C\}$. We define our forward verification rules in Sect. 4. To facilitate the illustration, we label the verification steps by 1), ..., 8). We mark the deployed verification rules in green. The verifier invokes the T.r.s to check language inclusions along the way.

1) **void send (int n){** (– *initialize the current effects state* –)
    $\{\Phi_C = \Phi_{pre}^{send(n)} = \text{True} \wedge \underline{\textbf{Ready}} \cdot \_^*\}$ [FV-Meth]

2)   **if(n==0){**
    $\{n = 0 \wedge \underline{\textbf{Ready}} \cdot \_^*\}$ [FV-If-Else]

3)   **event[Done]; }**
    $\{n = 0 \wedge \underline{\textbf{Ready}} \cdot \_^* \cdot \underline{\textbf{Done}}\}$ [FV-Event]

4)   **else{**
    $\{n \neq 0\}$ [FV-If-Else]

5)   **event[Send];**
    $\{n \neq 0 \wedge \underline{\textbf{Ready}} \cdot \_^* \cdot \underline{\textbf{Send}}\}$ [FV-Event]

6)   **send(n-1); }}**
    $rev(n \neq 0 \wedge \underline{\textbf{Ready}} \cdot \_^* \cdot \underline{\textbf{Send}}) \sqsubseteq rev(\Phi_{pre}^{send(n-1)})$ (-*check precondition-*)
    $\{n \neq 0 \wedge \underline{\textbf{Ready}} \cdot \_^* \cdot \underline{\textbf{Send}} \cdot \Phi_{post}^{send(n-1)}\}$ [FV-Call]

7) $\Phi_C' = (n = 0 \wedge \underline{\textbf{Ready}} \cdot \_^* \cdot \underline{\textbf{Done}}) \vee (n \neq 0 \wedge \underline{\textbf{Ready}} \cdot \_^* \cdot \underline{\textbf{Send}} \cdot \Phi_{post}^{send(n-1)})$

8) $\Phi_C' \sqsubseteq \Phi_{pre}^{send(n)} \cdot \Phi_{post}^{send(n)} \Leftrightarrow$ (– *check postcondition* –)
    $(n = 0 \wedge \underline{\textbf{Done}}) \vee (n \neq 0 \wedge \underline{\textbf{Send}} \cdot \Phi_{post}^{send(n-1)}) \sqsubseteq \Phi_{post}^{send(n)}$

Fig. 1. The forward verification example for method send.

The effects state 1) is obtained by initialising Φ_C from the precondition.

The effects states 2), 4) and 7) are obtained by [FV-If-Else], which adds the constraints from the conditionals into the current effects state, and unions the effects accumulated from two branches in the end. The effects states 3) and 5) are obtained by [FV-Event], which simply concatenates the triggered singleton event to the end of the current effects state. The effects state 6) is obtained by [FV-Call]. Before each method call, it checks whether the current state satisfies the precondition of the callee method. The rev function simply reverses the order

Table 2. The inclusion checking example on the postcondition of method **send**. I: The main rewriting proof tree (coming from the step 8) in Fig. 1); II: One sub-tree of the rewriting process.

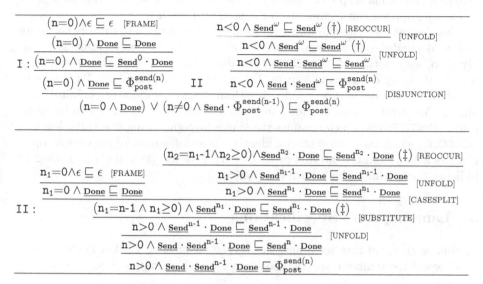

of effects sequences. If the precondition is not satisfied, then the verification fails, otherwise it concatenates the postcondition of the callee to the current effects.

While Hoare logics based on finite traces (terminating runs) [14] and infinite traces (non-terminating runs) [16] have been considered before, the reasoning on properties of mixed definitions is new. Prior effects in precondition is also new, allowing greater safety to be applied to sequential reactive controlling systems such as web applications, communication protocols and IoT systems.

2.3 The T.r.s

Our T.r.s is designed to check the inclusion between any two integrated dependent effects. We define its inference rules in Sect. 5. Here, we present the rewriting process on the postcondition checking of the method **send**. We mark the rules of some essential inference steps in green. Basically, our effects rewriting system decides effects inclusion through an iterated process of checking the inclusion of their partial derivatives. There are two important rules inherited from Antimirov and Mosses's algorithm: [DISPROVE], which infers false from a trivially inconsistent inclusion; and [UNFOLD], which applies Theorem 1 to generate new inclusions. $D_a(r)$ is the partial derivative of r w.r.t the event $\underline{a}$. Termination is guaranteed because the set of derivatives to be considered is finite, and possible cycles are detected using *memorization*.

Theorem 1 (Regular Expressions Inclusion). *For regular expressions r and s, $r \preceq s \Leftrightarrow (\forall a \in \Sigma).\ D_a(r) \preceq D_a(s)$.*

Intuitively, we use [DISPROVE] wherever the left-hand side (LHS) is *nullable*[1] while the right-hand side (RHS) is not. [DISPROVE] is essential because it is the heuristic refutation step to disprove the inclusion early, which leads to a great efficiency improvement compared to the standard methods.

Besides, we use symbolic values (assuming non-negative) to capture the finite traces, depended on program inputs. Whenever the symbolic value is possibly zero, we use the rule [CASESPLIT] to distinguish the zero (base) and non-zero (inductive) cases, as shown in Table 2-II. In addition, the T.r.s is obligated to reason about mixed inductive (finite) and coinductive (infinite) definitions. We achieve these features and still guarantee the termination by using rules: [SUBSTITUTE], which renames the symbolic terms using free variables; and [REOCCUR], which finds the syntactic identity, as a *companion*, of the current open goal, as a *bud*, from the internal proof tree [7]. (We use (†) and (‡) in Table 2 to indicate the pairing of buds with companions.)

3   Language and Specifications

In this section, we first introduce the target (sequential C-like) language and then depict the temporal specification language which supports our effects.

3.1   Target Language

The syntax of our core imperative language is given in Fig. 2 Here, we regard k and x are meta-variables. k^τ represents a constant of basic type τ. **var** represents the countably infinite set of arbitrary distinct identifiers. $\underline{a}$ refers to a singleton event coming from the finite set of events Σ. We assume that programs we use are well-typed conforming to basic types τ (we take () as the **void** type). A program $\mathcal{P}$ comprises a list of method declarations **meth***. Here, we use the $*$ superscript to denote a finite list (possibly empty) of items, for example, x^* refers to a list of variables, $x_1, ..., x_n$.

(*Program*)	$\mathcal{P}$ ::= meth*		(*Basic Types*)	τ ::= int | bool | void
(*Method Def.*)	meth ::= τ mn $(\tau$ x$)^*$ {requires Φ_{pre} ensures Φ_{post}} {e}			
(*Expressions*)	e ::= () | k^τ | x | τ x; e | mn(x*) | x:=e | e₁; e₂| **assert** Φ			
	| e₁ *op* e₂ | **event**[$\underline{a}$] | **if** v **then** e₁ **else** e₂			

k^τ : constant of type τ	x, mn ::∈ **var**	(Events)$\underline{a}$ ::∈ Σ

Fig. 2. A core imperative language.

Each method **meth** has a name **mn**, an expression-oriented body **e**, also is associated with a precondition Φ_{pre} and a postcondition Φ_{post} (the syntax of

---

[1] If the event sequence is possibly empty, i.e. contains ϵ, we call it nullable, formally defined in Definition 1.

effects specification Φ is given in Fig. 3). The language allows each iterative loop to be optimized to an equivalent tail-recursive method, where mutation on parameters is made visible to the caller. The technique of translating away iterative loops is standard and is helpful in further minimising our core language. Expressions comprise unit (), constants k, variables x, local variable declaration τ x; e, method calls $mn(x^*)$, variable assignments $x:=e$, expression sequences $e_1; e_2$, binary operations represented by e_1 op e_2, including $+$, $-$, $==$, $<$, etc, event raises expression **event**$[a]$, conditional expressions **if** v **then** e_1 **else** e_2, and the assertion constructor **assert**, parametrized with effects Φ.

3.2 The Specification Language

We plant the effects specifications into the Hoare-style verification system. We use {**requires** Φ_{pre} **ensures** Φ_{post}} to capture the precondition Φ_{pre} and the postcondition Φ_{post}, defined in Fig. 3

$$
\begin{array}{llll}
(\textit{Effects}) & \Phi & ::= & \pi \wedge es \mid \Phi_1 \vee \Phi_2 \mid \exists x.\Phi \\
(\textit{Event Seq.}) & es & ::= & \bot \mid \epsilon \mid \_ \mid a \mid es_1 \cdot es_2 \mid es_1 \vee es_2 \mid es_1 \wedge es_2 \mid \neg es \mid es^t \mid es^* \mid es^\omega \\
(\textit{Pure}) & \pi & ::= & \textbf{True} \mid \textbf{False} \mid A(t_1,t_2) \mid \pi_1 \wedge \pi_2 \mid \pi_1 \vee \pi_2 \mid \neg \pi \mid \pi_1 \Rightarrow \pi_2 \mid \forall x.\pi \mid \exists x.\pi \\
(\textit{Terms}) & t & ::= & n \mid x \mid t_1+t_2 \mid t_1-t_2
\end{array}
$$

$x ::\in \textbf{var}$ $n ::\in \mathbb{Z}$ $(\textit{Event})$ $a ::\in \Sigma$ $(\textit{Infinity})$ ω $(\textit{Kleene Star})$ $\star$

Fig. 3. Syntax of effects.

Effects can be a conditioned event sequence $\pi \wedge es$ or a disjunction of two effects $\Phi_1 \vee \Phi_2$, or an effect Φ existentially quantified over a variable x. Event sequences comprise *false* ($\bot$); an empty trace ϵ; the wild card $\_$ representing any single event; a single event a; sequences concatenation $es_1 \cdot es_2$; disjunction $es_1 \vee es_2$; conjunction $es_1 \wedge es_2$; negation $\neg es$; t times repetition of a trace, es^t, where t is a *term*; Kleene star, zero or many times (possibly infinite) repetition of a trace; and the infinite repetition of a trace, es^ω. However, for now, we restrict the nested usage of operators among $\neg$, t, $\star$ and ω.

We use π to donate a pure formula which captures the (Presburger) arithmetic conditions on program parameters. We use $A(t_1, t_2)$ to represent atomic formulas of two terms (including $=$, $>$, $<$, $\geq$ and $\leq$), A term can be a constant integer value n, an integer variable x which is an input parameter of the program and can be constrained by a pure formula. A term also allows simple computations of terms, t_1+t_2 and t_1-t_2.

3.3 Semantic Model of Effects

To define the model, **var** is the set of program variables, **val** is the set of primitive values, **es** is the set of event sequences (or event multi-trees, per se), indicating the sequencing constraints on temporal behaviour. Let $s, \varphi \models \Phi$ denote the model relation, i.e., the stack s and linear temporal events φ satisfy the temporal effects Φ, with s, φ from the following concrete domains: $s \triangleq var \to val$ and $\varphi \triangleq es$.

As shown in Fig. 4, we define the semantics of our effects. We use ++ to represent the append operation of two event sequences. We use [] to represent the empty sequence, [a] to represent the sequence only contains one element a.

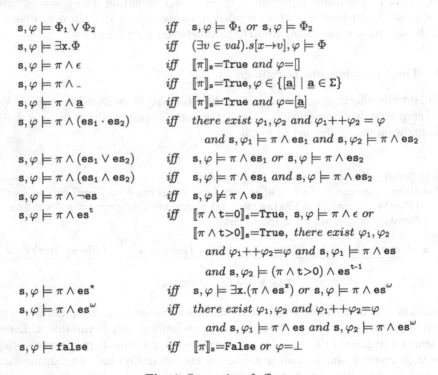

$$
\begin{aligned}
&s, \varphi \models \Phi_1 \vee \Phi_2 &&\textit{iff}\quad s, \varphi \models \Phi_1 \textit{ or } s, \varphi \models \Phi_2\\
&s, \varphi \models \exists x.\Phi &&\textit{iff}\quad (\exists v \in val).s[x\to v], \varphi \models \Phi\\
&s, \varphi \models \pi \wedge \epsilon &&\textit{iff}\quad [\![\pi]\!]_s = \text{True and } \varphi = []\\
&s, \varphi \models \pi \wedge \_ &&\textit{iff}\quad [\![\pi]\!]_s = \text{True}, \varphi \in \{[a] \mid a \in \Sigma\}\\
&s, \varphi \models \pi \wedge a &&\textit{iff}\quad [\![\pi]\!]_s = \text{True and } \varphi = [a]\\
&s, \varphi \models \pi \wedge (es_1 \cdot es_2) &&\textit{iff}\quad \textit{there exist } \varphi_1, \varphi_2 \textit{ and } \varphi_1 + + \varphi_2 = \varphi\\
&&&\qquad\textit{and } s, \varphi_1 \models \pi \wedge es_1 \textit{ and } s, \varphi_2 \models \pi \wedge es_2\\
&s, \varphi \models \pi \wedge (es_1 \vee es_2) &&\textit{iff}\quad s, \varphi \models \pi \wedge es_1 \textit{ or } s, \varphi \models \pi \wedge es_2\\
&s, \varphi \models \pi \wedge (es_1 \wedge es_2) &&\textit{iff}\quad s, \varphi \models \pi \wedge es_1 \textit{ and } s, \varphi \models \pi \wedge es_2\\
&s, \varphi \models \pi \wedge \neg es &&\textit{iff}\quad s, \varphi \not\models \pi \wedge es\\
&s, \varphi \models \pi \wedge es^t &&\textit{iff}\quad [\![\pi \wedge t = 0]\!]_s = \text{True}, s, \varphi \models \pi \wedge \epsilon \textit{ or }\\
&&&\qquad [\![\pi \wedge t > 0]\!]_s = \text{True}, \textit{ there exist } \varphi_1, \varphi_2\\
&&&\qquad\textit{and } \varphi_1 + + \varphi_2 = \varphi \textit{ and } s, \varphi_1 \models \pi \wedge es\\
&&&\qquad\textit{and } s, \varphi_2 \models (\pi \wedge t > 0) \wedge es^{t-1}\\
&s, \varphi \models \pi \wedge es^* &&\textit{iff}\quad s, \varphi \models \exists x.(\pi \wedge es^x) \textit{ or } s, \varphi \models \pi \wedge es^\omega\\
&s, \varphi \models \pi \wedge es^\omega &&\textit{iff}\quad \textit{there exist } \varphi_1, \varphi_2 \textit{ and } \varphi_1 + + \varphi_2 = \varphi\\
&&&\qquad\textit{and } s, \varphi_1 \models \pi \wedge es \textit{ and } s, \varphi_2 \models \pi \wedge es^\omega\\
&s, \varphi \models \text{false} &&\textit{iff}\quad [\![\pi]\!]_s = \text{False or } \varphi = \bot
\end{aligned}
$$

Fig. 4. Semantics of effects.

4   Automated Verification

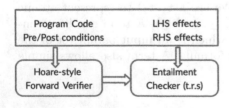

Fig. 5. Overview of verification.

An overview of our automated verification system is given in Fig. 5. It consists of a standard Hoare-style forward verifier (the front-end) and a T.r.s (the back-end). In this section, we mainly present the forward verifier, which invokes the back-end, by introducing a set of forward verification rules. Note that we allow the precondition of a method to be false. The body of any such method can always be successfully verified. This relaxation does not affect the soundness of our verification system. The inclusion checking process will be explained in Sect. 5.

$$\frac{\Phi_c'=\Phi_c \cdot \mathbf{a}}{\vdash \{\Phi_c\} \ \mathbf{event[a]} \ \{\Phi_c'\}} \ \text{[FV-Event]} \qquad \frac{\vdash \{\Phi_c\} \ e_1 \ \{\Phi_c'\} \qquad \vdash \{\Phi_c'\} \ e_2 \ \{\Phi_c''\}}{\vdash \{\Phi_c\} \ e_1; e_2 \ \{\Phi_c''\}} \ \text{[FV-Seq]}$$

$$\frac{\vdash \{v \wedge \Phi_c\} \ e_1 \ \{\Phi_c'\} \qquad \vdash \{\neg v \wedge \Phi_c\} \ e_2 \ \{\Phi_c''\}}{\vdash \{\Phi_c\} \ \mathbf{if} \ v \ \mathbf{then} \ e_1 \ \mathbf{else} \ e_2 \ \{\Phi_c' \vee \Phi_c''\}} \ \text{[FV-If-Else]}$$

$$\frac{\vdash \{\Phi_c\} \ e \ \{\Phi_c'\}}{\vdash \{\Phi_c\} \ \tau \ x; \ e \ \{\exists x.\Phi_c'\}} \ \text{[FV-Local]} \qquad \frac{\vdash rev(\Phi_c) \sqsubseteq rev(\Phi) \rightsquigarrow \gamma_R}{\vdash \{\Phi_c\} \ \mathbf{assert} \ \Phi \ \{\Phi_c\}} \ \text{[FV-Assert]}$$

$$\frac{\tau \ mn \ (\tau \ x)^* \ \{\mathbf{requires} \ \Phi_{pre} \ \mathbf{ensures} \ \Phi_{post}\} \ \{e\} \in \mathcal{P}}{\vdash rev(\Phi_c) \sqsubseteq rev([y^*/x^*]\Phi_{pre}) \rightsquigarrow \gamma_R \qquad \Phi_c' = \Phi_c \cdot [y^*/x^*]\Phi_{post}}{\vdash \{\Phi_c\} \ mn(y^*) \ \{\Phi_c'\}} \ \text{[FV-Call]}$$

$$\frac{\vdash \{\epsilon\} \ e \ \{\Phi_c\} \qquad \vdash \Phi_c \sqsubseteq \Phi_{post}}{\vdash \tau \ mn \ (\tau \ x)^* \ \{\mathbf{requires} \ \Phi_{pre} \ \mathbf{ensures} \ \Phi_{post}\} \ \{e\}} \ \text{[FV-Meth]}$$

Fig. 6. Some forward verification rules.

We present some of the forward verification rules in Fig. 6, which are used to systematically accumulate the effects based on the syntax of each statement. We use $\mathcal{P}$ to denote the program being checked. With pre/post conditions declared for each method in $\mathcal{P}$, we can apply modular verification to a method's body using Hoare-style triples $\vdash \{\Phi_C\} \ e \ \{\Phi_C'\}$, where Φ_C is the current effects and Φ_C' is the resulting effects by executing e. In [FV-If-Else], $(v \wedge \Phi_C)$ enforces v into the pure constraints of every traces in Φ_C, same for $(\neg v \wedge \Phi_C)$. In [FV-Call], we check whether the instantiated precondition of callee, $[y^*/x^*]\Phi_{pre}$, is satisfied by the $tail^2$ of current effects state, in which we use an auxiliary function rev to reverse the event sequences of effects. Then we obtain the next effects state by concatenating the instantiated postcondition, $[y^*/x^*]\Phi_{post}$, to the current effects state. (cf. step 6) in Fig. 1) In [FV-Meth], we initialize the current effects state using ϵ, accumulate the effects from the method body, to obtain Φ_C, and check inclusion between Φ_C and the declared specifications Φ_{post}[3].

5   Effects Inclusion Checker (the T.r.s)

The effects inclusion checking (an extension of the T.r.s proposed from [5]) will be triggered i) right before a method call, to check the satisfiability of the precondition; ii) after the forward verification, to check the satisfiability of the postcondition; and iii) when there is an assertion, to check the satisfiability of the asserted effects. As shown in Sect. 4, our forward verification generates effects inclusions of the form: $\Gamma \vdash \Phi_1 \sqsubseteq_V^\Phi \Phi_2 \rightsquigarrow \gamma_R$, a shorthand for: $\Gamma \vdash \Phi \cdot \Phi_1 \sqsubseteq \exists V. \ (\Phi \cdot \Phi_2) \rightsquigarrow \gamma_R$.

To prove such effects inclusions is to check whether all the possible event traces in the antecedent Φ_1 are legitimately allowed in the possible event traces from the consequent Φ_2, and (in case there are) to compute a residual effects

---

[2] We check the inclusion between the reversed current effects and precondition effects, meaning that, before calling a method, its required effects *has just happened*.

[3] Φ_{post} only needs to capture the effects from the current method body, excluding the history effects specified in Φ_{pre}.

γ_R (also known as "frame" in the frame inference) , which represents what was not consumed from the antecedent after matching up with the effects from the consequent. Γ is the proof context, i.e. a set of effects inclusions, Φ is the history of effects from the antecedent that have been used to match the effects from the consequent, and V is the set of existentially quantified variables from the consequent. Note that Γ, Φ and V are derived during the inclusion proof. The inclusion checking procedure is initially invoked with $\Gamma=\emptyset$, $\Phi=\text{True} \wedge \epsilon$ and $V=\emptyset$. We now briefly discuss the key steps and related inference rules that we may use in such an effects inclusion proof. Firstly, we present the reduction to eliminate the disjunctions from the antecedents and existential quantifiers. *(LHS refers to left-hand side, and RHS refers to right-hand side.)*

I. Effect Disjunction. An inclusion with a disjunctive antecedent succeeds if both disjunctions entail the consequent.

$$\frac{\Gamma \vdash \Phi_1 \sqsubseteq \Phi \rightsquigarrow \gamma_R^1 \qquad \Gamma \vdash \Phi_2 \sqsubseteq \Phi \rightsquigarrow \gamma_R^2}{\Gamma \vdash \Phi_1 \vee \Phi_2 \sqsubseteq \Phi \rightsquigarrow (\gamma_R^1 \vee \gamma_R^2)} \quad [\text{LHS-OR}]$$

II. Existential Quantifiers. Existentially quantified variables from the antecedent are simply lifted out of the inclusion relation by replacing them with fresh variables. On the other hand, we keep track of the existential variables coming from the consequent by adding them to V. *(u is a fresh variable)*

$$\frac{\Gamma \vdash [u/x]\Phi_1 \sqsubseteq_V^\Phi \Phi_2 \rightsquigarrow \gamma_R}{\Gamma \vdash \exists x. \ \Phi_1 \sqsubseteq_V^\Phi \Phi_2 \rightsquigarrow \gamma_R} \quad [\text{LHS-EX}] \qquad \frac{\Gamma \vdash \Phi_1 \sqsubseteq_{V \cup \{u\}}^\Phi ([u/x]\Phi_2) \rightsquigarrow \gamma_R}{\Gamma \vdash \Phi_1 \sqsubseteq_V^\Phi (\exists x. \ \Phi_2) \rightsquigarrow \gamma_R} \quad [\text{RHS-EX}]$$

Table 3. Some Normalization Lemmas for effects constructed by $\pi \wedge es$.

$es \vee es \to es$	$\epsilon^\omega \to \epsilon$	$(es_1 \cdot es_2) \cdot es_3 \to es_1 \cdot (es_2 \cdot es_3)$
$\bot \vee es \to es$	$es \wedge es \to es$	$(es_1 \vee es_2) \cdot es_3 \to es_1 \cdot es_3 \vee es_2 \cdot es_3$
$es \vee \bot \to es$	$es \wedge \bot \to \bot$	$es_1 \cdot (es_2 \vee es_3) \to es_1 \cdot es_2 \vee es_1 \cdot es_3$
$\epsilon \cdot es \to es$	$\bot^\omega \to \bot$	$es^\omega \cdot es_1 \to es^\omega$
$es \cdot \epsilon \to es$	$\epsilon^t \to \epsilon$	$\text{False} \wedge es \to \text{False} \wedge \bot$
$\bot \cdot es \to \bot$	$t{=}0 \wedge es^t \to \epsilon$	$es \wedge \epsilon \to \bot \quad (\delta_\pi(es){=}\text{false})$
$es \cdot \bot \to \bot$	$\bot^t \to \bot$	$es \wedge \epsilon \to \epsilon \quad (\delta_\pi(es){=}\text{true})$

III. Normalization. The rewriting of an inclusion between two quantifier-free effects starts with a general normalization for both the antecedent and the consequent. We assume that the effects formulae are tailored accordingly using the lemmas in Table 3, which are extended from the normalization rules suggested by Antimirov and Mosses, being able to further normalize our dependent effects.

IV. Substitution. In order to guarantee the termination, for both the antecedent and the consequent, a term $t_1 \oplus t_2$ will be substituted with a fresh variable u constrained with $u = t_1 \oplus t_2 \wedge u \geq 0$, where $\oplus \in \{+, -\}$. (cf. Table 2-II)

$$\frac{\pi' = (u = t_1 \oplus t_2 \wedge u \geq 0) \quad \Gamma \vdash (\pi_1 \wedge \pi') \wedge es_1^u \cdot es \sqsubseteq (\pi_2 \wedge \pi') \wedge es_2 \rightsquigarrow \gamma_R}{\Gamma \vdash \pi_1 \wedge (es_1^{t_1 \oplus t_2} \cdot es) \sqsubseteq \pi_2 \wedge es_2 \rightsquigarrow \gamma_R} \text{[LHS-SUB]}$$

$$\frac{\pi' = (u = t_1 \oplus t_2 \wedge u \geq 0) \quad \Gamma \vdash (\pi_1 \wedge \pi') \wedge es_1 \sqsubseteq (\pi_2 \wedge \pi') \wedge es_2^u \cdot es \rightsquigarrow \gamma_R}{\Gamma \vdash \pi_1 \wedge es_1 \sqsubseteq \pi_2 \wedge (es_2^{t_1 \oplus t_2} \cdot es) \rightsquigarrow \gamma_R} \text{[RHS-SUB]}$$

V. Case Split. Based on the semantics of the symbolic integer t, whenever it is possibly zero, we conduct a case split, to distinguish the zero (base) case, leads to an empty trace; and the non-zero (inductive) case. (cf. Table 2-II)

$$\text{[LHS-CASESPLIT]}$$
$$\frac{\Gamma \vdash ((\pi_1 \wedge t=0) \wedge es) \vee ((\pi_1 \wedge t > 0) \wedge es_1 \cdot es_1^{t-1} \cdot es) \sqsubseteq \pi_2 \wedge es_2 \rightsquigarrow \gamma_R}{\Gamma \vdash \pi_1 \wedge (es_1^t \cdot es) \sqsubseteq \pi_2 \wedge es_2 \rightsquigarrow \gamma_R}$$

$$\text{[RHS-CASESPLIT]}$$
$$\frac{\Gamma \vdash \pi_1 \wedge es_1 \sqsubseteq ((\pi_2 \wedge t=0) \wedge es) \vee ((\pi_2 \wedge t > 0) \wedge es_2 \cdot es_2^{t-1} \cdot es) \rightsquigarrow \gamma_R}{\Gamma \vdash \pi_1 \wedge es_1 \sqsubseteq \pi_2 \wedge (es_2^t \cdot es) \rightsquigarrow \gamma_R}$$

VI. Unfolding (Induction). Here comes the key inductive step of unfolding the inclusion. Firstly, we make use of the `fst` auxiliary function to get a set of events F, which are all the possibly *first* event from the antecedent. Secondly, we obtain a new proof context Γ' by adding the current inclusion, as an inductive hypothesis, into the current proof context Γ. Thirdly, we iterate each element **a** ($\underline{a} \in F$), and compute the partial derivatives (the *next-state* effects) of both the antecedent and consequent w.r.t **a**. The proof of the original inclusion succeeds if all the derivative inclusions succeeds.

$$\frac{F = \text{fst}_{\pi_1}(es_1) \quad \Gamma' = \Gamma, (\pi_1 \wedge es_1 \sqsubseteq \pi_2 \wedge es_2) \\ \forall \underline{a} \in F. \ (\Gamma' \vdash D_{\underline{a}}^{\pi_1}(es_1) \sqsubseteq D_{\underline{a}}^{\pi_2}(es_2))}{\Gamma \vdash \pi_1 \wedge es_1 \sqsubseteq \pi_2 \wedge es_2} \text{[UNFOLD]}$$

Next we provide the definitions and the key implementations[4] of Nullable, First and Derivative respectively. Intuitively, the Nullable function $\delta_\pi(es)$ returns a boolean value indicating whether $\pi \wedge es$ contains the empty trace; the First function $\text{fst}_\pi(es)$ computes a set of possible initial events of $\pi \wedge es$; and the Derivative function $D_{\underline{a}}^\pi(es)$ computes a next-state effects after eliminating one event **a** from the current effects $\pi \wedge es$.

---

[4] As the implementations according to basic regular expressions can be found in prior work [12]. Here, we focus on presenting the definitions and how do we deal with dependent values in the effects, as the key novelties of this work.

Definition 1 (Nullable). *Given any event sequence* es *under condition* π, *we define* $\delta_\pi(\text{es})$ *to be:*

$$\delta_\pi(\text{es}) : \text{bool} = \begin{cases} \text{true} & \text{if } \epsilon \in [\![\pi \wedge \text{es}_1]\!]_\varphi \\ \text{false} & \text{if } \epsilon \notin [\![\pi \wedge \text{es}_1]\!]_\varphi \end{cases}, \text{ where } \delta_\pi(\text{es}^t) = \text{SAT}(\pi \wedge (t=0))^5$$

Definition 2 (First). *Let* $\text{fst}_\pi(\text{es}) := \{\underline{a} \mid \underline{a} \cdot \text{es}' \in [\![\pi \wedge \text{es}]\!]\}$ *be the set of initial events derivable from event sequence* es *w.r.t. the condition* π.

$$\text{fst}_\pi(\text{es}_1 \cdot \text{es}_2) = \begin{cases} \text{fst}_\pi(\text{es}_1) \cup \text{fst}_\pi(\text{es}_2) & \text{if } \delta_\pi(\text{es}_1) = \text{true} \\ \text{fst}_\pi(\text{es}_1) & \text{if } \delta_\pi(\text{es}_1) = \text{false} \end{cases}$$

Definition 3 (Derivative). *The derivative* $D_{\underline{a}}^\pi(\text{es})$ *of an event sequence* es *w.r.t. an event* $\underline{a}$ *and the condition* π *computes the effects for the left quotient* $\underline{a}^{-1}[\![\pi \wedge \text{es}]\!]$, *where we define* $D_{\underline{a}}^\pi(\text{es}^t) = D_{\underline{a}}^{\pi \wedge t > 0}(\text{es}) \cdot \text{es}^{t-1}$.

$$D_{\underline{a}}^\pi(\text{es}_1 \cdot \text{es}_2) = \begin{cases} D_{\underline{a}}^\pi(\text{es}_1) \cdot \text{es}_2 \vee D_{\underline{a}}^\pi(\text{es}_2) & \text{if } \delta_\pi(\text{es}_1) = \text{true} \\ D_{\underline{a}}^\pi(\text{es}_1) \cdot \text{es}_2 & \text{if } \delta_\pi(\text{es}_1) = \text{false} \end{cases}$$

VII. Disprove (Heuristic Refutation). This rule is used to disprove the inclusions when the antecedent is nullable, while the consequent is not nullable. Intuitively, the antecedent contains at least one more trace (the empty trace) than the consequent.

$$\frac{\delta_{\pi_1}(\text{es}_1) \wedge \neg\delta_{\pi_1 \wedge \pi_2}(\text{es}_2)}{\Gamma \vdash \pi_1 \wedge \text{es}_1 \not\sqsubseteq \pi_2 \wedge \text{es}_2} \text{ [DISPROVE]}$$

VIII. Prove. We use three rules to prove an inclusion: (i) [PROVE] is used when there is a *subset* relation $\subseteq$ between the antecedent and consequent; (ii) [FRAME] is used when the consequent is empty, we prove this inclusion with a residue $\gamma_R{}^6$; and (iii) [REOCCUR] is used when there exists an inclusion hypothesis in the proof context Γ, which meets the conditions. It essentially assigns to the current unexpanded inclusion an interior inclusion with an identical sequent labelling.

$$\frac{\pi_1 \Rightarrow \pi_2 \quad \text{es}_1 \subseteq \text{es}_2}{\Gamma \vdash \pi_1 \wedge \text{es}_1 \sqsubseteq \pi_2 \wedge \text{es}_2} \text{ [PROVE]} \qquad \frac{\pi_1 \Rightarrow \pi_2 \quad \gamma_R = \pi_1 \wedge \text{es}_1}{\Gamma \vdash (\pi_1 \wedge \text{es}_1 \sqsubseteq \pi_2 \wedge \epsilon) \rightsquigarrow \gamma_R} \text{ [FRAME]}$$

$$\frac{\exists.(\pi_1' \wedge \text{es}_1' \sqsubseteq \pi_2' \wedge \text{es}_2') \in \Gamma \quad \pi_1 \Rightarrow \pi_1' \Rightarrow \pi_2' \Rightarrow \pi_2 \quad \text{es}_1 \subseteq \text{es}_1' \quad \text{es}_2' \subseteq \text{es}_2}{\Gamma \vdash \pi_1 \wedge \text{es}_1 \sqsubseteq \pi_2 \wedge \text{es}_2} \text{[REOCCUR]}$$

---

[5] The proof obligations are discharged using the Z3 SMT prover, while deciding the nullability of effects constructed by symbolic terms, represented by $\text{SAT}(\pi)$.

[6] A residue refers to the remaining event sequences from antecedent after matching up with the consequent. An inclusion with no residue means the antecedent completely/exactly matches with the consequent.

6   Implementation and Evaluation

To show the feasibility of our approach, we have implemented our effects logic using OCaml, on top of the HIP/SLEEK system [8]. The proof obligations generated by our verification are discharged using constraint solver Z3. Furthermore, we provide a web UI [2] to present more non-trivial examples. Next, we show case studies to demonstrate the expressive power of our integrated dependent effects.

6.1   Case Studies

i. Encoding LTL. Classical LTL extended propositional logic with the temporal operators $\mathcal{G}$ ("globally") and $\mathcal{F}$ ("in the future"), which we also write $\square$ and $\lozenge$, respectively; and introduced the concept of fairness, which ensures an infinite-paths semantics. LTL was subsequently extended to include the $\mathcal{U}$ ("until") operator and the $\mathcal{X}$ ("next time") operator. As shown in Table 4, we encode these basic operators into our effects, making it more intuitive and readable, mainly when nested operators occur. Furthermore, by putting the effects in the precondition, our approach naturally composites *past-time LTL* along the way.

Table 4. Examples for converting LTL formulae into Effects. ($\underline{\mathbf{A}}, \underline{\mathbf{B}}$ are events, n ≥ 0, m ≥ 0 are the default constraints.)

$\square \underline{\mathbf{A}} \equiv \underline{\mathbf{A}}^\star$	$\lozenge \underline{\mathbf{A}} \equiv \_^n \cdot \underline{\mathbf{A}}$	$\underline{\mathbf{A}} \, \mathcal{U} \, \underline{\mathbf{B}} \equiv \underline{\mathbf{A}}^n \cdot \underline{\mathbf{B}}$	$\underline{\mathbf{A}} \to \lozenge \underline{\mathbf{B}} \equiv \neg \underline{\mathbf{A}} \vee \_^n \cdot \underline{\mathbf{B}}$
$\mathcal{X} \underline{\mathbf{A}} \equiv \_ \cdot \underline{\mathbf{A}}$	$\square \lozenge \underline{\mathbf{A}} \equiv \_^n \cdot \underline{\mathbf{A}} \cdot (\_^m \cdot \underline{\mathbf{A}})^\star$	$\lozenge \square \underline{\mathbf{A}} \equiv \_^n \cdot \underline{\mathbf{A}}^\star$	$\lozenge \underline{\mathbf{A}} \vee \lozenge \underline{\mathbf{B}} \equiv \_^n \cdot \underline{\mathbf{A}} \vee \_^m \cdot \underline{\mathbf{B}}$

ii. Encoding μ-calculus. μ-calculus provides a single, elegant, uniform logical framework of great raw expressive power by using a least fixpoint (μ) and a greatest fixpoint (v). More specifically, it can express properties such as $vZ.P \wedge \mathcal{X}\mathcal{X}Z$, which says that there exists a path where the atomic proposition P holds at every even position, and any valuation can be used on odd positions. As we can see, such properties already go beyond the first order logic. In fact, analogously to our effects, the symbolic/constant values correspond to the least fixpoint (μ), referring to finite traces, and the constructor ω corresponds to the greatest fixpoint (v), referring to infinite traces. For example, we write $(\_ \cdot \underline{\mathbf{A}})^\omega$, meaning that the event $\underline{\mathbf{A}}$ recurs at every even position in an infinite trace.

iii. Kleene Star. By using $\star$, we make an approximation of the possible traces when the termination is non-deterministic. As shown in Fig. 7, a weaker specification of send(n) can be provided as **Send*** · **Done**, meaning that the repetition of event **Send** can be both finite and infinite, which is more concise than the prior work, also beyond μ-calculus. By supporting a variety

```
1  void send (int n){
2    if (...) {
3        event[Done];
4    }else{
5        event[Send];
6        send (n-1);
7  }}
```

Fig. 7. An unknown conditional

of specifications, we can make a trade-off between precision and scalability, which is important for realistic methodology on automated verification. For example, we can weaken precondition of server(n) (cf. Table 1) to $\Phi_{pre}^{server(n)} \triangleq True \wedge \epsilon$, and opt for either of the following two postcondition: $\Phi_{post1}^{server(n)} \triangleq n\geq0\wedge(\mathbf{Ready} \cdot \mathbf{Send}^n \cdot \mathbf{Done})^\omega$, or $\Phi_{post2}^{server(n)} \triangleq n\geq0\wedge(\mathbf{Ready} \cdot \mathbf{Send}^n \cdot \mathbf{Done})^\omega \vee n<0\wedge\mathbf{Ready} \cdot \mathbf{Send}^\omega$, with the latter being more complex but more precise.

iv. Beyond Regular, Context-Free and Context-Sensitive. The paradigmatic non-regular linear language: $n>0 \wedge \underline{a}^n \cdot \underline{b}^n$, can be naturally expressed by the depended effects. Besides, the effects can also express grammars such as $n>0 \wedge \underline{a}^n \cdot \underline{b}^n \cdot \underline{c}^n$, or $n>0 \wedge m>0 \wedge \underline{a}^n \cdot \underline{b}^m \cdot \underline{c}^n$, which are beyond context-free grammar. Those examples show that the traces which cannot be recognized even by push-down automata (PDA) can be represented by our effects. However, such specifications are significant, suppose we have a traffic light control system, we could have a specifications $n>0 \wedge m>0 \wedge (\mathbf{Red}^n \cdot \mathbf{Yellow}^m \cdot \mathbf{Green}^n)^\omega$, which specifies that (i) this is a continuous-time system which has an infinite trace, (ii) all the colors will occur at each life circle, and (iii) the duration of the green light and the red light is always the same. Moreover, these effects can not be translated into linear bounded automata (LBA) either, which equivalents to context-sensitive grammar, as LBA are only capable of expressing finite traces.

6.2 Experimental Results

We mainly compare our backend T.r.s with the mature model checker PAT [18], which implements techniques for LTL properties with fairness assumptions. We chose a realistic benchmark containing 16 IOT programs implemented in C for Arduino controlling programs [1]. For each of the programs, we (i) derive a number of temporal properties (for 16 distinct execution models, there are in total 235 properties with 124 valid and 111 invalid), (ii) express these properties using both LTL formulae and our effects, (iii) we record the total computation time using PAT and our T.r.s. Our test cases are provided as a benchmark [2]. We conduct experiments on a MacBook Pro with a 2.6 GHz Intel Core i7 processor.

As shown in Table 5, comparing the T.r.s to PAT, the total (dis-) proving time has been reduced by 31.7%. For that, we summarize the underlying reasons which lead to the improvement: (1)When the transition states of the models are small, the average execution time spent by the T.r.s is even less than the NFAs

Table 5. The experiments are based on 16 real world C programs, we record the lines of code (LOC), the number of testing temporal properties (#Prop.), and the (dis-) proving times (in milliseconds) using PAT and our T.r.s respectively.

Programs	LOC	# Prop.	PAT(ms)	T.r.s(ms)
1. Chrome_Dino_Game	80	12	32.09	7.66
2. Cradle_with_Joystick	89	12	31.22	9.85
3. Small_Linear_Actuator	180	12	21.65	38.68
4. Large_Linear_Actuator	155	12	17.41	14.66
5. Train_Detect	78	12	19.50	17.35
6. Motor_Control	216	15	22.89	4.71
7. Train_Demo_2	133	15	49.51	59.28
8. Fridge_Timer	292	15	17.05	9.11
9. Match_the_Light	143	15	23.34	49.65
10. Tank_Control	104	15	24.96	19.39
11. Control_a_Solenoid	120	18	36.26	19.85
12. IoT_Stepper_Motor	145	18	27.75	6.74
13. Aquariumatic_Manager	135	10	25.72	3.93
14. Auto_Train_Control	122	18	56.55	14.95
15. LED_Switch_Array	280	18	44.78	19.58
16. Washing_Machine	419	18	33.69	9.94
Total	2546	235	446.88	305.33

construction time, which means it is not necessary to construct the NFAs when a T.r.s solves it faster; (2)When the total states become larger, on average, the T.r.s outperforms automata-based algorithms, due to the significantly reduced search branches provided by the normalization lemmas; and (3)For the invalid cases, the T.r.s disproves them earlier without constructing the whole NFAs.

7   Related Work

Recently, temporal reasoning has garnered renewed importance for possibly non-terminating control programs with subtle use of recursion and non-determinism, as used in reactive or stream-based applications. In this section, we discuss the related works in the following two perspectives: (i) temporal verification and expressive effects; and (ii) efficient algorithms for language inclusion checking.

7.1   Verification and Expressive Effects

A vast range of techniques has been developed for the prediction of program temporal behaviors without actually running the system. One of the leading communities of temporal verification is automata-based model checking, mainly for finite-state systems. Various model checkers are based on some temporal logic specifications, such as LTL and CTL. Such tools extract the logic design from the program using modeling languages and verify specific assertions to guarantee various properties. However, classical model checking techniques usually require a manual modelling stage and need to be bounded when encountering non-terminating traces.

Meanwhile, to conduct temporal reasoning locally, there is a sub-community whose aim is to support temporal specifications in the form of *effects* via the type-and-effect system. The inspiration from this approach is that it leads to a modular and compositional verification strategy, where temporal reasoning can be combined together to reason about the overall program [10,13,17]. However, the temporal effects in prior work tend to coarsely over-approximate the behaviours either via ω-regular expressions [10] or by büchi automata [13]. One of the recent works [17] proposes the dependent temporal effects on program input values, which allows the reasoning on infinite input alphabet, but still loses the precision of the branching properties. The conventional effects have the form (Φ_u, Φ_v), which separates the finite and infinite effects. In this work, by integrating possibly finite and possibly infinite effects into a single disjunctive form with size properties, our integrated dependent effects eliminate the finiteness distinction, and enable an expressive modular temporal verification.

7.2   Efficient Algorithms for Language Inclusion Checking

Generally, it is unavoidable for any language inclusion checking solutions to have an exponential worst-case complexity. As there are no existing automata capable to express dependent effects, neither there exist corresponding inclusion checking algorithms. Here we reference two efficient prior works targeting basic regular sets: Antichain-based algorithms and the traditional T.r.s, which are both avoiding the explicit, complex translation from the NFAs into their minimal DFAs.

Antichain-based algorithm [9] was proposed for checking universality and language inclusion for finite word automata. By investigating the easy-to-check pre-order on set inclusion over the states powerset, Antichain is able to soundly prune the search space, therefore it is more succinct than the sets of states manipulated by the classical fixpoint algorithms. It significantly outperforms the classical subset construction, in many cases, it still suffers from the exponential blow up problem.

The main peculiarity of a purely algebraic T.r.s [5,6,12] is that it provides a reasoning logic for regular expression inclusions to avoid any kind of translation aforementioned. Specifically, a T.r.s takes finite steps to reduce $r \preceq t$ into its normal form $r' \preceq t'$ and the inclusion checking fails whenever $r' \preceq t'$ is not valid. A T.r.s is shown to be feasible and, generally, faster than the standard methods, because (i) it deploys the heuristic refutation step to disprove inclusions earlier; (ii) it prunes the search space by using fine-grained normalization lemmas. Overall, it provides a better average-case performance than those based on the translation to minimal DFAs. More importantly, a T.r.s allows us to accommodate infinite alphabets and capture size-dependent properties.

In this work, we choose to deploy an extended T.r.s, which composites optimizations from both Antichain-based algorithm and classical T.r.s. Having such a T.r.s as the back-end to verify temporal effects, one can benefit from the high efficiency without translating effects into automata. We generalize the Antimirov and Mosses's rewriting procedure [5], to be able to further reason about infinite traces, together with size properties and arithmetic constraints. One of the direct benefits granted by our effects logic is that it provides the capability to check the inclusion for possibly finite and infinite event sequences without a deliberate distinction, which is already beyond the strength of existing T.r.s [3,5,11,12].

8   Conclusion

We devise a concise and precise characterization of temporal properties. We propose a novel logic for effects to specify and verify the implementation of the possibly non-terminating programs, including the use of prior effects in preconditions. We implement the effects logic on top of the HIP/SLEEK system [8] and show its feasibility. Our work is the first solution that automate modular temporal verification using an expressive effects logic, which primarily benefits modern sequential controlling systems ranging over a variety of application domains.

Acknowledgement. This work is supported by the Academic Research Fund (AcRF) Tier-1 NUS research project R-252-000-A63-114.

References

1. Arduino. https://create.arduino.cc/projecthub/projects/tags/control
2. Online demo platform. http://loris-5.d2.comp.nus.edu.sg/EffectNew/index.html?ex=send_valid&type=c&options=sess
3. Almeida, M., Moreira, N., Reis, R.: Antimirov and Mosses's rewrite system revisited. Int. J. Found. Comput. Sci. **20**(04), 669–684 (2009)
4. Antimirov, V.: Partial derivatives of regular expressions and finite automata constructions. In: Mayr, E.W., Puech, C. (eds.) STACS 1995. LNCS, vol. 900, pp. 455–466. Springer, Heidelberg (1995). https://doi.org/10.1007/3-540-59042-0_96
5. Antimirov, V.M., Mosses, P.D.: Rewriting extended regular expressions. Theor. Comput. Sci. **143**(1), 51–72 (1995)
6. Bezem, M., Klop, J.W., de Vrijer, R.: Terese. Term Rewriting Systems. Cambridge Tracts in Theoretical Computer Science, vol. 55 (2003)
7. Brotherston, J.. Cyclic proofs for first-order logic with inductive definitions. In: Beckert, B. (ed.) TABLEAUX 2005. LNCS (LNAI), vol. 3702, pp. 78–92. Springer, Heidelberg (2005). https://doi.org/10.1007/11554554_8
8. Chin, W.-N., David, C., Nguyen, H.H., Qin, S.: Automated verification of shape, size and bag properties via user-defined predicates in separation logic. Sci. Comput. Program. **77**(9), 1006–1036 (2012)

9. De Wulf, M., Doyen, L., Henzinger, T.A., Raskin, J.-F.: Antichains: a new algorithm for checking universality of finite automata. In: Ball, T., Jones, R.B. (eds.) CAV 2006. LNCS, vol. 4144, pp. 17–30. Springer, Heidelberg (2006). https://doi.org/10.1007/11817963_5

10. Hofmann, M., Chen, W.: Abstract interpretation from büchi automata. In: Proceedings of the Joint Meeting of the Twenty-Third EACSL Annual Conference on Computer Science Logic (CSL) and the Twenty-Ninth Annual ACM/IEEE Symposium on Logic in Computer Science (LICS), p. 51. ACM (2014)

11. Hovland, D.: The inclusion problem for regular expressions. J. Comput. Syst. Sci. **78**(6), 1795–1813 (2012)

12. Keil, M., Thiemann, P.: Symbolic solving of extended regular expression inequalities. arXiv preprint arXiv:1410.3227 (2014)

13. Koskinen, E., Terauchi, T.: Local temporal reasoning. In: Proceedings of the Joint Meeting of the Twenty-Third EACSL Annual Conference on Computer Science Logic (CSL) and the Twenty-Ninth Annual ACM/IEEE Symposium on Logic in Computer Science (LICS), p. 59. ACM (2014)

14. Malecha, G., Morrisett, G., Wisnesky, R.: Trace-based verification of imperative programs with I/O. J. Symb. Comput. **46**(2), 95–118 (2011)

15. Murase, A., Terauchi, T., Kobayashi, N., Sato, R., Unno, H.: Temporal verification of higher-order functional programs. In: ACM SIGPLAN Notices, vol. 51, p. 57–68. ACM (2016)

16. Nakata, K., Uustalu, T.: A Hoare logic for the coinductive trace-based big-step semantics of while. In: Gordon, A.D. (ed.) ESOP 2010. LNCS, vol. 6012, pp. 488–506. Springer, Heidelberg (2010). https://doi.org/10.1007/978-3-642-11957-6_26

17. Nanjo, Y., Unno, H., Koskinen, E., Terauchi, T.: A fixpoint logic and dependent effects for temporal property verification. In: Proceedings of the 33rd Annual ACM/IEEE Symposium on Logic in Computer Science, pp. 759–768. ACM (2018)

18. Sun, J., Liu, Y., Dong, J.S., Pang, J.: PAT: towards flexible verification under fairness. In: Bouajjani, A., Maler, O. (eds.) CAV 2009. LNCS, vol. 5643, pp. 709–714. Springer, Heidelberg (2009). https://doi.org/10.1007/978-3-642-02658-4_59

A Reversible Operational Semantics for Imperative Programming Languages

Maribel Fernández[1(✉)] and Ian Mackie[2]

[1] Department of Informatics, King's College London, London, UK
`Maribel.Fernandez@kcl.ac.uk`
[2] University of Sussex, Brighton, UK

Abstract. Imperative programming languages are not reversible in general; however, there are well-known approaches to make them reversible, e.g., by storing computation histories or checkpointing. Another successful approach is based on designing restricted languages where all the commands are reversible (cf. Janus, R-WHILE). We present an alternative approach where we do not restrict the language. Instead, we modify the operational semantics (while preserving the meaning of programs) to obtain reversibility at both language level and computation level.

Keywords: Language-level reversibility · Reversible computation steps · Universal languages · Imperative programming

1 Introduction

This paper studies reversibility properties of imperative languages using formal specifications of the language operational semantics.

Reversibility has been studied at various abstraction layers (from hardware to software) since Landauer [17,18] demonstrated in 1961 that irreversible operations cause heat loss in computers. Although this effect was negligible in early computers, advances in low power computing and quantum computing triggered renewed interest in reversible computing and reversible programming languages (see [22] for a recent account of reversible computing foundations).

We focus on reversibility at programming language level, and consider two related notions: *source-code reversibility* and *computation-step reversibility*. The latter is usually defined as the property of being backwards deterministic, that is, every configuration has at most one predecessor [22]. Then every computation step can be undone (there is no information loss in computation steps). This is useful for example during program debugging [2]. Source-code reversibility, or *program inversion* (see, e.g., [8,11,12]), aims at defining, for each program P, a program that computes the inverse of P (in a sense to be made precise later).

Reversible models of computation (e.g., reversible Turing machines [21]) can be used to specify reversible algorithms and study their computability and complexity properties. For the latter, an alternative approach is based on the use of

© Springer Nature Switzerland AG 2020
S.-W. Lin et al. (Eds.): ICFEM 2020, LNCS 12531, pp. 91–106, 2020.
https://doi.org/10.1007/978-3-030-63406-3_6

concise programming languages with formal semantics [9,16,23,26]. This is the approach we follow in this paper.

Simple reversible imperative programming languages, such as R-WHILE [10] and Janus [19,27], have been used to study reversible programming. Janus is a high-level imperative language that supports deterministic forward and backward computation. It provides restricted (non-destructive) assignment[1], conditional and loop constructs, and mechanisms to call and uncall procedures. A more concise reversible imperative language, called R-CORE, uses a single reversible control flow construct (a loop but no conditional), a reversible assignment statement and a limited number of variables that can store tree data structures [11]. R-CORE has the same power of a reversible imperative language such as R-WHILE and Janus. Due to the restrictions in assignments, conditional and loops, these languages are not Turing complete [14,27]. However, they are reversible-Turing-complete (i.e., any computable reversible function can be programmed) and irreversible functions can be embedded into reversible ones[2] using well-known translations [6,17].

Since writing reversible embeddings of irreversible programs by hand can be difficult, Burhman et al [7] (see also [1]) suggest that the natural way is to compile irreversible programs to reversible ones. This paper is part of the effort to simplify the task of writing reversible programs. Here, instead of compiling we provide an operational semantics that similarly hides from the programmer the mechanisms that embed non-reversible computation into reversible one. We present a simple imperative programming language, RIMP, with unrestricted assignment, conditional and while-loop constructs, and provide a fine-grained operational semantics that ensures programs are reversible both at source-code level and at computation level. Thus, RIMP's operational semantics provides a formal specification of an interpreter for the language and a formal basis for the development of a debugger [2]. The advantages of incorporating the reversible embedding in the operational semantics of the language are twofold: on one hand, programmers can use the language in the standard way (all the commands behave as expected in an imperative language) and obtain reversibility "for free", on the other hand, this approach provides a uniform way of obtaining reversible versions of imperative languages and can be directly implemented in a semantic framework such as K [25].

Summarising, our main contributions are:

– We define a minimal imperative language with the standard syntax and specify a big-step operational semantics that ensures all programs can be inverted. We provide a function rev that, given a program P, produces a program P_r that performs the reverse of the computations of P. To be able to reverse assignments, each variable is represented using a pair consisting of a num-

---

[1] Assignments are non-destructive if the difference between the post- and pre-assignment values of the variable can be statically known, e.g., an assignment of the form $x := x + 2$ is non-destructive and can be reversed by the assignment $x := x - 2$.

[2] This does not mean they are universal: the reversible translation of the irreversible function is a different function, see [4] for more details.

ber and a stack that can be seen as a dynamic version of a non-destructive assignment (the stack can be omitted if all assignments for a given variable are non-destructive as in Janus). To be able to reverse while-loops, the big-step semantics uses counters. Since all assignments are reversible, we are able to deal with unrestricted conditionals (we use assignments to save the values of the variables used in the condition).

– We define an abstract machine equivalent to the standard one but with an extra stack and a switch to make the machine go forwards or backwards. The extra stack is used to store source code for backwards computations, not to store computation traces. The machine is deterministic in both directions.

Overview. In the next section we recall SIMP, a simple imperative language, used as a basis for the specification of RIMP in Sect. 3. Section 4 defines a source-code to source-code inversion function. Section 5 presents an abstract machine for RIMP, which is forward and backward deterministic. Section 6 discusses related work. Finally, we conclude in Sect. 7.

2   Preliminaries: SIMP

Programs in SIMP are commands (C) or integer expressions (E). For simplicity, we represent Booleans using integers (false is represented by 0, all other values represent true), however in examples we use true and false for clarity. The abstract syntax of SIMP is defined by the following grammar.

$$P ::= C \mid E$$
$$C ::= \mathsf{skip} \mid l := E \mid C; C \mid \mathsf{if}\ E\ \mathsf{then}\ C\ \mathsf{else}\ C \mid \mathsf{while}\ E\ \mathsf{do}\ C$$
$$E ::= \;!l \mid n \mid E\ op\ E \mid \neg E$$
$$op ::= + \mid - \mid * \mid / \mid > \mid < \mid = \mid \wedge$$

SIMP has sequencing (indicated by ;) and assignments. There is also a selector, a loop construct, and a skip instruction which will simply pass the control to the following statement. In the grammar above we assume that $n \in Z$ (the set of integers) and $l \in L = \{l_0, l_1, \ldots\}$ (a set of *locations* or *variables*). We only consider simple expressions, built out of numbers, variables and operators. The expression $!l$ denotes the value stored in l.

We only consider well-typed abstract syntax trees. As usual, we use infix notation (e.g., $E\ op\ E$ instead of $op(E, E)$), omitting parentheses when possible and using indentation to avoid ambiguity.

Example 1. Assuming a natural number n has been read and stored in the variable i_1, the following program *Fact* computes the factorial of n:

$$l := !i_1;\ factorial := 1;$$
$$\mathsf{while}\ !l > 0\ \mathsf{do}$$
$$(factorial := !factorial * !l;\ l := !l - 1)$$

The operational semantics of SIMP is defined by a transition system with:

- *Initial configurations* of the form $\langle P, s \rangle$ where P is a SIMP program and s is a store represented by a partial function from locations to integers.

  We denote by $dom(s)$ the set of locations where s is defined. Without loss of generality we assume s contains the input values for the program in a set of variables $i_1, \ldots, i_n$ which are not modified by P. The expression $s[l \mapsto n]$ denotes the function s' that coincides with s except that it maps l to the value n: $s[l \mapsto n](l) = n$ and $s[l \mapsto n](l') = s(l')$ if $l \neq l'$.

  Final configurations have the form $\langle n, s \rangle$ (where n is an integer), $\langle skip, s \rangle$, or are blocked configurations, such as $\langle !l, s \rangle$ where $l \notin dom(s)$. The first and third forms correspond to expressions and the second form to commands.

- An inductively defined *evaluation relation* $\langle P, s \rangle \Downarrow \langle P', s' \rangle$, where $\langle P', s' \rangle$ is a final configuration, see Fig. 1. In the rules to evaluate expressions we use $\overline{op}$ to denote standard machine operations, for example, $n_1 \overline{+} n_2$ represents the sum of n_1 and n_2, and $n_1 \overline{\wedge} n_2$ is 0 if one of the inputs is 0, 1 otherwise.

$$\frac{}{\langle c, s \rangle \Downarrow \langle c, s \rangle \ \text{ if } c \in Z} \ (\text{const}) \qquad \frac{}{\langle !l, s \rangle \Downarrow \langle n, s \rangle \ \text{ if } s(l) = n} \ (\text{var})$$

$$\frac{\langle E_1, s \rangle \Downarrow \langle b_1, s \rangle}{\langle \neg E_1, s \rangle \Downarrow \langle b, s \rangle \ \text{ if } b = not\ b_1} \ (\text{not}) \qquad \frac{\langle E_1, s \rangle \Downarrow \langle n_1, s \rangle \quad \langle E_2, s \rangle \Downarrow \langle n_2, s \rangle}{\langle E_1\ op\ E_2, s \rangle \Downarrow \langle n, s \rangle \ \text{ if } n = n_1\ \overline{op}\ n_2} \ (\text{op})$$

$$\frac{}{\langle skip, s \rangle \Downarrow \langle skip, s \rangle} \ (\text{skip}) \qquad \frac{\langle E, s \rangle \Downarrow \langle n, s \rangle}{\langle l := E, s \rangle \Downarrow \langle skip, s[l \mapsto n] \rangle} \ (:=)$$

$$\frac{\langle C_1, s \rangle \Downarrow \langle skip, s' \rangle \quad \langle C_2, s' \rangle \Downarrow \langle skip, s'' \rangle}{\langle C_1; C_2, s \rangle \Downarrow \langle skip, s'' \rangle} \ (\text{seq})$$

$$\frac{\langle E, s \rangle \Downarrow \langle \text{true}, s \rangle \quad \langle C_1, s \rangle \Downarrow \langle skip, s' \rangle}{\langle \text{if } E \text{ then } C_1 \text{ else } C_2, s \rangle \Downarrow \langle skip, s' \rangle} \ (\text{if}_\text{T}) \qquad \frac{\langle E, s \rangle \Downarrow \langle \text{false}, s \rangle \quad \langle C_2, s \rangle \Downarrow \langle skip, s' \rangle}{\langle \text{if } E \text{ then } C_1 \text{ else } C_2, s \rangle \Downarrow \langle skip, s' \rangle} \ (\text{if}_\text{F})$$

$$\frac{\langle E, s \rangle \Downarrow \langle \text{true}, s \rangle \ \langle C, s \rangle \Downarrow \langle skip, s_1 \rangle \ \langle \text{while } E \text{ do } C, s_1 \rangle \Downarrow \langle skip, s_2 \rangle}{\langle \text{while } E \text{ do } C, s \rangle \Downarrow \langle skip, s_2 \rangle} \ (\text{while}_\text{T})$$

$$\frac{\langle E, s \rangle \Downarrow \langle \text{false}, s \rangle}{\langle \text{while } E \text{ do } C, s \rangle \Downarrow \langle skip, s \rangle} \ (\text{while}_\text{F})$$

Fig. 1. Axioms and rules defining evaluation for SIMP

SIMP is universal but not reversible: for example, an assignment $l := 0$ cannot be reversed. One way to avoid this problem is to forbid destructive assignments. Alternatively, a more general notion of value can be used, as shown in the next section. However, to make the language reversible, we also need to be able to reverse conditionals and while-loops. These are generally irreversible so restrictions are imposed in reversible languages [10,19,27], or logs of computations are used to ensure reversibility [14,24]. We define reversible versions of these commands by renaming variables in conditions and using counters in loops.

3   RIMP: A Reversible Imperative Language

The language RIMP is a variant of SIMP with an extended syntax and modified operational semantics. Although the execution of programs in RIMP and SIMP is different, the results are equivalent as stated in Theorem 2.

The syntax of RIMP is the same as the syntax of SIMP, except that RIMP has an additional statement of the form $l =: E$, which we call *reverse assignment*. This is a key feature of RIMP.

Regarding conditionals, first we observe that any conditional can be transformed so that the variables used in the condition are not modified in the branches: if a program contains a command $C =$ if E then C_1 else C_2, where $l_1, \ldots, l_n$ are the variables used in E, then C can be replaced by a sequence of assignments $l'_i := !l_i$ for new variables $l'_1, \ldots, l'_n$ followed by a conditional if E' then C_1 else C_2, where E' coincides with E except that all occurrences of l_i are replaced by l'_i. By transforming conditionals in this way we will be able to define the reverse of a conditional, using the same semantic rules for the conditional as in SIMP.

Ensuring the while-loop is reversible is harder. To achieve reversibility, we will associate a different counter with each while-loop in the program. More precisely, we define a syntactic transformation, where the ith while-loop command while E do C occurring in the program (the order in which they are numbered is not important) is replaced by a sequence of commands as follows.

$$counter_i := 0;$$
$$\text{while } E \text{ do } (C; counter_i := \ !counter_i + 1)$$

Remark 1. *From now on, we assume that $counter_i$ is a protected name (not used by programmers) and RIMP programs have been processed to satisfy the above conditions, that is, in any command of the form   if E then C_1 else C_2 the variables in E are not modified by C_1 and C_2, and each while-loop uses a counter as specified above. This is not a restriction since any program can be translated into a program that satisfies these conditions.*

Example 2. The following program $\overline{Fact}$ is the translation of the program *Fact* given in Example 1 to compute the factorial of a number stored in the variable i_1.

$$l := !i_1; factorial := \ 1;$$
$$counter_1 := 0;$$
$$\text{while}_1 !l > 0 \text{do}$$
$$\quad (factorial := !factorial * !l; l := \ !l - 1;$$
$$\quad counter_1 := !counter_1 + 1)$$

As in Sect. 2, we specify the evaluation semantics of programs using configurations of the form $\langle P, s \rangle$, where s contains the input values for P in variables $i_1, \ldots, i_n$, which we assume are not modified by the program. However, we use the following set of runtime values in the store, where $n \in Z$:

$$v :: = 0 \mid +(n, v)$$

It is easy to define the integer associated with a runtime value:

$$[\![0]\!] = 0, \quad [\![+(n,v)]\!] = n + [\![v]\!]$$

and conversely, any number $n \in Z$ can be stored as a runtime value $rv(n)$:

$$rv(0) = 0, \quad rv(n) = +(n,0) \quad (n \neq 0).$$

The store will be represented by a function s that maps each variable to a pair (k,v) where $k = [\![v]\!]$. Although there is redundancy is this representation (we could use just v) we prefer to store also k to avoid recomputing $[\![v]\!]$. We write $s_1(l)$ and $s_2(l)$ to denote the first and second components of the pair $s(l)$, respectively (i.e., s_i is the composition of s and the ith projection).

Example 3. The pair $(3, +(2, +(1,0)))$ is valid since the runtime value $+(2, +(1,0))$ corresponds to the integer 3: $[\![+(2, +(1,0))]\!] = 3$. Different runtime values may be associated with the same integer, for example, $(3, +(3,0))$ is also valid. This is not a problem: different runtime values associated with the same integer correspond to different executions that produce the same number, as we will show later.

The evaluation relation for RIMP, denoted $\Downarrow_{\mathsf{RIMP}}$, associates each configuration $\langle P, s \rangle$ with its final result (assuming P is a terminating program). We define $\Downarrow_{\mathsf{RIMP}}$ inductively. The rules to evaluate expressions in RIMP are the same as in SIMP (see Fig. 1) except for axiom (var), which is replaced as follows:

$$\frac{}{\langle !l, s \rangle \Downarrow_{\mathsf{RIMP}} \langle n, s \rangle \text{ if} s_1(l) = n} \text{ (var)}$$

The rule to evaluate assignment statements $l := E$ in RIMP is different from the one in SIMP, as it uses runtime values.

$$\frac{\langle E, s \rangle \Downarrow_{\mathsf{RIMP}} \langle n, s \rangle}{\langle l := E, s \rangle \Downarrow_{\mathsf{RIMP}} \langle skip, s[l \mapsto (n, +(n_1, s_2(l)))] \rangle} (:=) \quad \text{where } n_1 = n - s_1(l)$$

This assignment command is equivalent to SIMP's, as shown below.

Lemma 1. *Let s be a SIMP store and $\overline{s}$ the store obtained by pairing each number k in s with $rv(k)$.*
$\langle l := E, s \rangle \Downarrow \langle skip, s' \rangle$ if and only if $\langle l := E, \overline{s} \rangle \Downarrow_{\mathsf{RIMP}} \langle skip, s'' \rangle$, where $s''_1 = s'$.
In particular $s'(l) = s''_1(l) = [\![s''_2(l)]\!] = n$, where $\langle E, s \rangle \Downarrow_{\mathsf{RIMP}} \langle n, s \rangle$.

Example 4. Consider again the program $\overline{Fact}$ of Example 2. Assume the input is 2, i.e., assume $s(i_1) = (2, +(2,0))$, $s(l) = s(factorial) = s(counter_1) = (0,0)$. Then $\langle \overline{Fact}, s \rangle \Downarrow_{\mathsf{RIMP}} \langle skip, s' \rangle$ where $s'_1(factorial) = 2$. The store s' contains the following values: $s'(i_1) = (2, +(2,0))$, $s'(l) = (0, +(-1, +(-1, +(2,0))))$, $s'(factorial) = (2, +(0, (+1, +(1,0))))$, $s'(counter_1) = (2, +(1, +(1, +(0,0))))$.

Although it is not intended for programmers to use reverse-assignment commands $x =: E$ in their programs, below we provide the rule to evaluate such commands. The idea is to define the semantics in such a way that this command reverses the last assignment $x := E$. The following rule achieves this effect.

$$\frac{\langle E, s' \rangle \Downarrow_{\mathsf{RIMP}} \langle n, s' \rangle}{\langle l =: E, s[l \mapsto (n, +(n_1, v))] \rangle \Downarrow_{\mathsf{RIMP}} \langle skip, s' \rangle} \; (=:) \quad \text{where } s' = s[l \mapsto (n - n_1, v)]$$

Given a program P in SIMP, let $\overline{P}$ be the translation of P such that no conditional command modifies the variables in the condition and while-loops use counters as specified above. The programs P and $\overline{P}$ produce equivalent results when executed using SIMP and RIMP evaluation rules, respectively. In this sense the translation preserves the semantics of the program.

Theorem 2. *Let P be a SIMP program, s a store, $\overline{P}$ the translation of P and $\overline{s}$ the store obtained by pairing each number k in s with $rv(k)$. $\langle P, s \rangle \Downarrow \langle u, s' \rangle$ if and only if $\langle \overline{P}, \overline{s} \rangle \Downarrow_{\mathsf{RIMP}} \langle u, s'' \rangle$. Moreover, for any variable l in $dom(s')$, $s''_1(l) = s'(l)$ (i.e., s' and s'' coincide in all the variables in $dom(s')$, but s'' may contain more variables).*

4   A Program Inverter for RIMP

In this section we define a function rev that takes a RIMP program P and produces a program P_r that computes the reverse of the computations generated by P. At this point, we should clarify that from a computability point of view, if P computes a function f, it is not the case that $rev(P)$ will compute f^{-1}. Indeed this would only be possible if f were injective. However, $rev(P)$ will be the inverse of P in the sense that any computation performed by P can be undone and the store returned to its initial state by executing $rev(P)$. The function rev is therefore a *program inverter* [10,14]. In the next section we study a different notion of reversibility, where instead of reversing at the level of the source code we reverse at the level of computation steps.

Let us define more precisely what the function rev should achieve. The following definition is adapted from the one stated for the R-WHILE program inverter (see Lemma 1 in [10]).

Definition 1 (Correctness of rev). *Given a program P, $rev(P)$ is correct if for any s, $\langle P, s \rangle \Downarrow \langle skip, s' \rangle$ implies $\langle rev(P), s' \rangle \Downarrow \langle skip, s'' \rangle$ where s'' and s are equivalent over $dom(s)$.*

It is well-known that to achieve correctness it is sufficient to define an operational semantics for P that checkpoints the execution or preserves a trace of each computation step [24]. We follow an alternative approach: The following syntax-directed function for RIMP programs, rev, relies on the use of runtime values for variables, under the assumption that conditionals and while-loops have been translated as explained above. The function rev is parametric on an index table, T, which indicates for each while-loop in P, its index i and its condition

E (the latter is used when applying rev a second time to get back to the original program).

$$
\begin{aligned}
rev(E) &= E \\
rev(x := E) &= x =: E \\
rev(x =: E) &= x := E \\
rev(\mathtt{skip}) &= \mathtt{skip} \\
rev(C_1; C_2) &= rev(C_2); rev(C_1) \\
rev(\mathtt{if}\ E\ \mathtt{then}\ C_1\ \mathtt{else}\ C_2) &= \mathtt{if}\ E\ \mathtt{then}\ rev(C_1)\ \mathtt{else}\ rev(C_2) \\
rev(\mathtt{while}_i\ E\ \mathtt{do}\ C) &= \mathtt{while}_i\ !counter_i > 0\ \mathtt{do}\ rev(C)\quad if\ counter_i \notin E \\
rev(\mathtt{while}_i\ !counter_i > 0\ \mathtt{do}\ C) &= \mathtt{while}_i\ E\ \mathtt{do}\ rev(C)\qquad\qquad if\ T(i) = E
\end{aligned}
$$

Example 5. The following program is obtained by applying rev to the program $\overline{Fact}$ given in Example 2:

$$
\begin{aligned}
&\mathtt{while}_1 !counter_1 > 0\,\mathtt{do} \\
&\quad (counter_1 =: \ !counter_1 + 1; \\
&\quad l =: \ !l - 1; factorial =: !factorial * \ !l); \\
&\quad counter_1 =: 0; \\
&\quad factorial =: 1; l =: !i_1
\end{aligned}
$$

Let s be a store such that $s(i_1) = (2, +(2, 0))$, $s(l) = s(factorial) = s(counter_1) = (0, 0)$. As indicated in Example 4, $\langle \overline{Fact}, s \rangle \Downarrow_{\mathsf{RIMP}} \langle skip, s' \rangle$ where $s'(i_1) = (2, +(2, 0))$, $s'(l) = (0, +(-1, +(-1, +(2, 0))))$, $s'(factorial) = (2, +(0, (+1, +(1, 0))))$, $s'(counter_1) = (2, +(1, +(1, +(0, 0))))$.

Now if we run $rev(\overline{Fact})$ in s', we get back to the initial store s: $\langle rev(\overline{Fact}), s' \rangle \Downarrow_{\mathsf{RIMP}} \langle skip, s \rangle$. Indeed, after executing the *while* loop, we obtain a store s'' where $s''(i_1) = (2, +(2, 0)), s''(l) = (2, +(2, 0)), s''(factorial) = (1, +(1, 0)), s''(counter_1) = (0, +(0, 0))$, and the three final reverse assignments leave the value $(0, 0)$ in $counter_1$, $factorial$ and l.

Note that $rev(rev(\overline{Fact})) = \overline{Fact}$. This is indeed a general property.

Property 1. The function rev is self-inverse: If P is a RIMP program as specified in Remark 1, then $rev(rev(P)) = P$.

The function rev is correct (see Definition 1).

Theorem 3. *Let P be a RIMP program as described in Remark 1. For any s, if $\langle P, s \rangle \Downarrow_{\mathsf{RIMP}} \langle u, s' \rangle$ then $\langle rev(P), s' \rangle \Downarrow_{\mathsf{RIMP}} \langle u, s'' \rangle$ where $s(l) = s''(l)$ for all $l \in dom(s)$.*

5   Reversing the Computations in RIMP

To define a notion of reversibility at computation-step level, we define a small-step semantics for RIMP by means of an abstract machine. For terminating programs, the abstract machine and the big-step evaluation semantics produce the same results (the big-step semantics is undefined for non-terminating programs).

The abstract machine for RIMP consists of five main elements:

1. a *control stack* c, where instructions are stored;
2. a *results stack*, where intermediate results of computations are stored;
3. an arithmetic unit, also called *processor*, which performs reversible arithmetic operations and comparisons;
4. a *store*, also called *memory*, modelled by a partial function m mapping locations to runtime values;
5. a *back stack*, which is used when computing backwards.

For simplicity, we assume the processor performs only integer-valued binary operations of addition, subtraction, multiplication and division, and always returns a result (division by zero produces a number rather than an error; we leave the treatment of errors for future work). As before, we represent the memory as a partial function, $dom(m)$ is the set of locations where m is defined.

Formally, an abstract machine is a transition system, and is therefore defined by a set of configurations and a transition relation. The configurations of the abstract machine for RIMP are tuples $\langle c, r, m, b \rangle$ of control stack, results stack, memory and back stack. Stacks are inductively defined: an empty stack is denoted by *nil*, and a non-empty stack $i \cdot c$ is obtained by pushing an element i on top of a stack c. The definition of the stacks c, r, b is given by the grammar:

$$c, b ::= nil \mid i \cdot c$$
$$i \quad ::= P \mid l \mid lab$$
$$r \quad ::= nil \mid P \cdot r \mid l \cdot r$$

where *lab* are instruction labels, P and l denote programs and locations (see the grammar in Sect. 2) and expressions are extended with underlined numbers, operators and variables (this will be used to distinguish backward and forward computation in the abstract machine). In other words, the control and back stack may be empty, or contain commands, expressions, locations and keywords such as *if* or *while*. In the same way, the results stack may be empty or contain commands, expressions or locations.

Initial configurations have the form $\langle P \cdot nil, nil, m, nil \rangle$, where we assume that P is a RIMP program.

The transition relation, denoted by $\rightarrow$, specifies how to execute commands and evaluate expressions. A transition $\langle c, r, m, b \rangle \rightarrow \langle c', r', m', b' \rangle$ corresponds to a step of computation of the abstract machine. There is a special transition *switch* to change the direction of computation. This can be done at any point in the computation.

$$\langle c, r, m, b \rangle \xrightarrow{switch} \langle b, r, m, c \rangle$$

Final configurations have the form $\langle nil, nil, m, b \rangle$, since the machine stops when the control stack is empty in which case the results stack is also empty. By executing a switch transition, the machine performs an additional set of computation steps to empty the back stack, returning to the initial configuration (the output of the program should be saved or printed first). No garbage is produced.

Tables 1, 2, 3 and 4 show the transition rules. Since the goal is to perform computations both forwards and backwards, we have more transition rules than in standard abstract machines for imperative languages. However, the machine does not store traces of computations, instead it ensures that when a command has been executed, its inverse is stored in the back stack (the inverse is a program, not a computation history).

The left-hand sides of rules could be simplified: for example, in rule *mun* (Table 1) it is not necessary for the pattern-matching algorithm to check that both occurrences of n are the same, one could simply use two different variables in the left-hand side, under the assumption that the rules are used only during executions that start in an initial configuration. We have kept the more detailed versions of the rules to help see the effect of backward steps.

Table 1. Rules for expressions

$$\langle n \cdot c, r, m, b \rangle \xrightarrow{num} \langle c, n \cdot r, m, \underline{n} \cdot b \rangle$$
$$\langle \underline{n} \cdot b, n \cdot r, m, c \rangle \xrightarrow{mun} \langle b, r, m, n \cdot c \rangle$$

$$\langle !l \cdot c, r, m, b \rangle \xrightarrow{var} \langle c, m_1(l) \cdot r, m, \underline{!l} \cdot b \rangle$$
$$\langle \underline{!l} \cdot b, n \cdot r, m, c \rangle \xrightarrow{rav} \langle b, r, m, !l \cdot c \rangle$$

$$\langle (E_1 \ oper \ E_2) \cdot c, r, m, b \rangle \xrightarrow{exp}$$
$$\langle E_1 \cdot E_2 \cdot oper \cdot c, r, m, exp \cdot \underline{E_1} \cdot \underline{E_2} \cdot b \rangle$$
$$\text{where } oper = op \text{ or } \overline{op}$$

$$\langle exp \cdot \underline{E_1} \cdot \underline{E_2} \cdot b, r, m, E_1 \cdot E_2 \cdot op \cdot c \rangle \xrightarrow{pxe} \langle b, r, m, (E_1 \ op \ E_2) \cdot c \rangle$$

$$\langle op \cdot c, n_2 \cdot n_1 \cdot r, m, \underline{E_2} \cdot \underline{E_1} \cdot exp \cdot \underline{E_1} \cdot \underline{E_2} \cdot b \rangle \xrightarrow{op} \langle c, n \cdot r, m, (E_1 op E_2) \cdot b \rangle$$
$$\text{where } n = n_1 \ \overline{op} \ n_2$$
$$\langle \underline{op} \cdot b, n_2 \cdot n_1 \cdot n \cdot r, m, \underline{E_2} \cdot \underline{E_1} \cdot exp \cdot \underline{E_1} \cdot \underline{E_2} \cdot c \rangle \xrightarrow{\overline{op}} \langle b, r, m, (E_1 op E_2) \cdot c \rangle$$
$$\text{where } n = n_1 \ \overline{op} \ n_2$$
$$\langle \neg E \cdot c, r, m, b \rangle \xrightarrow{neg} \langle E \cdot \neg \cdot c, r, m, neg \cdot \underline{E} \cdot b \rangle$$
$$\langle neg \cdot \underline{E} \cdot b, r, m, E \cdot c \rangle \xrightarrow{gen} \langle b, r, m, \neg E \cdot c \rangle$$

$$\langle \neg \cdot c, n \cdot r, m, \underline{E} \cdot neg \cdot \underline{E} \cdot b \rangle \xrightarrow{\neg} \langle c, n' \cdot r, m, (\neg E) \cdot b \rangle$$
$$\text{where } n' = not(n)$$
$$\langle \underline{\neg} \cdot b, n \cdot n' \cdot r, m, \underline{E} \cdot neg \cdot \underline{E} \cdot c \rangle \xrightarrow{\underline{\neg}} \langle b, r, m, (\neg E) \cdot c \rangle \quad \text{if } n' = not(n)$$

Example 6. Consider again the program $\overline{Fact}$ given in Example 2, and an initial configuration $c_0 = \langle \overline{Fact} \cdot nil, nil, m, nil \rangle$ where $m(i_1) = (2, +(2, 0))$, $m(l) = m(factorial) = m(counter_1) = (0, 0)$.

Table 2. Rules for skip, assignment and sequence commands

$$\langle \text{skip} \cdot c, r, m, b \rangle \xrightarrow{skip} \langle c, r, m, \text{skip} \cdot b \rangle$$

$$\langle (l := E) \cdot c, r, m, b \rangle \xrightarrow{asgn} \langle E \cdot !l \cdot := \cdot c, l \cdot r, m, asgn \cdot E \cdot b \rangle$$

$$\langle asgn \cdot E \cdot b, l \cdot r, m, E \cdot !l \cdot := c \rangle \xrightarrow{ngsa} \langle b, r, m, (l := E) \cdot c \rangle$$

$$\langle := \cdot c, n_2 \cdot n_1 \cdot l \cdot r, m, \underline{!l} \cdot E \cdot asgn \cdot E \cdot b \rangle \xrightarrow{:=}$$
$$\langle c, r, m[l \mapsto (n_1, +(n, m_2(l)))], (l =: E) \cdot b \rangle$$
$$\text{where } n = n_1 - n_2$$

$$\langle (l =: E) \cdot c, r, m[l \mapsto (n_1, +(n, v))], b \rangle \xrightarrow{asgn^r}$$
$$\langle E \cdot !l \cdot =: \cdot c, l \cdot r, m', asgn^r \cdot n \cdot E \cdot b \rangle$$
$$\text{where } m' = m[l \mapsto (n_1 - n, v)]$$

$$\langle asgn^r \cdot n \cdot E \cdot b, l \cdot r, m, E \cdot !l \cdot =: \cdot c \rangle \xrightarrow{ngsa^r}$$
$$\langle b, r, m[l \mapsto (m_1(l) + n, +(n, m_2(l)))], (l =: E) \cdot c \rangle$$

$$\langle =: \cdot c, n_2 \cdot n_1 \cdot l \cdot r, m', \underline{!l} \cdot E \cdot asgn^r \cdot n \cdot E \cdot b \rangle \xrightarrow{=:} \langle c, r, m', (l := E) \cdot b \rangle \quad \text{if } n = n_1 - n_2$$

$$\langle (C_1; C_2) \cdot c, r, m, b \rangle \xrightarrow{seq} \langle C_1 \cdot C_2 \cdot ; \cdot c, r, m, seq \cdot b \rangle$$

$$\langle seq \cdot b, r, m, C_1 \cdot C_2 \cdot ; \cdot c \rangle \xrightarrow{qes} \langle b, r, m, (C_1; C_2) \cdot c \rangle$$

$$\langle ; \cdot c, r, m, rev(C_2) \cdot rev(C_1) \cdot seq \cdot b \rangle \xrightarrow{;} \langle c, r, m, (rev(C_2); rev(C_1)) \cdot b \rangle$$

Below are the transitions from the initial configuration until the first assignment is fully evaluated. Here C is the program $\overline{Fact}$ without the first assignment.

$$c_0 \xrightarrow{seq} \langle (l := !i_1) \cdot C \cdot ; \cdot nil, nil, m, seq \cdot nil \rangle \xrightarrow{asgn}$$
$$\langle !i_1 \cdot !l \cdot := \cdot C \cdot ; \cdot nil, l \cdot nil, m, asgn \cdot !i_1 \cdot seq \cdot nil \rangle \xrightarrow{var}$$
$$\langle !l \cdot := \cdot C \cdot ; \cdot nil, 2 \cdot l \cdot nil, m, \underline{!i_1} \cdot asgn \cdot !i_1 \cdot seq \cdot nil \rangle \xrightarrow{var}$$
$$\langle := \cdot C \cdot ; \cdot nil, 0 \cdot 2 \cdot l \cdot nil, m, \underline{!l} \cdot !i_1 \cdot asgn \cdot !i_1 \cdot seq \cdot nil \rangle \xrightarrow{:=}$$
$$\langle C \cdot ; \cdot nil, nil, m[l \mapsto (2, +(2, 0))], (l =: !i_1) \cdot seq \cdot nil \rangle.$$

Note that the reverse of the assignment command executed has been stored in the back stack. Now applying rules $seq, asgn, num, var, :=$, the next assignment is evaluated, producing

$$\langle (counter_1 := 0; C') \cdot ; \cdot ; \cdot nil, nil, m[factorial \mapsto (1, +(1, 0)), l \mapsto (2, +(2, 0))],$$
$$(factorial =: 1) \cdot seq \cdot (l =: !i_1) \cdot seq \cdot nil \rangle$$
$$\text{where } C' =$$
$$\text{while}_1 \; !l > 0 \; \text{do} \; (factorial := !factorial * !l; l := !l - 1; counter_1 := !counter_1 + 1).$$

Further transitions produce $\langle C' \cdot ; \cdot ; \cdot ; \cdot nil, nil, m', b \rangle$, where
$m' = m[counter_1 \mapsto (0, 0), factorial \mapsto (1, +(1, 0)), l \mapsto (2, +(2, 0))]$ and
$b = (counter_1 =: 0) \cdot seq \cdot (factorial =: 1) \cdot seq \cdot (l =: !i_1) \cdot seq \cdot nil$.

Table 3. Rules for conditionals

$$\langle(\text{if } E \text{ then } C_1 \text{ else } C_2) \cdot c, r, m, b\rangle \xrightarrow{cond} \langle E \cdot \text{if} \cdot cond \cdot c, C_1 \cdot C_2 \cdot r, m, \underline{cond} \cdot b\rangle$$
$$\langle \underline{cond} \cdot b, C_1 \cdot C_2 \cdot r, m, E \cdot \text{if} \cdot cond \cdot c\rangle \xrightarrow{dnoc} \langle b, r, m, (\text{if } E \text{ then } C_1 \text{ else } C_2) \cdot c\rangle$$

$$\langle \text{if} \cdot cond \cdot c, \text{true} \cdot C_1 \cdot C_2 \cdot r, m, \underline{E} \cdot \underline{cond} \cdot b\rangle \xrightarrow{if_T} \langle C_1 \cdot cond \cdot c, C_1 \cdot C_2 \cdot r, m, E \cdot \underline{if} \cdot \underline{cond} \cdot b\rangle$$
$$\langle \underline{if} \cdot \underline{cond} \cdot b, \text{true} \cdot C_1 \cdot C_2 \cdot r, m, \underline{E} \cdot C_1 \cdot cond \cdot c\rangle \xrightarrow{fi_T} \langle \underline{E} \cdot \underline{cond} \cdot b, \text{true} \cdot C_1 \cdot C_2 \cdot r, m, \text{if} \cdot cond \cdot c\rangle$$

$$\langle \text{if} \cdot cond \cdot c, \text{false} \cdot C_1 \cdot C_2 \cdot r, m, \underline{E} \cdot \underline{cond} \cdot b\rangle \xrightarrow{if_F} \langle C_2 \cdot cond \cdot c, C_1 \cdot C_2 \cdot r, m, E \cdot \underline{if} \cdot \underline{cond} \cdot b\rangle$$
$$\langle \underline{if} \cdot \underline{cond} \cdot b, \text{false} \cdot C_1 \cdot C_2 \cdot r, m, \overline{E} \cdot C_2 \cdot cond \cdot c\rangle \xrightarrow{fi_F} \langle \underline{E} \cdot cond \cdot b, \text{false} \cdot C_1 \cdot C_2 \cdot r, m, \text{if} \cdot cond \cdot c\rangle$$

$$\langle cond \cdot c, C_1 \cdot C_2 \cdot r, m, rev(C) \cdot E \cdot \underline{if} \cdot \underline{cond} \cdot b\rangle \xrightarrow{endif} \langle c, r, m, (\text{if } E \text{ then } rev(C_1) \text{ else } rev(C_2)) \cdot b\rangle$$
$$\text{where } C \text{ is either } C_1 \text{ or } C_2$$

Table 4. Rules for loops

$$\langle(\text{while}_i \ E \text{ do } C) \cdot c, r, m, b\rangle \xrightarrow{loop}$$
$$\langle E \cdot \text{while}_i \cdot loop_i \cdot c, E \cdot C \cdot r, m, \underline{loop_i} \cdot b\rangle$$
$$\langle \underline{loop_i} \cdot b, E \cdot C \cdot r, m, E \cdot \text{while} \cdot loop_i \cdot c\rangle \xrightarrow{pool} \langle b, r, m, (\text{while}_i \ E \text{ do } C) \cdot c\rangle$$

$$\langle \text{while}_i \cdot loop_i \cdot c, \text{true} \cdot E \cdot C \cdot r, m, \underline{E} \cdot \underline{loop_i} \cdot b\rangle \xrightarrow{loop_T}$$
$$\langle C \cdot (\text{while}_i \ \overline{E \text{ do }} C) \cdot c, E \cdot C \cdot r, m, \text{true} \cdot \underline{while_i} \cdot \underline{loop_i} \cdot b\rangle$$
$$\langle \text{while}_i \cdot \underline{loop_i} \cdot b, \text{true} \cdot E \cdot C \cdot r, m, \underline{\text{true}} \cdot C \cdot (\text{while}_i \ E \text{ do } C) \cdot c\rangle \xrightarrow{pool_T}$$
$$\langle \underline{E} \cdot \underline{loop_i} \cdot b, \text{true} \cdot E \cdot C \cdot r, m, \text{while}_i \cdot loop_i \cdot c\rangle$$
$$\langle \text{while}_i \cdot loop_i \cdot c, \text{false} \cdot E \cdot C \cdot r, m, \underline{E} \cdot \underline{loop_i} \cdot b\rangle \xrightarrow{loop_F}$$
$$\langle \underline{loop_i} \cdot c, E \cdot C \cdot r, m, \text{false} \cdot \underline{while_i} \cdot \underline{loop_i} \cdot b\rangle$$
$$\langle \underline{while_i} \cdot \underline{loop_i} \cdot b, \text{false} \cdot E \cdot C \cdot r, m, \underline{\text{false}} \cdot loop_i \cdot c\rangle \xrightarrow{pool_F}$$
$$\langle \underline{E} \cdot \underline{loop_i} \cdot b, \text{false} \cdot E \cdot C \cdot r, m, \text{while}_i \cdot loop_i \cdot c\rangle$$
$$\langle loop_i \cdot c, E \cdot C \cdot r, m, \text{false} \cdot \underline{while_i} \cdot \underline{loop_i} \cdot b\rangle \xrightarrow{endw_F}$$
$$\langle loop_i \cdot c, 0 \cdot C_1 \cdot E \cdot C \cdot r, m, \underline{endw_i} \cdot b\rangle$$
$$\text{where } C_1 = rev(\text{while}_i \ E \text{ do } C)$$
$$\langle \underline{endw_i} \cdot b, 0 \cdot C_1 \cdot E \cdot C \cdot r, m, loop_i \cdot c\rangle \xrightarrow{wend_F}$$
$$\langle \text{false} \cdot \underline{while_i} \cdot \underline{loop_i} \cdot b, E \cdot C \cdot r, m, loop_i \cdot c\rangle$$
$$\langle loop_i \cdot c, n \cdot C_1 \cdot E \cdot C \cdot r, m, \underline{endw_i} \cdot rev(C) \cdot \text{true} \cdot \underline{while_i} \cdot \underline{loop_i} \cdot b\rangle \xrightarrow{endw_T}$$
$$\langle loop_i \cdot c, n+1 \cdot \overline{C_1} \cdot E \cdot C \cdot r, m, \underline{endw_i} \cdot b\rangle$$
$$\langle \underline{endw_i} \cdot b, n+1 \cdot C_1 \cdot E \cdot C \cdot r, m, loop_i \cdot c\rangle \xrightarrow{wend_T}$$
$$\langle \underline{endw_i} \cdot rev(C) \cdot \text{true} \cdot \underline{while_i} \cdot \underline{loop_i} \cdot b, n \cdot C_1 \cdot E \cdot C \cdot r, m, loop_i \cdot c\rangle$$
$$\langle loop_i \cdot c, n \cdot C_1 \cdot E \cdot C \cdot r, m, b\rangle \xrightarrow{endw} \langle c, r, m, C_1 \cdot b\rangle \quad \text{otherwise}$$
$$\text{i.e., } (endw_F), (endw_T) \text{ don't apply}$$

The machine now executes C'. First, rule *loop* is applied, producing the configuration c_1 below, where C_l is the loop body.

$$c_1 = \langle (!l > 0) \cdot while_1 \cdot loop_1 \cdot; \cdot; \cdot; \cdot nil, (!l > 0) \cdot C_l \cdot nil, m', loop_1 \cdot b \rangle \xrightarrow{exp}$$
$$\langle !l \cdot 0 \cdot > \cdot while_1 \cdot loop_1 \cdot; \cdot; \cdot; \cdot nil, (!l > 0) \cdot C_l \cdot nil, m', exp \cdot !l \cdot 0 \cdot loop_1 \cdot b \rangle \xrightarrow{var\ num}$$
$$\langle > \cdot while_1 \cdot loop \cdot; \cdot; \cdot; \cdot nil, 0 \cdot 2 \cdot (!l > 0) \cdot C_l \cdot nil, m', 0 \cdot !l \cdot exp \cdot !l \cdot 0 \cdot loop_1 \cdot b \rangle \xrightarrow{op}$$
$$\langle while_1 \cdot loop_1 \cdot; \cdot; \cdot; \cdot nil, \mathsf{true} \cdot (!l > 0) \cdot C_l \cdot nil, m', (!l{\geq}0) \cdot loop_1 \cdot b \rangle \xrightarrow{loop_T}$$
$$\langle C_l \cdot C' \cdot; \cdot; \cdot; \cdot nil, (!l > 0) \cdot C_l \cdot nil, m', \mathsf{true} \cdot while_1 \cdot loop_1 \cdot b \rangle.$$

The machine is now ready to execute the body of the loop and then repeat, until the condition is false, at which point a sequence of transitions $\xrightarrow{loop_F} \xrightarrow{endw_F} \xrightarrow{endw_T} \xrightarrow{endw_T} \xrightarrow{endw} \xrightarrow{;} \xrightarrow{;} \xrightarrow{;}$ leads to the final configuration:

$$\langle nil, nil, m'', rev(\overline{Fact}) \cdot nil \rangle \text{ where } m'' = m[factorial \mapsto (2, +(0, +(1, +(1, 0)))),$$
$$l \mapsto (0, +(-1, +(-1, +(2, 0)))), counter_1 \mapsto (2, +(1, +(1, +(0, 0))))]$$.

RIMP's abstract machine is switch-deterministic: for each configuration, there is at most one transition rule applicable in addition to switch.

Theorem 4 (Determinism). *For any configuration c of the RIMP abstract machine, there is at most one non-switch transition rule applicable to c.*

The abstract machine is reversible: at any point, the application of the switch rule triggers a change of direction, reversing the computation done. To prove this result, we use two properties: the first states that the machine correctly evaluates expressions and leaves the result at the top of the results stack. The second states that if P is a terminating program, and we start the machine at a configuration where P is at the top of the control stack, the machine performs a finite number of transitions and stops with $rev(P)$ in the back stack.

Lemma 2 (Correctness of the Abstract Machine). *For any RIMP expression E and command C:*

1. $\langle E \cdot c, r, m, b \rangle \rightarrow^* \langle c, n \cdot r, m, \underline{E} \cdot b \rangle$ *if and only if* $\langle E, m \rangle \Downarrow_{\mathsf{RIMP}} \langle n, m \rangle$.
2. $\langle C \cdot c, r, m, b \rangle \rightarrow^* \langle c, r, m', rev(C) \cdot b \rangle$ *if and only if* $\langle C, m \rangle \Downarrow_{\mathsf{RIMP}} \langle skip, m' \rangle$.

Theorem 5 (Reversible Computation). *Let $\langle c, r, m, b \rangle$ be a configuration obtained by applying transition rules starting from the initial configuration $\langle E \cdot nil, nil, m_0, nil \rangle$ (resp. $\langle C \cdot nil, nil, m_0, nil \rangle$), where E, C are a RIMP expression and command respectively. If $\langle c, r, m, b \rangle \rightarrow^* \langle c', r', m', b' \rangle$ then $\langle b', r', m', c' \rangle \rightarrow^* \langle b, r, m, c \rangle$.*

6 Related Work

Standard computation models (such as Turing machines and the λ-calculus) are not reversible: they can perform computation steps that destroy information. In fact, any non-injective function is irreversible. However, irreversible computation can be embedded into reversible computation by adding extra storage to save the intermediate states of the computation, as shown by Landauer [17,18] and Bennett [6]. Models of computation that are by construction reversible are also available (e.g., reversible Turing machines, reversible logic gates, see [21]). For a detailed discussion of the power of reversible Turing machines we refer to [4]. Perumalla [24] provides a detailed account of reversibility, including reversible programming languages (both language-level and computation level) and reversible hardware. In this paper, we focus only on reversibility of imperative languages and consider both source-code level and computation level reversibility.

Imperative languages are not reversible in general. There are two well-known approaches to transform irreversible languages into reversible ones: by storing snapshots of the memory (i.e., checkpointing) and by using commands to restore the state (the *control flow* approach). In this paper we propose a hybrid approach, based on the use of a representation of values that indicates how they were constructed. In a closely related work [14], a stack is associated with each variable and used to save all the previous values held by the variable. Our representation of values is equivalent.

Based on RIMP's big-step operational semantics we define a program inverter: a function *rev* that takes a program as input and outputs a program that performs the reverse computation of the input program. The function *rev* is analogous to the program inverters defined for reversible languages (see, e.g., [10]); however, since RIMP has general assignment and loop commands, the inversion relies on an augmented representation of values combined with the use of counters. It behaves like the function *inv* defined by Hoey et al [14], but we do not add stacks to reverse conditionals and while-loops. Instead, we transform the conditions in if-then-else commands to ensure the values are preserved so conditionals are reversible, and we associate a counter with each while-loop.

Reversible abstract machines have been extensively studied [22,27]. RIMP's abstract machine could be seen as an instance of interpreted-based reversal, however, unlike standard augmented interpreters that store a sequential log of all the operations executed and use the log to reverse the computation, the abstract machine does not store computation histories. Instead, it stores the source code of the reverse command (as defined by the *rev* function), once the command has been executed. The machine has forward and backward deterministic transition rules, so the direction of computation can be changed at any point. At the end of the execution of a command, the source code for the reverse command is in the back stack, which allows the machine to reverse the whole computation without storing histories. RIMP's abstract machine works as an interpreter when executing in forward mode but is also able to execute in backward mode, as a basis for a debugging tool.

We are currently exploring reversibility of RIMP at lower level. We have identified two directions: a compilation that targets a reversible assembly language in the style of PISA (see, e.g., [5]), inspired by [3]; and a token-based implementation, inspired by structural approaches to reversibility [1,20].

7   Conclusions and Future Work

We have discussed the design of a simple imperative language, RIMP, where programs can be inverted: the function *rev* translates a RIMP program into a program that performs the reverse computation. Using this feature we have built an abstract machine for RIMP where any computation step can be reversed (including the steps performed to evaluate expressions), without using computation logs to store all the computation history. Thus, RIMP's abstract machine can also be used as a debugger (indeed, one of the motivations for the study of reversibility is to provide foundations for debugging [2]).

In future work, we will develop a compiled version of RIMP, targeting a reversible low-level language, and analyse the amount of space used to make the programs reversible. We will also consider an extension of RIMP with local variable definitions and procedure calls. Another direction for future work is the addition of a concurrent operator, adapting the techniques used by Hoey et al [13–15] to reverse parallel programs. Finally, the approach presented in this paper could be implemented in a language framework such as K [25] to generate reversible versions of imperative languages in a uniform way.

References

1. Abramsky, S.: A structural approach to reversible computation. Theor. Comput. Sci. **347**(3), 441–464 (2005)
2. Agrawal, H., DeMillo, R.A., Spafford, E.H.: An execution-backtracking approach to debugging. IEEE Softw. **8**(3), 21–26 (1991)
3. Axelsen, H.B.: Clean translation of an imperative reversible programming language. In: Knoop, J. (ed.) CC 2011. LNCS, vol. 6601, pp. 144–163. Springer, Heidelberg (2011). https://doi.org/10.1007/978-3-642-19861-8_9
4. Axelsen, H.B., Glück, R.: On reversible Turing machines and their function universality. Acta Inf. **53**(5), 509–543 (2016)
5. Axelsen, H.B., Glück, R., Yokoyama, T.: Reversible machine code and its abstract processor architecture. In: Diekert, V., Volkov, M.V., Voronkov, A. (eds.) CSR 2007. LNCS, vol. 4649, pp. 56–69. Springer, Heidelberg (2007). https://doi.org/10.1007/978-3-540-74510-5_9
6. Bennett, C.: Logical reversibility of computation. IBM J. Res. Dev. **17**, 525–532 (1973)
7. Buhrman, H., Tromp, J., Vitányi, P.: Time and space bounds for reversible simulation. In: Orejas, F., Spirakis, P.G., van Leeuwen, J. (eds.) ICALP 2001. LNCS, vol. 2076, pp. 1017–1027. Springer, Heidelberg (2001). https://doi.org/10.1007/3-540-48224-5_82
8. Dijkstra, E.W.: Program inversion In: Bauer, F.L., et al. (eds.) Program Construction. LNCS, vol. 69, pp. 54–57. Springer, Heidelberg (1979). https://doi.org/10.1007/BFb0014657
9. Fernández, M.: Programming Languages and Operational Semantics - A Concise Overview. Undergraduate Topics in Computer Science. Springer, Heidelberg (2014). https://doi.org/10.1007/978-1-4471-6368-8
10. Glück, R., Yokoyama, T.: A linear-time self-interpreter of a reversible imperative language. Comput. Softw. **33**(3), 108–128 (2016)

11. Glück, R., Yokoyama, T.: A minimalist's reversible while language. IEICE Trans. **100-D**(5), 1026–1034 (2017)

12. Gries, D.: The Science of Programming. Texts and Monographs in Computer Science. Springer, Heidelberg (1981). https://doi.org/10.1007/978-1-4612-5983-1

13. Hoey, J., Ulidowski, I.: Reversible imperative parallel programs and debugging. In: Thomsen, M.K., Soeken, M. (eds.) RC 2019. LNCS, vol. 11497, pp. 108–127. Springer, Cham (2019). https://doi.org/10.1007/978-3-030-21500-2_7

14. Hoey, J., Ulidowski, I., Yuen, S.: Reversing imperative parallel programs. In: Peters, K., Tini, S. (eds.) Proceedings Combined 24th International Workshop on Expressiveness in Concurrency and 14th Workshop on Structural Operational Semantics, EXPRESS/SOS 2017. EPTCS, Berlin, Germany, 4th September 2017, vol. 255, pp. 51–66 (2017)

15. Hoey, J., Ulidowski, I., Yuen, S.: Reversing parallel programs with blocks and procedures. In: Pérez, J.A., Tini, S. (eds.) Proceedings Combined 25th International Workshop on Expressiveness in Concurrency and 15th Workshop on Structural Operational Semantics, EXPRESS/SOS 2018. EPTCS, Beijing, China, 3 September 2018, vol. 276, pp. 69–86 (2018)

16. Jones, N.D.: Computability and Complexity - From a Programming Perspective. Foundations of Computing Series. MIT Press, Cambridge (1997)

17. Landauer, R.: Irreversibility and heat generation in the computing process. IBM J. Res. Dev. **5**(3), 183–191 (1961)

18. Landauer, R.: Irreversibility and heat generation in the computing process. IBM J. Res. Dev. **44**(1), 261–269 (2000). Reprinted from IBM J. Res. Dev. 1961

19. Lutz, C., Derby, H.: Janus: a Time-reversible Language (1986)

20. Mackie, I.: A geometry of interaction machine for Gödel's system T. In: Kennedy, J., de Queiroz, R.J.G.B. (eds.) WoLLIC 2017. LNCS, vol. 10388, pp. 229–241. Springer, Heidelberg (2017). https://doi.org/10.1007/978-3-662-55386-2_16

21. Morita, K.: Universality issues in reversible computing systems and cellular automata. ENTCS **253**, 23–31 (2010)

22. Morita, K.: Theory of Reversible Computing. Monographs in Theoretical Computer Science. An EATCS Series. Springer, Heidelberg (2017). https://doi.org/10.1007/978-4-431-56606-9

23. Nielson, H.R., Nielson, F.: Semantics with Applications: An Appetizer. Undergraduate Topics in Computer Science. Springer, Heidelberg (2007). https://doi.org/10.1007/978-1-84628-692-6

24. Perumalla, K.S.: Introduction to Reversible Computing. Computational Science Series. CRC Press, Boca Raton (2014)

25. Rosu, G.: 𝕂: a semantic framework for programming languages and formal analysis tools. In: Pretschner, A., Peled, D., Hutzelmann, T. (eds.) Dependable Software Systems Engineering. NATO Science for Peace and Security Series - D: Information and Communication Security, vol. 50, pp. 186–206. IOS Press (2017)

26. Winskel, G.: The Formal Semantics of Programming Languages. Foundations of Computing. MIT Press, Cambridge (1993)

27. Yokoyama, T.: Reversible computation and reversible programming languages. Electr. Notes Theor. Comput. Sci. **253**(6), 71–81 (2010)

Parallel Chopped Symbolic Execution

Shikhar Singh$^{(\boxtimes)}$ and Sarfraz Khurshid

University of Texas, Austin, USA
shikhar_singh@utexas.edu, khurshid@ece.utexas.edu

Abstract. Symbolic execution, a well-known and widely studied software testing technique, faces scalability issues due to path explosion that limits its effectiveness. Recent work on *chopped symbolic execution* introduced the *Chopper* technique that allows the user to specify uninteresting parts of code that the symbolic analysis can try to ignore by focusing first on the essential parts. If necessary, the ignored parts are later explored once their impact on the main code under analysis becomes unavoidable. We introduce a parallel approach to chopped symbolic execution that integrates *path-based partitioning* with Chopper. Our tool, called *PChop*, speeds up chopped symbolic exploration by allowing multiple participating workers to explore non-overlapping regions of the code in parallel. We demonstrate the impact of our technique in a failure reproduction scenario, where we use both PChop and Chopper to re-create security vulnerabilities in the GNU libtasn1. The experimental results show that PChop is beneficial in situations where Chopper requires more than a minute to find the vulnerability when using a specific search strategy. For two vulnerabilities, PChop identified a previously undocumented code location to manifest each of them.

Keywords: Software testing · Symbolic execution · Parallel analysis · KLEE

1 Introduction

Symbolic execution, conceptualized, and demonstrated almost 40 years ago [4,16], is one of the most versatile and influential methodologies for analyzing software. The core of symbolic execution is a technique that undertakes a structured exploration of the execution paths which exist in the program being analyzed. A standard symbolic execution tool comprises of two main components. The first component constructs the path conditions, which are constraints on program inputs that cause the execution of a particular path. The second component is a mechanism to solve the path conditions and provide concrete values to the program inputs. Symbolic execution has found widespread application in test input generation. Solving path conditions for execution paths in a program yields a capable test suite that provides better code coverage. Advancements in SAT and SMT solving technology coupled with the rapid rise of computing power has paved the way for using symbolic execution in a diverse range of real-world

© Springer Nature Switzerland AG 2020
S.-W. Lin et al. (Eds.): ICFEM 2020, LNCS 12531, pp. 107–125, 2020.
https://doi.org/10.1007/978-3-030-63406-3_7

software. While symbolic execution presents itself as an attractive software analysis tool, it suffers from scalability issues. The main reasons for this drawback are the complexity of path conditions and the state-space explosion as software becomes more extensive and more expressive. These factors lead to prohibitively high exploration times, which hinders the adoption of this technology.

There have been several research endeavors to address these bottlenecks. Concolic execution, introduced in DART [15], combines concrete and symbolic execution to limit the path explosion problem. In this technique, the program runs with program inputs having concrete values. The symbolic path conditions for the execution path are recorded, and the last branch in the path condition is negated to execute a new path. Several tools extend concolic execution to target different programming environments and provide additional features [6,23,24]. DiSE [20], using an incremental approach, symbolically executes only the modified parts of the code. The compositional approach used in SMART [14] uses concolic execution for functions in isolation to reduce the number of paths. Several modern symbolic solvers incorporate the *Execution Generated Test* [8] approach where both concrete and symbolic states of a program are maintained. If an operation involves all concrete values, then it is executed normally, but in the presence of one or more symbolic variables, symbolic execution takes place. EXE [9] and KLEE [7] are two well-known tools in this category. KLEE is an open source symbolic execution tool that works on LLVM [1] generated bytecode and integrates with the LLVM architecture. KLEE, and tools built on top of KLEE have been used to test a wide range of software applications like computer vision [12], sensor networks [22], GPUs [19], device drivers [10], and online gaming [3]. KLEE is also used for automated debugging [29], thread scheduling [13], and exploit generation [2]. The distributed/parallel approach involves breaking down a sizeable symbolic execution problem into smaller ones and solving them simultaneously. A common technique to accomplish distribution is to divide program execution paths amongst several workers [5,11]. These paths are compactly represented using prefixes, which are bit-vectors that store a history of branching decisions (a *1* for a taken branch and *0* for a not-taken branch or vice-versa) from the program entry point up to a certain depth. Such prefixes can be communicated to workers to replay and extend further to explore deeper paths. *Chopped* symbolic execution [28] is a novel technique to mitigate the path-explosion problem. In this scheme, users can identify parts of code that are unimportant, and the symbolic analysis tries to avoid those parts. *Chopper* takes as input a list of function names and their call locations, determined by the user to be inessential. It skips over the function and continues with execution of the instruction following the call. To preserve the soundness of the analysis, Chopper lazily executes the skipped functions when their side-effects are observable by the non-skipped parts of the code. Chopper relies on static analyses to determine and resolve the side-effects of skipped function calls.

This paper proposes to tackle further the issue of scalability by developing a parallel version of Chopper called PChop. PChop utilizes a *path-prefix based partitioning scheme* to divide the program space into smaller non-overlapping regions. These smaller regions can be explored concurrently by multiple workers. Program regions are identified by prefixes that represent the path taken to reach them. As a result, a parallel framework requires a robust mechanism to generate these prefixes. In Chopper, symbolic execution can skip a function only to execute it at a later stage when its effect can no longer be ignored. This re-ordering of execution leads to the generation of inaccurate/invalid prefixes. In PChop, we resolve this issue by devising a new technique to generate valid and accurate prefixes for the execution paths.

This paper makes the following contributions.

- **Parallel Chopped Symbolic Execution.** We propose a parallel approach to Chopped symbolic execution that uses prefix-based partitioning to distribute work such that workers explore non-overlapping parts of the program space. We accomplish this by designing a chopping aware prefix generation scheme that accounts for skipping function calls and executing them out of program order only when their side-effects are observable.
- **Implementation.** We implement the proposed technique in our tool called $PChop^1$, which extends Chopper to enable parallel execution using message-passing interface(MPI).[2] The framework comprises a co-ordinator and several workers nodes which explore disjoint regions of the code in parallel.
- **Evaluation.** We evaluate and quantify the performance of the proposed scheme in the context of failure reproduction, which involves searching for documented vulnerabilities in GNU libtasn1. This library is used for serializing and de-serializing data according to Abstract Syntax Notation One (ASN.1) standard.[3] We study the time it takes to find the vulnerabilities with configurations comprising multiple workers and different search strategies.

2 Background

2.1 Parallel Symbolic Execution

A parallel symbolic execution scheme works by partitioning the program space and assigning them to the participating workers. A typical symbolic execution engine uses some kind of data structure to store and process constraints collected when exploring execution paths. We refer to these structures as *states*. At every branch point, two states are spawned, which represent the taken and not-taken branches. States can also be used to store path-prefix information as a sequence of bits which represent the branching history for that path. Let us assume that a *0* indicates the not taken(*false*) path and a *1* indicates the taken(*true*) path. Path-prefixes grow as exploration goes deeper into the program being analyzed. These states are assigned to workers, which, extend them by taking the exploration to deeper program paths and generating further states in the process.

---

[1] https://github.com/Shikhar8990/pChop.
[2] https://www.open-mpi.org/.
[3] https://www.gnu.org/software/libtasn1/.

The information about a state can be communicated to a node using one of two ways. The first method involves sending the path-conditions for the path represented by the state. The worker can then start symbolic execution using the path conditions as pre-conditions and generating states accordingly. Since no two distinct states would have identical path-conditions, this ensures no two workers explore the same regions in the program. A major disadvantage of this technique is that path constraints can become prohibitively long and complex for efficient communication. Alternatively, instead of constraints, path-prefixes representing states can be sent to the workers. In this case, a worker starts execution from the beginning and *replays* the path of its assigned prefix and then starts full symbolic execution. Replaying involves only collecting the constraints from the entry point and does not require any constraint solving. This scheme is more efficient as path-prefixes can be compactly represented as bit-vectors, which incur lower communication overheads.

2.2   *Chopping* in Symbolic Execution

The primary motivation behind techniques like the one used in Chopped symbolic execution is to make symbolic execution scalable by attempting to alleviate the path explosion problem. Chopper accomplishes this by focusing on *important* parts of the code while avoiding *uninteresting* parts as much as possible. The user is responsible for identifying the parts of the code to avoid. These uninteresting parts are specified as function calls in the program, which the analysis tries to overlook. Symbolic execution, in such a scenario, explores all possible paths in parts of the code deemed important and *skips* over unimportant parts. However, to make the analysis sound, parts that have been skipped may be executed lazily as their impact on the main code becomes apparent. Such techniques rely on static data flow analysis to determine the side-effects of a function. Chopper relies on a *whole program flow-insensitive, context-insensitive, and field-sensitive points-to analysis* to identify every location that may be accessed by a pointer [28]. A points-to analysis is used for recording all possible memory locations which may have been modified by a function. If symbolic exploration reaches a state that accesses (via a load instruction) a memory location whose contents are modified by a function (via a store instruction) skipped on the path, the state is suspended, and a recovery state is launched to capture the side-effects of that function. The state awaiting the results of the blocked load is marked as being dependent on the recovery state. The recovery state executes the skipped function call. If a branch causes the execution to fork in the recovery phase, the dependent state is also forked using the same branch condition. Eventually, one of the recovery states will execute the store instruction, which blocked the execution of the load instruction in the dependent state. Once the recovery state finishes exploring a path in the skipped function, its dependent state is resumed and can safely execute the load instruction. Algorithm 1 shows the basic workflow of Chopper. A state maintains its program counter, which points to the next instruction, a symbolic representation of the heap memory, and the constraints for the path. The algorithm begins the execution of the initial state, which

Algorithm 1. Simplified *Chopper* Loop [28]

```
 1:  s_o ← initial state
 2:  states ← list of active states
 3:  skippedFunc ← list of functions to be skipped
 4:  add s_o to states
 5:  while states is not empty or timeout do
 6:      s_curr ← select a state from states
 7:      inst ← next instruction to execute in s_curr
 8:      if inst is a function call instruction then
 9:          f ← target function
10:          if f is in skippedFunc then
11:              snapshot ← create a snapshot
12:              store tuple (snapshot, f) to a list snapshots for s_curr
13:          else
14:              execute the function call
15:      else if inst is Load then
16:          addr ← load address
17:          if value at addr may have been modified by one or more
                 functions skipped by s_curr then
18:              for each (snapshot, f) recorded by s_curr do
19:                  if (snapshot, f) may modify the value at addr then
20:                      suspend s_curr
21:                      recoveryState ← create from snapshot
22:                      link recoveryState to its dependent state s_curr
23:                      add recoveryState to list states
24:          else
25:              execute the load in s_curr
26:      else if inst is Store then
27:          addr ← store address
28:          execute the store in s_curr
29:          if s_curr is a recovery state then
30:              update the values at addr in dependent state
31:          else
32:              add addr to the list of addresses written by s_curr
33:      else if inst is Return then
34:          if s_curr is a recovery state and return belongs to a skipped function then
35:              terminate the s_curr
36:              dependentState ← get dependent state of recoveryState
37:              resume dependentState
38:              add dependentState to list states
39:          else
40:              execute return
41:      else if inst is Branch then
42:          if s_curr is a recovery state then
43:              cond ← branch condition
44:              depState ← dependent state of s_curr
45:              s'_curr ← forked recovery state for taken branch using cond
46:              depState' ← forked dependent state for taken branch using cond
47:              if both s'_curr and depState' are feasible then
48:                  add s'_curr to states
49:                  link s'_curr to its dependent state depState'
50:              else
51:                  Discard s'_curr and depState'
52:              Do the same for the fall-through branch
53:              Remove originating state s_curr from states
54:          else
55:              execute the branch normally
```

points to the first instruction in the code. As more states are added to the list as a result of branching, the search strategy determines which states are explored at every iteration of the loop (line 5). If the *inst* is a function call (line 8) and the target is a non-skipped function, normal symbolic execution of the function follows (line 14). When the call target is a skipped function, the current state of execution is stored as a *snapshot*. This snapshot preserves the symbolic state of the program right before the skipped function call. The snapshot is added to the list of snapshots for that state along with the function name (lines 11,12). On encountering a *load* instruction (line 15), an analysis of the type presented in [28] is used to determine if data at the address read by the load instruction may have been modified by one or more functions previously skipped by the state. If that is indeed the case, the relevant snapshot and function are retrieved (lines 18, 19), and the current state is suspended (line 20). A *recovery state* is created by cloning the snapshot. This state is added to the list of active states and is linked to its dependent state (lines 21–23). The recovery state reflects the program state right before the function call instruction that was overlooked by the suspended state. The recovery state executes the function call to explore the skipped function. If the load is not affected by the skipped functions, it is executed normally. A *store* instruction is processed in two steps. First, the memory is updated to register the store. Secondly, if a recovery state performs the store, the memory of the dependent state is also updated to reflect the store. In case s_{curr} is a normal state, the store address is recorded to maintain a list of memory locations modified by the normal state. Any modifications to these locations by earlier skipped functions are discarded. A *return* from a skipped function signals the end of a recovery phase. The recovery state is terminated, followed by the retrieval and resumption of its dependent state (lines 35–38). Return from a non-skipped function does not require any special provisions. A normal state, upon reaching a branch instruction (line 55), forks the execution to generate two new states. These new states capture the taken and not-taken paths. Branching for a recovery state is managed in several steps. First, the dependent state is retrieved (line 44). Then, both the recovery and the dependent states are forked to generate states for the taken path (*cond* is true). If both the newly forked states have feasible constraints, the forked recovery state (s'_{curr}) is added to the list of active states and is linked to its forked dependent state (*depState'*) (line 45–49). If one or both of the states have unsatisfiable constraints, they are discarded (line 51). The not-taken path is processed similarly. While describing the algorithm, we elided the details of the data flow analysis methodology and other features used in [28], as they are not pertinent to the current work.

3   Illustrative Example

This section introduces the core concepts of the proposed technique by working through a demonstrative example.

```
1 typedef struct student {
2       int id, feesPerCredit;
3       int gpa; //symbolic
4       int stateId; //symbolic
5       int credits; //symbolic
6 }student;
7 void calculateFeesPerCredit(student *s) {
8       if(s->stateId == 11) {
9             s->feesPerCredit = 400;
```

```
10        } else  if(s->stateId  ==  34)  {
11            s->feesPerCredit  =  450;
12        } else  {
13            s->feesPerCredit  =  600;
14        }
15   }
16   int  calculateFees(student*  s1)  {
17        calculateFeesPerCredit(s1);
18        if(s1->credits  >  9)  {
19            assert(s1->gpa  >  3);
20        }
21        if(s1->gpa  ==  4)  {
22            return  400;
23        } else  {
24            int  totalFees  =  s1->feesPerCredit*s1->credits;
25            return  totalFees;
26        }
27   }
28   int  main()  {
29        student  s1;
30        //initialize  s1  to  some  value
31        int  fees  =  calculateFees(&s1);
32        return  0;
33   }
```

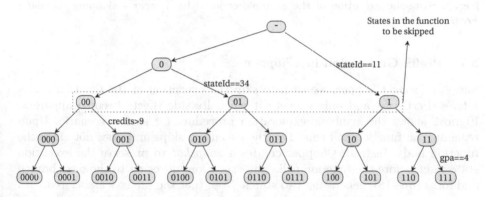

Fig. 1. Standard symbolic execution of the example code

Shown above is a simple C program to compute the tuition fees owed by a student enrolled in some university. Relevant information about a student is stored in *struct student*. The total fees is calculated based on the number of credits that the student is enrolling for and the fee per credit. The per-credit fee depends on the residency state of the student, which is identified by a unique *stateId*. A student enrolling for more than 9 credits requires a GPA of at least 3. A maximum possible GPA of 4 results in a tuition waiver and a flat fee is charged. Figure 1 shows the result of the standard symbolic execution of this program. Each state, shown as a gray box, is identified by its path-prefix. This execution results in a total of 12 terminal states. In a parallel setting comprising of n workers, a shallow symbolic exploration can be done to obtain n different states. Then their corresponding path-prefixes can be sent to the workers to explore further.

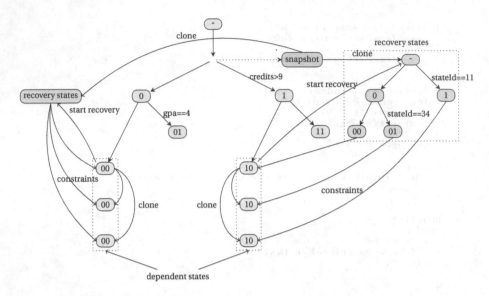

Fig. 2. Symbolic execution of the example code with *Chopper* - skipping *calculateFeesPerCredit*

3.1   Prefix Generation in *Chopper*

Suppose, using Chopper, we wish to skip the execution of the function *calculateFeesPerCredit* and only execute it when its side-effects become apparent. Figure 2 shows the symbolic exploration procedure for such a scenario. Upon reaching the function call (line 17), the execution skips and does not enter the function body. Instead, Chopper creates a *snapshot* to preserve the execution state right before the function call. The execution moves on to the next branch and forks (line 18), generating two states. Note that the prefixes associated with these states are different from the prefixes of the corresponding states in case of conventional non-skipped execution. The *true* side of the branch on line 21 can be executed without having to call the skipped function. However, the not-taken side requires the execution of *calculateFeesPerCredit*. As a result, the execution goes into recovery mode and suspends the state corresponding to the not-taken side of the branch. The snapshot captured earlier is used to generate a recovery state, which starts at the entry point of *calculateFeesPerCredit*. Every time the execution forks in the recovery region, the corresponding dependent states are replicated. The replicated states inherit the constraints and path-prefixes of the parent state. Once the recovery states reach the end of the function, the collected constraints are merged with those of the dependent states. The dependent states are then activated for further exploration. Since there are three unique paths in the skipped function, the dependent state is replicated twice, resulting in a total of 3 states to merge with each of the three recovery states. The recovery happens for 2 different paths, where memory locations modified by the *calculateFeesPerCredit* are accessed.

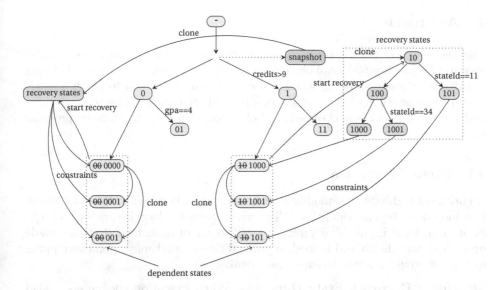

Fig. 3. Symbolic execution of the example code with *PChop* - skipping *calculate-FeesPerCredit*

3.2   Prefix Generation in *PChop*

A prefix based parallel execution scheme relies on the robustness of the path-prefix generation mechanism - no two states can have identical paths, and a prefix should represent the *actual path* taken by the execution. Symbolic execution with Chopper, when skipping a function call, violates both these conditions. The replicated dependent states all share the same path-prefixes, which leads to ambiguity in path-based parallelization. The first recovery state has an empty prefix since it is created from a snapshot of a state which witnessed no prior branches. However, this state executes after the exploration has already seen two branches (lines 18, 21). For recovery states, Chopper does not capture accurate branch histories in the non-recovery regions. In order to distribute states, path-prefixes should be generated in a way such that they capture execution in both normal and recovery modes. Figure 3 depicts the prefix generation process when using PChop on the same program, and skipping the same function. Prefix construction begins in the standard way with a 0 or 1 being appended to the path of the parent state for not-taken and taken branch states, respectively. However, when starting a recovery phase, instead of the first recovery state inheriting the prefix of the snapshot state, it acquires the prefix of the dependent state triggering the recovery. In the figure, state *10* triggers recovery, and the first recovery state gets a prefix of *10*. Subsequent recovery states also inherit and extend this prefix. At the end of the recovery phase, when the constraints of the recovery states are merged with the dependent states, the dependent states acquire the path-prefixes of their respective recovery states. As a result, all the states carry accurate branching histories from both non-recovery and recovery phases.

4   Approach

This section describes the proposed framework to integrate prefix-based parallel execution with chopped symbolic execution. We augment the original chopping algorithm to generate paths which reflect the branches taken to reach a state. These paths are then used to construct a prefix-based distribution scheme where multiple workers perform chopped symbolic execution in their allocated program regions.

4.1   Prefix Generation

Algorithm 2 highlights the modifications, made in PChop, to the Chopper execution loop described in Algorithm 1. The main execution loop is provided a *prefix* as an additional input. This prefix is a bit-vector of branching decisions made up to a certain depth and is used to guide different workers to non-overlapping regions of program space to explore in parallel.

Starting a Recovery State (Line 18). When execution encounters a load instruction that may have been previously modified by a skipped function call, a recovery state gets spawned from the relevant snapshot state. The recovery state, in this scheme, inherits the path history of the original state that encountered the blocking load (and is now suspended) and not the path history of the snapshot, which was the case in the original implementation. As a result, recovery states have a correct record of the execution path taken to reach them.

Returning from a Skipped Function (Line 27). A recovery state terminates on reaching the end of the skipped function, and its dependent state is resumed. The dependent state inherits the path taken by the corresponding recovery state. As a result, the non-recovery states have a record of the path taken in both recovery and non-recovery regions.

Branching (Lines 37, 40, 44, 47, 51, 52, 55 and 56). A branch in the execution results in the generation of two states forked from the parent state, one for each direction of the branch. These states are checked for feasibility to ensure that their path conditions are satisfiable. States representing infeasible program paths are discarded. To enforce non-overlapping execution by worker nodes, we ensure that every state follows the path restrictions defined by the prefix assigned to the worker. The function *allowBranch* takes as input, the current state depth, the prefix and a branch direction (1/0 for taken/not-taken) and evaluates to *true* if the path represented by the branch direction is allowed by the prefix. The equation below defines *allowBranch*. The term *prefix.length* denotes the length of the prefix (number of branches taken to generate the prefix) and *prefix[n]* represents the branch taken by the prefix at a depth of n. For example, a worker assigned a prefix of *0000* will only explore states representing not-taken branches up to a depth of 4 and can explore both taken and not-taken paths for any subsequent branches, provided the path conditions are feasible.

Algorithm 2. Augmented *Chopper* Loop to enable distributed execution

```
 1:  s_O ← initial state
 2:  prefix ← prefix assgined to the worker
 3:  states ← list of active states
 4:  skippedFunc ← list of functions to be skipped
 5:  add s_O to states
 6:  while states is not empty or timeout do
 7:      s_curr ← select a state from states
 8:      inst ← next instruction to execute in s_curr
 9:      if inst is Load then
10:          addr ← load address
11:          if value at addr may have been modified by one or more functions skipped by s_curr then
12:              for each (snapshot, f) recorded by s_curr do
13:                  if (snapshot, f) may modify the value at addr then
14:                      suspend s_curr
15:                      recoveryState ← create from snapshot
16:                      link recoveryState to its dependent state s_curr
17:                      add recoveryState to list states
18:                      recoveryState.path ← s_curr.path
19:          else
20:              execute the load in s_curr
21:      else if inst is Return then
22:          if s_curr is a recovery state and return belongs to a skipped function then
23:              terminate the s_curr
24:              dependentState ← get dependent state of recoveryState
25:              resume dependentState
26:              add dependentState to list states
27:              dependentState.path ← s_curr.path
28:          else
29:              execute return
30:      else if inst is Branch then
31:          cond ← branch condition
32:          s'_curr ← forked from s_curr for taken branch using cond
33:          s''_curr ← forked from s_curr for fall − through branch using !cond
34:          if s_curr is a recovery state then
35:              depState ← dependent state of s_curr
36:              depState' ← forked from depState for taken branch using cond
37:              if both s'_curr and depState' are feasible and allowBranch(s'_curr.depth, prefix, 1) then
38:                  add s'_curr to states
39:                  link s'_curr to its dependent state depState'
40:                  s'_curr.addToPath(1)
41:              else
42:                  Discard s'_curr and depState'
43:              depState'' ← forked from depState for fall − through branch using !cond
44:              if both s''_curr and depState'' are feasible and allowBranch(s''_curr.depth, prefix, 0) then
45:                  add s''_curr to states
46:                  link s''_curr to its dependent state depState''
47:                  s''_curr.addToPath(0)
48:              else
49:                  Discard s''_curr and depState''
50:          else
51:              if s'_curr is feasible and allowBranch(s'_curr.depth, prefix, 1) then
52:                  s'_curr.addToPath(1)
53:              else
54:                  Discard s'_curr
55:              if s''_curr is feasible and allowBranch(s''_curr.depth, prefix, 0) then
56:                  s''_curr.addToPath(0)
57:              else
58:                  Discard s''_curr
59:      Remove originating state s_curr from states
```

$$allowBranch(depth, prefix, branch) = \begin{cases} true, & depth \geq prefix.length \\ true, & depth < prefix.length \text{ and } branch == prefix[depth] \\ false, & depth < prefix.length \text{ and } branch! = prefix[depth] \end{cases}$$

4.2 Parallel Execution

The parallel framework comprises a coordinator and several worker nodes. The exploration occurs in two phases. In the first phase, the coordinator begins the symbolic execution of the given program. Not bound by a prefix, the coordinator is free to explore any feasible path (the prefix in line 2 of the algorithm is initialized to an empty bit-vector). The coordinator keeps a count of active states, which represent the leaf nodes of the exploration tree. The execution halts once an adequate number of active states are available. These active states act as roots of distinct sub-trees whose union represents the entire unexplored program space. The second phase begins with the coordinator distributing the paths corresponding to every active state amongst the workers. The workers start chopped symbolic execution guided by their assigned prefixes. For individual workers, states that violate the prefix bound are discarded (*allowBranch*). Load balancing happens via work-stealing; when a worker becomes idle, the coordinator instructs one of the busy workers to offload some of its active states and sends the corresponding prefixes to the idle worker. PChop allows workers to handle multiple prefixes at a time and in such cases, *allowBranch* evaluates to *true* if the branch direction is compatible with at least one of the prefixes.

5 Evaluation

The objective of our evaluation is to provide preliminary evidence of the benefits of our technique in the context of *failure reproduction*, where we use PChop to find and generate test cases for documented vulnerabilities. We hypothesize that using multiple workers can reduce the time it takes to reach the error-causing state and create a test case for the same.

5.1 Subjects

We use security vulnerabilities in the GNU libtasn1 for our experiments. This library is used for processing data in Abstract Syntax Notation One (ASN.1)

Table 1. Security vulnerabilities in *GNU libtasn1* [28]

Vulnerability	Version	C SLOC
CVE-2012-1569	2.11	24,448
CVE-2014-3467	3.5	22,091
CVE-2015-2806	4.3	28,115
CVE-2015-3622	4.4	28,109

Table 2. Search times *(hh:mm:ss)* to reproduce vulnerabilities in *GNU libtasn1*

Vulnerability	Search	Workers					
		1	*2*	*4*	*6*	*8*	*10*
CVE-2014-3467₁	*DFS*	00:00:02	00:00:03	00:00:04	00:00:03	00:00:04	00:00:07
	RAND	00:03:10	00:00:39	00:00:43	00:00:07	00:00:08	00:00:05
	BFS	00:00:02	00:00:03	00:00:03	00:00:04	00:00:04	00:00:07
CVE-2014-3467₂	*DFS*	00:00:48	00:00:53	00:00:59	00:01:09	00:01:25	00:01:36
	RAND	00:00:01	00:00:01	00:00:01	00:00:01	00:00:02	00:00:02
	BFS	00:00:48	00:00:52	00:00:59	00:01:08	00:01:30	00:01:04
CVE-2014-3467₃	*DFS*	00:00:04	00:00:05	00:00:05	00:00:04	00:00:04	00:00:07
	RAND	*timeout*	00:07:28	00:00:19	00:00:35	00:00:39	00:00:51
	BFS	00:00:04	00:00:05	00:00:03	00:00:04	00:00:02	00:00:07
CVE-2015-2806	*DFS*	00:10:14	00:05:14	00:02:22	00:01:27	00:01:16	00:01:39
	RAND	00:01:40	00:01:20	00:01:02	00:00:33	00:00:35	00:00:33
	BFS	00:10:14	00:04:16	00:02:28	00:04:32	00:03:42	00:01:32
CVE-2012-1569₁	*DFS*	00:00:07	00:00:08	00:00:10	00:00:13	00:00:08	00:00:13
	RAND	00:00:42	00:00:17	00:00:15	00:00:08	00:00:10	00:00:10
	BFS	00:00:06	00:00:08	00:00:10	00:00:10	00:00:05	00:00:10
CVE-2012-1569₂	*DFS*	00:00:16	00:00:18	00:00:14	00:00:18	00:00:09	00:00:19
	RAND	00:10:16	00:01:54	00:00:33	00:00:24	00:01:11	00:00:42
	BFS	00:00:16	00:00:18	00:00:19	00:00:28	00:00:16	00:00:16
CVE-2015-3622₁	*DFS*	00:05:16	00:05:51	00:02:07	00:02:22	00:05:35	00:04:16
	RAND	00:00:05	00:00:07	00:00:08	00:00:07	00:00:09	00:00:14
	BFS	00:05:19	00:05:54	00:04:00	00:05:22	00:03:28	00:03:41
CVE-2015-3622₂	*DFS*	00:05:30	00:06:01	00:04:29	00:02:58	00:06:53	00:04:23
	RAND	00:00:05	00:00:07	00:00:08	00:00:08	00:00:10	00:00:14
	BFS	00:05:29	00:06:06	00:04:00	00:02:38	00:04:02	00:04:24

format, and Distinguished Encoding Rules (DER) manipulation. GnuTLS uses
libtasn1 to manage X.509 digital certificates. The choice of the library as our
benchmark was motivated by its high usage, rich and complex code, and the fact
that Chopper is capable of symbolically analyzing it. All of the vulnerabilities we
use are due to out-of-bounds memory access. Table 1 provides further details. As
documented in [28], each of these vulnerabilities can be reproduced using a single
failure except CVE-2014-3467, where the failure can occur in three different
code locations. However, using PChop, we discovered one additional way each
to reproduce CVE-2012-1569 and CVE-2015-3622. The two new failures bring
the total number to eight.

5.2   Methodology

We adapt the driver used in [28] to exercise the library. The driver invokes functions in the API, similar to how an application would use the library. We follow

a methodology similar to the one used in [28] to determine which functions to skip for each vulnerability. We evaluate our technique using six parallel configurations comprising 1, 2, 4, 6, 8, and 10 workers and employ three search strategies - depth-first, breadth-first, and random-state search, resulting in a total of 18 unique configurations for each failure. Running a single worker is identical to running Chopper. Depth-first strategy, upon reaching a branching point, forks execution and follows one branch until a termination point is reached and then backtracks, generating deeper states in the process. Breadth-first search processes all states at a particular depth before proceeding to the next depth. Random-state search, as the name suggests, randomly picks a state to execute from the pool of active states. The execution starts with the master node generating initial states equal to the number of workers. Each worker is then given a single state, which is extended to explore deeper states. During work-stealing, idle workers can receive several states at a time from busy workers. The exploration continues until the vulnerability is found at the specified location or the search times out after 60 min. The search time for each vulnerability is compared across different configurations. PChop extends Chopper, which is based on KLEE (commit SHA b2f93ff). This version of KLEE uses LLVM 3.4. We use STP 2.3.3 as the SMT solver. PChop uses Open MPI version 1.10.2 to enable parallel execution. All the experiments were carried out on a 12 core Intel(R) Core(TM) i7-8700K CPU with 32Gb of memory, running Ubuntu 16.04 LTS.

5.3   Results

Table 2 shows search times to discover the vulnerabilities. The efficacy of this technique depends on the interplay between the prefix communication overheads and parallelism gained. Vulnerabilities that take longer to discover benefit more from our scheme than the ones, which Chopper discovers in a short amount of time. Overall, PChop reduces the search times in all configurations where Chopper takes more than one minute to locate the vulnerability. PChop especially benefits cases like CVE-2015-2806, where the search times across all three search policies are significant enough to justify the overheads of deploying a parallel technique like PChop. When detecting this particular vulnerability, PChop provides a speed-up of $8\times$, $3\times$ and $6.8\times$ for DFS, random-state search, and BFS respectively. In cases like CVE-2014-3467$_2$ where Chopper can recreate the vulnerability across all three search strategies in less than a minute, our system does not provide any improvement in performance. For the vulnerabilities examined in this paper, the choice of search strategy had a more dominating influence on search times as compared to the parallelization of the execution. For instance, in CVE-2014-3467$_1$, using BFS or DFS instead of a random-state drastically reduces the search time from 3 min to 2 s and no amount of parallelization using PChop could attain such a speed-up. Chopper discovers 7 out of 8 vulnerabilities fairly quickly using one of the three available search strategies. For such configurations, PChop does not provide any additional benefit. However, the development of search strategies for efficient exploration of programs is orthogonal to our proposed technique which enables parallel chopped symbolic execution and is agnostic to the search policy. PChop can be used as a stand-alone tool or as a complement to other means of accelerating the process of finding defects like the application multiple search strategies. The advantages of using PChop are evident in situations where a particular search strategy takes a significant amount of time to identify a vulnerability. For instance, when using a random-state search in the case of CVE-2012-3467[1], PChop offers a 38x speed-up with 10 workers. For CVE-2012 1569[2], employing a random-state search with 6 cores leads to the discovery of the vulnerability in 24 s as opposed to over 10 min taken by a single-core configuration. When using only DFS, discovering CVE-2014 3622[1] with PChop using 4 workers reduces the search time by 60%. In some cases, increasing the number of workers beyond a certain point lowers the performance. For instance, we witness an increase in the search time when going beyond 6 workers for CVE-2014-3622[2] with a DFS as well as BFS. A prefix provided to a worker from another worker as a result of work-stealing is beneficial if it represents a significant enough exploration space. When a substantial number of prefixes terminate at shallow depth, it causes more prefix transfers as the idle workers receive more work from busy workers. After a point, the communication overheads become more pronounced and are unable to be compensated by the added parallelism, which results in performance degradation.

6   Related Work

There have been several efforts to accomplish symbolic execution in a parallel/distributed setting. *Cloud9* [5], a well-known framework, defines region boundaries in terms of *fence nodes*, and the pool of states to be explored comprises the *candidate nodes*. Participating workers get a part of the execution tree, and work transfers involve sending explicit paths, represented as bit-vectors, of candidate of nodes which get added to the sub-tree of the worker receiving these paths. Our scheme is a variant of one used in tools like Cloud9, which also uses prefix information to distribute work. However, PChop's novelty lies in adapting and extending Chopper to build a prefix-based parallel execution tool, where user-defined regions of the code can be skipped. Ranged symbolic execution [25,26] partitions the program space using test inputs. A total ordering on tests is used to define ranges that start at a particular test $\tau1$ and end at a test $\tau2$ where $\tau2 > \tau1$ according to the ordering. A range comprises paths that lie between the two bounding tests. This idea is extended to devise a distributed approach where different workers explore ranges defined by a pair of tests. *Simple Static Partitioning(SSP)* [27] applies parallel symbolic execution on Java bytecode. This technique builds on top of Symbolic PathFinder(SPF) [21] as the symbolic execution framework. SSP performs a shallow symbolic search and collects path constraints for the explored paths. These constraints are then distributed among workers to act as pre-conditions for symbolic execution. Ranged symbolic execution and SSP represent ways of defining partitions for workers to explore in a parallel fashion, which is orthogonal to our goal of enabling parallel chopped symbolic execution. *DMC* [18] is a distributed approach to model counting, based on the *D4* [17] sequential model counter. DMC uses a master-worker configuration like PChop to enable multiple workers to compute the number of models of a given propositional formula.

7 Limitations

Program characteristics have a significant impact on the performance of a technique like PChop. As discussed in the evaluations, communication overheads can become prohibitively high if the transferred states terminate at shallow depths. Different applications exhibit distinct behavior, and it is challenging to make an assessment of which states to transfer in order to exploit maximum parallelism. We continue to explore the application of static analysis tools and heuristics to alleviate this issue. The evaluation presented in this paper used a multi-core processor with shared memory as the hardware platform. OpenMPI is this configuration, will use shared memory to pass messages between worker nodes. For the subjects evaluated, the parallelism gained from using up to 10 cores was sufficient to demonstrate the benefits of PChop. However, further scaling up the system by employing more workers in a *cluster* setting would use the network to exchange information. We plan to study the appropriate benchmarks that justify scaling to a cluster configuration and gaining insights into PChop's performance accounting for network overheads.

8 Conclusions

This paper presents a novel technique to parallelize chopped symbolic execution using a path-prefix based partitioning scheme. We extend Chopper to incorporate our prefix generation technique and develop an MPI based distribution framework. Our tool realizes chopped symbolic execution in a parallel setting where multiple worker nodes collaborate to explore a program by working on non-overlapping regions simultaneously. We evaluate our technique by recreating documented vulnerabilities in GNU libtasn1 and comparing the time it takes to find the issue. PChop is beneficial in situations where Chopper requires more than a minute to find the vulnerability when using a specific search strategy. For two vulnerabilities, PChop identified a previously undocumented code location to expose each of them.

Acknowledgements. This research was partially supported by the US National Science Foundation under Grant No. CCF-1704790.

References

1. Adve, V., Lattner, C., Brukman, M., Shukla, A., Gaeke, B.: LLVA: a low-level virtual instruction set architecture. In: Proceedings of the 36th Annual ACM/IEEE International Symposium on Microarchitecture (MICRO-36), San Diego, California, December 2003

2. Avgerinos, T., Cha, S.K., Rebert, A., Schwartz, E.J., Woo, M., Brumley, D.: Automatic exploit generation. Commun. ACM **57**(2), 74–84 (2014). https://doi.org/10.1145/2560217.2560219. http://doi.acm.org/10.1145/2560217.2560219

3. Bethea, D., Cochran, R.A., Reiter, M.K.: Server-side verification of client behavior in online games. ACM Trans. Inf. Syst. Secur. **14**(4), 32:1–32:27 (2008). https://doi.org/10.1145/2043628.2043633. http://doi.acm.org/10.1145/2043628.2043633

4. Boyer, R.S., Elspas, B., Levitt, K.N.: SELECT—a formal system for testing and debugging programs by symbolic execution. In: Proceedings of the International Conference on Reliable Software, pp. 234–245. ACM, New York (1975). https://doi.org/10.1145/800027.808445. http://doi.acm.org/10.1145/800027.808445

5. Bucur, S., Ureche, V., Zamfir, C., Candea, G.: Parallel symbolic execution for automated real-world software testing. In: Proceedings of the Sixth Conference on Computer Systems, EuroSys 2011, pp. 183–198. ACM, New York (2011). https://doi.org/10.1145/1966445.1966463. http://doi.acm.org/10.1145/1966445.1966463

6. Burnim, J., Sen, K.: Heuristics for scalable dynamic test generation. In: 2008 23rd IEEE/ACM International Conference on Automated Software Engineering, pp. 443–446, September 2008. https://doi.org/10.1109/ASE.2008.69

7. Cadar, C., Dunbar, D., Engler, D.: KLEE: unassisted and automatic generation of high-coverage tests for complex systems programs. In: Proceedings of the 8th USENIX Conference on Operating Systems Design and Implementation, OSDI 2008, pp. 209–224. USENIX Association, Berkeley (2008). http://dl.acm.org/citation.cfm?id=1855741.1855756

8. Cadar, C., Engler, D.: Execution generated test cases: how to make systems code crash itself. In: Godefroid, P. (ed.) SPIN 2005. LNCS, vol. 3639, pp. 2–23. Springer, Heidelberg (2005). https://doi.org/10.1007/11537328_2

9. Cadar, C., Ganesh, V., Pawlowski, P.M., Dill, D.L., Engler, D.R.: EXE: automatically generating inputs of death. In: Proceedings of the 13th ACM Conference on Computer and Communications Security, CCS 2006, pp. 322–335. ACM, New York (2006). https://doi.org/10.1145/1180405.1180445. http://doi.acm.org/10.1145/1180405.1180445

10. Chipounov, V., Candea, G.: Reverse engineering of binary device drivers with RevNic. In: Proceedings of the 5th European Conference on Computer Systems, EuroSys 2010, pp. 167–180. ACM, New York (2010). https://doi.org/10.1145/1755913.1755932. http://doi.acm.org/10.1145/1755913.1755932

11. Ciortea, L., Zamfir, C., Bucur, S., Chipounov, V., Candea, G.: Cloud9: a software testing service. SIGOPS Oper. Syst. Rev. **43**(4), 5–10 (2010). https://doi.org/10.1145/1713254.1713257. http://doi.acm.org/10.1145/1713254.1713257

12. Collingbourne, P., Cadar, C., Kelly, P.H.: Symbolic crosschecking of floating-point and SIMD code. In: Proceedings of the Sixth Conference on Computer Systems, EuroSys 2011, pp. 315–328. ACM, New York (2011). https://doi.org/10.1145/1966445.1966475. http://doi.acm.org/10.1145/1966445.1966475

13. Cui, H., Wu, J., Tsai, C.C., Yang, J.: Stable deterministic multithreading through schedule memoization. In: OSDI (2010)

14. Godefroid, P.: Compositional dynamic test generation. In: Proceedings of the 34th Annual ACM SIGPLAN-SIGACT Symposium on Principles of Programming Languages, POPL 2007, pp. 47–54. ACM, New York (2007). https://doi.org/10.1145/1190216.1190226. http://doi.acm.org/10.1145/1190216.1190226

15. Godefroid, P., Klarlund, N., Sen, K.: DART: directed automated random testing. SIGPLAN Not. **40**(6), 213–223 (2005). https://doi.org/10.1145/1064978.1065036. http://doi.acm.org/10.1145/1064978.1065036

16. King, J.C.: Symbolic execution and program testing. Commun. ACM **19**(7), 385–394 (1976). https://doi.org/10.1145/360248.360252. http://doi.acm.org/10.1145/360248.360252

17. Lagniez, J.M., Marquis, P.: An improved decision-DNNF compiler. In: Proceedings of the 26th International Joint Conference on Artificial Intelligence, IJCAI 2017, pp. 667–673. AAAI Press (2017). http://dl.acm.org/citation.cfm?id=3171642.3171738

18. Lagniez, J.M., Marquis, P., Szczepanski, N.: DMC: a distributed model counter. In: Proceedings of the 27th International Joint Conference on Artificial Intelligence, IJCAI 2018, pp. 1331–1338. AAAI Press (2018). http://dl.acm.org/citation.cfm?id=3304415.3304604

19. Li, G., Li, P., Sawaya, G., Gopalakrishnan, G., Ghosh, I., Rajan, S.: GKLEE: concolic verification and test generation for GPUs. ACM SIGPLAN Not. **47**(8), 215–224 (2012). https://doi.org/10.1145/2370036.2145844

20. Person, S., Yang, G., Rungta, N., Khurshid, S.: Directed incremental symbolic execution. In: Proceedings of the 32nd ACM SIGPLAN Conference on Programming Language Design and Implementation, PLDI 2011, pp. 504–515. ACM, New York (2011). https://doi.org/10.1145/1993498.1993558. http://doi.acm.org/10.1145/1993498.1993558

21. Păsăreanu, C.S., et al.: Combining unit-level symbolic execution and system-level concrete execution for testing NASA software. In: Proceedings of the 2008 International Symposium on Software Testing and Analysis, ISSTA 2008, pp. 15–26. ACM, New York (2008). https://doi.org/10.1145/1390630.1390635. http://doi.acm.org/10.1145/1390630.1390635

22. Sasnauskas, R., Link, J.A.B., Alizai, M.H., Wehrle, K.: KleeNet: automatic bug hunting in sensor network applications. In: Proceedings of the 6th ACM Conference on Embedded Network Sensor Systems, SenSys 2008, pp. 425–426. ACM, New York (2008). https://doi.org/10.1145/1460412.1460485. http://doi.acm.org/10.1145/1460412.1460485

23. Sen, K., Agha, G.: CUTE and jCUTE: concolic unit testing and explicit path model-checking tools. In: Ball, T., Jones, R.B. (eds.) CAV 2006. LNCS, vol. 4144, pp. 419–423. Springer, Heidelberg (2006). https://doi.org/10.1007/11817963_38

24. Sen, K., Marinov, D., Agha, G.: CUTE: a concolic unit testing engine for C. In: Proceedings of the 10th European Software Engineering Conference Held Jointly with 13th ACM SIGSOFT International Symposium on Foundations of Software Engineering, ESEC/FSE-13, pp. 263–272. ACM, New York (2005). https://doi.org/10.1145/1081706.1081750. http://doi.acm.org/10.1145/1081706.1081750

25. Siddiqui, J.H., Khurshid, S.: ParSym: parallel symbolic execution. In: 2010 2nd International Conference on Software Technology and Engineering, vol. 1, pp. V1-405–V1-409, October 2010. https://doi.org/10.1109/ICSTE.2010.5608866

26. Siddiqui, J.H., Khurshid, S.: Scaling symbolic execution using ranged analysis. In: Proceedings of the ACM International Conference on Object Oriented Programming Systems Languages and Applications, OOPSLA 2012, pp. 523–536. ACM, New York (2012). https://doi.org/10.1145/2384616.2384654. http://doi.acm.org/10.1145/2384616.2384654

27. Staats, M., Păsăreanu, C.: Parallel symbolic execution for structural test generation. In: Proceedings of the 19th International Symposium on Software Testing and Analysis, ISSTA 2010, pp. 183–194. ACM, New York (2010). https://doi.org/10.1145/1831708.1831732. http://doi.acm.org/10.1145/1831708.1831732

28. Trabish, D., Mattavelli, A., Rinetzky, N., Cadar, C.: Chopped symbolic execution. In: Proceedings of the 40th International Conference on Software Engineering, ICSE 2018, pp. 350–360. ACM, New York (2018). https://doi.org/10.1145/3180155.3180251. http://doi.acm.org/10.1145/3180155.3180251

29. Zamfir, C., Candea, G.: Execution synthesis: a technique for automated software debugging. In: Proceedings of the 5th European Conference on Computer Systems, EuroSys 2010, pp. 321–334. ACM, New York (2010). https://doi.org/10.1145/1755913.1755946. http://doi.acm.org/10.1145/1755913.1755946

Formal Methods and Machine Learning

PAC Learning of Deterministic One-Clock Timed Automata

Wei Shen[1] , Jie An[1] , Bohua Zhan[2,3](✉) , Miaomiao Zhang[1](✉),
Bai Xue[2,3] , and Naijun Zhan[2,3](✉)

[1] School of Software Engineering, Tongji University, Shanghai, China
{weishen,1510796,miaomiao}@tongji.edu.cn
[2] State Key Laboratory of Computer Science, Institute of Software, CAS,
Beijing, China
{bzhan,xuebai,znj}@ios.ac.cn
[3] University of Chinese Academy of Sciences, Beijing, China

Abstract. We study the problem of learning deterministic one-clock timed automata in the framework of PAC (probably approximately correct) learning. The use of PAC learning relaxes the assumption of having a teacher that can answer equivalence queries exactly, replacing it with approximate answers from testing on a set of samples. The framework provides correctness guarantees in terms of error and confidence parameters. We further discuss several improvements to the basic PAC algorithm. This includes a special sampling method, and the use of comparator and counterexample minimization to reduce the number of equivalence queries. We implemented a prototype for our learning algorithm, and conducted experiments on learning the TCP protocol as well as a number of randomly generated automata. The results demonstrate the effectiveness of our approach, as well as the importance of the various improvements for learning complex models.

Keywords: Timed automata · Active learning · Automata learning · Probably approximately correct learning

1 Introduction

In recent years, model learning [30] is emerging as a highly effective technique for learning black-box systems from system observations. It generally is divided into two categories: *active learning* and *passive learning*. Active learning under the L^* framework [7] can be viewed as an interaction between a *learner* and a *teacher*, where the learner asks *membership queries* and *equivalence queries* to a teacher who holds oracles to answer these queries. This is distinguished from passive learning, i.e., generating a model consistent with a given data set. Recently, active learning has been extended to many formal models.

This work has been partially funded by NSFC under grant No. 61972284, No. 61625206, No. 61732001 and No. 61836005, and by the CAS Pioneer Hundred Talents Program under grant No. Y9RC585036.

© Springer Nature Switzerland AG 2020
S.-W. Lin et al. (Eds.): ICFEM 2020, LNCS 12531, pp. 129–146, 2020.
https://doi.org/10.1007/978-3-030-63406-3_8

In previous work [5], we introduced active learning algorithms for deterministic one-clock timed automata (DOTA). There are two variants of the algorithm. The first variant is based on the assumption of a *smart teacher* who can provide clock-reset information along queries. The idea then is to use the reset information to convert the learning problem to that of learning the corresponding *reset-logical-timed language*, which can be solved following the approaches to learning symbolic automata [12, 20]. The second variant assumes only a *normal teacher* who does not provide reset information. The learner then needs to *guess* reset information on transitions discovered in the observation table. Due to these guesses, the second variant has exponential complexity in the size of the learned automata, while the first variant has polynomial complexity.

In both variants, we assumed that the equivalence queries can be answered exactly. In the experiments, this is implemented using a decision procedure for language inclusion. This kind of equivalence queries is difficult to realize in practical applications, as it essentially require a teacher to have the power to compare two systems exactly. This problem is addressed in [1] using conformance testing. Another way is to follow the PAC (probably approximately correct) framework, which is studied in existing work [7, 10, 21] for other kinds of models. Under this framework, for a given *error* ϵ and *confidence* δ, we can determine the number of test cases needed for each equivalence query. If the current hypothesis passes all test cases, then with probability $1 - \delta$, it agrees with the target model on at least $1 - \epsilon$ proportion of behaviours.

In this paper, we integrate PAC learning into the framework for learning DOTAs. This involves replacing the exact equivalence query with PAC-style equivalence query. To further reduce the number of such equivalence queries, we also integrate the idea of *comparators* [9, 28] into the learning framework. The comparator enforces that the quality of intermediate hypotheses obtained during learning does not decrease, by finding the smallest difference between successive hypotheses and then perform one membership query. This has the advantage of replacing some equivalence queries by membership queries, which accelerates the learning process. Replacing exact equivalence queries with PAC-style equivalence queries also introduces other problems. In particular, the distribution of inputs from which the test cases are sampled become very important. In general, sampling from a naïve uniform distribution of action and delay times is unlikely to yield good results, as too few of the samples are focused on the "interesting" parts of system behaviors. Hence, we design special sampling techniques adapted to our setting. Second, in contrast to exact decision procedures for equivalence which are likely to produce minimal counterexamples, there are no such guarantees for PAC-style testing. While this does not affect theoretical correctness of the algorithm, it can lead the algorithm to produce unnecessarily large learned models. Hence, we introduce a method for minimizing counterexamples that involves only membership queries to the teacher. In summary, the contributions of this paper are as follows.

- We describe the PAC learning of deterministic one-clock timed automata. In this setting, both membership and equivalence queries are conducted via testing, with PAC-style equivalence checking replacing exact equivalence queries.
- We accelerate learning by adding a comparator component to reduce the number of equivalence queries. We also propose approaches for better sampling and counterexample minimization to improve learning performance.
- We produce a prototype implementation of our methods, and perform experiments on a number of randomly generated automata, as well as a model of the functional specification of the TCP protocol. These experiments suggest that DOTAs can be learned under the more realistic assumptions of this paper.

The rest of the paper is organized as follows. In Sect. 2, we review the learning algorithm for deterministic one-clock timed automata and PAC learning of DFA. Section 3 describes the PAC learning framework for DOTA in detail, including improvements such as comparators, a special sampling method and the counterexample minimization. In Sect. 4, we extend this PAC framework to the case of normal teachers. The experimental results are reported in Sect. 5. Section 6 discusses related work. Finally, Sect. 7 concludes this paper.

2   Preliminaries

Let $\mathbb{N}$ be the natural numbers and $\mathbb{R}_{\geq 0}$ be the non-negative real numbers. We use $\top$ to stand for true and $\bot$ for false. Let $\mathbb{B} = \{\top, \bot\}$.

2.1   Deterministic One-Clock Timed Automata

In this paper, we consider a subclass of timed automata [2] that are deterministic and contain only a single clock, called *Deterministic One-Clock Timed Automata* (DOTA). Let c be the clock variable, denote by Φ_c the set of clock constraints of the form $\phi ::= \top \mid c \bowtie m \mid \phi \wedge \phi$, where $m \in \mathbb{N}$ and $\bowtie \in \{=, <, >, \leq, \geq\}$.

Definition 1 (One-clock timed automata). *A one-clock timed automata is a 6-tuple $\mathcal{A} = (\Sigma, Q, q_0, F, c, \Delta)$, where Σ is a finite set of actions, Q is a finite set of locations, q_0 is the initial location, $F \subseteq Q$ is a set of final locations, c is the unique clock and $\Delta \subseteq Q \times \Sigma \times \Phi_c \times \mathbb{B} \times Q$ is a finite set of transitions.*

A transition $\delta \in \Delta$ is a 5-tuple (q, σ, ϕ, b, q'), where $q, q' \in Q$ are the source and target locations, $\sigma \in \Sigma$ is an action, $\phi \in \Phi_c$ is a clock constraint, and b is the reset indicator. Such δ allows a jump from q to q' by performing an action σ if the current clock valuation ν satisfies the constraint ϕ. Meanwhile, clock c is reset to zero if $b = \top$ and remains unchanged otherwise. A *clock valuation* is a function $\nu : c \mapsto \mathbb{R}_{\geq 0}$ that assigns a non-negative real number to the clock. For $t \in \mathbb{R}_{\geq 0}$, let $\nu + t$ be the clock valuation with $(\nu + t)(c) = \nu(c) + t$. A *timed state* of $\mathcal{A}$ is a pair (q, ν), where $q \in Q$ and ν is a clock valuation. A *timed action* is a pair (σ, t) that indicates the action σ is applied after t time units since the occurrence of the previous action. A *run* ρ of $\mathcal{A}$ is a finite sequence

$\rho = (q_0, \nu_0) \xrightarrow{\sigma_1, t_1} (q_1, \nu_1) \xrightarrow{\sigma_2, t_2} \cdots \xrightarrow{\sigma_n, t_n} (q_n, \nu_n)$ where $\nu_0 = 0$, and for all $1 \leq i \leq n$ there exists a transitions $(q_{i-1}, \sigma_i, \phi_i, b_i, q_i) \in \Delta$ such that $\nu_{i-1} + t_i$ satisfies ϕ_i, and $\nu_i(c) = 0$ if $b_i = \top$, $\nu_i(c) = \nu_{i-1}(c) + t_i$ otherwise. The *timed trace* of a run ρ is a *timed word* trace$(\rho) = (\sigma_1, t_1)(\sigma_2, t_2) \ldots (\sigma_n, t_n)$.

Since time values t_i represent *delay* times, we call such a timed trace a *delay-timed word*, denoted as ω. If ρ is an accepting run of $\mathcal{A}$, trace(ρ) is called an *accepting timed word*. The *recognized timed language* of $\mathcal{A}$ is the set of accepting delay-timed words, i.e., $\mathcal{L}(\mathcal{A}) = \{trace(\rho) \mid \rho$ is an accepting run of $\mathcal{A}\}$. The corresponding *reset-delay-timed word* can be defined as $trace_r(\rho) = (\sigma_1, t_1, b_1)(\sigma_2, t_2, b_2) \cdots (\sigma_n, t_n, b_n)$, denoted as ω_r, where each b_i is the reset indicator for δ_i. The *recognized reset-timed language* $\mathcal{L}_r(\mathcal{A})$ is defined as $\{trace_r(\rho) \mid \rho$ is an accepting run of $\mathcal{A}\}$.

The delay-timed word $\omega = (\sigma_1, t_1)(\sigma_2, t_2) \cdots (\sigma_n, t_n)$ is observed outside, from the view of the global clock. On the other hand, the behaviour can also be observed inside, from the view of the local clock. This results in a *logical-timed word* of the form $\gamma = (\sigma_1, \mu_1)(\sigma_2, \mu_2) \cdots (\sigma_n, \mu_n)$ with $\mu_i = t_i$ if $i = 1 \vee b_{i-1} = \top$ and $\mu_i = \mu_{i-1} + t_i$ otherwise. We will denote the mapping from delay-timed words to logical-timed words above by Γ. Similarly, we introduce *reset-logical-timed word* $\gamma_r = (\sigma_1, \mu_1, b_1)(\sigma_2, \mu_2, b_2) \cdots (\sigma_n, \mu_n, b_n)$ as the counterpart of $\omega_r = (\sigma_1, t_1, b_1)(\sigma_2, t_2, b_2) \cdots (\sigma_n, t_n, b_n)$ in terms of the local clock. Without any substantial change, we can extend the mapping Γ to map reset-delay-timed words to reset-logical-timed words. The *recognized logical-timed language* of $\mathcal{A}$ is given as $L(\mathcal{A}) = \{\Gamma(trace(\rho)) \mid \rho$ is an accepting run of $\mathcal{A}\}$, and the *recognized reset-logical-timed language* of $\mathcal{A}$ as $L_r(\mathcal{A}) = \{\Gamma(trace_r(\rho)) \mid \rho$ is an accepting run of $\mathcal{A}\}$.

Definition 2 (Deterministic OTA). *An OTA is a deterministic one-clock timed automaton (DOTA) if there is at most one run for a given delay-timed word.*

We say a DOTA $\mathcal{A}$ is *complete* if for any location q and action σ, the constraints form a partition of $\mathbb{R}_{\geq 0}$. Any incomplete DOTA $\mathcal{A}$ can be transformed into a complete DOTA accepting the same timed language by adding a non-accepting *sink* location (see more details in [5]).

2.2   Exact Learning Algorithm for DOTAs

In this section, we describe the active learning problem for DOTA and the learning algorithms. We refer to [5] for more details. Active learning of a DOTA assumes the existence of a teacher who can answer two kinds of queries: membership and equivalence queries. We will consider two different settings, depending on whether the teacher also provides clock-reset information along with answers to queries.

A *smart teacher* permits a *logical*-timed word as input to a membership query, and returns whether the timed-word is accepted, as well as reset information at each transition along the trace. Moreover, if the equivalence query yields a counterexample, the counterexample is provided as a reset-delay-timed word. In practical applications, this corresponds to the case where some parts of the model (information of clock-reset) are known by testing or watchdogs (refer to the concept of testable system in [13,14]). This also conforms with the idea of combining black-box learning with white-box techniques, as exploited in [17].

A *normal teacher* corresponds to the usual case for active learning of automata. The teacher permits a delay-timed word as input to a membership query, and only returns whether the timed word is accepted. The equivalence query returns a delay-timed word as a counterexample in the non-equivalent case. The active learning problem in both settings is to learn DOTAs by asking only these two kinds of queries.

The algorithm converts the learning problem to that of learning the reset-logical-timed language, based on the following theorem in [5].

Theorem 1. *Given two DOTAs $\mathcal{A}$ and $\mathcal{B}$, if $L_r(\mathcal{A}) = L_r(\mathcal{B})$, then $\mathcal{L}(\mathcal{A}) = \mathcal{L}(\mathcal{B})$.*

In the smart teacher setting, the conversion is direct. The problem of learning the reset-logical-timed language follows existing techniques for learning symbolic automata. The algorithm maintains a *timed observation table* **T** to store answers from all previous queries. Once the learner has gained sufficient information, i.e., **T** is *closed* and *consistent*, a hypothesis $\mathcal{H}$ is constructed. Then the learner poses an equivalence query to the teacher to judge the equivalence between the hypothesis and the target model. If equivalent, the algorithm terminates with the answer $\mathcal{H}$. Otherwise, the teacher responds with a reset-delay-timed word ω_r as a counterexample. After processing ω_r, the algorithm starts a new round of learning. The whole procedure repeats until the teacher gives a positive answer for an equivalence query.

In the case of normal teacher, the learner needs to guess the reset information on each transition discovered in the observation table. At each iteration, the learner guesses all needed reset information and forms a number of table candidates. These table candidates are put into a priority queue, ordered by the number of needed guesses. Each iteration begins by taking the first table candidate from the queue. Operations on the table is then the same as the smart teacher case. Termination of the algorithm is due to the fact that the learner will eventually consider the case where all guesses are correct. Due to the needed guesses, the complexity of the algorithm is exponential in the size of the learned model.

2.3 PAC Learning of DFA

In reality, even in the case of DFA, it is difficult to implement teachers that can answer the equivalence query exactly. Hence, Angluin also introduced the concept of PAC learning for DFA in [7]. We review the basic ideas here.

Assume we are given a probability distribution $\mathcal{P}$ over elements of the language Σ^*. Fix a target regular language $L \subseteq \Sigma^*$. Let L_H be the recognized regular language of an hypothesis H. The quality of H is defined by its distance from L, that is, the probability of choosing a mismatched word $\omega \in \Sigma^*$ that belongs to one language but not the other. The set of all mismatched words is exactly the symmetric difference of the languages L and L_H. Hence, the distance is defined as $\mathcal{P}(L \oplus L_H)$, where $L \oplus L_H = L \backslash L_H \uplus L_H \backslash L$.

Definition 3 (PAC-style correctness for DFA). *Let ϵ be the error parameter and δ the confidence parameter. We say a learning algorithm is PAC(ϵ,δ)-correct if its output DFA hypothesis H satisfies $Pr(\mathcal{P}(L \oplus L_H) \leq \epsilon) \geq 1 - \delta$, where Pr represents the probability of the event $\mathcal{P}(L \oplus L_H) \leq \epsilon$.*

Under this setting, we replace exact equivalence checking, i.e, whether $L_H = L$, with the checking of approximate equivalence. In other words, we check approximate equivalence by randomly sampling test sequences according to a certain distribution. The minimum number of tests required for each equivalence query to ensure the above PAC-style correctness depends on the error and confidence parameters as well as the number of previous equivalence queries. This number was first introduced in [7] for learning DFA and then used in the PAC learning of symbolic automata [21].

Theorem 2. *The DFA learning algorithm PAC-learns a regular language L if the i-th equivalence query tests $r_i = \frac{1}{\epsilon} \left(\ln \frac{1}{\delta} + (i+1) \ln 2 \right)$ random words from a fixed distribution over Σ^* without finding a counterexample.*

3   PAC Learning of DOTA

In this section, we explain the PAC learning algorithm utilized to obtain a DOTA approximating the target timed language. In contrast to the learning algorithm given in [5], where equivalence checking is conducted between a hypothesis and the target model, here we allow more flexible implementation of the teacher via testing on the target system. In our PAC learning, membership queries as well as equivalence queries are conducted by testing on the implementation of the system.

3.1   PAC-Style Correctness

Let $\mathcal{P}$ be a probability distribution over elements of the delay-timed language $(\Sigma \times \mathbb{R}_{\geq 0})^*$. Again, let $\mathcal{L} \subseteq (\Sigma \times \mathbb{R}_{\geq 0})^*$ be the timed language of the target system, and $\mathcal{L}(\mathcal{H})$ be the timed language of the hypothesis $\mathcal{H}$. As before, the quality of $\mathcal{H}$ is defined as $\mathcal{P}(\mathcal{L} \oplus \mathcal{L}(\mathcal{H}))$, where $\mathcal{L} \oplus \mathcal{L}(\mathcal{H}) = \mathcal{L} \backslash \mathcal{L}(\mathcal{H}) \uplus \mathcal{L}(\mathcal{H}) \backslash \mathcal{L}$.

Definition 4 (PAC-style correctness for DOTA). *Let ϵ be the error parameter and δ the confidence parameter. We say a learning algorithm for DOTA is PAC(ϵ,δ)-correct if its output timed hypothesis $\mathcal{H}$ satisfies:*

$$Pr(\mathcal{P}(\mathcal{L} \oplus \mathcal{L}(\mathcal{H})) \leq \epsilon) \geq 1 - \delta, \tag{1}$$

where Pr represents the probability of the event $\mathcal{P}(\mathcal{L} \oplus \mathcal{L}(\mathcal{H})) \leq \epsilon$.

As before, PAC-style correctness can be obtained by performing a sufficient number of tests for each equivalence query. The main result for the DOTA case is given below, following [23].

Theorem 3. *The DOTA learning algorithm PAC-learns a timed language $\mathcal{L}$ if the i-th equivalence query tests*

$$r_i = \frac{1}{\epsilon} \left(\ln \frac{1}{\delta} + (i+1) \ln 2 \right) \tag{2}$$

random delay-timed words from a fixed distribution over $(\Sigma \times \mathbb{R}_{\geq 0})^*$ without finding a counterexample.

3.2 PAC-Style Equivalence Query

In this section, we present the overall procedure for the PAC-style equivalence query. The procedure is shown in Algorithm 1. Three improvements to the procedure will be discussed in the next three subsections.

The equivalence query accepts as input the hypothesis $\mathcal{H}$, the count i of the current query, the error parameter ϵ, and the confidence parameter δ. We first compute the number of samples needed according to Eq. (2). Then, we repeatly draw samples from a distribution. The choice of distribution is significant for the learning performance, and will be discussed in detail in Sect. 3.3. For each sample ω (a delay-timed word), we test it on both the target system $\mathcal{S}$ and the hypothesis $\mathcal{H}$ (testing on the target system uses a membership query). The test on $\mathcal{S}$ returns a pair v, ω_r, where v represents whether ω is an accepted timed word according $\mathcal{S}$, and ω_r is the reset-delay-timed word corresponding to ω. Likewise, the test on $\mathcal{H}$ returns a pair v', ω_r'. If $v \neq v'$, then ω is a counterexample to the equivalence between $\mathcal{H}$ and $\mathcal{S}$, and is returned directly. Otherwise, if all tests pass, we conclude $\mathcal{H}$ is $PAC(\epsilon, \delta)$-correct, based on Theorem 3.

Algorithm 1: PAC-style equivalence query **pac_equivalence($\mathcal{H}, i, \epsilon, \delta$)**

---

input : a hypothesis $\mathcal{H}$; the count i of current equivalent query; error parameter ϵ; confidence parameter δ.

output: *equivalent*: a boolean value to identify whether $\mathcal{H}$ passes all tests; *ctx*: a counterexample.

1 *equivalent* $\leftarrow \top$;
2 *counter* $\leftarrow 1$;
3 *testNum* $\leftarrow \frac{1}{\epsilon} \left(\ln \frac{1}{\delta} + (i+1) \ln 2 \right)$;
4 **while** *counter* $<$ *testNum* **do**
5      $\omega \leftarrow$ sample($\mathcal{P}$);   // $\mathcal{P}$ is a distribution over $(\Sigma \times \mathbb{R}_{\geq 0})^*$
6      $v, \omega_r \leftarrow$ test_dtw($\omega, \mathcal{S}$);   // test a timed word ω on system $\mathcal{S}$
7      $v', \omega_r' \leftarrow$ test_dtw($\omega, \mathcal{H}$);   // test a timed word ω on hypothesis $\mathcal{H}$
8   **if** $v \neq v'$ **then**
9            $equivalent \leftarrow \bot$; $ctx \leftarrow \omega_r$;
10   **return** *equivalent, ctx*;
11   *counter* $\leftarrow$ *counter* $+ 1$;
12 **return** *equivalent, ctx*

Two further improvements reduce the number of needed equivalence queries by adding a *comparator* (Sect. 3.4) and the *counterexample minimization* (Sect. 3.5).

3.3   Sampling Mechanism

The choice of the sampling distribution over $(\Sigma \times \mathbb{R}_{\geq 0})^*$ is important to whether PAC learning yields good results in real applications. While the theory guarantees the success of learning under any distribution, an inappropriate choice of distribution may lead to models that are not useful in practice. In particular, we observe that a naïve uniform distribution of action and time values is not useful in our case. The reason is that for many examples, e.g. the TCP protocol and the randomly generated automata on which we performed experiments, the vast majority of timed traces under uniform distribution are invalid for the automata. Hence, only a very small proportion lead to valid paths and test interesting behaviours of the system. This situation may also occur for other real-life systems. For many reactive systems and protocols, an input that is completely randomly generated will most likely be invalid in the current state, and hence will not test the interesting aspect of the system.

We address this problem by designing a custom sampling mechanism. Our aim is for one half of the overall distribution to consist of timed words that are guaranteed to be valid for the system. The other half consists of possibly invalid timed words, obtained from the valid ones by introducing a random change. In more detail, for both valid and possibly invalid timed traces, we first choose the length uniformly between 1 and an upper bound M (i.e. 1.5 times the number of locations in the experiments). For a given length, we could sample valid timed traces by repeatedly sampling random timed words, testing each on the system, and taking only the valid traces. This method is inefficient if the vast majority of timed words are invalid. We design a more efficient sampling method as follows. First, we perform a random walk on the locations of the system starting from the initial location. This gives a sequence of actions and bounds on the *logical* time of the timed trace. Next, we uniformly sample the logical time, subject to the obtained bounds, as well as the constraint that if the previous transition is not a reset, then the logical time should be greater than or equal to the previous logical time. To make sure that we will test traces with integer time values, we actually sample from the allowed *regions* of logical time, so that about half of sampled time values are integers. Otherwise, most of the sampled time values will contain fractions. Finally, the resulting logical-timed word is converted to delay-timed word, which is guaranteed to be valid. To sample possibly invalid timed traces of a given length, we first sample a valid timed trace of the same length using the above procedure, then randomly change one transition to a timed word with uniformly chosen action and time.

This sampling mechanism yield timed traces that are more likely to reflect interesting behaviours of the system. We note that while the sampling depends on the target system, it does not reveal the internal structure of the system to the learner. It only helps the learner by providing counterexamples that are

PAC Learning of DOTA

more likely to be relevant. In real applications, this sampling distribution can be approximated by sampling from user inputs (which are more likely to be valid) and their slight variations. Another way to approximate the distribution is to first sample random timed words, then remove most of the invalid ones as mentioned before. The target system continues to be viewed as a black-box. In Sect. 5, we will show that while the learning algorithm succeeds with any sampling distribution, the model learned using the distribution described above are far more likely to be completely correct (or at least very close to the target system from a human point of view) than using a naïve uniform distribution.

3.4 Comparator

During the learning process, the aforementioned algorithm generates a series of hypotheses. Ideally, we would prefer that each successive hypothesis gradually approaches the target system according to some measure. However, this may not be the case. As observed in [23] for symbolic automata, processing of counterexamples will generate two kinds of changes to the hypothesis. The first kind is called *expansive modification*, which means the latter hypothesis $\mathcal{H}'$ has more states and/or transitions than the former hypothesis $\mathcal{H}$. The second is called *non-expansive modification*, which implies that between the two hypotheses, only the symbols of the alphabet on the transitions differ. It is noted in [23] that $\mathcal{H}'$ is closer to the target system than $\mathcal{H}$.

However, in the case of expansive modification, this cannot be guaranteed. Vaandrager et al. showed in [9,28] that the successive hypothesis is not always better than the previous one, under a well-known metric based on minimal length counterexamples. To correct this, they proposed a modification to L^* to make sure that each *stable* hypothesis (see Definition 6) is at least as good as the previous one. Although the modification is for the DFA setting, we find that it is still applicable to the DOTA case. The distance metric to measure the quality of a hypothesis is defined as follows.

Definition 5 (Metric function). *Let $\mathcal{L}(\mathcal{H})$ and $\mathcal{L}(\mathcal{H}')$ be timed languages of two DOTAs $\mathcal{H}$ and $\mathcal{H}'$. The ultrametric function d is*

$$d\left(\mathcal{L}(\mathcal{H}), \mathcal{L}(\mathcal{H}')\right) = \begin{cases} 0 & \text{if } \mathcal{L}(\mathcal{H}) = \mathcal{L}(\mathcal{H}') \\ 2^{-n} & \text{otherwise,} \end{cases} \tag{3}$$

where n is the length of a minimal timed word that distinguishes $\mathcal{L}(\mathcal{H})$ and $\mathcal{L}(\mathcal{H}')$.

Definition 6 (Stable hypothesis). *Let $\mathcal{S}$ be the target system, and let $\mathcal{H}$ and $\mathcal{H}'$ be two hypotheses in the learning process. Then $\mathcal{H}'$ is called stable if $d(\mathcal{L}(\mathcal{H}), \mathcal{L}(\mathcal{S})) \geq d(\mathcal{L}(\mathcal{H}'), \mathcal{L}(\mathcal{S}))$.*

The procedure for finding stable hypotheses with a *comparator* is shown in Algorithm 2. For each newly learned hypothesis $\mathcal{H}'$, before asking the teacher an equivalence query, it is compared with the current stable hypothesis $\mathcal{H}$. This

---

Algorithm 2: Find new stable hypothesis **comparator**$(\mathcal{H}, \mathcal{H}')$

---

   input : current stable hypothesis $\mathcal{H}$; new hypothesis $\mathcal{H}'$.
   output: new stable hypothesis $\mathcal{H}$.
1   *compareFlag* ← ⊥;
2   **repeat**
       /* obtain minimal timed word ω that distinguishes $\mathcal{H}$ and $\mathcal{H}'$.   */
3 ω ← min_distinguishing_dtw$(\mathcal{H}, \mathcal{H}')$;
4 v, ω_r ← test_dtw$(\omega, \mathcal{S})$;   // test a timed word ω on system $\mathcal{S}$
5 v', ω'_r ← test_dtw$(\omega, \mathcal{H}')$;   // test a timed word ω on hypothesis $\mathcal{H}'$
6   **if** $v \neq v'$ **then**
7 ctx ← ω_r;   // found a counterexample
8   ctx_processing$(\mathbf{T}, ctx)$;   // handle the counterexample
9   Make table $\mathbf{T}$ closed and consistent;
10   Construct new hypothesis $\mathcal{H}'$;
11   **else**
12 $\mathcal{H}$ ← $\mathcal{H}'$;   // set $\mathcal{H}'$ as new stable hypothesis
13   *compareFlag* ← ⊤;
14   **until** *compareFlag* = ⊤;
15   **return** new stable hypothesis $\mathcal{H}$;

---

involves first generating a minimal-length sequence ω (a delay-timed word) distinguishing $\mathcal{H}$ and $\mathcal{H}'$, which can be achieved via a language equivalence checking since the model $\mathcal{H}$ and $\mathcal{H}'$ are known. Then ω is tested against the target system $\mathcal{S}$. If the result is inconsistent with that of $\mathcal{H}'$, the comparator found a counterexample to $\mathcal{H}'$ and returns the corresponding reset-delay-timed word ω_r to the learner to construct a new (and bigger) hypothesis. Otherwise (when the outputs are consistent), we promote $\mathcal{H}'$ to be the new stable hypothesis, and proceeds to perform a PAC-style equivalence query. This ensures that each stable hypothesis is at least as good as the previous one according to the metric function. It also has the practical effect of reducing the number of equivalence queries (replacing some of them by membership queries). This is particularly significant in the PAC learning setting as the number of tests of each equivalence query increases with the number of previously performed equivalence queries.

Because $\mathcal{H}$ and $\mathcal{H}'$ are both explicit DOTAs (in contrast to the target system which is a black box), finding the minimal distinguishing timed word between them can use the same timed language inclusion tests in [5, 24] (or using the technique of complementation and intersection of automata). The following theorem is adapted from [28].

Theorem 4. *The execution of Algorithm 2 terminates, and each stable hypothesis is at least as good as the previous one according to the metric function.*

3.5 Counterexample Minimization

When the equivalence query is answered using a decision procedure, the decision procedure can usually return counterexamples of small size. In fact, existing work on symbolic automata [23] introduces the concept of *helpful teacher* to indicate the ability of the teacher to return a minimal counterexample (which is a counterexample of minimal length and also minimal with respect to lexicographic order). Under this assumption, the learning algorithm for symbolic automata has better theoretical properties.

In the case of exact learning of DOTA, the correctness and termination of the algorithm [5] do not depend on being provided minimal counterexamples. However, the actual performance of the algorithm can still be significantly affected. In particular, if the counterexample is not minimal, it can lead to unnecessary splitting of edges in the learned model. For example, a guard $[5, \infty)$ on a transition can be unnecessarily split into $[5, 7)$ and $[7, \infty)$ on two transitions, if the learner is provided with a counterexample with time value 7 first, whereas directly providing a counterexample with time value 5 will not lead to splitting. This is particularly significant in the case of normal teacher, as its complexity is exponential in the number of edges in the learned model.

Hence, we propose a simple heuristic for improving a counterexample using only membership queries. First, when performing PAC-style equivalence queries, samples are tested in increasing order by length. When a minimal length counterexample (as a delay-timed word) is found, it is minimized according to lexicographic order as follows. We first run the timed word on the hypothesis, obtaining the corresponding logical-timed word. Then, for each transition of the logical-timed word starting from the beginning, we decrease the logical time step-by-step, at each step converting back to delay-timed word using the reset information and send the result as a membership query. The new delay-timed word is kept only if it is still a counterexample. Note this procedure finds locally minimal counterexamples, but is not guaranteed to find the globally minimal one.

3.6 The Whole Procedure

Integrating the previously introduced techniques, the overall learning framework is summarized in Algorithm 3. As described in Sect. 2.2, the learner performs several rounds of membership queries to make the observation table $\mathbf{T}$ prepared (closed and consistent) before constructing a new hypothesis. Then, the comparator is used to make sure that the current stable hypothesis always approaches the target system according to the metric function in Definition 5, which reduces the number of equivalence queries. On the stable hypothesis, PAC-style equivalence query is performed by testing. The whole procedure repeats until the PAC-style equivalence query terminates without finding a counterexample, so the hypothesis is considered correct with some probability of error. Since the new learning procedure only modifies the equivalence query, the main theoretical results from [5] still hold. This allows us to state the following main correctness theorem for the new procedure. Note that in [21,23] for the case of symbolic automata, termination is only with probability 1 if the alphabet is infinitely divisible. In our case, the endpoints of guards are integers, hence the algorithm is guaranteed to terminate.

Algorithm 3: PAC Learning of DOTAs

---

    input : timed observation table **T**; error ϵ; confidence δ.
    output: hypothesis $\mathcal{H}$, which is a PAC(ϵ,δ)-correct output for the target timed language $\mathcal{L}$.
1 Initialize timed observation table **T**;
2 Make **T** closed and consistent;
3 Construct a hypothesis $\mathcal{H}'$ from **T**;
4 $\mathcal{H} \leftarrow \mathcal{H}'$;   // initial stable hypothesis
5 $equivalent \leftarrow \perp$;
6 $i \leftarrow 0$;   // the number of PAC-style equivalence queries
7 **while** $equivalent = \perp$ **do**
8   **if** $i > 0$ **then**
9 $\mathcal{H} \leftarrow$ comparator($\mathcal{H}, \mathcal{H}'$);   // current stable hypothesis
10 $i \leftarrow i + 1$;
11 $equivalent, ctx \leftarrow$ pac_equivalence($\mathcal{H}, i, \epsilon, \delta$);   // PAC equivalence query
12   **if** $equivalent = \perp$ **then**
13   ctx_processing(**T**, ctx);   // handle counterexample
14   Make table **T** closed and consistent;
15   Construct a hypothesis $\mathcal{H}'$ from **T**;
16 **return** $\mathcal{H}$;

Theorem 5. *Algorithm 3 terminates after polynomial number of membership and PAC-style equivalence queries, and learns the target system in a probably approximately correct manner with error ϵ and confidence δ.*

4   Extending PAC Learning to Normal Teacher

In this section, we extend the algorithm given in [5] for the case of normal teacher to the PAC learning setting. The needed changes are similar to the smart teacher case, with each equivalence query for a hypothesis constructed from a prepared table candidate replaced by a PAC-style equivalence query. It should be noted that the count i of current equivalence query still increases with each query, regardless of the tree structure caused by the guesses. This can be justified as follows: in the derivation of Eq. (3), the number of needed queries is set so that the total probability of making a mistake (resulting in a model with error greater than ϵ) is at most δ, with $\delta/2^{i+1}$ being the bound on the probability of making a mistake at the i-th equivalence query. In the normal teacher setting, we should still accumulate the probabilities of making mistakes along different branches of the tree, so the derivation of Eq. (3) is still the same as before. As for the improvements reported in Sect. 3, they are still applied to the normal teacher setting. While in counterexample minimization, we run the timed word on the hypothesis, obtaining the corresponding logical-timed word based on the guessed resets.

The theoretical results (following [5]) are similar to the smart teacher case, except the complexity is now exponential due to the guessing of resets.

Theorem 6. *The learning process for the normal teacher terminates after exponential number of membership and PAC-style equivalence queries, and learns the target system in a probably approximately correct manner with error ϵ and confidence δ.*

In a variant of the above procedure, we can also group prepared table candidates by level, for example by the number of guesses made. If there are m_i tables at level i, then the number of samples for each PAC-style equivalence query at level i is modified to be $\frac{1}{\epsilon}(\ln\frac{1}{\delta}+(i+1)\ln 2+\ln m_i)$. We can also consider pruning the search tree by removing table candidates that appear to be less promising, for example with lower passing rate at the current iteration (which is similar to the genetic programming method in [26, 29]). With such a pruning method, we obtain a procedure that is sound but not necessarily complete or terminating.

5   Implementation and Experimental Results

In order to further investigate the efficiency and scalability of the proposed methods, we implemented a prototype in PYTHON and evaluated it on the functional specification of the TCP protocol and a set of randomly generated DOTAs. All of the experiments were carried out on a MacBook Pro with 8 GB RAM, Intel Core i5 with 2.7 GHz and running macOS Catalina 10.15.3. The tool and experiments are available in the tool page https://github.com/MrEnvision/learning_OTA_by_testing.

5.1   TCP Protocol

We refer to [5] for a state diagram specifying the state changes in the functional specification of the TCP protocol. It can be represented as a DOTA $\mathcal{A}$ (see Appendix D of [4]) with $|Q| = 11$ locations, $|\Sigma| = 10$ untimed actions, $|F| = 2$ final locations, and $|\Delta| = 19$ transitions with appropriately specified timing constraints including guards and resets. With our sampling method, comparator, and counterexample minimization, we run the prototype on this example 30 times with the error parameter $\epsilon = 0.001$ and confidence parameter $\delta = 0.001$ in the smart teacher setting. Our tool learned out 30 PAC(ϵ, δ)-correct DOTAs in which 28 models are exactly correct. In theory, the remaining two models should have at least 0.999 accuracy with confidence 0.999. In order to further check the quality of the remaining two models, we test them on 20000 more samples generated from the same distribution in the learning process. Both models have a passing rate of at least 0.9999. The minimum, mean and maximum numbers for membership and PAC equivalence queries are 608, 717.3, 912 and 18, 18.7, 20, respectively. The minimum, mean and maximum numbers of tests in the PAC equivalence queries are 107925, 122565.2 and 143806. The average time of learning is 138.9 s.

5.2   Random Experiments

We continue to use the random DOTAs in [5] to evaluate our PAC learning method. Additionally, we compare the performances with and without each of our three improvements, i.e. the specific sampling mechanism, the comparator and the counterexample minimization method.

Evaluation Results on Benchmark. With our specific sampling method, comparator, and counterexample minimization method, the experimental results on the benchmark are shown in Table 1. For each case, we run our tool 10 times and our tool learns all models in the corresponding PAC settings and sometimes generates a model which is exactly equivalent to the target model. The number of tests taken is also quite stable across the random trials, with minimum and maximum numbers usually within 50% of each other in each case.

Table 1. Experimental results on random examples for the smart teacher situation.

Case ID	$|\Delta|$	ϵ, δ	#Membership			#Equivalence			#Tests			n_{exact}	r_{pass}	t_{mean}
			N_{min}	N_{mean}	N_{max}	N_{min}	N_{mean}	N_{max}	N_{min}	N_{mean}	N_{max}			
4_4_20	18	0.001	167	173.1	181	28	29.3	30	418765	455798.8	487670	4	0.999945	90.2
4_4_20	18	0.01	140	161.5	178	23	26.7	29	26084	34647.1	41470	0	0.999460	34.5
7_2_10	18	0.001	471	561.1	781	28	31.6	39	333340	424286.5	592363	0	0.999964	88.6
7_2_10	18	0.01	375	487.4	717	23	26.5	31	21024	27676.6	36805	0	0.999695	24.8
7_4_10	26	0.001	746	766.5	796	46	47.7	51	533562	569403.8	618769	3	0.999995	133.8
7_4_10	26	0.01	729	778.0	853	46	48.0	50	49473	54829.8	63353	0	0.999960	59.8
7_6_10	32	0.001	676	832.7	1035	53	61.3	68	749773	1025486.9	1274129	4	1.0	341.5
7_6_10	32	0.01	678	807.7	998	54	58.2	63	72714	87215.3	101603	1	0.999870	137.3
7_4_20	26	0.001	419	442.2	480	41	42.4	43	599115	648487.5	690735	5	0.999986	160.7
7_4_20	26	0.01	382	451.6	733	36	38.8	42	44183	50828.7	62079	0	0.999860	101.0
10_4_20	36	0.001	682	935.5	1492	59	67.2	82	607149	816399.8	1233177	10	1.0	267.4
10_4_20	36	0.01	732	1029.4	1369	56	63.4	77	51185	69562.7	100264	2	0.999960	159.5

Case ID: n_m_κ, consisting of the number of locations, the size of the alphabet and the maximum constant appearing in the clock constraints, respectively, of the corresponding model.
$|\Delta|$: the number of transitions in the corresponding model.
ϵ, δ: the error and confidence parameters in PAC learning. (Here choose a same value.)
#Membership & #Equivalence & #Tests: the number of conducted membership queries, PAC-style equivalence queries and tests utilized in equivalence queries, respectively. N_{min}: the minimal, N_{mean}: the mean, N_{max}: the maximum.
n_{exact}: the number of exactly learned model.
r_{pass}: the average passing rate of the learned model on extra 20000 test cases randomly generated from the same distribution in the learning process.
t_{mean}: the average wall-clock time in seconds, including that taken by the learner and the teacher.

With/Without Specific Sampling Method. We evaluated our tool on the TCP protocol case study and the random examples by replacing the specific sampling method (Sect. 3.3) with sampling from a naïve uniform distribution. As expected, the algorithm also returns with models which are PAC(ϵ, δ)-correct outputs according to the naïve uniform distribution. However, the learned models sometimes have big differences with the target model even when choosing high accuracy and confidence. For example, when we choose $\epsilon = \delta = 0.001$ and sample testing timed words from the uniform distribution $U(1, 2 \cdot |Q|)$ in the TCP protocol case, the tool learned out models without some transitions back to the initial state which is one of the accepting states.

With/Without Comparator. As introduced in Sect. 3.4, the comparator could reduce the number of equivalence queries, and hence the number of test cases needed in such queries. We evaluated our tool without the comparator, and the number of PAC-style equivalence queries and test cases increased by 10% on average.

With/Without Counterexample Minimization. Figure 1 shows the experimental results with and without counterexample minimization for some of the randomly generated examples. We find that the number of PAC-style equivalence queries and tests increased by around 150% and 400% respectively. Hence, counterexample minimization improves the learning performance significantly on the random examples.

Evaluation on Random Example in Normal Teacher Setting. Finally, we evaluate the PAC-style learning method in the normal teacher situation. The results are shown in Table 2. As the method still depends on the quality of the provided counterexamples, a few of the cases can no longer be learned within the time limit of 2 min, compared to the case of exact equivalence query. Overall, the results still show that our method is effective in the normal teacher setting, which most importantly, provides a way to implement a teacher in practice.

6   Related Work

Various attempts have been carried out in the literature on learning timed models, which can be divided into two directions. The first direction is about passive learning. An algorithm was proposed to learn deterministic real-time automata in [33]. A passive learning algorithm for timed automata with one clock was further proposed in [32]. We furthermore refer the readers to [22,25] for learning specialized forms of practical timed systems in a passive manner. A common weakness of passive learning is that the generated model merely accepts all positive traces and rejects all negative ones for the given set of traces, without guaranteeing that it is a correct model of the target system. As to active learning, a learning algorithm for event recording automata [3] is proposed in [16]. The underlying learning algorithm has double-exponential complexity. In [19], Lin et al. proposed an efficient learning method for the same model. Learning techniques for symbolic automata are introduced in [12,20] and An et al. applied the techniques to learning real-time automata [6].

Recently, applying the ideas of PAC learning [31] to model learning is receiving increasing attention. Angluin introduced a PAC learning algorithm of DFA in [7]. In [21], Maler et al. applied PAC learning to symbolic automata. In [10], using PAC learning to obtain an approximate regular model of the set of feasible paths in a program, Chen et al. introduced a novel technique for verification and model synthesis of sequential programs. Another way to replace exact equivalence queries is conformance testing [8,18] via a finite number of testing queries. Well-known methods for conformance testing include W-method [11,15], UIO-method [27], etc. These methods can also be modified to test timed models [13,14]. In [29], Aichernig et al. introduced an approach to learn timed automata based on genetic programming. In subsequent work [26], they combined genetic programming with conformance testing to improve its performance.

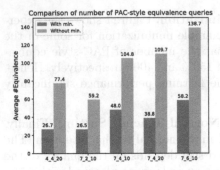 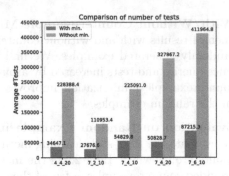

Fig. 1. Experimental results with and without counterexample minimization.

Table 2. Experimental results on random examples for the normal teacher situation.

Case ID	$|\Delta|_{\text{mean}}$	ϵ, δ	#Membership			#Equivalence			t_{mean}	$\#T_{explored}$	#Learnt	n_{exact}
			$N_{\min}$	N_{mean}	$N_{\max}$	$N_{\min}$	N_{mean}	$N_{\max}$				
3_2_10	4.8	0.001	63	142.0	346	5	7.6	12	4.8	96.3	9/10	6
4_2_10	6.8	0.001	128	224.2	394	6	13.0	19	10.3	200.2	9/10	6
5_2_10	8.8	0.001	155	308.1	534	9	15.0	20	12.6	292.6	7/10	7
6_2_10	11.9	0.001	96	446.0	661	9	16.0	22	19.9	454.4	7/10	4

#Membership & #Equivalence: the number of conducted membership and equivalence queries with the cached methods, respectively. $N_{\min}$: the minimal, N_{mean}: the mean, $N_{\max}$: the maximum.
$|\Delta|_{\text{mean}}$: the average number of transitions in the corresponding group.
$\#T_{explored}$: the average number of the explored table instances.
#Learnt: the number of the learnt DOTAs in the group (learnt/total).

7   Conclusion

In this paper, we presented a PAC learning algorithm for black-box systems that can be specified by DOTAs. We relax the ideal setting of a teacher that maintains oracles for both membership queries and exact equivalence queries. In our new setting, both membership and equivalence queries are conducted via testing, with PAC-style equivalence query replacing exact equivalence query. In addition, to reduce the number of equivalence queries, we introduced comparator into our learning framework. We also discussed the sampling approach, and a heuristic method to minimize counterexamples. A prototype is implemented in PYTHON, and is evaluated on the functional specification of the TCP protocol as well as a set of randomly generated examples. The experiments show the positive effects of each of the improvements on realistic examples. Possible future work includes extension to timed automata with multiple clocks.

References

1. Aichernig, B.K., Tappler, M.: Efficient active automata learning via mutation testing. J. Autom. Reason. **63**(4), 1103–1134 (2019)
2. Alur, R., Dill, D.L.: A theory of timed automata. Theor. Comput. Sci. **126**(2), 183–235 (1994)
3. Alur, R., Fix, L., Henzinger, T.A.: Event-clock automata: a determinizable class of timed automata. Theor. Comput. Sci. **211**(1), 253–274 (1999)
4. An, J., Chen, M., Zhan, B., Zhan, N., Zhang, M.: Learning one-clock timed automata (full version). arXiv:1910.10680 (2019)
5. An, J., Chen, M., Zhan, B., Zhan, N., Zhang, M.: Learning one-clock timed automata. In: Biere, A., Parker, D. (eds.) TACAS 2020. LNCS, vol. 12078, pp. 444–462. Springer, Cham (2020). https://doi.org/10.1007/978-3-030-45190-5_25
6. An, J., Wang, L., Zhan, B., Zhan, N., Zhang, M.: Learning real-time automata. Science China Information Sciences, in press. https://doi.org/10.1007/s11432-019-2767-4
7. Angluin, D.: Learning regular sets from queries and counterexamples. Inf. Comput. **75**(2), 87–106 (1987)
8. Berg, T., Grinchtein, O., Jonsson, B., Leucker, M., Raffelt, H., Steffen, B.: On the correspondence between conformance testing and regular inference. In: Cerioli, M. (ed.) FASE 2005. LNCS, vol. 3442, pp. 175–189. Springer, Heidelberg (2005). https://doi.org/10.1007/978-3-540-31984-9_14
9. van den Bos, P., Smetsers, R., Vaandrager, F.: Enhancing automata learning by log-based metrics. In: Ábrahám, E., Huisman, M. (eds.) IFM 2016. LNCS, vol. 9681, pp. 295–310. Springer, Cham (2016). https://doi.org/10.1007/978-3-319-33693-0_19
10. Chen, Y.F., et al.: PAC learning-based verification and model synthesis. In: ICSE 2016, pp. 714–724. IEEE (2016)
11. Chow, T.S.: Testing software design modeled by finite-state machines. IEEE Trans. Softw. Eng. **4**(3), 178–187 (1978)
12. Drews, S., D'Antoni, L.: Learning symbolic automata. In: Legay, A., Margaria, T. (eds.) TACAS 2017. LNCS, vol. 10205, pp. 173–189. Springer, Heidelberg (2017). https://doi.org/10.1007/978-3-662-54577-5_10
13. En-Nouaary, A., Dssouli, R., Khendek, F.: Timed WP-method: testing real-time systems. IEEE Trans. Softw. Eng. **28**(11), 1023–1038 (2002)
14. En-Nouaary, A., Dssouli, R., Khendek, F., Elqortobi, A.: Timed test cases generation based on state characterization technique. In: RTSS 1998, pp. 220–229. IEEE (1998)
15. Fujiwara, S., Bochmann, G.V., Khendek, F., Amalou, M., Ghedamsi, A.: Test selection based on finite state models. IEEE Trans. Softw. Eng. **17**(6), 591–603 (1991)
16. Grinchtein, O., Jonsson, B., Leucker, M.: Learning of event-recording automata. Theor. Comput. Sci. **411**(47), 4029–4054 (2010)
17. Howar, F., Jonsson, B., Vaandrager, F.: Combining black-box and white-box techniques for learning register automata. In: Steffen, B., Woeginger, G. (eds.) Computing and Software Science. LNCS, vol. 10000, pp. 563–588. Springer, Cham (2019). https://doi.org/10.1007/978-3-319-91908-9_26
18. Lee, D., Yannakakis, M.: Principles and methods of testing finite state machines-a survey. Proc. IEEE **84**(8), 1090–1123 (1996)

19. Lin, S.-W., André, É., Dong, J.S., Sun, J., Liu, Y.: An efficient algorithm for learning event-recording automata. In: Bultan, T., Hsiung, P.-A. (eds.) ATVA 2011. LNCS, vol. 6996, pp. 463–472. Springer, Heidelberg (2011). https://doi.org/10. 1007/978-3-642-24372-1_35

20. Maler, O., Mens, I.-E.: Learning regular languages over large alphabets. In: Ábrahám, E., Havelund, K. (eds.) TACAS 2014. LNCS, vol. 8413, pp. 485–499. Springer, Heidelberg (2014). https://doi.org/10.1007/978-3-642-54862-8_41

21. Maler, O., Mens, I.-E.: A generic algorithm for learning symbolic automata from membership queries. In: Aceto, L., Bacci, G., Bacci, G., Ingólfsdóttir, A., Legay, A., Mardare, R. (eds.) Models, Algorithms, Logics and Tools. LNCS, vol. 10460, pp. 146–169. Springer, Cham (2017). https://doi.org/10.1007/978-3-319-63121-9_8

22. Mediouni, B.L., Nouri, A., Bozga, M., Bensalem, S.: Improved learning for stochastic timed models by state-merging algorithms. In: Barrett, C., Davies, M., Kahsai, T. (eds.) NFM 2017. LNCS, vol. 10227, pp. 178–193. Springer, Cham (2017). https://doi.org/10.1007/978-3-319-57288-8_13

23. Mens, I.: Learning regular languages over large alphabets. (Apprentissage de langages réguliers sur des alphabets de grandes tailles). Ph.D. thesis, Grenoble Alpes University, France (2017). https://tel.archives-ouvertes.fr/tel-01792635

24. Ouaknine, J., Worrell, J.: On the language inclusion problem for timed automata: closing a decidability gap. In: Proceedings of the 19th IEEE Symposium on Logic in Computer Science, LICS 2004, pp. 54–63. IEEE Computer Society (2004)

25. Pastore, F., Micucci, D., Mariani, L.: Timed k-Tail: automatic inference of timed automata. In: Proceedings of 10th IEEE International Conference on Software Testing, Verification and Validation, ICST 2017, pp. 401–411. IEEE Computer Society (2017)

26. Pferscher, A., Aichernig, B., Tappler, M.: From passive to active: learning timed automata efficiently. In: NFM 2020 (2020). https://ti.arc.nasa.gov/events/nfm-2020/

27. Shen, Y.N., Lombardi, F., Dahbura, A.T.: Protocol conformance testing using multiple UIO sequences. IEEE Trans. Commun. 40(8), 1282–1287 (1992)

28. Smetsers, R., Volpato, M., Vaandrager, F.W., Verwer, S.: Bigger is not always better: on the quality of hypotheses in active automata learning. In: ICGI 2014, pp. 167–181 (2014). http://proceedings.mlr.press/v34/smetsers14a.html

29. Tappler, M., Aichernig, B.K., Larsen, K.G., Lorber, F.: Time to learn – learning timed automata from tests. In: André, É., Stoelinga, M. (eds.) FORMATS 2019. LNCS, vol. 11750, pp. 216–235. Springer, Cham (2019). https://doi.org/10.1007/ 978-3-030-29662-9_13

30. Vaandrager, F.: Model learning. Commun. ACM 60(2), 86–95 (2017)

31. Valiant, L.G.: A theory of the learnable. Commun. ACM 27(11), 1134–1142 (1984)

32. Verwer, S., De Weerdt, M., Witteveen, C.: The efficiency of identifying timed automata and the power of clocks. Inf. Comput. 209(3), 606–625 (2011)

33. Verwer, S., de Weerdt, M., Witteveen, C.: Efficiently identifying deterministic real-time automata from labeled data. Mach. Learn. 86(3), 295–333 (2011). https:// doi.org/10.1007/s10994-011-5265-4

Learning Fault Models of Cyber Physical Systems

Teck Ping Khoo[1]($\boxtimes$), Jun Sun[2], and Sudipta Chattopadhyay[1]

[1] Singapore University of Technology and Design, Singapore, Singapore
teckping_khoo@mymail.sutd.edu.sg, sudipta_chattopadhyay@sutd.edu.sg
[2] Singapore Management University, Singapore, Singapore
junsun@smu.edu.sg
https://www.smu.edu.sg/, https://www.sutd.edu.sg/

Abstract. Cyber Physical Systems (CPSs) comprise sensors and actuators which interact with the physical environment over a computer network to achieve some control objective. Bugs in CPSs can have severe consequences as CPSs are increasingly deployed in safety-critical applications. Debugging CPSs is therefore an important real world problem. Traces from a CPS can be lengthy and are usually linked to different parts of the system, making debugging CPSs a complex and time-consuming undertaking. It is challenging to isolate a component without running the whole CPS. In this work, we propose a model-based approach to debugging a CPS. For each CPS property, active automata learning is applied to learn a fault model, which is a Deterministic Finite Automata (DFA) of the violation of the property. The L* algorithm (L*) will find a minimum DFA given the queries and counterexamples. Short test cases can then be easily extracted from the DFA and executed on the actual CPS for bug rectification.

This is a black-box approach which does not require access to the PLC source code, making it easy to apply in practice. Where source code is available, the bug can be rectified. We demonstrate the ease and effectiveness of this approach by applying it to a commercially supplied miniature lift controlled by a Programmable Logic Controller (PLC). Two bugs were discovered in the supplier code. Both of them were patched with relative ease using the models generated. We then created 20 mutated versions of the patched code and applied our approach to these mutants. Our prototype implementation successfully built at least one model for each mutant corresponding to the property violated, demonstrating its effectiveness.

Keywords: Debugging · Active automata learning · L* algorithm · Programmable logic controllers

Cyber Physical Systems (CPSs), being distributed and embedded systems, are the drivers of modern applications such as smart buildings, smart healthcare,

Supported by TÜV SÜD Asia Pacific Pte Ltd.

S.-W. Lin et al. (Eds.): ICFEM 2020, LNCS 12531, pp. 147–162, 2020.
https://doi.org/10.1007/978-3-030-63406-3_9

highly automated driving and Industry 4.0. As such, bugs in CPSs can have severe or fatal consequences. Debugging CPSs is therefore an important real world problem with ongoing research efforts.

Existing methods for debugging CPSs fall into the category of simulation, offline debugging, and online debugging. Debugging by simulation works by injecting suspicious inputs into a CPS simulator and checking the output. Simulating the CPS generally requires developing a representative digital twin. It is usually hard to simulate the physical processes accurately. Offline debugging by log file analysis works by gathering large amounts of log files produced by the CPS. Normal and buggy traces are then compared to determine which variables are not changing in the expected way and causing the bug. Usually, the buggy traces mostly contain information irrelevant to the bug, and filtering them away can be difficult. Online debugging by setting breakpoints works by instrumenting a debugger with the CPS in real-time, and setting breakpoints in the CPS's program execution to determine the faulty input. Setting breakpoints may interfere with the buggy behavior being rectified. Additionally, for effective debugging, these breakpoints should be set in multiple components of the CPS. Getting logging to work in a distributed system is hard due to synchronization issues.

We aim to simplify the debugging of a CPS by developing a two-step methodology to build fault models of the CPS:

1. For each CPS property, develop an oracle which accepts a buggy sequence of inputs and rejects a normal one.
2. Apply active automata learning to build one DFA for each CPS property using its oracle, using suitable parameters, for debugging. Repeat Step 1 if needed till the fault model evolves into a sufficient representation of the bug.

L* [1] iteratively generates test sequences of inputs to the PLC, which may or may not lead to an error. The algorithm will automatically and systematically build a small DFA which generalizes all the various ways that the fault can be reproduced up to some number of steps. If none of the test sequences end in an error, then the returned DFA will simply have a single rejecting state. The returned DFA can provide a concise representation of the bug to the test engineer - instead of just knowing one sequence to reproduce the bug by testing, *the engineer now knows multiple shorter sequences to do so.*

We conducted a case study using a PLC-controlled miniature elevator system which was delivered with its specifications. Initial testing of this system revealed that it contained a number of bugs. For example, during some operation, it was possible for its doors to open while it was moving - a clear safety violation. Due to the system complexity, both the test engineers and the vendors have struggled to identify the cause of the bug for months. By specifying just two inputs, which are calling for levels 1 and 2 from the lift car, we were able to learn a fault model with only four states for this bug. After recovering the PLC source code from the PLC, we were able to fix the bug in a day.

In short, we make the following technical contributions:

1. We developed a two-steps model based approach to debugging a CPS. Given a particular property of the system, an extended L* algorithm is used to build a

minimum DFA which capture sequences of events which lead to the violation of this property, up to some number of steps and with suitable parameters. Bug-relevant short test cases can then be extracted from these models to aid in debugging the system.

2. We demonstrate the usefulness of this approach by applying it to study and patch multiple actual bugs in a miniature lift.
3. We demonstrate the effectiveness of our framework via comparison with random testing to fix the two actual CPS bugs. The comparison reveals that our framework consistently provided shorter test cases compared to random testing. Additionally, we statically analysed the source code of the PLC and mutated it to generate 20 bugs. Each mutant was created to trigger a violation of at least one of the ten CPS properties of interest. The expected fault models were all generated.
4. We share on how to select parameters when performing active automata learning on real systems.

Organization. The rest of this paper is organized as follows: Sect. 1 describes the system motivating our study. Section 2 gives an overview of our approach. Section 3 describes how we implemented our approach on the miniature lift. Section 4 poses and addresses some research questions. We evaluated our approach by applying it to debug some supplier PLC source code successfully. We also share the results of applying our approach to 20 mutations of the patched PLC source code. In Sect. 5 we review related work. Lastly, in Sect. 6 we conclude and provide some suggestions for further work.

1   System Description

The system under test is a fully functioning miniature lift developed for training purposes. This system was commercially purchased for the development of smart lift technologies. The system has four lift levels, a level sensor at each floor, a slow-down sensor in between each floor, a traction machine, a pulley system, door motors, buffer stops, and buttons for the lift car and at every floor for user input. The lift is controlled by a Mitsubishi FX3U-64M PLC and comes programmed as a double-speed lift. Upon moving off, a default normal speed will be used. If it reaches a slow-down sensor and if the next floor is to be fulfilled, a default slow speed shall be used. Each time the lift passes a slow-down sensor, the displayed floor will also be updated. This PLC has 32 input devices which are named as X0–X7, X10–X17, X20–X27, and X30 to X37. It has 32 output devices which are named as Y0–Y7, Y10–Y17, Y20–Y27, and Y30 to Y37.

Our approach does not require the source code. However, source code is needed for actual bug fixing. A Mitsubishi toolkit was used to extract the ladder logic source code from the PLC for analysis. This code comprises 1,305 rungs, Rungs 1 to 309 specifies the application, while the remaining rungs define 39 sub-routines named as P0 to P37, and P42. The comments for the program were not provided by the suppliers - as is a common practice for suppliers after

Table 1. PLC inputs of interest

	Purpose	Logic		Purpose	Logic
X17	L1 pressed	Normally Off	X1	Lift car is level with a floor	Normally Off
X20	L2 pressed	Normally Off	X2	Slowdown sensor active	Normally Off
X21	L3 pressed	Normally Off	X10	Lift car is at L4	Normally On, Off at L4
X23	L4 pressed	Normally Off	X11	Lift car is at L1	Normally On, Off at L1

Table 2. PLC Outputs of Interest

	Purpose		Purpose
Y2	Commands the doors to open	Y12	Switches the car L3 button light
Y3	Commands the doors to close	Y13	Switches the car L4 button light
Y6	Commands the lift to rise	Y30	Lights and dims the up display
Y7	Commands the lift to lower	Y31	Lights and dims the down display
Y4	Commands the lift to move slow	Y32	Shows L1 as the current floor
Y5	Commands the lift to move fast	Y32, Y33	Shows L3 as the current floor
Y10	Switches the car L1 button light	Y33	Shows L2 as the current floor
Y11	Switches the car L2 button light	Y34	Shows L4 as the current floor

system delivery, for protection of their intellectual property. Written approval to use their source code in a research paper was provided by the suppliers.

Table 1 summarizes the input devices, name, purpose and logic of the PLC's key inputs of interest, derived from both the system specifications as well as empirical observations. On the panel representing the lift car buttons, four of the inputs are for L1 to L4, and two are for door open and close. There is an "up" button on L1 and a "down" button on L4. There are "up" and "down" buttons on both L2 and L3, making a total of 12 user buttons. We selected only the four lift car buttons for L1 to L4 to reduce the experiments' complexity. Note that using these four buttons can already move the lift to all the four floors, as well as open and close the doors.

Table 2 provides a summary of the PLC's outputs of interest.

The system was originally purchased for the development of smart lifts technology - which could not proceed for a year due to the discovery of two bugs:

1. Occasionally, the lift doors can open while the lift is moving
2. Occasionally, the lift doors do not open after arriving at a floor

The suppliers were also unable to fix the bug despite extended manual debugging. This work was therefore motivated by actual limitations in debugging methodologies for CPS.

2   Overview

Figure 1 shows an overview of our approach. A fault model is learnt for each test oracle developed. Test cases are recovered from the fault model for debugging.

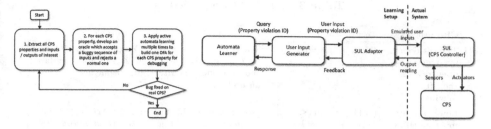

Fig. 1. Overview of approach   **Fig. 2.** Automata learning setup

2.1 Step 1 - Develop Oracles

Table 3 provides the system properties which we derive from the system specification and lift standards. The system inputs/outputs of interest are provided in Tables 1 and 2.

Testing requires a pass criteria, known as an oracle. We apply a *derived* test oracle, which categorizes buggy and normal behaviour by reading the outputs of the CPS. These output signals are systematically processed to evaluate real time state variables to determine if each oracle passed or failed. The last column of Table 3 provides the developed oracles corresponding to the system properties. Although this step is always system specific, it can be generalized to other CPSs by gathering the correct output signals and processing them according to the needs of the defined oracles.

2.2 Step 2 - Apply Active Automata Learning

Debugging assumes a fault which is reproducible using a minimal set of inputs. A key contribution of our work is the development of the framework to apply L* to a real system to learn a small DFA of the fault, which is beyond a straightforward deployment of the algorithm. Issues such as the modular design of the learning setup, equivalence query approximation, redundant membership queries and the message passing mechanism were addressed. Figure 2 shows the learning setup, which comprises three main parts - an Automata Learner, a User Input Generator, and a System Under Learning (SUL) Adaptor.

L* learns an unknown DFA using examples and counterexamples made up of an input alphabet Σ. L* will compute and pose membership queries to the SUL to keep an observation table closed and consistent. Once a closed and consistent observation table is achieved, L* generates a hypothesis automaton, for comparison with the actual SUL.

L* requires a *Minimally Adequate Teacher* (MAT) which knows the specification model of the SUL, and is able to exactly answer the equivalence query of whether the hypothesis automata and the SUL are equivalent. In practice, the actual system is the MAT. However, checking whether a hypothesis automaton is equivalent to the actual system is computationally complex. To overcome this,

Table 3. Identified CPS properties

	CPS property	Test oracle		CPS property	Test oracle
1	The lift doors must never be opened while the lift is moving	$(Y6 \vee Y7) \wedge \neg Y2$	6	The correct lift car buttons are always shown at most 1s after an update	Compare Y10, Y11, Y12, Y13 with emulated lift displays
2	Lower the lift must be off at most 1s after the lift reached L1	$(X11 \downarrow \wedge time(\leq 1s)) \wedge Y7 \downarrow$	7	Slow down the lift must be on at most 1s after the slow down sensor is activated, if the current floor is demanded	$((X2 \uparrow \wedge time(\leq 1s) \wedge curr\ flr\ demanded) \wedge \uparrow Y4$
3	Raise the lift must be off at most 1s after the lift reached L4	$(X10 \downarrow \wedge time(\leq 1s)) \wedge Y6 \downarrow$	8	Lower or raise the lift must be off at most 5s after slow down the lift is on	$(Y4 \uparrow \wedge time(\leq 5s)) \wedge (Y6 \downarrow \vee Y7 \downarrow)$
4	The correct floor is always shown at most 1s after an update	Compare Y32, Y33 and Y34 with emulated lift floor	9	If raise or lower the lift is off, it is always done at most 1s after the level sensor is activated	$(Y6 \downarrow \vee Y7 \downarrow) \Rightarrow (X1 \uparrow \wedge time(\leq 1s))$
5	The correct direction of travel is always shown at most 1s after an update	Compare Y30 and Y31 with emulated lift direction	10	Open the doors must be on at most 5s after the raise or lower the lift is off	$((Y6 \downarrow \vee Y7 \downarrow) \wedge time(\leq 5s)) \wedge Y2 \uparrow$

we implemented an approximate way of answering equivalence queries based on depth-bounded search. For each hypothesis automaton, *all* traces up to a maximum number of steps, which we denote as N, from the start state are extracted. In this algorithm, paths which end in an accepting state are not searched any further for new paths.

The User Input Generator will take the needed query from the learner and command the SUL Adaptor to execute the inputs one by one over the configured inter-input duration, τ. This parameter is both SUL and bug dependent. The value of τ must be realistic for actual CPS operation. Certain bugs, especially timing-related ones, can be triggered only if a specific sequence of inputs are injected fast enough. While the query is being executed, at any time, the SUL Adaptor can report back that the property being tested has been violated. In this case, subsequent remaining inputs of the query are not sent to the SUL Adaptor. Otherwise, if no fault has been detected, after the last input of the query has been executed, the SUL Adaptor will wait for the last I/O timeout of Ds. If there is still no fault detected, the SUL Adaptor will notify the User Input Generator that the last query has timed-out without fault.

During development, it was observed that on rare occasions, it is possible for a membership query to return true (or false) in one run but false (or true) in another run. This may be due to slight variances in hardware behavior (especially timings), or deeper issues in PLC coding, such as double coil syndrome [2]. We recognize that L* works only for deterministic systems. However, we observed that the non-deterministic behavior of our system is rarely observed, and therefore, our approach can still be applied but requires redundant membership queries for reliable model learning. A mechanism is implemented in the User Input Generator to provide more reliable membership query executions. All membership queries are executed at least twice. If both return the same result (both true or both false), it is fed back to the learner for continued model learning. However, if the results differ (one true and the other false), a third execution of the same query is done and its result is fed back to the learner. This reliability is achieved at the cost of doubling the query execution time, but is deemed to be worthwhile because L* will build a totally different model even if just one of the query results is different from a previous run.

The SUL Adaptor implements the actual execution of an input on the PLC, as well as the emulation of the sensor inputs. Note that the emulation is not needed if the actual CPS is being used to test the controller. In the running state, all the PLC outputs are read and the emulated lift states, which are the lift car and door positions, are updated based on these outputs. The property specified by the query received from the User Input Generator shall then be checked for violation. When either events - the needed property violation is detected or the query timed out - the SUL Adaptor will wait for reset input. It shall then inform the User Input Generator accordingly and wait for it to issue a command to execute a reset of the PLC. Once the command has been issued, the SUL Adaptor will reset the PLC and inform the User Input Generator after it is completed, so that the User Input Generator can send the next query. All the SUL Adaptor's relevant internal variables are reset as well, for a fresh cycle of query execution. In summary, Table 4 shows the parameters and their default values used by our framework and all experiments.

2.3   Illustration

We illustrate our framework using the first bug - that occasionally, the lift doors can open while the lift is moving. Throughout this paper, the default parameter values are $\Sigma = \{a, b, c, d\}$, $N = 3$, $\tau = 0.5$ s and $D = 8$ s, as shown in Table 4. The overheads incurred are shown in the last row of Table 11. Building these models required 351 queries which took almost two and a half hours. Table 5 shows the three automata built by L*. These DFAs were learnt by L* maintaining its membership tables, iteratively keeping it closed and consistent, and coming up with a hypothesis automaton when this is achieved. The short test cases generated from this DFA are ba, ca and da. Knowing that the initial state is at L1, and that the delay between inputs $\tau = 0.5$ s, the bug can be interpreted as being triggered after an input demanding that the lift move to some floor other than L1 (inputs b,c or d) is set, wait 0.5 s (the value of τ), and then press L1 (the input a). It can be inferred that the bug is due to a command to move the lift (inputs b, c or d) and the command to open the door (input a) being executed very near in time (0.5 s). A possible bug fix is to provide an interlock on these two commands, which was found to fix the bug. Further details about this bug fix can be found in Sect. 4.

Table 4. Parameters

Parameter	Meaning	Default
Σ	Automata Alphabet(set of inputs)	{a,b,c,d}
N	Maximum number of steps from the start state for equivalence query approximation	3
τ	Inter-input duration	0.5 s
D	Last I/O timeout	8 s

Table 5. Hypothesis fault models of Bug 1

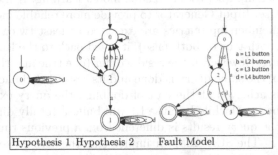

a = L1 button
b = L2 button
c = L3 button
d = L4 button

Hypothesis 1   Hypothesis 2   Fault Model

3   Implementation

This section provides details of the implementation of our approach to fix bugs found in the miniature lift system.

The overall learning system is run by a mini computer. This device uses the quad-core 64-bit 1.44 Ghz Intel Atom X5-Z8350 processor with 2 GB of RAM. Relay switches were used to switch the user and sensor input terminals on the PLC to 24V (on) and 0V (off), based on the learning traces provided by L*. A simple switch detection circuit was used to capture the PLC's outputs.

We adopt LearnLib [11] to implement our approach. LearnLib is a Java-based framework popular for active automata learning. We built the automata learner on top of LearnLib using Apache Maven [3] in the Eclipse IDE [4]. The parameters Σ and N are used by the Automata Learner. Table 6 shows the implemented alphabet Σ used by the Automata Learner. We have previously justified the use of these button inputs in the *System Description* section. The maximum number of steps from the start state, N, used for our equivalence query approximation, is 3. This is based on our observation that certain bugs in the SUL can already be triggered in two steps - we therefore only require the hypothesis and the unknown automata to be compared up to three steps to be able to get meaningful fault models.

The parameter τ, which is the inter-input duration, is used by the User Input Generator and is both SUL and bug dependent. We selected τ as 0.5 s after some testing, as this value is deemed to be essential to trigger certain bugs in the SUL. In general this is the minimum sampling duration, and in this case, a reasonable approximation for reproducing the bug.

The SUL Adaptor parameter D, which is the last I/O timeout, is used by the SUL Adaptor and is both SUL and bug dependent. We observed that the longest idling duration in the normal PLC operation, meaning that the PLC is no getting any input/output, is about 6 s. This is the period of time that the door has fully opened, and is waiting for its internal timer to expire, before being commanded to close the door. We need to set D to be longer than this duration to prevent cutting off the PLC's normal operation, and settled on $D = 8$ s.

The PLC has a pre-programmed reset state which shows only L1, provided X1, X3, X4, X5, X10, X16 and X22 are active. For L*, we require a means to reset the PLC before each query and selected the Mitsubishi proprietary MELSEC Communications Protocol (MC Protocol) [6].

We used MQTT as the transport protocol which delivers messages among the Automata Learner, User Input Generator and SUL Adaptor. MQTT is a lightweight protocol designed to be used by Internet-of-Things (IoT) devices. We selected it due to its ease of implementation and support for publish and subscribe. The selected MQTT broker is Mosquitto [7].

4   Research Questions and Experiments

In this section, we shall systematically evaluate the effectiveness and efficiency of our approach. We address the following research questions:

1. How effective is our approach in debugging a real CPS?
2. Does increasing the size of the alphabet Σ increase the time overhead significantly?
3. Can our approach effectively reduce the length of discovered buggy traces?
4. Can our approach find bugs effectively?

It is important to assess the effectiveness of our debugging framework on a real CPS, as a comparison with manual debugging. Studying the relationship between the size of the alphabet and the time overheads provides a practical bound on how many CPS inputs can be used to build fault models in a realistic time frame. Studying the reduction in the length of the discovered buggy traces provides a basis for comparing with normal testing. Finally, the effectiveness of our approach should be studied to prove that our approach can build fault models of bugs of a variety of nature.

As an optimization, a basic emulation of the lift sensor inputs to the PLC was developed to filter away irrelevant inputs caused by reading the actual inputs directly - therefore the emulation does not have to be very precise. The emulated lift's state variables are the car speed and position, door speed and position, buttons state, current floor and motion state.

4.1   How Effective Is Our Approach in Debugging a Real CPS?

We answer this question by using our framework to debug the two observed bugs in the lift controller. These bugs violates Properties 1 and 10 respectively. As a baseline, at least one other property which is not observed to be violated should be included in this experiment, and we randomly pick Property 2. We need to test that our framwork can build a "no fault model" for a specified property, meaning a DFA without any accepting states, if the property is never violated in all membership queries. If such a model cannot be built for a property, this means that the property is falsifiable based on the experimental parameters - at least one input sequence will cause a property violation.

<table>
<tr><td colspan="3">Table 6. Alphabet Σ</td></tr>
</table>

PLC Input	Purpose	Symbol
X17	Lift car L1 button	a
X20	Lift car L2 button	b
X21	Lift car L3 button	c
X23	Lift car L4 button	d

Table 7. Code versions

Code version	Representation
"A"	Supplier Code
"B"	Version "A" patched with the fix for Bug 1 (violation of Property 1)
"C"	Version "B" patched with the fix for Bug 2 (the violation of Property 10)

For this research question, we opted for a reduced alphabet $\Sigma = \{a, b\}$ for simplicity, meaning that we only press the lift car buttons for L1 and L2. This is deemed to be enough to trigger violations of Properties 1, 2, and 10. For clarity, we use a notation to represent the version of the code used for debugging, as shown in Table 7.

We use the notation $M_{code\_version, property}$ to denote the DFA built. For example, $M_{A,1}$ is the DFA built using code version "A" and set with property 1. Table 8 shows the models built.

Table 8. Fault models from code version "A"

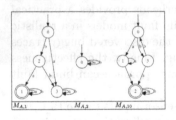

Table 9. Fault models from code version "B"

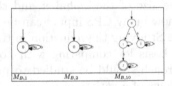

The regular expression for $M_{A,1}$ is $ba(a|b)*$. Interpreting this expression requires knowing that the fixed time interval between inputs, τ, is 0.5 s. This means that the steps to trigger this violation are: start from the reset state, press L2, wait for 0.5 s, press L1, and thereafter press 0 or more L1 or L2. The violation will be triggered after pressing the first L1. Using this knowledge, we were able to get many relevant, short traces for triggering the violation of Property 1. Moreover, by looking at $M_{A,1}$, it is clear that after the inputs ba, it does not matter how often or what inputs are provided to the system - the bug will be triggered. Knowing that the test starts when the lift is at L1, the input b causes Y6 to be activated (lift rise) while the input a will cause Y2 to be activated (doors open). The bug is patched by adding a check that the lift is not commanded to move up (Y6) or down (Y7) when it is being commanded to open its doors (Y2). In ladder logic, the symbol -||- represents a check that a device is switched on. The symbol -|/|- represents that it is switched off. Figure 3 shows the bug fix.

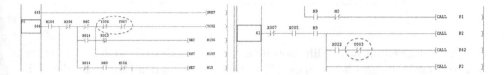

Fig. 3. Patch for Bug 1   **Fig. 4.** Patch for Bug 2

The model $M_{A,2}$ does not have an accepting state and is the "no fault" model. This is expected as the violation of Property 2 was not observed for code version "A". By observation, the controller is in a fault state after the violation of Property 1, ie after the lift door opens while the lift is in motion. This means that after the Bug 1 has occurred, L* will learn a model based on Bug 1 occurring first, followed by Bug 2. Therefore there is no value analysing $M_{A,10}$ at this stage - The model built from violating Property 10 should be analysed after Bug 1 is fixed.

Table 9 shows the models built after applying the patch for Bug 1 (and therefore getting code version "B") and running our framework.

Both $M_{B,1}$ and $M_{B,2}$ are now the "no fault" model. This confirms that code version "B" fixes Bug 1. For debugging Bug 2, which is the violation of Property 10, the reading of internal PLC device values is needed and we used MC protocol. From $M_{B,10}$, its regular expression is $(a+)b(a|b)*$. Bearing in mind that $\tau = 0.5$ s, the steps to trigger this violation are: start from the reset state, press L1 at least once, wait 0.5 s, press L2, then press 0 or more L1 or L2. By looking at $M_{B,10}$, it is clear that after the inputs ab, the bug will occur no matter how often or what inputs are provided. There must be some differing occurrence that a, b will cause, compared to another simple word like b, which is clearly rejected by $M_{B,10}$. On deeper analysis, the input a will open the door at L1. The bug happens when b is input 0.5 s after that. The bug does not happen if a does not occur before b. Some internal variable must have been set wrongly after a occurred - leading to the door being unable to open when the lift moved to L2 later on.

We used the discovered test cases to execute buggy runs of the PLC program, as well as some normal runs. For these runs, we used MC Protocol to log the PLC variables deemed needed for debugging. Both sets of logs were compared to identify variances. Analysis of the faulty runs uncovered that the device Y2 (to open the doors) was not activated due to the auxiliary device M104 being off. This was in turn due to the devices M105 and M106 being off, which was due to Y3 (door close) remaining active from L1 to L2, turning off only at L2. We guessed that to fix this bug, we need to add a check that Y3 needs to be off before the subroutine P42 (which moves the lift up or down) is called. Checking

Table 10. Fault models built from code version "C"

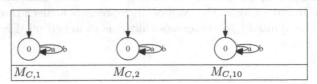

$M_{C,1}$ $M_{C,2}$ $M_{C,10}$

that Y3 is turned off before lift movement will turn on M105 and M106, which will turn on M104 and hence allow Y2 to be activated when the lift reaches L2. Figure 4 shows the bug fix.

Table 10 shows the models built after applying the patch for Bug 2 (and therefore getting code version "C") and running our framework:

As can be seen, running our framework on code version "C" yielded $M_{C,1}$, $M_{C,2}$ and $M_{C,10}$ which are all the "no fault" model. This confirms that code version "C" fixed Bug 2. From this effort, we are confident that our approach is able to fix actual CPS bugs.

4.2 Does Increasing the Size of the Alphabet Σ Increase the Time Overhead Significantly?

In order to answer this question, we ran our framework for the two actual bugs with varying alphabet sizes. As explained previously, Code version "A" was used to model Bug 1 while code version "B" was used to model Bug 2. Tables 11 and 12 show the results.

As expected, increasing the alphabet size increases the learning time significantly. As a rule, the choice of inputs should include only the ones which are deemed likely to cause the bug.

Table 13 shows the fault model of Bug 1 built from the respective alphabets, as well as the regular expression representing the model.

4.3 Can Our Approach Effectively Reduce the Length of Discovered Buggy Traces?

To address this question, we apply normal debugging on the two actual bugs. This is done by repeatedly sending inputs randomly picked from $\Sigma = \{a, b, c, d\}$ to the system. The interval between sending the inputs is randomly picked from 0.5 s to 30 s in steps of 0.5 s. These values are selected to simulate normal debugging inputs. When a bug is triggered, the system is reset and the process is repeated. The results of the tests are shown in Table 14.

Comparing these results with the alphabet $\Sigma = \{a, b, c, d\}$ in Tables 11 and 12, there is a reduction in the mean length of buggy queries. For Bug 1, normal debugging had a mean buggy query length of 215.6 while applying our framework required only 3.6. For Bug 2, the same measure was 55.6 for normal debugging and 4.1 for our framework. Therefore, while our framework requires upfront effort

Table 11. Alphabet size and overheads for actual Bug 1

Σ	# of Queries	# of States	Mean length of buggy queries	Total learning time
1 {a, b}	29	4	3.71	20.7 min
2 {a, b, c}	64	5	3.57	1 h 4.3 min
3 {a, b, c, d}	109	4	3.6	2 h 25.1 min

Table 12. Alphabet size and overheads for actual Bug 2

Σ	# of Queries	# of States	Mean Length of Buggy Queries	Total Learning Time
1 {a, b}	32	4	4.25	30.7 min
2 {a, b, c}	66	4	4.14	1 h 19.7 min
3 {a, b, c, d}	118	4	4.1	2 h 51.0 min

Table 13. Fault models of Bug 1 built from various alphabet sizes

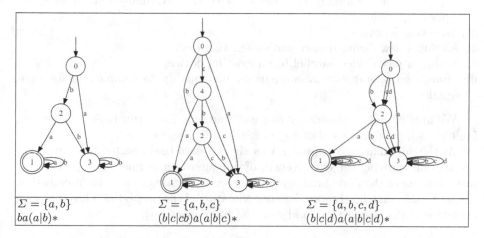

$\Sigma = \{a, b\}$	$\Sigma = \{a, b, c\}$	$\Sigma = \{a, b, c, d\}$
$ba(a|b)*$	$(b|c|cb)a(a|b|c)*$	$(b|c|d)a(a|b|c|d)*$

to be set up and tweaked correctly, it can be seen that the reduction in the mean length of buggy queries, as compared to normal, can be significant.

4.4   Can Our Approach Find Bugs Effectively?

The best way to measure the effectiveness of our framework is to apply it to a CPS with many actual bugs which affect the majority of the system requirements. However, despite our best efforts, we found only two actual bugs in the system and they pertained only to the lift and door motion. Therefore, we take code version "C" and mutated it 20 times. We did basic static analysis to ensure that each mutation causes at least one of the identified properties to be violated. This ensures that the mutations affect the majority of system requirements. To ensure that the mutation actually causes a bug, each mutation was tested on the actual system and the expected property was observed to be violated.

The static analysis and mutation were done by identifying a device directly or indirectly related to the bug, and applying some mutation to that device. The following shows the ways mutation was applied:

Table 14. Random testing results

	Bug 1	Bug 2
Number of buggy queries	9	12
Mean length of buggy queries	215.6	55.6
Total time taken	8 h 7 min	2 h 43 min

1. Replacing a device with another device
2. Replacing the "Normally On" device with the "Normally Off" device, i.e. replace -||- with -|/|-
3. Removing a device
4. Adding a new device in series to an existing device
5. Adding a new device parallel to an existing device
6. Change an operator from comparison for equality to comparison for non-equality

We applied our methodology to these mutants. Each run built at least one fault model, making a total of 36 models.

At the minimum, our approach was able to learn the expected fault model of the mutant, proving the effectiveness of our approach in finding bugs. In some instances, more than one fault model was learnt by a mutant - this means that the mutation can trigger more than one violation of the properties. Our approach therefore works as expected, and can find bugs effectively.

5   Related Work

From [8], the concept of Model Based Debugging assumes the existence of a system model which precisely captures the specified system behavior. A fault model is captured by directly observing the system. A comparison of the system model and the fault model will then yield insights into the explanation of the bug. Our work deviates slightly from the established concept - in that we do not have a system model, but rather, for example, a well-known proposition about the system that the lift doors cannot open while the lift is in motion.

From [9], the authors formulated a two-step framework for model based debugging of a PLC - In the first step, the desired, sequence of PLC outputs will be learnt by a Recurrent Neural Network (RNN). From [10], Aral et al. showed that an RNN can model an finite state machine. The captured buggy PLC output will be learnt by another RNN. In the second step, these two RNNs will then be used to train an Artificial Neural Network (ANN) which can then be used to debug the PLC. A small ladder logic diagram representing a clamp, punch and eject manufacturing system was used to demonstrate the concept. This methodology assumes the existence of the correctly specified system model, from which outputs can be recovered so as to build the specification-based RNN.

Marra et al. [12] reported their experience in applying online debugging of a CPS. The Pharo debugger [13] and the author's IDRA [14] remote debuggers were used to debug a CPS, which is a simple temperature sensing system built by the authors. The authors applied online debugging remotely, i.e. from another machine. They classified remote debugging into "traditional", represented by the use of the Pharo debugger, and "out-of-place", represented by the use of the IDRA debugger. The authors concluded that for this case study, using IDRA is faster than Pharo, at the expense of increased network activity.

6 Conclusion

We believe that bug reproduction is an important first step to debugging, especially for a graphical programming language like ladder logic which makes code step-through a painful experience due to its lack of familiar programming constructs. This paper reports our experience in applying a two-step methodology to determine the minimum sequence of inputs to reproduce a bug, by building a fault model of the system under testing. We believe that this methodology is applicable to other systems of varying nature, provided that the identification of the system properties of interest and the inputs/outputs is done correctly.

Testing the system for bug reproduction can be done either passively or actively, although the latter is preferred because system control brings with it the possibility of triggering the bug faster and expedites data collection. Moreover, system control is mandatory if the bug causes the system to become inoperable after occurrence, and such is the case for our miniature lift.

A simulator such as Safety Critical Application Development Environment (SCADE) with Design Verifier [5] can be explored in future. The combination of using graphical models to capture system logic and a proof assistant provides the possibility of exhaustively proving some system propositions. Active automata learning can also be applied to the system to learn a comprehensive system model. This allows testers to iteratively refine the system model. The resulting model can then be put to use for test case generation or system verification. A comparison of various approaches, such as the use of ANN or graph analysis, to capture a model of a PLC program should be done as well.

References

1. Angluin, D.: Learning regular sets from queries and counterexamples. Inf. Comput. **75**(2), 87–106 (1987). https://doi.org/10.1016/0890-5401(87)90052-6
2. Unknown. Double Coil Syndrome In Plc Ladder logic and how to cure it (2017). http://electrodoctrine.blogspot.com/2017/02/double-coil-syndrome-though-sound-like.html. Accessed 4 May 2020
3. Miller, F.P., Vandome, A.F., McBrewster, J.: Apache Maven. Alpha Press (2010)
4. Eclipse Foundation. The Platform for Open Innovation and Collaboration (2020). https://www.eclipse.org/. Accessed 4 May 2020
5. Inc ANSYS. SCADE Suite (2020). https://www.ansys.com/products/embedded-software/ansys-scade-suite. Accessed 4 May 2020

6. Mitsubishi. MELSEC Communication Protocol Reference Manual (2017). http://www.int76.ru/upload/iblock/9c0/q_l_series_reference_manual_communication_protocol_english_controller.pdf. Accessed 4 May 2020
7. Light. Mosquitto: server and client implementation of the MQTT protocol. J. Open Source Softw. **2**(13), 265 (2017). https://doi.org/10.21105/joss.00265. Accessed 4 May 2020
8. Mayer, W., Stumptner, M.: Model-based debugging - state of the art and future challenges. Electron. Notes Theoret. Comput. Sci. **174**(4), 61–82 (2007). ISSN 1571–0661, https://doi.org/10.1016/j.entcs.2006.12.030
9. Abdelhameed, M.M., Darabi, H.: Diagnosis and debugging of programmable logic controller control programs by neural networks. In: IEEE International Conference on Automation Science and Engineering, Edmonton, Alta, pp. 313–318 (2005). https://doi.org/10.1109/COASE.2005.1506788
10. Aral, K., Nakano, R.: Adaptive scheduling method of finite state automata by recurrent neural networks. In: Proceeding of the Fourth International Conference on Neural Information Processing, Dunedin, New Zealand, pp. 351–354 (1997)
11. Merten, M., Steffen, B., Howar, F., Margaria, T.: Next generation learnlib. In: Abdulla, P.A., Leino, K.R.M. (eds.) TACAS 2011. LNCS, vol. 6605, pp. 220–223. Springer, Heidelberg (2011). https://doi.org/10.1007/978-3-642-19835-9_18
12. Marra, M., et al.: Debugging cyber-physical systems with pharo: an experience report. In: Proceedings of the 12th edition of the International Workshop on Smalltalk Technologies (IWST 2017), p. 10. ACM, New York, Article 8 (2017). https://doi.org/10.1145/3139903.3139913
13. Pharo. Pharo: The Immersive Programming Experience. Pharo Board. https://pharo.org/web. Accessed 23 Sept 2019
14. Marra, M.: IDRA: An Out-of-place Debugger for non-stoppable Applications. http://soft.vub.ac.be/Publications/2017/vub-soft-ms-17-01.pdf. Accessed 23 Sept 2019

VARF: Verifying and Analyzing
Robustness of Random Forests

Chaoqun Nie, Jianqi Shi, and Yanhong Huang[✉]

Hardware/Software Co-design Technology and Application Engineering Research
Center, National Trusted Embedded Software Engineering Technology Research
Center, East China Normal University, Shanghai, China
chaoqun.nie@ntesec.ecnu.edu.cn, {jqshi,yhhuang}@sei.ecnu.edu.cn

Abstract. With the large-scale application of machine learning in various fields, the security of models has attracted great attention. Recent studies have shown that tree-based models are vulnerable to adversarial examples. This problem may cause serious security risks. It is important to verify the safety of models. In this paper, we study the robustness verification problem of Random Forests (RF) which is a fundamental machine learning technique. We reduce the verification problem of an RF model into a constraint solving problem solved by modern SMT solvers. Then we present a novel method based on the minimal unsatisfiable core to explain the robustness over a sample. Furthermore, we propose an algorithm for measuring Local Robustness Feature Importance (LRFI). The LRFI builds a link between the features and the robustness. It can identify which features are more important for providing robustness of the model. We have implemented these methods into a tool named VARF. We evaluate VARF on two public datasets, demonstrating its scalability and ability to verify large models.

Keywords: Formal verification · Random Forests · Robustness

1 Introduction

Machine learning (ML) has been widely used in many domains due to its outstanding performance. However, some popular machine learning models demonstrably lack reliability and security. For example, recent studies have proved that neural network models are susceptible to adversarial perturbations—a small input perturbation causes the model to produce an incorrect output [12,21,26]. This issue hinders the adoption of machine learning in many application domains. Therefore, the problem of verification of machine learning models has attracted the attention of AI and formal verification communities.

Formal methods play a vital role in the field of security verification. Verification techniques such as model checking and theorem proving have been successfully applied to find bugs in software, analyze hardware systems, and verify the security-related properties of models. Some ideas and methods have been proposed that address the verification of ML models by formal methods [13,18,25].

© Springer Nature Switzerland AG 2020
S.-W. Lin et al. (Eds.): ICFEM 2020, LNCS 12531, pp. 163–178, 2020.
https://doi.org/10.1007/978-3-030-63406-3_10

In the same vein, the goal of this work is to verify the robustness of random forests based on Satisfiability Modulo Theories (SMT) [1].

Random Forests (RF) [2] as an important example of tree-based models has been used in many security applications [9,15,19,22]. However, it is also vulnerable to adversarial perturbations [5,14,24,27]. In this paper, we not only effectively verify the robustness of RF, but also make a further study on the factors influencing the robustness. For example, which features have a greater impact on the robustness? Is there any difference in robustness between different classes of the model when their accuracy is similar? Through our experiments, we have discovered that there may be a difference in the robustness for different classes, which provides a good suggestion for other research related to model robustness verification [11,18,27]. We implemented our method in a tool named VARF and evaluated it on public datasets. The contributions of this paper are summarized as follows:

- We have developed the tool VARF for verifying the robustness of large random forests models.
- We propose a method for explaining the robustness over a sample by obtaining the robust feature set.
- We provide a method of measuring local robustness feature importance to reflect the impact of features on the robustness of classes.

The remainder of this paper is organized as follows. We survey related work in Sect. 2. Section 3 presents preliminary knowledge about robustness properties and satisfiability modulo theories. In Sects. 4 and 5, we encode random forests models and robustness properties into SMT formulas. In Sect. 6, we introduce the concept of robust feature set and local robustness feature importance in detail. Section 7 presents applications of our method on two case studies. Finally, we conclude in Sect. 8, which discusses the implications of our work and some ideas about future work.

2 Related Work

Security and interpretability of machine learning models are gaining attention in the research community. In the following, we group the related works in two categories: those that verify the tree-based models, and those that explain models.

We first review works related to the verification for tree-based models. The Silas is introduced by [4] for supporting logical analysis and verification of tree-based models. The Model Audit module of Silas can formally verify the model against user specifications. Sato et al. [24] leverage an SMT solver to extract the violation range in which the input value leads to the failure, then they create an input filter based on that range for preventing the failure occurring in the tree-based model. In their study, they focus on addressing the regression problem, whereas we are focused on classification. In [6], they formulate the verification problem of tree ensembles as a max-clique problem on a multi-partite graph. Then they further propose a multi-level algorithm based the boxicity of the graph to compute robustness bound. But we are concerned with the robustness of a given perturbation value. Einziger et al. [11] verify the robustness of gradient boosting trees using an SMT solver. Törnblom et al. [27] present a formal verification method for tree ensembles that leverage an abstraction-refinement approach to verify the robustness. The main disadvantage of their approach is low scalability.

For the interpretability of machine learning models, the authors of [3] propose a novel automated reasoning based approach which can extract valuable insights from machine learning models. Then the user can learn about the reason behind the decision-making of the models. Several researchers [8,29] try to approximate the complex model with a simpler model for providing a better understanding. Several local methods [17,23] try to probe the model's behaviour without needing to access the internal representation. They learn how the model's output changes over a perturbation distribution in the locality and infer the importance of varying the inputs from the resulting output values. In addition, example-based explanation methods [16,28] can select particular instances of the dataset to explain the behavior of machine learning models or to explain the underlying data distribution.

The goal of our work is not only to verify the robustness of random forests models but also to obtain more internal influence factors of the robustness. Notably, because our method is exact and does not rely on any approximations to the tree structure, the result of the verification is more accurate.

3 Preliminaries

In this section, we give several basic definitions of robustness properties and introduce some preliminary knowledge about satisfiability modulo theories.

3.1 Robustness Properties

Adversarial inputs enable adversaries to subvert the expected model behavior that leads to undesired consequences and could pose a security risk when these models are deployed in the real world. The robustness ensures that the decision of the model is invariant against small perturbations. More formally, let $M(x)$ represent the output of a model M on the input x and $label(x)$ be the true class of x.

Definition 1 (Adversarial Robustness). *A model M is $(\epsilon, p)-robust$ for an input x, if only if there does not exist an adversarial input x', $M(x) = label(x)$, $||x - x'||_p \leq \epsilon$, such that $M(x') \neq label(x)$.*

Here, the variable $label(x)$ indicates that we only consider the robustness of samples which are correctly predicted by model M. $||x - x'||_p \leq \epsilon$ restricts the distance between x and x' according to the norm p. In this paper, we consider the case of norm $p = \infty$, which bounds the maximum perturbation of each feature between x and x', has been considered frequently in the literature [5,6,11,18].

Another definition of robustness is proposed by [18]. It is called universal adversarial robustness. The property captures the robustness over a set of input values. Let N denote a set of input values, then we can define this similar property as follows:

Definition 2 (Universal Adversarial Robustness). *A model M is (ρ, ϵ, p)-universally robust over N, if it has at least $\rho \cdot |N|$ input values in N for which the (ϵ, p) − robust property holds.*

3.2   Satisfiability Modulo Theories

Satisfiability Modulo Theories (SMT) refer to the problem of determining whether a propositional formula is satisfiable with respect to some logical theory. A $\Sigma - theory$ T is a pair (Σ, A) where Σ is a signature and A is a class (in the sense of set theory) of Σ-models, that is closed under variable reassignment. A Σ-formula ϕ is T-satisfiable (resp., T-unsatisfiable) if it is satisfied by some (resp., no) interpretations in A. Furthermore, we use the linear real arithmetic theory in this paper. Then we extend the propositional formula with arithmetic terms and comparison operators. Let Ψ be an arithmetic term where c is a rational number constant. A Boolean formula F can be defined below:

$$\Psi := c \mid \Psi + \Psi \mid \Psi - \Psi \mid \Psi * \Psi \mid \Psi \div \Psi$$
$$F := \top \mid \bot \mid \Psi < \Psi \mid \Psi \le \Psi \mid \Psi = \Psi \mid \Psi > \Psi \mid \Psi \ge \Psi \mid \neg F \mid F \wedge F \mid F \vee F$$

A formula F is said to be satisfiable if F evaluates to True for some assignments. If there is no such assignment, we say that F is unsatisfiable.

4   Encoding of Decision Trees and Random Forests

This section provides the essential definitions of decision trees and their ensembles for classification. Then we consider the encoding of RF into Boolean formulae.

4.1   Decision Tree

Definition of Decision Tree. A decision tree T is an input-output model represented by a tree structure. It can be defined as a function $t : X^d \rightarrow Y^m$, from an input vector $x \in X^d$ where $x = <a_1, ..., a_d>$ taking its values to an output $y \in Y^m$. We denote by X^d the feature space and Y^m the outcome space. In this paper, we consider T as a binary classification tree.

The tree is composed of internal nodes and terminal nodes called leaves. Let N be the set of internal nodes and L be set of leaves. Any internal node $n \in N$ represents a subset of the space X^d, with the root node being X^d itself. Each node $n \in N$ is labeled with a univariate feature-threshold pair (a_i, η_i), and it uses the binary split $s_n = (a_i \leq \eta_i)$ to divide its subset into two subsets corresponding to their two children n_l and n_r (left child n_l and right child n_r). The leaves are labeled with the value of the output. The predicted class y for an input x is determined by the value of the leaf reached by x when it is propagated through the tree. In general, the value v_l of leaf l is a set of probabilities corresponding to each class such that $v_l = \{p_i | 0 \leq i \leq m, \sum_{i=0}^m p_i = 1\}$. Each p_i is a probability so it can't be larger than 1. Let $class(max(v_l))$ denote the class with the highest probability in v_l. Any input vector x is associated with a single leaf $l \in L$, such that $t(x) = y = class(max(v_l))$. In the tree T, every node has exactly one predecessor node, except for the root node n_0, which has no predecessor.

Boolean Formula of Decision Tree. Based on the structure of a decision tree T, we can encode it into a Boolean formula. First, we encode a single path in T, let $\omega(l)$ be the leaf formula of a leaf node l and N_l be the internal nodes set between the root node n_0 and the leaf l. Formally, the encoding of $\omega(l)$ can be defined as follows:

$$\omega(l): \bigwedge_{n \in N_l} (s_n) \wedge (o = v_l), s_n = \begin{cases} a_i \leq \eta_i & n_c = n_l \\ a_i > \eta_i & n_c = n_r \end{cases} \tag{1}$$

The variable o is used to constrain the leaf value v_l. The node n_c represents the child of node n, if n_c is the left child (resp., right child), the condition of node n should be $s_n = (a_i \leq \eta_i)$ (resp., $s_n = (a_i > \eta_i)$). Then we can define the tree's decision formula $\Pi(T)$. It can be defined as follows:

$$\Pi(T): \bigvee_{l \in L} \omega(l) \tag{2}$$

Intuitively, $\Pi(T)$ is a disjunction of leaf formulae, where each clause represents a concrete path to one of the leaves in T and its value. An important characteristic of our method is that it is exact and does not rely on any approximations to the tree structure.

4.2   Random Forests Classifier

Random Forests is a combination of decision trees such that each tree depends on the values of a random vector sampled independently. It uses averaging to improve the predictive accuracy and control over-fitting.

Definition of Random Forests Classifier. A random forests classifier C is a collection of k decision trees, that is $C = \langle T_1, ...T_k \rangle$. The predicted class is a vote by the trees in the forest. Without loss of generality, we consider the soft-voting case. For an input $x \in X^d$, the output of each tree is a set of probabilities corresponding to each class, then the ensemble takes predicted class with the highest mean probability estimate across the trees. We use $t_i(x)$ to denote predicted output of tree T_i and $t_i^j(x)$ to denote the probability of class j such that $\sum_{j=1}^{m} t_i^j(x) = 1$ where m is the number of classes. Then we can define the predicted class of C as follows:

$$C(x) = \underset{j}{argmax} \frac{1}{k} \sum_{i=1}^{k} t_i^j(x) \tag{3}$$

CNF Formula of Random Forests. The encoding of RF is a conjunction of encodings of its trees. We use variable o_i to constrain the output $t_i(x)$ of a tree T_i and o_i^j to constrain the probability $t_i^j(x)$ of class j. Let out be the constraint of the predicted class. The entire RF model can be encoded as a Boolean formula $R(x)$ as follows:

$$R(x) : \bigwedge_{i=1}^{k} \Pi(T_i) \wedge \left(out = \underset{j}{argmax} \frac{1}{k} \sum_{i=1}^{k} o_i^j \right) \tag{4}$$

It should be pointed out that the SMT solver can not directly deal with the $argmax$ function. We realized the $argmax$ through the basic functions provided by the solver.

5   Encoding of Robustness Properties

In the previous section, we have encoded the RF model into a CNF formula. Correspondingly, we further construct the Boolean formula of robustness property so that it can be verified on the SMT solver.

5.1   Verifying Adversarial Robustness

By Definition 1, we first encode the $\|x - x'\|_p \leq \epsilon$ into a Boolean formula. Formally, given an input $x = <a_1, ..., a_d>$, the maximum perturbation ϵ, an adversarial input x', then the perturbation constraint formula $\Delta(x, x', \epsilon)$ can be defined as follows:

$$\Delta(x, x', \epsilon) : \bigwedge_{i=1}^{d} |a_i - a_i'| \leq \epsilon \quad (a_i \in x, a_i' \in x') \tag{5}$$

We recall that the CNF formula $R(x)$ of RF contains a variable out. The value of out is the predicted class. So we only need to define $out \neq label(x)$ as the output constraint formula, where label(x) is the true class of x. Then the robustness verification problem of RF is transformed into finding whether there exists an assignment x' for a formula Φ, which is defined as follows:

$$\Phi : R(x') \wedge \Delta(x, x', \epsilon) \wedge (out \neq label(x)) \tag{6}$$

Theorem 1 *Given a random forests model $C = <T_1, ..., T_k>$, an input sample $x \in X^d$, its corresponding robustness formula is Φ. If Φ is satisfiable, then its true assignment $x' \in X^d$ is an adversarial input of the model, and the robustness property (cf. Definition 1) does not hold for model C and the input x. On the contrary, if Φ is unsatisfiable, then the model C is robust with respect to x.*

Proof Assuming that Φ is satisfiable, then there exist true assignments x' and $O = \{o_i | 1 \leq i \leq k\}$. By Formula (4) and (6), we can conclude that $(out \neq label(x))$ holds and every $\Pi(T_i)$ that appears in $R(x')$ holds. Without loss of generality, let us consider the formula $\Pi(T_1)$ of tree T_1 evaluates to True, there is a true assignment $o_1 \subset O$. We first need to prove that the predicted result of the tree T_1 for x' is the assignment o_1, that $t_1(x') = o_1$. By formula (2), there is at least one leaf formula that evaluates to True. Following the definition of the tree, each internal node has only one precursor node except the root node, so we can ensure there is only one leaf formula that evaluates to True. Assume the leaf formula is $w(l_0)$ and the value of the leaf l_0 is v_{l_0}. Then, let us consider the decision process for input x' in the tree T_1. When x' reaches an internal node n, if the feature $a' \in x'$ satisfies the condition $(s_n = (a' \leq \eta)) \in w(l_0)$, x' will be passed to the left child n_l or to the right child otherwise. Starting from the root node, applying the decision rule recursively from the root node, x' will end in the leaf l_0, then $t_1(x') = v_{l_0}$. By Formula (1), we have $o_1 = v_{l_0}$, then we can conclude that $t_1(x') = o_1$. Similarly, we can conclude $t_2(x') = o_2, ..., t_k(x') = o_k$. For the sake of description, we simplify Formula (3) as $C(x') = argmax(T(x'))$. By Formula (4), we have $out = argmax(O)$, then we can conclude that $C(x') = out$. Since $(out \neq label(x))$ is True, so the assignment x' is the adversarial input of the model C. Similarly, if Φ is unsatisfiable indicating there is no such an input x', such that the robustness holds. $\qquad\qquad\qquad\qquad\qquad\qquad\qquad\qquad\qquad\qquad\qquad\quad\square$

Then we can use the SMT solver to determine whether the formula Φ is satisfiable. An UNSAT result means that the property holds. A SAT result indicates that it does not hold and the solver provides a counterexample x'.

5.2 Verifying Universal Adversarial Robustness

By Definition 2, given an RF model C, a set of inputs N, for each $x_i \in N$, we can construct the formula of the adversarial robustness property Φ_i, and verify if at least ρ-fraction of the inputs are robust in N. The property can be encoded as:

$$\bigwedge_{i=1}^{|N|} (\Phi_i \Leftrightarrow q_i) \wedge \sum_{i=1}^{|N|} q_i \geq \rho \cdot |N| \qquad\qquad (7)$$

6 Robust Feature Set and Local Robustness Feature Importance

This section is concerned with the relationship between features and the robustness property. Firstly, we introduce the notion of robust feature set (RFS). The

RFS can be used to explain the robustness over a single sample. Then we propose an algorithm for computing the local robustness feature importance (LRFI) which reflects the impact of features on the robustness of classes.

6.1   Robust Feature Set

In the current verification of the robustness of tree-based models, when the robustness verification fails, the verifier will return a counterexample, but when the verification succeeds, no explanation information is given. So we purpose a method to explain why the sample is still identified correctly when features are permuted. In other words, we identify which features really affect the robustness of the model. As a similar study, Chen et al. [6] showed that their algorithm could find unimportant features, where any changes to one of those features alone cannot alter the prediction. Their findings suggest that for a sample, features may have different effects on its robustness. Based on our approach, we get a similar characteristic of features in a sample x by obtaining the *robust feature set* (RFS).

SMT solvers can produce minimal unsatisfiable cores (MUC) which is a subset of the original sub-formula. MUC is used to prove unsatisfiability. When we verify the robustness over sample x, we pass Φ into SMT solver, and an UNSAT result indicates that a property holds, the solver can return the MUC of Φ. Formally, we define the *robust feature set* as follows:

Definition 3 (Minimal Unsatisfiable Core). *Let F be a CNF formula and F_C be the set of conjuncts in F, $S \subseteq F_C$ is the MUC of F iff whenever F is unsatisfiable, S is unsatisfiable, and there is not $S'' \subset S$ that is also unsatisfiable.*

Definition 4 (Robust Feature Set). *Given an RF model C, an input $x = <a_1, ..., a_d>$ and the maximum perturbation ϵ. Let Φ be the robustness formula and Φ_c be the set of conjuncts in Φ, $\Delta(x, x', \epsilon) \subset \Phi$ be the perturbation constraint formula and Δ be the set of conjuncts in $\Delta(x, x', \epsilon)$. The RFS can be defined as follows:*

1. Φ is unsatisfiable and $S \subseteq \Phi_c$ is the MUC.
2. RFS = $\{a_i|$ a_i is the feature which appears in Δ_s where $\Delta_s \subseteq \Delta$ is the set of clauses existing in $S.\}$

Theorem 2 *Given an RF model C, an input $x \in X^d$ and the maximum perturbation ϵ. If the values of features in the RFS are fixed, the values of any other features are arbitrarily altered, the prediction result of this model on x will not change.*

Proof By Formula (4), we know that *out* is determined by $R(x')$ and $\Delta(x, x', \epsilon)$. With loss of generality, we can convert formula Φ to a formula $\Phi' := R(x') \wedge \Delta(x, x', \epsilon) \Rightarrow (out \neq label(x))$. The formula $R(x')$ depends on the structure of model C, when model C is given, $R(x')$ is fixed. In this case, the satisfiability of formula Φ can be considered as related to $\Delta(x, x', \epsilon)$ only, so we do not need to consider the case of $R(x')$ in this proof.

Let Φ_c be the set representation of the formula Φ'. Then Φ_c can be defined as follows: $\Phi_c = R \cup \Delta \Rightarrow \{o\}$. R is the set of conjuncts in formula $R(x')$, Δ is the set of conjuncts in formula $\Delta(x, x', \epsilon)$ where $\Delta = \{\delta_i | 0 \leq i \leq d, \delta_i = |a_i - a_i'| \leq \epsilon\}$ and $o = (out \neq label(x))$. Assume Φ_c is unsatisfiable and $S \subseteq \Phi_c$ is the MUC. First, we have $\Phi_c \backslash \{o\}$ is satisfiable. Obviously, there is at least one true assignment $x' = x$ that satisfies it. So o must exist in S, that is, $o \in S$. Let $R_s \subseteq R$ be the set of clauses existing in S and $\Delta_s \subseteq \Delta$ be the set of clauses existing in S. Then we have $S = R_s \cup \Delta_s \cup \{o\}$ and $\Phi_c \backslash S = (\Delta \backslash \Delta_s) \cup (R \backslash R_s)$.

By Definition 3 and 4, we can get the RFS which is a set of features that appear in Δ_s. Each feature $a_s \in RFS$ corresponds to a clause of Δ_s. Similarly, each feature $a_o \in X^d \backslash RFS$ also corresponds to a clause of $\Delta \backslash \Delta_s$. The Formula (5) represents the perturbation constraints on the features of input x, if $\delta \in \Delta$ evaluates to True, the perturbation value of the feature a cannot exceed ϵ. On the contrary, if δ evaluates to False, the perturbation value exceeds ϵ. So the True or False of the clause represents the perturbation range of the feature. According to the characteristics of MUS, we have every clause corresponding to each feature $a_o \in X^d \backslash RFS$ does not participate in the unsatisfiability of Φ. Since $S = R_s \cup \Delta_s \cup \{o\}$ is unsatisfiable, we can conclude every $\delta_s \in \Delta_s$ holds, that is, the perturbation value of each feature cannot exceed ϵ. Here we only consider the case where the value of feature is fixed such that every $\delta_s = |a_s - a_s'| = 0$ evaluates to True. Since $\Phi_c = R \cup \Delta \Rightarrow \{o\}$ is unsat, then $\Phi_c' = R \cup \Delta \Rightarrow \neg o$ is valid, $\neg o = (out = label(x))$, that is, the predicted result of the model for x is $label(x)$. □

According to the Theorem 2, if the values of the features in RFS are fixed, any perturbation outside the set cannot change the prediction. In other words, the features in RFS have a greater impact on the robustness over the sample for a disturbance value of ϵ. See Fig. 2.

6.2   Local Robustness Feature Importance

Based on the RFS, we can further analyze the influence of features on the robustness of a specific class (e.g. class "0" in the classification task of MNIST dataset), we introduced the *local robustness feature importance* (LRFI).

Algorithm 1 shows our process for computing LRFI of class y. As input, the algorithm takes an RF model C, a robust testing set N of the class y where robust means the verification results of inputs are UNSAT, the maximum perturbation ϵ, the feature set X^d. It returns LRFI of class y, and proceeds in three basic steps: (1) obtain all the RFS for the samples in testing set N according to Definition 4, then save them into a set S. (2) count the number of occurrences of each feature $a \in X^d$ in S. (3) apply min-max normalization to numbers, then return LRFI, which are normalized within the range [0,1]. Finally, the LRFI for class y is computed as the frequency of feature occurrence in the RFS of all the samples in N.

Algorithm 1: Local Robust Feature Importance of Class y

Input: An RF model C, a robust testing set $N = \{x_i | 0 \le i \le |N|, C(x_i) = y\}$,
     the maximum perturbation ϵ, the feature set $X^d = \{a_i | 0 \le i \le d\}$.

Output: $LRFI$ of class y.

```
 1 begin
 2 │   S ← ∅ ;                                              // S is a set
 3 │   V ← ∅ ;                                              // V is a set
 4 │   forall x ∈ N do
 5 │   │   Φ_x ← R(x') ∧ Δ(x, x', ε) ∧ (out = y) ;
 6 │   │   UNSAT ← solver(Φ_x) ;
 7 │   │   RFS_x ← get the robust feature set of x using Definition 4 ;
 8 │   │   add RFS_x to S ;
 9 │   end
10 │   forall a ∈ X^d do
11 │   │   n_a ← 0 ;         // n_a is the number of feature a occurrence in S
12 │   │   forall RFS_x ∈ S do
13 │   │   │   if a ∈ RFS_x then
14 │   │   │   │   n_a ← n_a + 1 ;
15 │   │   │   end
16 │   │   end
17 │   │   add (a, n_a) to V ;
18 │   end
   │   // obtain the minimum/maximum number of feature occurrences
19 │   min_n = MIN(V) ;
20 │   max_n = MAX(V) ;
21 │   forall (a, n_a) ∈ V do
22 │   │   n'_a ← (n_a − min_n)/(max_n − min_n) ;
23 │   │   add (a, n'_a) to LRFI ;
24 │   end
25 │   return LRFI
26 end
```

The LRFI reflects the influence of features on the robustness of this class in the model. The greater the importance value of features is, the greater the influence of features on the robustness of the class will be, on the contrary, the less the influence will be. Through our experiments, we find that the features altered around the basic shape of the class have a greater impact on its robustness. Compared with the feature located in the shape, the features around the shape are more likely to affect the robustness of the class. See Fig. 3.

7   Experiments and Analysis

We use the scikit-learn implementation of the random forests to deploy our method. We evaluate our methods by verifying the robustness property in two public large scale datasets: MNIST and Fashion-MNIST which can be found on OpenML [20]. Each dataset contains 70,000 images. The images are of size 28 × 28 pixels. Experiments were conducted on a machine with an Intel Core i7-5960X CPU and 32 GB RAM. We have implemented our method in VARF (Verify and Analysis Random Forests) tool based on Python, and the underlying SMT solver is z3 [10]. For each dataset, we randomized the dataset and split it into two subsets: a 80% training set, and a 20% test set. Then we randomly picked 100 images from the test set for each of the 10 classes, the size of each robustness test dataset is 1000. The timeout is 120 s for each instance to solve.

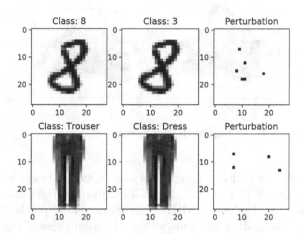

Fig. 1. Adversarial examples.

Figure 1 shows two examples that the adversarial robustness property does not hold for $\epsilon = 1$. The first column represents the original inputs, and the second shows the adversarial sample corresponding to the first. The altered pixels between them are marked in the third column. In the first example, an image of "8" is misclassified as "3". The second example, "Trouser" is misclassified as "Dress". As can be seen from these pictures, the differences are sometimes so small that they are indistinguishable for the human eye. So it is necessary to verify the robustness of RF models.

We show the samples which satisfy the adversarial robustness property with $\epsilon = 3$ from the two datasets in Fig. 2. These samples are correctly identified by the models. The picture on the right shows the RFS of the sample. We mark pixels of RFS with red rectangles. According to our conclusion, keeping the pixels in the robust feature set fixed and flipping any other pixels to any valid value cannot fool the model. According to the characteristic of the RFS, we can use our method to improve the efficiency of the adversarial sample generation technique [7].

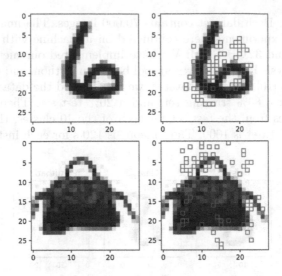

Fig. 2. Robust feature set.

Figure 3 shows the LRFI of different classes in two datasets with $\epsilon = 1$, the left displays the result of class "0" in MNIST and the right shows the result of class "Sneaker" in Fashion-MNIST. The more yellow pixels there are, the greater influence the feature has that affects the robustness of the class. It can be observed that the more influential features are distributed around the basic shape of the class. It's important to note that besides the two classes we present, the others also have the same characteristics.

The line chart Fig. 4 presents the robustness comparison of classes in the two datasets. The left part shows the results of MNIST. We can observe that there are several classes (e.g. class "0", "2", "6", "8") whose robustness rises slightly with the increasing number of trees. The results have an obvious fluctuation in the

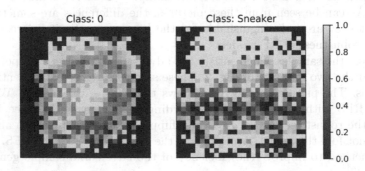

Fig. 3. Local robustness feature importance.

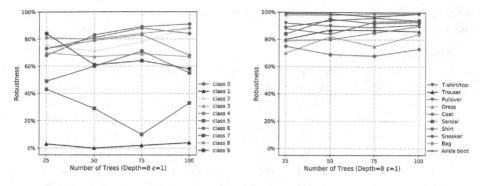

Fig. 4. Robustness of classes.

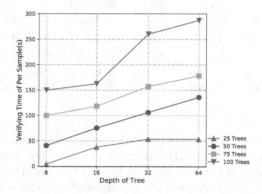

Fig. 5. Verifying time of our method on MNIST.

classes "4", "5", "7", "9". Besides, the robustness of class "1" always stays at a very low value. There is a significant difference between class "1" and the others. The gap is roughly between 40% and 80%. By contrast, the robustness of classes in the Fashion-MNIST (the right part) remains stable overall. However, the class "Shirt" is less robust than the others, and there is no such class whose robustness is very low robustness to pull down the overall robustness. Experimental results show that it is not accurate to focus on the robustness of the model as a whole. Furthermore, it indicates that the robustness verification of the model should be specific to each class to provide model users with a more helpful robustness testing result.

Table 1 summarizes the results for models trained with different parameters for the MNIST dataset. Note that for a fixed tree depth, the portion of failure is negatively correlated with the number of trees and the number of trees does not have an obvious influence on robustness. The verified portion ρ decreases with increasing ϵ because the adversary can leverage the larger ϵ value to construct adversarial images.

Table 1. The robustness of models trained with different parameters for the MNIST dataset.

Trees	Depth	Accuracy	$\epsilon = 1$			$\epsilon = 3$		
			Verified(ρ)	Timeout	Failed	Verified(ρ)	Timeout	Failed
25	5	84%	45.71%	0%	54.29%	9.64%	0.12%	90.24%
50	5	85%	54.68%	0%	45.32%	13.58%	2.69%	83.72%
75	5	86%	48.77%	5.61%	45.61%	9.24%	13.68%	77.08%
100	5	86%	54.07%	14.53%	31.40%	13.02%	21.74%	65.23%
25	8	91%	61.47%	0%	38.53%	9.88%	0.11%	90.01%
50	8	93%	61.02%	0%	38.98%	14.36%	3.02%	82.61%
75	8	92%	63.63%	5.32%	31.05%	12.81%	17.05%	70.14%
100	8	93%	63.48%	15.04%	21.48%	16.86%	24.81%	58.32%
25	10	93%	64.34%	0%	35.66%	14.18%	0%	85.82%
50	10	95%	63.21%	0%	36.79%	17.34%	0.53%	82.14%
75	10	94%	75.32%	5.32%	19.36%	13.83%	4.57%	81.60%
100	10	95%	66.84%	8.74%	24.42%	15.16%	14.21%	70.63%
100	32	96%	78.40%	0%	21.60%	11.70%	0%	88.30%
100	64	98%	54.78%	0%	45.22%	6.40%	0%	93.60%

Performance Analysis. In the paper [11], the authors purpose an optimization method named "safe pruning". The pruning can trim unreachable part of the search space to accelerate the verification for SMT solver. During the encoding of the model, the method removes all unsatisfiable leaf clauses with respect to the maximum perturbation ϵ. We adopt the method to enhance the scalability of VARF. In Fig. 5, it shows the average time of solved sample validation for different scale models. Solved in this context means that VARF can give a definite result instead of timeout for a sample. Obviously, with the increase of scale, the validation time also increases. In Table 1, the verification results of some samples are timeout, which means that SMT solver cannot give a definite result. It indicates the limitations of our method.

8   Conclusions and Future Work

By using our method, we can effectively verify the robustness of random forests models and propose a method to extract the robust feature set of a robust sample to explain the robustness. An algorithm of computing the local robustness feature importance is provided to demonstrate that the impact of features is different based on the robustness of classes. Furthermore, the generated antagonistic samples can be added to the training set to train more robust models.

There are some future work that we would like to explore. It should be possible to combine all the trees into one large tree, and simplify to a slightly smaller tree. Then we can verify the simplified tree, which may increase the scalability of our method. In addition, we will try to verify more reliability-related properties, such as liveness, whether the model will produce certain predicted results if certain features of the input are met.

Acknowledgments. This work is partially supported by STCSM Projects (No. 18QB1402000 and No. 18ZR1411600), SHEITC Project (2018-GYHLW-02012) and the Fundamental Research Funds for the Central Universities.

References

1. Barrett, C., Tinelli, C.: Satisfiability modulo theories. In: Clarke, E., Henzinger, T., Veith, H., Bloem, R. (eds.) Handbook of Model Checking, pp. 305–343. Springer, Heidelberg (2018). https://doi.org/10.1007/978-3-319-10575-8_11
2. Breiman, L.: Random forests. Mach. Learn. **45**(1), 5–32 (2001)
3. Bride, H., Dong, J., Dong, J.S., Hóu, Z.: Towards dependable and explainable machine learning using automated reasoning. In: Formal Methods and Software Engineering - 20th International Conference on Formal Engineering Methods, ICFEM 2018, Gold Coast, QLD, Australia, 12–16 November 2018, Proceedings, pp. 412–416 (2018). https://doi.org/10.1007/978-3-030-02450-5_25
4. Bride, H., Hou, Z., Dong, J., Dong, J.S., Mirjalili, S.M.: Silas: High performance, explainable and verifiable machine learning. CoRR abs/1910.01382 (2019). http://arxiv.org/abs/1910.01382
5. Chen, H., Zhang, H., Boning, D., Hsieh, C.J.: Robust decision trees against adversarial examples. In: Chaudhuri, K., Salakhutdinov, R. (eds.) Proceedings of the 36th International Conference on Machine Learning. Proceedings of Machine Learning Research, vol. 97, pp. 1122–1131. PMLR, Long Beach, California, USA, 09–15 June 2019. http://proceedings.mlr.press/v97/chen19m.html
6. Chen, H., Zhang, H., Si, S., Li, Y., Boning, D., Hsieh, C.J.: Robustness verification of tree-based models. In: Advances in Neural Information Processing Systems, pp. 12317–12328 (2019)
7. Cheng, M., Le, T., Chen, P., Zhang, H., Yi, J., Hsieh, C.: Query-efficient hard-label black-box attack: an optimization-based approach. In: 7th International Conference on Learning Representations, ICLR 2019, New Orleans, LA, USA, 6–9 May 2019. OpenReview.net (2019). https://openreview.net/forum?id=rJlk6iRqKX
8. Chu, L., Hu, X., Hu, J., Wang, L., Pei, J.: Exact and consistent interpretation for piecewise linear neural networks: a closed form solution. In: Proceedings of the 24th ACM SIGKDD International Conference on Knowledge Discovery and Data Mining (2018)
9. Cidon, A., Gavish, L., Bleier, I., Korshun, N., Schweighauser, M., Tsitkin, A.: High precision detection of business email compromise. In: 28th {USENIX} Security Symposium ({USENIX} Security 19), pp. 1291–1307 (2019)
10. de Moura, L., Bjørner, N.: Z3: an efficient SMT solver. In: Ramakrishnan, C.R., Rehof, J. (eds.) TACAS 2008. LNCS, vol. 4963, pp. 337–340. Springer, Heidelberg (2008). https://doi.org/10.1007/978-3-540-78800-3_24
11. Einziger, G., Goldstein, M., Sa'ar, Y., Segall, I.: Verifying robustness of gradient boosted models. In: Proceedings of the AAAI Conference on Artificial Intelligence, vol. 33, pp. 2446–2453 (2019)
12. Goodfellow, I.J., Shlens, J., Szegedy, C.: Explaining and harnessing adversarial examples. In: Bengio, Y., LeCun, Y. (eds.) 3rd International Conference on Learning Representations, ICLR 2015, San Diego, CA, USA, 7–9 May 2015, Conference Track Proceedings (2015). http://arxiv.org/abs/1412.6572

13. Huang, X., Kwiatkowska, M., Wang, S., Wu, M.: Safety verification of deep neural networks. In: Majumdar, R., Kunčak, V. (eds.) CAV 2017. LNCS, vol. 10426, pp. 3–29. Springer, Cham (2017). https://doi.org/10.1007/978-3-319-63387-9_1
14. Kantchelian, A., Tygar, J.D., Joseph, A.: Evasion and hardening of tree ensemble classifiers. In: International Conference on Machine Learning, pp. 2387–2396 (2016)
15. Kharraz, A., Robertson, W., Kirda, E.: Surveylance: automatically detecting online survey scams. In: 2018 IEEE Symposium on Security and Privacy (SP), pp. 70–86. IEEE (2018). https://doi.org/10.1109/SP.2018.00044
16. Kim, B., Koyejo, O., Khanna, R.: Examples are not enough, learn to criticize! criticism for interpretability. In: NIPS (2016)
17. Lundberg, S., Lee, S.I.: A unified approach to interpreting model predictions. In: NIPS (2017)
18. Narodytska, N., Kasiviswanathan, S., Ryzhyk, L., Sagiv, M., Walsh, T.: Verifying properties of binarized deep neural networks. In: Thirty-Second AAAI Conference on Artificial Intelligence (2018)
19. Nelms, T., Perdisci, R., Antonakakis, M., Ahamad, M.: Towards measuring and mitigating social engineering software download attacks. In: 25th {USENIX} Security Symposium ({USENIX} Security 16), pp. 773–789 (2016)
20. OpenML: openml.org. https://www.openml.org. Accessed 2020
21. Papernot, N., McDaniel, P., Jha, S., Fredrikson, M., Celik, Z.B., Swami, A.: The limitations of deep learning in adversarial settings. In: 2016 IEEE European symposium on security and privacy (EuroS&P), pp. 372–387. IEEE (2016)
22. Rafique, M.Z., Van Goethem, T., Joosen, W., Huygens, C., Nikiforakis, N.: It's free for a reason: exploring the ecosystem of free live streaming services. In: Proceedings of the 23rd Network and Distributed System Security Symposium (NDSS 2016), pp. 1–15. Internet Society (2016)
23. Ribeiro, M.T., Singh, S., Guestrin, C.: Anchors: high-precision model-agnostic explanations. In: AAAI (2018)
24. Sato, N., Kuruma, H., Nakagawa, Y., Ogawa, H.: Formal verification of decision-tree ensemble model and detection of its violating-input-value ranges. CoRR abs/1904.11753 (2019). http://arxiv.org/abs/1904.11753
25. Seshia, S.A., Sadigh, D.: Towards verified artificial intelligence. CoRR abs/1606.08514 (2016). http://arxiv.org/abs/1606.08514
26. Szegedy, C., et al.: Intriguing properties of neural networks. In: Bengio, Y., LeCun, Y. (eds.) 2nd International Conference on Learning Representations, ICLR 2014, Banff, AB, Canada, 14–16 April 2014, Conference Track Proceedings (2014). http://arxiv.org/abs/1312.6199
27. Törnblom, J., Nadjm-Tehrani, S.: An abstraction-refinement approach to formal verification of tree ensembles. In: Romanovsky, A., Troubitsyna, E., Gashi, I., Schoitsch, E., Bitsch, F. (eds.) SAFECOMP 2019. LNCS, vol. 11699, pp. 301–313. Springer, Cham (2019). https://doi.org/10.1007/978-3-030-26250-1_24
28. Wachter, S., Mittelstadt, B.D., Russell, C.: Counterfactual explanations without opening the black box: automated decisions and the GDPR. Eur. Econ.: Microeconomics Ind. Organ. eJournal (2017)
29. Zilke, J.R., Loza Mencía, E., Janssen, F.: DeepRED – rule extraction from deep neural networks. In: Calders, T., Ceci, M., Malerba, D. (eds.) DS 2016. LNCS (LNAI), vol. 9956, pp. 457–473. Springer, Cham (2016). https://doi.org/10.1007/978-3-319-46307-0_29

Formal Languages

Type-Based Declassification for Free

Minh Ngo[1,2], David A. Naumann[1], and Tamara Rezk[2(✉)]

[1] Stevens Institute of Technology, Hoboken, USA
[2] Inria, Sophia Antipolis, France
tamara.rezk@inria.fr

Abstract. This work provides a study to demonstrate the potential of using off-the-shelf programming languages and their theories to build sound language-based-security tools. Our study focuses on information flow security encompassing declassification policies that allow us to express flexible security policies needed for practical requirements. We translate security policies, with declassification, into an interface for which an unmodified standard typechecker can be applied to a source program—if the program typechecks, it provably satisfies the policy. Our proof reduces security soundness—with declassification—to the mathematical foundation of data abstraction, Reynolds' abstraction theorem.

1 Introduction

A longstanding challenge for software systems is the enforcement of security in applications implemented in conventional general-purpose programming languages. For high assurance, precise mathematical definitions are needed for policies, enforcement mechanism, and program semantics. The latter, in particular, is a major challenge for languages in practical use. In order to minimize the cost of assurance, especially over time as systems evolve, it is desirable to leverage work on formal modeling with other goals such as functional verification, equivalence checking, and compilation.

To be auditable by stakeholders, policy should be expressed in an accessible way. This is one of several reasons why types play an important role in many works on information flow (IF) security. For example, Flowcaml [33] and Jif [26] express policy using types that include IF labels. They statically enforce policy using dedicated IF type checking and inference. Techniques from type theory are also used in security proofs such as those for Flowcaml and the calculus DCC [1].

IF is typically formalized as the preservation of indistinguishability relations between executions. Researchers have hypothesized that this should be an instance of a celebrated semantics basis in type theory: relational parametricity [36]. Relational parametricity provides an effective basis for formal reasoning about program transformations ("theorems for free" [49]), representation independence and information hiding for program verification [6,25]. The connection between IF and relational parametricity has been made precise in 2015, for DCC, by translation to the calculus F_ω and use of the existing parametricity theorem

© Springer Nature Switzerland AG 2020
S.-W. Lin et al. (Eds.): ICFEM 2020, LNCS 12531, pp. 181–197, 2020.
https://doi.org/10.1007/978-3-030-63406-3_11

for F_ω [12]. The connection is also made, perhaps more transparently, in a translation of DCC to dependent type theory, specifically the calculus of constructions and its parametricity theorem [4].

In this work, we advance the state of the art in the connection between IF and relational parametricity, guided by three main goals. One of the goals motivating our work is to *reduce the burden of defining dedicated type checking, inference, and security proofs* for high assurance in programming languages. A promising approach towards this goal is the idea of leveraging type abstraction to enforce policy, and in particular, *leveraging the parametricity theorem to obtain security guarantees*. A concomitant goal is *to do so for practical IF policies* that encompass selective declassification, which is needed for most policies in practice. For example, a password checker program or a program that calculates aggregate or statistical information must be considered insecure without declassification.

To build on the type system and theory of a language without *a priori* IF features, policy needs to be encoded somehow, and the program may need to be transformed. For example, to prove that a typechecked DCC term is secure with respect to the policy expressed by its type, Bowman and Ahmed [12] encode the typechecking judgment by nontrivial translation of both types and terms into F_ω. Any translation becomes part of the assurance argument. Most likely, complicated translation will also make it more difficult to use extant type checking/inference (and other development tools) in diagnosing security errors and developing secure code. This leads us to highlight a third goal, needed to achieve the first goal, namely to *minimize the complexity of translation.*

There is a major impediment to leveraging type abstraction: few languages are relationally parametric or have parametricity theorems. The lack of parametricity can be addressed by focusing on well behaved subsets and leveraging additional features like ownership types that may be available for other purposes (e.g., in the Rust language). As for the paucity of parametricity theorems, we take hope in the recent advances in machine-checked metatheory, such as correctness of the CakeML and CompCert compilers, the VST logic for C, the relational logic of Iris. For parametricity specifically, the most relevant work is Crary's formal proof of parametricity for the ML module calculus [14].

Contributions. Our *first contribution* is to translate policies with declassification—in the style of relaxed noninterference [24]—into abstract types in a functional language, in such a way that typechecking the original program implies its security. For doing so, we neither rely on a specialized security type system [12] nor on modifications of existing type systems [15]. A program that typechecks may use the secret inputs parametrically, e.g., storing in data structures, but cannot look at the data until declassification has been applied. Our *second contribution* is to prove security by direct application of a parametricity theorem. We carry out this development for the polymorphic lambda calculus, using the original theorem of Reynolds. We also provide an extended version [29] that shows this development for the ML module calculus using Crary's theorem [14], enabling the use of ML to check security.

2   Background: Language and Abstraction Theorem

To present our results we choose the simply typed and call-by-value lambda calculus, with integers and type variables, for two reasons: (1) the chosen language is similar to the language used in the paper of Reynolds [36] where the abstraction theorem was first proven, and (2) we want to illustrate our encoding approach (Sect. 4) in a minimal calculus. This section defines the language we use and recalls the abstraction theorem, a.k.a. parametricity. Our language is very close to the one in Reynolds [36, Sect. 2]; we prove the abstraction theorem using contemporary notation.[1]

Language. The syntax of the language is as below, where α denotes a type variable, x a term variable, and n an integer value. A value is *closed* when there is no free term variable in it. A type is *closed* when there is no type variable in it.

$$\tau ::= \mathbf{int} \mid \alpha \mid \tau_1 \times \tau_2 \mid \tau_1 \to \tau_2 \qquad\qquad \text{Types}$$
$$v ::= n \mid \langle v, v \rangle \mid \lambda x : \tau.e \qquad\qquad\qquad \text{Values}$$
$$e ::= x \mid v \mid \langle e, e \rangle \mid \pi_i e \mid e_1 e_2 \qquad\qquad \text{Terms}$$
$$E ::= [.] \mid \langle E, e \rangle \mid \langle v, E \rangle \mid \pi_i E \mid E\,e \mid v\,E \qquad \text{Eval. Contexts}$$

We use small-step semantics, with the reduction relation $\twoheadrightarrow$ defined inductively by these rules.

$$\pi_i \langle v_1, v_2 \rangle \twoheadrightarrow v_i \qquad (\lambda x : \tau.e)v \twoheadrightarrow e[x \mapsto v] \qquad \frac{e \twoheadrightarrow e'}{E[e] \twoheadrightarrow E[e']}$$

We write $e[x \mapsto e']$ for capture-avoiding substitution of e' for free occurrences of x in e. We use parentheses to disambiguate term structure and write $\twoheadrightarrow^*$ for the reflexive, transitive closure of $\twoheadrightarrow$.

A *typing context* Δ is a set of type variables. A *term context* Γ is a mapping from term variables to types, written like $x : \mathbf{int}, y : \mathbf{int} \to \mathbf{int}$. We write $\Delta \vdash \tau$ to mean that τ is *well-formed w.r.t.* Δ, that is, all type variables in τ are in Δ. We say that e is *typable w.r.t.* Δ *and* Γ (denoted by $\Delta, \Gamma \vdash e$) when there exists a well-formed type τ such that $\Delta, \Gamma \vdash e : \tau$. The derivable typing judgments are defined inductively in Fig. 1. The rules are to be instantiated only with Γ that is well-formed under Δ, in the sense that $\Delta \vdash \Gamma(x)$ for all $x \in dom(\Gamma)$. When the term context and the type context are empty, we write $\vdash e : \tau$.

Logical Relation. The logical relation is a type-indexed family of relations on values, parameterized by given relations for type variables. From it, we derive a relation on terms. The abstraction theorem says the latter is reflexive.

---

[1] Some readers may find it helpful to consult the following references for background on logical relations and parametricity: [22, Chapt. 49], [25, Chapt. 8], [13, 31].

$$\text{FT-Int} \frac{}{\Delta, \Gamma \vdash n : \textbf{int}} \qquad\qquad \text{FT-Var} \frac{x : \tau \in \Gamma}{\Delta, \Gamma \vdash x : \tau}$$

$$\text{FT-Pair} \frac{\Delta, \Gamma \vdash e_1 : \tau_1 \qquad \Delta, \Gamma \vdash e_2 : \tau_2}{\Delta, \Gamma \vdash \langle e_1, e_2 \rangle : \tau_1 \times \tau_2} \qquad \text{FT-Prj} \frac{\Delta, \Gamma \vdash e : \tau_1 \times \tau_2}{\Delta, \Gamma \vdash \pi_i e : \tau_i}$$

$$\text{FT-Fun} \frac{\Delta, \Gamma, x : \tau_1 \vdash e : \tau_2}{\Delta, \Gamma \vdash \lambda x : \tau_1.e : \tau_1 \rightarrow \tau_2}$$

$$\text{FT-App} \frac{\Delta, \Gamma \vdash e_1 : \tau_1 \rightarrow \tau_2 \qquad \Delta, \Gamma \vdash e_2 : \tau_1}{\Delta, \Gamma \vdash e_1 \; e_2 : \tau_2}$$

Fig. 1. Typing rules

Let γ be a *term substitution*, i.e., a finite map from term variables to closed values, and δ be a *type substitution*, i.e., a finite map from type variables to closed types. In symbols:

$$\gamma ::= . \mid \gamma, x \mapsto v \qquad\qquad \text{Term Substitutions}$$
$$\delta ::= . \mid \delta, \alpha \mapsto \tau, \text{ where } \vdash \tau \qquad \text{Type Substitutions}$$

We say γ *respects* Γ (denoted by $\gamma \models \Gamma$) when $dom(\gamma) = dom(\Gamma)$ and $\vdash \gamma(x) : \Gamma(x)$ for any x. We say δ *respects* Δ (denoted by $\delta \models \Delta$) when $dom(\delta) = \Delta$. Let $Rel(\tau_1, \tau_2)$ be the set of all binary relations over closed values of closed types τ_1 and τ_2. Let ρ be an *environment*, a mapping from type variables to relations $R \in Rel(\tau_1, \tau_2)$. We write $\rho \in Rel(\delta_1, \delta_2)$ to say that ρ is compatible with δ_1, δ_2 as follows: $\rho \in Rel(\delta_1, \delta_2) \triangleq dom(\rho) = dom(\delta_1) = dom(\delta_2) \wedge \forall \alpha \in dom(\rho). \rho(\alpha) \in Rel(\delta_1(\alpha), \delta_2(\alpha))$. The logical relation is inductively defined in Fig. 2, where $\rho \in Rel(\delta_1, \delta_2)$ for some δ_1 and δ_2. For any τ, $[\![\tau]\!]_\rho$ is a relation on closed values. In addition, $[\![\tau]\!]_\rho^{ev}$ is a relation on terms.

Lemma 1. *Suppose that $\rho \in Rel(\delta_1, \delta_2)$ for some δ_1 and δ_2. For $i \in \{1, 2\}$, it follows that:*

- *if $\langle v_1, v_2 \rangle \in [\![\tau]\!]_\rho$, then $\vdash v_i : \delta_i(\tau)$, and*
- *if $\langle e_1, e_2 \rangle \in [\![\tau]\!]_\rho^{ev}$, then $\vdash e_i : \delta_i(\tau)$.*

We write $\delta(\Gamma)$ to mean a term substitution obtained from Γ by applying δ on the range of Γ, i.e.:

$$dom(\delta(\Gamma)) = dom(\Gamma) \text{ and } \forall x \in dom(\Gamma). \delta(\Gamma)(x) = \delta(\Gamma(x)).$$

Suppose that $\Delta, \Gamma \vdash e : \tau$, $\delta \models \Delta$, and $\gamma \models \delta(\Gamma)$. Then we write $\delta\gamma(e)$ to mean the application of γ and then δ to e. For example, suppose that $\delta(\alpha) = \textbf{int}$, $\gamma(x) = n$ for some n, and $\alpha, x : \alpha \vdash \lambda y : \alpha.x : \alpha \rightarrow \alpha$, then $\delta\gamma(\lambda y : \alpha.x) = \lambda y : \textbf{int}.n$. We write $\langle \gamma_1, \gamma_2 \rangle \in [\![\Gamma]\!]_\rho$ for some $\rho \in Rel(\delta_1, \delta_2)$ when $\gamma_1 \models \delta_1(\Gamma)$, $\gamma_2 \models \delta_2(\Gamma)$, and $\langle \gamma_1(x), \gamma_2(x) \rangle \in [\![\Gamma(x)]\!]_\rho$ for all $x \in dom(\Gamma)$.

$$\text{FR-INT}\ \frac{}{\langle n, n \rangle \in [\![\mathbf{int}]\!]_\rho} \qquad\qquad \text{FR-PAIR}\ \frac{\langle v_1, v_1' \rangle \in [\![\tau_1]\!]_\rho \qquad \langle v_2, v_2' \rangle \in [\![\tau_2]\!]_\rho}{\langle \langle v_1, v_2 \rangle, \langle v_1', v_2' \rangle \rangle \in [\![\tau_1 \times \tau_2]\!]_\rho}$$

$$\text{FR-FUN}\ \frac{\forall \langle v_1', v_2' \rangle \in [\![\tau_1]\!]_\rho.\langle v_1\ v_1', v_2\ v_2' \rangle \in [\![\tau_2]\!]_\rho^{\mathsf{ev}}}{\langle v_1, v_2 \rangle \in [\![\tau_1 \to \tau_2]\!]_\rho}$$

$$\text{FR-VAR}\ \frac{\langle v_1, v_2 \rangle \in R \in Rel(\tau_1, \tau_2)}{\langle v_1, v_2 \rangle \in [\![\alpha]\!]_{\rho[\alpha \mapsto R]}}$$

$$\text{FR-TERM}\ \frac{\vdash e_1 : \delta_1(\tau) \qquad \vdash e_2 : \delta_2(\tau) \qquad e_1 \to^* v_1 \qquad e_2 \to^* v_2 \qquad \langle v_1, v_2 \rangle \in [\![\tau]\!]_\rho}{\langle e_1, e_2 \rangle \in [\![\tau]\!]_\rho^{\mathsf{ev}}}$$

Fig. 2. The logical relation

Definition 1 (Logical equivalence). *Terms e and e' are logically equivalent at τ in Δ and Γ (written $\Delta, \Gamma \vdash e \sim e' : \tau$) if $\Delta, \Gamma \vdash e : \tau$, $\Delta, \Gamma \vdash e' : \tau$, and for all $\delta_1, \delta_2 \models \Delta$, all $\rho \in Rel(\delta_1, \delta_2)$, and all $\langle \gamma_1, \gamma_2 \rangle \in [\![\Gamma]\!]_\rho$, we have $\langle \delta_1\gamma_1(e), \delta_2\gamma_2(e') \rangle \in [\![\tau]\!]_\rho^{\mathsf{ev}}$.*

Theorem 1 (Abstraction [36]). *If $\Delta, \Gamma \vdash e : \tau$, then $\Delta, \Gamma \vdash e \sim e : \tau$.*

3   Declassification Policies

Confidentiality policies can be expressed by information flows of confidential sources to public sinks in programs. Confidential sources correspond to the secrets that the program receives and public sinks correspond to any results given to a public observer, a.k.a. the attacker. These flows can either be direct—e.g. if a function, whose result is public, receives a confidential value as input and directly returns the secret—or indirect—e.g. if a function, whose result is public, receives a confidential boolean value and returns 0 if the confidential value is false and 1 otherwise. Classification of program sources as confidential or public, a.k.a. *security policy*, must be given by the programmer or security engineer: for a given security policy the program is said to be secure for *noninterference* if public resources do not depend on confidential ones. Thus, noninterference for a program means total independence between public and confidential information. As simple and elegant as this information flow policy is, noninterference does not permit to consider as secure programs that purposely need to release information in a controlled way: for example a password-checker function that receives as confidential input a boolean value representing if the system password is equal to the user's input and returns 0 or 1 accordingly. In order to consider such intended dependences of public sinks from confidential sources, we need to consider more relaxed security policies than noninterference, a.k.a. *declassification policies*. Declassification security policies allow us to specify controlled ways to release confidential inputs [39].

Declassification policies that we consider in this work map confidential inputs to functions, namely *declassification functions*. These functions allow the programmer to specify what and how information can be released. The formal syntax for declassification functions in this work is given below,[2] where n is an integer value, and $\oplus$ represents primitive arithmetic operators.

$$
\begin{aligned}
\tau &::= \mathbf{int} \mid \tau \to \tau & \text{Types} \\
e &::= \lambda x : \tau.e \mid e\,e \mid x \mid n \mid e \oplus e & \text{Terms} \\
f &::= \lambda x : \mathbf{int}.e & \text{Declass. Functions}
\end{aligned}
$$

The static and dynamic semantics are standard. To simplify the presentation we suppose that the applications of primitive operators on well-typed arguments terminates. Therefore, the evaluations of declassification functions on values terminate. A policy simply defines which are the confidential variables and their authorized declassifications. For policies we refrain from using concrete syntax and instead give a simple formalization that facilitates later definitions.

Definition 2 (Policy). *A policy $\mathcal{P}$ is a tuple $\langle \mathbf{V}_\mathcal{P}, \mathbf{F}_\mathcal{P} \rangle$, where $\mathbf{V}_\mathcal{P}$ is a finite set of variables for confidential inputs, and $\mathbf{F}_\mathcal{P}$ is a partial mapping from variables in $\mathbf{V}_\mathcal{P}$ to declassification functions.*

For simplicity we require that if f appears in the policy then it is a closed term of type $\mathbf{int} \to \tau_f$ for some τ_f. In the definition of policies, if a confidential input is not associated with a declassification function, then it cannot be declassified.

Example 1 (Policy $\mathcal{P}_{OE}$ using f). Consider policy $\mathcal{P}_{OE}$ given by $\langle \mathbf{V}_{\mathcal{P}_{OE}}, \mathbf{F}_{\mathcal{P}_{OE}} \rangle$ where $\mathbf{V}_{\mathcal{P}_{OE}} = \{x\}$ and $\mathbf{F}_{\mathcal{P}_{OE}}(x) = f = \lambda x : \mathbf{int}.\, x \bmod 2$. Policy $\mathcal{P}_{OE}$ states that only the parity of the confidential input x can be released to a public observer.

4   Type-Based Declassification

In this section, we show how to encode declassification policies as standard types in the language of Sect. 2, we define and we prove our free theorem. We consider the termination-insensitive [30] information flow security property,[3] with declassification, called type-based relaxed noninterference (TRNI) and taken from Cruz et al. [15]. It is important to notice that our development, in this section, studies the reuse for security of standard programming languages type systems together with soundness proofs for security for free by using the abstraction theorem. In contrast, Cruz et al [15] use a modified type system for security and prove soundness from scratch, without apealing to parametricity.

Through this section, we consider a fixed policy $\mathcal{P}$ (see Definition 2) given by $\langle \mathbf{V}_\mathcal{P}, \mathbf{F}_\mathcal{P} \rangle$. We treat free variables in a program as inputs and, without loss of generality, we assume that there are two kinds of inputs: integer values, which are

---

[2] In this paper, the type of confidential inputs is **int**.

[3] Our security property is termination sensitive but programs in the language always terminate. In the extended version [29], in the development for ML, programs may not terminate and the security property is also termination sensitive.

considered as confidential, and declassification functions, which are fixed according to policy. A public input can be encoded as a confidential input that can be declassified via the identity function. We consider terms without type variables as source programs. That is we consider terms e s.t. for all type substitutions δ, $\delta(e)$ is syntactically the same as e.[4]

4.1 Views and Indistinguishability

In order to define TRNI we define two term contexts, called the confidential view and public view. The first view represents an observer that can access confidential inputs, while the second one represents an observer that can only observe declassified inputs. The views are defined using fresh term and type variables.

Confidential View. Let $\mathbf{V}_\top = \{x \mid x \in \mathbf{V}_\mathcal{P} \setminus dom(\mathbf{F}_\mathcal{P})\}$ be the set of inputs that cannot be declassified. First we define the encoding for these inputs as a term context:

$$\Gamma_{C,\top}^{\mathcal{P}} \triangleq \{x : \mathbf{int} \mid x \in \mathbf{V}_\top\}.$$

Next, we specify the encoding of confidential inputs that can be declassified. To this end, define $\langle\!\langle \_, \_ \rangle\!\rangle_C$ as follows, where $f : \mathbf{int} \to \tau_f$ is in $\mathcal{P}$.

$$\langle\!\langle x, f \rangle\!\rangle_C \triangleq \{x : \mathbf{int}, x_f : \mathbf{int} \to \tau_f\}$$

Finally, we write $\Gamma_C^{\mathcal{P}}$ for the term context encoding the confidential view for $\mathcal{P}$.

$$\Gamma_C^{\mathcal{P}} \triangleq \Gamma_{C,\top}^{\mathcal{P}} \cup \bigcup_{x \in dom(\mathbf{F}_\mathcal{P})} \langle\!\langle x, \mathbf{F}_\mathcal{P}(x) \rangle\!\rangle_C.$$

We assume that, for any x, the variable x_f in the result of $\langle\!\langle x, \mathbf{F}_\mathcal{P}(x) \rangle\!\rangle_C$ is distinct from the variables in $\mathbf{V}_\mathcal{P}$, distinct from each other, and distinct from $x_{f'}$ for distinct f'. We make analogous assumptions in later definitions.

   From the construction, $\Gamma_C^{\mathcal{P}}$ is a mapping, and for any $x \in dom(\Gamma_C^{\mathcal{P}})$, it follows that $\Gamma_C^{\mathcal{P}}(x)$ is a closed type. Therefore, $\Gamma_C^{\mathcal{P}}$ is well-formed for the empty set of type variables, so it can be used in typing judgments of the form $\Gamma_C^{\mathcal{P}} \vdash e : \tau$.

Example 2 (Confidential view). For $\mathcal{P}_{OE}$ in Example 1, the confidential view is:
$\Gamma_C^{\mathcal{P}_{OE}} = x : \mathbf{int}, x_f : \mathbf{int} \to \mathbf{int}$.

Public View. The basic idea is to encode policies by using type variables. First we define the encoding for confidential inputs that cannot be declassified. We define a set of type variables, $\Delta_{P,\top}^{\mathcal{P}}$ and a mapping $\Gamma_{P,\top}^{\mathcal{P}}$ for confidential inputs that cannot be declassified.

$$\Delta_{P,\top}^{\mathcal{P}} \triangleq \{\alpha_x \mid x \in \mathbf{V}_\top\} \qquad \Gamma_{P,\top}^{\mathcal{P}} \triangleq \{x : \alpha_x \mid x \in \mathbf{V}_\top\}$$

---

[4] An example of a term with type variables is $\lambda x : \alpha.x$. We can easily check that there exists a type substitutions δ s.t. $\delta(e)$ is syntactically different from e (e.g. for δ s.t. $\delta(\alpha) = \mathbf{int}$, $\delta(e) = \lambda x : \mathbf{int}.x$).

This gives the program access to x at an opaque type.

In order to define the encoding for confidential inputs that can be declassified, we define $\langle\!\langle \_, \_ \rangle\!\rangle_P$:

$$\langle\!\langle x, f \rangle\!\rangle_P \triangleq \langle \{\alpha_f\}, \{x : \alpha_f, x_f : \alpha_f \to \tau_f\}\rangle$$

The first form will serve to give the program access to x only via function variable x_f that we will ensure is interpreted as the policy function f. We define a type context $\Delta_P^{\mathcal{P}}$ and term context $\Gamma_P^{\mathcal{P}}$ that comprise the public view, as follows.

$$\langle \Delta_P^{\mathcal{P}}, \Gamma_P^{\mathcal{P}} \rangle \triangleq \langle \Delta_{P,\top}^{\mathcal{P}}, \Gamma_{P,\top}^{\mathcal{P}} \rangle \cup \bigcup_{x \in dom(\mathbf{F}_{\mathcal{P}})} \langle\!\langle x, \mathbf{F}_{\mathcal{P}}(x) \rangle\!\rangle_P,$$

where $\langle S_1, S_1' \rangle \cup \langle S_2, S_2' \rangle = \langle S_1 \cup S_2, S_1' \cup S_2' \rangle$.

Example 3 (Public view). For $\mathcal{P}_{OE}$, the typing context in the public view has one type variable: $\Delta_P^{\mathcal{P}_{OE}} = \alpha_f$. The term context in the public view is $\Gamma_P^{\mathcal{P}_{OE}} = x : \alpha_f,\ x_f : \alpha_f \to \mathbf{int}$.

From the construction, $\Gamma_P^{\mathcal{P}}$ is a mapping, and for any $x \in dom(\Gamma_P^{\mathcal{P}})$, it follows that $\Gamma_P^{\mathcal{P}}(x)$ is well-formed in $\Delta_P^{\mathcal{P}}$ (i.e. $\Delta_P^{\mathcal{P}} \vdash \Gamma_P^{\mathcal{P}}(x)$). Thus, $\Gamma_P^{\mathcal{P}}$ is well-formed in the typing context $\Delta_P^{\mathcal{P}}$. Therefore, $\Delta_P^{\mathcal{P}}$ and $\Gamma_P^{\mathcal{P}}$ can be used in typing judgments of the form $\Delta_P^{\mathcal{P}}, \Gamma_P^{\mathcal{P}} \vdash e : \tau$.

Notice that in the public view of a policy, types of variables for confidential inputs are not $\mathbf{int}$. Thus, the public view does not allow programs where concrete declassifiers are applied to confidential input variables even when the applications are semantically correct according to the policy (e.g. for $\mathcal{P}_{OE}$, the program $f\ x$ does not typecheck in the public view). Instead, programs should apply named declassifers (e.g. for $\mathcal{P}_{OE}$, the program $x_f\ x$ is well-typed in the public view).

Indistinguishability. The security property TRNI is defined in a usual way, using partial equivalence relations called indistinguishability. To define indistinguishability, we define a type substitution $\delta_{\mathcal{P}}$ such that $\delta_{\mathcal{P}} \models \Delta_P^{\mathcal{P}}$, as follows:

$$\text{for all } \alpha_x, \alpha_f \text{ in } \Delta_P^{\mathcal{P}}, \text{ let } \delta_{\mathcal{P}}(\alpha_x) = \delta_{\mathcal{P}}(\alpha_f) = \mathbf{int}. \tag{1}$$

The inductive definition of indistinguishability for a policy $\mathcal{P}$ is presented in Fig. 3, where α_x and α_f are from $\Delta_P^{\mathcal{P}}$. Indistinguishability is defined for τ s.t. $\Delta_P^{\mathcal{P}}, \Gamma_P^{\mathcal{P}} \vdash \tau$. The definitions of indistinguishability for $\mathbf{int}$ and $\tau_1 \times \tau_2$ are straightforward. We say that two functions are indistinguishable at $\tau_1 \to \tau_2$ if on any indistinguishable inputs they generate indistinguishable outputs. Since we use α_x to encode confidential integer values that cannot be declassified, any integer values v_1 and v_2 are indistinguishable, according to rule Eq-Var1. Notice that $\delta_{\mathcal{P}}(\alpha_x) = \mathbf{int}$. Since we use α_f to encode confidential integer values that can be declassified via f where $\vdash f : \mathbf{int} \to \tau_f$, we say that $\langle v_1, v_2 \rangle \in \mathcal{I}_V[\![\alpha_f]\!]$ when $\langle f\ v_1, f\ v_2 \rangle \in \mathcal{I}_E[\![\tau_f]\!]$.

$$\text{EQ-INT} \ \frac{}{\langle n, n \rangle \in \mathcal{I}_V[\![\mathbf{int}]\!]} \qquad \text{EQ-PAIR} \ \frac{\langle v_1, v_1' \rangle \in \mathcal{I}_V[\![\tau_1]\!] \qquad \langle v_2, v_2' \rangle \in \mathcal{I}_V[\![\tau_2]\!]}{\langle \langle v_1, v_2 \rangle, \langle v_1', v_2' \rangle \rangle \in \mathcal{I}_V[\![\tau_1 \times \tau_2]\!]}$$

$$\text{EQ-FUN} \ \frac{\forall \langle v_1', v_2' \rangle : \langle v_1', v_2' \rangle \in \mathcal{I}_V[\![\tau_1]\!].\langle v_1 \ v_1', v_2 \ v_2' \rangle \in \mathcal{I}_E[\![\tau_2]\!]}{\langle v_1, v_2 \rangle \in \mathcal{I}_V[\![\tau_1 \to \tau_2]\!]}$$

$$\text{EQ-VAR1} \ \frac{\vdash v_1, v_2 : \delta_\mathcal{P}(\alpha_x)}{\langle v_1, v_2 \rangle \in \mathcal{I}_V[\![\alpha_x]\!]} \qquad \text{EQ-VAR2} \ \frac{\vdash v_1, v_2 : \delta_\mathcal{P}(\alpha_f) \qquad \langle f \ v_1, f \ v_2 \rangle \in \mathcal{I}_E[\![\tau_f]\!]}{\langle v_1, v_2 \rangle \in \mathcal{I}_V[\![\alpha_f]\!]}$$

$$\text{EQ-TERM} \ \frac{\vdash e_1, e_2 : \delta_\mathcal{P}(\tau) \qquad e_1 \to^* v_1 \qquad e_2 \to^* v_2 \qquad \langle v_1, v_2 \rangle \in \mathcal{I}_V[\![\tau]\!]}{\langle e_1, e_2 \rangle \in \mathcal{I}_E[\![\tau]\!]}$$

Fig. 3. Indistinguishability

Example 4 (Indistinguishability). For $\mathcal{P}_{OE}$ (of Example 1), two values v_1 and v_2 are indistinguishable at α_f when both of them are even numbers or odd numbers.

$$\mathcal{I}_V[\![\alpha_f]\!] = \{\langle v_1, v_2 \rangle \mid \ \vdash v_1 : \mathbf{int}, \ \vdash v_2 : \mathbf{int}, \ (v_1 \ mod \ 2) =_{\mathbf{int}} (v_2 \ mod \ 2)\}.$$

We write $e_1 =_{\mathbf{int}} e_2$ to mean that $e_1 \to^* v$ and $e_2 \to^* v$ for some integer value v.

Term substitutions γ_1 and γ_2 are called *indistinguishable w.r.t.* $\mathcal{P}$ (denoted by $\langle \gamma_1, \gamma_2 \rangle \in \mathcal{I}_V[\![\mathcal{P}]\!]$) if the following hold.

- $\gamma_1 \models \delta_\mathcal{P}(\Gamma_P^\mathcal{P})$ and $\gamma_2 \models \delta_\mathcal{P}(\Gamma_P^\mathcal{P})$,
- for all $x_f \in dom(\Gamma_P^\mathcal{P})$, $\gamma_1(x_f) = \gamma_2(x_f) = f$,
- for all other $x \in dom(\Gamma_P^\mathcal{P})$, $\langle \gamma_1(x), \gamma_2(x) \rangle \in \mathcal{I}_V[\![\Gamma_P^\mathcal{P}(x)]\!]$.

Note that each γ_i maps x_f to the specific function f in the policy. Input variables are mapped to indistinguishable values.

We now define type-based relaxed noninterference w.r.t. $\mathcal{P}$ for a type τ well-formed in $\Delta_P^\mathcal{P}$. It says that indistinguishable inputs lead to indistinguishable results.

Definition 3. *A term e is TRNI$(\mathcal{P}, \tau)$ provided that $\Gamma_C^\mathcal{P} \vdash e$, and $\Delta_P^\mathcal{P} \vdash \tau$, and for all $\langle \gamma_1, \gamma_2 \rangle \in \mathcal{I}_V[\![\mathcal{P}]\!]$ we have $\langle \gamma_1(e), \gamma_2(e) \rangle \in \mathcal{I}_E[\![\tau]\!]$.*

Notice that if a term is well-typed in the public view then by replacing all type variables in it with **int**, we get a term which is also well-typed in the confidential view (that is, if $\Lambda_P^\mathcal{P}, \Gamma_P^\mathcal{P} \vdash e : \tau$, then $\Gamma_C^\mathcal{P} \vdash \delta(o) : \delta(\tau)$ where δ maps all type variables in $\Delta_P^\mathcal{P}$ to **int**). However, Definition 3 also requires that the term e is itself well-typed in the confidential view. This merely ensures that the definition is applied, as intended, to programs that do not contain type variables.

The definition of TRNI is indexed by a type for the result of the term. The type can be interpreted as constraining the observations to be made by the public observer. We are mainly interested in concrete output types, which express that the observer can do whatever they like and has full knowledge of the result. Put differently, TRNI for an abstract type expresses security under the assumption that the observer is somehow forced to respect the abstraction. Consider the policy $\mathcal{P}_{OE}$ (of Example 1) where x can be declassified via $f = \lambda x : \text{int}.x \bmod 2$. As described in Example 3, $\Delta_P^{\mathcal{P}_{OE}} = \alpha_f$ and $\Gamma_P^{\mathcal{P}_{OE}} = x : \alpha_f, \; x_f : \alpha_f \to \text{int}$. We have that the program x is $\text{TRNI}(\mathcal{P}_{OE}, \alpha_f)$ since the observer cannot do anything to x except for applying f to x which is allowed by the policy. This program, however, is not $\text{TRNI}(\mathcal{P}_{OE}, \text{int})$ since the observer can apply any function of the type $\text{int} \to \tau'$ (for some closed τ'), including the identity function, to x and hence can get the value of x.

Example 5. The program $x_f \; x$ is $\text{TRNI}(\mathcal{P}_{OE}, \text{int})$. Indeed, for any arbitrary $\langle \gamma_1, \gamma_2 \rangle \in \mathcal{I}_V[\![\mathcal{P}]\!]$, we have that $\gamma_1(x_f) = \gamma_2(x_f) = f = \lambda x : \text{int}.x \bmod 2$, and $\langle v_1, v_2 \rangle \in \mathcal{I}_V[\![\alpha_f]\!]$, where $\gamma_1(x) = v_1$ and $\gamma_2(x) = v_2$ for some v_1 and v_2. When we apply γ_1 and γ_2 to the program, we get respectively $v_1 \bmod 2$ and $v_2 \bmod 2$. Since $\langle v_1, v_2 \rangle \in \mathcal{I}_V[\![\alpha_f]\!]$, as described in Example 4, $(v_1 \bmod 2) =_{\text{int}} (v_2 \bmod 2)$. Thus, $\langle \gamma_1(x_f \; x), \gamma_2(x_f \; x) \rangle \in \mathcal{I}_E[\![\text{int}]\!]$. Therefore, the program $x_f \; x$ satisfies the definition of TRNI.

4.2   Free Theorem: Typing in the Public View Implies Security

In order to prove security "for free", i.e., as consequence of Theorem 1, we define $\rho_{\mathcal{P}}$ as follows:

- for all $\alpha_x \in \Delta_P^{\mathcal{P}}$, $\rho_{\mathcal{P}}(\alpha_x) = \mathcal{I}_V[\![\alpha_x]\!]$,
- for all $\alpha_f \in \Delta_P^{\mathcal{P}}$, $\rho_{\mathcal{P}}(\alpha_f) = \mathcal{I}_V[\![\alpha_f]\!]$.

It is a relation on the type substitution $\delta_{\mathcal{P}}$ defined in Eq. (1).

Lemma 2. $\rho_{\mathcal{P}} \in Rel(\delta_{\mathcal{P}}, \delta_{\mathcal{P}})$.

From Lemma 2, we can write $[\![\tau]\!]_{\rho_{\mathcal{P}}}$ or $[\![\tau]\!]_{\rho_{\mathcal{P}}}^{\text{ev}}$ for any τ such that $\Delta_P^{\mathcal{P}} \vdash \tau$. We next establish the relation between $[\![\tau]\!]_{\rho}^{\text{ev}}$ and $\mathcal{I}_E[\![\tau]\!]$: under the interpretation corresponding to the desired policy $\mathcal{P}$, they are equivalent. In other words, indistinguishability is an instantiation of the logical relation.

Lemma 3. *For any τ such that $\Delta_P^{\mathcal{P}} \vdash \tau$, we have $\langle v_1, v_2 \rangle \in [\![\tau]\!]_{\rho_{\mathcal{P}}}$ iff $\langle v_1, v_2 \rangle \in \mathcal{I}_V[\![\tau]\!]$, and also $\langle e_1, e_2 \rangle \in [\![\tau]\!]_{\rho_{\mathcal{P}}}^{\text{ev}}$ iff $\langle e_1, e_2 \rangle \in \mathcal{I}_E[\![\tau]\!]$.*

By analyzing the type of $\Gamma_P^{\mathcal{P}}(x)$, we can establish the relation of γ_1 and γ_2 when $\langle \gamma_1, \gamma_2 \rangle \in \mathcal{I}_V[\![\mathcal{P}]\!]$.

Lemma 4. *If $\langle \gamma_1, \gamma_2 \rangle \in \mathcal{I}_V[\![\mathcal{P}]\!]$, then $\langle \gamma_1, \gamma_2 \rangle \in [\![\Gamma_P^{\mathcal{P}}]\!]_{\rho_{\mathcal{P}}}$.*

The main result of this section is that a term is TRNI at τ if it has type τ in the public view that encodes the policy.

Theorem 2. *If e has no type variables and $\Delta_P^{\mathcal{P}}, \Gamma_P^{\mathcal{P}} \vdash e : \tau$, then e is $TRNI(\mathcal{P}, \tau)$.*

Proof. From the abstraction theorem (Theorem 1), for all $\delta_1, \delta_2 \models \Delta_P^P$, for all $\langle \gamma_1, \gamma_2 \rangle \in [\![\Gamma_P^P]\!]_\rho$, and for all $\rho \in Rel(\delta_1, \delta_2)$, it follows that

$$\langle \delta_1 \gamma_1(e), \delta_2 \gamma_2(e) \rangle \in [\![\tau]\!]_\rho^{ev}.$$

Consider $\langle \gamma_1, \gamma_2 \rangle \in \mathcal{I}_V [\![\mathcal{P}]\!]$. Since $\langle \gamma_1, \gamma_2 \rangle \in \mathcal{I}_V [\![\mathcal{P}]\!]$, from Lemma 4, we have that $\langle \gamma_1, \gamma_2 \rangle \in [\![\Gamma_P^P]\!]_{\rho_P}$. Thus, we have that $\langle \delta_P \gamma_1(e), \delta_P \gamma_2(e) \rangle \in [\![\tau]\!]_{\rho_P}^{ev}$. Since e has no type variable, we have that $\delta_P \gamma_i(e) = \gamma_i(e)$. Therefore, $\langle \gamma_1(e), \gamma_2(e) \rangle \in [\![\tau]\!]_{\rho_P}^{ev}$. Since $\langle \gamma_1(e), \gamma_2(e) \rangle \in [\![\tau]\!]_{\rho_P}^{ev}$, from Lemma 3, it follows that $\langle \gamma_1(e), \gamma_2(e) \rangle \in \mathcal{I}_E [\![\tau]\!]$. In addition, since e has no type variable and $\Delta_P^P, \Gamma_P^P \vdash e : \tau$, we have that $\delta_P(\Gamma_P^P) \vdash e : \delta_P(\tau)$ and hence, $\Gamma_C^P \vdash e$. Therefore, e is TRNI$(\mathcal{P}, \tau)$.

Example 6 (Typing implies TRNI). Consider the policy $\mathcal{P}_{OE}$. As described in Examples 2 and 3, the confidential view $\Gamma_C^{\mathcal{P}_{OE}}$ is $x : \text{int}, x_f : \text{int} \rightarrow \text{int}$ and the public view $\Delta_P^{\mathcal{P}_{OE}}, \Gamma_P^{\mathcal{P}_{OE}}$ is $\alpha_f, x : \alpha_f, x_f : \alpha_f \rightarrow \text{int}$. We look at the program $x_f \; x$. We can easily verify that $\Gamma_C^{\mathcal{P}_{OE}} \vdash x_f \; x : \text{int}$ and $\Delta_P^{\mathcal{P}_{OE}}, \Gamma_P^{\mathcal{P}_{OE}} \vdash x_f \; x : \text{int}$. Therefore, by Theorem 2, the program is TRNI$(\mathcal{P}_{OE}, \text{int})$.

Example 7. If a program is well-typed in the confidential view but not TRNI$(\mathcal{P}, \tau)$ for some τ well-formed in the public view of $\mathcal{P}$, then the type of the program in the public view is not τ or the program is not well-typed in the public view. In policy $\mathcal{P}_{OE}$, from Example 6, the public view is $\alpha_f, x : \alpha_f, x_f : \alpha_f \rightarrow \text{int}$. We first look at the program x that is not TRNI$(\mathcal{P}_{OE}, \text{int})$ since x itself is confidential and cannot be directly declassified. In the public view of the policy, the type of this program is α_f which is not **int**. We now look at the program $x \; mod \; 3$ that is not TRNI$(\mathcal{P}_{OE}, \alpha_f)$ since it takes indistinguishable inputs at α_f (e.g. 2 and 4) and produces results that are not indistinguishable at α_f (e.g. $2 = 2 \; mod \; 3$, $1 = 4 \; mod \; 3$, and $\langle 2, 1 \rangle \notin \mathcal{I}_V [\![\alpha_f]\!]$). We can easily verify that this program is not well-typed in the public view since the type of x in the public view is α_f, while mod expects arguments of the **int** type.

Remark 1 (Extension). Our encoding can be extended to support richer policies (details in appendix). To support policies where an input x can be declassified via two declassifiers $f : \text{int} \rightarrow \tau_f$ and $g : \text{int} \rightarrow \tau_g$ for some τ_f and τ_g, we use type variable $\alpha_{f,g}$ as the type for x and use $\alpha_{f,g} \rightarrow \tau_f$ and $\alpha_{f,g} \rightarrow \tau_g$ as types for x_f and x_g. To support policies where multiple inputs can be declassified via a declassifier, e.g. inputs x and y can be declassified via $f = \lambda z : \text{int} \times \text{int}.(\pi_1 z + \pi_2 z)/2$, we introduce a new term variable z which is corresponding to a tuple of two inputs x and y and we require that only z can be declassified. The type of z is α_f and two tuples $\langle v_1, v_2 \rangle$ and $\langle v_1', v_2' \rangle$ are indistinguishable at α_f when $f \langle v_1, v_2 \rangle = f \langle v_1', v_2' \rangle$.

5   Related Work

Typing Secure Information Flow. Pottier and Simonet [32] implement Flow-Caml [33], the first type system for information flow analysis dealing with a real-sized programming language (a large fragment of OCaml), and they prove soundness. In comparison with our results, we do not consider any imperative features; they do not consider any form of declassification, their type system significantly departs from ML typing, and their security proof is not based on an abstraction theorem. An interesting question is whether their type system can be translated to system F or some other calculus with an abstraction theorem. Flow-Caml provides type inference for security types. Our work relies on the Standard ML type system to enforce security. Standard ML provides type inference, which endows our approach with an inference mechanism. Barthe et al. [9] propose a modular method to reuse type systems and proofs for noninterference [40] for declassification. They also provide a method to conclude declassification soundness by using an existing noninterference theorem [37]. In contrast to our work, their type system significantly departs from standard typing rules, and does not make use of parametricity. Tse and Zdancewic [46] propose a security-typed language for robust declassification: declassification cannot be triggered unless there is a digital certificate to assert the proper authority. Their language inherits many features from System $F_{<:}$ and uses monadic labels as in DCC [1]. In contrast to our work, security labels are based on the Decentralized Label Model (DLM) [27], and are not semantically unified with the standard safety types of the language. The Dependency Core Calculus (DCC) [1] expresses security policies using monadic types indexed on levels in a security lattice with the usual interpretation that flows are only allowed between levels in accordance with the ordering. DCC does not include declassification and the noninterference theorem of [1] is proved from scratch (not leveraging parametricity). While DCC is a theoretical calculus, its monadic types fit nicely with the monads and monad transformers used by the Haskell language for computational effects like state and I/O. Algehed and Russo [5] encode the typing judgment of DCC in Haskell using closed type families, one of the type system extensions supported by GHC that brings it close to dependent types. However, they do not prove security. Compared with type systems, relational logics can specify IF policy and prove more programs secure through semantic reasoning [8,10,21,28], but at the cost of more user guidance and less familiar notations. Aguirre et al [2] use relational higher order logic to prove soundness of DCC essentially by formalizing the semantics of DCC [1].

Connections Between Secure IF and Type Abstraction. Tse and Zdancewic [45] translate the recursion-free fragment of DCC to System F. The main theorem for this translation aims to show that parametricity of System F implies noninterference. Shikuma and Igarashi identify a mistake in the proof [41]; they also give a noninterference-preserving translation for a version of DCC to the simply-typed lambda calculus. Although they make direct use of a specific logical relation, their results are not obtained by instantiating a parametricity theorem. Bowman and Ahmed [12] finally provide a translation from the recursion-free fragment of DCC to System F_ω, proving that parametricity implies noninterference, via a correctness theorem for the translation (which is akin to a full abstraction property). Bowman and Ahmed's translation makes essential use of the power of System

F_ω to encode judgments of DCC. Algehed and Bernardy [4] translate a label-polymorphic variant DCC (without recursion) into the calculus of constructions (CC) and prove noninterference directly from a parametricity result for CC [11]. The authors note that it is not obvious this can be extended to languages with nontermination or other effects. Their results have been checked in Agda and the presentation achieves elegance owing to the fact that parametricity and noninterference can be explicitly defined in dependent type theory; indeed, CC terms can represent proof of parametricity [11]. Our goals do not necessitate a system like DCC for policy, raising the question of whether a simpler target type system can suffice for security policies expressed differently from DCC. We answer the question in the affirmative, and believe our results for polymorphic lambda (and for ML) provide transparent explication of noninterference by reduction to parametricity. The preceding works on DCC are "translating noninterference to parametricity" in the sense of translating both programs and types. The implication is that one might leverage an existing type checker by translating both a program and its security policy into another program such that it's typability implies the original conforms to policy. Our work aims to cater more directly for practical application, by minimizing the need to translate the program and hence avoiding the need to prove the correctness of a translation. Cruz et al. [15] show that type abstraction implies relaxed noninterference. Similar to ours, their definition of relaxed noninterference is a standard extensional semantics, using partial equivalence relations. This is in contrast with Li and Zdancewic [24] where the semantics is entangled with typability.

Protzenko et al. [34] propose to use abstract types as the types for secrets and use standard type systems for security. This is very close in spirit to our work. Their soundness theorem is about a property called "secret independence", very close to noninterference. In contrast to our work, there is no declassification and no use of the abstraction theorem. Rajani and Garg [35] connect fine- and coarse-grained type systems for information flow in a lambda calculus with general references, defining noninterference (without declassification) as a step-indexed Kripke logical relation that expresses indistinguishability. Further afield, a connection between security and parametricity is made by Devriese et al [16], featuring a negative result: System F cannot be compiled to the the Sumii-Pierce calculus of dynamic sealing [43] (an idealized model of a cryptographic mechanism). Finally, information flow analyses have also been put at the service of parametricity [50].

Abstraction Theorems for Other Languages. Parametricity remains an active area of study [42]. Vytiniotis and Weirich [48] prove the abstraction theorem for R_ω, which extends F_ω with constructs that are useful for programming with type equivalence propositions. Rossberg et al [38] show another path to parametricity for ML modules, by translating them to F_ω. Crary's result [14] covers a large fragment of ML but without references and mutable state. Abstraction theorems have been given for mutable state, based on ownership types [6] and on more semantically based reasoning [3,7,17,44].

6 Discussion and Conclusion

In this work, we show how to express declassification policies by using standard types of the simply typed lambda calculus. By means of parametricity, we prove that type checking implies relaxed noninterference, showing a direct connection between declassification and parametricity. Our approach should be applicable to other languages that have an abstraction theorem (e.g [3,7,17,44]) with the potential benefit of strong security assurance from off-the-shelf type checkers. In particular, we demonstrate (in an extended version [29]) that the results can be extended to a large fragment of ML including general recursion. Although in this paper we demonstrate our results using confidentiality and declassification, our approach applies as well to integrity and endorsement, as they have been shown to be information flow properties analog to confidentiality [18–20,23].

The simple encodings in the preceding sections do not support computation and output at multiple levels. For example, consider a policy where x is a confidential input that can be declassified via f and we also want to do the computation $x + 1$ of which the result is at confidential level. Clearly, $x + 1$ is ill-typed in the public interface. We provide (in the extended version) more involved encodings supporting computation at multiple levels. To have an encoding that support multiple levels, we add universally quantified types $\forall \alpha . \tau$ to the language presented in Sect. 2. However, this goes against our goal of minimizing complexity of translation. Observe that many applications are composed of programs which, individually, do not output at multiple levels; for example, the password checker, and data mining computations using sensitive inputs to calculate aggregate or statistical information. For these the simpler encoding suffices.

Vanhoef et al. [47] and others have proposed more expressive declassification policies than the ones in Li and Zdancewic [24]: policies that keep state and can be written as programs. We speculate that TRNI for stateful declassification policies can be obtained for free in a language with state—indeed, our work provides motivation for development of abstraction theorems for such languages.

Acknowledgements. We thank anonymous reviewers for their suggestions. This work was partially supported by CISC ANR-17-CE25-0014-01, IPL SPAI, the European Union's Horizon 2020 research and innovation programme under grant agreement No 830892, US NSF CNS 1718713, and ONR N00014-17-1-2787.

References

1. Abadi, M., Banerjee, A., Heintze, N., Riecke, J.G.: A core calculus of dependency. In: ACM POPL, pp. 147–160 (1999)
2. Aguirre, A., Barthe, G., Gaboardi, M., Garg, D., Strub, P.: A relational logic for higher-order programs. PACMPL 1(ICFP), 21:1–21:29 (2017)
3. Ahmed, A., Dreyer, D., Rossberg, A.: State-dependent representation independence. In: ACM POPL, pp. 340–353 (2009)

4. Algehed, M., Bernardy, J.: Simple noninterference from parametricity. PACMPL **3**(ICFP), 89:1–89:22 (2019)
5. Algehed, M., Russo, A.: Encoding DCC in Haskell. In: Workshop on Programming Languages and Analysis for Security, pp. 77–89 (2017)
6. Banerjee, A., Naumann, D.A.: Ownership confinement ensures representation independence for object-oriented programs. J. ACM **52**(6), 894–960 (2005)
7. Banerjee, A., Naumann, D.A.: State based encapsulation for modular reasoning about behavior-preserving refactorings. In: Clarke, D., Noble, J., Wrigstad, T. (eds.) Aliasing in Object-Oriented Programming. Types, Analysis and Verification. LNCS, vol. 7850, pp. 319–365. Springer, Heidelberg (2013). https://doi.org/10.1007/978-3-642-36946-9_12
8. Banerjee, A., Naumann, D.A., Nikouei, M.: Relational logic with framing and hypotheses. In: FSTTCS. LIPIcs, vol. 65, pp. 11:1–11:16 (2016)
9. Barthe, G., Cavadini, S., Rezk, T.: Tractable enforcement of declassification policies. In: IEEE Computer Security Foundations Symposium, pp. 83–97 (2008)
10. Beckert, B., Ulbrich, M.: Trends in relational program verification. In: Müller, P., Schaefer, I. (eds.) Principled Software Development - Essays Dedicated to Arnd Poetzsch-Heffter on the Occasion of his 60th Birthday, pp. 41–58. Springer, Heidelberg (2018). https://doi.org/10.1007/978-3-319-98047-8_3
11. Bernardy, J.P., Jansso, P., Paterson, R.: Proofs for free: parametricity for dependent types. J. Func. Program. **22**(2), 107–152 (2012)
12. Bowman, W.J., Ahmed, A.: Noninterference for free. In: ICFP, pp. 101–113 (2015)
13. Crary, K.: Logical relations and a case study in equivalence checking. In: Pierce, B.C. (ed.) Advanced Topics in Types and Programming Languages, Chap. 6, pp. 245–289. The MIT Press (2005)
14. Crary, K.: Modules, abstraction, and parametric polymorphism. In: ACM POPL, pp. 100–113 (2017)
15. Cruz, R., Rezk, T., Serpette, B.P., Tanter, É.: Type abstraction for relaxed noninterference. In: ECOOP, pp. 7:1–7:27 (2017)
16. Devriese, D., Patrignani, M., Piessens, F.: Parametricity versus the universal type. PACMPL **2**(POPL), 38:1–38:23 (2018)
17. Dreyer, D., Neis, G., Rossberg, A., Birkedal, L.: A relational modal logic for higher-order stateful ADTs. In: ACM POPL, pp. 185–198 (2010)
18. Fournet, C., Guernic, G.L., Rezk, T.: A security-preserving compiler for distributed programs: from information-flow policies to cryptographic mechanisms. In: ACM Conference on Computer and Communications Security, CCS (2009)
19. Fournet, C., Planul, J., Rezk, T.: Information-flow types for homomorphic encryptions. In: ACM CCS, pp. 351–360 (2011)
20. Fournet, C., Rezk, T.: Cryptographically sound implementations for typed information-flow security. In: ACM POPL (2008)
21. Grimm, N., et al.: A monadic framework for relational verification: applied to information security, program equivalence, and optimizations. In: Certified Programs and Proofs, pp. 130–145 (2018)
22. Harper, R.: Practical Foundations for Programming Languages. Cambridge University Press (2016)
23. Li, P., Mao, Y., Zdancewic, S.: Information integrity policies. In: Proceedings of the Workshop on Formal Aspects in Security and Trust (FAST) (2003)
24. Li, P., Zdancewic, S.: Downgrading policies and relaxed noninterference. In: ACM POPL, pp. 158–170 (2005)
25. Mitchell, J.C.: Foundations for Programming Languages. MIT Press (1996)

26. Myers, A.C.: Jif homepage. http://www.cs.cornell.edu/jif/. Accessed July 2018
27. Myers, A.C., Liskov, B.: Protecting privacy using the decentralized label model. ACM Trans. Softw. Eng. Methodol. **9**, 410–442 (2000)
28. Nanevski, A., Banerjee, A., Garg, D.: Dependent type theory for verification of information flow and access control policies. ACM Trans. Program. Lang. Syst. **35**(2), 6 (2013)
29. Ngo, M., Naumann, D.A., Rezk, T.: Type-based declassification for free. CoRR abs/1905.00922 (2020). http://arxiv.org/abs/1905.00922
30. Ngo, M., Piessens, F., Rezk, T.: Impossibility of precise and sound termination-sensitive security enforcements. In: 2018 IEEE Symposium on Security and Privacy, SP. IEEE Computer Society (2018)
31. Pitts, A.M.: Typed operational reasoning. In: Pierce, B.C. (ed.) Advanced Topics in Types and Programming Languages, Chap. 7, pp. 245–289. The MIT Press (2005)
32. Pottier, F., Simonet, V.: Information flow inference for ML. In: ACM POPL, pp. 319–330 (2002)
33. Pottier, F., Simonet, V.: Flowcaml homepage. https://www.normalesup.org/simonet/soft/flowcaml/index.html. Accessed July 2018
34. Protzenko, J., et al.: Verified low-level programming embedded in F. PACMPL **1**(ICFP), 17:1–17:29 (2017)
35. Rajani, V., Garg, D.: Types for information flow control: labeling granularity and semantic models. In: IEEE Computer Security Foundations Symposium (2018)
36. Reynolds, J.C.: Types, abstraction and parametric polymorphism. In: IFIP Congress, pp. 513–523 (1983)
37. Rezk, T.: Verification of confidentiality policies for mobile code. Ph.D. thesis, University of Nice-Sophia Antipolis (2006)
38. Rossberg, A., Russo, C.V., Dreyer, D.: F-ing modules. J. Funct. Program. **24**(5), 529–607 (2014)
39. Sabelfeld, A., Sands, D.: Declassification: dimensions and principles. J. Comput. Secur. **17**(5), 517–548 (2009)
40. Fragoso Santos, J., Jensen, T., Rezk, T., Schmitt, A.: Hybrid typing of secure information flow in a JavaScript-like language. In: Ganty, P., Loreti, M. (eds.) TGC 2015. LNCS, vol. 9533, pp. 63–78. Springer, Cham (2016). https://doi.org/10.1007/978-3-319-28766-9_5
41. Shikuma, N., Igarashi, A.: Proving noninterference by a fully complete translation to the simply typed lambda-calculus. Logical Methods Comp. Sci. **4**(3) (2008)
42. Sojakova, K., Johann, P.: A general framework for relational parametricity. In: IEEE Symposium on Logic in Computer Science, pp. 869–878 (2018)
43. Sumii, E., Pierce, B.C.: A bisimulation for dynamic sealing. In: ACM POPL, pp. 161–172 (2004)
44. Timany, A., Stefanesco, L., Krogh-Jespersen, M., Birkedal, L.: A logical relation for monadic encapsulation of state: proving contextual equivalences in the presence of runST. Proc. ACM Program. Lang. **2**(POPL), 64:1–64:28 (2017)
45. Tse, S., Zdancewic, S.: Translating dependency into parametricity. In: International Conference on Functional Programming, pp. 115–125 (2004)
46. Tse, S., Zdancewic, S.: A design for a security-typed language with certificate-based declassification. In: Sagiv, M. (ed.) ESOP 2005. LNCS, vol. 3444, pp. 279–294. Springer, Heidelberg (2005). https://doi.org/10.1007/978-3-540-31987-0_20
47. Vanhoef, M., Groef, W.D., Devriese, D., Piessens, F., Rezk, T.: Stateful declassification policies for event-driven programs. In: IEEE Computer Security Foundations Symposium, pp. 293–307 (2014)

48. Vytiniotis, D., Weirich, S.: Parametricity, type equality, and higher-order polymorphism. J. Funct. Program. **20**(2), 175–210 (2010)
49. Wadler, P.: Theorems for free! In: International Conference on Functional Programming, pp. 347–359 (1989)
50. Washburn, G., Weirich, S.: Generalizing parametricity using information-flow. In: IEEE Symposium on Logic in Computer Science, pp. 62–71 (2005)

Four-Valued Monitorability of ω-Regular Languages

Zhe Chen[1,2,3]($\boxtimes$), Yunyun Chen[1], Robert M. Hierons[4], and Yifan Wu[1]

[1] College of Computer Science and Technology,
Nanjing University of Aeronautics and Astronautics,
Nanjing, People's Republic of China
zhechen@nuaa.edu.cn

[2] Shanghai Key Laboratory of Trustworthy Computing, Shanghai, China

[3] State Key Laboratory for Novel Software Technology, Nanjing University,
Nanjing, People's Republic of China

[4] Department of Computer Science, The University of Sheffield, Sheffield, UK
r.hierons@sheffield.ac.uk

Abstract. The use of runtime verification has led to interest in deciding whether a property is *monitorable*: whether it is always possible for the satisfaction or violation of the property to be determined after a finite future continuation during system execution. However, classical two-valued monitorability suffers from two inherent limitations, which eventually increase runtime overhead. First, no information is available regarding whether only one verdict (satisfaction or violation) can be detected. Second, it does not tell us whether verdicts can be detected starting from the current monitor *state* during system execution.

This paper proposes a new notion of four-valued monitorability for ω-languages and applies it at the state-level. Four-valued monitorability is more informative than two-valued monitorability as a property can be evaluated as a four-valued result, denoting that only satisfaction, only violation, or both are active for a monitorable property. We can also compute state-level weak monitorability, i.e., whether satisfaction or violation can be detected starting from a given state in a monitor, which enables state-level optimizations of monitoring algorithms. Based on a new six-valued semantics, we propose procedures for computing four-valued monitorability of ω-regular languages, both at the language-level and at the state-level. Experimental results show that our tool implementation MONIC can correctly, and quickly, report both two-valued and four-valued monitorability.

Keywords: Monitorability · ω-regular languages · Linear temporal logic · Multi-valued logics · Runtime verification.

Supported by the Joint Research Funds of National Natural Science Foundation of China and Civil Aviation Administration of China (No. U1533130) and the Open Project of Shanghai Key Lab. of Trustworthy Computing.

© Springer Nature Switzerland AG 2020
S.-W. Lin et al. (Eds.): ICFEM 2020, LNCS 12531, pp. 198–214, 2020.
https://doi.org/10.1007/978-3-030-63406-3_12

1   Introduction

Runtime Verification (RV) [6,29,32] is a lightweight formal technique in which program or system execution is monitored and analyzed. RV uses information extracted from an execution to check whether certain properties are satisfied or violated after a finite number of steps, possibly leading to online responses. In RV, properties are usually expressed using formalisms [26] such as Linear Temporal Logic (LTL) formulas [10,17,33,36], Nondeterministic Büchi Automata (NBAs), and ω-regular expressions, which represent ω-regular languages [7,15]. RV tools automatically synthesize monitors (i.e., code fragments) from formal specifications and then weave the code into the system through instrumentation [24,25,28]. The inserted code typically maintains a set of monitor objects that can detect property satisfaction or violation during system execution. Such approaches have been extended to parametric RV, in which properties are checked over every parameter instance (i.e., a combination of parameter values) by maintaining a monitor object for every parameter instance [11–13,27,34,38].

Figure 1 shows a monitor specification, written in the MOVEC language [13], for the parametric RV of an event-driven system that dispatches a variety of events (e.g., sensor status, keystrokes, program loadings etc.) to components (e.g., libraries, mobile apps, microservices etc.). Similar specifications can be written for other tools such as JavaMOP [11,34] and TraceMatches [4,5]. This specification defines a parametric monitor, named `priority`, which takes two parameters: a component ID c and an event ID e that should be instantiated with the values (i.e., actual arguments) generated by system execution. The specification body begins with four actions, which extract information regarding function calls: r records a component being registered to an event (it also creates a monitor object by instantiating the monitor parameters with the arguments of the call), u records an unregister, b records the broadcast of an event (the argument of the call) to all components, and n records a certain component being notified of a specific event. This specification is used to monitor system execution to check whether the property, specified as LTL formula $\phi_1 := (r \wedge Fu) \rightarrow ((\neg b \wedge \neg u)\, Un)\, Uu$, is satisfied or violated after a finite number of steps, i.e., any infinite future continuation makes the property satisfied or violated, respectively. The property requires that if a component c registers to an event e and unregisters later, then before the unregister, the event e cannot be broadcasted until c has been notified (i.e., c has a higher priority than unregistered components).

In practice, if the satisfaction or violation of a property is detected by a monitor object then an associated handler (i.e., a piece of code) is automatically triggered to perform some online response [11,13,34]. For example, Fig. 1 includes two handlers for the satisfaction (i.e., validation) and violation of the LTL formula: if the property is satisfied then a message is logged; if it is violated then an alarm is signaled and this prints the IDs of the component and the event. The two handlers may also be extended to more advanced operations, e.g., profiling and error recovery.

We may also monitor the system against other properties, e.g., $\phi_2 := Fr \rightarrow GFn$ that a component should receive notifications infinitely often after its

```
monitor priority(c,e) {
    creation action r(c,e) after call(% reg_component(% %:c, % %:e));
    action u(c,e) after call(% unreg_component(% %:c, % %:e));
    action b(e) before execution(% broadcast(% %:e));
    action n(c,e) after execution(% notify(% %:c, % %:e));

    ltl: (r && <>u) -> ((!b && !u) U n) U u;
    @validation {
        log("Priority applied: component %lu registers to event %lu.\n",
            monitor->c, monitor->e); }
    @violation {
        printf("Priority violated: component %lu registers to event %lu.\n",
            monitor->c, monitor->e); }
};
```

Fig. 1. A monitor specification with an LTL formula.

registration, $\phi_3 := r \to Fu$ that a component unregisters after its registration, and $\phi_4 := G(r \to \neg u\, Un)$ that a registered component receives at least one notification before its deregistration. The developer may also write handlers for the satisfaction and violation of each property.

When specifying properties, the developer is usually concerned with their monitorability [7,10,16,37], i.e., after any number of steps, whether the satisfaction or violation of the monitored property can still be detected after a finite future continuation. When writing handlers for these properties, the developer might consider the following question: *"Can the handlers for satisfaction and violation be triggered during system execution?"* We say that a verdict and its handler are *active* if there is some continuation that would lead to the verdict being detected and thus its handler being triggered. This question can be partly answered by deciding monitorability (with the traditional two-valued notion). For example, ϕ_2 (above) is non-monitorable, i.e., there is some finite sequence of steps after which no verdict is active. Worse, ϕ_2 is also weakly non-monitorable [14], i.e., no verdict can be detected after any number of steps. Thus writing handlers for ϕ_2 is a waste of time as they will never be triggered. More seriously, monitoring ϕ_2 at runtime adds no value but increases runtime overhead. In contrast, ϕ_1, ϕ_3 and ϕ_4 are monitorable, i.e., some verdicts are always active. Thus their handlers must be developed as they may be triggered. However, this answer is still unsatisfactory, as the existing notion of monitorability suffers from two inherent limitations: *limited informativeness* and *coarse granularity*.

Limited Informativeness. The existing notion of monitorability is not sufficiently informative, as it is two-valued, i.e., a property can only be evaluated as monitorable or non-monitorable. This means, for a monitorable property, we only know that some verdicts are active, but no information is available regarding whether only one verdict (satisfaction or violation) is active. As a result, the developer may still write unnecessary handlers for inactive verdicts. For example,

ϕ_1, ϕ_3 and ϕ_4 are monitorable. We only know that at least one of satisfaction and violation is active, but this does not tell us which ones are active and thus which handlers are required. As a result, the developer may waste time in handling inactive verdicts, e.g., the violation of ϕ_3 and the satisfaction of ϕ_4. Thus, the existing answer is far from satisfactory.

Limited informativeness also weakens the support for property debugging. For example, when writing a property the developer may expect that both verdicts are active but a mistake may lead to only one verdict being active. The converse is also the case. Unfortunately, these kinds of errors cannot be revealed by two-valued monitorability, as the expected property and the written (erroneous) property are both monitorable. For example, the developer may write formula ϕ_4 while having in mind another one $\phi_5 := r \rightarrow \neg u\,Un$, i.e., what she/he really wants is wrongly prefixed by one G. These two formulas cannot be discriminated by deciding two-valued monitorability as both are monitorable.

Coarse Granularity. The existing notion of monitorability is defined at the language-level, i.e., a property can only be evaluated as monitorable or not as a whole, rather than a notion for (more fine-grained) states in a monitor. This means that we do not know whether satisfaction or violation can be detected *starting from the current state* during system execution. As a result, every monitor object must be maintained during the entire execution, again increasing runtime overhead. For example, $\phi_6 := GFr \vee (\neg n \rightarrow X\neg b)$ is weakly monitorable, thus all its monitor objects (i.e., instances of the Finite State Machine (FSM) in Fig. 2), created for every pair of component and event, are maintained.

Note that parametric runtime verification is NP-complete for detecting violations and coNP-complete for ensuring satisfaction [12]. This high complexity primarily comes from the large number of monitor objects maintained for all parameter instances [12,13,34]. For state-level optimizations of monitoring algorithms, if no verdict can be detected starting from the current state of a monitor object, then the object can be switched off and safely removed to improve runtime performance. For example, in Fig. 2, only satisfaction can be detected starting from states P1,

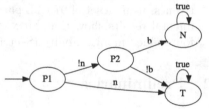

Fig. 2. A monitor for LTL formula $\phi_6 := GFr \vee (\neg n \rightarrow X\neg b)$. Each transition is labeled with a propositional formula denoting a set of satisfying states. For example, "!n" denotes $\{\emptyset, \{r\}, \{b\}, \{r,b\}\}$ and "true" denotes all states.

P2 and T, whereas no verdict can be detected starting from state N. Thus a monitor object can be safely removed when it enters N. Unfortunately, the existing notion does not support such optimizations.

Our Solution. In this paper, we propose a new notion of four-valued monitorability for ω-languages, and apply it at the state-level, overcoming the two limitations discussed above. First, the proposed approach is more informative than two-valued monitorability. Indeed, a property can be evaluated as a four-valued result, denoting that *only satisfaction, only violation, or both are active* *for a monitorable property*. Thus, if satisfaction (resp. violation) is inactive, then writing handlers for satisfaction (resp. violation) is not required. This can also enhance property debugging. For example, ϕ_4 and ϕ_5 can now be discriminated by their different monitorability results, as ϕ_4 can never be satisfied but ϕ_5 can be satisfied and can also be violated. Thus, additional developer mistakes can be revealed. Second, we can compute state-level weak monitorability, i.e., whether satisfaction or violation can be detected starting from a given state in a monitor. For example, in Fig. 2, N is weakly non-monitorable, thus a monitor object can be safely removed when it enters N, achieving a state-level optimization.

In summary, we make the following contributions.[1]

- We propose a new notion of four-valued monitorability for ω-languages (Sect. 3), which provides more informative answers as to which verdicts are active. This notion is defined using six types of prefixes, which complete the classification of finite sequences.
- We propose a procedure for computing four-valued monitorability of ω-regular languages, given in terms of LTL formulas, NBAs or ω-regular expressions (Sect. 4), based on a new six-valued semantics.
- We propose a new notion of state-level four-valued weak monitorability and its computation procedure for ω-regular languages (Sect. 5), which describes which verdicts are active for a state. This can enable state-level optimizations of monitoring algorithms.
- We have developed a new tool, MONIC, that implements the proposed procedure for computing monitorability of LTL formulas. We evaluated its effectiveness using a set of 97 LTL patterns and formulas ϕ_1 to ϕ_6 (above). Experimental results show that MONIC can correctly report both two-valued and four-valued monitorability (Sect. 6).

2   Preliminaries

Let AP be a non-empty finite set of *atomic propositions*. A *state* is a complete assignment of truth values to the propositions in AP. Let $\Sigma = 2^{AP}$ be a finite *alphabet*, i.e., the set of all states. Σ^* is the set of finite words (i.e., sequences of states in Σ), including the empty word ϵ, and Σ^ω is the set of infinite words. We denote atomic propositions by p, q, r, finite words by u, v, and infinite words by w, unless explicitly specified. We write a finite or infinite word in the form $\{p, q\}\{p\}\{q, r\} \cdots$, where a proposition appears in a state iff it is assigned true. We drop the brackets around singletons, i.e., $\{p, q\}p\{q, r\} \cdots$.

An ω-*language* (i.e., a linear-time infinitary property) L is a set of infinite words over Σ, i.e., $L \subseteq \Sigma^\omega$. Linear Temporal Logic (LTL) [33,36] is a typical representation of ω-regular languages. LTL extends propositional logic, which uses *boolean connectives* $\neg$ (not) and $\wedge$ (conjunction), by introducing *temporal connectives* such as $\boldsymbol{X}$ (next), $\boldsymbol{U}$ (until), $\boldsymbol{R}$ (release), $\boldsymbol{F}$ (future, or eventually) and

---

[1] A longer version of this paper (with all proofs) is available at https://arxiv.org/abs/2002.06737.

G (globally, or always). Intuitively, $X\phi$ says that ϕ holds at the next state, $\phi_1 U\phi_2$ says that at some future state ϕ_2 holds and before that state ϕ_1 always holds. Using the temporal connectives X and U, the full power of LTL is obtained. For convenience, we also use some common abbreviations: *true, false,* standard boolean connectives $\phi_1 \vee \phi_2 \equiv \neg(\neg\phi_1 \wedge \neg\phi_2)$ and $\phi_1 \rightarrow \phi_2 \equiv \neg\phi_1 \vee \phi_2$, and additional temporal connectives $\phi_1 R\phi_2 \equiv \neg(\neg\phi_1 U\neg\phi_2)$ (the dual to U), $F\phi \equiv true\, U\phi$ (ϕ eventually holds), and $G\phi \equiv \neg F\neg\phi$ (ϕ always holds). We denote by $L(\phi)$ the ω-language accepted by a formula ϕ.

Let us recall the classification of prefixes that are used to define the three-valued semantics and two-valued monitorability of ω-languages.

Definition 1 (Good, bad and ugly prefixes [8,31]**).** *A finite word $u \in \Sigma^*$ is a good prefix for L if $\forall w \in \Sigma^\omega.uw \in L$, a bad prefix for L if $\forall w \in \Sigma^\omega.uw \notin L$, or an ugly prefix for L if no finite extension makes it good or bad, i.e., $\not\exists v \in \Sigma^*.\forall w \in \Sigma^\omega.uvw \in L$ and $\not\exists v \in \Sigma^*.\forall w \in \Sigma^\omega.uvw \notin L$.*

In other words, good and bad prefixes *satisfy* and *violate* an ω-language in some finite number of steps, respectively. We denote by $good(L)$, $bad(L)$ and $ugly(L)$ the set of good, bad and ugly prefixes for L, respectively. Note that they do not constitute a complete classification of finite words. For example, any finite word of the form $p \cdots p$ is neither a good nor a bad prefix for $p\, Uq$, and also is not an ugly prefix as it can be extended to a good prefix (ended with q) or a bad prefix (ended with $\emptyset$).

Definition 2 (Three-valued semantics [10]**).** *Let $\mathbb{B}_3$ be the set of three truth values: true $\top$, false $\bot$ and inconclusive ?. The truth value of an ω-language $L \subseteq \Sigma^\omega$ wrt. a finite word $u \in \Sigma^*$, denoted by $[u \models L]_3$, is $\top$ or $\bot$ if u is a good or bad prefix for L, respectively, and ? otherwise.*

Note that the inconclusive value does not correspond to ugly prefixes. Although an ugly prefix always leads to the inconclusive value, the converse does not hold. For example, $[p \cdots p \models L(p\,Uq)]_3 = ?$ but $p \cdots p$ is not an ugly prefix.

Bauer et al. [10] presented a monitor construction procedure that transforms an LTL formula ϕ into a three-valued monitor, i.e., a deterministic FSM that contains $\top$, $\bot$ and ? states, which output $\top$, $\bot$ and ? after reading over good, bad and other prefixes respectively. For example, in Fig. 2, state T is a $\top$ state, whereas the remaining states are all ? states. This construction procedure requires 2ExpSpace. It has been shown that the three-valued monitor can be used to compute the truth value of an ω-language wrt. a finite word [10], which is the output of the corresponding monitor after reading over this word.

Lemma 1. *Let $M = (Q, \Sigma, \delta, q_0, \mathbb{B}_3, \lambda_3)$ be a three-valued monitor for an ω-language $L \subseteq \Sigma^\omega$, where Q is a finite set of states, Σ is a finite alphabet, $\delta : Q \times \Sigma \mapsto Q$ is a transition function, $q_0 \in Q$ is an initial state, $\mathbb{B}_3$ is an output alphabet and $\lambda_3 : Q \rightarrow \mathbb{B}_3$ is an output function. For any $u \in \Sigma^*$, $[u \models L]_3 = \lambda_3(\delta(q_0, u))$.*

Definition 3 (Two-valued monitorability [7,10,37]**).** *An ω-language* $L \subseteq \Sigma^\omega$ *is u*-monitorable *for* $u \in \Sigma^*$, *if* $\exists v \in \Sigma^*$ *s.t. uv is a good or bad prefix, and* monitorable *if it is u-monitorable for every* $u \in \Sigma^*$.

In other words, L is *u-monitorable* if u has a *good* or *bad extension*. L is *monitorable* if every finite word has a good or bad extension. Note that an ugly prefix can never be extended to a good or bad prefix. Thus, L is *non-monitorable* iff there exists an ugly prefix for L.

3   Four-Valued Monitorability

In this section, we propose a new notion of four-valued monitorability, to provide more informative answers to monitorability checking. As we promised, it can indicate whether only satisfaction, only violation, or both are active for a monitorable property. Two-valued monitorability cannot achieve this because its definition only requires that all finite words (i.e., u in Definition 3) can be extended to good or bad prefixes (which witness satisfaction or violation, respectively), but does not discriminate between them on the types and number of the verdicts that the extensions of each finite word can witness. To address this limitation, our approach aims to discriminate accordingly these finite words by inspecting which types of prefixes they can be extended to.

To achieve this objective, we first need to propose a new classification of prefixes, as the traditional classification (as the good, the bad and the ugly) is not satisfactory due to incompleteness, i.e., it does not include the finite words that are neither good nor bad but can be extended to good or bad prefixes. Thus we introduce the notions of positive, negative and neutral prefixes, in addition to good, bad and ugly prefixes, to complete the classification.

Definition 4 (Positive, negative and neutral prefixes). *A finite word* u *is*

- a positive prefix *for* L *if it is not good, but some finite extension makes it good but never bad, i.e.,* $\exists w \in \Sigma^\omega.uw \notin L$, $\exists v \in \Sigma^*.\forall w \in \Sigma^\omega.uvw \in L$, *and* $\not\exists v \in \Sigma^*.\forall w \in \Sigma^\omega.uvw \notin L$,
- a negative prefix *for* L *if it is not bad, but some finite extension makes it bad but never good, i.e.,* $\exists w \in \Sigma^\omega.uw \in L$, $\exists v \in \Sigma^*.\forall w \in \Sigma^\omega.uvw \notin L$, *and* $\not\exists v \in \Sigma^*.\forall w \in \Sigma^\omega.uvw \in L$, *or*
- a neutral prefix *for* L *if some finite extension makes it good and some makes it bad, i.e.,* $\exists v \in \Sigma^*.\forall w \in \Sigma^\omega.uvw \in L$ *and* $\exists v \in \Sigma^*.\forall w \in \Sigma^\omega.uvw \notin L$.

We denote by $posi(L)$, $nega(L)$ and $neut(L)$ the set of positive, negative and neutral prefixes for L, respectively. It is easy to see that the three new sets of prefixes and the three traditional sets of good, bad and ugly prefixes are mutually disjoint. An interesting fact, as shown by the following theorem, is that the six sets of prefixes exactly constitute the complete set of finite words. Furthermore, the six types of prefixes directly correspond to the six-valued semantics (cf. Definition 5). This completes the classification of prefixes.

Theorem 1. $good(L) \cup bad(L) \cup posi(L) \cup nega(L) \cup neut(L) \cup ugly(L) = \Sigma^*$.

The traditional three-valued semantics can identify only good and bad prefixes with the truth values $\top$ and $\bot$ respectively, whereas all the prefixes of the other four types are given the same value ?. To discriminate them, we further divide the value ? into four truth values.

Definition 5 (Six-valued semantics). *Let $\mathbb{B}_6$ be the set of six truth values: true $\top$, false $\bot$, possibly true $\mp$, possibly false $\pm$, possibly conclusive $+$ and inconclusive $\times$. The truth value of an ω-language $L \subseteq \Sigma^*$ wrt. a finite word $u \in \Sigma^*$, denoted by $[u \models L]_6$, is $\top$, $\bot$, $\mp$, $\pm$, $+$ or $\times$ if u is a good, bad, positive, negative, neutral or ugly prefix for L, respectively.*

Note that the six-valued semantics models a rigorous correspondence between truth values and prefix types. Unlike the three-valued semantics, the inconclusive value now exactly corresponds to ugly prefixes.

The definition of four-valued monitorability is built on the following notion of four-valued u-monitorability which is used to discriminate finite words by inspecting which types of prefixes they can be extended to.

Definition 6 (Four-valued u-monitorability). *An ω-language $L \subseteq \Sigma^\omega$ is*

- weakly positively u-monitorable *for $u \in \Sigma^*$, if $\exists v \in \Sigma^*$, s.t. uv is a good prefix.*
- weakly negatively u-monitorable *for $u \in \Sigma^*$, if $\exists v \in \Sigma^*$, s.t. uv is a bad prefix.*
- positively u-monitorable *if it is weakly positively, but not weakly negatively, u-monitorable. (u has only good extensions, thus u is a good/positive prefix.)*
- negatively u-monitorable *if it is weakly negatively, but not weakly positively, u-monitorable. (u has only bad extensions, thus u is a bad/negative prefix.)*
- neutrally u-monitorable *if it is both weakly positively and weakly negatively u-monitorable. (u has both good and bad extensions, thus u is a neutral prefix.)*
- not u-monitorable *if it is neither weakly positively nor weakly negatively u-monitorable. (u has neither good nor bad extension, thus u is an ugly prefix.)*

In other words, the traditional u-monitorability is split into two parts, i.e., weakly positive and weakly negative u-monitorability. As a result, L is u-monitorable iff L is positively, negatively or neutrally u-monitorable.

Definition 7 (Four-valued monitorability). *An ω-language $L \subseteq \Sigma^\omega$ is*

- positively monitorable *if it is positively u-monitorable for every $u \in \Sigma^*$.*
- negatively monitorable *if it is negatively u-monitorable for every $u \in \Sigma^*$.*
- neutrally monitorable *if it is u-monitorable for every $u \in \Sigma^*$, and is neutrally ϵ-monitorable for the empty word ϵ.*
- non-monitorable *if it is not u-monitorable for some $u \in \Sigma^*$.*

In other words, the set of monitorable ω-languages is divided into three classes, i.e., positively, negatively and neutrally monitorable ones. Note that the definition of neutral monitorability consists of two conditions, of which the first ensures that L is monitorable while the second ensures that both of satisfaction and violation can be detected after some finite sequences of steps. We denote the four truth values (positively, negatively, neutrally and non-monitorable) by $M_\top$, $M_\perp$, M_+ and $M_\times$, respectively.

We can validate that four-valued monitorability indeed provides the informativeness we require, as described in Sect. 1, by showing the following theorem, that the truth values $M_\top$, $M_\perp$, and M_+ indicate that only satisfaction, only violation, and both can be detected after some finite sequences of steps, respectively. This theorem can be proved by Definitions 7 and 6, in which u is substituted by the empty word ϵ.

Theorem 2. *If an ω-language $L \subseteq \Sigma^\omega$ is*

- $M_\top$ *then* $\exists u \in \Sigma^*.\forall w \in \Sigma^\omega.uw \in L$ *and* $\nexists u \in \Sigma^*.\forall w \in \Sigma^\omega.uw \notin L$.
- $M_\perp$ *then* $\exists u \in \Sigma^*.\forall w \in \Sigma^\omega.uw \notin L$ *and* $\nexists u \in \Sigma^*.\forall w \in \Sigma^\omega.uw \in L$.
- M_+ *then* $\exists u \in \Sigma^*.\forall w \in \Sigma^\omega.uw \in L$ *and* $\exists u \in \Sigma^*.\forall w \in \Sigma^\omega.uw \notin L$.

Let us consider some simple but essential examples regarding basic temporal connectives. More examples, such as the formulas used in Sect. 1, will be considered in Sect. 6.

- Formula $\boldsymbol{F}p$ is positively monitorable, as any finite word can be extended to a good prefix (ended with p) but never a bad prefix. This means that only satisfaction, but no violation, of the property can be detected after some finite sequences of steps.
- Formula $\boldsymbol{G}p$ is negatively monitorable, as any finite word can be extended to a bad prefix (ended with $\emptyset$) but never a good prefix. This means that only violation, but no satisfaction, of the property can be detected after some finite sequences of steps.
- Formula $p\,\boldsymbol{U}q$ is neutrally monitorable, as it is monitorable and ϵ (more generally, any finite word of the form $p \cdots p$) can be extended to both a good prefix (ended with q) and a bad prefix (ended with $\emptyset$). This means that both of satisfaction and violation of the property can be detected after some finite sequences of steps.
- Formula $\boldsymbol{GF}p$ is non-monitorable, as any finite word can never be extended to a good or bad prefix, due to the infinite continuations $\emptyset\emptyset \cdots$ and $pp \cdots$ respectively. This means that neither satisfaction nor violation of the property can be detected.

4   Computing Four-Valued Monitorability

In this section, we propose a procedure for computing the four-valued monitorability of ω-regular languages, based on the six-valued semantics.

The first step is a monitor construction procedure that transforms an LTL formula into a six-valued monitor, i.e., a deterministic FSM which outputs $\top$, $\bot$, $\mp$, $\pm$, $+$ and $\times$ after reading over good, bad, positive, negative, neutral and ugly prefixes respectively. For example, in Fig. 2, states P1, P2 and N are all ? states under the three-valued semantics. After refining the output function with the six-valued semantics, states P1 and P2 become $\mp$ states, whereas state N becomes a $\times$ state.

The construction procedure first constructs a three-valued monitor, using the traditional approach which requires 2ExpSpace [10]. Then we refine its output function, assigning new outputs to ? states. Specifically, our procedure traverses all the states in the monitor, and for each state, starts another nested traversal to check whether a $\top$ state or a $\bot$ state is reachable. A ? state is assigned output $\mp$ if $\top$ states are reachable but no $\bot$ state is, $\pm$ if $\bot$ states are reachable but no $\top$ state is, $+$ if both $\top$ and $\bot$ states are reachable, or $\times$ if neither is reachable. This refinement step can be done in polynomial time and NLSpace (using the three-valued monitor as the input). Thus, constructing a six-valued monitor requires also 2ExpSpace. Let us formalize the above construction procedure.

Definition 8. *Let $M = (Q,\ \Sigma,\ \delta,\ q_0,\ \mathbb{B}_3,\ \lambda_3)$ be a three-valued monitor for an ω-language $L \subseteq \Sigma^\omega$. The corresponding six-valued monitor $M' = (Q,\ \Sigma,\ \delta,\ q_0,\ \mathbb{B}_6,\ \lambda)$ is obtained by refining the output function λ_3 of M as in Fig. 3.*

$$\text{for any } q \in Q, \lambda(q) = \begin{cases} \top, \text{if } \lambda_3(q) = \top \\ \bot, \text{if } \lambda_3(q) = \bot \\ \mp, \text{if } \begin{cases} \lambda_3(q) \neq \top \\ \exists v \in \Sigma^*.\ \delta(q,v) = q' \wedge \lambda_3(q') = \top, \text{ and} \\ \forall v \in \Sigma^*.\ \delta(q,v) = q' \rightarrow \lambda_3(q') \neq \bot \end{cases} \\ \pm, \text{if } \begin{cases} \lambda_3(q) \neq \bot \\ \exists v \in \Sigma^*.\ \delta(q,v) = q' \wedge \lambda_3(q') = \bot, \text{ and} \\ \forall v \in \Sigma^*.\ \delta(q,v) = q' \rightarrow \lambda_3(q') \neq \top \end{cases} \\ +, \text{if } \begin{cases} \exists v \in \Sigma^*.\ \delta(q,v) = q' \wedge \lambda_3(q') = \top, \text{ and} \\ \exists v \in \Sigma^*.\ \delta(q,v) = q' \wedge \lambda_3(q') = \bot \end{cases} \\ \times, \text{if } \begin{cases} \forall v \in \Sigma^*.\ \delta(q,v) = q' \rightarrow \lambda_3(q') \neq \top, \text{ and} \\ \forall v \in \Sigma^*.\ \delta(q,v) = q' \rightarrow \lambda_3(q') \neq \bot \end{cases} \end{cases}$$

Fig. 3. The output function λ.

We can show the following lemma, that the six-valued monitor can be used to compute the truth value of an ω-language wrt. a finite word. This lemma can be proved by Definitions 5 and 2, Lemma 1 and Definition 8.

Lemma 2. *Let $M = (Q,\ \Sigma,\ \delta,\ q_0,\ \mathbb{B}_6,\ \lambda)$ be a six-valued monitor for an ω-language $L \subseteq \Sigma^\omega$. For any $u \in \Sigma^*$, $[u \models L]_6 = \lambda(\delta(q_0, u))$.*

As a property of the six-valued monitor, the following theorem shows that each state in a monitor can be reached by exactly one type of prefixes (by Lemma 2 and Definition 5).

Theorem 3. *Let $M = (Q, \Sigma, \delta, q_0, \mathbb{B}_6, \lambda)$ be a six-valued monitor for an ω-language $L \subseteq \Sigma^\omega$. For a state $q \in Q$, $\lambda(q)$ equals $\top, \bot, \mp, \pm, +$ or $\times$, iff it can be reached by good, bad, positive, negative, neutral or ugly prefixes, respectively.*

Based on the six-valued monitor, the second step determines the four-valued monitorability of an ω-language L by checking whether its monitor has some specific reachable states. The monitorability of L is $M_\top$ iff neither $\times$ nor $\bot$ states are reachable (thus neither $\pm$ nor $+$ states are reachable), $M_\bot$ iff neither $\times$ nor $\top$ states are reachable (thus neither $\mp$ nor $+$ states are reachable), M_+ iff no $\times$ state is reachable but a $+$ state is reachable (thus both $\top$ and $\bot$ states are reachable), and $M_\times$ iff a $\times$ state is reachable. These rules can be formalized:

Theorem 4. *Let $M = (Q, \Sigma, \delta, q_0, \mathbb{B}_6, \lambda)$ be a six-valued monitor for an ω-language $L \subseteq \Sigma^\omega$. The monitorability of L, denoted by $\eta(L)$, is:*

$$\eta(L) = \begin{cases} M_\top, \text{ iff } \forall u \in \Sigma^*.\ \delta(q_0, u) = q' \to \lambda(q') \neq \times \land \lambda(q') \neq \bot \\ M_\bot, \text{ iff } \forall u \in \Sigma^*.\ \delta(q_0, u) = q' \to \lambda(q') \neq \times \land \lambda(q') \neq \top \\ M_+, \text{ iff } \begin{cases} \forall u \in \Sigma^*.\ \delta(q_0, u) = q' \to \lambda(q') \neq \times, \text{ and} \\ \exists u \in \Sigma^*.\ \delta(q_0, u) = q' \land \lambda(q') = + \end{cases} \\ M_\times, \text{ iff } \exists u \in \Sigma^*.\ \delta(q_0, u) = q' \land \lambda(q') = \times \end{cases}$$

The above checking procedure can be done in linear time and NLSpace by traversing all the states of monitor. However, note that this procedure is performed after constructing the monitor. Thus, when an ω-regular language L is given in terms of an LTL formula, the four-valued monitorability of L can be computed in 2ExpSpace; the same complexity as for two-valued monitorability. As we will see in Sect. 6, the small size of standard LTL patterns means that four-valued monitorability can be computed in very little time

Now consider other representations of ω-regular languages. If L is given in terms of a Nondeterministic Büchi Automata (NBA), we first explicitly complement the NBA, and the rest of the procedure stays the same. However, the complement operation also involves an exponential blowup. If L is given in terms of an ω-regular expression, we first build an NBA for the expression, which can be done in polynomial time, and the rest of the procedure is the same as for NBA. Hence, independent of the concrete representation, four-valued monitorability of an ω-regular language can be computed in 2ExpSpace, by using the monitor-based procedure.

5   State-Level Four-Valued Weak Monitorability

In this section, we apply four-valued monitorability at the state-level, to predict whether satisfaction and violation can be detected *starting from a given state in a monitor.* Recall that the notions of monitorability (cf. Definitions 3 and 7) are defined using the extensions to good and bad prefixes. However, good and bad prefixes are defined for an ω-language, not for a state. Thus such definitions cannot be directly applied at the state-level. Instead, we define state-level monitorability using the reachability of $\top$ and $\bot$ states, which are equivalent notions to good and bad prefixes according to Theorem 3.

Another note is that the resulting state-level monitorability is too strong to meet our requirements, because it places restrictions on all the states reachable from the considered state. For example, in Fig. 2, we require discriminating states P1 and P2 from state N, as satisfaction can be detected starting from P1 and P2, but neither satisfaction nor violation can be detected starting from N. However, P1, P2 and N are all non-monitorable as neither $\top$ states nor $\bot$ states are reachable from N (in turn, reachable from P1 and P2). To provide the required distinction, we should use a weaker form of state-level monitorability as follows.

Definition 9 (State-level four-valued weak monitorability). *Let $M = (Q, \Sigma, \delta, q_0, \mathbb{B}_6, \lambda)$ be a six-valued monitor. A state $q \in Q$ is*

- *weakly $M_\top$ if a $\top$ state but no $\bot$ state is reachable from q.*
- *weakly $M_\bot$ if a $\bot$ state but no $\top$ state is reachable from q.*
- *weakly M_+ if both a $\top$ state and a $\bot$ state are reachable from q.*
- *weakly $M_\times$ if neither $\top$ states nor $\bot$ states are reachable from q.*

A state is *weakly monitorable*, iff it is weakly positively, negatively or neutrally monitorable. For example, in Fig. 2, states P1, P2 and T are all weakly positively monitorable as T is a reachable $\top$ state, while state N is weakly non-monitorable. Thus, states P1 and P2 can now be discriminated from state N.

We can validate that state-level four-valued weak monitorability can indeed predict whether satisfaction and violation can be detected *starting from a given state*, as anticipated in Sect. 1, by showing the following theorem, that the truth values $M_\top$, $M_\bot$, M_+ and $M_\times$ indicate that only satisfaction, only violation, both and neither can be detected, respectively. This theorem can be proved by Definition 9 and Theorem 3.

Theorem 5. *Let $M = (Q, \Sigma, \delta, q_0, \mathbb{B}_6, \lambda)$ be a six-valued monitor. Suppose a state $q \in Q$ can be reached from q_0 by reading $u \in \Sigma^*$, i.e., $\delta(q_0, u) = q$. If q is*

- *weakly $M_\top$ then $\exists v \in \Sigma^*.\forall w \in \Sigma^\omega.uvw \in L \wedge \nexists v \in \Sigma^*.\forall w \in \Sigma^\omega.uvw \notin L$.*
- *weakly $M_\bot$ then $\exists v \in \Sigma^*.\forall w \in \Sigma^\omega.uvw \notin L \wedge \nexists v \in \Sigma^*.\forall w \in \Sigma^\omega.uvw \in L$.*
- *weakly M_+ then $\exists v \in \Sigma^*.\forall w \in \Sigma^\omega.uvw \in L \wedge \exists v \in \Sigma^*.\forall w \in \Sigma^\omega.uvw \notin L$.*
- *weakly $M_\times$ then $\nexists v \in \Sigma^*.\forall w \in \Sigma^\omega.uvw \in L \wedge \nexists v \in \Sigma^*.\forall w \in \Sigma^\omega.uvw \notin L$.*

The four truth values can be used in state-level optimizations of monitoring algorithms:

- If a state is weakly positively (resp. negatively) monitorable, then a monitor object can be safely removed when it enters this state, provided that only violation (resp. satisfaction) handlers are specified, as no handler can be triggered.

– If a state is weakly neutrally monitorable, then a monitor object must be preserved if it is at this state as both satisfaction and violation can be detected after some continuations.
– If a state is weakly non-monitorable, then a monitor object can be safely removed when it enters this state as no verdict can be detected after any continuation.

Besides, a monitor object can also be removed when it enters a $\top$ state or a $\bot$ state, as any finite or infinite continuation yields the same verdict.

Let us consider the relationship between the language-level monitorability and the state-level weak monitorability. The following lemma shows that the monitorability of an ω-language depends on the weak monitorability of all the reachable states of its monitor. This means, if an ω-language is non-monitorable, then its monitor contains a reachable weakly non-monitorable state.

Lemma 3. *Let* $M = (Q, \Sigma, \delta, q_0, \mathbb{B}_6, \lambda)$ *be a six-valued monitor for an ω-language* $L \subseteq \Sigma^\omega$. L *is monitorable iff every reachable state of M is weakly monitorable.*

Let us consider how one can compute the state-level four-valued weak monitorability for each state in a six-valued monitor. We first formalize a mapping from truth values to weak monitorability, and then show that the state-level weak monitorability can be quickly computed from the output of the state.

Definition 10 (Value-to-weak-monitorability). *Let* $vtom : \mathbb{B}_6 \mapsto \mathbb{M}_4$ *be the* value-to-weak-monitorability operator *that converts a truth value in $\mathbb{B}_6$ into the corresponding result of weak monitorability in* $\mathbb{M}_4 = \{M_\top, M_\bot, M_+, M_\times\}$, *defined as follows:* $vtom(\top) = vtom(\mp) = M_\top$, $vtom(\bot) = vtom(\pm) = M_\bot$, $vtom(+) = M_+$ *and* $vtom(\times) = M_\times$.

Theorem 6. *Let* $M = (Q, \Sigma, \delta, q_0, \mathbb{B}_6, \lambda)$ *be a six-valued monitor for an ω-language* $L \subseteq \Sigma^\omega$. *The four-valued weak monitorability of $q \in Q$ equals* $vtom(\lambda(q))$.

6   Implementation and Experimental Results

We have developed a new tool, MONIC, that implements the proposed procedure for computing four-valued monitorability of LTL formulas. MONIC also supports deciding two-valued monitorability. We have evaluated its effectiveness using a set of LTL formulas, including formulas ϕ_1 to ϕ_6 (used in Sect. 1) and Dwyer et al.'s 97 LTL patterns [10,18]. The tool implementation MONIC and the dataset of LTL formulas are available at https://github.com/drzchen/monic. The evaluation was performed on an ordinary laptop, equipped with an Intel Core i7-6500U CPU (at 2.5GHz), 4GB RAM and Ubuntu Desktop (64-bit).

The result on formulas ϕ_1 to ϕ_6 shows that: ϕ_1 is neutrally monitorable, ϕ_2 is non-monitorable, ϕ_3 is positively monitorable, ϕ_4 is negatively monitorable, ϕ_5 is neutrally monitorable, and ϕ_6 is non-monitorable (but weakly monitorable).

Thus, the violation of ϕ_3 and the satisfaction of ϕ_4 can never be detected, whereas both verdicts are active for ϕ_1 and ϕ_5. Further, ϕ_4 and ϕ_5 can be discriminated by their different monitorability results.

We also ran MONIC on Dwyer et al.'s specification patterns [10,18], of which 97 are well-formed LTL formulas. The result shows that 55 formulas are monitorable and 42 are non-monitorable. For those monitorable ones, 6 are positively monitorable, 40 are negatively monitorable and 9 are neutrally monitorable. Our result disagrees with the two-valued result reported in [10] only on the 6th LTL formula listed in the Appendix of [10]. More precisely, MONIC reports negatively monitorable, whereas the result in [10] is non-monitorable. The formula is as follows (! for ¬, & for ∧, | for ∨, -> for →, U for U, <> for F, [] for G):

```
[](("call" & <>"open") ->
  ((!"atfloor" & !"open") U
  ("open" | (("atfloor" & !"open") U
    ("open" | (("atfloor" & !"open") U
      ("open" | (("atfloor" & !"open") U
        ("open" | (!"atfloor" U "open")))))))))) .
```

A manual inspection of its monitor (in Fig. 4) shows that our result is correct. Indeed, state F is a ⊥ state, and states N1 to N7 are all ± states that can reach the ⊥ state F.

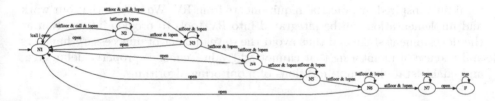

Fig. 4. The monitor of an LTL pattern.

Finally, the above results for ϕ_1 to ϕ_6 and the 97 LTL patterns were computed in 0.03 and 0.07 s, with 16 MB and 20 MB memory consumed, respectively (all reported by GNU time). To conclude, the results show that MONIC can correctly report both two-valued and four-valued monitorability of typical formulas in very little time.

7 Related Work

Monitorability is a principal foundational question in RV because it delineates which properties can be monitored at runtime. The classical results on monitorability have been established for ω-languages, especially for LTL [7,10,37]. Francalanza and Aceto et al. have studied monitorability for the Hennessy-Milner logic with recursion, both with a branching-time semantics [1,21–23] and with a linear-time semantics [2]. There exist some variants of monitorability as well. For example, monitorability has been considered over unreliable communication channels which may reorder or lose events [30]. However, all of the existing works only consider two-valued notions of monitorability at the language-level.

Monitorability has been studied in other contexts. For example, a topological viewpoint [16] and the correspondence between monitorability and the classifications of properties (e.g., the safety-progress and safety-liveness classifications) [19,20,35] have been established. A hierarchy of monitorability definitions (including monitorability and weak monitorability [14]) has been defined wrt. the operational guarantees provided by monitors [3].

A four-valued semantics for LTL [8,9] has been proposed to refine the three-valued semantics [10]. It divides the inconclusive truth value ? into two values: *currently true* and *currently false*, i.e., whether the finite sequence observed so far satisfies the property based on a finite semantics for LTL. Note that it provides more information on what has already been seen, whereas our six-valued semantics describes what verdicts can be detected in the future continuation.

8   Conclusion

We have proposed four-valued monitorability and the corresponding computation procedure for ω-regular languages. Then we applied the four-valued notion at the state-level. To our knowledge, this is the first study of multi-valued monitorability, inspired by practical requirements from RV. We believe that our work and implementation can be integrated into RV tools to provide information at the development stage and thus avoid the development of unnecessary handlers and the use of monitoring that cannot add value, enhance property debugging, and enable state-level optimizations of monitoring algorithms.

References

1. Aceto, L., Achilleos, A., Francalanza, A., Ingólfsdóttir, A.: A framework for parameterized monitorability. In: Baier, C., Dal Lago, U. (eds.) FoSSaCS 2018. LNCS, vol. 10803, pp. 203–220. Springer, Cham (2018). https://doi.org/10.1007/978-3-319-89366-2_11
2. Aceto, L., Achilleos, A., Francalanza, A., Ingólfsdóttir, A., Lehtinen, K.: Adventures in monitorability: from branching to linear time and back again. In: Proceedings of the ACM on Programming Languages,(POPL 2019), vol. 3, pp. 52:1–52:29 (2019)
3. Aceto, L., Achilleos, A., Francalanza, A., Ingólfsdóttir, A., Lehtinen, K.: An operational guide to monitorability. In: Ölveczky, P.C., Salaün, G. (eds.) SEFM 2019. LNCS, vol. 11724, pp. 433–453. Springer, Cham (2019). https://doi.org/10.1007/978-3-030-30446-1_23
4. Allan, C., et al.: Adding trace matching with free variables to AspectJ. In: Proceedings of OOPSLA 2005, pp. 345–364. ACM (2005)
5. Avgustinov, P., Tibble, J., de Moor, O.: Making trace monitors feasible. In: Proceedings of OOPSLA 2007, pp. 589–608. ACM (2007)

6. Bartocci, E., Falcone, Y., Francalanza, A., Reger, G.: Introduction to runtime verification. In: Bartocci, E., Falcone, Y. (eds.) Lectures on Runtime Verification. LNCS, vol. 10457, pp. 1–33. Springer, Cham (2018). https://doi.org/10.1007/978-3-319-75632-5_1

7. Bauer, A.: Monitorability of ω-regular languages. CoRR abs/1006.3638 (2010)

8. Bauer, A., Leucker, M., Schallhart, C.: The good, the bad, and the ugly, but how ugly is ugly? In: Sokolsky, O., Taşıran, S. (eds.) RV 2007. LNCS, vol. 4839, pp. 126–138. Springer, Heidelberg (2007). https://doi.org/10.1007/978-3-540-77395-5_11

9. Bauer, A., Leucker, M., Schallhart, C.: Comparing LTL semantics for runtime verification. J. Log. Comput. **20**(3), 651–674 (2010)

10. Bauer, A., Leucker, M., Schallhart, C.: Runtime verification for LTL and TLTL. ACM Trans. Softw. Eng. Methodol. (TOSEM) **20**(4), 14 (2011)

11. Chen, F., Rosu, G.: MOP: an efficient and generic runtime verification framework. In: Proceedings of OOPSLA 2007, pp. 569–588. ACM (2007)

12. Chen, Z.: Parametric runtime verification is NP-complete and coNP-complete. Inf. Process. Lett. **123**, 14–20 (2017)

13. Chen, Z., Wang, Z., Zhu, Y., Xi, H., Yang, Z.: Parametric runtime verification of C programs. In: Chechik, M., Raskin, J.-F. (eds.) TACAS 2016. LNCS, vol. 9636, pp. 299–315. Springer, Heidelberg (2016). https://doi.org/10.1007/978-3-662-49674-9_17

14. Chen, Z., Wu, Y., Wei, O., Sheng, B.: Deciding weak monitorability for runtime verification. In: Proceedings of ICSE 2018, pp. 163–164. ACM (2018)

15. d'Amorim, M., Roşu, G.: Efficient monitoring of ω-Languages. In: Etessami, K., Rajamani, S.K. (eds.) CAV 2005. LNCS, vol. 3576, pp. 364–378. Springer, Heidelberg (2005). https://doi.org/10.1007/11513988_36

16. Diekert, V., Leucker, M.: Topology, monitorable properties and runtime verification. Theor. Comput. Sci. **537**, 29–41 (2014)

17. Drusinsky, D.: The temporal rover and the ATG rover. In: Havelund, K., Penix, J., Visser, W. (eds.) SPIN 2000. LNCS, vol. 1885, pp. 323–330. Springer, Heidelberg (2000). https://doi.org/10.1007/10722468_19

18. Dwyer, M.B., Avrunin, G.S., Corbett, J.C.: Patterns in property specifications for finite-state verification. In: Proceedings of ICSE 1999, pp. 411–420. ACM (1999)

19. Falcone, Y., Fernandez, J.-C., Mounier, L.: Runtime verification of safety-progress properties. In: Bensalem, S., Peled, D.A. (eds.) RV 2009. LNCS, vol. 5779, pp. 40–59. Springer, Heidelberg (2009). https://doi.org/10.1007/978-3-642-04694-0_4

20. Falcone, Y., Fernandez, J.C., Mounier, L.: What can you verify and enforce at runtime? Int. J. Softw. Tools Technol. Transf. (STTT) **14**(3), 349–382 (2012). https://doi.org/10.1007/s10009-011-0196-8

21. Francalanza, A.: A theory of monitors. In: Jacobs, B., Löding, C. (eds.) FoSSaCS 2016. LNCS, vol. 9634, pp. 145–161. Springer, Heidelberg (2016). https://doi.org/10.1007/978-3-662-49630-5_9

22. Francalanza, A., et al.: A foundation for runtime monitoring. In: Lahiri, S., Reger, G. (eds.) RV 2017. LNCS, vol. 10548, pp. 8–29. Springer, Cham (2017). https://doi.org/10.1007/978-3-319-67531-2_2

23. Francalanza, A., Aceto, L., Ingólfsdóttir, A.: Monitorability for the Hennessy-Milner logic with recursion. Formal Methods Syst. Design **51**(1), 87–116 (2017). https://doi.org/10.1007/s10703-017-0273-z

24. Geilen, M.: On the construction of monitors for temporal logic properties. Electr. Notes Theor. Comput. Sci. **55**(2), 181–199 (2001)

25. Havelund, K.: Runtime verification of C programs. In: Suzuki, K., Higashino, T., Ulrich, A., Hasegawa, T. (eds.) FATES/TestCom -2008. LNCS, vol. 5047, pp. 7–22. Springer, Heidelberg (2008). https://doi.org/10.1007/978-3-540-68524-1_3

26. Havelund, K., Reger, G.: Runtime verification logics a language design perspective. In: Aceto, L., Bacci, G., Bacci, G., Ingólfsdóttir, A., Legay, A., Mardare, R. (eds.) Models, Algorithms, Logics and Tools. LNCS, vol. 10460, pp. 310–338. Springer, Cham (2017). https://doi.org/10.1007/978-3-319-63121-9_16

27. Havelund, K., Reger, G., Thoma, D., Zălinescu, E.: Monitoring events that carry data. In: Bartocci, E., Falcone, Y. (eds.) Lectures on Runtime Verification. LNCS, vol. 10457, pp. 61–102. Springer, Cham (2018). https://doi.org/10.1007/978-3-319-75632-5_3

28. Havelund, K., Roşu, G.: Synthesizing monitors for safety properties. In: Katoen, J.-P., Stevens, P. (eds.) TACAS 2002. LNCS, vol. 2280, pp. 342–356. Springer, Heidelberg (2002). https://doi.org/10.1007/3-540-46002-0_24

29. Havelund, K., Roşu, G.: Runtime verification - 17 years later. In: Colombo, C., Leucker, M. (eds.) RV 2018. LNCS, vol. 11237, pp. 3–17. Springer, Cham (2018). https://doi.org/10.1007/978-3-030-03769-7_1

30. Kauffman, S., Havelund, K., Fischmeister, S.: Monitorability over unreliable channels. In: Finkbeiner, B., Mariani, L. (eds.) RV 2019. LNCS, vol. 11757, pp. 256–272. Springer, Cham (2019). https://doi.org/10.1007/978-3-030-32079-9_15

31. Kupferman, O., Vardi, M.Y.: Model checking of safety properties. Formal Methods Syst. Design 19(3), 291–314 (2001). https://doi.org/10.1023/A:1011254632723

32. Leucker, M., Schallhart, C.: A brief account of runtime verification. J. Logic Algebraic Program. 78(5), 293–303 (2009)

33. Manna, Z., Pnueli, A.: The Temporal Logic of Reactive and Concurrent Systems: Specification. Springer, Heidelberg (1992). https://doi.org/10.1007/978-1-4612-0931-7

34. Meredith, P.O., Jin, D., Griffith, D., Chen, F., Rosu, G.: An overview of the MOP runtime verification framework. Int. J. Softw. Tools Technol. Transf. (STTT) 14(3), 249–289 (2012). https://doi.org/10.1007/s10009-011-0198-6

35. Peled, D., Havelund, K.: Refining the safety–liveness classification of temporal properties according to monitorability. In: Margaria, T., Graf, S., Larsen, K.G. (eds.) Models, Mindsets, Meta: The What, the How, and the Why Not?. LNCS, vol. 11200, pp. 218–234. Springer, Cham (2019). https://doi.org/10.1007/978-3-030-22348-9_14

36. Pnueli, A.: The temporal logic of programs. In: Proceedings of FOCS 1977, pp. 46–57. IEEE Computer Society (1977)

37. Pnueli, A., Zaks, A.: PSL model checking and run-time verification via testers. In: Misra, J., Nipkow, T., Sekerinski, E. (eds.) FM 2006. LNCS, vol. 4085, pp. 573–586. Springer, Heidelberg (2006). https://doi.org/10.1007/11813040_38

38. Rosu, G., Chen, F.: Semantics and algorithms for parametric monitoring. Log. Methods Comput. Sci. 8(1), 1–47 (2012)

Other Applications of Formal Methods

Formally Verified Trades in Financial Markets

Suneel Sarswat[(✉)] and Abhishek Kr Singh

Tata Institute of Fundamental Research, Mumbai, India
suneel.sarswat@gmail.com, abhishek.uor@gmail.com

Abstract. We introduce a formal framework for analyzing trades in financial markets. These days, all big exchanges use computer algorithms to match buy and sell requests and these algorithms must abide by certain regulatory guidelines. For example, market regulators enforce that a matching produced by exchanges should be *fair, uniform* and *individual rational.* To verify these properties of trades, we first formally define these notions in a theorem prover and then develop many important results about matching demand and supply. Finally, we use this framework to verify properties of two important classes of double sided auction mechanisms. All the definitions and results presented in this paper are completely formalized in the Coq proof assistant without adding any additional axioms to it.

1 Introduction

In this paper, we introduce a formal framework for analyzing trades in financial markets. Trading is a principal component of all modern economies. Over the past few centuries, more and more complex instruments are being introduced for trade in the financial markets. All big stock exchanges use computer algorithms to match buy requests (demand) with sell requests (supply) of traders. Computer algorithms are also used by traders to place orders in the markets (known as *algorithmic trading*). With the arrival of computer assisted trading, the volume and liquidity in the markets have increased drastically, and as a result, the markets have become more complex.

Software programs that enable the whole trading process are extremely complex and have to meet high efficiency criteria. Furthermore, to increase the confidence of traders in the markets, the market regulators set stringent safety and fairness guidelines for these software. Traditionally, to meet such criteria, software development has extensively relied on testing the programs on large data sets. Although testing is helpful in identifying bugs, it cannot guarantee the absence of bugs. Even small bugs in the trading software can have a catastrophic effect on the overall economy. An adversary might exploit a bug to his benefit and to the disadvantage of other genuine traders. These events are certainly undesirable in a healthy economy.

Recently, there have been various instances [17,19,20] of violation of the trading rules by the stock exchanges. For example, in [20], a regulator noted:

© Springer Nature Switzerland AG 2020
S.-W. Lin et al. (Eds.): ICFEM 2020, LNCS 12531, pp. 217–232, 2020.
https://doi.org/10.1007/978-3-030-63406-3_13

"NYSE Arca failed to execute a certain type of limit order under specified market conditions despite having a rule in effect that stated that NYSE Arca would execute such orders"[1]. This is an instance of a program not meeting its specification. Here the program is a matching algorithm used by the exchange and the regulatory guidelines are the broad specifications for the program. Note that, in most of the cases, the guidelines stated by the regulators are not a complete specification of the program. Moreover, there is no formal guarantee that these guidelines are consistent. These are some serious issues potentially compromising the safety and integrity of the markets.

Recent advances in formal methods in computer science can be put to good use in ensuring safe and fair financial markets. During the last few decades, formal method tools have been increasingly successful in proving the correctness of large software and hardware systems [7,9,10,12]. While model checking tools have been used for the verification of hardware, the use of interactive theorem provers have been quite successful in the verification of large software. A formal verification of financial algorithms using these tools can be helpful in the rigorous analysis of market behavior at large. The matching algorithms used by the exchanges (venues) are at the core of the broad spectrum of algorithms used in financial markets. Hence, a formal framework for verifying matching algorithms can also be useful in verifying other algorithms used in financial markets. This need has also been recognized by Passmore and Ignatovich [15]. They state

> Indeed, if venues are not safe, fair and correct, e.g., if one can exploit flaws in the venue matching logic to jump the queue and have their orders unfairly prioritized over others, then "all bets are off" as one ascends the stack to more complex algorithms.

In this work, we make significant progress in addressing this need, including completely formalizing the matching algorithm used in the pre-markets. Before we describe our full contribution, we first briefly describe trading at an exchange.

1.1   An Overview of Trading at an Exchange

An exchange is an organized financial market. There are various types of exchanges: stock exchange, commodity exchange, foreign exchange etc. An exchange facilitates trading between buyers and sellers for the products which are registered at the exchange. A potential trader, a buyer or a seller, places orders in the markets for a certain product. These orders are matched by the stock exchange to execute trades. Most stock exchanges hold trading in two main sessions: pre-market (or call auction session) and continuous market (or regular trading session) (See [6] for details on the market microstructure).

The pre-market session reduces uncertainty and volatility in the market by discovering an opening price of the product. During the pre-market session, an exchange collects all the buy requests (bids) and sell requests (asks) for a fixed

---

[1] The New York Stock Exchange and the Archipelago Exchange merged together to form NYSE Arca, which is an exchange where both stocks and options are traded.

duration of time. At the end of this duration the exchange matches these buy and sell requests at a single price using a matching algorithm. In the continuous market session, the incoming buyers and sellers are continuously matched to each other. An incoming bid (ask), if matchable, is immediately matched to the existing asks (bids). Otherwise, if the bid (ask) is not matchable, it is placed in a priority queue prioritized first by price and then by time. A trader can place orders of multiple quantity of each product to trade during both the sessions. In the continuous market session, unless otherwise specified, an order of multiple units of a product can be partially executed, that too potentially at different trade prices. In the pre-market session, an order of multiple units can always be partially executed and all trades occur at a single price, namely the opening price. In this work, we will be concerned primarily with the pre-market session where orders can always be partially executed, which is also the case for most orders in the continuous market session. Hence, for simplicity of analysis, it suffices to assume that each order is of a single unit of a single product; a multiple quantity order can always be treated as a bunch of orders each with a single quantity and the analysis for a single product will apply for all the products individually. As a result, note that a single trader who places an order of multiple units is seen as multiple traders ordering a single unit each. In both sessions of trades multiple buyers and sellers are matched simultaneously. A mechanism used to match multiple buyers and sellers is known as a double sided auction [5].

In double sided auctions, an auctioneer (e.g. exchanges) collects buy and sell requests over a period of time. Each potential trader places the orders with a limit price: below which a seller will not sell and above which a buyer will not buy. The exchange at the end of this time period matches these orders based on their limit prices. This entire process is completed using a double sided auction matching algorithm. Designing algorithms for double sided auctions is well studied topic [13,14,21]. A major emphasis of many of these studies have been to either maximize the number of matches or maximize the profit of the auctioneer. In the auction theory literature, the profit of an auctioneer is defined as the difference between the limit prices of matched bid-ask pair. However, most exchanges today earn their profit by charging transaction costs to the traders. Therefore, maximizing the number of matches increases the profit of the exchange as well as the liquidity in the markets. There are other important properties, like fairness, uniformity and individual rationality, besides the number of matches which are considered while evaluating the effectiveness of a matching algorithm. However, it is known that no single algorithm can possess all of these properties [13,21].

1.2 Our Contribution

Our main goal through this work is to show effectiveness of formal methods in addressing real needs in financial markets and hopefully, along with subsequent works, this will lead to fully-verified real trading systems. In this work, we formally define various notions from auction theory relevant for the analysis of trades in financial markets. We define notions like bids, asks and matching in the Coq proof assistant. The dependent types of Coq turn out to be very useful in giving concise representation to these notions, which also reflects their natural definitions. After preparing the basic framework, we define important properties of matching in a double sided auction: fairness, uniformity and individual rationality. These properties reflect various regulatory guidelines for trading. Furthermore, we formally prove some results on the existence of various combinations of these properties. For example, a maximum matching always exists which is also fair. These results can also be interpreted as consistency proofs for various subsets of regulatory guidelines. We prove all these results in the constructive setting of the Coq proof assistant without adding any additional axioms to it. These proofs are completed using computable functions which computes the actual instances (certificate). We also use computable functions to represent various predicates on lists. Finally, we use this setting to verify properties of two important classes of matching algorithms: uniform price and maximum matching algorithms.

We briefly describe the main results formalized in this work. To follow the discussion below, recall that each bid and each ask is of a single quantity, and hence the problem of pairing bids and asks can be seen as a matching problem between all bids and all asks with additional price constraints.

Upper Bound on Matching Size: After formalizing the various notions, we first show that these definitions are also useful in formalizing various theorems on double sided auctions by formalizing a combinatorial result (Theorem 1) which gives a tight upper bound on the total number of possible trades (size of a maximum matching). For a given price, the demand (supply) is the total number of buyers (sellers) willing to trade at that price. Theorem 1 states that for any price p, the total number of trades is at most the sum of the demand and supply at price p. To prove Theorem 1, we first formalize Lemmas 1–3.

Properties of Matchings: We next formalize theorems relating to three important properties of matchings: fairness, uniformity and individual rationality. Before explaining the theorems, we first explain these terms.

A matching is *unfair* if there exists two buyers who had different bids and the lower bid buyer gets matched but not the higher bid one. Similarly, it could be unfair if a more competitive seller is left out. If a matching is not unfair, then it is *fair*.

A matching is *uniform* if all trades happen at the same price and is *individually rational* if for each matched bid-ask pair the trade price is between the bid and ask limit prices. In the context of formal markets, the trade price is always between the limit prices of the matched bid-ask pair. Note that, during the premarket session, a single price is discovered, and thus the exchange is required to produce a uniform matching for this session of trading.

Theorem 2 states that there exists an algorithm that can convert any matching into individual rational. This can be achieved by assigning the trade prices as the middle values between the limit prices of matched bid-ask pairs.

Theorem 3 states that given a matching there exists a fair matching of the same cardinality. We use two functions *Make_FOB* and *Make_FOA* which successively makes the matching fair on the bids and then the asks, thus resulting in a fair matching. The proof of Theorem 3, which is based on induction, uses Lemmas 4–9 and is quite technically subtle, as induction fails when we try to use it directly (see the discussion below Lemma 4), and we need to first prove intermediate Lemmas 4 and 5 before we can use induction. In addition, we exhibit (see Fig. 4) individual rational matchings to show that they cannot be both uniform and maximum simultaneously.

Matching Algorithms: Finally, we formalize two important matching algorithms: *produce_ MM* and *produce_ UM*.

Theorem 4 shows that produce_MM always outputs a maximum matching. Composing *Make_ FOB*, *Make_ FOA* (from Theorem 3) and *produce_ MM* (Theorem 4), we can show that there exists an algorithm that outputs a maximum matching which is also fair (Theorem 5).

The *produce_ UM* algorithm is implemented by the exchanges for opening price discovery, and Theorem 6 states that *produce_ UM* outputs a maximum-cardinality matching amongst all uniform matchings. We can compose *Make_ FOA*, *Make_ FOB* (Theorem 5) and *produce_ UM* (Theorem 6) to get an algorithm that produces a maximum matching amongst all uniform matchings that is also fair. Instead, we directly prove that the matching produced by *produce_ UM* is also fair by first proving Lemmas 11 and 10. This completely formalizes the matching algorithm used by the exchanges during the pre-market session of trading.

Finally we observe that while our work is useful for continuous markets, it does not completely formalize trades during the continuous market session. This requires further work as the lists continuously get updated during this session of trading and the order types are also more involved. See the discussion in Conclusion and Future Works (Sect. 4).

1.3   Related Work

There is no prior work known to us which formalizes double-sided auction mechanism used by the exchanges. Passmore and Ignatovich in [15] highlight the significance, opportunities and challenges involved in formalizing financial markets. Their work describes in detail the whole spectrum of financial algorithms that need to be verified for ensuring safe and fair markets. Matching algorithms used by the exchanges are at the core of this whole spectrum. Another important work in formalization of trading using model checking tools is done by Iliano *et al.* [4]. They use concurrent linear logic (CLF) to outline two important properties of a trading system: the market is never in a locked-or-crossed state, and the trading always take place at best bid or best ask limit price. They also highlight the limitation of CLF in stating and proving properties of trading systems.

On the other hand, there are quite a few works formalizing various concepts from auction theory [3,11,18]. Most of these works focus on the Vickrey auction mechanism. In a Vickrey auction, there is a single seller with different items and multiple buyers with valuations for each subset of item. Each buyer places bids for every combination of the items. At the end of the bidding, the aim of the seller is to maximize the total value of the items by suitably assigning the items to the buyers. Financial derivatives and other type of contracts are also formalized in [2,8].

1.4   Organization of the Paper

In Sect. 2, we formally define the essential components of trading at an exchange. In particular, we define some important properties of matchings and prove Theorems 1–3. In Sect. 3, we present a maximum matching algorithm (*produce_ MM*) which produces a maximum matching which is fair. We also present an equilibrium price matching algorithm (*produce_ UM*) which is used for price discovery in financial markets. We also specify and prove some correctness properties for these algorithms (Theorems 4–7). We summarize the work in Sect. 4 with an overview of future works. The Coq code for this work is available at [1], which can be compiled on the latest version of Coq (8.10.1).

2   Modeling Trades at Exchanges

An auction is a competitive event, where goods and services are sold to the most competitive participants. The priority among participating traders is determined by various attributes of the bids and asks (e.g. price, time etc). This priority can be finally represented by ordering them in a list.

2.1   Bid, Ask and Limit Price

In any double sided auction multiple buyers and sellers place their orders to buy or sell a unit of an underlying product. The auctioneer matches these buy-sell requests based on their *limit prices*. While the limit price for a buy order (i.e. *bid*) is the price above which the buyer does not want to buy the item, the limit price of a sell order (i.e. *ask*) is the price below which the seller does not want to sell the item. If a trader wishes to buy or sell multiple units, he can create multiple bids or asks with different *ids*. We can express bids as well asks using records containing two fields.

```
Record Bid: Type:= Mk_bid { bp:> nat; idb: nat }.
Record Ask: Type:= Mk_ask { sp:> nat; ida: nat }.
```

For a bid b, (bp b) is the limit price and (idb b) is its unique identifier. Similarly for an ask a, (sp a) is the limit price and (ida a) is the unique identifier of a. Note that the limit prices are natural numbers when expressed in the monetary unit of the lowest denomination (like cents in USA). Also note the use of coercion :> in the first field of *Bid* which declares bp as an implicit function that is applied to any term of type *Bid* appearing in a context requiring a natural number. Hence from now on we can simply use b instead of (bp b) for the limit price of b. Similarly, we use a for the limit price of an ask a.

Since equality for both the fields of *Bid* as well as *Ask* is decidable (i.e. `nat: eqType`), the equality on *Bid* as well as *Ask* can also be proved to be decidable. This is achieved by declaring two canonical instances `bid_eqType` and `ask_eqType` which connect *Bid* and *Ask* to the `eqType`.

2.2 Matching Demand and Supply

All the buy and sell requests can be assumed to be present in list B and list A, respectively. At the time of auction, the auctioneer matches bids in B to asks in A. We say a bid-ask pair (b, a) is *matchable* if $b \geq a$ (i.e. $bp\ b \geq sp\ a$). Furthermore, the auctioneer assigns a trade price to each matched bid-ask pair which results in a matching M. We define a matching as a list whose entries are of type `fill_type`.

```
Record fill_type: Type:=  Mk_fill {bid_of: Bid; ask_of: Ask; tp: nat}
```

In a matching M, a bid or an ask appears at most once. There might be some bids in B which are not matched to any asks in M and some asks in A which are not matched to any bids in M. The list of bids present in M is denoted by B_M and the list of asks present in M is denoted by A_M. For example in Fig. 1 the bid with limit price 37 is not present in B_M.

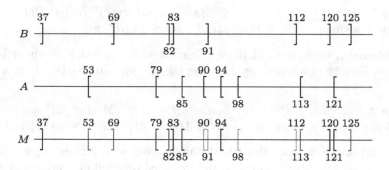

Fig. 1. Bids in B and asks in A are represented using close and open brackets respectively, and a matched bid-ask pair in M is assigned the same colors. (Color figure online)

More precisely, for a given list of bids B and list of asks A, M is a matching iff, (1) All the bid-ask pairs in M are matchable, (2) B_M is duplicate-free, (3) A_M is duplicate-free, (4) $B_M \subseteq B$, and (5) $A_M \subseteq A$.

Definition 1. *matching_in B A M := All_matchable M* $\wedge$ *NoDup B_M* $\wedge$ *NoDup A_M* $\wedge$ *$B_M \subseteq B$* $\wedge$ *$A_M \subseteq A$.*

The term *NoDup B_M* in the above definition indicates that each bid is a request to trade one unit of the item and the items are indivisible. We use the term $B_M \subseteq B$ to express that each element in the list B_M comes from the list B.

Let $B(\geq p)$ represents the bids in B whose limit price is greater than or equal to a given price p. In other words, the quantity $|B(\geq p)|$ represents the total demand of the product at a given price p in the market. Similarly, we can use $A(\leq p)$ to represent all the asks in A whose limit price is less than or equal to the given price p. Hence, the quantity $|A(\leq p)|$ represents the total supply of the product at the given price p.

Although, in general we can not say much about the relationship between the total demand (i.e. $|B(\geq p)|$) and supply (i.e. $|A(\leq p)|$) at an arbitrary price p, we can certainly prove the following important result about the matched bid ask pairs.

Lemma 1. *buyers_above_ge_sellers (M: list fill_type) (B: list Bid) (A: list Ask):* $\forall p,\ matching\_\ in\ B\ A\ M \rightarrow |B_M(\geq p)| \geq |A_M(\geq p)|.$

Lemma 1 claims that in any valid trade output M and for a given price p, the total volume of bids willing to buy at or above the price p is equal to or higher than the total volume of asks willing to sell at a limit price at least p.

Similarly, we prove Lemma 2 which states that, In a matching M, the total volume of bids willing to buy at or below a price p is equal to or smaller than the total volume of asks willing to sell at a limit price at most p.

Lemma 2. *sellers_below_ge_buyers (M: list fill_type) (B: list Bid) (A: list Ask):* $\forall p,\ matching\_\ in\ B\ A\ M \rightarrow |B_M(\leq p)| \leq |A_M(\leq p)|.$

Additionally, we have the following lemma which provides an upper bound on the cardinality of a matching M using $|B_M(\geq p)|$ and $|A_M(\leq p)|$ at a price p.

Lemma 3. *maching_buyer_right_plus_seller_left (M: list fill_type) (B:list Bid) (A:list Ask):* $\forall p,\ (matching\_\ in\ B\ A\ M) \rightarrow |M| \leq |B_M(\geq p)| + |A_M(\leq p)|.$

It is important to note that the total demand at a certain price p in the market is always greater or equal to the matched demand at a price p or above (i.e. $|B(\geq p)| \geq |B_M(\geq p)|$). Similarly, for total supply at a price p we have $|A(\leq p)| \geq |A_M(\leq p)|$. These facts when put together with Lemma 3 can help us prove the following result.

Theorem 1. *bound_on_M (M: list fill_type) (B:list Bid) (A:list Ask):* $\forall p,$ $(matching\_\ in\ B\ A\ M) \rightarrow |M| \leq |B(\geq p)| + |A(\leq p)|.$

It states that no matching M can achieve a trade volume higher than the sum of the total demand and supply in the market at any given price.

2.3   Individually Rational Trades

An auctioneer assigns a trade price to each matched bid-ask pair. Since the limit price for a buyer is the price above which she does not want to buy, the trade price for this buyer is expected to be below her limit price. Similarly, the trade price for the seller is expected to be above his limit price. Therefore, in any matching it is desired that the trade price of a bid-ask pair lies between their limit prices. A matching which has this property is called an *individual rational (IR)* matching.

Definition 2. *Is_IR* $M := \forall m, m \in M \rightarrow ((bid\_of\ m) \geq tp\ m) \wedge (tp\ m \geq (ask\_of\ m))$.

Note that any matching can be converted to an IR matching without altering its bid-ask pair (See Fig. 2). Hence we have the following result,

Theorem 2. *exists_IR_matching:* $\forall M\ B\ A,\ matching\_in\ B\ A\ M \rightarrow (\exists\ M',\ B_M = B'_M \wedge A_M = A'_M \wedge matching\_in\ B\ A\ M' \wedge Is\_IR\ M')$.

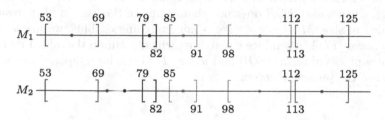

Fig. 2. The colored dots represent trade prices for matched bid-ask pairs. Matching M_2 is not IR but M_1 is IR, even though both the matchings contain exactly the same bid-ask pairs. (Color figure online)

2.4   Fairness in Competitive Markets

A bid with higher limit price is considered more *competitive* compared to bids with lower limit prices. Similarly, an ask with lower limit price is considered more competitive compared to asks with higher limit prices. In a competitive market, more competitive traders are prioritized for matching. A matching which prioritizes more competitive traders is called a *fair* matching.

Definition 3. *fair_on_bids* $M\ B := \forall b\ b',\ b \in B \wedge b' \in B \rightarrow b > b' \rightarrow b' \in B_M \rightarrow b \in B_M$.

Definition 4. *fair_on_asks* $M\ A := \forall s\ s',\ s \in A \wedge s' \in A \rightarrow s < s' \rightarrow s' \in A_M \rightarrow s \in A_M$.

Definition 5. *Is_fair* $M\ B\ A := fair\_on\_asks\ M\ A \wedge fair\_on\_bids\ M\ B$.

Here, the predicate *fair_on_bids M B* states that the matching M is fair for the list of buyers B. Similarly, the predicate *fair_on_asks M A* states that the matching M is fair for the list of sellers A. A matching which is fair on bids as well as asks is expressed using the predicate *Is_fair M B A*. Now we can state and prove the following result which states that a fair matching can always be achieved without compromising the cardinality of the matching.

Theorem 3. *exists_fair_matching (Nb: NoDup B) (Na: No Dup A): matching_in B A M* → (∃ *M', matching_in B A M'* ∧ *Is_fair M' B A* ∧ $|M| = |M'|$).

Proof Idea. We prove this statement by converting a matching into a fair matching without changing its cardinality. In order to achieve this we use functions *make_FOB* and *make_FOA* (See Fig. 3). The function *make_FOB* produces a matching which is fair on bids from an input matching M and a list of bids B both of which are sorted in decreasing order of their bid prices (Lemma 8). Moreover, since *make_FOB* does not change any of the asks in M, it results in a matching of size $|M|$. Once we get a fair matching on bids, we use a similar function *make_FOA* to produce a matching which is fair on the asks. Finally, the correctness proofs of *make_FOB* and *make_FOA* can be composed to complete the proof of the present theorem.   □

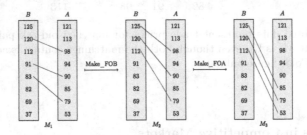

Fig. 3. The dotted lines represent matched bid-ask pairs. The function *make_FOB* changes M_1 into a fair matching on bids M_2, whereas *make_FOA* changes M_2 into a fair matching on asks M_3.

The functions *make_FOB* and *make_FOA* are both recursive in nature and have identical definitions. Therefore, it is sufficient to discuss the properties of *make_FOB* which is defined recursively as follows.

```
Fixpoint Make_FOB (M) (B):= match (M,B) with
    |(nil,_) => nil
    |(m::M',nil) => nil
    |(m::M',b::B') =>  (Mk_fill b (ask_of m) (tp m))::(Make_FOB M' B')
    end.
```

In each step the function *make_FOB* picks the top bid-ask pair, say (b, a) in M_1 and replaces b with the most competitive bid available in B, resulting in a matching M_2 (See Fig. 3). Note that *make_FOB* does not change any of the asks in M. Moreover, due to the recursive nature of *make_FOB* on B, a bid is not repeated in the process of replacement (i.e., B_{M_2} is duplicate-free). Therefore, we would like to have the following lemma.

Lemma 4. $\forall M \ B,$ *(Sorted $\downarrow_{bp} M$)* $\rightarrow$ *(Sorted $\downarrow_{bp} B$)* $\rightarrow$ *matching_in B A M* $\rightarrow$ *fair_on_bids (Make_FOB M B) B.*

Induction Failure: The function *make_FOB* is recursive on both B and M, and hence a proof of this lemma is expected using an inductive argument on the structure of B. Although the theorem is true, an attempt to prove it using induction on B will fail. Let $M = (b_1, a_1) :: (b_2, a_2) :: M''$ and $B = b_2 :: b_1 :: B''$, where both B and M are sorted by decreasing bid prices and $(bp \ b_1) = (bp \ b_2)$. After the first iteration, the *make_FOB* will calls itself on $M' = (b_2, a_2) :: M''$ and $B' = (b_1 :: B'')$. In the inductive proof, in order to use the induction hypothesis we need to prove that M' is a matching for the list of bids in B'. This is clearly not true since $B_{M'}$ is not a subset of B' since $b_2 \notin B'$ but $b_2 \in B_{M'}$. This complication arises because we are dealing with all the information contained in the bids while the proof requires reasoning only based on their limit prices. We resolve this difficulty by systematically mapping the properties of M, B and A to the properties of their corresponding price columns. For example, we have the following result on the prices of B.

Lemma 5. *sorted_nodup_is_sublistB:* $\forall B_1 \ B_2,$ *NoDup B_1* $\rightarrow$ *NoDup B_2* $\rightarrow$ *Sorted $\downarrow_{bp} B_1$* $\rightarrow$ *Sorted $\downarrow_{bp} B_2$* $\rightarrow$ $B_1 \subset B_2$ $\rightarrow$ *sublist $P_{B_1} \ P_{B_2}$.*

Here, P_B is projection of the limit prices of bids in B. The term (*sublist P_{B_1} P_{B_2}*) represents the sub-sequence relation between the lists P_{B_1} and P_{B_2}. Furthermore, we have the following lemmas specifying the sub-list relation between lists.

Lemma 6. *sublist_intro1:* $\forall a,$ *sublist l s* $\rightarrow$ *sublist l (a::s).*

Lemma 7. *sublist_elim3a:* $\forall a \ e,$ *sublist (a::l) (e::s)* $\rightarrow$ *sublist l s.*

Note the recursive nature of the *sublist* relation on both its arguments, as evident in Lemma 7. It makes inductive reasoning feasible for the statements where *sublist* is in the antecedent. Hence, we use the sublist relation to state and prove the following result.

Lemma 8. *mfob_fair_on_bid M B: (Sorted $\downarrow_{bp} M$)* $\rightarrow$ *(Sorted $\downarrow_{bp} B$)* $\rightarrow$ *sublist $P_{B_M} \ P_B$* $\rightarrow$ *fair_on_bids (Make_FOB M B) B.*

Similarly, we can state and prove the following result which specifies the function *make_FOA*.

Lemma 9. *mfob_fair_on_ask M A: (Sorted $\uparrow_{sp} M$)* $\rightarrow$ *(Sorted $\uparrow_{sp} A$)* $\rightarrow$ *sublist $P_{A_M} \ P_A$* $\rightarrow$ *fair_on_asks (Make_FOA M A) A.*

Since the fair matching is obtained by composing the functions *Make_FOA* and *Make_FOB*, we can combine the proofs of Lemma 9 and Lemma 8 to obtain the complete proof of Theorem 3.

2.5   Liquidity and Perceived-Fairness in the Markets

The liquidity in any market is a measure of how quickly one can trade in the market without much cost. One way to increase the liquidity is to maximize the number of matched bid-ask pairs. For a given list of bids B and list of asks A we say a matching M is a maximum matching if no other matching M' on the same B and A contains more matched bid-ask pairs than M.

Definition 6. *$Is\_MM\ M\ B\ A := (matching\_in\ B\ A\ M) \wedge (\forall M', matching\_in$
$B\ A\ M' \rightarrow |M'| \leq |M|)$.*

Designing a mechanism for a maximum matching is an important aspect of a double sided auction. In certain situations, to produce a maximum matching, bid-ask pairs must be assigned different trade prices (Fig. 4). However, different prices simultaneously for the same product leads to dissatisfaction amongst some of the traders. A mechanism which clears all the matched bid-ask pairs at a single trade price is called a *uniform matching* (or *perceived-fairness*).

Fig. 4. The only individually rational matching of size two is not uniform.

3   Optimizing Trades in Financial Markets

In Sect. 2.5, we observed that a maximum matching may not be a uniform matching. In this Section, we present two broad classes of double sided auction mechanisms: a maximum matching mechanism and a uniform price mechanism. While the maximum matching mechanism tries to maximize the overall volume of the trade, the uniform price mechanism tries to obtain a uniform matching of maximum possible cardinality.

3.1   A Maximum Matching Mechanism

We will now discuss a matching mechanism which produces maximum trade volume while maintaining the fairness criterion. This scheme produces the same output as the one proposed in [14]. However, there are some important differences in both mechanisms. The algorithm suggested in [14] is a non recursive method which generates the final trade in two steps; the algorithm first determines the cardinality n of a maximum matching on the given set of bids and asks and then in the next step it produces a fair matching of cardinality n. On the other hand, we use a recursive function *produce_MM* on the lists of bids and asks to produce a maximum matching which is then converted into a fair matching using the already defined function *make_FOA* (See Fig. 5(a)). We follow this approach because it allows us to easily compose the correctness proof of these individual functions to validate the properties of the final trade generated by the whole mechanism.

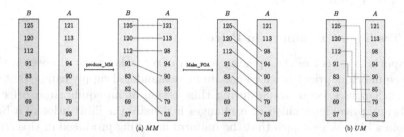

Fig. 5. (a) At each iteration *produce_MM* selects a most competitive available bid and then pairs it with the largest matchable ask. The output of this function is already fair on bids. In the second step, the function *make_FOA* converts this output into fair matching. (b) Maximum matching amongst uniform. Note that, the size of both the matchings are different.

```
Fixpoint produce_MM (B) (A) := match (B, A) with
  |(nil, _) => nil
  |(b::B', nil) => nil
  |(b::B', a::A') =>  match (a <= b) with
     |true => {|bid_of:=b; ask_of:=a; tp:=(bp b)|}::(produce_MM B' A')
     |false => produce_MM B A'
    end
  end.
```

The correctness proof of *produce_MM* is obtained using an inductive argument on the structure of the input lists. At each iteration *produce_MM* generates a matchable bid-ask pair (See Fig. 5(a)). Due to the recursive nature of function *produce_MM* on both B and A, it never pairs any bid with more than one ask. This ensures that the list of bids in matching (i.e. B_M) is duplicate-free. Note that *produce_MM* tries to match a bid until it finds a matchable ask. The function terminates when either all the bids are matched or it encounters a bid for which no matchable ask is available. The following theorem states that the function *produce_MM* produces a maximum matching when both B and A are sorted in a decreasing order of the limit prices.

Theorem 4. *produce_MM_is_MM (Nb: NoDup B) (Na: NoDup A): Sorted* $\downarrow_{bp} B \rightarrow$ *Sorted* $\downarrow_{sp} A \rightarrow$ *Is_MM (produce_MM B A) B A.*

The detailed proof of the above theorem can be found at [16].

Now that we proved the maximality property of *produce_MM* we can produce a fair as well as maximum matching by applying the functions *Make_FOA* and *Make_FOB* to the output of *produce_MM*. More precisely, for a given list of bids B and list of asks A, we have the following result stating that there exists a matching which is both maximum and fair.

Theorem 5. *exists_fair_maximum (B: list Bid)(A: list Ask)*: $\exists$ M, *(Is_fair M B A $\wedge$ Is_MM M B A)*.

3.2 Trading at Equilibrium Price

An important aspect of the opening session of a market is to discover a single price (equilibrium price) at which maximum demand and supply can be matched. Most exchanges execute trade during this session at an equilibrium price. An equilibrium price determined at exchanges is usually the limit price of a bid or ask from a bid-ask pair such that the uniform matching produced in this session remains individual rational. We will now describe a function *produce_UM* which produces an individually rational matching which is fair and maximum among all uniform matchings.

```
Fixpoint pair_uniform (B:list Bid) (A:list Ask):=  match (B,A) with
   |(nil, _) => nil
   |(_,nil)=> nil
   |(b::B',a::A') => match (a <= b) with
            |false => nil
            |true =>{|bid_of:= b;ask_of:= a; tp:=(bp b)|}::pair_uniform B' A'
         end
      end.
Definition uniform_price B A := bp (bid_of (last (pair_uniform B A))).
Definition produce_UM B A:=
replace_column (pair_uniform B A) (uniform_price B A).
```

The function *pair_uniform* output bid-ask pairs, *uniform_price* computes the uniform price and finally *produce_UM* produces a uniform matching. The function *pair_uniform* is recursive and matches the largest available bid in B with the smallest available ask in A at each iteration (See Fig. 5(b)). This function terminates when the most competitive bid available in B is not matchable with any available ask in A.

The following theorem states that the function *produce_UM* produces a maximum matching among all uniform matchings when the list of bids B is sorted in a decreasing order of the limit prices and the list of asks A is sorted in an increasing order of the limit prices.

Theorem 6. *UM_is_maximal_Uniform (B: list Bid) (A:list Ask)*: *Sorted* $\downarrow_{bp}$ B $\rightarrow$ *Sorted* $\uparrow_{sp}$ A $\rightarrow$ $\forall M$, *Is_uniform* M $\rightarrow$ $|M| \leq |produce\_UM\ B\ A|$.

The detailed proof of the above theorem can be found at [16].

Next, we prove that the *produce_UM* generates a maximum matching among all uniform matchings which is also fair when the list of bids B is sorted in a decreasing order of the limit prices and the list of asks A is sorted in an increasing order of the limit prices. In order to prove this, we first prove the following two lemmas.

Lemma 10. *UM_pair_fair_on_asks (B: list Bid) (A:list Ask): Sorted $\downarrow_{bp}$ B $\rightarrow$ Sorted $\uparrow_{sp}$ A $\rightarrow$ fair_on_asks (pair_uniform B A) A.*

Lemma 11. *UM_pair_fair_on_bids (B: list Bid) (A:list Ask): Sorted $\downarrow_{bp}$ B $\rightarrow$ Sorted $\uparrow_{sp}$ A $\rightarrow$ fair_on_bids (pair_uniform B A) B.*

Theorem 7. *UM_fair (B: list Bid) (A:list Ask)(m:fill_type): Sorted $\downarrow_{bp}$ B $\rightarrow$ Sorted $\uparrow_{sp}$ A $\rightarrow$ Is_fair (produce_ UM B A) B A.*

The proof of Theorem 7 is similar to the proof of Theorem 3 once we use Lemmas 10 and 11.

4   Conclusion and Future Works

In this work, we developed a formal framework to verify important properties of matching algorithms used by the exchanges. These algorithms use double sided auctions to match multiple buyers with multiple sellers during different sessions of trading. We presented correctness proofs for two important classes of double sided auction mechanisms: uniform price algorithms and maximum matching algorithms.

An important direction of future work is the individual analysis of various orders types which are important for the continuous markets (e.g. limit orders, market orders, stop-loss orders, iceberg orders, fill or kill (FOK), immediate or cancel (IOC) etc.). This would require maintaining a priority queue based on the various attributes of these orders. A formal analysis of these order attributes together with the verification of trading mechanisms can provide a formal foundation which will be useful in the rigorous analysis of other market behaviors at large. Also for continuous markets, due to the various order types, it becomes important to consider multiple unit orders which requires more work. Moreover, the insights gained from these attempts to formalize the overall trading mechanism can be helpful in developing robust as well as efficient trading systems of the future which can be used directly at the exchanges.

References

1. Coq formalization. https://github.com/suneel-sarswat/auction
2. Bahr, P., Berthold, J., Elsman, M.: Certified symbolic management of financial multi-party contracts. In: Proceedings of the 20th International Conference on Functional Programming, pp. 315–327. ACM (2015)
3. Caminati, M.B., Kerber, M., Lange, C., Rowat, C.: Sound auction specification and implementation. In: Proceedings of the Sixteenth ACM Conference on Economics and Computation, pp. 547–564. ACM (2015)

4. Cervesato, I., Khan, S., Reis, G., Zunic, D.: Formalization of automated trading systems in a concurrent linear framework. In: Linearity-TLLA@FLoC. EPTCS, vol. 292, pp. 1–14 (2018)

5. Friedman, D.: The double auction market institution: a survey. Double Auct. Mark.: Inst. Theor. Evid. **14**, 3–25 (1993)

6. Harris, L.: Trading and Exchanges: Market Microstructure for Practitioners. Oxford University Press, New York (2003)

7. Henzinger, T.A., Jhala, R., Majumdar, R., Sutre, G.: Software verification with BLAST. In: Ball, T., Rajamani, S.K. (eds.) SPIN 2003. LNCS, vol. 2648, pp. 235–239. Springer, Heidelberg (2003). https://doi.org/10.1007/3-540-44829-2_17

8. Peyton Jones, S., Eber, J.-M., Seward, J.: Composing contracts: an adventure in financial engineering. In: Proceedings 5th International Conference on Functional Programming, pp. 280–292 (2000)

9. Burch, J.R., Clarke, E.M., McMillan, K.L.: Sequential circuit verification using symbolic model checking. In: 27th Design Automation Conference (1990)

10. Klein, G., Elphinstone, K., Heiser, G., Andronick, J., et al.: seL4: formal verification of an OS kernel. In: Proceedings of the ACM SIGOPS 22nd Symposium on Operating Systems Principles, pp. 207–220. ACM (2009)

11. Lange, C., et al.: A qualitative comparison of the suitability of four theorem provers for basic auction theory. In: Carette, J., Aspinall, D., Lange, C., Sojka, P., Windsteiger, W. (eds.) CICM 2013. LNCS (LNAI), vol. 7961, pp. 200–215. Springer, Heidelberg (2013). https://doi.org/10.1007/978-3-642-39320-4_13

12. Leroy, X.: A formally verified compiler back-end. J. Autom. Reason. **43**(4), 363 (2009). https://doi.org/10.1007/s10817-009-9155-4

13. McAfee, R.P.: A dominant strategy double auction. J. Econ. Theory **56**(2), 434–450 (1992)

14. Niu, J., Parsons, S.: Maximizing matching in double-sided auctions. In: International Conference on Autonomous Agents and Multi-Agent Systems, AAMAS 2013, Saint Paul, MN, USA, 6–10 May 2013, pp. 1283–1284 (2013)

15. Passmore, G.O., Ignatovich, D.: Formal verification of financial algorithms. In: de Moura, L. (ed.) CADE 2017. LNCS (LNAI), vol. 10395, pp. 26–41. Springer, Cham (2017). https://doi.org/10.1007/978-3-319-63046-5_3

16. Sarswat, S., Kr Singh, A.: Formally verified trades in financial markets. arXiv preprint arXiv:2007.10805 (2020)

17. Securities Exchange Board of India (SEBI). Order in the matter of NSE Colocation, 30 April 2019

18. Tadjouddine, E.M., Guerin, F., Vasconcelos, W.: Abstracting and verifying strategy-proofness for auction mechanisms. In: Baldoni, M., Son, T.C., van Riemsdijk, M.B., Winikoff, M. (eds.) DALT 2008. LNCS (LNAI), vol. 5397, pp. 197–214. Springer, Heidelberg (2009). https://doi.org/10.1007/978-3-540-93920-7_13

19. U.S. Securities and Exchange Commission (SEC). NYSE to Pay US Dollar 14 Million Penalty for Multiple Violations, 6 March 2018. https://www.sec.gov/news/press-release/2018-31

20. U.S. Securities and Exchange Commision (SEC). SEC Charges NYSE for Repeated Failures to Operate in Accordance With Exchange Rules, 1 May 2014. https://www.sec.gov/news/press-release/2014-87

21. Wurman, P.R., Walsh, W.E., Wellman, M.P.: Flexible double auctions for electronic commerce: theory and implementation. Decis. Supp. Syst. **24**(1), 17–27 (1998)

Formalizing the Transaction Flow Process of Hyperledger Fabric

Xiangyu Chen[1], Ximeng Li[3(✉)], Qianying Zhang[2], Zhiping Shi[1],
and Yong Guan[3]

[1] Beijing Key Laboratory of Electronic System Reliability and Prognostics,
Capital Normal University, Beijing, China
chenxiangyu980723@163.com, shizp@cnu.edu.cn
[2] Beijing Engineering Research Center of High Reliable Embedded System,
Capital Normal University, Beijing, China
qyzhang@cnu.edu.cn
[3] Beijing Advanced Innovation Center for Imaging Theory and Technology,
Capital Normal University, Beijing, China
{lixm,guanyong}@cnu.edu.cn

Abstract. Blockchains leverage the synergy of technologies from networking, cryptography, distributed protocols, security policies, and computer programming, to provide guarantees such as distributed consensus and tamper-resistance over records of data and activities. The interaction of diverse technical elements in a blockchain could create obstacles in precisely understanding the workings of it, and the guarantees delivered by it. We help overcome these obstacles in the case of the transaction flow process of the Hyperledger Fabric blockchain, through theorem-proving techniques. The transaction flow process is an overarching architectural component for the handling of transactions in Hyperledger Fabric. We formalize the transaction flow, and prove that it preserves distributed consensus, in the Coq proof assistant. Our development complements existing formalizations of consensus mechanisms for blockchain systems.

1 Introduction

A blockchain is a globally shared, distributed digital ledger [24]. The ledger typically contains a chain of blocks holding records of data and activities. A series of properties are typically enforced about the ledger: distributed consensus, tamper-resistance, repudiation-resistance, traceable provenance of data and activities, etc. These properties make the blockchain an ideal choice for trustworthily managing the relations of production in the information era.

Despite the simplicity of the blockchain concept as a distributed data structure, the enforcement of the blockchain properties is really achieved through a fusion of diverse technological elements – computer networks, cryptographic algorithms, distributed protocols, security policies, computer programs, etc. The need for proper synergy between all these technological elements renders the blockchain arguably one of the most sophisticated IT innovations ever made.

© Springer Nature Switzerland AG 2020
S.-W. Lin et al. (Eds.): ICFEM 2020, LNCS 12531, pp. 233–250, 2020.
https://doi.org/10.1007/978-3-030-63406-3_14

Hyperledger Fabric [8] is the prototypical example of permissioned blockchain system – the permission to participate in the blockchain network is obtained through explicit authentication. Hyperledger Fabric features a novel execute-order-validate paradigm in the handling of tasks. This parallelizes the execution of tasks and the recording of executed tasks in the blockchain, which increases efficiency while maintaining consensus. Hyperledger Fabric has been widely adopted and adapted by businesses throughout the world for blockchain-enabled applications [1].

The aforementioned execute-order-validate paradigm manifests itself in the transaction flow process – the process by which the transactions (roughly the tasks) are proposed, executed, ordered, entered into blocks, and recorded on the network nodes. The transaction flow process threads through almost all the major technical elements of Hyperledger Fabric. Hence, a precise grasp of the transaction flow is key to understanding how the main technical elements of this system play together, and how the key blockchain properties (e.g., consensus) emerge out of this interplay. However, due to the conceptual complexity involved, and the occasional vagueness of natural languages for the documentation [6], it is non-trivial to achieve the desired precision level in the understanding.

It is well-known that the use of formal methods often helps articulate the design of IT systems (e.g., [18]). For blockchain systems specifically, there have been several efforts formalizing a core part of the architecture – the consensus mechanism. Pîrlea and Sergey [19] formalize a generic model of blockchain consensus. Fernández Anta et al. [12] formalize distributed ledger objects and their implementations, establishing several consistency guarantees. Wilcox et al. [21] and Woos et al. [23] formalize the Raft protocol and prove that it achieves state machine replication across the network. Buterin and Griffith [11], as well as Hirai [3], formalize the Casper protocol and prove its key safety and liveness properties. Maung Maung Thin et al. [17] formally analyze the safety properties of the Tendermint protocol. The focus of these existing developments is on consensus mechanisms, rather than blockchain architectures in which these mechanisms are employed (together with other technical ingredients).

In this work, we formalize the transaction flow process of Hyperledger Fabric through theorem-proving techniques. Our formalization articulates how the major technical elements of this blockchain system are brought together by this process, in the handling and recording of tasks. These technical elements include: a heterogeneously structured network with nodes in different roles, policies governing the validity of executions, summaries of the effects of code execution, and mechanisms for ordering and validating transactions. We illustrate the formalization using an application scenario where the pricing information about cars is managed using the Hyperledger Fabric blockchain. In addition, we formally prove that the distributed consensus over the ledger is preserved under the transaction flow. Last but not least, we mechanize our development [5] in the Coq proof assistant [2]. Our concrete technical contributions thus include:

- a formalization of the transaction flow process of Hyperledger Fabric;
- a formal proof that the transaction flow preserves distributed consensus;
- a mechanization of the formal model and proof in the Coq proof assistant.

In this paper, our formalization is presented in a set-theoretic language. No prior knowledge about a specific formalism is needed to understand it. The mechanization in Coq provides strong evidence on the sanity of this formalization and the correctness of the formal proof.

Other Related Work. Apart from the formalization of mechanisms for blockchain consensus, there are mainly two other classes of existing work related to ours. One is on formal models about the timing aspect of the Hyperledger Fabric transaction flow. Stochastic Reward Nets and Generalised Stochastic Petri Nets are used to help analyze the main factors affecting the transaction throughput, and optimize the performance [20,25]. The other class is on the formalization and verification of blockchain programs. The specific developments here include the formal verification of chaincode (e.g., [10]) in Hyperledger Fabric, and of smart contracts (e.g., [7,9,13–16]) in Ethereum [22].

Structure. In Sect. 2, we introduce the central architectural concepts, and the transaction flow process of Hyperledger Fabric. In Sect. 3, we formalize the architectural entities of Hyperledger Fabric, including transactions, blocks, network nodes, etc. In Sect. 4, we present the formalization of the transaction flow process as a transition system. In Sect. 5, we formalize the preservation of the consensus over the ledger under the transaction flow, and briefly discuss our development in Coq. In Sect. 6, we conclude our development.

2   The Architecture of Hyperledger Fabric

2.1   The Central Concepts

The network of Hyperledger Fabric is formed by peer nodes and orderers. A *peer node* (or *peer* in short) holds a copy of the distributed ledger. This ledger consists of the *blockchain*, and the *world state* that maps the variables relevant to any business logics executed to their values. The business logics are expressed in *smart contracts*, and a group of smart contracts fulfilling a common purpose is wrapped in a *chaincode* that is deployed on peers [6]. The execution of an operation in a smart contract, and its outcome, are represented as a *transaction*. The transactions are proposed by *clients* via interactions with the peers. These transactions are recorded in the blocks of the blockchain, in some order. This order is determined by the *ordering service* run by the *orderers*.

2.2   The Transaction Flow

The transaction flow process in Hyperledger Fabric is illustrated in Fig. 1. The figure is adapted from similar illustrations in [8] and [6].

A client proposing a transaction first sends a number of *transaction proposals* – each to a peer. For the first peer, this is depicted by $A \rightarrow B$ in Fig. 1. A transaction proposal contains the operation of a smart contract that the client intends to invoke. A peer receiving a transaction proposal may execute the operation, and respond to the client with an endorsement on the transaction proposal and the execution result $(B \rightarrow C \rightarrow D)$. After the client collects enough endorsements on its transaction proposal (as per a policy called the endorsement policy), it may create a transaction (at E). The transaction is sent to the ordering service $(E \rightarrow F)$, which places the transaction in a block $(F \rightarrow G)$. The block can then be integrated into the ledger of any peer, after the peer validates the block $(G \rightarrow H \rightarrow J$ and $G \rightarrow I \rightarrow K)$.

This process is coined as *execute-order-validate*. It allows for the concurrent execution of different transactions (in the form of transaction proposals) at different subsets of peers, and for the execution and ordering of transactions to be performed concurrently. Below, we explain the individual stages of this process.

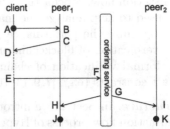

Fig. 1. The transaction flow of hyperledger fabric

A Client Proposes a Transaction. A client proposing a transaction submits a transaction proposal to a number of peers (represented for one of the peers by $A \rightarrow B$ in Fig. 1). These peers will check the validity of the transaction proposal and respond correspondingly to the client.

The Peers Endorse on the Transaction Proposal. A peer receiving the transaction proposal executes the operation of the target smart contract in the world state local to the peer. If nothing goes wrong in the execution, the peer generates an endorsement on the proposal. This endorsement contains a *readset* that records which variables are read in the execution, and which versions of them are read. Here, the version number of a variable increases with updates of the variable. The endorsement also contains a *writeset* that records which variables are updated in the execution, and the new values of these variables. Hence, the readset and the writeset constitute a summary of the execution of the invoked operation. That is, if the operation is executed with each variable at the version according to the readset, then the execution updates each variable to the value according to the writeset, incrementing the version number of the variable. If the peer decides to endorse on the transaction proposal, it responds to the client sending the proposal with its endorsement $(C \rightarrow D$ in Fig. 1).

The Client Generates a Transaction. The client waits for enough endorsements (according to the endorsement policy of the smart contract invoked) to be received for its transaction proposal. The client then composes and sends a transaction to the ordering service $(E \rightarrow F$ in Fig. 1). This transaction carries information about its original proposal, and all the endorsements by the peers. The readsets and writesets in the endorsements need to agree. The values on which they agree are used as the readset and the writeset of the overall transaction.

The Orderers Enter the Transaction into a Block. The ordering service puts the transaction received from the client into a block, along with a number of other transactions received from any clients ($F \rightarrow G$ in Fig. 1). In doing so, the ordering service implements a system-wide order among transactions. The block contains the hash of the list of transactions in it, and the hash of the list of transactions in the previous block. The block is eventually delivered to the peers.

The Peers Validate and Integrate the Block. Upon receiving a block created by the ordering service, a peer validates the transactions in the block, appends the block to its copy of the blockchain (if the block header contains proper hash values), and updates its local record of the world state by integrating the effects of the valid transactions in the block. In validating a transaction, it is checked whether the endorsements in the transaction satisfy the endorsement policy for the smart contract invoked. Although the check is supposed to be already performed by the client generating the transaction, this client is not trusted in doing it properly. It is also checked whether the variables in the local world state have equal version numbers to those in the readset of the transaction. This is to ensure that there have not been further updates to the world state after the initial execution of the invoked operation by the peers (as represented by $B \rightarrow C$). Such potential updates would invalidate the writeset. A transaction passing both checks is valid, and the writeset of the transaction is used to update the world state. Invalid transactions get marked in the block and their effects are discarded.

3 Formalizing the Architectural Entities

We formalize the main entities involved in the transaction flow of Hyperledger Fabric, including different kinds of network nodes, transaction proposals, endorsements, transactions, ledgers, blocks, world states, etc.

3.1 Sets and Elements for the Entities

We start by introducing the sets and meta-variables that constitute the basis of our formalization. These include client identifiers $cid \in CId$, peer identifiers $pid \in PId$, chaincode identifiers $ccid \in CcId$, public keys $pk \in PK$, hash values $h \in H$, and keys $k \in K$ that are mapped to values in world states. In addition, we use t to range over the set $T := \{tt, ff\}$ of truth values, and n to range over the set $\mathbb{N}$ of natural numbers.

We present the definitions modeling the main entities involved in the transaction flow in Table 1. If an entity is modeled by a tuple, we give the name of each component that can be used to refer to the component. This name may differ from the meta-variable ranging over the domain of the component in general.

The definitions given in Table 1 are explained as follows. A *client* (c) is modeled by a timestamp ts counting the number of transactions proposed, a list $txps$

Table 1. The main entities involved in the transaction flow

	Sets	Elements
Clients	$C := TS \times TxP^* \times (H \to Ed^*)$	$c := (ts, txps, edm)$
Peers	$P := PK \times (CcId \to (EP \times Op^*)_\perp) \times$	$p := (pk, ep\_cc, lg, txps, op\_sem)$
	$Lg \times TxP^* \times (Op \to \Sigma \to (R \times W)_\perp)$	
Ordering services	$O := BS \times BN \times H \times Tx^* \times (BN \to B_\perp)$	$o := (bsz, lbn, lbh, txs, bm)$
Trans. proposals	$TxP := CId \times CcId \times Op \times TS$	$txp := (cid, ccid, op, ts)$
Endorsements	$Ed := Ed_0 \times Sig$	$ed := (ed_0, sig)$
Endorsed data	$Ed_0 := PId \times CcId \times Op \times R \times W$	$ed_0 := (pid, ccid, op, r, w)$
Transactions	$Tx := CcId \times Op \times R \times W \times Ed^*$	$tx := (ccid, op, r, w, eds)$
Ledgers	$Lg := B^* \times (CcId \to \Sigma_\perp)$	$lg := (blks, wss)$
Blocks	$B := BH \times Tx^* \times T^*$	$b := (bh, txs, flags)$
Block headers	$BH := BN \times H \times H$	$bh := (bn, cbh, pbh)$
Endors. policies	$EP := Sig^* \to T$	$ep \in EP$
Signatures	$Sig := PK \times H$	$sig := (pk, h)$
World states	$\Sigma := K \to (V \times Vr)_\perp$	$\sigma \in \Sigma$
Values	$V := \mathbb{N} \cup (K \to V_\perp)$	$v \in V$
Read sets	$R := K \to Vr_\perp$	$r \in R$
Write sets	$W := K \to (\{ff\} \cup \{tt\} \times V_\perp)$	$w \in W$
Hash functions	$HF := (TxP \cup Ed_0 \cup Tx^*) \to H$	$hf \in HF$
Timestamps	$TS := \mathbb{N}$	$ts \in TS$
Block sizes	$BS := \mathbb{N}$	$bsz \in BS$
Block numbers	$BN := \mathbb{N}$	$bn \in BN$
Version numbers	$Vr := \mathbb{N}$	$vr \in Vr$

of transaction proposals sent but not yet endorsed on by enough peers, and a function edm from each hash value of a transaction proposal to a list of endorsements that have been received for the proposal. A *peer* (p) is modeled by a public key pk identifying the peer, a function ep_cc mapping each chaincode identifier to an optional pair consisting of the endorsement policy for the chaincode and the list of operations in the chaincode, a ledger lg, a list $txps$ of transaction proposals not yet processed by the peer, and a function op_sem that interprets each operation of a smart contract in a given world state as a readset and a writeset. The *ordering service* (o) is modeled by the size bsz of each block to be formed, the block number lbn for the last block formed, the hash value lbh of the transactions in the last block formed, a list txs of pending transactions to be assembled into blocks, and a function bm mapping each block number to an optional block having that block number. A *transaction proposal* (txp) is modeled by a client identifier cid for the client generating the proposal, a chaincode identifier $ccid$ for the chaincode to be invoked in the transaction, the operation op invoked, and the timestamp ts of the client when it sends the transaction proposal. An *endorsement* (ed) is modeled by the endorsed data ed_0, and a signature sig on the endorsed data by the endorsing peer. The endorsed data (ed_0) consists of the peer identifier pid for the endorsing peer, the chaincode identifier $ccid$ for the chaincode invoked, the operation op invoked, and the readset r and writeset w generated by executing (or simulating) the operation. A *transaction* (tx) is modeled by a chaincode identifier $ccid$ for the chaincode invoked in the transaction, the operation op in the chaincode that is invoked, a readset r and a writeset w constituting a summary of the executional effects of the chaincode, and a list eds of endorsements that made the transaction possible. A *ledger* (lg) is modeled by a list $blks$ of blocks (i.e., a blockchain), and a function wss mapping each chaincode identifier to the world state of the chaincode. A *block* (b) is modeled by a block header bh, a list txs of transactions contained in the block, and a list $flags$ of truth values indicating the validity of the individual transactions. A *block header* (bh) is modeled by a block number bn, a hash value cbh for the list of transactions in the current block, and a hash value pbh for the previous block. An *endorsement policy* (ep) is modeled by a function mapping each list of signatures produced by endorsing peers to a truth value indicating whether these endorsing peers are enough to qualify a transaction. A *signature* (sig) is modeled by a public key pk that can be used to verify the signature, and a hash value h representing the data that is signed. A *world state* (σ) is modeled by a function mapping each key to an optional pair of the value and version number for the key. A *value* (v) may be a natural number, or a function mapping each key to an optional value. A *readset* (r) is modeled as a function mapping each key to an optional version number. A *writeset* (w) is modeled as a function mapping a key to $f\!f$ if the key is unaffected, to a pair of the form (tt, v) if the key is updated to v, or to a pair of the form $(tt, \bot)$ if the key is deleted.

3.2   Inspection and Update of the Entities

We make extensive use of lists, tuples, and functions in our formalization. We introduce the notation used in the presentation for the inspection and manipulation of these structures.

For a *list* $as \in A^*$, we write $|as|$ for the length of as, and (abuse notation to) write $a \in as$ for the membership of a in as, and $as \setminus a$ for the list as' obtained by removing the first occurence of a in as. We write $firstn(as, n)$ (where $n \in \{0, \ldots, |as|\}$) for the list consisting of the first n elements of as, in their original order. We write $skipn(as, n)$ (where $n \in \{0, \ldots, |as|\}$) for the list obtainable by removing the first n elements from as. For two lists as_1 and as_2 in A^*, we write $as_1 {}^{\wedge} as_2$ for the concatenation of as_1 and as_2. For a *tuple* $\tau = (\nu_1, \ldots, \nu_n)$ where $\nu_1, \ldots, \nu_n$ are the meta-variables for the components of τ (see Table 1), we write $\tau.\nu_i$ (where $i \in \{1, \ldots, n\}$) for the i-th component of τ. For a *function* $f \in A \to A'$, we write $f\,a$ for the application of f on a. We sometimes represent a function f by the λ-expression $\lambda a.f\,a$.

We use *path expressions* to help specify the update of entities with nested functions and tuples. The update of the part of the entity e referred to by the path expression ξ to a is denoted by $e[\xi := a]$. Here, ξ is given by

$$\xi ::= .\nu\ \xi \mid d\ \xi \mid \epsilon$$

In the above, d is a meta-variable ranging over the domain of some function, and ν is the name of a tuple component. Neither d nor ν contains any function application or component referencing in itself. For example, $o[.bm\ bn := b]$ represents the ordering service that is like o, except that the block mapped to from bn by the component named bm is b. Formally, $e[\xi := a]$ gives the entity e' that is the same as e, except that $e'[\![\xi]\!]$ has the value a. Here, $e[\![\xi]\!]$ represents the result of interpreting the path expression ξ relative to e. This interpretation is given by $e[\![.\nu\ \xi]\!] := (e.\nu)[\![\xi]\!]$, $e[\![d\ \xi]\!] := (e\ d)[\![\xi]\!]$, and $e[\![\epsilon]\!] := e$. We have the example derivation $o[\![.bm\ bn]\!] = (o.bm)[\![bn\ \epsilon]\!] = ((o.bm)\ bn)[\![\epsilon]\!] = (o.bm)\ bn$. The update expression $e[\xi := a]$ is used in Sect. 4.2 where the dynamics of the transaction flow is formalized.

3.3 Illustrative Examples

To help with the understanding of our formalization, we use a running example for illustration. In this example, the information about the pricing of cars is managed on a blockchain. For simplicity, we consider a single type of cars from a single producer, with the price of the cars recorded on a single peer node, and operated on by a single client. Through proposed transactions, this client may set the price of the cars to some fixed value, or to a discount price.

Example 1 (Endorsement policy). For the aforementioned scenario, we consider the endorsement policy $ep_\star \in EP$ given by $ep_\star\ sigs := (\exists h : (pk_\star, h) \in sigs)$. Here, $pk_\star$ is the public key of the (only) peer. Hence, the endorsement by the peer is required on each transaction proposal, under this endorsement policy. $\square$

Example 2 (Operations). The operations setting the price of the cars and applying deductions on the prices are captured by the list $ops_\star := [set\_op, dc\_op]$. The operation set_op sets the price to 6000\$. The operation dc_op applies a 10% deduction to the price. The intuitive meanings of the two operations are captured by the function $op\_sem_\star \in Op \to \Sigma \to (R \times W)_\perp$, given by

$$op\_sem_\star := (\lambda op.\lambda\sigma.\perp)[\,set\_op := (\lambda\sigma.(r_s, w_s)),\ dc\_op := (\lambda\sigma.(r_d, w_d))\,]$$

Here, $r_s = \lambda k.\perp$, $w_s = (\lambda k.\perp)[price := (tt, 6000)]$, $r_d = (\lambda k.\perp)[price := (\sigma\ price).vr]$, and $w_d = (\lambda k.\perp)[price := (tt, (\sigma\ price).v * 0.9)]$. Interpreting each operation in a world state yields a pair of a readset and a writeset. The operation set_op involves no reading of the world state. This is captured by the readset r_s mapping each key to $\perp$. The writeset w_s yielded by this operation indicates that the value for the key $price$ is affected (tt), and is set to 6000. The operation dc_op reads the current price of the cars. This is captured by the readset r_d mapping $price$ to its version number in the given world state σ. The writeset w_d for this operation reflects that the value for the key $price$ is set to 90% of its original value in the given world state σ. $\square$

Example 3 (Transaction). Consider a transaction tx_1 invoking the operation set_op. Then, tx_1 is of the form $(ccid_\star, set\_op, r_s, w_s, [ed_1])$, where $ed_1 = (ed_{10}, (pk_\star, hf_\star ed_{10}))$, $ed_{10} = (pid_\star, ccid_\star, set\_op, r_s, w_s)$, $pid_\star$ is the identifier of the only peer, $ccid_\star \in CcId$ is the identifier for the car-pricing chaincode, and ed_1 is the endorsement by the peer on the transaction. ☐

Example 4 (Peer). Consider the situation where one single block b_1 containing the single transaction tx_1 has been created by the ordering service, and integrated into the ledger on the peer. The state of the peer can be modeled as

$$p_\star := (pk_\star, ep\_cc_\star, lg_\star, [], op\_sem_\star)$$

where $ep\_cc_\star = (\lambda ccid. \bot)[ccid_\star := (ep_\star, ops_\star)]$, $lg_\star = ([b_1], (\lambda ccid.\lambda k.\bot)[ccid_\star := (\lambda k.\bot)[price := (6000, 1)]])$, and $b_1 = ((0, hf_\star [tx_1], hf_\star []), [tx_1], [tt])$. Here, the ledger $lg_\star$ contains the blockchain $[b_1]$. The list $[tt]$ in b_1 reflects that tx_1 is valid. The ledger $lg_\star$ also contains a mapping giving the world state of the chaincode. This world state maps the key *price* to the value 6000 and the version 1. ☐

Example 5 (Ordering service). The state of the ordering service is modeled as

$$o_\star := (1, 0, hf_\star [tx_1], [], (\lambda bn.\bot)[0 := ((0, hf_\star [tx_1], hf_\star []), [tx_1], [])])$$

Hence, the block size is 1, the block number of the last block is 0, the last block hash is $hf_\star [tx_1]$, the list of pending transactions is the empty list and the block number 0 is mapped to the only block that has been created, i.e., $((0, hf_\star [tx_1], hf_\star []), [tx_1], [])$. This block is the same as b_1 in Example 4 except that the list of validity flags is empty. This is because the validity flags are generated after the validation of the block at the peer, while the block recorded in the ordering service is not yet processed by the peer. ☐

Example 6 (Client). The state of the client is modeled by $c_\star := (1, [], \lambda h.[])$. Hence, the timestamp of the client is currently 1, after the increment when proposing the first transaction, tx_1. The list of pending transaction proposals is empty, for the only generated proposal has been handled, with its corresponding transaction created. Finally, the only endorsement on the transaction proposal has been cleared after the transaction is created. This is reflected by $\lambda h.[]$ that maps each transaction proposal hash to the empty list of endorsements. ☐

4 Formalizing the Transaction Flow

In this section, we formalize the dynamics of the transaction flow process of Hyperledger Fabric as a transition system.

4.1 Specification of the Transition Relation

We formally model a processing step in the transaction flow with a transition relation. It is represented using the notation $hf \vdash \langle \kappa, \rho, o \rangle \xrightarrow{\alpha} \langle \kappa', \rho', o' \rangle$.

This notation says: The network state $\langle \kappa, \rho, o \rangle$ is updated to the network state $\langle \kappa', \rho', o' \rangle$ after a transition step performing the action α, and using hf for the hashing operations potentially involved. Here, $\kappa, \kappa' \in CId \rightarrow C_\perp$ capture the states of the clients, $\rho, \rho' \in PId \rightarrow P_\perp$ capture the states of the peers, and $o, o' \in O$ capture the states of the ordering service. The set Act of actions is given by

$$Act := \{\, cli\_prop(cid, pids) \mid cid \in CId \wedge pids \in PId^* \,\} \cup$$
$$\{\, peer\_resp(pid, cid) \mid pid \in PId \wedge cid \in CId \,\} \cup \{\, peer\_dprop(pid) \mid pid \in PId \,\} \cup$$
$$\{\, cli\_trans(cid) \mid cid \in CId \,\} \cup \{\, cli\_dprop(cid) \mid cid \in CId \,\} \cup$$
$$\{\, os\_blk() \,\} \cup \{\, peer\_blk(pid) \mid pid \in PId \,\}$$

With $cli\_prop(cid, pids)$, we model the action of a client sending a transaction proposal to a number of peers. The client has client identifier cid, and the transaction proposal is sent to all peers with peer identifiers in the list $pids$. With $peer\_resp(pid, cid)$, we model the action of a peer responding to a transaction proposal with an endorsement. The peer has the peer identifier pid, and the response is sent to the client with the client identifier cid. With $peer\_dprop(pid)$, we model the action of a peer not endorsing a transaction proposal, and dropping the transaction proposal correspondingly. With $cli\_trans(cid)$, we model the action of a client sending a transaction to the ordering service, after having collected enough endorsements on one of its transaction proposals. With $cli\_dprop(cid)$, we model the action of a client dropping a transaction proposal due to the inability to collect enough endorsements on the transaction proposal. With $os\_blk()$, we model the action of the ordering service forming a new block. With $peer\_blk(pid)$, we model the action of a peer validating a block and incorporating the block into the ledger on the peer.

4.2   Conditions for the Transitions

We specify the sufficient conditions for the different kinds of transitions to take place, i.e., conditions for $hf \vdash \langle \kappa, \rho, o \rangle \xrightarrow{\alpha} \langle \kappa', \rho', o' \rangle$ to hold with different values for α. When multiple conditions hold simultaneously, any of the corresponding transitions may happen, reflecting the nondeterminism of the transaction flow.

The condition for the transition representing a client sending a transaction proposal is specified as

$$\exists cid \in CId, c \in C, pids \in PId^*, ccid \in CcId, op \in Op, txp \in TxP :$$
$$c = \kappa\ cid\ \wedge\ txp = (cid, ccid, op, c.ts)\ \wedge$$
$$\kappa' = \kappa[cid.txps := c.txps^{\smallfrown}[txp],\ cid.ts := c.ts + 1]\ \wedge$$
$$\rho' = \rho[pid.txps := (\rho\ pid).txps^{\smallfrown}[txp]]_{pid \in pids}\ \wedge\ o' = o\ \wedge\ \alpha = cli\_prop(cid, pids)$$

Hence, a client with client identifier cid may send a transaction proposal txp to the peers with peer identifiers in $pids$, if txp contains the current timestamp $c.ts$ of the client. In addition, txp contains some chaincode identifier $ccid$ for the chaincode to be invoked, and some operation op in the chaincode. The transaction proposal txp is entered into the list of pending transaction proposals of the client, and into the lists of the pending transaction proposals of all the targeted peers when the transaction proposal arrives at these peers. Finally, the timestamp of the client is incremented to signal the proposal of a new transaction.

The condition for the transition representing a peer responding to a transaction proposal with an endorsement is specified as

$$\exists cid \in CId, pid \in PId, p \in P, txp \in TxP, r \in R, w \in W,$$
$$ep \in EP, ops \in Op^*, h \in H, ed_0 \in Ed_0, sig \in Sig :$$
$$\rho \; pid = p \; \wedge \; txp \in p.txps \; \wedge \; txp.cid = cid \; \wedge \; h = hf \; txp \; \wedge$$
$$p.ep\_cc \; txp.ccid = (ep, ops) \; \wedge \; txp.op \in ops \; \wedge$$
$$p.op\_sem \; txp.op \; (p.lg.wss \; txp.ccid) = (r, w) \; \wedge$$
$$ed_0 = (pid, txp.ccid, txp.op, r, w) \; \wedge \; sig = (p.pk, \; hf \; ed_0) \; \wedge$$
$$\kappa' = \kappa[cid.edm \; h := ((\kappa \; cid).edm \; h)^\wedge[(ed_0, sig)]] \; \wedge$$
$$\rho' = \rho[pid.txps := p.txps \setminus txp] \; \wedge \; o' = o \; \wedge \; \alpha = peer\_resp(pid, cid)$$

Hence, a peer with peer identifier pid may respond (with an endorsement) to a transaction proposal txp from the client with client identifier cid, if txp is in the peer's list of pending transaction proposals ($p.txps$), the operation requested in txp (i.e., $txp.op$) is supported by the chaincode, and the execution of the operation in the local world state for the chaincode yields the readset r and the writeset w. The peer then signs on the data relevant to txp and the outcome of the execution consisting of r and w. Essentially, it produces a signature that can be verified by the public key of the peer. Finally, txp is removed from the peer's pending list, and the endorsement (ed_0, sig) is added to the list of endorsements kept for the hash value of txp by the client. The client may check this list to see if enough endorsements have been collected for a transaction proposal.

The condition for the transition representing a client composing and sending a transaction after having collected enough endorsements is specified as

$$\exists pid \in PId, p \in P, cid \in CId, c \in C, txp \in TxP, h \in H,$$
$$ep \in EP, ops \in Op^*, eds \subset Ed^*, tx \in Tx :$$
$$\kappa \; cid = c \; \wedge \; txp \in c.txps \; \wedge \; h = hf \; txp \; \wedge$$
$$\rho \; pid = p \; \wedge \; p.ep\_cc \; txp.ccid = (ep, ops) \; \wedge$$
$$c.edm \; h = eds \; \wedge \; ep \; (map \; \lambda ed.(ed.sig) \; eds) = tt \; \wedge$$
$$(\exists r, w : (\forall ed \in eds : ed.r = r \wedge ed.w = w) \; \wedge \; tx = (txp.ccid, txp.op, r, w, eds)) \; \wedge$$
$$\kappa' = \kappa[cid.txps := (\kappa \; cid).txps \setminus txp, \; cid.edm \; h := []] \; \wedge$$
$$\rho' = \rho \; \wedge \; o' = o[.txs := o.txs^\wedge[tx]] \; \wedge \; \alpha = cli\_trans(cid)$$

Hence, a client with client identifier cid may compose and send a transaction to the ordering service if it has collected enough endorsements on a transaction proposal txp (with hash value h), such that the endorsement policy ep for the chaincode invoked in txp is satisfied. This endorsement policy is kept on some peer. Furthermore, all the endorsements that lead to the satisfaction of ep have the same readset and writeset. Moreover, the transaction tx is formed to contain the readset and writeset, as well as the endorsements. Finally, the txp that is the basis of the new transaction is removed from the pending list in the client, the corresponding list of endorsements is emptied, and the new transaction tx is added into the list of pending transactions in the ordering service.

The condition for the transition representing the ordering service creating a block from a sequence of transactions is specified as

$$\exists bh \in BH, bn \in BN, h, h' \in H, b \in B:$$

$|o.txs| \geq o.bsz \;\wedge\; bn = o.lbn + 1 \;\wedge\; o.bm\; bn = \bot \;\wedge$

$h = hf\; firstn(o.txs, o.bsz) \;\wedge\; h' = o.lbh \;\wedge$

$bh = (bn, h, h') \;\wedge\; b = (bh, firstn(o.txs, o.bsz), [\,]) \;\wedge$

$o' = o[\,.lbn := o.lbn + 1, .lbh := h, .txs := skipn(o.txs, o.bsz), .bm\; bn := b] \;\wedge$

$\kappa' = \kappa \;\wedge\; \rho' = \rho \;\wedge\; \alpha = os\_blk()$

Hence, the ordering service may create a new block if the number of pending transactions $|o.txs|$ has exceeded the block size $o.bsz$, and the ordering service has not recorded any block with some block number bn that is greater than that of the last block by one. The new block b contains the first $o.bsz$ transactions in the list of pending transactions recorded in the ordering service. Furthermore, b contains in its header the new block number bn, the hash h of the list of transactions in b, and the hash h' of the last block. The new block b has an empty list of validity flags upon creation. Finally, the last block number is incremented in the ordering service, the last block hash is updated to the hash for b, the transactions that have been added into b are removed from the pending list, and b is mapped from its block number in the ordering service.

The condition for the transition representing a peer integrating a block into its ledger is specified as

$$\exists pid \in PId, p \in P, b', b'' \in B, epmp \in (CcId \rightarrow EP_\bot), flags \in T^*, wss' \in (CcId \rightarrow \Sigma_\bot):$$

$\rho\; pid = p \;\wedge\; b' = o.bm\; b'.bh.bn \;\wedge$

$\left[\begin{array}{l} p.lg.blks = [\,] \wedge b'.bh.bn = 0 \;\vee \\ \exists b, blks' : p.lg.blks = blks'^\frown[b] \wedge b'.bh.bn = b.bh.bn + 1 \wedge b'.bh.pbh = b.bh.cbh \end{array} \right] \wedge$

$epmp = ep\text{-}of(p.ep\_cc) \;\wedge\; txs\_validate(b'.txs, epmp, p.lg.wss) = (flags, wss') \;\wedge$

$b'' = (b'.bh, b'.txs, flags) \wedge$

$\kappa' = \kappa \;\wedge\; \rho' = \rho[pid.lg := ((p.lg.blks)^\frown[b''], wss')] \;\wedge\; o' = o \;\wedge\; \alpha = peer\_blk(pid)$

where $ep\text{-}of(ep\_cc)\; ccid := \begin{cases} ep & \text{if } ep\_cc\; ccid = (ep, ops) \\ \bot & \text{if } ep\_cc\; ccid = \bot \end{cases}$

Hence, a peer with identifier pid may integrate a new block into its ledger, if some block b' is mapped from its block number in the ordering service, its block number is greater than the block number of the current last block in the ledger of the peer by one, and b' contains a previous block hash that is equal to the block hash of the current last block. The list of transactions in b' is validated, generating a list of truth values as the validity flags for these transactions. Finally, the new block with these validity flags (b'') is appended to the blockchain of the peer, and the local record of world states on the peer are updated to those resulting from the validation. In the above, the function $txs\_validate$ is in $Tx^* \times (CcId \rightarrow EP_\perp) \times (CcId \rightarrow \Sigma_\perp) \rightarrow (T^* \times (CcId \rightarrow \Sigma_\perp))$. It models the validation of a list of transactions under an initial series of endorsement policies and world states for the chaincodes. The function yields a sequence of validity flags for the validated transactions, and a final series of world states for the chaincodes.

For space reasons, the definition of $txs\_validate$, and the conditions for the transitions with the actions $peer\_dprop(pid)$ and $cli\_dprop(cid)$ are omitted. All these technical elements are covered by the Coq development [5].

We remark that the transition system captures the concurrency in the handling of transactions through an interleaving semantics. For instance, after a transition for the proposal of a transaction, and before the corresponding transitions for the endorsement of this proposal, there can be other transitions for the endorsement of other transaction proposals, the creation of new blocks, etc.

4.3   Illustrative Examples

We elaborate on the car-pricing scenario discussed in Sect. 3.3, to illustrate the formalization of the transaction flow process. In Sect. 3.3, the network modeled is in a state where the blockchain contains a single block with a single transaction. In this section, we consider the proposal and processing of a second transaction that attempts to set the price of the cars to the discount price.

Example 7 (Proposal of transaction). The client sends a transaction proposal to the peer, invoking the operation dc_op. This is captured by the transition $hf_\star \vdash \langle \kappa_1, \rho_1, o_1 \rangle \xrightarrow{cli\_prop(cid_\star, [pid_\star])} \langle \kappa_2, \rho_2, o_2 \rangle$. Here, κ_1, ρ_1 and o_1 are such that $\kappa_1 \; cid_\star = c_\star$, $\rho_1 \; pid_\star = p_\star$, and $o_1 = o_\star$ (see Example 4, Example 5, and Example 6 for the definitions of $p_\star$, $o_\star$, and $c_\star$). The transaction proposal sent is of the form $(cid_\star, ccid_\star, dc\_op, 1)$. □

Example 8 (Response to proposal). The peer responds to the transaction proposal with an endorsement. This is captured by the transition $hf_\star \vdash \langle \kappa_2, \rho_2, o_2 \rangle \xrightarrow{peer\_resp(pid_\star, cid_\star)} \langle \kappa_3, \rho_3, o_3 \rangle$ for some κ_3, ρ_3, and o_3. The response of the peer is of the form $(ed_{20}, (pk_\star, hf_\star \; ed_{20}))$ where ed_{20} is the tuple

$$(pid_\star, ccid_\star, dc\_op, (\lambda k.\perp)[price := 1], (\lambda k.\perp)[price := (tt, 5400)])$$

Here, the readset $(\lambda k.\perp)[price := 1]$ reflects that the execution of the operation dc_op in the local world state of the peer reads version 1 of the key *price*. The writeset reflects that the execution of this operation writes the value 5400 (the discount price) to the key *price*. □

Example 9 (Sending of transaction). The client creates and sends a transaction after making sure that the endorsement policy for the chaincode containing the operation dc_op is satisfied. This is captured by the transition $hf_\star \vdash \langle \kappa_3, \rho_3, o_3 \rangle \xrightarrow{cli\_trans(cid_\star)} \langle \kappa_4, \rho_4, o_4 \rangle$ for some κ_4, ρ_4, and o_4. This transition takes place because the endorsement policy $ep_\star$ (see Example 1) is evaluated to tt on the list of signatures extracted from the list of endorsements $[(ed_{20}, (pk_\star, hf_\star\ ed_{20}))]$. The transaction created, denoted by tx_2, is

$$(ccid_\star, dc\_op, (\lambda k.\bot)[price := 1], (\lambda k.\bot)[price := (tt, 5400)], [(ed_{20}, (pk_\star, hf_\star\ ed_{20}))])$$

Furthermore, $o_4.txs$ is the singleton list $[tx_2]$ – the transaction tx_2 is entered into the pending list of transactions of the ordering service, after this transition. □

Example 10 (Block creation). The ordering service creates a new block after receiving the new transaction. This is captured by the transition $hf_\star \vdash \langle \kappa_4, \rho_4, o_4 \rangle \xrightarrow{os\_blk()} \langle \kappa_5, \rho_5, o_5 \rangle$, for some κ_5, ρ_5, and o_5. This transition takes place because $o_4.bsz = 1$ and $|o_4.txs| = 1 \geq o_4.bsz$. That is, there are sufficiently many pending transactions in the ordering service to form a new block. The block formed is $b_{20} = ((1, hf_\star\ [tx_2], hf_\star\ [tx_1]), [tx_2], [])$. The block header contains the block number 1, the hash value for the transactions $[tx_2]$ in the block, and the hash value for the transactions $[tx_1]$ in the previous block. The list of validity flags is empty, for the block is not yet validated. After this transition, $o_5.lbn$ is 1 – the block number of the last generated block. In addition, $o_5.lbh$ is $hf_\star\ [tx_2]$ – the block hash for the last generated block. Moreover, the list $o_5.txs$ of pending transactions is empty. Lastly, $o_5.bm$ maps block number 1 to b_{20}. □

Example 11 (Block validation). The peer incorporates the new block into its ledger after validating the new block. This is captured by the transition $hf_\star \vdash \langle \kappa_5, \rho_5, o_5 \rangle \xrightarrow{peer\_blk(pid_\star)} \langle \kappa_6, \rho_6, o_6 \rangle$ for some κ_6, ρ_6, and o_6. The transition takes place because $o_5.bm$ maps 1 to some block b_{20}, b_{20} has a block number that is greater than the current last block in the ledger of the peer by 1, and b_{20} has a previous block hash that equals the block hash of the last block in the ledger.

The version number of $price$ is 1 in the peer state $(\rho_5\ pid_\star)$. This is in accordance with the readset of tx_2. Hence, tx_2 is found to be valid. A new series wss' of world states is generated after the validation of tx_2 – the only transaction in the block. After this transition, we have $(\rho_6\ pid_\star).lg = ([b_1, b_2], wss')$, where $b_2 = ((1, hf_\star\ [tx_2], hf_\star\ [tx_1]), [tx_2], [tt])$. This reflects that the new block is integrated into the ledger on the peer, and the transaction in this block is valid. □

Now, the process involving the execution, ordering, and validation of the new transaction is completed. In the ledger of the peer, the world state records the new price for the cars, 5400$. The corresponding key is updated to version 2.

5   Proving Preservation of Consensus

We show that the consistency of the ledgers on the different peers is preserved by the evolvement of the network state, as is driven by the transaction flow.

The consistency of the ledgers on the peers is captured by the predicate $cl \in HF \times (CId \rightarrow C_\perp) \times (PId \rightarrow P_\perp) \times O \rightarrow T$. This predicate is given by

$$cl(hf, \kappa, \rho, o) :=$$

$$\forall pid_1, pid_2 \in PId, p_1, p_2 \in P :$$

$$pid_1 \neq pid_2 \land \rho\, pid_1 = p_1 \land \rho\, pid_2 = p_2 \Rightarrow$$

$$\left[\begin{array}{l} ep\text{-}of(p_1.ep\_cc) = ep\text{-}of(p_2.ep\_cc) \\[4pt] \land \left[\begin{array}{l} |p_1.lg.blks| \leq |p_2.lg.blks| \Rightarrow \\[3pt] \left[\begin{array}{l} p_1.lg.blks = firstn(p_2.lg.blks, |p_1.lg.blks|) \\[3pt] \land \left[\begin{array}{l} \exists \rho', \kappa', o', p'_1, k = |p_2.lg.blks| - |p_1.lg.blks| : \\[3pt] hf \vdash \langle \kappa, \rho, o \rangle \xrightarrow{\;peer\_blk(pid_1)\;}_k \langle \kappa', \rho', o' \rangle \land \rho'\, pid_1 = p'_1 \land p'_1.lg = p_2.lg \end{array} \right] \end{array} \right] \end{array} \right] \end{array} \right]$$

Here, the notation $hf \vdash \langle \kappa, \rho, o \rangle \xrightarrow{\;peer\_blk(pid_1)\;}_k \langle \kappa', \rho', o' \rangle$ represents a transition sequence of length k, where each transition performs the action $peer\_blk(pid_1)$. Hence, the ledgers on different peers (with identifiers pid_1 and pid_2) are consistent in a network state $\langle \kappa, \rho, o \rangle$, if the following conditions are met. Firstly, the endorsement policies kept on the peers for the same chaincode are the same. Secondly, of the blockchains on the two peers, the shorter one is a prefix of the other. Thirdly, the peer with the shorter chain is able to catch up with the other peer on the ledger by performing k transition steps integrating further blocks. Here, k is the difference in the length of the two blockchains.

The preservation of ledger consistency is captured by the following theorem.

Theorem 1. *If $cl(hf, \kappa, \rho, o)$ holds, and $hf \vdash \langle \kappa, \rho, o \rangle \xrightarrow{\alpha} \langle \kappa', \rho', o' \rangle$ holds, then $cl(hf, \kappa', \rho', o')$ holds.*

The proof [5] of this theorem is by a case analysis on the action α. The theorem demonstrates that the interaction of the diverse technical artifacts, such as endorsement policies, summaries of code execution in terms of readsets and writesets, hash-connected blocks, and versioned key-value stores, really fulfills the basic requirement of maintaining consensus in a blockchain system. In the case of Hyperledger Fabric, the transaction flow builds on the order of transactions delivered by the ordering service, to provide system-level consensus guarantees.

Mechanization in Coq. We mechanize Theorem 1 and its proof in Coq 8.9.0. This is based on our mechanization of the formal model for the Hyperledger Fabric transaction flow. Here, the basic entities such as transaction proposals, transactions, and network nodes, are mechanized using the inductive datatypes and records of Coq. The transition system for the transaction flow is mechanized as an inductive proposition. The proof itself is mechanized by establishing 41 lemmas on the preservation of the states of peers and the ordering service under different kinds of transition steps, and the preservation of the similarity between these states. A more elaborate version of the illustrative example with two peers is covered in the mechanization. The overall mechanization [5] totals about 3.2k LoCs (excluding comments, and imported infrastructure definitions, lemmas and tactics [4]). It greatly raises the confidence level on the sanity of the formal model, and of its link to distributed consensus.

6   Conclusion

Hyperledger Fabric is the prototypical permissioned blockchain system extensively adopted for commercial applications. The transaction flow process is an overarching architectural component of Hyperledger Fabric. It embodies the execute-order-validate paradigm of this system. It also shows how different technical components, such as policies, protocols, cryptographic mechanisms, and code execution, are jointly employed in the handling of transactions in a heterogeneously structured network. The conceptual complexity in the transaction flow process, together with the lack of formal description, leads to obstacles in precisely understanding how the process works, and renders it non-trivial to confidently assert the satisfaction of key blockchain properties such as consensus.

In this paper, we formalize the transaction flow process of Hyperledger Fabric, prove that the process preserves distributed consensus, and mechanize the development in the Coq proof assistant. The formalized transaction flow process is shared between the most recent versions of Hyperledger Fabric (2.x) and older versions of this system (1.4.x). The formalization rigorously describes how the different types of network nodes (i.e., peers, orderers, and clients) participate in a multi-stage process involving hashing, timestamping, policy checking and code execution, to handle transactions concurrently, and to maintain consensus over the distributed ledger. Our formalization is illustrated with a rich series of examples in a scenario where pricing information about cars is managed on a blockchain. Our mechanization of the formal model in Coq significantly increases the confidence level on the sanity of the formalization and the proofs. Potential directions for future work include the establishment of further properties of the formal model, and the provision of a formal account on the relationship between our development and existing formalizations of consensus mechanisms for blockchain systems, e.g., in terms of refinement.

Acknowledgement. This work was supported by the National Natural Science Foundation of China (61876111, 61602325, 618770400, 62002246), the general project KM202010028010 of Beijing Municipal Education Commission, and the Youth Innovative Research Team of Capital Normal University. The authors thank the anonymous reviewers for their valuable comments.

References

1. Companies using Hyperledger Fabric. https://101blockchains.com/hyperledger-fabric/
2. The Coq proof assistant. https://coq.inria.fr/
3. A repository for PoS related formal methods. https://github.com/palmskog/pos
4. Software foundations. https://softwarefoundations.cis.upenn.edu/
5. Formalization of transaction flow process of Hyperledger Fabric in Coq (2020). https://github.com/lixm/hf-trans-flow
6. Hyperledger Fabric documentation (2020). https://buildmedia.readthedocs.org/media/pdf/hyperledger-fabric/latest/hyperledger-fabric.pdf
7. Amani, S., Bégel, M., Bortin, M., Staples, M.: Towards verifying Ethereum smart contract bytecode in Isabelle/HOL. In: CPP 2018, pp. 66–77 (2018)
8. Androulaki, E., Barger, A., Bortnikov, V., Cachin, C., et al.: Hyperledger fabric: a distributed operating system for permissioned blockchains. In EuroSys 2018, pp. 30:1–30:15 (2018)
9. Banach, R.: Verification-led smart contracts. In: Bracciali, A., Clark, J., Pintore, F., Rønne, P.B., Sala, M. (eds.) FC 2019. LNCS, vol. 11599, pp. 106–121. Springer, Cham (2020). https://doi.org/10.1007/978-3-030-43725-1_9
10. Beckert, B., Herda, M., Kirsten, M., Schiffl, J.: Formal specification and verification of Hyperledger Fabric chaincode. In: SDLT 2018 (2018)
11. Buterin, V., Griffith, V.: The Casper finality gadget. CoRR, abs/1710.09437
12. Fernández Anta, A., Georgiou, C., Konwar, K., Nicolaou, N.: Formalizing and implementing distributed ledger objects. In: NETYS 2018, pp. 19–35 (2018)
13. Grishchenko, I., Maffei, M., Schneidewind, C.: A semantic framework for the security analysis of Ethereum smart contracts. In: POST 2018, pp. 243–269 (2018)
14. Hirai, Y.: Defining the ethereum virtual machine for interactive theorem provers. In: Brenner, M., et al. (eds.) FC 2017. LNCS, vol. 10323, pp. 520–535. Springer, Cham (2017). https://doi.org/10.1007/978-3-319-70278-0_33
15. Jiao, J., Kan, S., Lin, S.-W., Sanan, D., Liu, Y., Sun, J.: Semantic understanding of smart contracts: executable operational semantics of Solidity. In: S&P 2020 (2020)
16. Li, X., Shi, Z., Zhang, Q., Wang, G., Guan, Y., Han, N.: Towards verifying ethereum smart contracts at intermediate language level. In: Ait-Ameur, Y., Qin, S. (eds.) ICFEM 2019. LNCS, vol. 11852, pp. 121–137. Springer, Cham (2019). https://doi.org/10.1007/978-3-030-32409-4_8
17. Thin, W.Y.M.M., Dong, N., Bai, G., Dong, J.: Formal analysis of a proof-of-stake blockchain. In: ICECCS 2018, pp. 197–200 (2018)
18. Nielson, F., Nielson, H.R.: Formal Methods - An Appetizer. Springer, Heidelberg (2019). https://doi.org/10.1007/978-3-030-05156-3
19. Pîrlea, G., Sergey, I.: Mechanising blockchain consensus. In: CPP 2018, pp. 78–90 (2018)
20. Sukhwani, H., Wang, N., Trivedi, K.S, Rindos, A.: Performance modeling of Hyperledger Fabric (permissioned blockchain network). In: NCA 2018, pp. 1–8 (2018)
21. Wilcox, J.R., et al.: Verdi: a framework for implementing and formally verifying distributed systems. In: PLDI 2015, pp. 357–368 (2015)
22. Wood, G.: Ethereum: a secure decentralised generlised transaction ledger. https://gavwood.com/paper.pdf

23. Woos, D., Wilcox, J.R., Anton, S., Tatlock, Z., Ernst, M.D., Anderson, T.E.: Planning for change in a formal verification of the Raft consensus protocol. In: CPP 2016, pp. 154–165 (2016)
24. Yaga, D., Mell, P., Roby, N., Scarfone, K.: Blockchain technology overview. Technical report, NISTIR 8202 (2018)
25. Yuan, P., Zheng, K., Xiong, X., Zhang, K., Lei, L.: Performance modeling and analysis of a Hyperledger-based system using GSPN. Comput. Commun. **153**, 117–124 (2020)

Embedding Approximation in Event-B: Safe Hybrid System Design Using Proof and Refinement

Guillaume Dupont[1(✉)], Yamine Aït-Ameur[1], Neeraj K. Singh[1],
Fuyuki Ishikawa[2], Tsutomu Kobayashi[3], and Marc Pantel[1]

[1] INPT-ENSEEIHT/IRIT, University of Toulouse, Toulouse, France
{guillaume.dupont,yamine,nsingh,marc.pantel}@enseeiht.fr
[2] National Institute of Informatics, Tokyo, Japan
f-ishikawa@nii.ac.jp
[3] Japan Science and Technology Agency, Saitama, Japan
t-kobayashi@nii.ac.jp

Abstract. Hybrid systems consist of a discrete part (controller) that interacts with a continuous physical part (plant). Formal verification of such systems is complex and challenging in order to handle both the discrete objects and continuous objects, such as functions and differential equations for modelling the physical part, for synthesising hybrid controllers. In many cases, where the continuous component model uses complex differential equations, a well-defined *approximation* operation involves simplifying it. The aim of this approximation is to ease the development of the controller, which would not be feasible with the actual differential equation. We claim this approximation operation can be treated as an extension of the discrete refinement operation, as long as all the necessary mathematical concepts are formalised. This paper extends the Event-B's refinement which is capable of expressing an approximation between two hybrid systems as a refinement relation. We encode this *approximate refinement* relationship in Event-B, relying on its deductive reasoning enhanced by the theory of approximation based on the notion of approximate (bi-)simulation. New proof obligations resulting from this *approximate refinement* are highlighted. Finally, we illustrate how it applies to a case study borrowed from literature.

1 Introduction

Hybrid systems consist of both discrete and continuous dynamic behaviour, where discrete elements interact with physical environment [3]. Due to this dual nature, the verification of such systems is complex; it requires the capability to

Supported by the ANR DISCONT Project (https://discont.loria.fr), Grant Number ANR-17-CE25-0005.
Supported by JST, ACT-I, Grant Number JPMJPR17UA.

handle and reason on continuous behaviour defined as functions and differential equations for modelling the physical part, in addition to the usual discrete behaviour of the controller.

Many formal approaches for hybrid systems design and verification have been developed. The most popular methods are hybrid automata [3], hybrid programs [21,22], hybrid model checking [4,13,14,18], proof and refinement approaches using continuous action systems [5], Event-B [23], hybrid Event-B [6] and hybrid CSP [8,19]. These approaches model both discrete and continuous behaviours in a single integrated modelling language.

Such methods are generally based on concurrently modelling a discrete controller component and a plant's continuous dynamics, i.e. the regulated phenomena. The controller usually encodes a mode automaton with discrete state variables, describing changes and controller decisions. On the other side, the physics of the controlled plant is expressed using continuous state variables evolving according to differential equations.

Motivation of the Paper. In many cases where the continuous part involves complex differential equations, the design of such systems requires additional engineering steps because the continuous behaviour needs to be approximated. The objective of this approximation is to ease the verification of the developed hybrid system or to implement the controller, which would not be feasible nor verifiable with the actual complex differential equation. Linearisation is one such case of approximation. The complex differential equations are refined using a well-defined *approximation* operation. Indeed, when a linear differential equation is available, many useful mathematical results can be applied and verification techniques (e.g. model checking) can be used. Nowadays, in many formal method settings, the preliminary steps leading to the approximated system are mathematically well-founded, but not formally handled by the underlying formal modelling language. This activity remains a mathematical development.

State of the Art. The proposed approach relies on the work of Girard and Pappas in [15,17] where the notion of approximate (bi-)simulation has been introduced. In this study, rather than using classical simulation relations [20], the authors weakened this definition by introducing a relation between safely approximated versions of the observed state variables. The main purpose of this work is to enable the use of hybrid model checkers to perform formal verification. In order to be handled by the intended hybrid model checker, the complex differential equations of the original hybrid system are reformulated (simplified) using an approximation. The safety of the defined approximation guarantees that the properties checked on the obtained approximated hybrid system are also the properties of the original one. Although the defined approximation is mathematically sound, the method did not explicitly formalise the properties of the given approximation or the properties of the original hybrid system.

Our Claim. We claim that this approximation operation, its properties and the corresponding design steps can be *explicitly* handled as an extension of the exact refinement operation, provided that all the required mathematical concepts are also explicitly formalised. We show that the Event-B method and its associated integrated development environment Rodin is capable to handle this formalisation. The defined approximate refinement relationship weakens the exact relationship available in many state-based formal methods like ASM, Z, VDM and Event-B. Moreover, this formalisation offers other capabilities such as checking other properties like invariants preservation and guard strengthening.

Objective of the Paper. In the same state of mind as our previous work [10,11], we propose an extension of Event-B's refinement capable of expressing an approximation between two hybrid systems as a refinement relation. We encode, in a generic framework, this *approximate refinement* relation in Event-B, relying on its deductive reasoning enhanced by a theory of approximation we defined, and on the notion of approximate (bi-)simulation of [15,17]. New proof obligations resulting from this *approximate refinement* are highlighted. Finally, we show how it applies to a case study borrowed from literature.

Organisation of this Paper. Next section gives a short presentation of Event-B (completed in Appendix A). The hybrid systems modelling features we formalise are presented in Sect. 3 and the generic hybrid systems Event-B model, relying on these features, is sketched in Sect. 4. Our framework for approximated refinement, formalised in Event-B, is presented in Sect. 5. A case study showing how our approach applies is developed in Sect. 6. Finally, a conclusion and future research directions are described in the last section.

2 Event-B: A Refinement and Proof State Based Method

In this section, we recall basic notions of Event-B [1]. The approach we follow in this work is state-based and relies on a set of events that describe state changes. The Event-B method [1] supports the development of *correct-by-construction* complex systems. First order logic and set theory are used as the core modelling language. The design process consists of a series of refinements of an abstract model (specification) leading to the final concrete model. Refinement progressively contributes to add system design decisions.

Event-B *Machines* formalise models described as state-transitions systems and a set of proof obligations are automatically generated for each model. A proof system is associated to it, with proof rules for each concept.

In the following, superscripts ^{A} and ^{C} denote abstract and concrete features respectively.

Contexts (Table 1.a). *Contexts* are the static part of a model. They set up all the definitions, axioms and theorems needed to describe the required concepts. *Carrier sets s, constants c, axioms A* and *theorems T_{ctx}* are introduced.

Machines (Table 1.b). *Machines* describe the dynamic part of a model as a transition system, where a set of guarded events modifies a set of variables (states).

Table 1. Model structure

Context	Machine	Refinement
CONTEXT Ctx	**MACHINE** M^A	**MACHINE** M^C
SETS s	**SEES** Ctx	**REFINES** M^A
CONSTANTS c	**VARIABLES** x^A	**VARIABLES** x^C
AXIOMS A	**INVARIANTS** $I^A(x^A)$	**INVARIANTS** $J(x^A, x^C) \wedge I^C(x^C)$
THEOREMS T_{ctx}	**THEOREMS** $T_{mch}(x^A)$	...
END	**VARIANT** $V(x^A)$	**EVENTS**
	EVENTS	**EVENT** evt^C
	EVENT evt^A	**REFINES** evt^A
	ANY α^A	**ANY** α^C
	WHERE $G^A(x^A, \alpha^A)$	**WHERE** $G^C(x^C, \alpha^C)$
	THEN	**WITH**
	$x^A :\mid BAP^A(\alpha^A, x^A, x^{A'})$	$x^{A'}, \alpha^A: W(\alpha^A, \alpha^C, x^A, x^{A'}, x^C, x^{C'})$
	END	**THEN**
	...	$x^C :\mid BAP^C(\alpha^C, x^C, x^{C'})$
		END
		...
(a)	(b)	(c)

Variables x, invariants $I(x)$, theorems $T_{mch}(x)$, variants $V(x)$ and events evt (possibly guarded by G and/or parameterised by α) are defined in a machine. They use Before-After Predicates (BAP), expressed in first order logic, to record variable changes. *Invariants* and *theorems* formalise system safety while *variants* define convergence properties (reachability).

Refinements (Table 1.c). A system is gradually designed by introducing properties (functionality, safety, reachability) at various abstraction levels. A *Refinement* decomposes a *machine*, a state-transitions system, into a less abstract one, with more design decisions (refined states and events), moving from an abstract level to a less abstract one (simulation relationship). Property preservation is ensured by a gluing invariant relating abstract and concrete variables.

Proof Obligations (PO) and Property Verification. To establish the correctness of an Event-B model (*machine* or *Refinement*) POs are automatically generated, that need to be proved.

Extensions with Mathematical Theories. In order to handle theories beyond set theory and first order logic, an Event-B extension to support externally defined mathematical theories has been proposed in [2]. It offers the capability to introduce new datatypes through the definition of new types, sets operators, theorems and associated rewrite and inference rules all packed in so-called *theories*.

Event-B and its IDE Rodin. It offers resources for model edition, automatic PO generation, project management, refinement and proof, model checking, model animation and code generation. Several provers, like SMT solvers, are plugged into Rodin. A useful extension with theories is available as a plug-in [7].

3   Hybrid Systems Modelling Features

Modelling hybrid systems requires to handle continuous behaviours. We thus need to access specific mathematical objects and properties, not natively available in Event-B. These concepts such as differential equations and their associated properties have been modelled through an intensive use of Event-B theories and have been used to model various case studies found in [9–11].

Below, we recall some basic features of these theories and introduce the new theory of approximation needed to formalise approximate refinement.

3.1   A Theory of Continuous Mathematics

In order to deal with continuous objects, theories have been defined for continuous functions, (ordinary) differential equations as well as for their properties. They are used throughout the defined models. Some of those concepts as they are used in this paper are recalled below.

Time. A notion of time is needed to define continuous behaviours. We thus introduce dense time $t \in \mathbb{R}^+$, modelled as a continuously evolving variable.

System state. According to the architecture of hybrid systems, we have identified two types of states.

- **Discrete state** $x_s \in STATES$ is a variable that represents the controller's internal state. It evolves in a point-wise manner with instantaneous changes.
- **Continuous state** $x_p \in \mathbb{R}^+ \rightarrow S$ represents the plant's state and evolves continuously. It is modelled as a function of time with values in space S.
  In the following, we use x to denote the union of discrete and continuous state variables.
- **Continuous gluing invariant** is defined with the generic form $x_p^A \in \mathcal{O} \circ x_p^C$ where $\mathcal{O} \in S^C \leftrightarrow S^A$ is a relation linking abstract and continuous state-spaces. This invariant glues the abstract x_p^A and concrete x_p^C continuous variables. It is qualified as *exact* since it maps concrete values in S^C to abstract values in S^A using the $\in$ operator. Definition of an approximate gluing invariant, extending exact one, is presented later in this paper.

Hybrid Modelling Features. Modelling hybrid systems requires to introduce multiple basic operators and primitives defined below.

- **Feasible**$(x_s, x_p, D, \mathcal{P}, \mathcal{I})$, the feasible predicate states that, given x_s and x_p, there exists $x_p' \in D \rightarrow S$ such that $\mathcal{P}(x_s, x_p, x_p')$ holds and $\forall t^* \in D, x_p'(t^*) \in \mathcal{I}$. In state x_s, the predicate $\mathcal{P}$ holds for x_p and its next value x_p' on time interval D fulfils the constraint $\mathcal{I}$. It defines the feasibility condition of a continuous state change, i.e. continuous before-after predicate defined below.
- **DE**(S) type for differential equations, the solutions of which evolve in set S
- **ode**(f, η_0, t_0) is the ODE[1] $\dot{\eta}(t) = f(\eta(t), t)$ with initial condition $\eta(t_0) = \eta_0$

---

[1] Ordinary Differential Equation.

- **solutionOf**$(D, \eta, \mathcal{E})$ is the predicate stating that function η is a solution of equation $\mathcal{E}$ on subset D
- **Solvable**$(D, \mathcal{E}, \mathcal{I})$ is the predicate stating that equation $\mathcal{E}$ has a solution defined on subset D so that the solution satisfies the constraint $\mathcal{I}$

Continuous Assignment. Continuous variables are essentially functions of time and are at least defined on $[0, t]$ (where t is the current time). Updating such variables, thus, requires to (1) make the time progress from t to $t' > t$, and (2) to append to the already existing function a new piece corresponding to its extended behaviour (on $[t, t']$) while ensuring its "past" (i.e. whatever happened on $[0, t]$) remains unchanged.

Similarly to the classic Event-B's before-after predicate (BAP), we define a *continuous before-after predicate* (*CBAP*) operator, denoted $:|_{t \to t'}$, as follows[2]:

$$x_p :|_{t \to t'} \mathcal{P}(x_s, x_p, x'_p) \,\&\, \mathcal{I} \equiv [0, t] \lhd x' = [0, t] \lhd x \qquad (PP)$$

$$\wedge \, \mathcal{P}(x_s, [t, t'] \lhd x_p, [t, t'] \lhd x'_p) \qquad (PR)$$

$$\wedge \, \forall t^* \in [t, t'], x'_p(t^*) \in \mathcal{I} \qquad (LI)$$

We note $CBAP(x_s, x_p, x'_p) \equiv PP(x_p, x'_p) \wedge PR(x_s, x_p, x'_p) \wedge LI(x_p, x'_p)$. The operator consists of 3 parts: past preservation and coherence at assignment point (PP), before-after predicate on the added section (PR), and local invariant preservation (LI). The discrete state variables x_s do not change in the interval $[t, t']$ but the predicate $\mathcal{P}$ may use it for control purposes.

For convenience, we introduce the following shortcut derived from the above definition, and that represents continuous evolution along a solvable differential equation $\mathcal{E} \in \mathbf{DE}(S)$: $x :\sim_{t \to t'} \mathcal{E} \,\&\, \mathcal{I} \equiv x :|_{t \to t'} \mathbf{solutionOf}([t, t'], x', \mathcal{E}) \,\&\, \mathcal{I}$.

3.2   A Theory of Approximation

In addition to the continuous mathematical objects of Sect. 3.1, a theory of approximation is required to implement approximate refinement in Event-B.

Formal Definitions. In the following, we introduce the necessary concepts and operators related to approximation and used throughout this paper. Let us assume (E, d) to be a metric space with distance d.

Approximation $(\approx^\delta)$. Let $x, y \in E$ and $\delta \in \mathbb{R}^+$. We say that x approximately equals to y by δ (or x is a δ-approximation of y) iff $x \approx^\delta y \equiv d(x, y) \leq \delta$.

δ-expansion. Let $S \subseteq E$ and $\delta \in \mathbb{R}^+$. The δ-expansion of S, noted $\mathcal{E}_\delta(S)$, is defined as $\mathcal{E}_\delta(S) = \{y \in E \mid \exists x \in S, x \approx^\delta y\} = \{y \in E \mid \exists x \in S, d(x, y) \leq \delta\}$.

δ-membership $(\in^\delta)$. Let $\delta \in \mathbb{R}^+$, $S \subseteq E$ and $x \in E$. x belongs to S up to δ, denoted $x \in^\delta S$, iff x belongs to the δ-expansion of S. We write $x \in^\delta S \equiv x \in \mathcal{E}_\delta(S) \equiv \exists y \in S, d(x, y) \leq \delta$.

---

[2] The $\lhd$ operator denotes the domain restriction operator; e.g.: $A \lhd f$ is the function defined at most on A, with the same values as f.

Operators Extensions. For convenience, this definition is extended as follows.

– Let $f \in F \to E$ and $X \subseteq F$, then $f \in_X^\delta S \equiv \forall x \in X, f(x) \in^\delta S$
– Let $\Sigma \in F \to \mathbb{P}(E)$ (multivalued function), then $f \in_X^\delta \Sigma \equiv \forall x \in X, f(x) \in^\delta \Sigma(x)$

Note that, when X is not given, the operator is applied on the function's domain of definition (i.e., $X = \mathrm{dom}(f)$).

Table 2. Approximation theory excerpt

| THEORY ApproximationBase
TYPE PARAMETERS F
. . .
AXIOMATIC DEFINITIONS
  OPERATORS
    DeltaApproximation <predicate>
      (δ: $\mathbb{R}^+$, a: F, b: F)
    AXIOMS
— *commutativity , reflexivity ,* . . . | THEORY Approximation
IMPORT THEORY ApproximationBase
TYPE PARAMETERS E , F
OPERATORS
  — *Definition of* $f \approx_{D_E}^\delta g$
  FDeltaApproximation <predicate>
    (D_E: $\mathbb{P}(E)$, δ: $\mathbb{R}^+$,
     f: $E \nrightarrow F$, g: $E \nrightarrow F$)
    well−definedness condition
      $D_E \subseteq \mathrm{dom}(f), D_E \subseteq \mathrm{dom}(g)$
    $\forall x \cdot x \in D_E \Rightarrow$
      DeltaApproximation($\delta, f(x), g(x)$)
  . . . |

Note: δ-approximation ($\approx^\delta$) (resp. δ-membership ($\in^\delta$)) is a weak version of equality (resp. set membership). Indeed, when $\delta = 0$, by the separation property of distance d, we obtain $x \approx^0 y \equiv d(x,y) \leq 0 \equiv x = y$. It follows that for any $S \subseteq E$, $\mathcal{E}_0(S) = S$ and thus $x \in^0 S \equiv x \in S$.

Implementation Using Theories. The above defined operators and concepts have been implemented in two Event-B theories (*ApproximationBase* and *Approximation*) from which an excerpt is given in Table 2. Typically, approximation ($\approx^\delta$) is expressed algebraically through the *DeltaApproximation* operator, while its function-lifted version is implemented as the *FDeltaApproximation* operator.

All the theories presented above can be accessed from https://irit.fr/~Guillaume.Dupont/models.php

4 Modelling Hybrid Systems Using Event-B

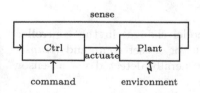

Fig. 1. Generic hybrid system representation

In our previous work [11], we proposed a generic approach to model hybrid systems within Event-B. This approach relies strongly on modelling features presented in Sect. 3 and it is based on a generic model, instantiated using refinement.

This generic model is based on the classical hybrid system architecture pattern shown in Fig. 1. In this model, *controllers* are characterised by discrete state variables while *plants* (the continuous phenomenon being controlled) are modelled using continuous state variables, which evolution is described using differential equations. Sensors are able to determine the plant's state and influence the controller's state according to it; conversely, actuators are able to temper the plant's state following a controller order. Besides, user commands or internal calculus may also change the controller's state. Similarly, the plant's environment may impact its evolution.

Below, we recall the generic model at the heart of our approach. More details as well as various case studies can be found in [9–11] and all the developed models are accessible at https://irit.fr/~Guillaume.Dupont/models.php.

4.1   Generic Model and Its Refinement

As mentioned in Sect. 3.1, the generic model defines three variables: time, discrete state and continuous state. Following the architecture pattern of Fig. 1, it revolves around 4 events, modelling the different aspects of a hybrid system. This model and its refinement are presented below. Due to space limitations, only sensing and actuation events are presented. They are representative of the two other categories of events (transitions in the controller and environment changes). More details can be found in [9–11].

Machine Header. The abstract machine is defined in a quite straightforward way. Time (t), discrete x_s and continuous x_p states are introduced in *inv1-inv3*. Invariant `inv4` expresses the continuous state to be defined (at least) always on $[0, t]$. `inv5` shows additional safety properties regarding the continuous state.

MACHINE M^A	MACHINE M^C REFINES M_A
VARIABLES t, x_s^A, x_p^A	VARIABLES t, x_s^C, x_p^C
INVARIANTS	INVARIANTS
inv1: $t \in \mathbb{R}^+$	inv2: $x_s^C \in STATES^C$
inv2: $x_s^A \in STATES^A$	inv3: $x_p^C \in \mathbb{R} \nrightarrow S^C$
inv3: $x_p^A \in \mathbb{R} \nrightarrow S^A$	inv4: $[0, t] \subseteq dom(x_p^C)$
inv4: $[0, t] \subseteq dom(x^A)$	inv5: $\forall t^* \cdot t^* \in [0, t] \Rightarrow x_p^C(t^*) \in \mathcal{I}^C$
inv5: $\forall t^* \cdot t^* \in [0, t] \Rightarrow x_p^A(t^*) \in \mathcal{I}^A$	inv6: $x_p^A \in \mathcal{O} \circ x_p^C$
	inv7: $J_s(x_s^C, x_s^A)$

When refining *machine M^A* by M^C, *gluing invariants* (`inv6` and `inv7`) relate abstract and concrete state variables. Discrete state variables are glued as in traditional discrete refinement (`inv7` gluing invariant $J_s(x_s^C, x_s^A)$), and the continuous variables, following the definition of Sect. 3.1, are glued using an observation relation $\mathcal{O} \in S^C \leftrightarrow S^A$. In addition, event guards $G^A(x_s^A)$ and $G^A(x_p^A)$ may be strengthened as $G^C(x_s^C)$ and $G^C(x_p^C)$.

Transition and Sense Events. These events model changes in the controller induced either as a result of an internal calculus or a user command (*transitions*) or as a result of changes in the plant, generally detected via a sensor (*sense*). They only modify the discrete state x_s.

Sensing events are guarded by a predicate on the current continuous state $(x_p(t) \in \mathcal{G})$ representing the actual sensing.

EVENT Sense^A	EVENT Sense^C REFINES Sense^A
WHEN	WHEN
grd1: $x_p^A(t) \in \mathcal{G}^A$	grd1: $x_p^C(t) \in \mathcal{G}^C$
THEN	THEN
act1: $x_s^A :\in STATES$	act1: $x_s^C :\in STATES$
END	END

Behave and Actuate Events. These events model changes in the plant, either caused by the environment (*behave*) or induced by actuators to which the controller issued a command (*actuate*) depending on its state (guard grd1).

An actuation typically occurs after a *sense* or *transition* event has been triggered. They update the behaviour of the continuous state using the CBAP operator defined in Sect. 3.1.

EVENT Actuate^A	EVENT Actuate^C REFINES Actuate^A
ANY t_p	ANY t_p
WHEN	WHEN
grd1: $t_p \in \mathbb{R} \wedge t_p > t$	grd1: $t_p \in \mathbb{R} \wedge t_p > t$
grd2: $G_s^A(x_s^A)$	grd2: $G_s^C(x_s^C)$
grd3: **Feasible**$(x_p^A, [t, t_p], \mathcal{P}^A, \mathcal{I}^A)$	grd3: **Feasible**$(x_p^C, [t, t_p], \mathcal{P}^C, \mathcal{I}^C)$
grd4: $x_p^A(t) \in \mathcal{I}^A$	grd4: $x_p^C(t) \in \mathcal{I}^C$
THEN	WITH $x_p^{A'} \in \mathcal{O} \circ x_p^{C'}$
act1: $x_p^A :|_{t \to t_p} \mathcal{P}^A(x_s^A, x_p^A, x_p^{A'}) \& \mathcal{I}^A$	THEN
END	act1: $x_p^C :|_{t \to t_p} \mathcal{P}^C(x_s^C, x_p^C, x_p^{C'}) \& \mathcal{I}^C$
	END

Transition and *Sense* are *discrete* events: they are instantaneous, while *Actuate* and *Behave* are *continuous* events: they represent a continuous phenomenon that lasts from time t to t_p, a time during which no other event can occur while time progresses. Note that because t and t_p are reals, they can be infinitely close from each other, meaning the constraint that nothing happens on this time interval can always be satisfied (provided we find t_p close enough to t).

4.2 Proof Obligations

The proof obligations related to the defined generic model and to the refinement operation are defined in Table 3. For the continuous events, the *CBAP* predicates (*PP*, *PR* and *LI*) are involved in the proof obligations of the simulation and invariant preservation.

Note that, based on the definition of the gluing invariant, a witness is explicitly defined in the refinement for each continuous event as $x_p^{A'} \in \mathcal{O} \circ x_p^{C'}$. Because the abstract variable $x_p^{A'}$ is no more available in the refinement, this witness ensures the second part of the invariant preservation PO's right hand side (as $x_p^{A'} \in \mathcal{O} \circ x_p^{C'}$ appears on both sides of the implication).

4.3 Instantiation of the Generic Model

The generic model is instantiated using refinement: the concrete system's behaviour is modelled with events that refine one of the four generic events and variables are substituted using gluing invariants and witnesses.

Table 3. Refinement POs for the generic model: case of Exact refinement

(5) Event Simulation (SIM)	$A \wedge x_p^A \in \mathbb{R} \nrightarrow S^A \wedge [0,t] \subseteq \mathrm{dom}(x_p^A) \wedge x_p^C \in \mathbb{R} \nrightarrow S^C \wedge [0,t] \subseteq \mathrm{dom}(x_p^C)$ $\wedge x_p^A \in \mathcal{I}^A \wedge x_p^C \in \mathcal{I}^C \wedge x_p^C(t) \in \mathcal{G}^C$ $\wedge x_p^A \in \mathcal{O} \circ x_p^C \wedge x_p^{A'} \in \mathcal{O} \circ x_p^{C'}$ $\wedge PP(x^C, x^{C'}) \wedge PR(x^C, x^{C'}) \wedge LI(x^C, x^{C'})$ $\Rightarrow PR(x^A, x^{A'}) \wedge LI(x^A, x^{A'})$
(6) Guard Strengthening (GS)	$A \wedge x_p^A \in \mathbb{R} \nrightarrow S^A \wedge [0,t] \subseteq \mathrm{dom}(x_p^A) \wedge x_p^C \in \mathbb{R} \nrightarrow S^C \wedge [0,t] \subseteq \mathrm{dom}(x_p^C)$ $\wedge x_p^A \in \mathcal{I}^A \wedge x_p^C \in \mathcal{I}^C$ $\wedge x_p^A \in \mathcal{O} \circ x_p^C \wedge x_p^{A'} \in \mathcal{O} \circ x_p^{C'}$ $\wedge x_p^C(t) \in \mathcal{G}^C \Rightarrow x_p^A(t) \in \mathcal{G}^A$
(7) Invariant preservation (INV)	$A \wedge x_p^A \in \mathbb{R} \nrightarrow S^A \wedge [0,t] \subseteq \mathrm{dom}(x_p^A) \wedge x_p^C \in \mathbb{R} \nrightarrow S^C \wedge [0,t] \subseteq \mathrm{dom}(x_p^C)$ $\wedge x_p^A \in \mathcal{I}^A \wedge x_p^C \in \mathcal{I}^C \wedge x_p^C(t) \in \mathcal{G}^C \wedge x_p^A \in \mathcal{O} \circ x_p^C \wedge x_p^{A'} \in \mathcal{O} \circ x_p^{C'}$ $\wedge PP(x^C, x^{C'}) \wedge PR(x^C, x^{C'}) \wedge LI(x^C, x^{C'})$ $\Rightarrow x_p^{C'} \in \mathbb{R} \nrightarrow S^C \wedge [0,t'] \subseteq \mathrm{dom}(x_p^{C'}) \wedge x_p^{C'} \in \mathcal{I}^C \wedge x_p^{A'} \in \mathcal{O} \circ x_p^{C'}$

Exact refinement for continuous variables has been successfully used in the development of complex systems including automatic car stop [11], signalized left turn assist [9] or water tank control [10].

5 Our Framework

5.1 Limitations: Exact vs Approximate Refinement

The refinement presented above relies on an exact set-membership as the core of its gluing invariant (i.e. $x_p^A \in \mathcal{O} \circ x_p^C$). There is no *deviation* nor any approximation. Abstract and concrete variables are linked by relation $\mathcal{O}$.

However, it becomes really restrictive in the case where an exact gluing invariant is not available. Usually this is the case when *approximations* are introduced i.e. when transforming a complex differential equation into a linear one or when reducing its order, solutions are close enough but *not* equal; it prohibits the use of exact refinement.

We claim that such development can be handled by specifying a weaker gluing invariant in relation with approximation.

5.2 Approximate Refinement

When introducing approximation, it is important to guarantee that the properties of the original system are preserved in the approximate one. The definition of a weaker gluing invariant involving a relation with approximation will handle such a preservation using re-defined refinement POs.

We propose to weaken the defined refinement relationship introduced in Sect. 4. For this, we strongly rely on the seminal work of Girard and Pappas [15–17], who defined the notion of approximate simulation.

We define a gluing invariant of the form $J(x_p^A, x_p^C) \wedge x_p^A \in^\delta \mathcal{O} \circ x_p^C$. Here $x_A \in^\delta \mathcal{O} \circ x_C$ links safely abstract x_p^A and concrete x_p^C continuous variables by an approximation relation and J is a predicate defining additional gluing properties.

In addition to formalising in Event-B the approximate simulation, we show that the proposed approach offers two additional capabilities 1) *strengthening event transitions* and 2) *defining gluing invariants ensuring properties preservation*. Note that these two capabilities are not explicitly handled in Girard and Pappas definitions. Moreover, the proof obligations associated to these capabilities are also produced.

5.3 Formalising Approximate Refinement in Event-B

Relying on the theory of approximation presented in Sect. 3.2, we design an approximate refinement of the generic model of hybrid systems (recalled in Sect. 4). This refinement consists of refining the abstract variable x_p^A with an approximated concrete variable x_p^C; events are neither added nor removed.

MACHINE M_A	MACHINE M_C REFINES M_A
VARIABLES t, x_s^A, x_p^A	VARIABLES t, x_s^C, x_p^C
INVARIANTS	INVARIANTS
inv1: $t \in \mathbb{R}^+$	inv2: $x_s^C \in STATES^C$
inv2: $x_s^A \in STATES$	inv3: $x_p^C \in \mathbb{R} \nrightarrow S^C$
inv3: $x_p^A \in \mathbb{R} \nrightarrow S^A$	inv4: $[0,t] \subseteq \mathrm{dom}(x_p^C)$
inv4: $[0,t] \subseteq \mathrm{dom}(x_p^A)$	inv5: $\forall t^* \cdot t^* \in [0,t] \Rightarrow x_p^C(t^*) \in \mathcal{I}^C$
inv5: $\forall t^* \cdot t^* \in [0,t] \Rightarrow x_p^A(t^*) \in \mathcal{I}^A$	inv6: $x_p^A \in^\delta \mathcal{O} \circ x_p^C$
	inv7: $J_s(x_s^C, x_s^A)$

Machine Header. Both abstract and concrete machines define their own state variables, including time t. The only difference here is the gluing invariant for continuous variables (**inv6**) which follows the approximate gluing invariant $x_p^A \in^\delta \mathcal{O} \circ x_p^C$ defined previously.

EVENT Sense$_A$	EVENT Sense$_C$ REFINES
WHEN	Sense$_A$
grd1: $x_p^A(t) \in \mathcal{G}^A$	WHEN
THEN	grd1: $x_p^C(t) \in \mathcal{G}^C$
act1: $x_s^A :\in STATES$	THEN
END	act1: $x_s^C :\in STATES$
	END

Sense Event. Sensing event is similar to the one of exact refinement. Extra care should be taken to handle continuous state variables in the guard. Indeed, we need to make sure that the concrete constraint $x_p^C \in \mathcal{G}^C$ is strong enough to imply $x_p^A \subset \mathcal{G}^A$, taking the approximation into account (GS proof obligation). It needs a guard that is stronger than it would be for exact refinement, so that it still holds when the modelled system drifts away from a realistic state.

Actuate Events. Actuation events are also similar to the exact refinement ones. The main difference is the witness for $x_p^{A'}$, which is updated using the gluing invariant $x_p^A \in^\delta \mathcal{O} \circ x_p^C$. As mentioned before, this witness ensures gluing invariant preservation (INV proof obligation).

Again, due to space limitation, the whole event-B models are not given, but they are accessible at https://irit.fr/~Guillaume.Dupont/models.php.

EVENT Actuate$_A$	EVENT Actuate$_C$ REFINES Actuate$_A$
ANY t_p	ANY t_p
WHEN	WHEN
grd1: $t_p \in \mathbb{R} \wedge t_p > t$	grd1: $t_p \in \mathbb{R} \wedge t_p > t$
grd2: $x_s = State$	grd2: $x_s = State$
grd3: **Feasible**$(x_p^A, [t, t_p], \mathcal{P}^A, \mathcal{I}^A)$	grd3: **Feasible**$(x_p^C, [t, t_p], \mathcal{P}^C, \mathcal{I}^C)$
grd4: $x_p^A(t) \in \mathcal{I}^A$	grd4: $x_p^C(t) \in \mathcal{I}^C$
	WITH $x_p^{A'} \in^\delta \mathcal{O} \circ x_p^{C'}$
THEN	THEN
act1: $x_p^A :|_{t \rightarrow t_p} \mathcal{P}^A(x_s^A, x_p^A, x_p^{A'}) \& \mathcal{I}^A$	act1: $x_p^C :|_{t \rightarrow t_p} \mathcal{P}^C(x_s^C, x_p^C, x_p^{C'}) \& \mathcal{I}^C$
END	END

5.4 Proof Obligations: Revisited for Approximate Refinement

The POs associated to the generic model described in Sect. 5.3 related to approximate refinement are presented in Table 4. These POs are close to those in Table 3 obtained for the exact refinement.

Table 4. Refinement POs for the generic model: case of approximate refinement

(5) Event Simulation (SIM)	$A \wedge x_p^A \in \mathbb{R} \nrightarrow S^A \wedge [0, t] \subseteq \text{dom}(x_p^A) \wedge x_p^C \in \mathbb{R} \nrightarrow S^C \wedge [0, t] \subseteq \text{dom}(x_p^C)$ $\wedge x_p^A \in \mathcal{I}^A \wedge x_p^C \in \mathcal{I}^C \wedge x_p^C(t) \in \mathcal{G}^C$ $\wedge x_p^A \in^\delta \mathcal{O} \circ x_p^C \wedge x_p^{A'} \in^\delta \mathcal{O} \circ x_p^{C'}$ $\wedge PP(x^C, x^{C'}) \wedge PR(x^C, x^{C'}) \wedge LI(x^C, x^{C'})$ $\Rightarrow PR(x^A, x^{A'}) \wedge LI(x^A, x^{A'})$
(6) Guard Strengthening (GS)	$A \wedge x_p^A \in \mathbb{R} \nrightarrow S^A \wedge [0, t] \subseteq \text{dom}(x_p^A) \wedge x_p^C \in \mathbb{R} \nrightarrow S^C \wedge [0, t] \subseteq \text{dom}(x_p^C)$ $\wedge x_p^A \in \mathcal{I}^A \wedge x_p^C \in \mathcal{I}^C$ $\wedge x_p^A \in^\delta \mathcal{O} \circ x_p^C \wedge x_p^{A'} \in^\delta \mathcal{O} \circ x_p^{C'}$ $\wedge x_p^C(t) \in \mathcal{G}^C \Rightarrow x_p^A(t) \in \mathcal{G}^A$
(7) Invariant preservation (INV)	$A \wedge x_p^A \in \mathbb{R} \nrightarrow S^A \wedge [0, t] \subseteq \text{dom}(x_p^A) \wedge x_p^C \in \mathbb{R} \nrightarrow S^C \wedge [0, t] \subseteq \text{dom}(x_p^C)$ $\wedge x_p^A \in \mathcal{I}^A \wedge x_p^C \in \mathcal{I}^C \wedge x_p^C(t) \in \mathcal{G}^C \wedge x_p^A \in^\delta \mathcal{O} \circ x_p^C$ $\wedge PP(x^C, x^{C'}) \wedge PR(x^C, x^{C'}) \wedge LI(x^C, x^{C'})$ $\Rightarrow x_p^{C'} \in \mathbb{R} \nrightarrow S^C \wedge [0, t'] \subseteq \text{dom}(x_p^{C'}) \wedge x_p^{C'} \in \mathcal{I}^C \wedge x_p^{A'} \in^\delta \mathcal{O} \circ x_p^{C'}$

All the POs of Table 4 use the gluing invariant $x_p^A \in^\delta \mathcal{O} \circ x_p^C$ as hypothesis. The INV invariant PO states that the invariant is preserved. Note that the definitions, by the system designer, of the suited approximation δ and of the observation relation $\mathcal{O}$ are key issues. Indeed, the whole proof process relies on these definitions.

5.5 Exact Refinement as a Particular Case of Approximate Refinement

Remind that approximation as given in Sect. 3.2 with $\delta = 0$ becomes $x \approx^0 y$, which is equivalent to $d(x, y) \leq 0$. As a distance is positive and definite, this actually entails $x = y$. In other words, "0-approximation" is equality.

Moreover, for any $S \subseteq E$, $\mathcal{E}_0(S) = S$, and it follows that $x \in^\delta S \equiv x \in S$. Table 5 shows that exact refinement is derived from approximate refinement when $\delta = 0$. In particular, as mentioned by Girard and Pappas in [15–17] classical simulation is obtained when $\delta = 0$ (SIM proof obligation in Table 3).

Table 5. Exact and approximate refinement

	Exact	Approximate
Observation map	$\mathcal{O} \in S^C \leftrightarrow S^A$	
Gluing invariant	$x_p^A \in \mathcal{O} \circ x_p^C$	$x_p^C \in^\delta \mathcal{O} \circ x_p^C$
Pointwise predicate	$x_p^A(t) \in \mathcal{O}[\{x_p^C(t)\}]$	$x_p^A(t) \in^\delta \mathcal{O}[\{x_p^C(t)\}]$

6   Case Study

As a way to validate our approach and as a red wire through the paper, we propose to solve a case study. This problem was first presented by [12] and [15].

6.1   Problem Statement

Initial Problem. The system is a robot identified by its 2-dimension position p^C and speed v^C corresponding to two state variables evolving in $\mathbb{R} \times \mathbb{R}$ equipped with some norm $\| \cdot \|$. The robot can move in any direction of the plane. Its goal is to visit multiple targets (a set of points T_i in the space) while remaining in the specified area. The robot controls its speed and direction, modelled as a vector $u^C \in \mathbb{R} \times \mathbb{R}$. The actual physics of the robot follows a 4th order, linear differential equation with a *complex* control.

If we consider $\eta^C = \begin{bmatrix} v_x^C & v_y^C & p_x^C & p_y^C \end{bmatrix}^\top$ as system's continuous state, then the equation $\dot{\eta}^C = f^C(\eta^C, u^C)$, where f^C is a linear function, describes the behaviour of the robot.

Approximation. Although previous equation $\dot{\eta}^C = f^C(\eta^C, u^C)$ describes the actual behaviour of the robot, this system is quite complicated to deal with. However, to prove that the robot visits target points and remains in the specified area, it is actually sufficient to consider the approximated system described by $\dot{p}^A = u^A$, where p^A is the approximated position of the robot.

The obtained 2nd order linear system assumes that the robot directly controls its speed modelled as $u^A \in \mathbb{R} \times \mathbb{R}$. It is possible to write this equation as a controlled ODE $\dot{\eta}^A(t) = f^A(\eta^A(t), u^A(t))$ with $\eta^A = \begin{bmatrix} p_x^A & p_y^A \end{bmatrix}$.

In [12], the authors proved that the two defined systems are actually δ-bisimilar provided that $\delta = 2\nu$, $\|u^C\| \leq \nu$ and $\|u^A\| \leq \mu$ with μ, ν such that $\frac{\nu}{2}(1 + 4K + 2\sqrt{1 + 4K}) \leq \mu$ (with K a coefficient used in f^C).

6.2   System Requirements

Let us consider a given target point $T \in \mathbb{R}^2$ and a control u^A, then the robot shall fulfill the following requirements. The robot shall be able to

REQ1 move toward the current target point T.
REQ2 sense that its position is close to target point T up to $\tau > 0$ written as $\|T - p^A(t)\| < \tau$ in which case the target is considered to be visited
REQ3 obtain a new target point and to replay the same process to reach it
SAF1 remain in the designated circular area of radius $A > 0$ and centred around $(0,0)$, i.e. $\forall t^* \in [0,t], \|p^A(t)\| < A$.

Note that, in order for the robot to be able to visit target T, it must initially be within the designated area close enough but not outside ($\|T\| < A - \tau$).

6.3   Refinement Strategy

We have formalised this problem using the approximate refinement relationship defined in Sect. 5. We first consider the approximated system and prove that it fulfils the requirements. Then, another refinement introduces the complex dynamics. When this refinement is proved then the robot still behaves correctly.

Starting from the generic model (Sect. 4.1), the second step is a first (exact) refinement of the generic model where the system (robot) is modelled and basic requirements are handled. It defines the continuous state $x_p^A = p^A$, which evolves according to the simple differential equation $\dot{p}^A = u^A$.

The third step introduces *approximate* refinement as a second refinement. It enriches the simple model, of the previous refinement, to make it closer to reality. It defines the continuous state $x_p^C = (p^C, v^C)$ and the gluing invariant $p^A \approx^\delta p^C \equiv x_p^A \in^\delta \mathcal{O} \circ x_p^C$ where δ and $\approx^\delta$ are respectively defined in Sects. 6.1 and 3.2. Here, $\mathcal{O} = \mathrm{prj}_1$ is the first canonical projection operator used to observe p^c.

6.4   Event-B Development

This case study has been entirely developed in Event-B using Rodin with the help of the theories defined in Sect. 4 and based on the generic model recalled in the same section. We show below the *Actuation* event and its refinement. The witness WITH clause ensures the correctness of the refinement. A concrete position p^C approximating the abstract one p^A is given as witness. In addition, act1 introduces a different differential equation defining the evolution of p^C. This differential equation maintains the approximation relation, which is proved via the PO 7 (INV) of Table 4.

actuate_movement REFINES Actuate	actuate_movement REFINES actuate_movement

ANY t_p
 WHEN
    grd1: $t_p \in \mathbb{R}^+ \wedge t_p > t$
    grd2: $\|p^A(t) - T\| > \tau \wedge \|p^A(t)\| < A$
    grd3: **Solvable**$([t, t_p], \mathbf{ode}(f^A(\cdot, u^A),$
         $p^A(t), t), \|p^A(t) - T\| > \tau \wedge$
         $\|p^A(t)\| < A)$
 WITH $x'_p = x^{A\prime}$
 THEN
    act1: $p^A :\sim_{t \to t_p} \mathbf{ode}(f^A(\cdot, u^A), p^A(t), t)$
         $\& \|p^A(t) - T\| > \tau \wedge \|p^A(t)\| < A$
 END
	ANY t_p
	 WHEN
	    grd1: $t_p \in \mathbb{R}^+ \wedge t_p > t$
	    grd2: $\|p^C(t) - T\| > \tau + \delta \wedge \|p^C(t)\| < A - \delta$
	    grd3: **Solvable**$([t, t_p], \mathbf{ode}(f^C(\cdot, u^C),$
	         $(v^C(t) \mapsto p^C(t)), t),$
	         $\|p^C(t) - T\| > \tau + \delta \wedge$
	         $\|p^C(t)\| < A - \delta)$
	 WITH $p^{A\prime} \approx^\delta_{[0, t_p]} p^{C\prime}$
	 THEN
	    act1: $p^C, v^C :\sim_{t \to t_p} \mathbf{ode}(f^C(\cdot, u^C),$
	         $(v^C(t) \mapsto p^C(t)), t)$
	         $\& \|p^C(t) - T\| > \tau + \delta \wedge$
	         $\|p^C(t)\| < A - \delta$
	 END

The proofs entailed by approximate refinement are not a lot more complicated than for hybrid systems that use exact refinement. The hardest POs are event simulation (SIM) and feasibility i.e. existence of a witnesses (see Table 4).

Due to space limitation, we do not show the whole Event-B model. The complete Event-B model corresponding to this case study can be found at https://irit.fr/~Guillaume.Dupont/models.php.

7 Conclusion

After defining a generic model for the stepwise development of hybrid systems models using an *exact* refinement relationship, this paper presented an extension of this approach. This extension consists of formalising another refinement relation relying on a safe *approximation* between abstract and refined states. The introduction of this *approximate refinement relation* expands the range of hybrid systems that can be developed within our approach. Moreover, the *exact refinement* is directly entailed by this *approximate refinement*.

The approach we followed consists in producing a generic model, completely formalised and proved. As shown is Sect. 6, this generic model can be instantiated for specific case studies. Many of the proofs already completed at the generic level are preserved, and only the proofs related to the instantiations need to be achieved, by providing witnesses.

This work has opened several new research directions and questions. First, the definition of a library of generic models refining the one presented in this paper can be defined with particular differential equation patterns along with the corresponding approximation to be used for specific systems. It will reduce the proof effort from the user side. Another research direction is to develop theory for handling multi-dimensional state-space. This notion of approximate refinement may be applied in other areas and state based systems where states are approximately observed, in particular for data oriented models.

References

1. Abrial, J.R.: Modeling in Event-B: System and Software Engineering. Cambridge University Press, Cambridge (2010)
2. Abrial, J.R., Butler, M., Hallerstede, S., Leuschel, M., Schmalz, M., Voisin, L.: Proposals for mathematical extensions for Event-B. Technical report (2009). http://deploy-eprints.ecs.soton.ac.uk/216/
3. Alur, R., Courcoubetis, C., Henzinger, T.A., Ho, P.-H.: Hybrid automata: an algorithmic approach to the specification and verification of hybrid systems. In: Grossman, R.L., Nerode, A., Ravn, A.P., Rischel, H. (eds.) HS 1991-1992. LNCS, vol. 736, pp. 209–229. Springer, Heidelberg (1993). https://doi.org/10.1007/3-540-57318-6_30
4. Asarin, E., Dang, T., Maler, O.: The d/dt tool for verification of hybrid systems. In: Brinksma, E., Larsen, K.G. (eds.) CAV 2002. LNCS, vol. 2404, pp. 365–370. Springer, Heidelberg (2002). https://doi.org/10.1007/3-540-45657-0_30
5. Back, R.-J., Petre, L., Porres, I.: Generalizing action systems to hybrid systems. In: Joseph, M. (ed.) FTRTFT 2000. LNCS, vol. 1926, pp. 202–213. Springer, Heidelberg (2000). https://doi.org/10.1007/3-540-45352-0_17
6. Banach, R., Butler, M., Qin, S., Verma, N., Zhu, H.: Core hybrid Event-B I: single hybrid event-B machines. Sci. Comput. Programm. **105**, 92–123 (2015)
7. Butler, M.J., Maamria, I.: Practical theory extension in Event-B. In: Theories of Programming and Formal Methods - Essays Dedicated to Jifeng He on the Occasion of His 70th Birthday, pp. 67–81 (2013)
8. Chaochen, Z., Ji, W., Ravn, A.P.: A formal description of hybrid systems. In: Alur, R., Henzinger, T.A., Sontag, E.D. (eds.) HS 1995. LNCS, vol. 1066, pp. 511–530. Springer, Heidelberg (1996). https://doi.org/10.1007/BFb0020972
9. Dupont, G., Aït-Ameur, Y., Pantel, M., Singh, N.K.: Hybrid systems and Event-B: a formal approach to signalised left-turn assist. In: Abdelwahed, E.H., et al. (eds.) MEDI 2018. CCIS, vol. 929, pp. 153–158. Springer, Cham (2018). https://doi.org/10.1007/978-3-030-02852-7_14
10. Dupont, G., Aït-Ameur, Y., Pantel, M., Singh, N.K.: Handling refinement of continuous behaviors: a refinement and proof based approach with Event-B. In: 13th International Symposium on Theoretical Aspects of Software Engineering, pp. 9–16. IEEE Computer Society Press (2019)
11. Dupont, G., Aït-Ameur, Y., Pantel, M., Singh, N.K.: Proof-based approach to hybrid systems development: dynamic logic and event-B. In: Butler, M., Raschke, A., Hoang, T.S., Reichl, K. (eds.) ABZ 2018. LNCS, vol. 10817, pp. 155–170. Springer, Cham (2018). https://doi.org/10.1007/978-3-319-91271-4_11
12. Fainekos, G.E., Girard, A., Pappas, G.J.: Hierarchical synthesis of hybrid controllers from temporal logic specifications. In: Hybrid Systems: Computation and Control, 10th International Workshop, HSCC 2007, Proceedings, pp. 203–216 (2007)
13. Frehse, G.: PHAVer: algorithmic verification of hybrid systems past HyTech. Int. J. Softw. Tools Technol. Transfer **10**(3), 263–279 (2008)
14. Frehse, G., et al.: SpaceEx: scalable verification of hybrid systems. In: Gopalakrishnan, G., Qadeer, S. (eds.) CAV 2011. LNCS, vol. 6806, pp. 379–395. Springer, Heidelberg (2011). https://doi.org/10.1007/978-3-642-22110-1_30
15. Girard, A., Julius, A.A., Pappas, G.J.: Approximate simulation relations for hybrid systems. Disc. Event Dyn. Syst. **18**(2), 163–179 (2008)

16. Girard, A., Pappas, G.J.: Approximate bisimulation relations for constrained linear systems. Automatica **43**(8), 1307–1317 (2007)
17. Girard, A., Pappas, G.J.: Approximation metrics for discrete and continuous systems. lIEEE Trans. Autom. Control **52**(5), 782–798 (2007)
18. Henzinger, T.A.: The theory of hybrid automata. In: Inan, M.K., Kurshan, R.P. (eds.) Verification of Digital and Hybrid Systems, NATO ASI Series, vol. 170, pp. 265–292. Springer, Heidelberg (2000). https://doi.org/10.1007/978-3-642-59615-5_13
19. Jifeng, H.: From CSP to hybrid systems. In: Roscoe, A.W. (ed.) A Classical Mind, pp. 171–189. Prentice Hall International (UK) Ltd. (1994)
20. Milner, R.: An algebraic definition of simulation between programs. Technical report, Stanford, CA, USA (1971)
21. Platzer, A.: Differential dynamic logic for hybrid systems. J. Autom. Reason. **41**(2), 143–189 (2008). https://doi.org/10.1007/s10817-008-9103-8
22. Platzer, A., Quesel, J.-D.: KeYmaera: a hybrid theorem prover for hybrid systems (System Description). In: Armando, A., Baumgartner, P., Dowek, G. (eds.) IJCAR 2008. LNCS (LNAI), vol. 5195, pp. 171–178. Springer, Heidelberg (2008). https://doi.org/10.1007/978-3-540-71070-7_15
23. Su, W., Abrial, J.R., Zhu, H.: Formalizing hybrid systems with Event-B and the rodin platform. Sci. Comput. Programm. **94**(Part 2), 164–202 (2014). Abstract State Machines, Alloy, B, VDM, and Z

Formal Foundations for Intel SGX Data Center Attestation Primitives

Muhammad Usama Sardar$^{(\boxtimes)}$, Rasha Faqeh, and Christof Fetzer

Chair of Systems Engineering, Institute of Systems Architecture,
Faculty of Computer Science, Technische Universität Dresden, Dresden, Germany
muhammad_usama.sardar@mailbox.tu-dresden.de,
{rasha.faqeh,christof.fetzer}@tu-dresden.de

Abstract. Intel has recently offered third-party attestation services, called Data Center Attestation Primitives (DCAP), for a data center to create its own attestation infrastructure. These services address the availability concerns and improve the performance as compared to the remote attestation based on Enhanced Privacy ID (EPID). Practical developments, such as Hyperledger Avalon, have already planned to support DCAP in their roadmap. However, the lack of formal proof for DCAP leads to security concerns. To fill this gap, we propose an automated, rigorous, and sound formal approach to specify and verify the remote attestation based on Intel SGX DCAP under the assumption that there are no side-channel attacks and no vulnerabilities inside the enclave. In the proposed approach, the data center configuration and operational policies are specified to generate the symbolic model, and security goals are specified as security properties to produce verification results. The evaluation of non-Quoting Verification Enclave-based DCAP indicates that the confidentiality of secrets and integrity of data is preserved against a Dolev-Yao adversary in this technology. We also present a few of the many inconsistencies found in the existing literature on Intel SGX DCAP during formal specification.

Keywords: Remote attestation · Data centers · Formal verification · Trusted execution environment · Intel SGX · Data center attestation primitives

1 Introduction

Public cloud environments offer a cost-effective solution to deploy application services. However, today's real-world applications often deal with sensitive data that must be protected, such as highly valued intellectual property. The adoption of public clouds is limited due to the uncertainty of the adequate protection of such data and application execution [4]. Trusted Execution Environments (TEEs) [43] with enhanced security measures have recently emerged as a promising approach to increase the confidence of the security of the data and the execution in the cloud. Several TEE implementations with varying scope have been

© Springer Nature Switzerland AG 2020
S.-W. Lin et al. (Eds.): ICFEM 2020, LNCS 12531, pp. 268–283, 2020.
https://doi.org/10.1007/978-3-030-63406-3_16

developed, such as Intel Software Guard Extensions (SGX) [16], AMD Secure Processor [33] and ARM TrustZone [42]. Intel SGX is one of the most widely used TEEs in practice. It enables an application to create secure containers, called enclaves, to run computations on the cloud with hardware-enforced confidentiality and integrity guarantees. The data and computation inside enclaves are inaccessible to untrusted entities, including the operating system and other low-level software [36].

In order to enhance confidence that the intended software is securely running inside an enclave on a fully updated Intel SGX enabled platform at the latest security level, Intel SGX provides an attestation mechanism [3]. There are two types of enclave attestation in Intel SGX: *Local or intra-platform attestation* and *remote or inter-platform attestation* [3]. Local attestation allows an enclave to prove its identity to another enclave on the same platform. If an enclave proves its identity to a remote party, it is referred to as remote attestation (RA). In a nutshell, the remote host creates a cryptographic report (i.e., Quote) that is signed by a hardware-specific key. The report contains information about the enclave creation, including software, hardware, and configurations of the remote host.

Intel currently offers two types of RA, i.e., Enhanced Privacy ID (EPID) [32] and Data Center Attestation Primitives (DCAP) [45]. In RA based on EPID, the relying party verifies the Quote at runtime by contacting Intel Attestation Service (IAS), which confirms that the enclave runs a particular piece of code on a genuine Intel SGX enabled platform. Recently, third-party attestation, called DCAP [45], has been supported by Intel SGX to provide an architecture to benefit from RA without having Intel to validate the attestations at runtime. Thus, a data center can create its attestation infrastructure using classical public-key algorithms, such as the Elliptic Curve Digital Signature Algorithm (ECDSA) or Rivest-Shamir-Adleman (RSA) algorithm. DCAP has many benefits over EPID. For instance, by caching the verification data in a data center caching service, internet-based services are not required at runtime. This alone leads to improved availability and performance compared to EPID. Moreover, it improves privacy by making trust decisions in-house [45].

The security analysis of a TEE that supports attestation is typically performed informally using testing for a specific adversary model. Although such an analysis is suitable to show the presence of security errors, it cannot be used to prove their absence [50]. If left in the system, these errors may have serious consequences, for instance, significant damage to the finances and reputation of a company, and even deaths. To overcome this limitation of testing, rigorous and sound formal methods have been utilized to analyze the security goals on an abstract model. For instance, Intel developed formal tools, namely Deductive Verification Framework (DVF) [21], iPave [19] and Accordion [36], for establishing formal correctness of SGX. However, the verification using these tools does not cover the attestation process, which is a crucial part of Intel SGX for practical use [3]. Intel also provides formal proofs for EPID [11,12]. Subramanyan et al. [46] presented a formalization of attestation for an idealized abstract platform and semi-automated verification approach to establish the identity of the enclave. Specifically, the authors assume axioms about the correctness of Intel SGX RA. We complemented these works by focusing on the symbolic verification of the cryptographic protocol in the RA based on EPID in our recent work [44].

To the best of our knowledge, there is no publicly available formal proof for RA based on Intel SGX DCAP. The proof is crucially essential for safety-critical use cases, where the availability of cloud services is indispensable. With this motivation, our work presents the specification and fully automated verification of RA based on Intel SGX DCAP using a popular automatic symbolic protocol verifier, ProVerif [9]. Intel SGX does not include defense against the software side-channel adversary as the security objective [31], so we do not consider side-channel attacks in this work, and assume that there are no vulnerabilities inside the enclave. In our approach, the data center configuration and operational policies are specified to create a symbolic model. The security goals are specified as security properties. The cryptographic protocol verification may result in proof of security goals or detection of an attack.

The rest of the paper is organized as follows: We present the existing approaches for the formal verification of Intel SGX in Sect. 2. Section 3 expounds on our proposed approach for the specification of the system model and security goals. Next, we analyze confidentiality and integrity properties for attestation in the non-Quoting Verification Enclave (non-QVE) based Intel SGX DCAP [25], as an industrial case study in Sect. 4. We also point out a few discrepancies discovered in the literature of Intel SGX DCAP during specification. Finally, we conclude the paper in Sect. 5 with some future directions of research.

2   Related Work

In this section, we present the formal verification efforts related to Intel SGX in general. In Sect. 2.1, we give an overview of the formalization of secure remote execution by a group of researchers at the University of California, Berkeley and Massachusetts Institute of Technology, Cambridge [46]. Then we present the formalizations by Intel in Sect. 2.2. Finally, we summarize the discussion in Sect. 2.3.

2.1   Secure Remote Execution

Subramanyan et al. [46] presented a formal definition for secure remote execution of enclaves and its decomposition into three main properties, namely confidentiality, integrity, and secure measurement. The proposed verification methodology is based on an idealized abstraction of enclave platforms, called Trusted Abstract Platform (TAP), along with a parameterized adversary model. Using an intermediate verification language, Boogie [6], the authors prove that TAP satisfies the requirements for secure remote execution. Additionally, they utilize the stuttering simulation [13] to prove that Intel SGX and MIT Sanctum [17] implementations refine TAP under certain parameterizations of the adversary.

Thus, the results can be used to compare security guarantees of different enclave platforms.

However, this verification approach is semi-automated, as the user has to find the correct inductive invariants manually to prove the properties. In this case, 935 such annotations were required. This manual effort to re-prove each time a software policy is updated makes it difficult for runtime verification. Specifically, for Intel SGX, the authors ignore the details of RA and instead assume various axioms.

Compared with this work, our proposed approach is based on a fully automated verification, where new updates in the operational policies of RA can be proved to be secure without the need for inductive invariants. Moreover, we complement the work by providing proofs of RA in Intel SGX.

2.2 Formalizations by Intel

To the best of our knowledge, Intel has not published any work on the formal verification of RA based on DCAP. However, Intel has described some works, e.g., [27], on the formal verification of Intel SGX focusing on the enclave page management and page table translations tracking [39]. Intel addresses the verification in two steps: first, to prove the sequential correctness, and second, to prove that SGX is linearizable [36]. Some undiscovered bugs were identified in both steps [27].

Intel verifies the correctness of Intel SGX in the sequential (or single-threaded) setting by using DVF, which is a language and Satisfiability Modulo Theories (SMT)-based deductive verification tool developed at Intel [21]. DVF models a system as a transition system consisting of states and transitions. An execution is an interleaving of transitions [47]. DVF supports Hoare-style and assume-guarantee reasoning. It maps proof obligations into the multisorted first-order logic supported by modern SMT solvers [21], e.g., Yices SMT solver. The properties verified are SGX invariants, security properties for enclave confidentiality and enclave data integrity, and lifecycle properties. Critical bugs were identified during this verification [27].

DVF has a couple of limitations. First, it does not model concurrency, whereas SGX has 22 instructions that share the concurrent data structure, some of which contain as many as 50 interleaving points [36]. Second, the verification is semi-automated and includes a painful process of manually generating the auxiliary invariants [15].

To address concurrency issues, Intel considers linearizability [22] as a correctness condition. Intel uses iPave [19] to prove SGX linearizability, and finds the linearization point using heuristics [36]. The properties, such as system invariants or per-state assertion, can be specified [27]. The graphical iFlow model is converted to XML representation. iPave contains two compilers. The first compiler translates XML representation to a new logical formalism, called a Logic Sequence Diagram (LSD) [19]. The second compiler translates the LSD to a symbolic finite state machine (FSM) with guarded transitions between states. Bounded model checking [7,8] for task-reachability and termination analysis can then be performed on the resulting FSM. However, Intel provides no information about k-bound used for this verification.

Intel identified critical security bugs in SGX using iPave, proving the linearizability of SGX instructions using the assertion analysis and proving some SGX invariants, e.g., a pending page is never cached [27]. However, the framework has some limitations. Non-determinism cannot be modeled in iPave since disjunctive transitions are not currently supported due to performance reasons [19]. Moreover, the graphical input leads to a heavy translation burden which is frequently a source of modeling errors. Finally, because of the lack of abstraction mechanism, it is not easy to experiment with it using various SGX configurations [36].

To address the last two issues mentioned above, a compiler, known as Accordion [36], was developed at Intel to verify linearizability automatically via model checking. Accordion is implemented as an embedded domain-specific language [20] in Haskell [38]. Each SGX instruction is specified as a function with necessary arguments. The syntax is close to the informal specification language used by the SGX architects. Intel reports that the bugs previously found by iPave could be replicated in Accordion. However, no new bugs were discovered.

Accordion, like iPave, does not support non-determinism. DVF, on the other hand, supports non-determinism but not concurrency. In comparison to Intel approaches, our proposed approach supports non-determinism as well as concurrency. Finally, Intel is secretive about their validation processes, as neither proofs nor tools are available to the public, which limits the confidence of the user. ProVerif, used in our proposed approach, is an open-source tool. Our verification results are available within seconds, making it suitable for deployment in an untrusted setting, such as a public cloud. The trade-off that our proposed approach makes is the relatively low implementation details because the focus is on the symbolic protocol verification. The comparison is summarized in Table 1.

2.3 Discussion

The focus of the verification in all of Intel's works is on the enclave page management and page table translations tracking [39], whereas the important process of RA remains unverified. Subramanyan et al. [46] present a semi-automated approach towards RA for single-threaded enclaves where they use various axioms for RA in Intel SGX. Other formalizations of RA also exist, e.g., [14,37,40], but these are not in the context of hardware-based TEE. The verification of trusted hardware-based RA in Intel SGX poses new challenges. We complemented these verification efforts by providing automated symbolic verification of RA based

Table 1. Comparison of the proposed approach with Intel's related work

Tool	Concurrency	Non-determinism	Open-source	Implementation details
DVF [21]	No	Yes	No	High
iPave [19]	Yes	No	No	High
Accordion [36]	Yes	No	No	High
Proposed	Yes	Yes	Yes	Low

on EPID in our previous work [44]. In this work, we focus on the symbolic verification of RA based on DCAP.

3   Proposed Approach

In this section, we present our formal framework in detail. Fig. 1 shows the high-level workflow of our approach, which is based on ProVerif [9]. A *data center configuration* captures the behavior of the entities in Intel SGX DCAP. *Operational policies* represent the cryptographic protocols used for communication among the entities. Based on the data center configuration and operational policies, we specify the attestation protocol in the ProVerif's specification language, a dialect of the applied pi-calculus [1,2]. ProVerif automatically translates the protocol into a set of Horn clauses [48]. Horn clauses are first-order logical formulas of the form $F_1 \wedge ... \wedge F_n \Rightarrow F$, where $F_1, ..., F_n$ and F are facts.

We specify the security goals, e.g., confidentiality and integrity, as security properties in ProVerif. ProVerif automatically translates these properties into derivability queries on the Horn clauses. ProVerif uses a sound and complete (see [9] for a proof) algorithm based on *resolution with free selection* [5] to determine whether a fact is derivable from the clauses. If the fact is not derivable, then the desired security property is proved. If the fact is derivable, then ProVerif attempts to reconstruct an attack at the pi-calculus level. If this attack reconstruction succeeds, the attack against the considered property is detected. If the attack reconstruction fails because of the abstractions in the Horn clause representation, ProVerif cannot decide whether the property is satisfied or not. The main abstraction done by ProVerif is that clauses can be applied any number of times, so the repetitions (or not) of actions are ignored.

3.1   Symbolic Model

A formal model for a data center with Intel SGX is generated by producing a parallel composition of the replication of communicating processes. Each process models a core entity involved in RA. The replication allows each process to produce an unbounded number of sessions with other processes. The entities involved are defined in the data center configuration. For RA based on DCAP, we describe the data center model as the tuple: (App, Enc, QE, PCE, RP, DCS), where App refers to the SGX application, Enc represents an SGX application enclave, which is an isolation environment provided by Intel SGX to perform some security-critical operation in an encrypted area of the memory. QE and PCE represent Intel provided architecture enclaves, called Quoting Enclave (QE) and Provisioning Certification Enclave (PCE), respectively. QE generates the attestations to be verified, and PCE is the local certificate authority that issues certificates for QE. QE and PCE are provided as Quote Generation Library based on ECDSA. The user platform consists of the entities Enc, App, QE, and PCE, as shown in Fig. 2. RP represents the relying party that performs the attestation verification. The data center can have a caching service, represented by DCS,

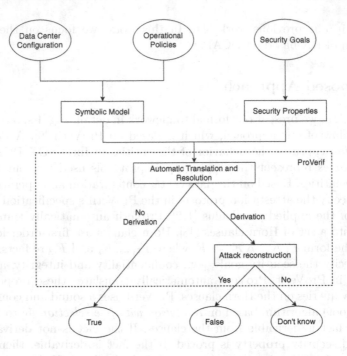

Fig. 1. The workflow of the proposed approach.

which provides the data required for attestation generation and verification, such as certificates, revocation lists for certificates, and Trusted Computing Base (TCB) information.

Operational policies capture both computations and communication done by all core entities defined in the data center configuration. The computations are modeled using constructors [9], and the communications are modeled using channels. Both constructors and channels are public by default. However, a constructor can optionally be defined as private if the adversary is unable to perform the computation done by the constructor. Similarly, a channel can optionally be defined as private to model a secure channel.

3.2 Adversary Model

ProVerif considers a very powerful symbolic adversary with Dolev-Yao [18] capabilities, i.e., an adversary has full control of the communication channels. It can read, modify, delete, and inject messages. It can also manipulate data, e.g., compute the ith element of a tuple; and decrypt messages if it has the necessary keys. Initially, all variables and constructors that are not declared private are also in the knowledge of the adversary. ProVerif assumes the cryptographic primitives to be perfect. However, the proposed approach can be extended to consider cryptographic primitives by integrating with tools such as CryptoVerif [10].

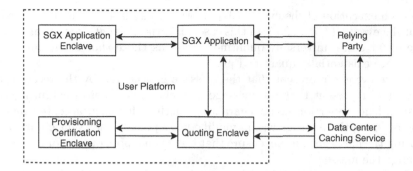

Fig. 2. The remote attestation for Intel SGX DCAP.

We use the non-determinism in ProVerif to model different choices of actions available to the adversary, so all possible combinations of actions are covered. Exhaustive analysis of such non-determinism is impractical in functional testing-based analysis and is one of our approach's strengths.

3.3   Security Properties

In the context of RA in a data center, confidentiality and integrity are generally the most critical security goals. We use reachability and correspondence assertions [49] to formalize these proof obligations.

Confidentiality. Confidentiality is the state of being secret from the attacker [35]. In the context of RA, one can analyze whether secret keys and data in plaintext remain out of knowledge of the attacker. Similar to [44], this can be formalized in ProVerif as a reachability property of the form:

$$\text{query (attacker (s)).} \tag{1}$$

In (1), s represents a free name or a term in plaintext built by a constructor application to the variables.

Integrity. Integrity is the state of being unmodified by an attacker [35]. In the context of RA, one can analyze the integrity of the messages sent among the various entities. This can be formalized using injective correspondence assertions [9], which are of the form:

$$\begin{aligned} &\text{query } x_1 : t_1, ..., x_n : t_n; \\ &\text{event } (e(M_1, ..., M_j)) \texttt{==>inj-event } (e'(N_1, ..., N_k)). \end{aligned} \tag{2}$$

In (2), $M_1, ..., M_j, N_1, ..., N_k$ are optional terms built by the application of constructors to the variables $x_1, ..., x_n$ of types $t_1, ..., t_n$ and e, e' are declared as events. These events do not affect on attacker capabilities. The query is satisfied if, for each execution of the event $e(M_1, ..., M_j)$, there is a distinct earlier execution of the event $e'(N_1, ..., N_k)$. In this case, all variables that occur as arguments to the event e are universally quantified, whereas those that occur only in the event e' are existentially quantified [9].

Let the event e represent that the message is accepted by the receiver, and the event e' represent that the message is unchanged. Then, such an injective correspondence assertion could guarantee whether, for each accepted message by the receiver, the message was unmodified. By placing the event e' just before accepting the message, one can ensure that there is no more option for an attacker to change the message.

Additionally, we verify that the event e is actually reachable. This is because if the event e is not executed, the injective assertions would still return true. In this case, it is due to the reason that the event was never executed.

4 Industrial Case Study: Non-QVE Based DCAP

There are two main types of RA based on DCAP, i.e., QVE based and non-QVE based DCAP [25]. In this section, we present the formalization of the non-QVE based DCAP. For a symbolic model generation, we elaborate on the data center configuration and operational policies in Sect. 4.1. Then we specify confidentiality and integrity as the security goals of the data center in Sect. 4.2.

4.1 Symbolic Model Generation

We combine various Intel documentation, mainly [3, 16, 24–26, 28–31, 34, 45], to extract the operational policies of non-QVE based DCAP. An abstracted form of these policies for Quote generation is depicted in Fig. 3. RA in Intel SGX is done in two phases. The first phase is the local attestation in the user platform. An SGX application requests QE for the target information. This is formalized as a function of arity zero. QE responds by sending the Provisioning Certification Key (PCK) certificate ID structure pck_cert_id to the Quote Provider Library, which sends back the TCB and QE certification data. QE obtains the QE Seal key from the hardware using EGETKEY instruction [28] and uses this along with the TCB received to derive an ECDSA key, called Attestation Key (AK). QE sends public part of AK pk_AK, its identity QE_ID and TCB to the PCE for certification. PCE uses the TCB to derive its key, called PCK. PCE signs the information received from QE with PCK to form a certificate-like structure cert and sends it along with the public key pk_PCK back to QE. Next, QE forms its target information structure qe_target_info and sends it to the requesting SGX application. The application forwards it to its enclave.

The SGX application enclave calls the EREPORT instruction to create a cryptographic Report, which consists of report body, value for key wear-out protection, and Message Authentication Code (MAC) [41] over report body. The structure of the Report is similar to that of RA based on EPID, presented in [44]. The report body comprises the security version number (SVN) of the processor

(CPUSVN), enclave information from SGX Enclave Control Structure (SECS), and the data provided by the user (REPORTDATA). The enclave information from SECS includes its identity, i.e., MRENCLAVE. The Report also includes the value for key wear-out protection. Finally, the Report has a MAC over the report body. AES128-CMAC, a block cipher-based MAC based on 128-bit AES, is used as the MAC algorithm [3]. The key used for this MAC computation is derived using parameters, such as value for key wear-out protection, and information of target enclave from the so-called TARGETINFO structure [28].

The application enclave sends the Report to the SGX application. The SGX application forwards the Report to QE, which receives a cryptographic key, called report key, by calling the EGETKEY instruction. It then verifies the Report using the report key. Since QE and SGX application enclaves are on the same platform, this attestation is referred to as local attestation.

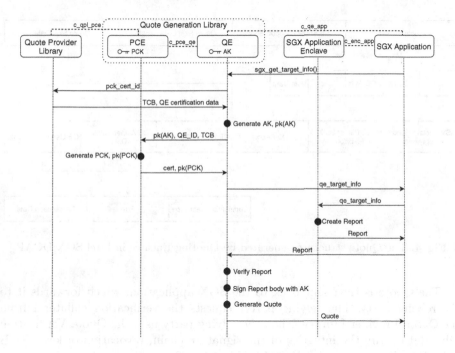

Fig. 3. Channels and process flow of the Quote generation for Intel SGX DCAP.

If the local attestation succeeds, QE signs report body with AK and creates a so-called Quote, which can be verified by the relying party in the second phase. The structure of Quote, depicted in Fig. 4, is based on the description given in Intel's ECDSA Quote Library API [25]. An abstracted implementation in ProVerif's specification language is as follows:

$$out(c\_app,((TCB,QE\_ID),rptbody,sig\_len(sign\_data),$$
$$(sign(rptbody,AK),Pub\_AK,QE\_auth\_data,QE\_cert\_data))). \tag{3}$$

In (3), out represents a keyword for sending a message over the channel $\mathtt{qe\_app}$ between SGX application and its enclave. The variable TCB represents the current TCB (QE SVN and PCE SVN) and QE_ID represents the identity of QE sent in the user data field. The variable rptbody represents the report body of ISV enclave. The function sig_len takes as input the signature data sign_data, and generates its length. The function sign(rptbody,AK) generates the signature over report body using the attestation key AK. Pub_AK is the public part of AK. The variables QE_auth_data and QE_cert_data represent the variable-length QE authentication and certification data structures, respectively. The variable QE_cert_data consists of certification data type, size, and certification data. For brevity, QE Report and QE Report signature are omitted in (3). For our implementation in ProVerif, all communication channels are considered untrusted and all constructors are taken as public.

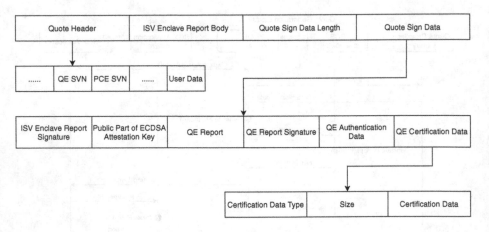

Fig. 4. The Quote structure generated by Quoting Enclave in Intel SGX DCAP.

The Quote is then sent back to the SGX application, which forwards it to the relying party. The relying party requests the verification collateral from the Quote Provider Library. Then the relying party uses the Quote Verification Library to verify the integrity of the signature chain, revocation of keys, TCB in chain, QE source, and ISV enclave identity [29,45].

One of the biggest challenges in the formalization is the presence of various discrepancies in the explanation of Intel SGX literature. An exhaustive list of inconsistencies discovered is out of the scope of this paper. Since the remote attestation based on DCAP also uses the same Report structure as that of EPID, it includes the same discrepancies as mentioned in [44]. Notably, the most cited document on Intel SGX [16] also contains inconsistencies. Additionally, we provide a couple of instances specific to DCAP:

1. The description of QE certification data structure in the Quote is inconsistent, e.g., QE_ID is missing (for reference, see Appendix A.4) in [25].

2. The literature contains some ambiguous statements, such as "The QE Report is a report when the QE Report is certified." in [25].

Such discrepancies clearly advocate the need for a precise and unambiguous description of RA. Such a description would help formalize RA in more detail.

4.2 Formalization and Verification of Properties

We use the formalization presented in Sect. 3.3 to represent the security properties of non-QVE based DCAP.

Confidentiality. The side-channel software attacks are not considered part of the security objectives of Intel SGX DCAP [31]; therefore, we do not consider it in this work. Similar to EPID-based RA in Intel SGX [44], we verify the following two important confidentiality properties for non-QVE based RA in the Intel SGX DCAP:

1. We analyze whether the secret sent by the relying party is leaked to the adversary in plaintext. This is formalized by replacing s in (1) by the free name representing the secret sent by the remote challenger in plaintext. Verification results from ProVerif confirm that only the encrypted contents of the secret are visible to the adversary.
2. We consider whether the adversary can get the report key. This is formalized by replacing s in (1) by the term constructor for the report key with the arguments of specification of QE and value for key wear-out protection. ProVerif results confirm that the adversary cannot access the report key.

Integrity. We analyze the following two integrity properties with injective correspondence assertions [9], utilizing the formalizations presented in Sect. 3.3:

1. We analyze whether the Report's integrity is maintained when it reaches its destination, i.e., QE (See Fig. 3). We utilize (2) with the variables of report body, value for key wear-out protection, report key, and MAC. The event $e(M_1, ..., M_j)$ in (2) is replaced by the event ReportAccepted with the arguments report body, value for key wear-out protection, report key and MAC. The event ReportAccepted is executed whenever QE accepts a Report. Moreover, the event $e'(N_1, ..., N_k)$ in (2) is replaced by the event ReportBodyCorrect with the argument report body. The event ReportBody-Correct is executed whenever the contents of the report body are unmodified just before the acceptance. Thus, we analyze whether, for each occurrence of ReportAccepted, there is a distinct earlier occurrence of the event ReportBodyCorrect with the same report body. Here, the arguments report body, value for key wear-out protection, report key, and MAC are universally quantified. ProVerif results confirm that the Report's integrity is preserved, and an adversary is unable to get a modified Report to be accepted by QE.

2. We analyze whether the Quote's integrity is maintained when it reaches its destination, i.e., the relying party. In this case, we utilize (2) with the variables of the report body. The events $e(M_1, ..., M_j)$ and $e'(N_1, ..., N_k)$ in (2) are replaced by the events QuoteVerified and QuoteCorrect with the argument report body, respectively. The event QuoteVerified is executed whenever the relying party verifies a Quote. The event QuoteCorrect is executed when a Quote remains unmodified just before the verification by the relying party. Thus, we analyze whether, for each occurrence of QuoteVerified, there is a distinct earlier occurrence of the QuoteCorrect event with the same report body. Here, the argument report body is universally quantified. Thus, the property ensures that for every Quote that is verified, there is a distinct corresponding Quote with correct contents. ProVerif results confirm that the Quote's integrity is preserved, and an adversary is unable to get a modified Quote to be accepted by the relying party.

As mentioned in Sect. 3.3, we also verify that the events ReportAccepted and QuoteVerified are actually reachable. ProVerif returns a counter-example in each case showing the trace in which these events are reached. This confirms that these events are executable, and queries for integrity are valid.

The verification is performed using ProVerif version 2.01 on Ubuntu 18.04 LTS on an Intel Core i7-6700 quad-core machine with a processor base frequency of 3.40 GHz with 32 GB of RAM. The average verification time to prove all the above properties in this experimental setup is 50 ms. This shows the scalability of the proposed approach, and the convenience to schedule the verification task in the design process.

5 Conclusion

The remote attestation process in Intel SGX is a critical process in which a relying party establishes trust in a remote platform and enclave. We propose a formal approach for the specification and symbolic verification of third-party attestation based on Intel SGX DCAP. We adopt Intel SGX threat model which does not consider side-channel attacks [31] and assume that there are no vulnerabilities inside the enclave. Under these assumptions, we prove in a popular symbolic protocol verifier, ProVerif, that the remote attestation based on Intel SGX DCAP preserves the confidentiality of secrets and integrity of the verifying data (Report and Quote), against a Dolev-Yao adversary. The specification helped discover various inconsistencies in the existing literature of Intel SGX DCAP. For the future, it will be interesting to formally evaluate the effectiveness of the mitigation mechanism for Intel SGX in the presence of side-channels for practical applications, such as Hyperledger Avalon [23].

Acknowledgments. We would like to thank Do Le Quoc for his feedback on this work.

References

1. Abadi, M., Blanchet, B., Fournet, C.: The applied pi calculus: mobile values, new names, and secure communication. J. ACM (JACM) **65**(1), 1–41 (2017)
2. Abadi, M., Fournet, C.: Mobile values, new names, and secure communication. ACM SIGPLAN Not. **36**(3), 104–115 (2001)
3. Anati, I., Gueron, S., Johnson, S., Scarlata, V.: Innovative technology for CPU based attestation and sealing. In: International Workshop on Hardware and Architectural Support for Security and Privacy, 2013. ACM, New York (2013). https://software.intel.com/en-us/articles/innovative-technology-for-cpu-based-attestation-and-sealing
4. Avram, M.G.: Advantages and challenges of adopting cloud computing from an enterprise perspective. Procedia Technol. **12**, 529–534 (2014)
5. Bachmair, L., Ganzinger, H.: Resolution theorem proving. In: Handbook of Automated Reasoning, pp. 19–99. Elsevier (2001)
6. Barnett, M., Chang, B.-Y.E., DeLine, R., Jacobs, B., Leino, K.R.M.: Boogie: a modular reusable verifier for object-oriented programs. In: de Boer, F.S., Bonsangue, M.M., Graf, S., de Roever, W.-P. (eds.) FMCO 2005. LNCS, vol. 4111, pp. 364–387. Springer, Heidelberg (2006). https://doi.org/10.1007/11804192_17
7. Biere, A., Cimatti, A., Clarke, E.M., Fujita, M., Zhu, Y.: Symbolic model checking using SAT procedures instead of BDDs. In: Design Automation Conference, pp. 317–320. ACM/IEEE (1999)
8. Biere, A., Cimatti, A., Clarke, E., Zhu, Y.: Symbolic model checking without BDDs. In: Cleaveland, W.R. (ed.) TACAS 1999. LNCS, vol. 1579, pp. 193–207. Springer, Heidelberg (1999). https://doi.org/10.1007/3-540-49059-0_14
9. Blanchet, B.: Modeling and verifying security protocols with the applied pi calculus and ProVerif. Found. Trends Priv. Secur. **1**(1–2), 1–135 (2016)
10. Blanchet, B.: CryptoVerif: a computationally-sound security protocol verifier. Technical report (2017)
11. Brickell, E., Li, J.: Enhanced privacy ID: a direct anonymous attestation scheme with enhanced revocation capabilities. In: Privacy in Electronic Society, pp. 21–30. ACM (2007)
12. Brickell, E., Li, J.: Enhanced privacy ID from bilinear pairing for hardware authentication and attestation. In: Social Computing, pp. 768–775. IEEE (2010)
13. Browne, M.C., Clarke, E.M., Grümberg, O.: Characterizing finite Kripke structures in propositional temporal logic. Theor. Comput. Sci. **59**(1–2), 115–131 (1988)
14. Cabodi, G., Camurati, P., Loiacono, C., Pipitone, G., Savarese, F., Vendraminetto, D.: Formal verification of embedded systems for remote attestation. WSEAS Trans. Comput. **14**, 760–769 (2015)
15. Conchon, S., Roux, M.: Reasoning about universal cubes in MCMT. In: Ait-Ameur, Y., Qin, S. (eds.) ICFEM 2019. LNCS, vol. 11852, pp. 270–285. Springer, Cham (2019). https://doi.org/10.1007/978-3-030-32409-4_17
16. Costan, V., Devadas, S.: Intel SGX explained. IACR Cryptology ePrint Archive (2016)
17. Costan, V., Lebedev, I., Devadas, S.: Sanctum: minimal hardware extensions for strong software isolation. In: USENIX Security Symposium, pp. 857–874 (2016)
18. Dolev, D., Yao, A.: On the security of public key protocols. IEEE Trans. Inf. Theory **29**(2), 198–208 (1983)
19. Fraer, R., et al.: From visual to logical formalisms for SoC validation. In: Formal Methods and Models for Codesign (MEMOCODE), pp. 165–174. ACM/IEEE (2014)

20. Gill, A.: Domain-specific languages and code synthesis using Haskell. Queue **12**(4), 30–43 (2014)
21. Goel, A., Krstic, S., Leslie, R., Tuttle, M.: SMT-based system verification with DVF. In: Satisfiability Modulo Theories, vol. 20, pp. 32–43. EasyChair (2013)
22. Herlihy, M.P., Wing, J.M.: Linearizability: a correctness condition for concurrent objects. ACM Trans. Program. Lang. Syst. **12**(3), 463–492 (1990)
23. Hyperledger: Hyperledger Avalon (2020). https://www.hyperledger.org/use/avalon. Accessed 24 July 2020
24. Intel: Attestation service for Intel® Software Guard Extensions (Intel® SGX): API documentation. https://api.trustedservices.intel.com/documents/sgx-attestation-api-spec.pdf, revision 6.0. Accessed 24 July 2020
25. Intel: Intel®Software Guard Extensions (Intel®SGX) Data Center Attestation Primitives: ECDSA Quote Library API, March 2020–08 July 2020. https://download.01.org/intel-sgx/sgx-dcap/1.7/linux/docs/Intel_SGX_ECDSA_QuoteLibReference_DCAP_API.pdf. Accessed 24 July 2020
26. Intel: SGX Data Center Attestation Primitives. https://github.com/intel/SGXDataCenterAttestationPrimitives. Accessed on 24 July 2020
27. Intel: Intel®Software Guard Extensions (Intel® SGX), June 2015. https://software.intel.com/sites/default/files/332680-002.pdf, revision 1.1. Accessed 24 July 2020
28. Intel: Intel® 64 and IA-32 architectures: software developer's manual. Order Number: 325462–071US, October 2019. https://software.intel.com/sites/default/files/managed/39/c5/325462-sdm-vol-1-2abcd-3abcd.pdf. Accessed 24 July 2020
29. Intel: Intel® SGX data center attestation primitives (Intel® SGX DCAP) (2019). https://download.01.org/intel-sgx/sgx-dcap/1.7/linux/docs/Intel_SGX_DCAP_ECDSA_Orientation.pdf, revision 08–07-2020, Accessed 24 July 2020
30. Intel: Intel®PCK Certificate and Certificate Revocation List Profile Specification, March 2020. https://download.01.org/intel-sgx/sgx-dcap/1.7/linux/docs/Intel_SGX_PCK_Certificate_CRL_Spec-1.4.pdf, revision 1.4, 30 March 2020, updated 08–07-2020. Accessed 24 July 2020
31. Intel: Intel®Software Guard Extensions (Intel®SGX): developer guide, April 2020. https://download.01.org/intel-sgx/sgx-linux/2.9.1/docs/Intel_SGX_Developer_Guide.pdf, revision 2.9.1, April 2020. Accessed 24 July 2020
32. Johnson, S., Scarlata, V., Rozas, C., Brickell, E., Mckeen, F.: Intel® Software Guard Extensions: EPID provisioning and attestation services (2016), https://software.intel.com/content/www/us/en/develop/download/intel-sgx-intel-epid-provisioning-and-attestation-services.html
33. Kaplan, D.: AMD x86 memory encryption technologies. USENIX Association, Austin, TX, August 2016
34. Knauth, T., Steiner, M., Chakrabarti, S., Lei, L., Xing, C., Vij, M.: Integrating remote attestation with transport layer security. arXiv preprint:1801.05863 (2018)
35. Lee, E.A., Seshia, S.A.: Introduction to Embedded Systems: A Cyber-Physical Systems Approach. MIT Press, Cambridge (2017)
36. Leslie-Hurd, R., Caspi, D., Fernandez, M.: Verifying linearizability of Intel® software guard extensions. In: Kroening, D., Păsăreanu, C.S. (eds.) CAV 2015. LNCS, vol. 9207, pp. 144–160. Springer, Cham (2015). https://doi.org/10.1007/978-3-319-21668-3_9
37. Lugou, F., Apvrille, L., Francillon, A.: SMASHUP: a toolchain for unified verification of hardware/software co-designs. J. Cryptograph. Eng. **7**(1), 63–74 (2017)
38. Marlow, S., et al.: Haskell 2010 language report (2010). https://www.haskell.org/onlinereport/haskell2010

39. McKeen, F., et al.: Intel® software guard extensions (Intel® SGX) support for dynamic memory management inside an enclave. In: Hardware and Architectural Support for Security and Privacy, pp. 1–9. ACM (2016)

40. Nunes, I.D.O., Eldefrawy, K., Rattanavipanon, N., Steiner, M., Tsudik, G.: VRASED: a verified hardware/software co-design for remote attestation. In: 28th USENIX Security Symposium, pp. 1429–1446. USENIX Association, Santa Clara (2019)

41. Paar, C., Pelzl, J.: Understanding Cryptography: A Textbook for Students and Practitioners. Springer, Cham (2009)

42. Pinto, S., Santos, N.: Demystifying ARM TrustZone: a comprehensive survey. ACM Comput. Surv. (CSUR) 51(6), 1–36 (2019)

43. Sabt, M., Achemlal, M., Bouabdallah, A.: Trusted execution environment: what it is, and what it is not. In: Trustcom/BigDataSE/ISPA, vol. 1, pp. 57–64. IEEE (2015)

44. Sardar, M.U., Quoc, D.L., Fetzer, C.: Towards formalization of EPID-based remote attestation in Intel SGX, Euromicro Conference on Digital System Design (To appear, 2020)

45. Scarlata, V., Johnson, S., Beaney, J., Zmijewski, P.: Supporting third party attestation for Intel® SGX with Intel® data center attestation primitives. White paper (2018)

46. Subramanyan, P., Sinha, R., Lebedev, I., Devadas, S., Seshia, S.A.: A formal foundation for secure remote execution of enclaves. In: SIGSAC Conference on Computer and Communications Security, pp. 2435–2450. ACM (2017)

47. Tuttle, M.R., Goel, A.: Protocol proof checking simplified with SMT. In: Network Computing and Applications, pp. 195–202. IEEE (2012)

48. Weidenbach, C.: Towards an automatic analysis of security protocols in first-order logic. CADE 1999. LNCS (LNAI), vol. 1632, pp. 314–328. Springer, Heidelberg (1999). https://doi.org/10.1007/3-540-48660-7_29

49. Woo, T.Y.C., Lam, S.S.: A semantic model for authentication protocols. In: IEEE Computer Society Symposium on Research in Security and Privacy, pp. 178–194, May 1993

50. Zeller, A.: Why Programs Fail: A Guide to Systematic Debugging. Elsevier (2009)

Short Papers

Short Papers

Towards Modeling and Verification of the CKB Block Synchronization Protocol in Coq

Hao Bu and Meng Sun[✉]

School of Mathematical Sciences, Peking University, Beijing 100871, China
{buhao,sunm}@pku.edu.cn

Abstract. The Nervos CKB (Common Knowledge Base) is the base layer of a new kind of blockchain. The CKB block synchronization protocol provides a set of rules that participating nodes must obey while synchronizing their blocks. This protocol mainly consists of three parts: connecting header, downloading block and accepting block. In this paper, we model the CKB block synchronization protocol in Coq and verify the correctness of the protocol. Our model takes the communication between nodes and the reliability of implementation into consideration to reflect a more realistic environment faced by the blockchain. We prove the soundness and the completeness of the protocol under several reliability and consistency assumptions. We also prove that without some of these assumptions, the protocol may fail to guarantee the correctness of block synchronization. Our formal verification can ensure the security of the protocol and provide ways to prevent potential attacks.

Keywords: Blockchain · Block synchronization protocol · Verification · Coq

1 Introduction

First introduced in 2008, Bitcoin [8] is the first public permissionless blockchain. Although it has been successfully applied in various domains, Bitcoin suffers from the problem of scalability. To alleviate this problem, people have proposed many solutions in recent years such as Bitcoin Lightning [10], Polkadot [12] and Bitcoin Cash [3]. These solutions can be roughly divided into two categories: *on-chain scaling* and *off-chain scaling*. On-chain scaling focuses on increasing the supply of block space, but it has to compromise on security and decentralization. Off-chain scaling solutions use two layers: Layer 1 guarantees the security of the blockchain and layer 2 brings nearly unlimited space for transactions.

The Nervos Network [11] is a new blockchain ecosystem using off-chain scaling to address the challenges faced by blockchains like Bitcoin and Ethereum. CKB is layer 1 of the Nervos Network and it contains a collection of protocols. An application of blockchains can contain many nodes. When a node generates new

© Springer Nature Switzerland AG 2020
S.-W. Lin et al. (Eds.): ICFEM 2020, LNCS 12531, pp. 287–296, 2020.
https://doi.org/10.1007/978-3-030-63406-3_17

blocks, it may push an announcement to other nodes. Upon receiving the message from peers, the node will perform a round of block synchronization to update the status of newly generated blocks. The CKB block synchronization protocol [4] contains the rules that describe the steps of synchronization.

The correctness of a protocol is of vital importance. Many protocols are error-prone, and people have found vulnerabilities on protocols that have been considered to be correct for many years [2]. The model checking approach models protocols as transition systems and uses graph algorithms to check all branches automatically. There are many works on verifying protocols by model checking such as [5–7]. However, the number of blocks in a blockchain has no upper bound, and commonly used model checkers sometimes can only provide very limited results for that. These results usually cannot reflect the unbounded properties of protocols. On the other hand, theorem proving can yield precise results even for potentially unbounded models, which makes it suitable for verifying blockchain-related protocols. For example, the consistency of a blockchain-based distributed consensus protocol is verified in [9] using Coq.

In this paper, we use Coq to model and verify the CKB block synchronization protocol. This protocol mainly consists of three parts: *connecting header*, *downloading block* and *accepting block*. Because the protocol simply behaves as the sequence of these three parts, we can model and verify the three parts separately. We use *List* in the Coq standard library to model the chain of blocks and a chain of blocks can be modeled as a list of numbers in Coq, where different numbers denote different status. Because the protocol may be deployed in quite complex environments, we take the reliability of communication and implementation into consideration. This protocol is a relatively abstract description rather than a concrete implementation, where the details of communication and implementation are unspecified, so we use *Prop* in Coq to represent abstract characters like the reliability of communication. Then we use axioms to model the concrete behavior of these abstract characters. A chain is defined to be *valid* if it *should* be accepted by the protocol, and *accepted* if it *would* be accepted by the protocol. We prove that under some reliability and consistency assumptions, the protocol is both sound and complete, that is, a chain is valid if and only if it is accepted. Furthermore, we simulate potential attacks under which some of the reliability assumptions may be violated. We prove that without these assumptions, the protocol may accept invalid chains and reject valid chains, thus unreliable.

This paper is organized as follows. After this general introduction, we give a brief description of the block synchronization and the CKB block synchronization protocol in Sect. 2. Section 3 presents the modeling and verification of the protocol in Coq. In Sect. 4 we simulate potential attacks on the protocol. Finally, Sect. 5 concludes the paper with some further research directions.

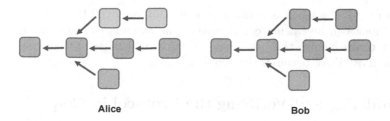

Fig. 1. Local status trees of two nodes.

2   Preliminaries

2.1   The Block Synchronization

Blocks in a blockchain may have different status, for simplicity, we assume that a block can be *valid, invalid* or *unknown*. An application of blockchains can contain a lot of nodes, and due to the asynchrony of nodes, the same block may have different status in different nodes. Each node has its local status tree to record the status of blocks in the blockchain. Figure 1 shows the local status trees of two nodes named Alice and Bob, and we use the color red, green and grey to denote the status invalid, valid and unknown respectively.

A chain is valid if all its blocks are valid, and we use *best chain* to denote the valid chain with the most accumulated PoW (Proof of Work). When a node generates new blocks and its best chain changes, it pushes an announcement to other nodes. When a node receives a block synchronization message, it performs synchronization with all other nodes which have changed their best chains since the last synchronization. The purpose of block synchronization is to compare the best chains of other nodes with its own, and the chain with the most PoW will become its new best chain.

2.2   The CKB Block Synchronization Protocol

The CKB block synchronization protocol is divided into three parts: connecting header, downloading block and accepting block. These three parts are executed one by one and a chain can enter the next stage only if it passes the current stage.

The connecting header stage is the first stage and headers of all blocks in the candidate best chain will be downloaded and verified. If a block has already been valid in the local status tree, it will not be downloaded and verified again. The format of received headers will be checked first, then the contents of headers.

In the downloading block stage, complete blocks in the candidate best chain will be downloaded. Earlier blocks will be downloaded and verified first, and if a block is verified to be invalid, the chain will be rejected without downloading or verifying later blocks.

The accepting block stage is the last stage. Blocks of the candidate best chain will be verified one by one until all blocks are verified to be valid or any invalid block is found. If a block is verified to be invalid, only the PoW before the first invalid block can be calculated. If none of the candidates has more PoW than the best chain before, the best chain remains unchanged. Otherwise, the one with the most PoW becomes the new best chain.

3　Modeling and Verifying the Protocol in Coq

In this section, we model and verify the three parts of the block synchronization protocol respectively. For simplicity, we name two nodes Alice and Bob, and Alice will download Bob's best chain and verify it. We use numbers 1, 2 and 3 to denote the invalid, unknown and valid block respectively. The complete Coq specification of the protocol and detailed proofs of theorems can be found in [1].

3.1　Connecting Header Stage

In the connecting header stage, Bob sends the headers of his best chain to Alice. Those blocks which are already valid in Alice's local status tree will not be sent and only the unique part is sent. In this stage, a block is valid means that its header is valid. The verification of the received message is divided into two parts. First the format will be checked:

1. The blocks in the message are continuous.
2. All blocks in the message and the parent block of the first block are not invalid in Alice's local status tree.
3. The status of the parent block of the first block is not unknown in Alice's local status tree.

After that, the contents of headers will be checked by a checker. The chain is accepted if the format and the contents are both valid.

As Bob may be a malicious attacker, the block in Bob's valid chain may be invalid actually. The global status tree is introduced to record the real status of blocks. Every block in the global status tree is either valid or invalid.

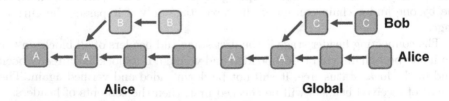

Fig. 2. Alice's local status tree and the global status tree.

Figure 2 shows Alice's local status tree and the global status tree. The chain ends with "Alice" denotes Alice's best chain and the chain ends with "Bob" denotes Bob's best chain. The blocks marked with "A" are the overlap part of two chains. The blocks with "B" and "C" denote the unique part of Bob's best chain in Alice's local status tree and the global status tree respectively. In the above algorithm, Bob sends blocks with "C" to Alice.

To prove the algorithm, we need to make some assumptions first. For example, we assume that all valid blocks in the global status tree are not invalid in Alice's local status tree. Otherwise, Alice's local status tree conflicts with the global, which means Alice is an illegal node. We are not interested in illegal nodes as their behavior is unpredictable. The consistency between Alice and the global can be captured by the following axiom:

```
Axiom consistent_chain: valid_list list_C ->
valid_or_unknown_list list_B.
```

The following axiom models the checker of the algorithm. If the checker is reliable, the output result should be valid if and only if the input message is valid. The communication between nodes can be modeled in a similar way.

```
Axiom reliable_output: reliable_checker ->
(valid_list input <-> valid_list output).
```

Bob's best chain is valid if both list_A and list_C are valid. If the format is correct and the output of the checker is valid, the chain will be accepted.

```
Definition B_valid:= valid_list list_A /\ valid_list list_C.
Definition B_accepted:= correct_format /\ (valid_list output).
```

Now we can formally prove the soundness and completeness of the algorithm under the reliability assumptions by proving the following theorem. It states that Bob's best chain is accepted by the algorithm if and only if it is valid.

```
Theorem correctness_of_connecting_header:
reliable_communication /\ reliable_checker ->
(B_valid <-> B_accepted).
```

3.2 Downloading Block Stage

After the headers are downloaded and verified to be valid, Alice will request complete blocks of Bob's best chain. Earlier blocks will be downloaded and verified first. The latter block will be verified only after the former block has been verified to be valid. In this stage, a block is valid means that its content is valid. The algorithm has three possible results:

- **ACCEPT:** All blocks are downloaded and verified to be valid, then the candidate best chain is accepted and can enter the next stage.

- **REJECT:** There is a block which is downloaded and verified to be invalid, then later blocks in the chain will be ignored. The candidate best chain will be rejected and will not enter the next stage.
- **TIMEOUT:** The download of a block times out. In this situation, the validity of the candidate best chain cannot be decided and the node will try later again.

Similar to the previous stage, we are interested in Bob's best chain in both Alice's local status tree and the global status tree. Alice's local status tree will update following the execution of the algorithm and Fig. 3 is a snapshot of Bob's best chain in the two status trees when the algorithm terminates.

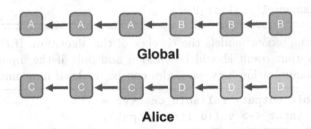

Global

Alice

Fig. 3. Bob's best chain in two status trees.

In Fig. 3, the fourth block is found to be invalid, so the fifth and sixth blocks will not be verified and the candidate best chain is rejected. The blocks marked with "A" and "C" stand for those that have been downloaded and verified to be valid when the algorithm terminates, and the blocks with "B" and "D" stand for those that have not been verified to be valid. We use list_A to list_D to represent these chains and we use list_0 to represent Bob's best chain in the global status tree.

We use several axioms to represent the consistency of these lists. For example, as list_0 is the join of list_A and list_B, we can derive the following axiom.

```
Axiom consistent_list0AB: (list_0 = list_A <-> list_B = nil) /\
(valid_list list_0 <-> valid_list list_A /\ valid_list list_B).
```

We model the implementation and the checker of the algorithm in a similar way to the previous stage. For example, if the checker is reliable, the validity of list_C should be the same as list_A's.

```
Axiom reliable_listAC: reliable_checker -> list_A = list_C.
```

We then formally define the three possible results of the algorithm:

```
Definition ACCEPT:= list_D = nil.
Definition REJECT:= ~list_D = nil /\ hd 0 list_D = 1.
Definition TIMEOUT:= ~list_D = nil /\ hd 0 list_D = 2.
```

Bob's best chain is valid if list_0 is valid. When the result of the algorithm is ACCEPT, the chain is accepted.

```
Definition B_valid:= valid_list list_0.
Definition B_accepted:= ACCEPT.
```

We can now prove the soundness of the algorithm.

```
Theorem soundness_of_downloading_block: reliable_checker /\
reliable_implement -> (B_accepted -> B_valid).
```

This theorem states that if the algorithm accepts a chain, then we can be sure this chain is valid, under the assumptions that the checker and implementation are reliable. However, we cannot promise that a valid chain will actually be accepted by the algorithm. It is because the download of blocks may time out, in which case the algorithm cannot decide the validity of the input chain.

To prove the completeness of the algorithm, we need to assume the termination of the algorithm.

```
Axiom one_of_three: algorithm_termination ->
(ACCEPT /\ ~TIMEOUT /\ ~REJECT)\/(~ACCEPT /\ TIMEOUT /\ ~REJECT)
\/(~ACCEPT /\ ~TIMEOUT /\ REJECT).
```

Moreover, we assume that the node can successfully download the block eventually, even if it may encounter some TIMEOUT before. With these assumptions, we can prove the completeness of the algorithm.

```
Theorem completeness_of_downloading_block: reliable_checker /\
reliable_implement /\ algorithm_termination /\ ~TIMEOUT ->
(B_valid -> B_accepted).
```

3.3 Accepting Block Stage

In this stage, the verification will be performed from earlier blocks to later blocks one by one. If a block is found to be invalid, the blocks after it will not be verified. However, unlike the previous stage, we do not reject a chain immediately when we find an invalid block in it. Instead, blocks before the first invalid block can still constitute a candidate best chain.

Fig. 4. Bob's best chain in Alice's local status tree.

Figure 4 shows Bob's best chain in Alice's local status tree. The fourth block is the first invalid one, so the fifth and sixth blocks are ignored without verifying. The first three blocks with "A" constitute the candidate best chain of Bob.

As the synchronization is performed with all other nodes which have changed their best chains since the last synchronization, there may be more than one node synchronizing with Alice. Therefore, there may be several candidate best chains passing all the verification before. If none of these candidates contains more PoW than Alice's original best chain, Alice's best chain will remain unchanged and all candidates are rejected. Otherwise, the one with the most PoW contained becomes Alice's new best chain.

We use an ensemble to represent the PoW of all candidates, and we declare `init` to be the PoW of Alice's original best chain. Without loss of generality, we assume that Bob contains the most PoW among all candidates.

```
Parameter L: Ensemble nat.
Parameter init: nat.
Axiom B_is_max_in_L: max_num B L.
```

We declare the proposition `reliable_checker` and we assume when it holds, the above algorithm will be faithfully implemented.

```
Axiom correct_implement: reliable_checker ->
(REJECT_ALL <-> forall x,L x -> x <= init) /\
(ACCEPT_B <-> L B /\ B > init /\
forall x, (L x /\ ~x = B -> x < B)) /\
(ACCEPT_OTHER <-> exists x, (L x /\ ~x = B /\
x > init /\ forall y, (L y /\ ~x = y) -> y < x)).
```

We can prove the correctness of the algorithm.

```
Theorem correctness_of_accepting_block: reliable_checker ->
(init >= B -> REJECT_ALL) /\ (init < B -> ACCEPT_B).
```

We can also prove that if the algorithm is implemented correctly, all candidates except Bob will be rejected.

```
Theorem reject_other: reliable_checker -> ~ACCEPT_OTHER.
```

4   Attack Simulation

In this section we simulate potential attacks on the protocol. Many assumptions have been used in Sect. 3, which mainly include the reliability of the checker, communication and implementation as well as the consistency between chains. We have proved the protocol is correct under these assumptions.

However, in practical applications, the situation is much more complicated. The implementation may contain flaws and malicious attackers may tamper the communication. In this section, we simulate these potential attacks and observe the behavior of the protocol under attacks.

We have mentioned in Sect. 3 that the behavior of Alice will be unpredictable if it is not consistent with the global. To formally prove it, we remove the consistency assumption between list_B and list_C. Furthermore, we make some technical modification to several definitions in Sect. 3.

Now we can prove that although the checker and communication are still reliable, the algorithm without the consistency assumption is no longer correct. Specifically, it may reject a valid chain.

```
Theorem error_without_consistent_between_listBC:
reliable_communication /\ reliable_checker ->
exists list_B, (B_valid -> ~(B_accepted list_B)).
```

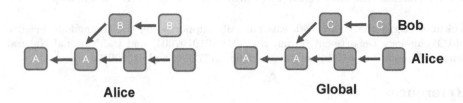

Fig. 5. A counterexample where the algorithm cannot perform correctly.

The proof of this theorem is constructive and can be intuitively illustrated by Fig. 5. Because Alice is not necessarily consistent with the global, a globally valid block can be invalid in Alice's local status tree. Under this condition, although Bob's best chain is valid, it cannot pass the format check and will be rejected.

Similarly, if the communication is not reliable, the message Bob sends may be distorted and different from the message Alice receives. If the checker is not reliable, it may decide an invalid block to be valid, thus making the protocol unreliable. Their formal statements are similar to the previous one and are omitted here.

These reliability and consistency assumptions rely on concrete implementation of the algorithm, which is beyond the scope of this abstract protocol. Therefore, the above potential attacks cannot be avoided by simply modifying the protocol. When we actually deploy the protocol into applications, we should carefully verify the implementation and ensure these assumptions to be met.

5   Conclusion and Future Work

In this paper we formally model the CKB block synchronization protocol in Coq. To reflect the complicated environment where the protocol is deployed, we integrate the reliability of implementation and communication into our model. The protocol is just an abstract description of block synchronization and does not include concrete implementation, therefore, we use *Prop* in Coq to represent the reliability and consistency properties involved and we use axioms to model the behavior of these properties. We then strictly prove the soundness and completeness of the protocol in Coq, which means the protocol is correct under several reliability and consistency assumptions. Furthermore, we simulate potential attacks by removing some of these assumptions. We prove that without these assumptions, the protocol may fail to correctly perform the block synchronization. The proofs of attack simulations are constructive and can therefore be used to test the concrete implementation of the protocol.

The CKB block synchronization protocol also contains some parallel algorithm optimization to make full use of resource. We have only modeled and verified the original algorithm in this paper. In the future, we plan to model and verify the optimized algorithm to provide enhanced security assurance. In addition, we are also planning to extend this approach to investigate other protocols in CKB, such as the transaction filter protocol and the CKB consensus protocol.

Acknowledgments. This work was partially supported by the Guangdong Science and Technology Department (Grant no. 2018B010107004) and the National Natural Science Foundation of China under grant no. 61772038 and 61532019.

References

1. The source code of proofs in this paper. https:// github. com/ H- Bu/ CKB-verification
2. Bhargavan, K., Blanchet, B., Kobeissi, N.: Verified models and reference implementations for the TLS 1.3 standard candidate. In: 2017 IEEE Symposium on Security and Privacy, pp. 483–502. IEEE (2017)
3. Bitcoin Cash. https:// www. bitcoincash. org
4. CKB block synchronization protocol. https:// github. com/ nervosnetwork/ rfcs/ blob/ master/ rfcs/ 0004- ckb- block- sync/ 0004- ckb- block- sync. md
5. Fiterău-Broştean, P., Janssen, R., Vaandrager, F.: Combining model learning and model checking to analyze TCP implementations. In: Chaudhuri, S., Farzan, A. (eds.) CAV 2016. LNCS, vol. 9780, pp. 454–471. Springer, Cham (2016). https:// doi. org/ 10. 1007/ 978- 3- 319- 41540- 6_25
6. Havelund, K., Skou, A., Larsen, K.G., Lund, K.: Formal modeling and analysis of an audio/video protocol: an industrial case study using UPPAAL. In: Proceedings Real-Time Systems Symposium, pp. 2–13. IEEE (1997)
7. Lu, Y., Sun, M.: Modeling and verification of IEEE 802.11i security protocol in UPPAAL for Internet of Things. Int. J. Softw. Eng. Knowl. Eng. **28**(11–12), 1619–1636 (2018)
8. Nakamoto, S.: Bitcoin: a peer-to-peer electronic cash system (2008). https:// bitcoin. org/ bitcoin. pdf
9. Pîrlea, G., Sergey, I.: Mechanising blockchain consensus. In: Proceedings of the 7th ACM SIGPLAN International Conference on Certified Programs and Proofs, pp. 78–90. ACM (2018)
10. Poon, J., Dryja, T.: The bitcoin lightning network: scalable off-chain instant payments (2016). https:// www. bitcoinlightning. com/ wp- content/ uploads/ 2018/ 03/ lightning- network- paper. pdf
11. The Nervos Network. https:// www. nervos. org
12. Wood, G.: Polkadot: vision for a heterogeneous multi-chain framework (2016). https:// polkadot. network/ PolkaDotPaper. pdf

Accurate Abstractions for Controller Synthesis with Non-uniform Disturbances

Yunjun Bai[1(✉)] and Kaushik Mallik[2]

[1] SKLCS, Institute of Software Chinese Academy of Sciences, University of Chinese
Academy of Sciences, Beijing, China
baiyj@ios.ac.cn
[2] MPI-SWS, Kaiserslautern, Germany
kmallik@mpi-sws.org

Abstract. Abstraction-Based Controller Synthesis (ABCS) is an emerging field for automatic synthesis of correct-by-design controllers for non-linear dynamical systems in the presence of bounded disturbances. Existing ABCS techniques assume a global (state-independent) and uniform upper bound on disturbances. This can be overly pessimistic, resulting in a failure to find a controller. In this paper, we extend ABCS to accurately compute abstractions for system models with state and input-dependent non-uniform disturbances. This requires a subtle assume-guarantee style computation of the state evolution and the estimation of the error. We empirically show the benefit of our approach with significantly smaller amount of non-determinism in the abstract transitions.

1 Introduction

Abstraction-based controller synthesis (ABCS) is a fully automated controller synthesis technique for non-linear, continuous dynamical systems with respect to temporal control objectives [4,8,9,14,16,18]. In ABCS, first, the original non-linear dynamical system, under a sampled-time semantics, is approximated by a simpler finite-state system, called the *abstraction*. Second, using automata-theoretic algorithms for reactive synthesis [11], an appropriate two-player game is solved on the abstraction to compute an *abstract controller*. Finally, the abstract controller is *refined* to a sampled-time controller for the original continuous system. The correctness of the refinement process, and thus correctness of ABCS, depends on an alternating refinement or feedback refinement relation [1,10,14,16] between the original continuous system and the abstraction.

A simple and effective abstraction procedure is to partition the state and the input spaces using disjoint hypercubes, which form the state and input spaces of the finite-state abstraction. For every abstract state and input pair, the (non-deterministic) transitions of the abstraction provides an over-approximation of the possible states that can be reached under the effect of the continuous dynamics in the presence of disturbances. This algorithm has been implemented in several tools [9,12,17].

© Springer Nature Switzerland AG 2020
S.-W. Lin et al. (Eds.): ICFEM 2020, LNCS 12531, pp. 297–307, 2020.
https://doi.org/10.1007/978-3-030-63406-3_18

Existing abstraction techniques work on systems whose dynamics can be modeled as the differential inclusion

$$\dot{x} \in f(x, u) + [\![-d, d]\!],$$

where d represents a constant upper-bound on the disturbances which the system may experience. One important shortcoming of such techniques is the use of a global, state-independent, uniform upper bound on the disturbances. In real-world applications, such a global worst-case view often leads to an unnecessarily pessimistic abstraction, which could result in failure of controller synthesis. Consider for example a simple path planning problem for a robot in a space filled with obstacles (Fig. 1). Assume that the disturbance models how slippery the floor is. If it is observed that the floor is very slippery in some part (e.g. the cross-hatched region in Fig. 1) of the state space, even if this part is less critical and obstacle-free, the present state-of-the-art would assume that the floor is very slippery *everywhere*. This pessimism might cause a significant reduction in the size of the controller domain, especially in the critical obstacle-filled parts of the state space.

In this paper, we extend ABCS to system models with *state and input-dependent disturbance*:

$$\dot{x} \in f(x, u) + [\![-d(x, u), d(x, u)]\!].$$

The advantage of this generalization is two fold: First, it increases the accuracy of ABCS and the chances of a successful controller synthesis, even when the existing approaches fail. For example, in Fig. 1 the small purple region is the domain of the controller obtained using one of the existing approaches, whereas the large green region is the domain of the controller obtained using our proposed abstraction method. Second, our generalization enables localized incremental updates of the existing abstraction when the underlying disturbance model either changes locally over time, or is updated during runtime through learning-based exploration of the state space. The problem of exploration has recently gained popularity in the context of machine-learning and robotics applications, as it turns out that in most cases only approximate models of the system and the environment are known apriori, and a more precise model is learnt during runtime [5–7,13]. Existing ABCS techniques are not suitable for dynamic changes in the underlying model. Thus, any change in the model involves a complete re-computation of the whole abstraction and the associated controller. We show in a companion paper [3] how the method presented in this paper is instrumental for locally adapting an existing abstraction under changing disturbances. The adaptation algorithm propagates the effect of changes backwards, and selectively re-computes transitions only for those abstract states which might have been affected by this change. We do not discuss this application of adaptive re-computation of abstractions any further in this paper.

Technically, for construction of abstraction, the extension to state- and input-dependent disturbances is non-trivial for the following reason. The key step in the abstraction process is the estimation of a *growth bound* which is an upper-bound on the maximum perturbation of a nominal trajectory under the influence of disturbance. When the disturbance does not depend on the system's state, the growth bound can be computed independently of the system's state trajectories by solving the initial value problem for an auxiliary linear ordinary differential equation [10,16].

However, for state-dependent distur-bances, the dynamics of the growth bound is non-linear, and is coupled with the state trajectories of the system. We show a new algorithm that jointly computes state trajectories and growth bounds. The joint evolution means that there is a cyclic dependency between the size of the initial hyper-rectangle from which the trajectory starts and the size of the growth bound. A sim-ple numerical integration procedure can be unsound unless the disturbance on the dynamics between two integration points is estimated soundly. We show how the cycle can be broken by locally approximating the disturbance by an upper bound in an assume-guarantee fashion and provide an algorithm to approximate the growth bound to any desired accuracy. Due to space limita-tion we omit all the proofs; the proofs can be found in the extended version of this paper [2].

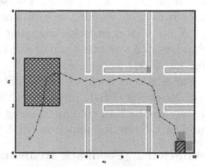

Fig. 1. State space of a vehicle (descrip-tion in [2]) assigned with a reach-avoid task. The goal and the obstacles are indicated using the hatched region in the bottom right and the gray rectan-gles, respectively. The region in cross-hatch has higher disturbance ($d = 0.1$) than the rest ($d = 0.05$). The purple and the green region represent the controller domains due to a uniform worst case dis-turbance (existing approaches) and state-dependent disturbances (our algorithm), respectively.

We have implemented our algorithm on top of SCOTS v0.2 [17]. We empir-ically show, through a number of case studies, that a state-dependent model of disturbances can lead to more precise abstractions. In fact, in our examples, the global upper bound was too conservative to find a controller.

2   Preliminaries

2.1   Notation

We use the notation $\mathbb{R}$, $\mathbb{R}_{>0}$, and $\mathbb{N}$ to denote the set of reals, the set of positive reals, and the set of natural numbers (excluding 0) respectively. Given a set A and an $n \in \mathbb{N}$, we use A^n to denote the cartesian product $\times_n A$. Given any vector $x \in A^n$, we use x_i to denote the element in the i-th dimension of x. For any function $f \colon A \to B$, we write dom f to denote the domain of f.

2.2   Systems and Refinement

A *system* $S = (X, U, F)$ consists of a state space X, an input space U, and a transition relation $F \subseteq X \times U \times X$. A system is called *finite* if X and U are finite sets. A *run* of a system is a finite or infinite sequence $\xi = x_0 x_1 \ldots$ such that for every i-th element in the sequence, with $i \geq 0$, there is an $u_i \in U$ such that $(x_i, u_i, x_{i+1}) \in F$. The set of runs of S is denoted $\mathcal{B}(S)$ and the set of runs of S starting from a state $x \in X$ is denoted $\mathcal{B}(S)(x)$. A *controller* $C : X \to U$ is a function mapping states to inputs which restricts the set of behaviors of a system: a run $\xi = x_0 x_1 \ldots$ is *compatible* with C if for every i, we have $(x_i, C(x_i), x_{i+1}) \in F$.

For ABCS to work, we need a suitable notion of abstraction. *Feedback Refinement Relations* (FRR) provide such a notion [1,16]. Here we omit the details of how an abstraction computed using FRR can be used in ABCS, which can be found in the original paper on FRR-based symbolic control [16].

Definition 1 (Feedback Refinement Relations). *Let $S_i = (X_i, U, F_i)$ for $i \in \{1, 2\}$ be two systems on the same set of inputs. Let $\pi_i : X_i \to 2^U$ be the mapping $\pi_i(x) = \{u \in U \mid \exists x' \in X_i \cdot (x, u, x') \in F_i\}$ giving the set of allowed inputs in state x of S_i. A feedback refinement relation from S_1 to S_2 is a relation $Q \subset X_1 \times X_2$ such that for all $x_1 \in X_1$ there is an $x_2 \in X_2$ such that $(x_1, x_2) \in Q$, and for all $(x_1, x_2) \in Q$, the following holds:*

(i) $\pi_2(x_2) \subseteq \pi_1(x_1)$ and
(ii) for all $u \in \pi_2(x_2)$ and for all $x_1' \in X_1$ such that $(x_1, u, x_1') \in F_1$, there is an $x_2' \in X_2$ such that $(x_2, u, x_2') \in F_2$ and $(x_1', x_2') \in Q$.

We use $S_1 \preccurlyeq_Q S_2$ to represent that Q from S_1 to S_2 is an FRR. We say S_2 is an *abstraction* of S_1 if there is an FRR Q such that $S_1 \preccurlyeq_Q S_2$. It is well known that if $S_1 \preccurlyeq_Q S_2$ then any controller $C : X_2 \to U$ solving a (suitably projected) control problem on S_2 can be refined to a controller solving the control problem on S_1 [1]. In this paper we focus on computing an abstraction; we refer to the standard reactive synthesis literature [11,15] for the details of the synthesis algorithms.

2.3   Time-Sampled Control Systems

We consider continuous-time *control systems* $\Sigma = (X, U, d, f)$, where $X = \mathbb{R}^n$ is the state space, $U \subset \mathbb{R}^m$ is the input space, $d : X \times U \to X$ is a function having continuous first order derivative in the first argument which models the upper-bound of the state dependent disturbances, and $f : X \times U \to X$ is the unperturbed system dynamics. The overall dynamics is expressed by the following differential inclusion:

$$\dot{x} \in f(x, u) + [\![-d(x, u), d(x, u)]\!]. \tag{1}$$

Since the set of disturbances $[\![-d(x, u), d(x, u)]\!]$ at any given state $x \in X$ and input $u \in U$ is symmetric about the origin, hence without loss of generality we assume that $d(x, u)$ is positive for all $x \in X$ and input $u \in U$. We assume that f is explicitly known and is continuously differentiable in x for all $u \in U$. The set $[\![-d(x, u), d(x, u)]\!]$ represents the set of all possible disturbances capturing the unmodeled dynamics and environmental uncertainties. Given an initial state $x_0 \in X$, a constant control input[1] $u \in U$ for time $\tau \in \mathbb{R}_+$ and any interval $I \subset [0, \tau]$, the evolution of Σ in I is given by the continuous trajectory $\xi_u : I \to X$ which satisfies $\dot{\xi}_u(t) \in f(\xi_u(t), u) + [\![-d(\xi_u(t), u), d(\xi_u(t), u)]\!]$. Moreover we define the *nominal trajectory* $\varphi_{x_0 u} : I \to X$, which satisfies the unperturbed differential equation $\dot{\varphi}_{x_0 u}(t) = f(\varphi_{x_0 u}(t), u)$ and $\varphi_{x_0 u}(0) = x_0$.

Given a fixed time sampling parameter $\tau > 0$, we define a system $\Sigma_\tau = (X, U, f_\tau)$ that represents the *sampled-time representation* of a control system Σ, where $f_\tau \subseteq X \times U \times X$ is the transition relation such that for all $(x, u, x') \in X \times U \times X$, we have $(x, u, x') \in f_\tau$ if and only if there is a solution of (1) for the constant input u such that $\xi(0) = x$ and $\xi(\tau) = x'$. The state space of Σ_τ is still infinite; our goal is to obtain a *finite-state* abstraction $\widehat{\Sigma}$ of Σ_τ.

3   Computation of Abstraction

3.1   A Generic Construction

Fix a control system $\Sigma = (X, U, d, f)$ and its sampled-time representation $\Sigma_\tau = (X, U, f_\tau)$ for a fixed sampling time $\tau > 0$. Our goal is to compute a finite-state abstraction $\widehat{\Sigma} = (\widehat{X}, \widehat{U}, \widehat{f})$. We work in the usual setting of ABCS, where an abstraction is obtained by first partitioning the state space and input space of Σ_τ into finitely many hypercubes, and then over-approximating the transitions to obtain the desired finite-state abstraction $\widehat{\Sigma}$.

We consider abstract state spaces defined by hyper-rectangular covers. A *hyper-rectangle* $[\![a, b]\!]$ with $a, b \in (\mathbb{R} \cup \{\pm\infty\})^n$ defines the set $\{x \in \mathbb{R}^n \mid a_i \leq x_i \leq b_i$ for $i \in \{1, \ldots, n\}\}$; it is non-empty if $a < b$. For $\eta \in \mathbb{R}^n_{>0}$, we say that a hyper-rectangle $[\![a, b]\!]$ has diameter $\eta \in (\mathbb{R}_{>0} \cup \{\pm\infty\})^n$ if for each $i \in \{1, \ldots, n\}$, we have $|b_i - a_i| = \eta_i$. The *center* of a non-empty hyper-rectangle $[\![a, b]\!]$, written $ctr([\![a, b]\!])$, is the point $(\frac{1}{2}(b_1 - a_1), \frac{1}{2}(b_2 - a_2), \ldots, \frac{1}{2}(b_n - a_n))$.

A set C of hyper-rectangles is called a *cover* of the state space X if every $x \in X$ belongs to some hyper-rectangle in C.

In the following, we make the standard assumption that there is a compact subset $X' \subseteq X$ of the state space that is of interest to the control problem. Given a discretization parameter $\eta \in \mathbb{R}^n_{>0}$, the abstract state space $\widehat{X}$ is a (finite) cover of the compact set X' with hyper-rectangles of diameter η together with a finite number of hyper-rectangles (some are unbounded) which cover $X \setminus X'$.

The abstract transition relation $\widehat{f}$ is defined as an over-approximation of the reachable states in a single time sampling period τ. The over-approximation is formalized by a *growth bound*.

---

[1] We restrict our notation to piecewise constant control inputs as more general control inputs will be unnecessary for the later part.

Definition 2 (Growth bound). *Let $\Sigma = (X, U, d, f)$ be a control system. Given a fixed sampling time $\tau > 0$ and sets $K \subset X$ and $U' \subset U$, a growth bound is a map $\beta_\tau : \mathbb{R}^n \times \mathbb{R}^n_{>0} \times U' \to \mathbb{R}^n_{>0}$ satisfying the following conditions:*

(i) $\beta_\tau(p, r, u) \geq \beta_\tau(p, r', u)$ whenever $r \geq r'$ and $u \in U'$;
(ii) for all $p \in K$ and $u \in U'$, $[0, \tau] \subset dom\, \varphi_{pu}$, and if ξ_u is a trajectory of (1) on $[0, \tau]$ with $\xi_u(0) \in K$ then

$$| \xi_u(\tau) - \varphi_{pu}(\tau) | \leq \beta_\tau(p, |\xi_u(0) - p|, u) \tag{2}$$

holds component-wise. Recall that $\varphi_{pu}(t)$ denotes the nominal trajectory starting from state p.

Definition 2 is an adaptation of the growth bound introduced by Resissig et al. [16]; the difference is that our growth bound also depends on the initial state of the nominal trajectory. The intuition behind this extra requirement is that the deviation of the actual trajectory from the nominal trajectory may not be independent of the path of the state trajectory in our case. This will be clear in the subsequent development.

Given the notion of state space partition and growth bound, we can now define the finite-state abstraction as follows:

Definition 3. *Let $\Sigma = (X, U, d, f)$ be a control system, let $\tau > 0$ be a sampling time, $\eta \in \mathbb{R}^n_{>0}$ a discretization parameter, and $\beta_\tau : \mathbb{R}^n \times \mathbb{R}^n_{>0} \times \widehat{U} \to \mathbb{R}^n_{>0}$ a growth bound. A finite-state abstraction $\widehat{\Sigma} = (\widehat{X}, \widehat{U}, \widehat{f})$ of Σ_τ consists of a finite set $\widehat{X}$ which forms a cover of X with hyper-rectangles of diameter η, a finite set $\widehat{U} \subseteq U$ of inputs, and a transition relation $\widehat{f} \subseteq \widehat{X} \times \widehat{U} \times \widehat{X}$ which satisfies, for all $\widehat{x}, \widehat{x}' \in \widehat{X}$ and $\widehat{u} \in \widehat{U}$, $(\widehat{x}, \widehat{u}, \widehat{x}') \in \widehat{f}$ if and only if*

$$\left(\varphi_{ctr(\widehat{x})\widehat{u}}(\tau) + [\![-\gamma, \gamma]\!] \right) \cap \widehat{x}' \neq \emptyset, \tag{3}$$

where $\gamma = \beta_\tau(ctr(\widehat{x}), \frac{1}{2}\eta, \widehat{u})$.

The following theorem is adapted from [16, Theorem VIII.4].

Theorem 1. *For every control system $\Sigma = (X, U, d, F)$, for every sampling time τ, state discretization η, and growth bound β, we have $\Sigma_\tau \preccurlyeq_Q \widehat{\Sigma}$, through the Feedback Refinement Relation $(x, \widehat{x}) \in Q$ if and only if $x \in \widehat{x}$.*

Thus, given parameters τ and η, in order to compute an abstraction, we have to show how to compute a suitable growth bound.

3.2 Growth Bound Computation

We now present a specific way of computing the growth bound $\beta_\tau(\cdot, \cdot, \cdot)$, which is motivated by the growth bound used in [16] for the case of uniform disturbance.

Given that f is continuously differentiable, we can define a certain upper bound on the speed of deviation of two perturbed trajectories of the system Σ, which is formalized in the following definition. We use $D_j f_i$ to denote the partial derivative with respect to the j-th component of the first argument of f_i.

Definition 4. *For a given control system $\Sigma = (X, U, d, f)$, let $K \subseteq K' \subseteq X$ be sets, where K' is convex, such that for all $u \in U'$ and for all $t \in [0, \tau]$, $\xi_u(0) \in K$ implies $\xi_u(t) \in K'$. Define the parametrized matrix $L : U' \to \mathbb{R}^{n \times n}$ which satisfies*

$$L_{i,j}(u) \geq \begin{cases} \sup_{x \in K'} D_j f_i(x, u) & \text{if } i = j, \\ \sup_{x \in K'} |D_j f_i(x, u)| & \text{otherwise.} \end{cases} \tag{4}$$

In the following, we use the maximum disturbance functions $w(t; p, u, z(t)) := \sup\{d(x', u) \mid x' \in [\varphi_{pu}(t) - z(t), \varphi_{pu}(t) + z(t)]\}$ and $w_{\max}(u) = \sup\{d(x, u) \mid x \in X\}$. Note that we use semicolon in the function argument to separate variables (symbols preceding the semicolon) from parameters (symbols following the semicolon). The following theorem establishes a way of sound computation of the growth bound.

Theorem 2. *Fix a time-sampling parameter $\tau > 0$. Let $\Sigma = (X, U, d, f)$ be a control system, and $z : \mathbb{R}_{>0} \to X$ be a solution to the initial value problem:*

$$\dot{z}(t) = L(u)z(t) + \overline{w}(t; u), \quad z(0) = r \tag{5}$$

where for all $t \in [0, \tau]$, $\overline{w}(t; u) \geq w(t; p, u, z(t))$. Then any trajectory $\xi_u(\cdot)$ of Σ with $|\xi_u(0) - p| \leq r$ is continuable to $[0, \tau]$, and $|\xi_u(t) - \varphi_{pu}(t)| \leq z(t)$ holds for all $t \in [0, \tau]$. In particular, $\beta_\tau(p, r, u) = z(\tau)$ is a growth bound of (1) on K, U' associated with τ.

In the following, we write $z_{\max}(\cdot; r, u)$ for the solution of the IVP (5) when $\overline{w}(\cdot; u) = w_{\max}(u)$ and write $z^*(\cdot; p, r, u)$ for the solution when $\overline{w}(\cdot; u) = w(\cdot; p, u, z(\cdot))$. Note that in either case, existence and uniqueness of the solution is guaranteed by the continuity of both the r.h.s. and the first order partial derivative of the r.h.s. w.r.t. $z(t)$; the non-trivial latter case follows from the fact that the function $d(\cdot, u)$ has continuous first order derivative.

Unfortunately, when $\overline{w}(t; u) = w(t; p, u, z(t))$, (5) is a highly non-linear ODE, and it is difficult to obtain a closed form solution for $z(t)$,

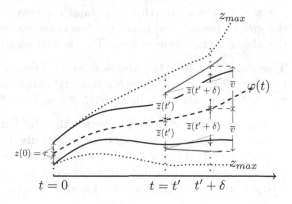

Fig. 2. Growth bound computation The dashed line shows the nominal trajectory and the solid lines show the ideal growth bound z^*. The dotted lines show the upper bound $z_{\max}$. Having computed $\bar{z}$ at time t', we want to compute $\bar{z}$ at time $t' + \delta$. The green lines show that it is unsound to use $\bar{z}(t')$ to compute a bound on the disturbance in the interval $[t', t' + \delta)$. Instead, we compute $\bar{v}$ using the estimate $\bar{z}(t')$ and the upper bound $w_{\max}$ on the error (the red lines). Using $\bar{v}(t' + \delta)$, we estimate $\bar{z}(t' + \delta)$ soundly.

if it exists at all. On the other hand, numerical computation of $z(t)$ will be unsound due to the unavoidable time-discretization: At any given time-step k, w will be estimated based on the disturbances seen upto the previous time-step $k-1$, which could be smaller than the actual disturbances seen in the interval $((k-1)h, kh]$, where h is the step size of the numerical solver (see Fig. 2).

For these reasons, we only give an algorithm that approximates the value of $z^*(t; p, r, u)$ by $\overline{z}(t; p, r, u, \delta)$ for a fixed parameter $\delta \in (0, \tau]$, such that the approximation $\overline{z}(\tau; p, r, u, \delta)$ is a sound growth bound of (1) and the approximation error can be made arbitrarily small. (Soundness of $\overline{z}(\tau; p, r, u, \delta)$ as a growth bound essentially prove that the numerical solution that we present later is also sound.) We introduce a conservative over-approximation of $w(t; p, u, z(t))$ that does not depend on $z(t)$, and the conservatism can be made arbitrarily small by tuning δ. This is based on an an assume-guarantee style decomposition of the computation of $w(t; p, u, z(t))$. For any $t \geq 0$, define $t^- := \max\{0, t - \delta\}$. *Assume* that for any given $t \geq 0$, the value of $\overline{z}(t^-; p, r, u, \delta)$ is already known, and in particular, $\overline{z}(0; p, r, u, \delta) = r$. Then we can *guarantee* that the over-approximation of the maximum disturbance seen at time t is $\overline{v}(t; p, r, u, \delta) :=$ $\sup\{d(x') \mid \varphi_{pu}(t) - \epsilon \leq x' \leq \varphi_{pu}(t) + \epsilon\}$, where $\epsilon = z_{\max}(\delta^-; \overline{z}(t^-; p, r, u, \delta), u)$ and $\delta^- = \min\{t, \delta\}$. Figure 2 shows the calculations.

We write $\overline{z}(\cdot; p, r, u, \delta)$ for the solution of the IVP (5) when $\overline{w}(\cdot; u)$ is set to $\overline{v}(\cdot; p, r, u, \delta)$. Note that existence and uniqueness of the solution is guaranteed, because the right hand side is both continuous and has continuous first order partial derivative with respect to $z(t)$: the proof is trivial when we note that $\overline{v}(t; \cdot, \cdot, \cdot, \delta)$ is independent of $\overline{z}(t; \cdot, \cdot, \cdot, \delta)$. For every $\delta > 0$, the solution $\overline{z}(\tau; p, r, u, \delta)$ is a growth bound, and the smaller the value of δ, the tighter is the growth bound, and hence the less conservative (i.e. less non-determinism) is the abstract transition system. This is formalized using the following theorem.

Theorem 3. *Using the notation as in Theorem 2, for all $\delta > 0$ and for all $t \in [0, \tau]$, $\overline{v}(t; p, r, u, \delta) \geq w(t; p, u, z^*(t))$. Moreover, for all $t \in [0, \tau]$ and for all $\varepsilon > 0$, there exists a $\delta > 0$, s.t. $|\overline{z}(t; p, r, u, \delta) - z^*(t; p, r, u)| < \varepsilon$.*

It is easy to see from Theorem 3 that by fixing $t = \tau$, we can always find a small enough $\delta > 0$ to get an arbitrarily tight and sound growth bound $\beta_\tau(p, r, u) = \overline{z}(\tau; p, r, u, \delta)$. Moreover, it can be shown that if $L(u)$ is a non-negative matrix, then a δ corresponding to $t = \tau$ and $\epsilon > 0$ ensures that $|\overline{z}(t; p, r, u, \delta) - z^*(t; p, r, u)| < \varepsilon$ for all $t \in [0, \tau]$.

3.3   ComputeAbs: Abstraction Algorithm

The abstraction algorithm COMPUTEABS iterates over all the abstract state-input pairs $(\widehat{x}, \widehat{u}) \in \widehat{X} \times \widehat{U}$. For each pair, it computes the set of transitions $(\widehat{x}, \widehat{u}, \widehat{x}')$ using an ODE solver in the following way.

First, for all $(\widehat{x}, \widehat{u})$, the disturbance function d is over-approximated using a piecewise constant function $\widehat{d} : \widehat{X} \times \widehat{U} \to \mathbb{R}^n$ defined as

$$\widehat{d}(\widehat{x}, \widehat{u}) := \sup_{x' \in \widehat{x}}\{d(x', \widehat{u})\}. \tag{6}$$

Second, a numerical ODE solver is used to jointly solve the IVP for the dynamics and the growth bound:

$$\dot{x}(t) = f(x(t), u), \quad x(0) = ctr(\widehat{x}) \tag{7}$$

$$\dot{z}(t) = L(u)z(t) + \widehat{w}(t; u), \quad z(0) = \frac{1}{2}\eta \tag{8}$$

where $\widehat{w}(t; u)$ approximates $\overline{w}(t; u)$ as described below.

The numerical algorithm used in our implementation is based on 4th order Runge-Kutta method. The ODE solver uses a fixed step size $h > 0$. For soundness, we need to make sure that the distance between two consecutive intermediate points obtained during the numerical solution of the IVP are not separated by a distance more than the discretization η. The following condition ensures this property:

$$\eta \geq \sup_{x,u} |f(x, u)| \times h. \tag{9}$$

Using the notation used in Theorem 3 we set $\delta = h$. This sets $\delta^- = \delta = h$, $t^- = t - \delta = t - h$ (note that each time point t equals kh for some $k \in \mathbb{N}$) and $\epsilon = z_{\max}(\delta^-; z^*(t - h; p, r, u), u)$. Finally, we define

$$\widehat{w}(t; u) = \sup_{\widehat{x}'}\{\widehat{d}(\widehat{x}', u) \mid \widehat{x}' \in \widehat{X} \text{ s.t. } \widehat{x}' \cap (x(t) + [\![-r(t) - \epsilon, r(t) + \epsilon]\!]) \neq \emptyset\}$$

Table 1. Experimental results for four different system models described in the extended version [2]: Comparison of SCOTSv0.2 and COMPUTEABS in terms of number of transitions (top) and computation time (bottom).

Case Study		SCOTSv0.2	COMPUTEABS	relative
Vehicle (3d)	# transitions	3.123×10^7	2.921×10^7	55%
	time (sec.)	16.81	24.64	0.7×
Manipulator(4d)	# transitions	1.244×10^9	1.048×10^9	84%
	time (sec.)	735.65	1012.34	0.7×
Cancer treatment(3d)	# transitions	8.301×10^8	7.263×10^8	88%
	time (sec.)	28.28	78.56	0.4×
Aircraft landing (3d)	# transitions	5.530×10^9	2.047×10^9	37%
	time (sec.)	264.099	528.62	0.5×

Based on the solution $(x(\tau), z(\tau))$ returned by the ODE solver, the abstraction algorithm adds transitions $(\widehat{x}, \widehat{u}, \widehat{x}')$ for every $\widehat{x}, \widehat{x}' \in \widehat{X}$ and every $\widehat{u} \in \widehat{U}$ such that $\widehat{x}' \cap [x(\tau) + -z(\tau), x(\tau) + z(\tau)] \neq \emptyset$.

4 Experimental Results

We implemented COMPUTEABS as an extension of SCOTSv0.2 [17], and evaluated the algorithms on 4 benchmark examples to show the effectiveness of our method. A performance comparison between COMPUTEABS and the original SCOTSv0.2 is summarized in Table 1; the details of the systems' models can be found in the extended version [2]. All the experiments were performed on an Intel(R) Xeon(R) Processor E7-8857 v2 (3.00 GHz) with 16 GB memory. Since we focus on the abstraction step of ABCS in this paper, no data related to synthesis is presented. However, we emphasize that the number of abstract transitions is a good indicator for the chances of successful synthesis. More transitions indicates a less accurate abstraction making the synthesis harder.

References

1. Alur, R., Henzinger, T.A., Kupferman, O., Vardi, M.Y.: Alternating refinement relations. In: Sangiorgi, D., de Simone, R. (eds.) CONCUR 1998. LNCS, vol. 1466, pp. 163–178. Springer, Heidelberg (1998). https://doi.org/10.1007/BFb0055622
2. Bai, Y., Mallik, K.: Accurate abstractions for controller synthesis with non-uniform disturbances (2019). https://people.mpi-sws.org/~kmallik/uploads/NonUniformGrowthBound.pdf
3. Bai, Y., Mallik, K., Schmuck, A., Zufferey, D., Majumdar, R.: Incremental abstraction computation for symbolic controller synthesis in a changing environment. In: 2019 IEEE 58th CDC, pp. 6261–6268 (2019)
4. Belta, C., Yordanov, B., Gol, E.A.: Formal Methods for Discrete-Time Dynamical Systems. Springer, Cham (2017)
5. Berkenkamp, F., Moriconi, R., Schoellig, A.P., Krause, A.: Safe learning of regions of attraction for uncertain, nonlinear systems with gaussian processes. In: CDC 2016, pp. 4661–4666. IEEE (2016)
6. Berkenkamp, F., Turchetta, M., Schoellig, A., Krause, A.: Safe model-based reinforcement learning with stability guarantees. In: Advances in Neural Information Processing Systems, pp. 908–918 (2017)
7. Fisac, J.F., Akametalu, A.K., Zeilinger, M.N., Kaynama, S., Gillula, J., Tomlin, C.J.: A general safety framework for learning-based control in uncertain robotic systems. arXiv preprint arXiv:1705.01292 (2017)
8. Girard, A.: Controller synthesis for safety and reachability via approximate bisimulation. Automatica 48(5), 947–953 (2012)
9. Hsu, K., Majumdar, R., Mallik, K., Schmuck, A.: Multi-layered abstraction-based controller synthesis for continuous-time systems. In: HSCC 2018, pp. 120–129. ACM (2018)
10. Liu, J., Ozay, N.: Finite abstractions with robustness margins for temporal logic-based control synthesis. Nonlinear Anal.: Hybrid Syst. 22, 1–15 (2016)
11. Maler, O., Pnueli, A., Sifakis, J.: On the synthesis of discrete controllers for timed systems. In: Mayr, E.W., Puech, C. (eds.) STACS 1995. LNCS, vol. 900, pp. 229–242. Springer, Heidelberg (1995). https://doi.org/10.1007/3-540-59042-0_76
12. Mazo Jr., M., Davitian, A., Tabuada, P.: PESSOA: a tool for embedded controller synthesis. In: Touili, T., Cook, B., Jackson, P. (eds.) CAV 2010. LNCS, vol. 6174, pp. 566–569. Springer, Heidelberg (2010). https://doi.org/10.1007/978-3-642-14295-6_49

13. Moldovan, T.M., Abbeel, P.: Safe exploration in Markov decision processes. arXiv preprint arXiv:1205.4810 (2012)

14. Nilsson, P., Ozay, N., Liu, J.: Augmented finite transition systems as abstractions for control synthesis. Discrete Event Dyn. Syst. **27**(2), 301–340 (2017). https://doi.org/10.1007/s10626-017-0243-z

15. Pnueli, A., Rosner, R.: On the synthesis of a reactive module. In: POPL 1989, pp. 179–190. ACM (1989)

16. Reissig, G., Weber, A., Rungger, M.: Feedback refinement relations for the synthesis of symbolic controllers. TAC **62**(4), 1781–1796 (2017)

17. Rungger, M., Zamani, M.: SCOTS: a tool for the synthesis of symbolic controllers. In: HSCC, pp. 99–104. ACM (2016)

18. Tabuada, P.: Verification and Control of Hybrid Systems: A Symbolicapproach. Springer, Cham (2009). https://doi.org/10.1007/978-1-4419-0224-5

Formalising Privacy-Preserving Constraints in Microservices Architecture

Inna Vistbakka[1] and Elena Troubitsyna[2(✉)]

[1] Åbo Akademi University, Turku, Finland
inna.vistbakka@abo.fi
[2] KTH – Royal Institute of Technology, Stockholm, Sweden
elenatro@kth.se

Abstract. Microservices is an architectural style that promotes structuring an application as a collection of loosely coupled fine-grained services. Since each microservice typically accesses different data, while composing complex applications it is hard to monitor which data are getting accessed in the entire application workflow. This raises a serious concern over the privacy protection especially in such a domain as health care. In this paper, we propose a formal Event-B based approach to analysing privacy preservation constraints in the applications developed in the microservices architectural style.

Keywords: Privacy · Modelling · Microservices · Event-B · Verification

1 Introduction

In accordance to the General Data Protection Regulation (GDPR) [4], companies require to preserve privacy while handling personal user information. This is an especially important issue in the healthcare domain, which inherently handles a lot of sensitive personal data.

In this paper, we propose a formal approach to verifying privacy-preservation constraints in the microservices-based development. Microservices [6] is a popular architectural style that promotes building applications as an orchestration of loosely coupled fine-grained services. The approach supports modularity, continuous integration and parallel independent work by multiple developers. Typically an application – an orchestrated complex service – is composed of several microservices. It might access a large variety of data. Therefore, ensuring privacy protection in complex workflows inherent to microservices architectures constitutes a serious technical challenge.

In this paper, we rely on a formal modelling in Event-B [2] with the associated prover and model checker provided by the Rodin platform [10] to formally define and verify the privacy preservation constraints. In the static part of the Event-B specification, we define both – the microservices in terms of their data access and the intended overall structure of the microservices architecture. In the

© Springer Nature Switzerland AG 2020
S.-W. Lin et al. (Eds.): ICFEM 2020, LNCS 12531, pp. 308–317, 2020.
https://doi.org/10.1007/978-3-030-63406-3_19

dynamic part, we defined privacy preservation constraints and verified whether the scenarios that the analysed application intends to support, preserve privacy constraints. Model checking is used then to generate all feasible scenario execution traces under the constraints defined in the context. Each scenario can either preserve or violate privacy constraints, where a breach of privacy is defined as a reachability problem. As a result, we can explicitly identify the causes of potential privacy breaches, as well as propose and verify corrective solutions.

2   Privacy Issues in Modern Software Design

MicroService Architecture (MSA) [6] (sometimes referred to as fine-grained service-oriented architecture) – is a new architectural style, which quickly grows in popularity. MSA advocates development of applications as an orchestration of loosely-coupled services of small granularity. MSA supports continuous integration and shorter development cycles. Among other benefits is a flexibility in programming language selection and enhanced service scalability.

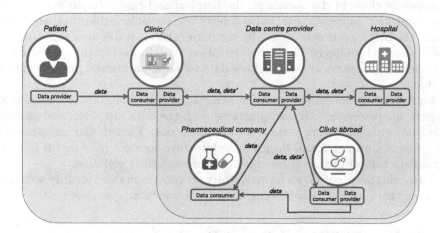

Fig. 1. Example: electronic health records handling with disclosures

Companies from different domains, including healthcare, have started to adopt MSA to respond more rapidly to the ever-changing demands of the business. However, even though MSA style offers many benefits in terms of flexibility and agility, it inevitable possesses the problem associated with its distributed and data-intensive nature – privacy protection of handled data, which is especially acute in the healthcare sector.

The applications developed for the healthcare domain have stringent requirements imposed on the patient's privacy, personal data protection and their misuse. Each patient should be able to individually make a decision about which data can be disclosed to which party. Any application or a company that handles such data should guarantee that these constrains are preserved.

Next we present an example, adopted from [18] which illustrates privacy protection issues in the healthcare domain. First, we give a high level description of the workflow and then discuss it from the MSA point of view.

We assume that a patient needs a medical treatment abroad. A clinic in the homeland has taken an x-ray image of the patient and has shared it (disclosed to) the data center collecting EHRs. The data center collects EHRs from different organisations. Moreover, it also shares, i.e., discloses, them with other organisations, such as clinics, health insurance agencies, and pharmaceutical companies.

An interaction of a patient with an organisation starts from the verification of patient's digital identity and selection of data privacy protection policy. For instance, since the x-ray should be taken in the clinic in the homeland but the treatment to be received at a hospital and clinic abroad, a patient agrees that the clinic in the homeland discloses the digital identity, history of disease and x-ray image to the clinic and hospital abroad. The disclose is agreed to be handled by a datacenter in the homeland. Any other additional disclosures are not permitted.

Figure 1 illustrates the possible interactions with different organisations, which might be involved in our example. It shows the authorized disclosures between the clinic in the homeland, the hospital and clinic abroad via the data center provider. Moreover, Fig. 1 also depicts two possible non-authorized disclosures. The first violation is caused by the data center – it discloses the data to a pharmaceutical company. The second violation is performed by the clinic abroad, which after the treatment also discloses data to a non-authorized pharmaceutical company.

Each organisation in our example handles patient's data using a number of different microservices. All manipulations with the data are performed on multiple platforms and using various web applications. Though the unauthorized disclosure is not intentional, the given architecture does not have means to monitor satisfaction of privacy constraints and prevent their violation.

To tackle this problem, we formalise privacy constraints and identify scenarios violating them using Event-B – the framework which we overview next.

3   Background: Event-B and ProB

Event-B is a state-based formal approach that promotes the correct-by-construction development and formal verification by theorem proving [2]. In Event-B, a system model is specified as an *abstract state machine*. An abstract state machine encapsulates the model state, represented as a collection of variables, and defines the events – the operations over the states, i.e., it describes the dynamic system behaviour. The variables are strongly typed by the constraining predicates that, together with other important system properties, are defined as model *invariants*. Usually, a machine has an accompanying component, called a *context*, which includes user-defined sets, constants and their properties given as a list of model axioms.

The dynamic behaviour of the system is defined by a collection of atomic *events*. Generally, an event has the following form:

$$e \mathrel{\widehat{=}} \textbf{any } a \textbf{ where } G_e \textbf{ then } R_e \textbf{ end},$$

where e is the event's name, a is the list of local variables, G_e is the event guard, and R_e is the event action. The guard is a predicate over the local variables of the event and the state variables of the system. The guard defines the conditions under which the event is *enabled*. If several events are enabled at the same time, any of them can be chosen for execution nondeterministically.

Modelling, refinement and verification in Event-B is supported by an automated tool – Rodin platform [10]. The platform provides the designers with an integrated extendable modelling environment, supporting automatic generation and proving of the proof obligations. The ProB extension [7] of Rodin supports automated consistency checking of Event-B machines via model checking, constraint based checking, and animation. In the next section, we formulate the main steps of the verification process and demonstrate its application to the EHR example.

4 Verification of Privacy-Preserving Constrains in MSA Using Event-B

Event-B offers a convenient separation of models of static and dynamic aspects of system behaviour within the unified and hence, semantically coherent specification. This allows us to represent the static and dynamic concepts within the same specification in a consistent way.

In the static part of the specification – context – we aim at defining the mathematical constructs required to represent the microservices architecture under study. An excerpt from the specification pattern of the context is shown in Fig. 2. We define the set of all microservices names (ids) as an abstract constant set *MS*. The abstract types of data, to be handled by the desired application, are defined by the abstract set *DATA_TYPE*. Similarly, the names of all the relevant organisations are defined in the abstract set *ORG*.

In the **CONSTANTS** clause, we have an opportunity to explicitly define the static relationships between the abstract sets as the corresponding constants that are defined in as the axioms in the **AXIOMS** clause. We adopt *Consumer-Producer* pattern for modelling a microservice. Hence, for each microservice we define an abstract relation *Cons_Data*, which maps the microservice name to the set of data types in the abstract set *DATA_TYPE*, which the microservice can consume, i.e., define which data are disclosed to this microservice. Similarly, we define the abstract relation *Prod_Data*, which maps the microsevice name to the set of data types, which the microservice exposes to the other microservices.

The abstract constant *DOMAIN* defines the association between the (names of) organisation and the microservices. The abstract relation *O_PERM* defines the permissions for a certain subset of data – a subset of *DATA_TYPE*, to be exposed to each particular organisation.

```
CONTEXT MSA_context
SETS MS, DATA_TYPE, ORG, ...
CONSTANTS Cons_Data, Prod_Data, DOMAIN, O_PERM, ...
AXIOMS
  axm1: MS ≠ ∅
  axm2: DATA_TYPE ≠ ∅
  axm3: ORG ≠ ∅
  axm4: Cons_Data ∈ MS → ℙ(DATA_TYPE)
  axm5: Prod_Data ∈ MS → ℙ(DATA_TYPE)
  axm6: DOMAIN ∈ ORG → ℙ(MS)
  axm7: O_PERM ∈ ORG → ℙ(DATA_TYPE)
  axm8: ScenarioSeq = {...}
  ...
END
```

Fig. 2. The excerpt of context MSA_context

The introduced definitions formally specify the microservices architectures and privacy constraints. As a result of development or verification, new microservices might be introduced, existing modified or privacy policy changed.

To enable a lightweight verification process, in the context, we also statically define the scenario, which should run in our microservices architecture. It is defined as a sequence of (names of) microservices.

In the machine, we define the variables representing the scenarios as a sequence of microservices, progress of a scenario execution as well as the "accumulated" knowledge – the subset of data that is getting exposed to each microservice in the scenario. The types of the introduced variables are defined in the **INVARIANTS** clause. The most interesting part of the invariants is our privacy preservation condition (3), which now can be checked for each scenario that we intend to verify.

The verification process relies on proofs and model checking. Proofs allow us to verify consistency of the introduced constants and correctness of the specification as such. Model checking is used to iteratively check the desired scenarios. We aim at verifying that none of the scenarios modelled as a sequence of microservices violates the invariant. The summary of the proposed verification process in Event-B is given below.

4.1   Approach Description

The proposed approach consists of the following steps:

- *Step 1.* Define (or subsequently modify) the corresponding Event-B *context* component, containing the (types of) involved data elements (in **SETS** and **CONSTANTS** clauses) and the involved static relationships between them (in **AXIOMS** clause). The generic pattern for specifying microservices architecture in the context given in Fig. 2.
- *Step 2.* In the dynamic part, create an abstract Event-B machine that defines the dynamic part of the model. Define the desired privacy preservation constraints as a part of the model invariant. Explicitly model the progress of

execution of the chosen scenario by defining the events that modify the variables representing the current step and the name of the microservice involved into execution of this step. In the model context, define (or modify the definition of) the scenario to be verified as a sequence of microservices. Verify consistency and correctness of the specification by invoking the prover integrated into the Rodin platform.

– *Step 3.* Simulate an execution of a chosen scenario in Event-B machine part by invoking model checker ProB integrated into the Rodin platform. Each scenario can either preserve or violate privacy constraints, where a breach of privacy is defined as a reachability problem. Any violations of the privacy constraints lead to deadlocking the model. If a deadlock is found then diagnose the problem by exploring the found counterexample: the execution step of the scenario and the name of the corresponding microservice. Otherwise, go to *Step 5.*

– *Step 4:* Propose a solution to rectify the found problem. It would require to make some changes in the data access rights of some microservices. Feasibility and effectiveness of such changes can be immediately checked using the modified specification. Return to the *Step 2* for necessary modifications of one or several definitions.

– *Step 5:* The verified scenario preserves the defined privacy preservation policy. If all the desired scenarios associated with a given application have been verified then the current specification of the data access of the involved microservices preserves the desired privacy constraints and the current version of the application can be safely (from the privacy point of view) deployed. Otherwise, go to *Step 2* to define and verify another scenario.

Next we further elaborate on the proposed approach by applying it to the example – handling EHRs.

4.2 Application of the Approach to the EHR Example

To illustrate our approach, we take our EHR example discussed in Sect. 2. The involved workflow and possible interactions with different organisations are depicted in Fig.1.

Let us consider the following scenario defined as a sequence of microservices:

$$(\text{WebP\_App}, \text{HC\_Adm}, \text{DCP\_Mng}, \text{PCU\_PA}) \tag{1}$$

Here WebP_App stands for a patient Web application service, HC_Adm is a patient administrative service associated with a home patient's clinic, DCP_Mng is a data collection service of a data center provider organisation, and PCU_DA denotes a data analytic service associated with a pharmaceutical company.

To verify whether this scenario satisfies the privacy-preserving constraints (defined as **axm4** and **inv6**), we follow the steps of the approach described in Sect. 4.1. First, we define the static part of our Event-B model – the context

```
CONTEXT EHR_context
SETS MS, DATA_TYPE, ORG, S
CONSTANTS Cons_Data, Prod_Data, DOMAIN, O_PERM, ScenarioSeq, ScenarioCur...
AXIOMS
axm1:  MS = {WebP_App, HC_Adm, DCP_Mng, HA_Mng, PCU_DA, CA_Mng, ...}
axm2:  DATA_TYPES = {UPRI_CR, LabResUs, ImgUs, IdUss, ... }
axm3:  ORG = {Pat, HC, DCP, CA, HA, PCU}
axm4:  O_PERM = {Pat ↦ {UPRI_CR, LabResUs, ImgUs}, HC ↦ {UPRI_CR, LabResUs, ...}, ...}
...
axm7:  ScenarioSeq ∈ S → (ℕ ↦MS)
axm8:  ScenarioSeq = {s₁ ↦ {1 ↦ WebP_App, 2 ↦ HC_Adm, 3 ↦ DCP_Mng, 3 ↦ PCU_DA}, ...}
axm9:  ScenarioCur ∈ ℕ ↦MS
axm10:  ScenarioCur = {1 ↦ WebP_App, 2 ↦ HC_Adm, 3 ↦ DCP_Mng, 3 ↦ PCU_DA}
...
```

Fig. 3. Case study: context definition

component (see Fig. 3). The involved structures (sets of microservices, organisations, data types, etc.) are defined (by **axm1–axm3**) by instantiating with the example-specific details the generic specification pattern presented in Fig. 3.

Then we create an abstract Event-B machine model (see Fig. 4). Here we define the artefacts required to model the dynamic aspect, e.g., accumulated data elements *Cons_Data_Known*, a current scenario sequence *SimScenarioCur*, etc. We introduce them as model variables and formulate their properties in the **INVARIANTS** clause.

Next, we define the scenario sequence to be checked as a constant *ScenarioCur* in the model context (see Fig. 3). In the machine part of the Event-B specification of EHR, we simulate this scenario execution by storing a scenario steps in *SimScenarioCur* variable as well as saving the consumed data for every involved in a scenario microservice in *Cons_Data_Known* variable.

To verify a scenario in a traceable manner and facilitate diagnosing the problems, we define a number of events – start, next, compl – that simulate the scenario execution (see Fig. 4). The sequence of microservices is built by starting from the first microservices (modelled by the event start) and simulating the execution sequence leading to the last microservices (modelled by the event next). The scenario execution process is completed when the last (in the current scenario sequence) microservice is executed (modelled by the event compl).

The invariant property **inv7:** *finish = TRUE ⇒ SimScenarioCur=ScenarioCur* states that if the scenario execution has been completed then the scenario contains all the steps (i.e., is equal to the executed steps). In the case when the resulting command sequence *SimScenarioCur* does not match to the required sequence, a violation is found by model checking. Consequently, the found scenario sequence becomes an input for the analysis in *Step 4.*

For instance, in our example, while checking a scenario (1), we have found a deadlock – the scenario deadlocks on the execution of the last miscroservice of a pharmaceutical company, where microservice *ms_c=PCU_DA*. The analysis

```
MACHINE  EHR_machine_1
SEES  EHR_context
VARIABLES  Cons_Data_Known, SimScenarioCur, finish, num
INVARIANTS
...
inv4:  Cons_Data_Known ∈ MS → ℙ(DATA_TYPE) // stores accumulated data elements
inv5:  SimScenarioCur ∈ ℕ ⇸ MS                  // stores a current scenario sequence
inv6:  ∀ms. ms ∈ ran(ScenarioCur)⇒Cons_Data_Known(ms) ⊄ O_PERM(DOMAIN⁻¹({ms})
inv7:  finish=TRUE ⇒ SimScenarioCur=ScenarioCur
...
EVENTS
...
start ≙
  any  ms_p, ms_c, org_c, data
  where  num=0 ∧ ms_p = ScenarioCur(1) ∧ ms_c = ScenarioCur(2) ∧
         ms_c ∈ DOMAIN(org_c)  ∧ data ⊆ Prod_Data(ms_p) ∧
         Cons_Data(ms_c) ⊆ O_PERM(org_c)  ∧ ...
  then
         SimScenarioCur := {1 ↦ ms_p, 2 ↦ ms_c}
         Cons_Data_Known(ms_c) := data
         num := num + 1
         finish := bool(num = card(ScenarioCur))
  end
next ≙
  any  ms_p, ms_c, org_c, data
  where  finish = FALSE ∧ num > 0 ∧
         ms_p = ScenarioCur(num+1) ∧ ms_c = ScenarioCur(num+1) ∧
         ms_c ∈ DOMAIN(org_c)  ∧ data ⊆ Prod_Data(ms_p) ∧
         Cons_Data(ms_c) ⊆ O_PERM(org_c) ∧
         Cons_Data(ms_c) ⊆ Prod_Data(ms_p)  ∧ ...
  then
         SimScenarioCur := SimScenarioCur ∪ {num + 1 ↦ ms_p}
         Cons_Data_Known(ms_c) := Cons_Data(ms_c) ∪ data
         num := num + 1
         finish := bool(num = card(ScenarioCur))
  end
...
END
```

Fig. 4. Case study: excerpt of the machine EHR_machine_1

discovered that a pharmaceutical company gets access to the data type *ImgUs*, which is not allowed by the privacy-preserving constraints.

At the current stage, we assume that the changes in the data access rely on the manual inspection of the identified disclosures. However, model animation can significantly facilitate this process by allowing us to replay the identified disclosures scenario and considering consumed and produces data of each microservice individually.

5   Related Work and Conclusions

A comprehensive overview of the state-of-the-art in privacy research is presented in [11]. Various aspects of reasoning about privacy have been also actively studied within the formal methods community. Agrafiotis et al. [3] rely on Hoare logic to detect and resolve ambiguities in privacy requirements. In particular, they also consider the problem of inconsistency with the privacy constraints caused by an aggregation of data. Abe and Simpson [1] use Z to model system–environment interactions and ProZ to verify whether such interactions can trigger a transition to an undesired privacy-violating state. Privacy is addressed from the "data in the system" perspective, which allows the authors to specify privacy preservation constraints as the model invariant. In our work, we also define privacy as an invariant property of the model.

A data-flow oriented approach to graphical and formal modelling of privacy and security constraints has been proposed in [12–14,17]. These works use the graphical modelling to represent system architecture and the data flow. The diagrams are translated into a formal modelling framework Event-B, to verify the impact of privacy violations and security attacks on the behaviour of the system.

A role-based access control (RBAC) is a popular mechanism for privacy assurance. A contract-based approach to modelling and verification of RBAC for cloud was proposed in [8]. An approach to integrating UML modelling and formal modelling in Event-B to reason about behaviour and properties of web-services was proposed in [9]. A domain-specific language for modelling role-based access control and translating graphical models in Event-B was proposed in [15] and formalised in [16]. A similar approach for service-oriented architectures was proposed in [5].

In the approach discussed in this paper, we focus on representing a microservices architecture and the privacy policy in connection to the organisational domain, to which a microservice belongs. It enables a more straightforward analysis of the required privacy constraints in the development process.

In this paper, we proposed a formal approach to verifying privacy-preservation constraints in the applications developed in the microservices architectural style. We demonstrated how to formally specify microservices and the overall architecture to enable lightweight but rigorous analysis of privacy policy preservation. Our approach supports a clear traceability between the high level privacy description – the user's consent to disclose particular data to certain organisations – and the formal specification of the privacy preserving constraints.

The automated tool support – the Rodin platform – have been critical for implementing our approach. The provers have been used to verify consistency of the architectures and Pro-B model checker to verify scenarios. As a future work, we are planning to investigate the idea of integrating different privacy enhancing mechanisms into the specifications of microservices architectures to enable a formal verification of privacy of the resultant solutions.

References

1. Abe, A., Simpson, A.: Formal models for privacy. In: Proceedings of EDBT/ICDT 2016, CEUR Workshop Proceedings, vol. 1558, CEUR-WS.org (2016)

2. Abrial, J.-R.: Modeling in Event-B. Cambridge University Press, Cambridge (2010)
3. Agrafiotis, I., Creese, S., Goldsmith, M., Papanikolaou, N.: Applying formal methods to detect and resolve ambiguities in privacy requirements. In: Fischer-Hübner, S., Duquenoy, P., Hansen, M., Leenes, R., Zhang, G. (eds.) Privacy and Identity 2010. IAICT, vol. 352, pp. 271–282. Springer, Heidelberg (2011). https://doi.org/10.1007/978-3-642-20769-3_22
4. European Commission: Proposal for a General Data Protection Regulation. Codecision legislative procedure for a regulation 2012/0011 (COD), European Commission. Brussels, Belgium, January 2012
5. Laibinis, L., Troubitsyna, E., Leppänen, S.: Service-oriented development of fault tolerant communicating systems: refinement approach. IJERTCS **1**(2), 61–85 (2010)
6. Fowler, M., Lewis, J.: Microservices: a definition of this new architectural term. https://martinfowler.com/articles/microservices.ml. Accessed 01 Apr 2019
7. ProB. Animator and Model Checker. https://www3.hhu.de/stups/prob/index.php/. Accessed 01 Apr 2019
8. Rauf, I., Troubitsyna, E.: Generating cloud monitors from models to secure clouds. In: DSN 2018, IEEE Computer Society (in print, 2018)
9. Rauf, I., Vistbakka, I., Troubitsyna, E.: Formal verification of stateful services with REST APIs using Event-B. In: IEEE ICWS 2018. IEEE (in print, 2018)
10. Rodin. Event-B platform. http://www.event-b.org/
11. Spiekermann, S., Cranor, L.F.: Engineering privacy. IEEE Trans. Softw. Eng. **35**(1), 67–82 (2009)
12. Tarasyuk, A., Troubitsyna, E., Laibinis, L.: Formal modelling and verification of service-oriented systems in probabilistic event-B. In: Derrick, J., Gnesi, S., Latella, D., Treharne, H. (eds.) IFM 2012. LNCS, vol. 7321, pp. 237–252. Springer, Heidelberg (2012). https://doi.org/10.1007/978-3-642-30729-4_17
13. Troubitsyna, E., Laibinis, L., Pereverzeva, I., Kuismin, T., Ilic, D., Latvala, T.: Towards security-explicit formal modelling of safety-critical systems. In: Skavhaug, A., Guiochet, J., Bitsch, F. (eds.) SAFECOMP 2016. LNCS, vol. 9922, pp. 213–225. Springer, Cham (2016). https://doi.org/10.1007/978-3-319-45477-1_17
14. Troubitsyna, E., Vistbakka, I.: Deriving and formalising safety and security requirements for control systems. In: Gallina, B., Skavhaug, A., Bitsch, F. (eds.) SAFECOMP 2018. LNCS, vol. 11093, pp. 107–122. Springer, Cham (2018). https://doi.org/10.1007/978-3-319-99130-6_8
15. Vistbakka, I., Barash, M., Troubitsyna, E.: Towards creating a DSL facilitating modelling of dynamic access control in event-B. In: Butler, M., Raschke, A., Hoang, T.S., Reichl, K. (eds.) ABZ 2018. LNCS, vol. 10817, pp. 386–391. Springer, Cham (2018). https://doi.org/10.1007/978-3-319-91271-4_28
16. Vistbakka, I., Troubitsyna, E.: Modelling and verification of dynamic role-based access control. In: Atig, M.F., Bensalem, S., Bliudze, S., Monsuez, B. (eds.) VECoS 2018. LNCS, vol 11181, pp. 48–63. Springer, Cham (2018). https://doi.org/10.1007/978-3-030-00359-3_4
17. Vistbakka, I., Troubitsyna, E., Kuismin, T., Latvala, T.: Co-engineering safety and security in industrial control systems: a formal outlook. In: Romanovsky, A., Troubitsyna, E.A. (eds.) SERENE 2017. LNCS, vol. 10479, pp. 96–114. Springer, Cham (2017). https://doi.org/10.1007/978-3-319-65948-0_7
18. Wohlgemuth, S., Echizen, I., Sonehara, N., Müller, G.: Tagging disclosures of personal data to third parties to preserve privacy. In: Rannenberg, K., Varadharajan, V., Weber, C. (eds.) SEC 2010. IAICT, vol. 330, pp. 241–252. Springer, Heidelberg (2010). https://doi.org/10.1007/978-3-642-15257-3_22

Algebraic Approach for Confidence Evaluation of Assurance Cases

Yoriyuki Yamagata[1(✉)] and Yutaka Matsuno[2]

[1] National Institute of Advanced Industrial Science and Technology (AIST),
1-8-31 Midorigaoka, Ikeda, Osaka 563-8577, Japan
yoriyuki.yamagata@aist.go.jp
[2] College of Science and Technology, Nihon University,
Chiba 7-24-1, Narashinodai, Funabashi 274-8501, Japan
matsuno.yutaka@nihon-u.ac.jp

Abstract. This paper presents a preliminary study on a method to evaluate the confidence of assurance cases using an abstract algebra mapped to a partial order. Unlike conventional quantitative methods for confidence evaluation, our approach is purely qualitative and employs a small number of axioms. It does not rely on numerical parameters that are difficult to determine in practice. Furthermore, our method can be regarded as an abstraction over numerical methods that use probability. To illustrate that our method provides a rigorous foundation for the qualitative evaluation of assurance cases, we give a sufficient condition for a multi-legged argument to improve confidence. Finally, we use our method to evaluate a concrete goal structuring notation (GSN) diagram that argues that a computer simulation of a biological system is reliable. These findings suggest that methods based on abstract axioms are viable approaches for confidence evaluation of assurance cases.

Keywords: Assurance case · Goal structuring notation (GSN) ·
Confidence · Formal semantics

1 Introduction

Creating and evaluating assurance cases are challenging tasks. The concept of assurance cases is given an abstract definition such as "A reasoned and compelling argument, supported by a body of evidence, that a system, service or organization will operate as intended for a defined application in a defined environment" [2]. By such an abstract definition, virtually all artifacts of the target system could be parts of the assurance case. In an automotive assurance case guideline [10], it is noted that "the question of when to stop adding further detail to an assurance case is not one that can be easily answered." An important issue is understanding how much *confidence* one can have in the claim and how different arguments contribute to such confidence, given a claim and a supporting argument [6].

© Springer Nature Switzerland AG 2020
S.-W. Lin et al. (Eds.): ICFEM 2020, LNCS 12531, pp. 318–327, 2020.
https://doi.org/10.1007/978-3-030-63406-3_20

Goal structuring notation (GSN) [2] is a widely used graphical notation for assurance cases. A GSN diagram starts with a top goal of a claim to be argued, such as "System X is safe." Each goal is decomposed into sub-goals via a strategy node, which explains why the sub-goals are sufficient to support the goal, and finally, into directly verifiable evidence. A GSN diagram also documents the assumptions and contexts for an assurance case. This study uses GSN diagrams for presenting assurance cases.

Previous studies on the confidence of assurance cases were mostly based on numerical evaluations. A drawback of numerical evaluations is that the results depend on the numerical parameters used in the evaluation, whose appropriateness is difficult to verify. Thus, a widely applicable quantitative method for the confidence evaluation of assurance cases remains to be established.

This paper proposes a method to evaluate the confidence of assurance cases using an abstract algebra mapped to a partial order. This method has several advantages over numerical methods. First, the proposed method is defined using a small number of axioms without numerical parameters; thus, the results have a clear meaning. Second, the proposed method is based on weaker assumptions and is more general than numerical methods. Finally, the proposed framework can be regarded as an abstraction over (previously proposed) probability methods of confidence evaluation. Although our axioms are still weak for fine confidence evaluation, we believe that the method based on abstract axioms is shown to be a viable research direction.

The remainder of this paper is organized as follows. Section 2 reviews related studies. Section 3 gives the definition of GSN diagrams. Section 4 defines an abstract algebra of "states" and introduces our evaluation method. Section 5 relates our method to probabilistic evaluation. Section 6 describes the application of our method to *multi-legged arguments* [3] and gives a sufficient condition for a multi-legged argument to improve confidence. Section 7 analyzes a concrete GSN diagram that argues the correctness of a computer simulation of a biological process, namely lymphoid tissue formation. Finally, Sect. 8 states the conclusions and explores possible extensions of our framework.

2   Related Work

Developing an evaluation method for an assurance case is a current research objective, and various approaches have been proposed for this purpose. Studies on evaluating assurance cases are mainly concerned with the term *confidence*, i.e., how stakeholders gain sufficient confidence for the dependability of the system from the assurance cases. In [4], probability was used to calculate the confidence in assurance cases. Using the probabilistic framework, Bloomfield et al. [3] showed that independent multi-legged arguments increase the confidence of assurance cases. Other approaches include using Baconian probability [14] and the Dempster–Shafer theory (DST) [13]. The Baconian approach considers the doubts eliminated by the claims and evidence in a case with eliminative induction. DST supports the assignment of weights (i.e., mass) to a combination of possible events, rather than only assigning weights (probabilities) to each event, as is done in standard probability theory. In [9], Rushby noted that the interpretation of assurance cases could be "inductive," i.e., the conjunction of sub-claims strongly suggests that the claim is true, or it could be "deductive," i.e., the conjunction implies (or entails or proves) the claim, and he emphasized that for evaluating assurance cases, the inductive nature of assurance cases must be considered.

The method proposed in this paper is based on an abstract algebra and a partial order; thus, it is purely qualitative. We do not regard the qualitative nature of our method as a drawback, because the reasoning of assurance cases is inherently qualitative: assurance cases are written in natural language (even using graphical notations) and thus exhibit a qualitative nature. Our method provides a rigorous theoretical foundation for the qualitative evaluation of assurance cases. Furthermore, it can be regarded as an abstraction of other methods. In Sect. 5, we show that all evaluation methods based on probability are special cases of our method if they obey the axioms of probability and certain weak conditions.

3   Goal Structuring Notation (GSN)

GSN is a graphical notation for representing an informal argument. The argument is constructed in a top-down manner, in which a "goal," i.e., a final claim, is gradually elaborated as sub-goals and directly verifiable evidence.

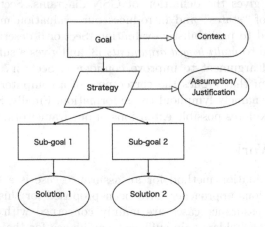

Fig. 1. GSN components

A GSN diagram is constructed with the following types of nodes. A goal is a claim to be demonstrated. A strategy is a method for deriving a goal, which decomposes the goal into several sub-goals (premises). A (sub-)goal may be demonstrated by direct evidence (solution). A context indicates an environment that specifies how a goal is interpreted. An assumption and a justification are underlying reasons why a strategy is correct and taken for granted. We use the notation ⋄, which indicates an "undeveloped" argument, i.e., an argument that is not completed.

To facilitate the formal analysis, we introduce a term notation for GSN diagrams. In the definition, we omit the context and assumption nodes for simplicity of presentation.

Definition 1 (Term notations for GSN diagrams D, modified from [8]).

$$D ::= \langle g, \diamond \rangle \tag{1}$$
$$| \ \langle g, e \rangle \tag{2}$$
$$| \ \langle g, \text{OR}, (D_1, \ldots, D_n) \rangle \tag{3}$$
$$| \ \langle g, \text{st}, (D_1, \ldots, D_n) \rangle \tag{4}$$

$\langle g, \diamond \rangle$ is an undeveloped argument, and $\langle g, e \rangle$ is an argument directly derived from an evidence e. $\langle g, \text{OR}, (D_1, \ldots, D_n) \rangle$ is a *multi-legged* argument, in which the same conclusion is obtained using different diagrams $D_1, \ldots, D_n$. We discuss multi-legged arguments in Sect. 6. $\langle g, \text{st}, (D_1, \ldots, D_n) \rangle$ is an argument derived from $D_1, \ldots, D_n$ using a strategy st.

4   Truthmaker Semantics and Confidence

4.1   Truthmakers

Classical logic assumes the principle of bivalence: the statement either holds or not, and there is no middle ground. However, the goals of GSN may not be interpreted to have just two truth values because we may not have sufficient information to determine the truth values. To interpret the goals of GSN, we adopt a radically different approach called *truthmaker semantics* [5], which has recently been developed in the field of logic.

Truthmaker semantics assumes that the world consists of objects called *truthmakers* that make a statement true. For example, the truthmaker of the statement "New York is rainy" is the rain in New York.

Truthmakers have a mereological structure [11], which represents a part-whole relation between two truthmakers. For example, the rain in New York is a part of the rain and wind in New York. The part-whole relation between the truthmakers forms an order relation. Further, we may amalgamate two truthmakers, say, the rain in New York and the wind in New York. The amalgamation of two truthmakers is represented by a binary operation ⊕.

Depending on their mereological structure, truthmakers obey different sets of axioms. In this study, we employ a small set of axioms to interpret a wide variety of confidence evaluations. Let S (a state-space) be a set of truthmakers that we consider.

Definition 2. *Let S be a state space. Then, S has the element 0, the binary operator ⊕, and the order relation ⊑ such that*

1. *(Unit)* $0 \oplus s = s \oplus 0 = s$.
2. *(Commutativity)* $s_1 \oplus s_2 = s_2 \oplus s_1$, $s_1, s_2 \in \mathcal{S}$.
3. *(Mereological order)* $s_1 \sqsubseteq s_2 \iff \exists s_3 \in \mathcal{S}, s_1 \oplus s_3 = s_2$.
4. *(Common part)* there is a minimum $s_1 \sqcap s_2$ for $s_1, s_2 \in \mathcal{S}$.

We often call truthmakers *states*, because truthmakers represent "the state of affairs" in the world.

There is a natural model of axioms in Definition 2 as sets of *evidence*. Let $\mathcal{E}$ be a set (of *evidence*).

Proposition 1 (Semantics of evidence). *Let $\mathcal{S}$ be the power set of $\mathcal{E}$. Let 0 be the empty set $\emptyset$, $\oplus$ be the set-theoretic union $\cup$, $\sqsubseteq$ be the inclusion $\subseteq$, and $\sqcap$ be the intersection $\cap$. Then, $\mathcal{S}$ satisfies the axioms in Definition 2.*

Proof. (Axiom 1.) $\emptyset \cup s = s \cup \emptyset = s$. (Axiom 2.) $s_1 \cup s_2 = s_2 \cup s_1$. (Axiom 3.) Let $s_2 \backslash s_1$ be the set subtraction $s_2 \cap s_1^c$. Then, $s_1 \cup (s_2 \backslash s_1) = s_2$. (Axiom 4.) $s_1 \cap s_2$ is the minimum of s_1 and s_2 with respect to the order $\subseteq$.

In particular, the axioms of Definition 2 are consistent, because they have a model.

4.2 Frame, Interpretation, and Confidence

A *frame* determines how a GSN diagram is interpreted as an inference on truthmakers (in the state space $\mathcal{S}$). First, we define when two states are *orthogonal*.

Definition 3. *Two states s_1 and s_2 are* orthogonal *if $s_1 \not\sqsubseteq s_2$ and $s_2 \not\sqsubseteq s_1$. If all the elements of S are mutually orthogonal, S is said to be orthogonal as well.*

Let the set of evidence $\mathcal{E} \subseteq \mathcal{S}$ be orthogonal. Note that $\mathcal{E}$ is different from $\mathcal{E}$ in Proposition 1

Definition 4. *A tuple $\langle \mathcal{S}, \mathcal{E}, \mathrm{st} \rangle$ is called a* frame.

 - $\mathcal{S}$ is a state space.
 - $\mathcal{E} \subseteq \mathcal{S}$ is the set of evidence.
 - st is a set of strategies, which are monotone functions from $\mathcal{S}$ to $\mathcal{S}$.

We assume the following properties.

1. For any evidence e, strategy st, and state s, $e \sqsubseteq \mathrm{st}(s)$ only when $e \sqsubseteq s$.
2. st contains a special strategy id called the identity strategy. id is the identity function on the state space $\mathcal{S}$.

Independence of evidence means that all the evidence must be independently verified. We use this property to show that having multiple evidence increases confidence. Property 1 states that no strategy can infer the evidence unless that evidence is already verified.

Using a frame, we interpret a GSN diagram and its validity.

Definition 5 (Interpretation of a GSN diagram). *We assume that a goal g is an element of $\mathcal{S}$ such that $g \neq 0$ and evidence e is an element of $\mathcal{E}$.*

$$[\![\langle g, \diamond \rangle]\!]\rho := 0 \tag{5}$$

$$[\![\langle g, e \rangle]\!]\rho := e \in \mathcal{E} \tag{6}$$

$$[\![\langle g, \mathrm{OR}, (D_1, \dots, D_n) \rangle]\!] := [\![D_1]\!] \sqcap \cdots \sqcap [\![D_n]\!] \tag{7}$$

$$[\![\langle g, \mathrm{st}, (D_1, \dots, D_n) \rangle]\!] := \mathrm{st}([\![D_1]\!] \oplus \cdots \oplus [\![D_n]\!]) \tag{8}$$

Definition 6 (Validity of a GSN diagram). *Let D be a diagram. For a state $s \in \mathcal{S}$, we say that D justifies s whenever $s \sqsubseteq [\![D]\!]$. D is valid if the goal g of D is justified by D.*

The distinction between inductive and deductive inferences [9] can be defined as follows.

Definition 7 (Inductive and deductive strategies). *If a strategy $\mathrm{st} \in \mathbf{st}$ satisfies $\mathrm{st}(s) \sqsupseteq s$ for all $s \in \mathcal{S}$, st is said to be* inductive. *If $\mathrm{st} \in \mathbf{st}$ satisfies $\mathrm{st}(s) \sqsubseteq s$ for all $s \in \mathcal{S}$, st is said to be* deductive.

Definition 8. *Confidence $\mathcal{C}$ is any partial order. Confidence evaluation θ is a mapping from $\mathcal{S}$ to $\mathcal{C}$ such that for any $s_1, s_2 \in \mathcal{S}$, if $s_1 \sqsubseteq s_2$, then $\theta(s_2) \leq \theta(s_1)$. If, for any $s_1 \sqsubset s_2$, $\theta(s_2) < \theta(s_1)$ holds, then θ is said to be* strict.

If $s_1 \sqsubseteq s_2$, s_2 has less confidence because it states more details about the state of the world compared to s_1.

Theorem 1. *If D is a valid GSN diagram and g is a goal of D, then $\theta(g) \geq \theta([\![D]\!])$.*

Proof. Since $g \sqsubseteq [\![D]\!]$.

5 Relation to Probabilistic Evaluation

Probability is widely used for the confidence evaluation of GSN diagrams [3,4, 6,13,14]. Although different methods and assumptions have been used to assign probability in the literature, they all satisfy the axioms of probability.

In this section, we show that our axioms are satisfied with any probabilistic evaluation with natural assumptions. Therefore, our axioms can be used to analyze the properties that hold for any probabilistic evaluation.

Theorem 2. *Let $\langle \Omega, \mathcal{F}, P \rangle$ be a probability space, where Ω is the set of all samples, $\mathcal{F}$ the set of all possible samples and P a probability measure on them. Then, $\mathcal{F}$ can be regarded as a state space by $X \sqsubseteq Y \iff X \supseteq Y$, $X \oplus Y := X \cap Y$ $0 := \Omega$.*

Proof. We check only axiom 3 in Definition 2. If $X \sqsubseteq Y$, then $X \supseteq Y$. Then, $X \oplus Y = X \cap Y = Y$. Conversely, if $X \cap Z = Y$, then $Y \subseteq X$. Therefore, $X \sqsubseteq Y$.

Theorem 3. *A probability measure $P : \mathcal{F} \to [0,1]$ is a confidence evaluation. If, for non-empty X, $P(X) > 0$ holds, then P is a strict confidence evaluation.*

Proof. If $X \sqsubseteq Y$, then $X \supseteq Y$. Therefore, $P(X) \geq P(Y)$. Further, if $X \sqsubset Y$, then $X \supset Y$. Therefore, there is a non-empty set Z such that $Y \cup Z = X$ and $Y \cap Z = \emptyset$. By the axiom of probability, $P(Y) + P(Z) = P(X)$. If $P(Z) > 0$, then $P(Y) < P(X)$.

We say that P is strict if, for any non-empty X, $P(X) > 0$.

Theorem 4. *Let $E_1, \ldots, E_n$ be independent (in the sense of probability theory) events that are not equal to Ω. If P is strict, then $\mathcal{E} = \{E_1, \ldots, E_n\}$ forms a set of evidence.*

Proof. Let $A \backslash B = A \cap B^c$ be a set subtraction. First, note that $P(E_i) \neq 1$ because $\Omega \backslash E_i$ is non-empty. Assume that $E_1 \sqsubseteq E_2$. Then, $E_1 \supseteq E_2$ holds. Therefore, $P(E_1 \cap E_2) = P(E_2) \neq P(E_1)P(E_2)$ because $P(E_2) \neq 1$. This contradicts the independence of E_1 and E_2.

Theorem 5. *Let $\mathbf{st}$ be a set of monotone functions over 2^Ω such that $\mathrm{st} \in \mathbf{st}$ satisfies $X \supseteq \mathrm{st}(X)$ and $P(\mathrm{st}(X) \mid E) \leq P(X \mid E)$ for any evidence E. Then, $\langle \Omega, \mathcal{E}, \mathbf{st} \rangle$ is a frame.*

Proof. We only need to prove that $E \sqsubseteq \mathrm{st}(X)$ only when $E \subseteq X$. Assume that $E \sqsubseteq \mathrm{st}(X)$. Then, $P(\mathrm{st}(X) \mid E) = 1$ because $E \supseteq \mathrm{st}(X)$. Because $P(\mathrm{st}(X) \mid E) \leq P(X \mid E) = 1$, $E \sqsubseteq X$.

6   Multi-legged Argument

Bloomfield et al. [3] argued that multi-legged arguments can increase confidence. In this section, we present a sufficient condition for multi-legged arguments to increase confidence.

A multi-legged argument can be written using the OR construct, as shown in Fig. 2.

Theorem 6. *If $[\![D_1]\!]$ and $[\![D_2]\!]$ are independent and a confidence evaluation θ is strict, having a multi-legged argument increases confidence.*

Proof.
$$\theta([\![D]\!]) = \theta([\![D_1]\!] \sqcap [\![D_2]\!]) > \theta([\![D_1]\!]), \theta([\![D_2]\!]) \tag{9}$$
because $[\![D_1]\!] \sqcap [\![D_2]\!] \sqsubset [\![D_1]\!], [\![D_2]\!]$.

The next theorem gives sufficient conditions of D_1 and D_2, which makes Theorem 6 hold.

Theorem 7. *Suppose that the following conditions hold:*

- *D_1 and D_2 contain only inductive inferences.*

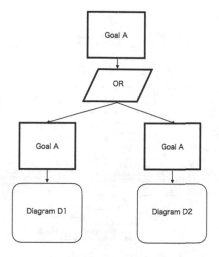

Fig. 2. Multi-legged argument D

- For set $E(D_1)$ of the evidence of D_1 and $E(D_2)$ of the evidence of D_2, neither $E(D_1) \subseteq E(D_2)$ nor $E(D_2) \subseteq E(D_1)$ holds.
- D_1 and D_2 do not use a multi-legged argument.

Then, the multi-legged argument using D_1 and D_2 increases confidence.

Proof. There is evidence that $e \notin E(D_1)$ whereas $e \notin E(D_2)$. By induction on D_1, $e_1 \sqsubseteq [\![D_1]\!]$. Here, we use the fact that D_1 has no multi-legged argument. If D_1 has a multi-legged argument, $e \sqsubseteq [\![D_1]\!]$ may not hold. By property 1 of Definition 4, we can show that $e \not\sqsubseteq [\![D_2]\!]$ by induction on D_2. Therefore, $[\![D_1]\!] \not\sqsubseteq [\![D_2]\!]$. By a similar argument, $[\![D_2]\!] \not\sqsubseteq [\![D_1]\!]$. Therefore, $[\![D_1]\!]$ and $[\![D_2]\!]$ are independent. By Theorem 6, we obtain the conclusion of the theorem.

7 Concrete Example

In this section, we analyze a part of the concrete GSN diagram shown in Fig. 3, which argues the correctness of a computer simulation of a biological process, namely lymphoid tissue formation. Using our framework, we can clarify the nature of arguments and suggest further improvement.

Figure 3 shows the argument for claim 1.1.4: "simulation captures cell aggregation emergent behavior at 72 h." Claim 1.1.4 is derived from three strategies; thus, we can regard the argument as a multi-legged argument. As discussed in Sect. 6, if each argument is based on different sets of evidence, contains only inductive strategies, and does not contain another multi-legged argument, then a multi-legged argument improves confidence.

However, claim 1.1.4.3.1 in Fig. 3 uses the opinions of domain experts as the only evidence. Because claim 1.1.4.1.1 also uses the opinions of domain experts,

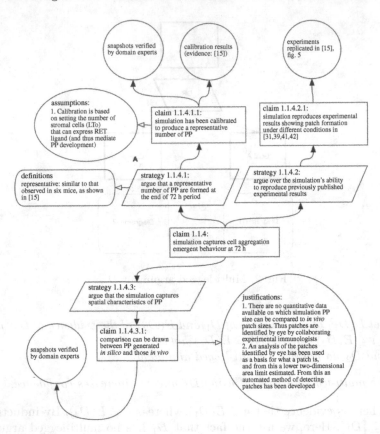

Fig. 3. GSN used for justification of a biological simulation (claim 1.1.4) [1] (Licensed under the Creative Commons Attribution 4.0 International License)

the evidence used in claim 1.1.4.3.1 might be contained in that of claim 1.1.4.1.1, which violates the condition presented in Sect. 6. Therefore, the multi-legged argument based on claims 1.1.4.1.1 and 1.1.4.3.1 may not increase the confidence of claim 1.1.4. An explicit description of the opinion of domain experts would increase the confidence of the argument by differentiating the evidence used by claims 1.1.4.1.1 and 1.1.4.3.1.

8   Conclusion and Future Work

This paper presented a framework for interpreting and evaluating assurance cases in an abstract manner. Unlike numerical evaluation methods, our method is purely qualitative, which we consider an advantage because the reasoning of assurance cases is inherently qualitative. We demonstrated that our method can provide a rigorous theoretical foundation for the qualitative evaluation of assurance cases, using multi-legged arguments (Sect. 6) and a concrete case study

(Sect. 7) as examples. Furthermore, we showed that probabilistic evaluations are special cases of our method in Sect. 5.

In the future, we plan to investigate additional axioms to realize a finer confidence evaluation. Further, we plan to investigate the relation of our method to other methods, especially the Dempster–Shafer theory.

References

1. Alden, K., Andrews, P.S., Polack, F.A., Veiga-Fernandes, H., Coles, M.C., Timmis, J.: Using argument notation to engineer biological simulations with increased confidence. J. R. Soc. Interface **12**(104), 20141059 (2015)
2. Assurance Case Working Group: Goal structuring notation community standard version 2, January 2018. https://scsc.uk/r141B:1
3. Bloomfield, R., Littlewood, B.: Multi-legged arguments: the impact of diversity upon confidence in dependability arguments. In: Proceedings of the International Conference on Dependable Systems and Networks, June 2014, pp. 25–34 (2003)
4. Bloomfield, R.E., Littlewood, B., Wright, D.: Confidence: its role in dependability cases for risk assessment. In: Proceedings of The 37th Annual IEEE/IFIP International Conference on Dependable Systems and Networks, DSN 2007, Edinburgh, UK, 25–28 June 2007, pp. 338–346. IEEE Computer Society (2007)
5. Fine, K.: Truthmaker Semantics. A Companion to the Philosophy of Language, February 2017, pp. 556–577 (2017)
6. Guiochet, J., Do Hoang, Q.A., Kaaniche, M.: A model for safety case confidence assessment. In: Koornneef, F., van Gulijk, C. (eds.) SAFECOMP 2015. LNCS, vol. 9337, pp. 313–327. Springer, Cham (2015). https://doi.org/10.1007/978-3-319-24255-2_23
7. Maksimov, M., Kokaly, S., Chechik, M.: A survey of tool-supported assurance case assessment techniques. ACM Comput. Surv. **52**(5), 1–34 (2019)
8. Matsuno, Y.: A Design and implementation of an assurance case language. In: Proceedings - 44th Annual IEEE/IFIP International Conference on Dependable Systems and Networks, DSN 2014, pp. 630–641 (2014)
9. Rushby, J.: Assurance and assurance cases. In: Pretschner, A., Peled, D., Hutzelmann, T. (eds.) Dependable Software Systems Engineering (Marktoberdorf Summer School Lectures, 2016), NATO Science for Peace and Security Series D, pp. 207–236, vol. 50. IOS Press, October 2017
10. The MISRA consortium: Guidelines for automotive safety arguments (2019)
11. Varzi, A.: Mereology. In: Zalta, E.N. (ed.) The Stanford Encyclopedia of Philosophy. Metaphysics Research Lab, Stanford University, spring 2019 (2019)
12. Wang, R., Guiochet, J., Motet, G., Schön, W.: Modelling confidence in railway safety case. Saf. Sci. **110**(December), 286–299 (2018)
13. Wang, R., Guiochet, J., Motet, G., Schön, W.: Safety case confidence propagation based on dempster-shafer theory. Int. J. Approx. Reason. **107**, 46–64 (2019)
14. Weinstock, C.B., Goodenough, J.B., Klein, A.Z.: Measuring assurance case confidence using baconian probabilities. In: 2013 Proceedings of ASSURE 2013, pp. 7–11, IEEE Computer Society, San Francisco (2013)

Correction to: Formal Methods and Software Engineering

Shang-Wei Lin⑩, Zhe Hou⑩, and Brendan Mahony

Correction to:
S.-W. Lin et al. (Eds.): *Formal Methods and Software Engineering*, **LNCS 12531,**
https://doi.org/10.1007/978-3-030-63406-3

In the original version the surname of the editor Brendan Mahony has been misspelled. This has been now corrected.

The updated version of the book can be found at
https://doi.org/10.1007/978-3-030-63406-3

Doctoral Symposium Paper

Verification of a TLSF Algorithm in Embedded System

Li Shaofeng[1,2(✉)] ⓘ, Qiao Lei[2], and Yang Mengfei[3]

[1] School of Computer Science and Technology, Xidian University, Xi'an, China
Isfmoon@163.com
[2] Beijing Institute of Control Engineering, Beijing China
[3] China Academy of Space Technology, Beijing China

Abstract. Space embedded operating system is a typical safety-critical system. Due to the harsh environment outside the space, its system resources are very limited. Memory is a basic resource for system program operation. Therefore, effective memory management is a very important module. In the early space embedded system, the program is simple to run. At the same time, in order to ensure the certainty of system operation, static memory management methods are mostly used, which leads to the system not being flexible enough and the memory usage rate is relatively low. Therefore, it is necessary to use dynamic memory management to manage memory, but the uncertainty of its execution makes it less used in embedded systems. This paper uses formal verification to prove a dynamic memory algorithm implemented in a space embedded system Management—the correctness of the TLSF algorithm.

Keywords: Memory management · TLSF algorithm · Formal verification

1 Background

The TLSF algorithm [1] adopts the principle of better matching, combining the two mechanisms of packet free linked list and bitmap matching to quickly locate the appropriate memory block. Because its execution time is O(1) level of order of magnitude, it has been widely used in the resource-constrained embedded field. However, for a safety-critical system, safety and reliability are the most critical considerations. At present, there are many verification works [2, 3] for the TLSF algorithm, but there is no verification work designed for requirements. If the design of an algorithm starting from the wrong requirements, then even it the code is implemented correctly, problems will occur at a certain moment. Therefore, this paper prove the requirements of the memory management module is correct, which is apply algorithm of TLSF in the space embedded system.

The allocation and de-allocation of memory in the TLSF algorithm is based on area-based memory allocation and recovery. Each allocated object is a continuous area in memory, and the memory is recovered by destroying the area and releasing all

Supported by the National Natural Science Foundation of China: 61632005.

objects in it. This continuous memory area is also called a memory block. The block header of the memory block fully contains the information of the memory block. Considering the related operations of memory allocation, a memory block is represented by the following five-tuple: $mb \triangleq \langle bst, bad, bsi, pbl, fbl \rangle$. Bst refers to the state of the memory block, bad refers to the start address of the memory block, bsi refers to the size of the memory block, pbl refers to the physical previous memory block of the memory block, and fbl refers to the adjacent block of relative value on the free block list.

The TLSF algorithm uses a 32-bit bitmap to quickly determine the range of the memory block size to be found, and then uses the corresponding memory block list to quickly find the memory block that meets the requirements. Given the size of a required memory block, the algorithm quickly locates a memory block list through a two-level 32-bit bitmap, and then returns the first memory block of the memory block list to the application for use. The index structure of a TLSF algorithm uses the quadruple $S \triangleq \langle bBS, fl, sl, BL \rangle$, where bBS is the size of the largest block in memory, BL is the list of free memory blocks, fl and sl are the secondary positioning of the system 32-level bitmap. The fl is a 32-bit number, and the sl is an array composed of multiple 32-bit numbers.

Therefore, after executing any function of the memory management module, the memory index structure S can be used to represent all the free memory of the system at this time. Based on this observation, the function of the memory management module can be abstracted as a change to S. This article verify an implemented of TLSF algorithm to prove its correctness.

2   Verification

The two main functions of the memory management algorithm are allocation and release. Allocation refers to the allocation of appropriate memory blocks to the application program according to the requirements of the application program. Release refers to free the memory block used by the application program which has been used up, and the block will be used for other applications. This section takes the allocation and release functions of the TLSF algorithm as examples to prove the correctness of its function design.

2.1   Global Nature

The operation of memory management behavior for memory blocks should satisfy the following properties:

- inv1: The memory block whose status is occupied cannot be reallocated.
- inv2: The memory block that is free cannot be released.
- inv3: Any two adjacent memory blocks cannot overlap.
- inv4: There is at least one non-free block between two free blocks.
- inv5: There is no adjacent free blocks.
- inv6: If there is a continuous address space of N bytes in the memory area, any

allocation request with a memory size of less than or equal to N bytes can be satisfied.

- inv7: The difference between the memory block allocated to the application and the memory size required by the application will not exceed a certain fixed value.
- inv8: Any memory space that has been freed can be allocated.
- inv9: The size of the smallest free block of memory is greater than or equal to a certain fixed value.
- inv10: Any allocated memory space can be released.

The above properties must be met during the implementation of the memory management TLSF algorithm. One of the memory blocks b directly represents its memory block address, sta(b) represents the state of the memory block, and size(b) refers to the size of the memory block. M refers to the size of the smallest memory block allowed by the system, alloc(s) and free(b) represent the memory block of the allocated size s and the released memory block b, and right(b) refers to the next memory of the physical memory. Block, left(b) refers to the previous memory block of b in physical memory.

The above properties must be met during the implementation of the memory management TLSF algorithm. One of the memory blocks b directly represents its memory block address, sta(b) represents the state of the memory block, and size(b) refers to the size of the memory block. M refers to the size of the smallest memory block allowed by the system, alloc(s) and free(b) represent the memory block of the allocated size s and the released memory block b, and right(b) refers to the next memory of the physical memory. Block, left(b) refers to the previous memory block of b in physical memory.

2.2 The Function of Allocate

In the process of allocating memory, in addition to satisfying the global properties of Sect. 3.1, there are also some local properties that need to be satisfied.

Theorem updateGe: forall size:N, update(size)¿size.
Theorem checkFL: forall size:N,
 $MBS < size < mSize \rightarrow getFL(size) < FL \wedge getSL(size) < SL$
Theorem slGrow: forall fl sl:N,
 $getGE_slMap(fl, sl) > 0 \rightarrow getSL(getGE_slMap(fl, sl)) \geq sl$
Theorem flGrow : forall fl:N, getGEFL(fl)¿fl
Theorem blsize: forall bl:BL,size(rm(bl))−size(bl) 1
Theorem bl2nil: $forall bl : BL, size(bl) = 1 \rightarrow rm(bl) = nil$

Among them, updateGe means that the size after the update process must be greater than the original size. In the search process, checkFL refers to the property that the value of the secondary index calculated according to the application program satisfies, and slGrow and flGrow refer to the calculation according to the application program After the secondary index has no suitable free blocks, it is the property that is satisfied when searching for free blocks in a higher range. blsize and bl2nil refer to the local properties that the size of the free block list satisfies in the process remove.

2.3   The Function of Release

In the process of releasing the memory block, in addition to satisfying the global properties of Sect. 3.1, there are also some local properties that need to be satisfied.

Theorem noFreeAdB: $forall b : mb, b' = merge(b) \rightarrow right(b').bst = 1 \wedge left(b').bst = 1$.
Theorem inBblsize: $forall(b : mb)(bl : BL), size(insert(b, bl)) = size(bl) + 1$.
Theorem nil2bl: $forall(b : mb), size(insert(b, nil)) = 1$.

Among them, noFreeAdB means that after the memory block b is merged, the memory before and after the new memory block b'must be occupied. InBblsize and nil2bl, after inserting a free memory block in a free memory block list, the number of nodes in the free memory block list is increased by 1.

3   Conclusion and Future Work

Each function of the memory management module is verified at the design layer. While satisfying the global properties of the memory management module proposed in Sect. 3.1, it also satisfies the local properties of some functions. All verification work is performed in the interactive theorem proving tool Coq.

Aiming at the key embedded operating system, this paper proposes a three-layer verification and development framework for requirements, design, and code based on the actual needs of the space field. Future considerations This verification development framework will be more widely promoted and applied to the development of systems in other critical areas, and related verification strategies will be abstracted, and the common parts of verification will be extracted and encapsulated as a verification framework to facilitate verification in other fields.

References

1. Masmano, M., Ripoll, I., Crespo, A., Real, J.: TLSF: a new dynamic memory allocator for real-time systems. In: Euromicro Conference on Real-time Systems. IEEE Computer Society (2004)
2. Fang, B., Sighireanu, M., Pu, G., Su, W., Abrial, J.-R., Yang, M., Qiao, L.: Formal modelling of list based dynamic memory allocators. Sci. China Inf. Sci. 61(12), 1–16 (2018). https://doi.org/10.1007/s11432-017-9280-9
3. Zhang, Yu., Zhao, Y., Sanan, D., Qiao, L., Zhang, J.: A verified specification of TLSF memory management allocator using state monads. In: Guan, N., Katoen, J.-P., Sun, J. (eds.) SETTA 2019. LNCS, vol. 11951, pp. 122–138. Springer, Cham (2019). https://doi.org/10.1007/978-3-030-35540-1_8

Author Index

Printed in the United States
By Bookmasters

Printed in the United States
By Bookmasters